International Library of Criminology, Criminal Justice and Penology – Second Series

Series Editors: Gerald Mars and David Nelken

Titles in the Series:

Gender and Prisons
Dana Britton

Quantitative Methods in Criminology
Shawn Bushway and David Weisburd

Detecting Deception
David Canter and Donna Youngs

Offender Profiling
David Canter and Michael Davis

Insurgent Terrorism
Gerald Cromer

Crime and Security
Benjamin Goold and Lucia Zedner

Recent Developments in Criminological Theory
Stuart Henry

Gun Crime
Richard Hobbs and Robert Hornsby

The Criminology of War
Ruth Jamieson

The Impact of HIV/AIDS on Criminology and Criminal Justice
Mark M. Lanier

Burglary
Robert Mawby

Domestic Violence
Mangai Natarajan

Women Police
Mangai Natarajan

Crime and Immigration
Graeme Newman and Joshua Freilich

Crime and Social Institutions
Richard Rosenfeld

The Death Penalty, Volumes I and II
Austin Sarat

Gangs
Jacqueline Schneider and Nick Tilley

Corporate Crime
Sally Simpson and Carole Gibbs

Crime and Deviance in Cyberspace
David Wall

Green Criminology
Nigel South and Piers Beirne

Surveillance and Social Control
Dean Wilson and Clive Norris

Quantitative Methods in Criminology

Quantitative Methods in Criminology

Edited by

Shawn Bushway
University of Maryland, USA

and

David Weisburd
Hebrew University of Jerusalem and University of Maryland, USA

ASHGATE

Published by
Ashgate Publishing Limited
Gower House
Croft Road
Aldershot
Hants GU11 3HR
England

Ashgate Publishing Company
Suite 420
101 Cherry Street
Burlington, VT 05401-4405
USA

Ashgate website: http://www.ashgate.com

British Library Cataloguing in Publication Data
Quantitative methods in criminology. – (International
  library of criminology, criminal justice and penology.
  Second series)
  1. Criminal statistics 2. Criminology – Mathematical models
  I. Bushway, Shawn II. Weisburd, David
  364'.0727

Library of Congress Control Number: 2005925058

ISBN 0 7546 2446 3

Printed in Great Britain by The Cromwell Press, Trowbridge, Wiltshire

Contents

PART IV   DESCRIPTIVE ANALYSIS OF QUANTITATIVE DATA

PART V   CAUSAL MODELLING

Acknowledgements

The editors would like to thank Nancy Morris for her thoughtful assistance in preparing this book for publication.

The editors and publishers would also like to thank the following for permission to use copyright material.

American Academy of Political and Social Science for the essays: Albert D. Biderman and Albert J. Reiss Jr (1967), 'On Exploring the "Dark Figure" of Crime', *Annals of the American Academy of Political and Social Science*, **374**, pp. 1–15; David Weisburd, Cynthia M. Lum and Anthony Petrosino (2001), 'Does Research Design Affect Study Outcomes in Criminal Justice?', *Annals of the American Academy of Political and Social Science*, **578**, pp. 50–70.

American Psychological Association for the essay: Mark W. Lipsey and David B. Wilson (1993), 'The Efficacy of Psychological, Educational, and Behavioral Treatment: Confirmation from Meta-Analysis', *American Psychologist*, **48**, pp. 1181–209. Copyright © 1993 American Psychological Assocation.

American Society of Criminology for the essays: David P. Farrington, Rolf Loeber, Magda Stouthamer-Loeber, Welmoet B. van Kammen and Laura Schmidt (1996), 'Self-reported Delinquency and a Combined Delinquency Seriousness Scale Based on Boys, Mothers, and Teachers: Concurrent and Predictive Validity for African-Americans and Caucasians', *Criminology*, **34**, pp. 493–517. Copyright © 1996 American Society of Criminology; Arnold Barnett, Alfred Blumstein and David P. Farrington (1989), 'A Prospective Test of a Criminal Career Model', *Criminology*, **27**, pp. 373–88. Copyright © 1989 American Society of Criminology; David Weisburd, Shawn Bushway, Cynthia Lum and Sue-Ming Yang (2004), 'Trajectories of Crime at Places: A Longitudinal Study of Street Segments in the City of Seattle', *Criminology*, **42**, pp. 283–321. Copyright © 2004 American Society of Criminology.

American Sociological Association for the essay: Lawrence W. Sherman and Richard A. Berk (1984), 'The Specific Deterrent Effects of Arrest for Domestic Assault', *American Sociological Review*, **49**, pp. 261–72.

Crime Justice Press for the essay: David M. Kennedy, Anthony A. Braga and Anne M. Piehl (1998), 'The (Un)known Universe: Mapping Gangs and Gang Violence in Boston', in *Crime Mapping and Crime Prevention*, D. Weisburd and T. McEwen (eds), *Crime Prevention Studies*, **7**, pp. 219–62.

University of Chicago Press for the essay: David Weisburd with Anthony Petrosino and Gail Mason (1993), 'Design Sensitivity in Criminal Justice Experiments', *Crime and Justice*, **17**, pp. 337–79.

Preface to the Second Series

The first series of the International Library of Criminology, Criminal Justice and Penology has established itself as a major research resource by bringing together the most significant journal essays in contemporary criminology, criminal justice and penology. The series made available to researchers, teachers and students an extensive range of essays which are indispensable for obtaining an overview of the latest theories and findings in this fast changing subject. Indeed the rapid growth of interesting scholarly work in the field has created a demand for a second series which like the first consists of volumes dealing with criminological schools and theories as well as with approaches to particular areas of crime, criminal justice and penology. Each volume is edited by a recognised authority who has selected twenty or so of the best journal articles in the field of their special competence and provided an informative introduction giving a summary of the field and the relevance of the articles chosen. The original pagination is retained for ease of reference.

The difficulties of keeping on top of the steadily growing literature in criminology are complicated by the many disciplines from which its theories and findings are drawn (sociology, law, sociology of law, psychology, psychiatry, philosophy and economics are the most obvious). The development of new specialisms with their own journals (policing, victimology, mediation) as well as the debates between rival schools of thought (feminist criminology, left realism, critical criminology, abolitionism etc.) make necessary overviews that offer syntheses of the state of the art.

GERALD MARS
Visiting Professor, Brunel University, Middlesex, UK

DAVID NELKEN
Distinguished Professor of Sociology, University of Macerata, Italy;
Distinguished Research Professor of Law, University of Cardiff, Wales;
Honorary Visiting Professor of Law, LSE, London, UK

Introduction

Introduction

When we began the process of identifying the main contributions to quantitative criminology, a more general question emerged that is perhaps unusual in the series of readers of which our book is a part. Is there a quantitative criminology, or are quantitative methods in criminology simply the direct application of approaches from other disciplines such as economics, psychology or sociology? The question of what falls within the domain of quantitative criminology is an important issue to discuss at the outset and one that was central to our approach to selecting essays for inclusion in this volume.

Deciding that quantitative criminology is simply about the application of methods from other fields would not necessarily rule out the importance of attention to quantitative methods in criminology. Indeed, the description of the *Journal of Quantitative Criminology*, an important catalyst for advancing quantitative criminology, notes on its website that the journal 'focuses on research advances from such fields as statistics, sociology, geography, political science, economics, and engineering' as they are applied to criminological problems. But we ultimately decided that wholesale importation of statistical techniques will be of limited value because the questions asked in criminology are different from the questions asked in other fields. Successful application of statistical techniques depends on an acute awareness of the methodological and measurement issues that arise in criminology and criminal justice. Therefore, quantitative criminology as a subfield also needs to serve an introspective role. Quantitative criminology in this sense is not simply about importing techniques from other fields, but about recognizing the need to adapt such approaches to criminological data and questions. Following this approach, for example, the new *Journal of Experimental Criminology* notes, on its website, that it is 'committed to the advancement of the science of systematic reviews and experimental methods in criminology and criminal justice'.

In our view, the development of a quantitative criminology also implies an additional type of scientific advance. The process of adapting methods to fit the unique features of criminological data and questions ultimately leads to the development of new methods and measures which better serve the purposes of the field. It is not enough to apply methods; it is essential to explore new methods that may be essential to solving the statistical and methodological problems that criminological data raise. In its fully mature form, quantitative criminology as a subfield must serve not only as a translator of techniques but as a source of new techniques and methods that serve to answer the questions that arise in our field. And, in this context, we would expect that criminological innovations in statistics and research methods would also have an impact on the approaches that are used in other fields. This, of course, would bring us full circle with criminology not only drawing its methods from other disciplines, but other disciplines drawing insights from quantitative criminology.

These observations led us to what we define below as the three 'Is' of quantitative criminology: *importation* of techniques from other fields; *introspection* with regard to their application to specific criminological problems; and *innovation* in the development of new methodological and statistical approaches. In this volume we show that quantitative criminology has reached a maturity that may surprise many scholars from other fields and indeed many criminologists. Criminologists have not only drawn sophisticated and cutting-edge approaches from other fields, they have given significant attention to the ways in which such approaches must be adapted to fit criminological problems. Such introspection is no longer novel in criminology and criminal justice, it is expected by peer reviewers and journal editors. Even the development of completely new approaches to quantitative problems can be found in criminology today. As we illustrate in our discussion below, in the case of developmental criminology, quantitative criminology is taking a leadership role in advancing approaches in other fields.

Below we turn to a more detailed examination of the roles of importation, introspection and innovation in quantitative criminology. We then introduce the essays included in our volume and discuss why we consider them to be important in a reader that defines the main themes of quantitative criminology.

The Three Is of Quantitative Criminology: Importation, Introspection and Innovation

Authors of essays that employ sophisticated or innovated statistical methods are accustomed to editorial reviews which end with: 'This article is too statistical; it would be a better fit at the *Journal of Quantitative Criminology*.' The *Journal of Quantitative Criminology*, which only began publication in 1985, can at times feel like a quantitative ghetto, where good but challenging work is read by only a few other specialists often trained in other disciplines. This holding of quantitative methods at arm's length is reflected in the fact that the *Journal of Quantitative Criminology* is not sponsored by either of the main criminological associations. In contrast, the national organizations of the other mainstream social sciences – psychology, sociology and economics – all sponsor methodological journals. Perhaps reflecting an emerging trend in the recognition of the centrality of methods to problems in criminology and criminal justice, the Campbell Collaboration Crime and Justice Group in cooperation with the Academy of Experimental Criminology have recently joined to sponsor a new quantitative journal, the *Journal of Experimental Criminology*.

Although quantitative criminology did not begin as a central component of the discipline of criminology and criminal justice, any anecdotal survey of the mainstream criminological journals would demonstrate the increased importance of sophisticated statistical methods in criminology. This is partly because many talented scholars trained in other disciplines have been brought to the schools and departments teaching criminology or have begun to examine criminological problems, partly the result of increased statistical training in criminology departments, and partly because federal funders, such as the National Institute of Justice, the National Science Foundation and the National Institute of Drug Abuse, have come to demand of criminologists approaches that can meet the standards of rigorous scientific review.

In this context, the growth of quantitative criminology began in good part as an 'importation' of techniques from other fields. This importation was an efficient way of increasing knowledge, especially in a young field like criminology and criminal justice. But the wholesale adoption of concepts from one field ultimately has limitations, because the field of criminology and criminal justice, like any area, has its own unique data and questions which cannot be solved by a 'one size fits all' approach to quantitative analysis. The best statistical models are ones that match the reality of the processes generating the data.

For example, consider ordinary least squares regression or OLS which has played a central role in criminological analysis at least since the 1970s. This approach allowed researchers not only to define the size and significance of effects in observational data, but also to control for possible confounding due to relationships among independent variables. The importation of OLS techniques from economics was an important advance over models based on simple comparisons of means or cross-tabulations. Even today, OLS often serves as the starting point for criminology graduate students learning statistics. But OLS methods could not simply be 'imported' from economics, because the variables that are of interest in economics and those of interest in criminology are often very different. In economics, the focus of causal analysis is most often on continuous dependent variables such as dollars earned or hours worked. In criminology, the focus of causal analysis is often on discrete dependent variables such as recidivism or crime counts. OLS will often provide misleading results when the dependent variables examined are not measured as continuous variables.

Today, a researcher would be very unlikely to have an essay accepted for publication in which OLS regression was used for analysing whether a convicted offender was sentenced to prison or not. In this case, the researcher would be expected to use maximum likelihood techniques such as logistic or probit regression. This example illustrates the fact that methods imported from other fields must often be examined critically when adapted to the field of criminology. As a result, we believe that the development of a sophisticated quantitative criminology demands not only importation, but also 'introspection'. Scholars must examine carefully how criminological assumptions and problems differ from those in the fields from which approaches are adopted. In this sense, they must not only know the techniques, but must also understand them well enough to see where they are inappropriate or where they must be adapted to specific criminological problems.

For quantitative criminology to reach a level of sophistication that methods in other fields have gained, criminologists must understand the strengths and weaknesses of the methods at hand. Researchers are often all too eager to adopt technical solutions to pervasive problems like selection bias in mechanistic ways – ways that the originators of the technique would likely disavow and perhaps not even recognize. For example, Berk (1983) imported the Heckman selection technique into sociology and criminology from economics. Over time, the use of the Heckman approach has become standard practice in sentencing research, despite the fact that Heckman only intended it to be an approximation for a more detailed approach which at the time (1979) was too time-consuming to compute on the average computer. Moreover, simulation data has shown that the method often causes more problems than it solves (Stolzenberg and Relles, 1990). It is ironic that the use of the Heckman selection procedure is now growing in criminology while researchers in economics rarely, if ever, use the technique.

To be fair, statistical sophistication in criminology has grown markedly over the last few years, and the Heckman technique is perhaps an extreme example. Consider as a counter example, Wayne Osgood's use of negative binomial regression in his 2000 essay included as the final chapter in this volume. The explicit intention of the essay was to import the negative binomial model, which was well developed in statistics, into criminology in order to deal with the unique features of aggregate crime data. The essay has been cited 16 times at the time of writing, and a search of the Criminal Justice Periodicals database reveals four essays since 2000 which cite Osgood and include the term 'negative binomial' in the abstract. This is a good example of the process of dissemination working in the way it should. A quantitative criminologist notes a problem in the criminology literature, introduces a method from another field which might be useful for solving the problem, and then researchers begin to apply the technique to appropriate problems.

As the techniques begin to become more complicated, the burden increases on the empirical researcher to be able to understand advanced statistical techniques. And this is not simply the process of understanding how to use a specific computer software package. In a practice not unique to criminology, researchers often refer to software packages (HLM, LISREL) rather than the underlying statistical models that they apply. While these packages are useful tools, they, like any tool, are ultimately only as good as the user who applies them. And the artful user needs to understand the basic statistical models underlying the software package. For example, hierarchical linear modelling was developed to deal with data that has nested levels, most notably data on individuals that come from common schools or classrooms. Yet, one does not need HLM to deal with this problem – one can simply include a dummy variable for each school or classroom into a standard regression to control for any common error problems. The approach embedded in HLM, the random effects method, is more efficient (that is, it results in smaller standard errors) and facilitates more sophisticated analysis than can be accomplished using simple dummy variables, but it also requires more assumptions. All too often, this trade-off is not understood by empirical criminologists and the result is a kind of desultory application without understanding.

At the bare minimum, therefore, criminologists should strive to be competent analysts, capable of taking techniques from other fields and adapting them to fit criminological questions. But, ultimately, this tailoring should not be the purview of a select few 'quantitative criminologists', but of all researchers who use quantitative methods to study questions in criminology and criminal justice. We refer to this type of researcher as an empirical criminologist and believe that the vast majority of academic criminologists fall within this category. This need should ultimately cause us to change how we educate our graduate students. Researchers engaged in theory testing need both an intimate knowledge of the assumptions of theory and of the statistical techniques used to model that theory. We also believe that the quantitative criminologists who often teach statistical courses in departments can no longer be excused for 'dumbing down' statistics classes because of the perceived limitations of criminology students. Criminology and criminal justice, as a field, must deal with the fact that competent empirical analysis in criminology requires a sophisticated understanding of statistical models by the average empirical researcher who uses these techniques.

But if empirical researchers should be competent in the application of statistical methods without specializing in quantitative criminology, is there a need for quantitative criminologists? We believe that as the field as a whole becomes more sophisticated, there will be a growing need for a subset of researchers who develop techniques and methods that directly respond to the needs of the field. The methods for solving key questions in criminology may not be found in methods developed for sociology or economics. Our problems are sometimes unique, and in this case a real quantitative criminology will have to look within itself to find creative answers to difficult statistical questions. And, indeed, as the field has matured, there is clear evidence that researchers are in fact beginning to do just that, particularly in the field of developmental criminology. For example, semi-parametric trajectory analysis has its roots in economics. However, the problems that are faced in criminology demand not simply an introspection and thoughtful adoption of such approaches, but also the development of new methods of conceptualizing and analysing developmental data.

Originally, Daniel Nagin and Kenneth Land (1993) imported the semi-parametric approach from economics as yet another way of controlling for unobserved differences in people, which might explain perceived causal relationships between observed variables. Over time, they have developed the technique to study developmental trajectories of crime in a way that matches the language of developmental theory. This type of trajectory analysis is a direct response to the plaintive request of researchers such as Hagan and Palloni (1988) who explicitly called for techniques which allowed for the testing of the theoretical ideas in developmental criminology. The 1996 essay included in this volume by Land and Nagin (Chapter 17) is, in our opinion, the paper where these ideas started to develop more completely and true innovation began. We have also included two essays in this volume which, we believe, illustrate the way in which this technique has been applied to truly advance understanding in criminology. The first, by Shawn Bushway, Terence Thornberry and Marvin Krohn (Chapter 18) applies the use of trajectories to the study of desistance. The essay demonstrates how this method represents an innovation over previous methods used to study desistance. The second essay by David Weisburd, Shawn Bushway, Cynthia Lum and Sue-Ming Yang (Chapter 19) is the first to apply the trajectory technique to study crime at small units of geography over time. The use of trajectory analysis allowed these researchers to identify a diversity of trends in crime across street segments in Seattle in the 1990s, and led them to speculate on whether the crime drop in American cities was restricted to very specific places and was not common across the city landscape as has generally been assumed. But the Nagin and Land approach has not been limited to use in criminology. There are now well over 50 essays that use this innovative approach that have been published in criminology, sociology and psychology. The Nagin and Land approach is also described in a well-known volume in developmental science published by the American Psychological Association, *New Methods for the Analysis of Change* by Linda M. Collins and Aline G. Sayers (2001).

The remainder of this volume serves to celebrate and commemorate what we hope is a 'coming of age' of quantitative criminology as an established subfield in criminology. We have chosen ground-breaking essays from the past that have been responsible for new waves of criminological research and we have also identified more recent essays which could serve as benchmarks for future criminologists. All the essays reflect one of the three Is: importation, introspection and innovation. Some contain aspects of all three basic traits, while others tend to focus on one or the other. We have chosen to organize the essays into five basic sections that cover the broad array of concerns that quantitative criminology addresses: Research Design and Study Outcomes, Quantitative Issues in Sampling, Issues in Measurement, Descriptive Analysis of Quantitative Data, and Causal Modelling. We discuss our choices in some detail below.

Research Design and Study Outcomes

Often, the first choice that empirical criminologists face in a research programme is to define the research design of their study. Generally, research designs can be divided into three classes: randomized experiments; quasi-experiments; and observational or non-experimental studies. Each approach seeks to solve the problem of how we can make causal links between independent and dependent variables.

For much of the history of criminology, researchers have relied on observational methods drawn primarily from sociology and economics. In such methods, the researcher collects information from the field, observes the phenomenon under study, and then attempts to use statistical techniques to solve problems of confounding that might occur. For example, if a researcher was interested in defining the effect of imprisonment on recidivism he or she could not simply look at how those sentenced to prison compared on subsequent criminal behaviour as contrasted with those not sentenced to prison. Clearly there are factors that would confound this comparison, such as the fact that a custodial sentence is more likely if an offender has a prior criminal record or has committed a more serious crime. Using observational methods, the researcher would seek to identify such confounding variables and then to neutralize their impact through the use of statistical modelling techniques such as multiple regression. Much of the efforts of quantitative criminology over the last half-century have been directed at overcoming biases that are common in observational studies.

However, in fields like medicine and psychology, researchers have long used experimental methods to establish causal relationships. In this case, through the use of random allocation of subjects to treatment and control groups, the researcher is able to assume that most potential threats to the validity of causal observations are overcome. Lawrence Sherman and Richard Berk (Chapter 1) provide an important example of the importation of this approach into criminology in their essay 'The Specific Deterrent Effects of Arrest for Domestic Assault'. The study, conducted in 1984, not only showed that large-scale criminological experiments could be carried out in criminal justice agencies, but also provided an example of how strong experimental methods could be applied in crime and justice field settings despite the special problems likely to be encountered in carrying out randomized experiments in criminal justice. This experiment is far from the first in criminology; indeed, one of the first major criminological studies was the Cambridge Summerville Youth Study which began in the 1930s. However, it spawned a new generation of experimental criminological research in the United States and more recently in other countries including Australia and the United Kingdom.

Richard Berk, Heather Ladd, Heidi Graziano and Jong-Ho Baek (Chapter 2) provide a more recent example of the use of innovative experimental methods within a criminal justice setting in their (2003) study testing inmate classification systems. Inmate classification is an example of the everyday use of quantitative methods in the criminal justice system. The use of an experiment to test the quality of a new version of an inmate classification system in an important criminal justice system like California reflects the growing maturity of quantitative criminology. We see no reason why this type of experimental approach cannot be replicated any time new systems are implemented in the criminal justice system and we look forward to the time when such careful practice is the rule and not the exception.

David Weisburd, Cynthia Lum and Anthony Petrosino (Chapter 3) attempt to learn more about the applications of different criminological approaches by comparing experimental, quasi-experimental and non-experimental studies that were identified in the Maryland Report (Sherman *et al.*, 1997). The Maryland Report provides a systematic sample of crime and justice studies, and allowed the authors to ask the question: 'Does research design affect study outcomes in criminal justice?' This study is an example of 'introspection' and suggests that specific biases may be apparent in criminal justice studies that are not found in other fields.

The final essay in Part I, by Mark Lipsey and David Wilson (1993), uses 'meta-analysis' to examine the effectiveness of psychological, educational and behavioural treatment. We chose to place it in this section because it reflects another approach to defining causality in criminal justice studies, and because it reflects the importation of a new approach to crime and justice study. Meta-analysis is a form of observational study, which uses 'studies' as a unit of analysis. By statistically analysing a broad group of studies within a single explanatory framework, meta-analysis seeks to overcome the simplistic use of single studies (which are, in some sense, individual case studies) to draw wide causal inferences. Meta-analysis also forces researchers to focus on the magnitude of average effects, rather than only on the statistical significance of outcomes. As a result, the essay represents not only an importation of a significant new design approach, but also includes a good deal of introspection about the specific methods used in the studies. This essay is often used in other fields as a model for the meta-analytic approach, and Lipsey and Wilson have become leaders in the development of meta-analytic statistical methods across a series of other disciplines.

Quantitative Issues in Sampling

Perhaps the single most important development in criminology in the last 30 years is the development of explicitly criminological data sets such as the National Crime Victimization Survey, National Youth Survey and the Rochester Youth Development Study. But these new data sources have issues that arise with respect to the creation of representative populations. The first essay in Part II by Robert Brame and Raymond Paternoster (Chapter 5) discusses two issues that arise in longitudinal data: attrition, in which dropping out is systematic; and selective non-answers, in which people do not answer certain questions. The authors show that, even in the simplest cases, these types of problem can lead to substantial bias in inference. The authors explore the use of various correction procedures imported directly from statistics and conclude with a note of caution about ignoring missing data problems. This essay demonstrates the importance of having sophisticated quantitative criminologists who can serve as a bridge between what is happening in statistics and specific applications in criminology.

The second paper in this section (Weisburd, 1993) explores design issues that arise in criminal justice experiments, focusing on the problem of statistical power. Weisburd identifies a paradox in experimental studies in crime and justice that suggests caution in the simple application of design assumptions to crime and justice data. Perhaps the most common approach used in the social sciences and medicine for increasing the statistical power of experimental (and indeed non-experimental) studies is to increase the sample size of experimental and control groups. Weisburd, however, finds that increasing sample size will often paradoxically lead to a decline in the actual statistical power in a study. This is because the introduction of additional cases in crime and justice studies often results in the weakening of other design components of these studies.

The final essay in Part II by Douglas Smith and Raymond Paternoster (Chapter 7) deals with selection into administrative data sets which are becoming increasingly common in criminology as technology makes them more accessible. Individuals are not randomly selected into different parts of the criminal justice system, but are assigned by actors in the criminal justice system on the basis of characteristics that are not always measured in the data. This paper is one of the few studies in criminology to effectively use instrumental variable methods developed in economics to address an important substantive question – whether or not incarceration leads to deviance amplification. Smith and Paternoster make a strong case for the substantive importance of statistical controls for selection artifacts.

Issues in Measurement

Quantitative criminology must also continue to be an area that supports the validation of measures and data sources. The measurement of crime has been the subject of a rich set of essays, some of which we include in this book. The comparison of self-reports and official records, the discussion of the problems with disaggregated UCR data, and the potential problem of survey fatigue in longitudinal data are all very important topics that have been brought to the field's attention by quantitative criminologists. Although this area of criminology tends to be less 'sexy', it is no less important. And criminology deserves some credit in this area. In economics, by contrast, researchers often take the data as given and do not question its validity. The essays in Part III are very careful reviews of the type of data that is used in everyday quantitative analysis. We hope that quantitative criminologists continue to explore and document the strengths and weaknesses of the data used in the field. As even the most sophisticated technique is completely dependent on the quality of the data used in estimation, we take it as a given that introspection about the data must take place at the same time that innovative new techniques are developed to analyse the data.

The first two essays in Part III are among the first to draw attention to the problems involved in relying on official records to measure crime. In their classic (1963) analysis of the use of official statistics, John Kitsuse and Aaron Cicourel (Chapter 8) raise a fundamental question for criminological researchers. Do the data that we gain from the criminal justice system reflect the theoretical questions that criminologists are really interested in? Even today, some researchers use criminal justice statistics to define criminality ignoring the fact that they are socially constructed and reflect not only offending but also the myriad of discretionary decisions made in the criminal justice system. This essay was ground-breaking in its recognition of the importance of understanding the history and context of the data that empirical criminologists use. The second essay, by Albert Biderman and Albert J. Reiss (Chapter 9), written in 1967, also examines the gap between the data available to researchers and the reality of the phenomena they seek to describe. This essay was among the first to recognize the 'dark figure of crime' and broke new ground in its attempt to add sophistication to the ways in which criminologists understand criminality and the criminal justice system. Biderman and Reiss argue that '[criminological] data are not some objectively observable universe of "criminal acts," but rather those events defined, captured, and processed as such by some institutional mechanism' (p. 215). This observation remains one of the most important cautions for criminological research.

Michael Geerken's essay (Chapter 10) extends that concern about official records to the use of rap sheets to compile 'lifetime' pictures of crime. Geerken compares the data from the New Orleans local police with the state and federal repositories and reveals substantial variation, depending on the source. The comparison shows that there can be a fairly large number of false negatives at the local level and that this false negative rate has a racial component based on mobility. Whites tend to be more mobile than blacks and are therefore more likely to show up in the state system than in the New Orleans system. This essay shows that reliance on the New

Orleans system would lead to the misleading conclusion that black robbers have longer rapsheets than do white robbers.

During the 1980s, the concerns raised by researchers about official data led to an increase in self-reported offending measures. Not surprisingly, the self-reported measures have been found to have specific limitations as well. The (1992) essay by Julie Horney and Ineke Marshall (Chapter 11) deals with the resolution of a question about self-reported offending rates. Specifically, some researchers were concerned that the high-profile Rand Inmate Surveys led to inflated measures of the offending rate. The authors conducted a random experiment in which two groups of inmates reported their past offending in two ways – the Rand method and a newer approach based on an event history calendar. The methods led to similar results. This essay is noteworthy for the way in which it uses rigorous methods to address a measurement issue.

Janet Lauritsen's (1998) essay (Chapter 12) is another exploration of self-reported offending in longitudinal data. She demonstrates that there are apparently survey fatigue/testing effects in the National Youth Survey, whereby people start lying in response to criminal history questions – seemingly aware that there will be a long list of follow-up questions if they respond accurately by reporting criminal involvement. Regardless of age, there is a constant decrease in reported delinquency from wave to wave that cannot be accounted for by period effects.

Finally, the essay by David Farrington, Rolf Loeber, Magda Stouthamer-Loeber, Welmoet Van Kammen and Laura Schmidt (Chapter 13) is included because it represents an important example of validity testing using multiple reporting sources, including self report and official record data. The authors' conclusions support the use of self-reported crime scales, but also encourage the use of additional information when available. There are other noteworthy examples of this type of introspective validity testing, including Krohn, Stern, Thornberry and Jang's (1992) comparison of parental and student perceptions of family life and Wiersema, Loftin and McDowall's (2000) comparison of homicide reports at the city level from the Supplemental Homicide Reports and the National Vital Statistics System.

Descriptive Analysis of Quantitative Data

Although causal analysis is generally considered the central concern of statistical methods, we are struck by the growing importance of careful description in criminology. We have already discussed three of the essays which deal with developmental trajectories in the body of the text (Chapters 17, 18, 19). We have chosen to include three other very different essays to emphasize the diversity of approaches that people have taken to describe data in criminology. Michael Maltz's essay (Chapter 14) demonstrates the utility of using graphs to display information. The essay by David Kennedy, Anthony Braga and Anne Piehl (Chapter 15) demonstrates the application of crime mapping to the problem of gang violence. This essay is part of an impressive crime prevention programme in Boston, but our interest here is in highlighting crime mapping as a descriptive technique that has gained widespread acceptance in applied policing.

The essay by Arnold Barnett, Alfred Blumstein and David Farrington (Chapter 16) is included as a clear example of the criminal career model that has had such a strong influence in developmental criminology and, indeed, criminology more generally. This method, which was directly imported from operations research, played an important role in identifying key concepts and encouraging the collection of new longitudinal data. This essay fits a simple two-parameter model (rate of offending and desistance probability) to two groups of offenders using data to age 25, and predicts desistance. It then compares its prediction to reality, using data to age 32. Despite the simplicity of the models, the essay shows that basic descriptive analysis can provide powerful and comprehensive descriptions of crime characteristics

Causal Modelling

As we noted above, causal analysis has, from the outset, been a central concern in criminological research. In Part I we identified ground-breaking essays that utilize innovative experimental designs to solve threats to valid causal inferences. In Part V we present essays that rely on observational statistical methods to model criminological problems or the effects of criminal justice interventions. Such techniques have advanced significantly over the past two decades.

The essay by Ian Ayres and Steven Levitt (Chapter 20) is included for two reasons. First, it is a substantively interesting and important essay that uses strong empirical methods. It demonstrates fairly convincingly that car theft declines with the onset of Lojack, an automobile anti-theft device. Second, the essay is not written by criminologists but by economists. The number of economists who are studying crime has been growing, led by Steve Levitt, a prominent young economist at the University of Chicago. The main strength of this new breed of economists is causal analysis. We think that there is much promise for the advancement of quantitative criminology in the collaboration between criminologists and economists (see also Bushway and Reuter, 2005).

In Chapter 21 David McDowall, Colin Loftin and Brian Wiersema use an interrupted time series research design, which is a strong but underutilized technique in criminology. Theirs is also an important study in that it pools data from multiple studies to increase statistical power. The essay by David Greenberg (Chapter 22) also examines issues in time series data. Indeed, many of the key conceptual and empirical issues that arise in time series research are raised in an interesting substantive context in this study. Both essays demonstrate an impressive understanding of state-of-the-art statistical methods developed in statistics and econometrics.

Conclusions

The essays in this volume illustrate the ways in which importation, introspection and innovation have been used to create a subfield which we term 'quantitative criminology'. The advances in quantitative criminology over the last three decades have been as dramatic as, if not more dramatic than, those of other areas of criminology, and we think that we are likely to see even more interest in quantitative criminology in the coming decades. If we are right in our view, then we would expect not only greater sophistication in criminology journals, and more emphasis on methodological and statistical training in criminology and criminal justice programmes, but also the emergence of a cadre of quantitative criminologists who will play a leadership role more generally in the development of quantitative methods in the social sciences. These trends which are already apparent, suggest that the future of quantitative criminology is a bright one. We hope that this edited volume will provide a benchmark for a new generation of quantitative criminologists who will play a leadership role not only in exploring and understanding crime and justice, but also in advancing quantitative methods in our field.

References

Berk, Richard (1983), 'An Introduction to Sample Selection Bias in Sociological Data', *American Sociological Review*, **48**, pp. 386–98.

Bushway, Shawn and Reuter, Peter (2005), 'Collaborating with Economists', *The Criminologist*, **30**, pp. 1–3.

Collins, Linda M. and Sayers, Aline G. (2001), *New Methods for the Analysis of Change*, New York: American Psychological Association.

Hagan, John and Palloni Alberto (1988), 'Crimes as Social Events in the Life Course: Reconceiving a Criminological Controversy', *Criminology*, **26**(1), pp. 87–100.

Krohn, Marvin D., Stern, Susan B., Thornberry, Terence P. and Jang, Sung Joon (1992), 'The Measurement of Family Process Variables: An Examination of Adolescent and Parent Perceptions of Family Life on Delinquent Behavior', *Journal of Quantitative Criminology*, **8**, pp. 287–315.

Nagin, Daniel S. and Land, Kenneth (1993), 'Age, Criminal Careers and Population Heterogeneity: Specification and Estimation of a Nonparametric Mixed-Poisson Model', *Criminology*, **31**, pp. 327–62.

Sherman, Lawrence W., Gottfredson, Denise C., MacKenzie, Doris L., Eck, John E., Reuter, Peter and Bushway, Shawn D. (1997), *Preventing Crime: What Works, What Doesn't, What's Promising*, Washington DC: US Department of Justice, National Institute of Justice.

Stolzenberg R.M. and Relles, D.A. (1990), 'Theory Testing in a World of Constrained Research Design', *Sociological Methods & Research*, **18**, pp. 395–415.

Wiersema, Brian, Loftin, Colin and McDowall, David (2000), 'A Comparison of Supplemental Homicide Reports and National Vital Statistics System Homicide Estimates for U.S. Counties', *Homicide Studies*, **4**, pp. 317–40.

Part I
Research Design and Study Outcomes

[1]

THE SPECIFIC DETERRENT EFFECTS OF
ARREST FOR DOMESTIC ASSAULT*

LAWRENCE W. SHERMAN   RICHARD A. BERK
University of Maryland. College Park   *University of California. Santa Barbara*
and Police Foundation

with

42 Patrol Officers of the Minneapolis Police Department,
Nancy Wester, Donileen Loseke, David Rauma, Debra Morrow, Amy Curtis,
Kay Gamble, Roy Roberts, Phyllis Newton, and Gayle Gubman

The specific deterrence doctrine and labeling theory predict opposite effects of punishment on individual rates of deviance. The limited cross-sectional evidence available on the question is inconsistent, and experimental evidence has been lacking. The Police Foundation and the Minneapolis Police Department tested these hypotheses in a field experiment on domestic violence. Three police responses to simple assault were randomly assigned to legally eligible suspects: an arrest; "advice" (including, in some cases, informal mediation); and an order to the suspect to leave for eight hours. The behavior of the suspect was tracked for six months after the police intervention, with both official data and victim reports. The official recidivism measures show that the arrested suspects manifested significantly less subsequent violence than those who were ordered to leave. The victim report data show that the arrested subjects manifested significantly less subsequent violence than those who were advised. The findings falsify a deviance amplification model of labeling theory beyond initial labeling, and fail to falsify the specific deterrence prediction for a group of offenders with a high percentage of prior histories of both domestic violence and other kinds of crime.

Sociologists since Durkheim ([1893] 1972:126) have speculated about how the punishment of individuals affects their behavior. Two bodies of literature, specific deterrence and labeling, have developed competing predictions (Thorsell and Klemke, 1972). Durkheim, for example, implicitly assumed with Bentham that the pains of punishment deter people from repeating the crimes for which they are punished, especially when punishment is certain, swift and severe. More recent work has fostered the ironic view that punishment often makes individuals more likely to commit crimes because of altered interactional structures, foreclosed legal opportunities and secondary deviance (Lemert,

1951, 1967; Schwartz and Skolnick, 1962; Becker, 1963).

Neither prediction can muster consistent empirical support. The few studies that allege effects generally employ weak designs in which it is difficult, if not impossible, to control plausibly for all important factors confounded with criminal justice sanctions and the rule-breaking behavior that may follow. Thus, some claim to show that punishment deters individuals punished (Clarke, 1966; F.B.I., 1967:34–44; Cohen and Stark, 1974:30; Kraut, 1976; Murray and Cox, 1979; McCord, 1983), while others claim to show that punishment increases their deviance (Gold and Williams, 1969; Shoham, 1974; Farrington, 1977; Klemke, 1978). Yet all of these studies suffer either methodological or conceptual flaws as tests of the effects of punishment (Zimring and Hawkins, 1973; Gibbs, 1975; Hirschi, 1975; Tittle, 1975), especially the confounding of incarceration with attempts to rehabilitate and the frequent failure to differentiate effects for different types of offenders and offenses (Lempert, 1981–1982).

Perhaps the strongest evidence to date comes from a randomized experiment conducted by Lincoln et al. (unpubl.). The experiment randomly assigned juveniles, who had already been apprehended, to four different treatments ranked in their formality: release; two types of diversion; and formal

---

* Direct all correspondence to: Lawrence W. Sherman, Police Foundation, 1909 K Street N.W., Washington, D.C. 20006.

This paper was supported by Grant #80–IJ–CX–0042 to the Police Foundation from the National Institute of Justice, Crime Control Theory Program. Points of view or opinions stated in this document do not necessarily represent the official position of the U.S. Department of Justice, the Minneapolis Police Department, or the Police Foundation.

We wish to express our thanks to the Minneapolis Police Department and its Chief, Anthony V. Bouza, for their cooperation, and to Sarah Fenstermaker Berk, Peter H. Rossi, Albert J. Reiss, Jr., James Q. Wilson, Richard Lempert, and Charles Tittle for comments on an earlier draft of this paper.

charging. The more formal and official the processing, the more frequent the repeat criminality over a two-year follow-up period. This study supports labeling theory for arrested juveniles, although it cannot isolate the labeling or deterrent effects of arrest per se.

In all likelihood, of course, punishment has not one effect, but many, varying across types of people and situations (Chambliss, 1967; Andenaes, 1971). As Lempert (1981–1982:523) argues, "it is only by attending to a range of such offenses that we will be able to develop a general theory of deterrence." The variables affecting the deterrability of juvenile delinquency, white-collar crime, armed robbery and domestic violence may be quite different. Careful accumulation of findings from different settings will help us differentiate the variables which are crime- or situation-specific and those which apply across settings.

In this spirit, we report here a study of the impact of punishment in a particular setting, for a particular offense, and for particular kinds of individuals. Over an eighteen-month period, police in Minneapolis applied one of three intervention strategies in incidents of misdemeanor domestic assault: arrest; ordering the offender from the premises; or some form of advice which could include mediation. The three interventions were assigned randomly to households, and a critical outcome was the rate of repeat incidents. The relative effect of arrest should hold special interest for the specific deterrence–labeling controversy.

POLICING DOMESTIC ASSAULTS

Police have been typically reluctant to make arrests for domestic violence (Berk and Loseke, 1981), as well as for a wide range of other kinds of offenses, unless victims demand an arrest, the suspect insults the officer, or other factors are present (Sherman, 1980). Parnas's (1972) qualitative observations of the Chicago police found four categories of police action in these situations: negotiating or otherwise "talking out" the dispute; threatening the disputants and then leaving; asking one of the parties to leave the premises; or (very rarely) making an arrest.

Similar patterns are found in many other cities. Surveys of battered women who tried to have their domestic assailants arrested report that arrest occurred in 10 percent (Roy, 1977:35) or 3 percent (see Langley and Levy, 1977:219) of the cases. Surveys of police agencies in Illinois (Illinois Law Enforcement Commission, 1978) and New York (Office of the Minority Leader, 1978) found explicit policies against arrest in the majority of the agencies surveyed. Despite the fact that violence is reported to be present in one-third (Bard and Zacker, 1974) to two-thirds (Black, 1980) of all domestic disturbances police respond to, police department data show arrests in only 5 percent of those disturbances in Oakland (Hart, n.d., cited in Meyer and Lorimer, 1977:21), 6 percent of those disturbances in a Colorado city (Patrick et al., n.d., cited in Meyer and Lorimer, 1977:21) and 6 percent in Los Angeles County (Emerson, 1979).

The best available evidence on the frequency of arrest is the observations from the Black and Reiss study of Boston, Washington and Chicago police in 1966 (Black, 1980:182). Police responding to disputes in those cities made arrests in 27 percent of violent felonies and 17 percent of the violent misdemeanors. Among married couples (Black, 1980:158), they made arrests in 26 percent of the cases, but tried to remove one of the parties in 38 percent of the cases.

An apparent preference of many police for separating the parties rather than arresting the offender has been attacked from two directions over the last fifteen years. The original critique came from clinical psychologists, who agreed that police should rarely make arrests (Potter, 1978:46; Fagin, 1978:123–24) in domestic assault cases, and argued that police should mediate the disputes responsible for the violence. A highly publicized demonstration project teaching police special counseling skills for family crisis intervention (Bard, 1970) failed to show a reduction in violence, but was interpreted as a success nonetheless. By 1977, a national survey of police agencies with 100 or more officers found that over 70 percent reported a family crisis intervention training program in operation. While it is not clear whether these programs reduced separation and increased mediation, a decline in arrests was noted for some (Wylie et al., 1976). Indeed, many sought explicitly to reduce the number of arrests (University of Rochester, 1974; Ketterman and Kravitz, 1978).

By the mid-1970s, police practices were criticized from the opposite direction by feminist groups. Just as psychologists succeeded in having many police agencies respond to domestic violence as "half social work and half police work," feminists began to argue that police put "too much emphasis on the social work aspect and not enough on the criminal" (Langley and Levy, 1977:218). Widely publicized lawsuits in New York and Oakland sought to compel police to make arrests in every case of domestic assault, and state legislatures were lobbied successfully to reduce the evidentiary requirements needed for police to make arrests for misdemeanor domestic assaults. Some legislatures are now considering statutes requiring police to make arrests in these cases.

The feminist critique was bolstered by a study (Police Foundation, 1976) showing that for 85 percent of a sample of spousal homicides, police had intervened at least once in the preceding two years. For 54 percent of the homicides, police had intervened five or more times. But it was impossible to determine from the cross-sectional data whether making more or fewer arrests would have reduced the homicide rate.

In sum, police officers confronting a domestic assault suspect face at least three conflicting options, urged on them by different groups with different theories. The officers' colleagues might recommend forced separation as a means of achieving short-term peace. Alternatively, the officers' trainers might recommend mediation as a means of getting to the underlying cause of the "dispute" (in which both parties are implicitly assumed to be at fault). Finally, the local women's organizations may recommend that the officer protect the victim (whose "fault," if any, is legally irrelevant) and enforce the law to deter such acts in the future.

RESEARCH DESIGN

In response to these conflicting recommendations, the Police Foundation and the Minneapolis Police Department agreed to conduct a randomized experiment. The design called for random assignment of arrest, separation, and some form of advice which could include mediation at the officer's discretion. In addition, there was to be a six-month follow-up period to measure the frequency and seriousness of domestic violence after each police intervention. The advantages of randomized experiments are well known and need not be reviewed here (see, e.g., Cook and Campbell, 1979).

The design only applied to simple (misdemeanor) domestic assaults, where both the suspect and the victim were present when the police arrived. Thus, the experiment included only those cases in which police were empowered (but not required) to make arrests under a recently liberalized Minnesota state law; the police officer must have probable cause to believe that a cohabitant or spouse had assaulted the victim within the last four hours (but police need not have witnessed the assault). Cases of life-threatening or severe injury, usually labeled as a felony (aggravated assault), were excluded from the design for ethical reasons.

The design called for each officer to carry a pad of report forms, color coded for the three different police actions. Each time the officers

encountered a situation that fit the experiment's criteria, they were to take whatever action was indicated by the report form on the top of the pad. We numbered the forms and arranged them in random order for each officer. The integrity of the random assignment was to be monitored by research staff observers riding on patrol for a sample of evenings.

After police action was taken, the officer was to fill out a brief report and give it to the research staff for follow-up. As a further check on the randomization process, the staff logged in the reports in the order in which they were received and made sure that the sequence corresponded to the original assignment of treatments.

Anticipating something of the victims' background, a predominantly minority, female research staff was employed to contact the victims for a detailed face-to-face interview, to be followed by telephone follow-up interviews every two weeks for 24 weeks. The interviews were designed primarily to measure the frequency and seriousness of victimizations caused by the suspect after the police intervention.[1] The research staff also collected criminal justice reports that mentioned the suspect's name during the six-month follow-up period.

CONDUCT OF THE EXPERIMENT

As is common in field experiments, implementation of the research design entailed some slippage from the original plan. In order to gather data as quickly as possible, the experiment was originally located in the two Minneapolis precincts with the highest density of domestic violence crime reports and arrests. The 34 officers assigned to those areas were invited to a three-day planning meeting and asked to participate in the study for one year. All but one agreed. The conference also produced a draft order for the chief's signature specifying the rules of the experiment. These rules created several new situations to be excluded from the experiment, such as if a suspect attempted to assault police officers, a victim persistently demanded an arrest, or if both parties were injured. These additional exceptions, unfortunately, allowed for the possibility of differential attrition from the separation and mediation treatments. The im-

---

[1] The protocols were based heavily on instruments designed for an NIMH-funded study of spousal violence conducted by Richard A. Berk, Sarah Fenstermaker Berk, and Ann D. Witte (Center for Studies of Crime and Delinquency, Grant #MH-34616–01). A similar protocol was developed for the suspects, but only twenty-five of them agreed to be interviewed.

plications for internal validity are discussed later.

The experiment began on March 17, 1981, with the expectation that it would take about one year to produce about 300 cases (it ran until August 1, 1982, and produced 330 case reports.) The officers agreed to meet monthly with the project director (Sherman) and the project manager (Wester). By the third or fourth month, two facts became clear: (1) only about 15 to 20 officers were either coming to meetings or turning in cases; and (2) the rate at which the cases were turned in would make it difficult to complete the project in one year. By November, we decided to recruit more officers in order to obtain cases more rapidly. Eighteen additional officers joined the project, but like the original group, most of these officers only turned in one or two cases. Indeed, three of the original officers produced almost 28 percent of the cases, in part because they worked a particularly violent beat, and in part because they had a greater commitment to the study. Since the treatments were randomized by officer, this created no internal validity problem. However, it does raise construct validity problems to which we will later return.

There is little doubt that many of the officers occasionally failed to follow fully the experimental design. Some of the failures were due to forgetfulness, such as leaving the report pads at home or at the police station. Other failures derived from misunderstanding about whether the experiment applied in certain situations; application of the experimental rules under complex circumstances was sometimes confusing. Finally, from time to time there were situations that were simply not covered by the experiment's rules.

Whether any officers intentionally subverted the design is unclear. The plan to monitor randomization with ride-along observers broke down because of the unexpectedly low incidence of cases meeting the experimental criteria. The observers had to ride for many weeks before they observed an officer apply one of the treatments. We tried to solve this problem with "chase-alongs," in which the observers rode in their own car with a portable police radio and drove to the scene of any domestic call dispatched to any officer in the precinct. Even this method failed.

Thus, we are left with at least two disturbing possibilities. First, police officers anticipating (e.g., from the dispatch call) a particular kind of incident, and finding the upcoming experimental treatment inappropriate, may have occasionally decided to void the experiment. That is, they may have chosen to exclude certain cases in violation of the experimental design. This amounts to differential attrition,

which is clearly a threat to internal validity. Note that if police officers blindly decided to exclude certain cases (e.g., because they did not feel like filling out the extra forms on a given day), all would be well for internal validity.

Second, since the recording officer's pad was supposed to govern the actions of each pair of officers, some officers may also have switched the assignment of driver and recording officer after deciding a case fit the study in order to obtain a treatment they wanted to apply. If the treatments were switched between driver and recorder, then the internal validity was again threatened. However, this was almost certainly uncommon because it was generally easier not to fill out a report at all than to switch.

Table 1 shows the degree to which the treatments were delivered as designed.[2] Ninety-nine percent of the suspects targeted for arrest actually were arrested, while only 78 percent of those to receive advice did, and only 73 percent of those to be sent out of the residence for eight hours were actually sent. One explanation for this pattern, consistent with the experimental guidelines, is that mediating and sending were more difficult ways for police to control the situation, with a greater likelihood that officers might resort to arrest as a fallback position. When the assigned treatment is arrest, there is no need for a fallback position. For example, some offenders may have refused to comply with an order to leave the premises.

Such differential attrition would potentially bias estimates of the relative effectiveness of arrest by removing uncooperative and difficult offenders from the mediation and separation treatments. Any deterrent effect could be underestimated and, in the extreme, artifactual support for deviance amplification could be found. That is, the arrest group would have too many "bad guys" *relative* to the other treatments.

We can be more systematic about other factors affecting the movement of cases away from the designed treatments. The three delivered treatments represent a polychotomous outcome amenable to multivariate statistical analysis. We applied a multinominal logit formulation (Amemiya, 1981:1516–19; Maddala, 1983:34–37), which showed that the designed treatment was the dominant cause of the treatment actually received (a finding suggested by Table 1). However, we also found that five other variables had a statistically sig-

---

[2] Sixteen cases were dropped because no treatment was applied or because the case did not belong in the study (i.e., a fight between a father and son).

Table 1. Designed and Delivered Police Treatments in Spousal Assault Cases

Designed Treatment	Delivered Treatment			
	Arrest	Advise	Separate	Total
Arrest	98.9%	0.0%	1.1%	29.3%
	(91)	(0)	(1)	(92)
Advise	17.6%	77.8%	4.6%	34.4%
	(19)	(84)	(5)	(108)
Separate	22.8%	4.4%	72.8%	36.3%
	(26)	(5)	(83)	(114)
Total	43.4%	28.3%	28.3%	100%
	(136)	(89)	(89)	(314)

nificant effect on "upgrading" the separation and advice treatments to arrests: whether police reported the suspect was rude; whether police reported the suspect tried to assault one (or both) of the police officers; whether police reported weapons were involved; whether the victim persistently demanded a citizen's arrest; and whether a restraining order was being violated. We found no evidence that the background or characteristics of the suspect or victim (e.g., race) affected the treatment received.

Overall, the logit model fit the data very well. For well over 80 percent of the cases, the model's predicted treatment was the same as the actual treatment (i.e., correct classifications), and minor alterations in the assignment threshold would have substantially improved matters. Moreover, a chi-square test on the residuals was not statistically significant (i.e., the observed and predicted treatments differed by no more than chance). In summary, we were able to model the assignment process with remarkable success simply by employing the rules of the experimental protocol (for more details, see Berk and Sherman, 1983).

We were less fortunate with the interviews of the victims: only 205 (of 330, counting the few repeat victims twice) could be located and initial interviews obtained, a 62 percent completion rate. Many of the victims simply could not be found, either for the initial interview or for follow-ups: they either left town, moved somewhere else or refused to answer the phone or doorbell. The research staff made up to 20 attempts to contact these victims, and often employed investigative techniques (asking friends and neighbors) to find them. Sometimes these methods worked, only to have the victim give an outright refusal or break one or more appointments to meet the interviewer at a "safe" location for the interview.

The response rate to the bi-weekly follow-up interviews was even lower than for the initial interview, as in much research on women crime victims. After the first interview, for which the victims were paid $20, there was a gradual falloff in completed interviews with

each successive wave; only 161 victims provided all 12 follow-up interviews over the six months, a completion rate of 49 percent. Whether paying for the follow-up interviews would have improved the response rate is unclear; it would have added over $40,000 to the cost of the research. When the telephone interviews yielded few reports of violence, we moved to conduct every fourth interview in person, which appeared to produce more reports of violence.

There is absolutely no evidence that the experimental treatment assigned to the offender affected the victim's decision to grant initial interviews. We estimated a binary logit equation for the dichotomous outcome: whether or not an initial interview was obtained. Regressors included the experimental treatments (with one necessarily excluded), race of the victim, race of the offender, and a number of attributes of the incident (from the police sheets). A joint test on the full set of regressors failed to reject the null hypothesis that all of the logit coefficients were zero. More important for our purposes, none of the t-values for the treatments was in excess of 1.64; indeed, none was greater than 1.0 in absolute value. In short, while the potential for sample selection bias (Heckman, 1979; Berk, 1983) certainly exists (and is considered later), that bias does not stem from obvious sources, particularly the treatments. This implies that we may well be able to meaningfully examine experimental effects for the subset of individuals from whom initial interviews were obtained. The same conclusions followed when the follow-up interviews were considered.

In sum, despite the practical difficulties of controlling an experiment and interviewing crime victims in an emotionally charged and violent social context, the experiment succeeded in producing a promising sample of 314 cases with complete official outcome measures and an apparently unbiased sample of responses from the victims in those cases.

RESULTS

The 205 completed initial interviews provide some sense of who the subjects are, although the data may not properly represent the characteristics of the full sample of 314. They show the now familiar pattern of domestic violence cases coming to police attention being disproportionately unmarried couples with lower than average educational levels, disproportionately minority and mixed race (black male, white female), and who were very likely to have had prior violent incidents with police intervention. The 60 percent suspect unemployment rate is strikingly high in a community

Table 2. Victim and Suspect Characteristics: Initial Interview Data and Police Sheets

	Victims	Suspects
A. Unemployment		
Victims 61%		
Suspects 60%		
B. Relationship of Suspect to Victim		
Divorced or separated husband	3%	
Unmarried male lover	45%	
Current husband	35%	
Wife or girlfriend	2%	
Son, brother, roommate, other	15%	
C. Prior Assaults and Police Involvement		
Victims assaulted by suspect, last six months	80%	
Police intervention in domestic dispute,		
last six months	60%	
Couple in Counseling Program	27%	
D. Prior Arrests of Male Suspects		
Ever Arrested For Any Offense	59%	
Ever Arested For Crime Against Person	31%	
Ever Arrested on Domestic Violence Statute	5%	
Ever Arrested On An Alcohol Offense	29%	
E. Mean Age		
Victims 30 years		
Suspects 32 years		
F. Education	Victims	Suspects
< high school	43%	42%
high school only	33%	36%
> high school	24%	22%
G. Race	Victims	Suspects
White	57%	45%
Black	23%	36%
Native American	18%	16%
Other	2%	3%

N = 205 (Those cases for which initial interviews were obtained)

with only about 5 percent of the workforce unemployed. The 59 percent prior arrest rate is also strikingly high, suggesting (with the 80 percent prior domestic assault rate) that the suspects generally are experienced lawbreakers who are accustomed to police interventions. But with the exception of the heavy representation of Native Americans (due to Minneapolis' unique proximity to many Indian reservations), the characteristics in Table 2 are probably close to those of domestic violence cases coming to police attention in other large U.S. cities.

Two kinds of outcome measures will be considered. One is a *police-recorded "failure"* of the offender to survive the six-month follow-up period without having police generate a written report on the suspect for domestic violence, either through an offense or an arrest report written by any officer in the department, or through a subsequent report to the project research staff of a randomized (or other) intervention by officers participating in the experiment. A second kind of measure comes from the *interviews with victims*, in which victims were asked if there had been a repeat incident with the same suspect, broadly defined to include an actual assault, threatened assault, or property damage.

The two kinds of outcomes were each formulated in two complementary ways: as a dummy variable (i.e., repeat incident or not) and as the amount of time elapsed from the treatment to either a failure or the end of the follow-up period. For each of the two outcomes, three analyses were performed: the first using a linear probability model; the second using a logit formulation; and the third using a proportional hazard approach. The dummy outcome was employed for the linear probability and logit analyses, while the time-to-failure was employed for the proportional hazard method.[3]

Given the randomization, we began in traditional analysis of variance fashion. The official measure of a repeat incident was regressed on the treatment received for the sub-

---

[3] In addition to the linear probability model, the logit and proportional hazard formulations can be expressed in forms such that the outcome is a probability (e.g., the probability of a new violent incident). However, three slightly different response functions are implied. We had no theoretical basis for selecting the proper response function, and consequently used all three. We expected that the substantive results could be essentially invariant across the three formulations.

Table 3. Experimental Results for Police Data

Variable	Linear		Logistic		Proportional Hazard Rate	
	Coef	t-value	Coef	t-value	Coef	t-value
Intercept (separate)	0.24	5.03*	−1.10	−4.09*	—	—
Arrest	−0.14	−2.21*	−1.02	−2.21*	−0.97	−2.28*
Advise	−0.05	−0.79	−0.31	−0.76	−0.32	−0.88
	F = 2.01		Chi-square = 5.19		Chi-square = 5.48	
	P = .07		P = .07		P = .06	
N = 314						

  * $p < .05$. two-tailed test.

set of 314 cases (out of 330) that fell within the definition of the experiment. Compared to the baseline treatment of separation, which had the highest recidivism rate in the police data, the arrest treatment reduced repeat occurrences by a statistically significant amount ($t = -2.38$). Twenty-six percent of those separated committed a repeat assault, compared to 13 percent of those arrested. The mediation treatment was statistically indistinguishable from the other two. To help put this in perspective, 18.2 percent of the households failed overall.

The apparent treatment effect for arrest in this conventional analysis was suggestive, but there was a danger of biased estimates from the "upgrading" of some separation and advise treatments. In response, we applied variations on the corrections recommended by Barnow et al. (1980: esp. 55). In brief, we inserted instrumental variables in place of the delivered treatments when the treatment effects were analyzed. These instruments, in turn, were constructed from the multinomial logit model described earlier.[4]

Table 3 shows the results of the adjusted models. The first two columns report the results for the linear probability approach. Again, we find a statistically significant effect for arrest ($t = -2.21$). However, it is well known that the linear probability model will produce inefficient estimates of the regression coefficients and biased (and inconsistent) estimates of the standard errors. Significance tests, therefore, are suspect. Consequently, we also estimated a logit model, with pretty much the same result. At the mean of the endogenous variable (i.e., 18.2 percent), the logit coefficient for arrest translates into nearly the same effect (i.e., −.15) found with the linear probability model ($t = -2.21$).

One might still object that the use of a dummy variable outcome neglects right-hand censoring. In brief, one cannot observe failures that occur after the end of the experimental period, so that biased (and inconsistent) results follow. Thus, we applied a proportional hazard analysis (Lawless, 1982: Ch. 7) that adjusts for right-hand censoring. In this model the time-to-failure dependent variable is transformed into (roughly) the probability at any given moment during the six-month follow-up period of a new offense occurring, given that no new offenses have yet been committed. The last two columns of Table 3 indicate that, again, an effect for arrest surfaces ($t = -2.28$). The coefficient of −0.97 implies that compared to the baseline of separation, those experiencing an arrest were less likely to commit a new battery by a multiplicative factor of .38 (i.e., e raised to the −0.97 power). If the earlier results are translated into comparable terms, the ·effects described by the proportional hazard formulation are the largest wé have seen (see footnote 4). But the major message is that the arrest effect holds up under three different statistical methods based on slightly different response functions. Overall, the police data indicate that the separation treatment produces the highest recidivism, arrest produces the lowest, with the impact of "advise" (from doing nothing to mediation) indistinguishable from the other two effects.

Table 4 shows the results when self-report data are used. A "failure" is defined as a new assault, property destruction or a threatened assault. (Almost identical results follow from a definition including only a new assault.) These results suggest a different ordering of the effects, with arrest still producing the lowest recidivism rate (at 19%), but with advice producing the highest (37%).

Overall, 28.9 percent of the suspects in Table 4 "failed." Still, the results are much the same as found for the official failure measure. However, given the effective sample of 161, we are vulnerable to sample selection bias. In response, we applied Heckman's (1979) sample selection corrections. The results were virtually ᵢunchanged (and are therefore not reported).

---

[4] We did *not* simply use the conditional expectations of a multinomial logit model. We used an alternative procedure to capitalize on the initial random assignment. The details can be found in Berk and Sherman (1983).

Table 4. Experimental Results for Victim Report Data

Variable	Linear		Logistic		Proportional Hazard Rate	
	Coef	t-value	Coef	t-value	Coef	t-value
Intercept (advise)	0.37	5.54*	−0.53	−1.70	—	—
Arrest	−0.18	−2.00*	−0.94	−2.01*	−0.82	−2.05*
Separate	−0.04	−0.35	−0.15	−0.10	−0.27	−0.09
	F = 2.31		Chi-square = 4.78		Chi-square = 4.36	
	P = .10		P = .09		P = .11	

N = 161 (Those cases for which *all* follow-up interviews were obtained)

* p < .05, two-tailed test.

An obvious rival hypothesis to the deterrent effect of arrest is that arrest incapacitates. If the arrested suspects spend a large portion of the next six months in jail, they would be expected to have lower recidivism rates. But the initial interview data show this is not the case: of those arrested, 43 percent were released within one day, 86 percent were released within one week, and only 14 percent were released after one week or had not yet been released at the time of the *initial* victim interview. Clearly, there was very little incapacitation, especially in the context of a six-month follow-up. Indeed, virtually all those arrested were released before the first follow-up interview. Nevertheless, we introduced the length of the initial stay in jail as a control variable. Consistent with expectations, the story was virtually unchanged.

Another perspective on the incapacitation issue can be obtained by looking at repeat violence which occurred shortly after the police intervened. If incapacitation were at work, a dramatic effect should be found in households experiencing arrest, especially compared to the households experiencing advice. Table 5 shows how quickly the couples were reunited, and of those reunited in one day, how many of them, according to the victim, began to argue or had physical violence again. It is apparent that *all* of the police interventions effectively stopped the violence for a 24-hour period after the couples were reunited. Even the renewed quarrels were few, at least with our relatively small sample size. Hence, there is again no evidence for an incapacitation effect. There is

also no evidence for the reverse: that arrested offenders would take it out on the victim when the offender returned home.

DISCUSSION AND CONCLUSIONS

The experiment's results are subject to several qualifications. One caution is that both kinds of outcome measures have uncertain construct validity. The official measure no doubt neglects a large number of repeat incidents, in part because many of them were not reported, and in part because police are sometimes reluctant to turn a family "dispute" into formal police business. However, the key is whether there is *differential* measurement error by the experimental treatments; an undercount randomly distributed across the three treatments will not bias the estimated experimental effects (i.e., only the estimate of the intercept will be biased). It is hard to imagine that differential undercounting would come solely from the actions of police, since most officers were not involved in the experiment and could not have known what treatment had been delivered.

However, there might be differential undercounting if offenders who were arrested were less likely to remain on the scene after a new assault. Having been burned once, they might not wait around for a second opportunity. And police told us they were less likely during the follow-up period (and more generally) to record an incident if the offender was not present. For example, there would be no arrest forms since the offender was not available to arrest. If all we had were the official outcome

Table 5. Speed of Reunion and Recidivism by Police Action

Police Action	Time of Reunion				New Quarrel Within A Day	New Violence Within A Day
	Within One Day	More than One Day but Less Than One Week	Longer or No Return	(N)		
Arrested (and released)	38%	30%	32%	(N=76)	(2)	(1)
Separated	57%	31%	10%	(N=54)	(6)	(3)
Advised	—	—	—	(N=72)	(4)	(1)

N = 202 (Down from the 205 in Table 2 due to missing data)

measures, there would be no easy way to refute this possibility. Fortunately, the self-report data are *not* vulnerable on these grounds, and the experimental effects are found nevertheless.

It is also possible that the impact for arrest found in the official outcome measure represents a reluctance of *victims* to call the police. That is, for some victims, the arrest may have been an undesirable intervention, and rather than face the prospect of another arrest from a new incident, these victims might decide not to invoke police sanctions. For example, the arrest may have cost the offender several days' work and put financial stress on the household. Or the offender may have threatened serious violence if the victim ever called the police again. However, we can again observe that the self-report data would not have been vulnerable to such concerns, and the experimental effects were found nevertheless. The only way we can see how the self-report data would fail to support the official data is if respondents in households experiencing arrest became more hesitant to admit to *interviewers* that they had been beaten a second time. Since there was no differential response rate by treatment, this possibility seems unlikely. If the arrested suspects had intimidated their victims more than the other two treatment groups, it seems more likely that such intimidation would have shown up in noncooperation with the interviews than in differential underreporting of violence in the course of the interviews.

This is not to say that the self-report data are flawless; indeed there is some reason to believe that there was undercounting of new incidents. However, just as for the official data, unless there is differential undercounting by the experimental treatments, all is well. We can think of no good reasons why differential undercounting should materialize. In summary, internal validity looks rather sound.

The construct validity of the treatments is more problematic. The advice and separation interventions have unclear content. Perhaps "good" mediation, given consistently, would fare better compared to arrest. The more general point is that the treatment effects for arrest are only relative to the impact of the other interventions. Should their content change, the relative impact of arrest could change as well.

Likewise, we noted earlier that a few officers accounted for a disproportionate number of the cases. What we have been interpreting, therefore, as results from different intervention strategies could reflect the special abilities of certain officers to make arrest particularly effective relative to the other treatments. For example, these officers may have been less skilled in mediation techniques. However, we re-estimated the models reported in Tables 3 and 4, including an interaction effect to capture the special contributions of our high-productivity officers. The new variable was not statistically significant, and the treatment effect for arrest remained.

Finally, Minneapolis is hardly representative of all urban areas. The Minneapolis Police Department has many unusual characteristics, and different jurisdictions might well keep suspects in custody for longer or shorter periods of time. The message should be clear: external validity will have to wait for replications.

Despite these qualifications, it is apparent that we have found no support for the deviance amplification point of view. The arrest intervention certainly did not make things worse and may well have made things better. There are, of course, many rejoinders. In particular, over 80 percent of offenders had assaulted the victims in the previous six months, and in over 60 percent of the households the police had intervened during that interval. Almost 60 percent of the suspects had previously been arrested for something. Thus, the counterproductive consequences of police sanction, if any, may for many offenders have already been felt. In labeling theory terms, secondary deviation may already have been established, producing a ceiling for the amplification effects of formal sanctioning. However, were this the case, the arrest treatment probably should be less effective in households experiencing recent police interventions. No such interaction effects were found. In future analyses of these data, however, we will inductively explore interactions with more sensitive measures of police sanctioning and prior criminal histories of the suspects.

There are, of course, many versions of labeling theory. For those who theorize that a metamorphosis of self occurs in response to official sanctions over a long period of time, our six-month follow-up is not a relevant test. For those who argue that the development of a criminal self-concept is particularly likely to occur during a lengthy prison stay or extensive contact with criminal justice officials, the dosage of labeling employed in this experiemnt is not sufficient to falsify that hypothesis. What this experiment does seem to falsify for this particular offense is the broader conception of labeling implicit in the prior research by Lincoln et al. (unpubl.), Farrington (1977) and others: that for every possible increment of criminal justice response to deviance, the more increments (or the greater the formality) applied to the labeled deviant, the greater the likelihood of subsequent deviation. The absolute strength of the dosage is irrelevant to this hypothesis, as long as some variation in dosage is present. While the experiment does not falsify all possible "labeling theory" hypotheses, it does at least seem to falsify this one.

The apparent support for deterrence is perhaps more clear. While we certainly have no evidence that deterrence will work in general, we do have findings that swift imposition of a sanction of temporary incarceration may deter male offenders in domestic assault cases. And we have produced this evidence from an unusually strong research design based on random assignment to treatments. In short, criminal justice sanctions seem to matter for this offense in this setting with this group of experienced offenders.

A number of police implications follow. Perhaps most important, police have historically been reluctant to make arrests in domestic assault cases, in part fearing that an arrest could make the violence worse. Criminal justice sanctions weakly applied might be insufficient to deter and set the offender on a course of retribution. Our data indicate that such concerns are by and large groundless.

Police have also felt that making an arrest was a waste of their time: without the application of swift and severe sanctions by the courts, arrest and booking had no bite. Our results indicate that only three of the 136 arrested offenders were formally punished by fines or subsequent incarceration. This suggests that arrest and initial incarceration alone may produce a deterrent effect, regardless of how the courts treat such cases, and that arrest makes an independent contribution to the deterrence potential of the criminal justice system. Therefore, in jurisdictions that process domestic assault offenders in a manner similar to that employed in Minneapolis, we favor a *presumption* of arrest; an arrest should be made unless there are good, clear reasons why an arrest would be counterproductive. We do not, however, favor *requiring* arrests in all misdemeanor domestic assault cases. Even if our findings were replicated in a number of jurisdictions, there is a good chance that arrest works far better for some kinds of offenders than others and in some kinds of situations better than others.[5] We feel it best to leave police a loophole to capitalize on that variation. Equally important, it is widely recognized that discretion is inherent in police work. Simply to impose a requirement of arrest, irrespective of the features of the immediate situation, is to invite circumvention.

---

[5] Indeed, one of the major policy issues that could arise from further analysis of the interaction effects would be whether police discretion should be guided by either achieved or ascribed relevant suspect characteristics.

REFERENCES

Amemiya, Takeshi
 1981 "Qualitative response models: a survey." Journal of Economic Literature 19:1483–1536.
Andenaes, Johannes
 1971 "Deterrence and specific offenses." University of Chicago Law Review 39:537.
Bard, Morton
 1970 "Training police as specialists in family crisis intervention." Washington, D.C.: U.S. Department of Justice.
Bard, Morton and Joseph Zacker
 1974 "Assaultiveness and alcohol use in family disputes—police perceptions." Criminology 12:281–92.
Barnow, Burt S., Glen G. Cain and Arthur S. Goldberger
 1980 "Issues in the analysis of selectivity bias." Pp. 53–59 in Ernst W. Stromsdorfer and George Farkas (eds.), Evaluation Studies Review Annual, Volume 5. Beverly Hills: Sage.
Becker, Howard
 1963 The Outsiders. New York: Free Press.
Berk, Richard A.
 1983 "An introduction to sample selection bias in sociological data." American Sociological Review, 48:386–98.
Berk, Richard A. and Lawrence W. Sherman
 1983 "Police responses to family violence incidents: an analysis of an experimental design with incomplete randomization." Unpublished manuscript, Department of Sociology, University of California at Barbara.
Berk, Sarah Fenstermaker and Donileen R. Loseke
 1981 "Handling family violence: situational determinants of police arrest in domestic disturbances." Law and Society Review 15:315–46.
Black, Donald
 1980 The Manners and Customs of the Police. New York: Academic Press.
Chambliss, William
 1967 "Types of deviance and the effectiveness of legal sanctions." Wisconsin Law Review 1967:703–19.
Clarke, Ronald V. G.
 1966 "Approved school boy absconders and corporal punishment." British Journal of Criminology: 6:364–75.
Cohen, Lawrence E. and Rodney Stark
 1974 "Discriminatory labeling and the five-finger discount." Journal of Research in Crime and Delinquency 11:25–39.
Cook, Thomas D. and Donald T. Campbell
 1979 Quasi-Experimentation: Design and Analysis Issues for Field Settings. Chicago: Rand McNally.
Durkheim, Emile
 [1893] Selected Writings. Edited with an Intro-
 1972 duction by Anthony Giddens. [Selection from Division of Labor in Society, 6th edition, 1960 (1893)] Cambridge: Cambridge University Press.
Emerson, Charles D.
 1979 "Family violence: a study by the Los

Angeles County Sheriff's Department."
Police Chief 46(6):48–50.

Fagin, James A.
1978 "The effects of police interpersonal communications skills on conflict resolution."
Ph.D. Dissertation, Southern Illinois University Ann Arbor: University Microfilms.

Farrington, David P.
1977 "The effects of public labeling." British Journal of Crininology 17:112–25.

Federal Bureau of Investigation
1967 Uniform Crime Reports. Washington, D.C.: U.S. Department of Justice.

Gold, Martin and Jay Williams
1969 "National study of the aftermath of apprehension." Prospectus 3:3–11.

Gibbs, Jack P.
1975 Crime, Punishment and Deterrence. New York: Elsevier.

Heckman, James
1979 "Sample selection bias as a specification error." Econometrica 45:153–61.

Hirschi, Travis
1975 "Labeling theory and juvenile delinquency: an assessment of the evidence." Pp. 181–203 in Walter R. Gove (ed.), The Labeling of Deviance. New York: Wiley.

Illinois Law Enforcement Commission
1978 "Report on technical assistance project—domestic violence survey." (Abstract). Washington, D.C.: National Criminal Justice Reference Service.

Ketterman, Thomas and Marjorie Kravitz
1978 Police Crisis Intervention: A Selected Bibliography. Washington, D.C.: National Criminal Justice Reference Service.

Klemke, Lloyd W.
1978 "Does apprehension for shoplifting amplify or terminate shoplifting activity?" Law and Society Review 12:391–403.

Kraut, Robert E.
1976 "Deterrent and definitional influences on shoplifting." Social Problems 23:358–68.

Langley, Richard and Roger C. Levy
1977 Wife Beating: The Silent Crisis. New York: E. P. Dutton.

Lawless, Jerald F.
1982 Statistical Models and Methods for Lifetime Data. New York: Wiley.

Lemert, Edwin M.
1951 Social Pathology. New York: McGraw-Hill.
1967 Human Deviance, Social Problems and Social Control. Englewood Cliffs, NJ: Prentice-Hall.

Lempert, Richard.
1981– "Organizing for deterrence: lessons from
1982 a study of child support." Law and Society Review 16:513–68.

Lincoln, Suzanne B., Malcolm W. Klein, Katherine S. Teilmann and Susan Labin
un- "Control organizations and labeling theory:
publ. official versus self-reported delinquency." Unpublished manuscript, University of Southern California.

Maddala, G. S.
1983 Limited, Dependent and Qualitative Vari-

ables in Econometrics. Cambridge: Cambridge University Press.

McCord, Joan
1983 "A longitudinal appraisal of criminal sanctions." Paper presented at the IXth International Congress on Criminology, Vienna, Austria, September.

Meyer, Jeanie Keeny and T. D. Lorimer
1977 Police Intervention Data and Domestic Violence: Exploratory Development and Validation of Prediction Models. Report prepared under grant #RO1MH27918 from National Institute of Mental Health. Kansas City, Mo., Police Department.

Murray, Charles A. and Louis A. Cox, Jr.
1979 Beyond Probation. Beverly Hills: Sage.

Office of the Minority Leader, State of New York
1978 Battered Women: Part I (Abstract). Washington, D.C.: National Criminal Justice Reference Service.

Parnas, Raymond I.
1972 "The police response to the domestic disturbance." Pp. 206–36 in Leon Radzinowicz and Marvin E. Wolfgang (eds.), The Criminal in the Arms of the Law. New York: Basic Books.

Police Foundation
1976 Domestic Violence and the Police: Studies in Detroit and Kansas City. Washington, D.C.: The Police Foundation.

Potter, Jane
1978 "The police and the battered wife: the search for understanding." Police Magazine 1:40–50.

Roy, Maria (ed.)
1977 Battered Women. New York: Van Nostrand Reinhold.

Schwartz, Richard and Jerome Skolnick
1962 "Two studies of legal stigma." Social Problems 10:133–42.

Sherman, Lawrence W.
1980 "Causes of police behavior: the current state of quantitative research." Journal of Research in Crime and Delinquency 17:69–100.

Shoham, S. Giora
1974 "Punishment and traffic offenses." Traffic Quarterly 28:61–73.

Thorsell, Bernard A. and Lloyd M. Klemke
1972 "The labeling process: reinforcement and deterrent." Law and Society Review 6:393–403.

Tittle, Charles
1975 "Labeling and crime: an empirical evaluation." Pp. 157–79 in Walter R. Gove (ed.), The Labeling of Deviance. New York: Wiley.

University of Rochester
1974 "FACIT—Family Conflict Intervention Team Experiment—Experimental Action Program." (Abstract). Washington, D.C.: National Criminal Justice Reference Service.

Wylie, P. B., L. F. Basinger, C. L. Heinecke and J. A. Reuckert
1976 "Approach to evaluating a police program

of family crisis interventions in sex demonstration cities—Final report." (Abstract). Washington, D.C.: National Criminal Justice Reference Service.

Zimring, Franklin E. and Gordon T. Hawkins
1973 Deterrence: The Legal Threat in Crime Control. Chicago: University of Chicago Press.

[2]

A RANDOMIZED EXPERIMENT TESTING INMATE CLASSIFICATION SYSTEMS*

RICHARD A. BERK
HEATHER LADD
HEIDI GRAZIANO
JONG-HO BAEK
    UCLA

Research Summary:

In California, incarceration in the state prison system is in part organized by security level. The higher the security level, the more restrictive the setting. Upon arrival at a reception center, new inmates are scored within a classification system that is used to determine the appropriate level of security. In this paper, we report on the development and testing of a new inmate classification scoring system. Over 20,000 inmates took part in a randomized experiment in which half were assigned to their housing using the existing scoring system and half were assigned to their housing using the new scoring system. There were two key outcomes: (1) potential mismatches between the number of inmates assigned to different security levels and the available beds and (2) reports of inmate misconduct.

Policy Implications:

We conclude there to be some potential crowding problems, but that the new scoring system is much better than the old scoring system in sorting inmates by the likelihood of misconduct. We also conclude that some predictors popular in the past are no longer effective (e.g., marital status), while some new predictors are extremely powerful (e.g., gang activity), and that one can build in a number of mandatory housing placements (e.g., for sex offenders) and not degrade the overall effectiveness of the new classification system. Finally, the new classification system is shown to be more user-friendly than the existing classification system and well received by the staff responsible for implementing it.

KEYWORDS: Experiments, Prisons, Security, Classification

---

* The research reported in this paper would have been impossible without the talents and efforts of our colleagues at the California Department of Corrections: George Lehman, Maureen Tristan, Gloria Rea, Penny O'Daniel, Micki Mitchell, Mark Cook, Martha Oyog, and Terrence Newsome. They implemented the experiment and the data collection, as well as provided extensive comments on an earlier draft of this paper.

216   BERK ET AL.

The California Department of Corrections (CDC) currently houses approximately 160,000 inmates in 33 institutions, 16 community correctional facilities (CCFs), 41 camps, and 8 prisoner mother facilities across the state. These facilities differ in many ways, including architectural design and construction, staffing, and program availability. However, they are each mandated to ensure public safety and institutional security.

A wide variety of housing options are provided within four levels of security. Inmates deemed to be most problematic are placed in the most restrictive settings requiring celled housing, a lethal perimeter, controlled movement, and armed supervision within the housing units and dining halls. Inmates identified as less dangerous to staff, other inmates, and the public are placed in less restrictive facilities, which can include dormitory housing, a nonlethal perimeter, and unarmed oversight.

Each housing option has a designated security level. The CDC uses an inmate classification score system to evaluate each inmate's need for supervision. The fundamental goal of the CDC classification system is to place an inmate in the least restrictive security level consistent with internal security and public safety. Although the average cost for housing an inmate in CDC is over $25,000 a year, costs for more restrictive level of housing are significantly more expensive.

An earlier study conducted for CDC (Berk and de Leeuw, 1998) evaluated the existing inmate classification score system by which inmates were classified and then placed in different levels of security. Although the data suggested that overall the procedures were placing inmates roughly consistent with Department's expectations, there was also evidence that improvements in the system could be made.

In this paper, we address how the inmate classification system was revised and then describe a randomized experiment to test the new system against the old one. Over 20,000 inmates took part in the experiment, which included two years of follow-up data. Key outcomes to be examined were the amount and type of misconduct in prison[1] and the implications of the new system for prison crowding; would the current distribution of beds by security levels suffice if inmates were distributed to levels differently? The study is one of the largest randomized trials ever undertaken, and certainly the very largest criminal justice randomized experiment. We will focus not just on the design, but also on its implementation in a prison setting where placement decisions can have very serious consequences. Finally, we report the central findings and policy implications.

---

1. These can range from minor violations, such as failing to cooperate during a head count, to very serious violations such as battery on a correctional officer, staff, or another prisoner, selling drugs, or trying to escape.

SUMMARY OF THE CDC'S CURRENT CLASSIFICATION SYSTEM

Most inmates begin their sentences at a reception center, where, for each, a substantial amount of background information is collected on a standardized form, the CDC Form 839, "CDC Classification Score Sheet," commonly referred to as a CDC form 839 or simply "839." Much of the case factor information collected is thought to be related to the propensity for misconduct: sentence length, disciplinary history, work history, age, prior incarcerations, and much more. The 839 assigns points to each of the background items. An inmate's total number of points constitutes a "classification score," which in turn, is used to help determine placements in one of four security levels. A higher score is supposed to reflect a greater proclivity to engage in misconduct or to attempt an escape and, therefore, the need for a higher level of security. For about 75% of inmates, placement in a security level is fully determined by the classification score. Inmates who score between 0 and 18 are placed in level I, 19 and 27 are placed in level II, 28 and 51 go to level III, and above 52 are placed in level IV.

Alternatively, about 25% of inmates are placed in a security level that is not necessarily consistent with classification scores. When the classification score is thought to not properly reflect the level of risk the inmate poses, an "administrative placement" can follow. Approval to place an inmate in a security inconsistent with an inmate's classification score requires the "endorsement" of a department official (a Classification Staff Representative or CSR).

An administrative placement considers both temporary and permanent case factors affecting inmate safety. An administrative placement is temporary when the administrative determinant is subject to time constraints, a potential change in case factors, or the receipt of additional information. For example, an inmate may be placed in a higher level of security pending the resolution of an active law enforcement felony hold likely to be exercised. Similarly, when an inmate's classification score falls within a security level that does not have available bed space, an inmate may receive a "population override" to an open bed in a security level above the level indicated by the classification score. This override is eliminated when beds at the original security level are available.

An administrative placement can also take special note of inmates who are convicted of sex crimes, particularly violent crimes, or crimes for which the sentence is life without the possibility of parole (LWOPs). Such inmates are placed in at least level III facilities regardless of their classification score. Part of the rationale is the jeopardy to public safety that may

218   BERK ET AL.

follow should such an inmate escape. There is also the belief that the inmates serving LWOP feel they have little to lose.

Finally, inmates are sometimes placed in one of two kinds of special facilities that do not formally correspond to a single security level. Inmates otherwise eligible for minimum-security custody who have classification scores consistent with a level I or level II security level are eligible for placement at a CCF (Community Correctional Facility). Placement in a Security Housing Unit (SHU) is based on a departmental determination that the inmate's behavior endangers the safety of others or the security of the institution.[2] Placement in SHU is not based on the inmates classification score.

CHANGES TO THE EXISTING SYSTEM

Previous research (Berk and de Leeuw, 1998) coupled with less formal reviews internal to CDC led to a number of revisions of the existing inmate classification score instrument. The elimination of some items and the addition of others were suggested to better identify inmates with a proclivity for misconduct.

Several items were removed because they had no demonstrable association with misconduct in prison. The eliminated "stability factors" included an inmate's marital status, employment, education, and military service. Items indicating a successful escape were removed for the same reason coupled with the fact that successful escapes are very rare. Finally, whether or not an inmate had adjusted successfully to dormitory living in a past incarceration was removed. After years of severe crowding and the use of buildings not designed for housing inmates, it was no longer clear what inferences could be drawn.

Variables added because they were shown to be strongly related to misconduct included street gang or disruptive group activity, diagnosis of mental illness at a CDC reception center, age when first arrested, and prior incarceration. The earlier research and the day-to-day experiences of prison staff made clear that this meant young inmates with long arrest histories, gang activity, and/or a mental illness diagnosis.

Finally, modifications were made to the scoring of existing items. First, the weight given to length-of-sentence was reduced, because the association between misconduct and length of sentence was very weak, after accounting for other background items such as age. Second, because there was a strong association between age and misconduct, more weight was given to the younger ages (measured at arrival to a reception center) shown to be most problematic.

---

2. From the California Code of Regulations, Title 15, section 3341.5(c)

INMATE CLASSIFICATION 219

Project staff also recommended the implementation of "mandatory minimum scores." The mandatory minimum score integrates administrative determinants representing certain permanent case factors into the inmate classification scoring system. As such, they are a threshold score overriding the classification score otherwise calculated for an inmate. The goal is to make such places more objective. For example, regardless of the calculated classification score, an LWOP inmate will be given at least 52 points leading to level IV housing. The mandatory minimums were as follows:

- 52 points: inmates sentenced to death
- 52 points: LWOP inmates
- 28 points: Inmates serving multiple life terms or life with specific circumstances
- 19 points: Inmates with a history of escape
- 19 points: U.S. Immigration and Naturalization hold
- 19 points: Inmates committed for specific sex offenses or sex related behavior
- 19 points: Inmates found to be violent felons per statutory requirements
- 19 points: Inmates determined to meet criteria as a high notoriety inmate
- 19 points: Inmate serving a life sentence

Once changes in the items were determined, an effort was made to design the forms implementing the changes that would be easier to use and would, ideally, produce more accurate information. A number of different formats were proposed, each carefully reviewed by CDC staff experienced in how such forms are used in the field. Several of the most promising forms were field tested by institutional staff. In the end, there was a broad consensus that in addition to the technical improvements in the instrument, the new forms were far more user friendly than the existing forms.

In short, the primary goals of the new classification score system were to better predict inmate misconduct and place them accordingly. In addition, the new scoring system was designed to be easier to administer and less prone to recording and arithmetic errors.

PAST STUDIES

Inmate classification systems, serving a variety of purposes, have long been part of the penal scene in the United States (Brennan, 1987). "Objective" classification systems, roughly like the one used in California, are a more recent development, but are now common across the country. A nearly universal question is how well objective classification systems work.

Much has been written on objective classification systems, including

220   BERK ET AL.

their development and evaluation, (Alexander and Austin, 1992; Austin, 1986; Brennan, 1987; Kane, 1986; Hardyman et al., 2000; Hardyman and Adams-Fuller, 2001). There are, however, few reports of experimental evaluations of these systems. Of the evaluations that have been done, most have not been experimental in nature and several were flawed because of small and biased samples (Alexander and Austin, 1992).

For example, in 1987, the Washington Department of Corrections initiated one of the better randomized experiments using 488 medium custody inmates to test the effectiveness of a Prison Management Classification (PMC) system. The goals of the new system were to improve safety and operations (Austin et al., 1993). The research results suggested that the new system worked reasonably well. Unfortunately, all experimental inmates were assigned to a new facility, so it was not clear how much of the treatment was the classification system and how much the new housing.

Quasi-experiments are more common. Thus, two quasi-experimental studies of classification were completed in Tennessee (Baird, 1993). The first, in 1984, compared the behavior of inmates classified to different levels, but all were treated as minimum custody. A key finding was that many more inmates than originally thought could be classified as minimum custody without affecting public and prison safety. In 1991, a follow-up study was completed reviewing the behavior of inmates classified as minimum custody but, for lack of beds, placed as medium custody. By and large, the original conclusions were still valid.

There seem to be four conclusions from past research: (1) There are a number of reasons a priori for favoring objective classification systems, (2) existing objective systems are broadly similar, (3) rigorous evaluations of the systems are highly unusual, and (4) the weight of the research evidence suggests objective systems, although superior to less formal procedures, could certainly be improved. All four conclusions are consistent with the rationale for the work reported here.

STUDY DESIGN AND RATIONALE

Some Legal and Political Issues

Clearly, a study testing a new way to assign inmates to different security levels entails substantial risks for prisoners and prison staff. These were carefully weighed against the potential benefits for a classification system that was safer and more cost-effective. On balance, CDC administrators felt the potential benefits were substantially greater than the potential costs. Because statutes governing CDC's implementation of regulatory changes allow discretion in conducting "pilot studies" involving no more than 10% of the total inmate population, the state regulatory office approved a two-year pilot project to test the revised inmate classification score forms. Plans for the study were thoroughly reviewed by stakeholders, including CDC administrators, representatives of prison employee bargaining unions, several other California State agencies, California State legislative offices, and a wide variety of other interested parties. There was widespread agreement that the study was worth doing.

SELECTION OF SUBJECTS

Power analyses were undertaken that were unusually well informed because of the previous research cited above. A key concern was to have a sufficient number of level IV inmates because analyses by security level were anticipated, and level IV inmates typically constitute only about 5% of the inmate population. Overall attrition had to be addressed as well because time served by level I and II inmates was commonly less than the length of the two-year follow-up. Finally, it was necessary to anticipate how the random assignment would be implemented. In particular, the implementation would have to fit as snugly as possible within the existing administrative structure to minimize disruptions, errors, and workload. Thus, for example, it was not practical to recruit a special group of reception center staff to implement the experiment, in part because a means would have had to be found to send a subset of incoming inmates to those staff members without raising undue concerns. Moreover, any alteration in existing intake procedures risked affecting other reception center activities (e.g., medical exams). In the end, it was decided that we would simply include all new felony commitments for six months as our subject pool, which ruled out such options as oversampling the relatively rare level IV prisoners.[3]

These and other considerations led to a target sample size of 20,000 new felony commitments overall, with half to be placed under the experimental classification score system and half under the existing classification score system. All new felon commitments arriving at the CDC Reception Center between November 1, 1998 and April 30, 1999 were included in the study for an actual sample size of 21,734. One important asset of this approach was that the target sample size was reached as soon as possible, which meant that the follow-up data collection could be ended at the shortest possible time. Another advantage was that for a well-defined period, the

---

3. There were many potential complications associated with oversampling. For example, one would have to compute a classification score first to determine who the level IV inmates were. And because computing that score was the major administrative burden in study implementation, oversampling would not actually save significant time or resources. We settled on collecting a sufficiently large sample overall to have the requisite number of level IV inmates.

entire reception process could be put on special footing. This simplified implementation enormously.

RANDOMIZATION AND PLACEMENT OF THE INMATES

CDC ID numbers were used to divide the subjects into experimental (new classification score system) and control (existing classification score system) groups. Unique ID numbers are assigned sequentially at each reception center. Inmates receiving odd prison numbers were assigned to the experimental group, and inmates receiving even numbers were assigned to the control group. All subjects were informed verbally and in writing that they were part of a study on the CDC classification system. Each inmate also received a copy of the classification score forms used to determine his or her classification score and was advised in writing that the assigned correctional counselor would be able to provide answers to most questions. Further, the inmates were advised that they could review the complete manual on the use of experimental classification score form. Project staff provided a copy of the manual for each facility law library to which inmates had access. During the project period, the CDC received no reported cases of inmates challenging participation in the study.

An intake classification score form, called CDC Form 839 (or "an 839"), was filled out for each inmate in the study. The control group version was used to record and tabulate intake information for the control group (color-coded yellow), from which placements were determined. The experimental group version played the same role for the experimental group (color-coded orange). However, both forms were filled out for all subjects, even though only one form would guide placement. The rationale was to permit answers to counterfactual "what if" questions, such as how a particular type of experimental inmate would have been placed under the existing classification score system. We will exploit such counterfactual information below.

DATA COLLECTION

Inmate intake forms were key-entered so that a machine-readable file was produced. Also key-entered were CDC "reclassification" forms (CDC Form 840, called an "840"). About a year after reception, the performance of each inmate is reviewed, and an 840 filled out. Because the CDC requires that inmates be evaluated at least annually, the classification score, housing assignment, and performance of each inmate are reviewed by a classification committee to update the 840. Recorded are both favorable and unfavorable behavior and points assessed as a result of disciplinary violations during the preceding period.

The annual review is designed to evaluate the inmate's behavior, update

INMATE CLASSIFICATION 223

the classification score, and consider any need for a change in placement. An inmate who is free of any disciplinary actions and demonstrates positive participation in an inmate program during the period reviewed earns points that are deducted from the classification score. Conversely, an inmate who has been found guilty of one or more disciplinary violations during the period of review has points added.

Point reductions often result in a transfer to a lower security level when the inmate's score falls within a range associated with such a level. A score increase can have the opposite impact. If an inmate completes his or her sentence and is released to parole before the annual reclassification review, the inmate may have no 840.[4] Thus, an inmate may have no 840, one 840, or several.

The 840s used for the experimental subjects were largely the same as the 840 used for the control subjects. The main difference was to increase a bit the weight given to inmate behavior since the last review so that good conduct could be better rewarded. For both the experimental and control inmates, the 840s permit one to determine how an inmate's classification score changes over time.

The 840s document the endorsement of an inmate to a different facility or to a different security level within an institutional complex. With the use of the CDC Movement History File, which essentially records an inmate's placements over time, and the endorsed location documented on the 840, one can determine how and when a change in the classification score translates into a change in housing.

To further supplement the data on the 839 and 840, data were extracted and key-entered from the CDC Form 115, "Rules Violation Report" (called a "115"). A 115 is initiated when staff observe an inmate engaged in some form of prison misconduct. Inmate disciplinary violations range from minor violation such as failing to report to an assignment to serious violations such as battery on a correctional officer or on another inmate, trafficking in drugs, or attempting an escape.

For the experiment, project staff audited every 115 received by any of the 21,734 inmates during the 24 months they were part of the study. Project staff compiled and entered data to record the date of the misconduct, a description of the specific act, the inmate's housing location and security level at the time of the incident, the determination of whether the violation was serious or only "administrative," the "division level" if the 115

---

4. Inmates returned to complete their sentences continued to be included in the study. Their classification scores were updated on an 840. Inmates returned with a new conviction and sentence were not included in the study because they were, in effect, a new admission after the study intake period.

was serious, the mental health status of the inmate at the time of the violation, and whether the violation was drug-related and/or alcohol-related.[5]

STUDY IMPLEMENTATION

Pages could be written about how the study was implemented. For this paper, three points can be made. First, project personnel worked closely with CDC staff to provide thorough training in the new instrument. In addition, a special manual was provided to all and a hotline established where pressing questions could be quickly answered.

Second, the randomization process was regularly monitored by on-site observation and statistical analyses of preliminary data. No important problems were uncovered during the six months of intake.

Third, all intake forms were thoroughly reviewed as part of routine CDC procedure with supplemental reviews by project staff. Project staff were stationed at the reception facilities during the six months of intake for a minimum of three days a week. As time permitted, cases completed by reception center personnel were given a complete review by project staff. After all forms were later key-entered, the project staff audited nearly 100% of all 839s and 840s. Finally, all intake forms were subject to a number of logical checks with specially written computer algorithms. If errors were found through any of these processes, the case file was reviewed and corrections were made. In addition, records were kept of the corrections made to determine if there were systematic errors in the data collection process. No such errors were found.

FINDINGS

In this paper, we only consider the results for the 19,318 male inmates in the study. Approximately 90% of all recent CDC inmates are male, and levels of housing security only apply to male inmates; there really are no security levels for female prisoners. Although classification scores are computed on all inmates, only for males do the scores have important placement implications. In short, the experiment only has relevance to male inmates.

Data on Randomization

If the experiment was implemented as designed, there should be equal numbers of inmates in the two groups, experimental and control, and the com-position of those groups will be effectively the same. Our data indicate that this was the case. There are 9,662 inmates in the experimental

---

5. Serious offenses recorded on the 115 are placed in one of several broad categories, such as "narcotics trafficking." These are called "division levels."

INMATE CLASSIFICATION 225

group and 9,656 inmates in the control group. The expected 50-50 split is approximated extremely well. Composition of the two groups was also very similar. For example, there were 1,811 gang members among the experimental group and 1,792 gang members among the control group. That is a split of 50.3% versus 49.7%. Another way to show the split is that 18.7% of the experimental group and 18.6% of the control group are gang members. Consider the number of inmates under 21 years of age. There are 1,179 such inmates in the experimental group versus 1,160 in the control group. That is a 50.0% to 49.6% split. A total of 12.2% of the experimentals and 12.0% of the controls were under the age of 21. Regardless of the background variable chosen, the two groups were balanced. The experimental and control groups were effectively identical.

FIGURE 1. PLACEMENT SCORE DISTRIBUTIONS FOR CONTROLS (MALE SAMPLE)

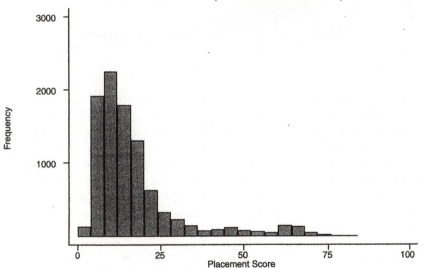

TREATMENT EFFECTS ON THE SIZE AND MIX OF INMATE POPULATIONS

Figures 1 and 2 show the score distributions for the control and experimental groups, respectively. Both distributions are skewed to the right with the mass of data below a score of 25, as would be expected. Most inmates are incarcerated for a relatively short period of time and are not high risk. Low classification scores follow. The two score distributions are much the same, except that the experimental scores are shifted a bit to the right.

FIGURE 2. PLACEMENT SCORE DISTRIBUTION FOR EXPERIMENTALS (MALE SAMPLE)

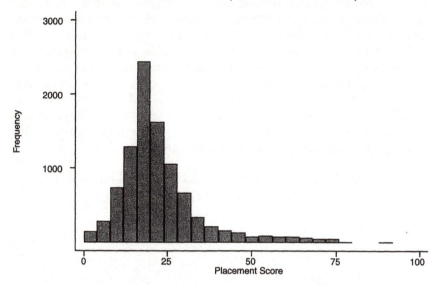

If one compares scores by initial endorsed placement level, it is easily seen that the shift in scores for the experimental inmates is primarily in the lower levels. For example, within level I, the median score increases from 11 to 15 and the mean from 12 to 15. Level II shows a slight difference favoring the experimental group, but levels III and IV have similar central tendencies for the experimental and control groups. Note that these are aggregate results and do not imply that the new forms simply increased lower scores a few points on the average. We will see shortly that a lot more is going on.

ITEMS MOST AFFECTING THE CLASSIFICATION SCORE DISTRIBUTIONS

Which items in the classification score were driving these score totals? Note that the importance of an item in practice is a function of the weight given to that item in the scoring system and the amount of empirical variation in that item among incoming prisoners. We computed the average percentage that each item contributed to the total score. The analysis was done separately in each security level in part because average overall scores that served as the base vary substantially by level.

For the control inmates, the story is simple. Points awarded for longer sentences dominate the classification score. It accounts for about 28% of the score in level I and about 80% in level IV. Even for level I inmates, term length is more than twice as important as any other item. By design,

INMATE CLASSIFICATION   227

the new system was intended to make term length far less important, and increase the impact of other items; term length was in past studies not found to be nearly as useful an indicator of misconduct as its weight suggested. What actually happened?

For the experimental inmates, in level I, more than half the total score on the average was determined by the inmate's age at first arrest and at reception. Another 25% was explained by points awarded for longer sentences. Having no serious misconduct charges during prior incarcerations was responsible for 12% of the total. None of the other score variables individually contributed more than 5%. The story in level II was much the same.

The overall pattern in level III was similar to that of levels II and I, except that on the average, 34% of the total score was explained by sentence and another 31% of the variation was explained by the age of the inmate at first arrest. Having no serious misconduct charges during prior incarcerations counted for 5% of the total. Points given for being a gang member starts to count in level III, explaining 8% of the total score.

In level IV, 62% of the total score on the average is determined by sentence length. This is reasonable because inmates assigned to level IV generally commit the worst crimes, thereby receiving the longest sentences.

In short, the score distributions are determined by relatively few classification items. Term length dominated the old classification system. Under the new system, the impact of points for longer sentences are far less important. New items included to better predict misconduct take up the slack.

Impact on the Placement of Inmates

One of the key issues raised by the experiment was the potential impact of the new classification form on initial placement. Table 1 shows the actual placements for the experimental and control groups.[6] Note that we have included for now Reception Center (RC) placements, which represent the few inmates who were not placed in a regular CDC prison.[7] We have also at this point included CCF, which are level I placements, and SHU placements, which, as we mentioned earlier, are formally outside of the classification system. Later analyses will focus on the four security

6. Technically, the "initial placement" is actually an inmate's "endorsed location."

7. The majority of inmates paroling from RC, who are not placed in a regular housing unit, are inmates who complete their sentences while in RC and are, therefore, released from RC to parole. A few have pending court obligations and are ordered back to a county jail for another offense.

levels because placement in those levels is what the experiment was meant to address, and it is those levels that affect the vast majority of inmates.

TABLE 1. INITIAL PLACEMENTS FOR THE EXPERIMENTALS AND CONTROLS SEPARATELY (MALE SAMPLE)

Initial Placement	Controls	Experimentals	Total
RC	2.25%	2.55%	2.40% (463)
CCF	15.82%	13.82%	14.82% (2863)
Level I	33.51%	25.54%	29.53% (5705)
Level II	30.36%	31.92%	31.14% (6016)
Level III	12.55%	21.42%	16.99% (3282)
Level IV	5.24%	4.46%	4.85% (937)
SHU	0.26%	0.29%	0.27% (55)
Total	100% (9656)	100% (9662)	100% (19318)

For the experimental group, there is a significant decline in the relative size of the level I population from about 34% to 26% and a significant increase in the relative size of the level III population from about 13% to 21%. Given the large sample sizes, such disparities are easily large enough to reject the null hypothesis of no difference. How might such a shift come about?

Recall that all inmates were scored under both systems. Thus, for every placement, there is considerable information on the hypothetical placement that could have been made but was not. That is, for all experimental inmates, we have information on how they would have been placed under the existing classification system, and for all control inmates, we have information on how they would have been placed under the revised classification system.

Table 2 is constructed by comparing the actual placement of each inmate to the hypothetical placement (i.e., without population overrides) under the classification system that was not applied to them. The table shows that although there is some displacement of inmates, overall, the majority of inmates would receive the same initial placement under either system. The major exception for the experimental group is in level III where only 53% of the inmates would have been placed the same under the original system.

If one goes a step farther and tabulates for the experimental group, the actual placement against what the placement would have been under the existing classification system (table not shown), it is readily apparent that although some inmates are placed very differently under the new system

INMATE CLASSIFICATION 229

TABLE 2. PERCENTAGE OF EXPERIMENTAL AND CONTROL INMATES FOR WHOM THE ACTUAL INITIAL PLACEMENT WAS THE SAME AS THE HYPOTHETICAL INITIAL PLACEMENT (MALE SAMPLE)

Initial Placement	Experimentals	Controls
RC	100.00%	100.00%
CCF	99.93%	94.24%
Level I	97.33%	68.20%
Level II	81.06%	83.19%
Level III	52.51%	85.40%
Level IV	88.63%	81.23%
SHU	100.00%	100.00%

(e.g., in level IV instead of level I), a majority who are placed differently shift up or down one level. Thus, for example, of the level III inmates who would have been placed differently, 62% would have been placed in level II, and 28% would have been placed in level I.

From Table 2, it is level I for the control group where the major changes occur; only 68% would have been placed in the same level under both systems. Tabulating for the controls the actual placement against the placement that would have occurred under the new system (table not shown) again shows that the majority of those inmates who would have been placed differently, would have changed only one level. Thus, for example, of those level I inmates who would have been placed differently, 71% would have been placed in level II, and 26% would have been placed in level III. Clearly, there is an important shift upward overall under the new system from level I to levels II and III. As before, given the very large sample sizes, all such percentage comparisons easily lead to a rejection of the null hypothesis of no difference.

Shifts of the sort just described can have important implications for crowding insofar as the new classification system allocates inmates initially in a manner inconsistent with available beds. Equally important is how the new distribution of inmates affects which kind of inmates are sent to which kinds of facilities. For example, is the new system really placing "gang-bangers" in more secure settings, as intended?

We focus here on levels I and III because that is where differences in placements between the new and existing system are most pronounced. For level III placements, 25% of the control group were linked to gang activity compared to 44% of the experimental group; 39% of the control group were under 27 compared to 58% of the experimental group; 17% of

the control group were under the age of 21 compared to 29% of the experimental group. Finally, 17% of the control group had a history of mental
illness compared to 13% of the experimental group. All but the last of
these patterns are consistent with the intent of the new classification system. For inmates with a history of mental illness, it is likely that there are
other common features of such individuals that were both unanticipated
and mitigated the impact of the mental illness designation.

For level I placements, 17% of the control group were determined to be
involved in street gang activity compared with 6% of the experimental
group. In addition, 32% of the control group were under the age of 27
compared to 19% of the experimental group; 12% of the control group
were under the age of 21 compared with 4% of the experimental group.
Finally, 2.4% of the control group had mental illness status compared with
1.3% of the experimental group. The pattern for level I inmate is less dramatic than for level III inmates, primarily because it was relatively rare to
find in level I institutions many inmates with gang activity or a history of
mental illness. However, the impact on age is apparent: Younger inmates
are generally shifted upward under the experimental classification score
system.

IMPACT ON THE MIX OF INMATES

Given the impacts of the new classification system on initial placement,
what might the longer term implications be? Recall that misconduct can
lead to movement to higher security levels, whereas good conduct can lead
to movement into lower security levels. Using 24 months of data from the
Movement Files, one can see how the populations in the different levels
will change over time. Figure 3 contains seven graphs showing the number
of experimental and control inmates in each placement location for the
length of the follow-up period. There is one graph each for the RC, CCF,
SHU, and each of the four security levels I through IV.

1. The RC population drops to zero for both the experimental and
   control groups by month 6 as would be expected because the RC is
   the holding place for the inmates until assignment to a bed in one
   of the institutions. Both groups show the same distribution over
   the 24 months.
2. The population in the CCF increases until about month 6, at which
   time the population starts to decrease. This is, of course, a necessary consequence of the six-month intake at the beginning of the
   study. There are a maximum of about 200 more inmates in the control group than in the experimental group, but the control group
   exits the CCF more quickly. Thus, by the end of the study, the
   numbers of inmates are approximately equal for the two groups.

INMATE CLASSIFICATION   231

FIGURE 3. THE NUMBER OF INMATES IN EACH LOCATION BY MONTH AFTER ADMISSION (MALE SAMPLE)

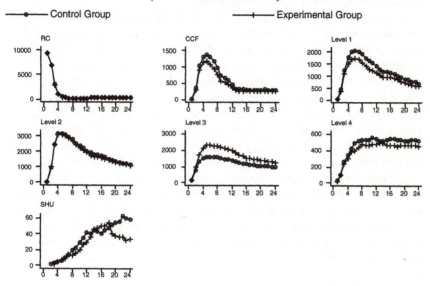

3. For level I, we again see an increase in the number of inmates till month 6 for both groups of inmates. There are approximately 200 more control inmates in level I than in experimental at that point. The gap between the two groups closes over time so, by month 24, the numbers are practically the same.

4. Level II shows the increase to month 6 followed by a decrease to month 24. However, the distributions for the two groups are basically the same.

5. Level III shows an increase in population until month 6, with the experimental group having about 500 more inmates than the control. The gap between the two groups closes as the distributions decrease. It appears that if the trend was to continue, the numbers of control and experimental inmates should be approximately equal by month 30.

6. Level IV shows an increase in population until month 6 and then tapers off but does not decrease as might be expected. There are about 100 more controls than experimentals, a gap that is roughly constant over the length of the study.

7. SHU has such small numbers that the graph contains no reliable information.

One message from Figure 3 is that differences in placement patterns for

232   BERK ET AL.

the experimental and control inmates generally decrease over time. This would make sense if the net percentage of inmates leaving a given level were about the same for both groups. The group with the greater initial number would shrink faster toward zero.

Another message is that during the follow-up period, a substantial fraction of the inmates in the study were released from prison because their terms expired. Indeed, about a quarter of the experimental inmates and about a quarter of the control inmates were released on parole within a year after they arrived at a CDC reception center. By the end of the second year, those figures were approximately 80% each. This "attrition" was fully expected based on CDC's own studies, and it was one of the reasons why such a large sample of inmates was required. But movement of inmates out of prison needs to be considered part of the explanation for the declining curves in addition to movement to other security levels.[8] The major exception is level IV inmates, most of whom remain in level IV for the entire 24 months of the study. This too is really no surprise because level IV placements depend substantially on term length, and inmates with long terms to serve are assigned a large number of points. It would take the typical level IV inmates several years of good behavior to significantly reduce their point totals.[9]

MISCONDUCT

COMPARING MISCONDUCT FOR THE EXPERIMENTAL AND CONTROL INMATES

One of the central issues of the study in-custody misconduct: Would the new forms better sort inmates into different categories of risk and then after placement reduce, or at least not increase, the amount of misconduct? We looked at misconduct in a number of ways. To begin, using whether or not an inmate had a CDC Form 115 during the 2-year study, we compared the experiences of inmates placed by the new and existing procedures. For the experimental group, 34.4% engaged in misconduct compared to 34.9% for the control group. Clearly, there were no important overall differences.

There are two broad types of 115s: "administrative" and "serious." Administrative 115s range from not reporting on time for a class or a job to failure to comply with departmental grooming standards. Serious 115s range from possession of a deadly weapon to manslaughter or murder. Administrative 115s were recorded for 13.9% of the experimental inmates

---

8. Note that the attrition did not differ for the experimental and control groups. Thus, the attrition does not affect the study of treatment effects.
9. The very large point total also are usually well above the threshold between a level III placement and a level IV placement.

and 14.4% of the control inmates. Serious 115s were recorded for 20.4% of the experimental and 20.5% of the control inmates. There are once again no important differences.

Although the majority of inmates did not engage in misconduct during the 24 months we have observed, some received more than one 115. When using the total number of 115s committed as the outcome, the conclusions are the same: The control and experimental inmates each have about half of the total number of 115s and of the administrative and serious 115s as well.

Given the substantial changes in how the inmates were placed under the new forms, the lack of any important differences in misconduct between the experimental and control inmates may seem somewhat perplexing. In an effort to better understand, we examined misconduct for the experimentals and controls as a function of initial placement. Table 3 shows the results.

TABLE 3. PERCENTAGE OF EXPERIMENTAL AND CONTROL INMATES ENGAGING IN MISCONDUCT BY INITIAL PLACEMENT (MALE SAMPLE)

Initial Placement	Experimentals	Controls
Level I	29%	34%
Level II	30%	33%
Level III	53%	48%
Level IV	50%	52%

Table 3 reveals some modest differences in the amount of misconduct for the control and experimental groups. The experimentals and controls are most alike in levels II and IV. In level I, the control group engages in somewhat more misconduct. In level III, the experimental group engages in somewhat more misconduct. These findings are not surprising given that one of the goals of the new system was to place inmates at high risk for in-custody misconduct into more secure settings. Thus, although the overall levels of misconduct are about the same for the inmates placed under the new and existing classification system, the new system shifted the misconduct into the higher security levels, especially level III.[10]

INCLUDING THE ROLE OF CLASSIFICATION SCORE AND PLACEMENT

But, there is much more to the story. Misconduct is a function of an

---

10. Note that because most inmates are in level I or II housing, the misconduct percentages in those levels largely determine the overall misconduct rate.

inmate's proclivity to get into trouble and the nature of the setting in which he is placed. One needs to try to separate these two distinct effects. Indeed, a failure to do so has been a major flaw in much past research.

Using a generalized regression discontinuity design (Berk and de Leeuw, 1998), one can consider misconduct as a function of initial placement and classification score. In this instance, the design leads naturally to a logistic regression with placement and classification score as predictors. For the inmates placed by their classification score into one of the four security levels, estimates of the effect of placement are in principle unbiased without including any other covariates. This may seem counterintuitive, but the underlying rationale has been accepted for well over a generation (Campbell and Stanley, 1963). A formal proof and further details can be found in Berk and de Leeuw (1998).

Tables 4 and 5 show the results of logistic regressions using the existence of a CDC Form 115 as the response variable and initial placement and classification score as the explanatory variables. Table 4 reports the results for the experimental group, and Table 5 reports the results for the control group. For both regressions, level I serves as the reference category for security level. Only placements into one of the four security levels are included in the analysis because these are the placements linked to classification score. By the same reasoning, all mandatory minimum placements are excluded for the experimental inmates, and all administrative placements are excluded for the control inmates. Placements made outside of the inmate classification system and not relevant to how well the classification score works.

TABLE 4. MISCONDUCT LOGISTIC REGRESSION FOR EXPERIMENTAL INMATES—MALES ONLY WITH MANDATORY PLACEMENTS EXCLUDED (N = 6121)

Predictor	Coefficient	S. E.	Multiplier
Score	0.080	0.005	1.09
Level II	−0.08	0.075	0.92
Level III	−0.27	0.117	0.76
Level IV	−2.99	0.27	0.05
Constant	−2.25	0.010	–

From Table 4, we see for the experimental inmates, an odds multiplier for classification score of 1.09. This means that for each additional point received, an inmate's odds of misconduct are multiplied by a factor of 1.09. This may seem like a small effect, but from one level to the next, inmates'

TABLE 5. MISCONDUCT LOGISTIC REGRESSION FOR CONTROL INMATES—MALES ONLY WITH ADMINISTRATIVE PLACEMENTS EXCLUDED (N = 5177)

Predictor	Coefficient	S. E.	Multiplier
Score	0.059	0.005	1.06
Level II	0.05	0.095	1.05
Level III	−0.78	0.163	0.46
Level IV	−2.27	0.295	0.10
Constant	−1.38	0.075	–

scores can vary by 20 points or more. Consider two inmates who differ in score by 20 points. For the inmate with the higher score, the odds of misconduct are 5.60 times greater (i.e., $1.09^{20} = 5.60$) than for the inmate with the lower score.

Table 5 contains the parallel analysis for the control inmates. One can see that classification score is less effective in sorting inmates by the risk of misconduct; the odds multiplier of 1.06. This difference (1.09 versus 1.06) may seem unimportant, but it is significant when comparing inmates with substantial differences in score. For the experimental group, 20 additional points translates into a risk of misconduct that is 5.60 times larger. For the control inmates, the 20 additional points translates into risk that is only 3.20 times greater. Clearly, the new classification system makes greater distinctions between inmates with respect to the risk of misconduct.[11]

The experiment was not designed to study the impact of placement on misconduct, and therefore, any such analysis must be interpreted with caution; there was no random assignment to security level. Still the apparent impact of security level broadly makes sense.

One can see from Table 4, that level IV compared to level I has a substantial impact on the odds of misconduct. An initial placement in level IV rather than level I reduces the odds of misconduct by a factor of 0.05. This is a large reduction, roughly equivalent to the increase in the risk of misconduct associated 33 addition classification points (i.e., $0.06^{-1} \approx 16.7 \approx 1.09^{33}$). However, consistent with the findings in Table 3, such reductions are not large enough to compensate for the increases in risk compared to level I. The classification scores of level IV inmates are generally more

---

11. Analyses of misconduct versus classification score were also undertaken for each level individually. A "matching" analysis of this sort (rather than relying on covariance adjustments) is a more robust analysis, made possible here by the large samples. In each case, the experimental score performed better at sorting inmates by their level of risk.

than 33 points greater than the classification scores of level I inmates. Hence, it is not surprising to find one of the very highest rates of misconduct in level IV facilities.

In Table 4, there is also evidence of a far smaller "suppressor effect" in III when compared to level I. The coefficients are over twice the standard error, and the multiplier large enough to be of some practical interest (0.76). Still, CDC officials are quick to point out that although there is somewhat greater control over inmates in level III compared to level I, level IV housing is substantially more restrictive than the lower levels. In short, under the revised classification system, the suppressor effects are consistent with the way CDC currently allocates its social control resources.

For the control inmates, Table 5 shows that under the existing classification system, there is also a strong suppressor effect in level IV compared to level I. There is also apparently an important suppressor effect for level III for the control inmates, although it is much smaller than the suppressor effect for level IV. The pattern of suppressor effects when the control inmates are compared to the experimental inmates is consistent with what we learned earlier; the revised classification system shifts a more difficult class of inmate up to level III. One might well expect, therefore, a reduction in the effectiveness of level III placements.

With the findings in Tables 4 and 5 in place, we can now return to the issue of why the overall rates of misconduct were effectively the same for the experimental and control inmates. For both the experimental and control inmates, the largest suppressor effect by far was found for level IV. Yet, most inmates placed differently under the revised system were shuffled among levels I, II, and III. Relative to level I, there are no suppressor effects in level II. Although there is some evidence of suppressor effects in level III, most inmate placements were to levels I and II. Hence, overall rates of misconduct for the experimental and control inmates would be determined primarily by characteristics of the offender, not security arrangements. And random assignment made the mix of offenders under the experimental condition comparable on the average to the mix of offenders under the control condition.

It is important to stress that we have examined the impact of initial placement only. About half the inmates in the study remained in their initial placements until the 12-month evaluation, and about a third remained in their initial placements during a 2-year follow-up. Ideally, one might like to explore the impact of each placement. Unfortunately, this is extremely difficult to do because one would have to determine the time spent in each and then allow for different placement sequences. For example, six months in a level III facility followed by six months in a level IV facility implies something very different from six months in a level IV

INMATE CLASSIFICATION 237

facility followed by six months in a level III facility. Clearly, there would be a large number of possible sequences of placements, and even with our large sample size, statistical power would be very low. But once again, the goal of the experiment was not to examine in great detail the effect of placements on misconduct. Whatever we are able to learn about such processes is a bonus.

Finally, the analyses reported in Tables 4 and 5 undertaken again using as the outcome a serious 115 only. Do the revised classification scores sort inmates better than the existing classification scores when the outcome is serious misconduct alone? Although the number of serious 115s is somewhat smaller and as a result, the statistical analyses are less reliable, the results are much the same. Tables 6 and 7 indicate that the revised system outperforms the existing system even when serious misconduct is the sole concern; the odds multiplier for the revised scores is 1.06, whereas the odds multiplier for the existing scores is 1.04. For differences in inmates'

TABLE 6. SERIOUS MISCONDUCT LOGISTIC REGRESSION FOR EXPERIMENTAL INMATES— MALES ONLY WITH MANDATORY PLACEMENTS EXCLUDED (N = 6121)

Predictor	Coefficient	S. E.	Multiplier
Score	0.060	0.005	1.06
Level II	0.30	0.087	1.35
Level III	0.30	0.126	1.35
Level IV	−1.23	0.274	0.29
Constant	−2.80	0.108	−

TABLE 7. SERIOUS MISCONDUCT LOGISTIC REGRESSION FOR CONTROL INMATES—MALES ONLY WITH ADMINISTRATIVE PLACEMENTS EXCLUDED (N = 5177)

Predictor	Coefficient	S. E.	Multiplier
Score	0.039	0.006	1.04
Level II	0.38	0.107	1.46
Level III	0.04	0.175	1.04
Level IV	−0.56	0.308	0.57
Constant	−2.13	0.085	−

238   BERK ET AL.

scores of 20 points, the odds of serious misconduct under the revised system are 3.21 times larger. For the existing scores, the odds of serious misconduct are 2.19 times larger. There is also strong evidence for important
suppressor effects in level IV, but these are a somewhat weaker than
found for all misconduct. Serious misconduct may be more difficult to contain under existing staffing and institutional arrangements. No evidence is
found for suppressor effects in level III. Again, serious misconduct may be
less amenable to control.

UNPACKING THE ITEMS IN THE CLASSIFICATION SCORE

We were also interested in knowing which items used to construct the
classification score are most strongly associated with future misconduct.
The logistic regressions in Tables 4 and 5 were rerun with the classification
score items substituted for overall classification score. The six items that
seem to be most strongly associated with any misconduct were age of first
arrest, age at reception, mental illness, prior jail sentences, a prior sentence with the California Youth Authority, and a prior CDC sentence.
Gang activity almost made the cut, but was highly correlated with the variables corresponding to age and added little new information. When serious misconduct is used as the response variable, gang activity becomes an
important predictor even with the age variables included. In contrast to
the implications of old system, points computed from the nominal sentence length were found to be unimportant in predicting misconduct. In
short, inmates who are engaged in gang activity, young, and who have long
histories of contact with the criminal justice system tended to get in the
most trouble. Mental illness also counts. Once these variables are factored
in, other items such as offense type and sentence length do not contribute
much. We also find no evidence that earlier good behavior predicts less
misconduct. Points for successful completion of a prior minimum custody
incarceration and having no serious disciplinaries in the last 12 months
were not associated with less misconduct. One implications is that in the
future it might be possible to further simplify how the classification score
is calculated.

RECLASSIFICATION

Finally, we turn to what might be learned from CDC form 840. Recall
that such forms are filled out as a routine matter approximately every 12
months while an inmate is incarcerated. They are also filled out if there is
any reason, such as inmate misconduct, to compute a new classification
score.

The revised classification system did not make important changes in the
840 form. The main alteration was to allow classification points to be

deducted a bit more rapidly when there was no reported misconduct. In fact, this is what the data show. A regression of each inmate's 840 score on his 839 score showed that for both the experimentals and controls, the regression coefficient was effectively 1.0. This is not surprising because few classification scores change dramatically between the two assessments. For the control inmates, the intercept was about −2.0. The classification score had declined on the average by about 2 points. For the experimental inmates, the intercept was a little smaller than −4.0. The classification score had declined on the average by about 4 points. With the average classification score in our data of less than 20, during the first year or so, the classification score for the control inmates dropped by about 10% while the classification score for the experimental inmates dropped by about 20%. This is just about what the new forms were designed to accomplish.

CONCLUSIONS AND POLICY IMPLICATIONS

It would seem that there are a number of conclusions whose policy implications are relatively straightforward, as follows:

1. The experiment was well executed. Indeed, it was in many ways a textbook example of a very large field experiment. Working in a total institution like a prison surely helps, but the CDC also invested considerable resources in the project. There was also the key advantage of several preliminary studies. The moral is clear: Large-scale randomized experiments can be conducted well in prison settings when there is the commitment to do so. And because randomized experiments are widely understood to be the "gold standard" in program evaluation when causal inference is central, randomized experiments should always be seriously considered when the effectiveness of prison programs is of interest.

2. The revised inmate classification forms were well received by prison staff. Anecdotal evidence indicates that the new forms were more user friendly than the old forms. Quality control oversight indicated that the new forms were also less prone to recording and computational errors. Finally, the new forms were also preferred by the CDC staff bargaining organizations. In short, staff "buy-in" did not seem to be a problem.

3. Given the prison setting, it is difficult to know what conclusions to draw from the absence of any challenge to the revised forms or the experiment from inmates or inmate advocacy groups. Perhaps the earlier meetings with stakeholders helped. Or perhaps, the changes in the classification forms were too small to seem important.

4. Converting placement "overrides" under the existing system to

"mandatory minimums" under the revised system proved to be a simple and effective means to make explicit decisions that previously had been difficult to track. Mandatory minimums made the new system more "transparent."

5. Under the revised system, inmates who engaged in gang activities, who were young, and who had had long histories of contact with the criminal justice system were anticipated to be among the most likely to get into trouble. Mental health problems could also be an important factor. In fact, the data from the experimental group supported the use of these indicators. Gang activity and mental illness were not considered in the old classification system, and age was not weighted as heavily.

6. A number of classification indicators popular with corrections officials and prison researchers a generation ago were discarded: marital status, education, service in the military, and employment history. In fact, they were virtually unrelated to prison misconduct among the control group.

7. The majority of inmates had the same endorsed placements under the existing and revised systems. For those with different placements, the placement shifts were typically one level. Thus, the new classification system was by design and, in fact, a refinement of the existing procedures, not a wholesale reformulation. Given that earlier research had shown the existing classification procedures to be functioning reasonably well, both the plan and the outcome made sense. This argues more generally for the usefulness of preliminary studies.

8. Overall, there was under the revised system a net decline in the population initially assigned to level I facilities and a net increase in the population initially assigned to level III facilities. The net decline in level I and increase in level III dissipated over time, so the net changes in population distributions did not accumulate. Neither result was surprising once the revised instrument was designed. Still, there may well be a need to reconfigure some facilities in response to these modest population shifts. And therein lies an important lesson: with housing pure and simple such a critical component of any prison system, it is very difficult to tinker with any feature of prison life and not affect the fit between the number of beds and inmate needs.

9. The revised classification score sorted inmates substantially better by level of risk. Thus, there was clear evidence that one can improve on an inmate classification system that was already well respected by prison administrators across the country.

INMATE CLASSIFICATION 241

10. The revised classification score sorted inmates substantially better by level of risk when serious misconduct was the sole concern, not all misconduct. That is, the revised classification score works better than the existing classification score in predicting serious misconduct.

11. Under both the existing and revised classification systems, there was strong evidence for "suppressor effects" in level IV compared to all other endorsed placements. The architectural design of prisons coupled with staffing and administrative procedures really matter for the safety of inmates and staff and indeed more generally, if order is to be maintained.

12. Under the revised classification system, inmate scores declined a bit more quickly over time. Consequently, downward movement to lower levels of security will occur more rapidly.

The California Department of Corrections is currently making plans to implement the revised classification system. Drafts of new administrative procedures have been written, materials for retraining intake staff have been designed, and "sign-off" has been achieved throughout the Department. There have also been meetings with stakeholders explaining the changes underway and the research supporting these changes. It is likely that the revised system will become the operational system by early 2003.

REFERENCES

Alexander, Jack and James Austin
   1992   Handbook for Evaluating Prison Classifications Systems. San Francisco: National Council on Crime and Delinquency.

Austin, James
   1986   Evaluating how well your classification system is operating: A practical approach. In Lawrence A. Bennett (ed.), Crime & Delinquency 32, No. 3. Newbury Park, CA: Sage.

Austin, James, Christopher Baird, and Deborah Neuenfeldt
   1993   Classification for internal management purposes: The Washington experience. In Classification: A tool for managing today's offenders. Laurel, MD: American Correctional Association.

Baird, Christopher
   1993   Objective classification in Tennessee: Management, effectiveness, and planning issues. In Classification: A Tool for Managing Today's Offenders. Laurel, MD: American Correctional Association.

Berk, Richard A. and Jan de Leeuw
   1998   An evaluation of California's inmate classification system using a generalized regression discontinuity design. Journal of the American Statistical Association 94:1045–1052.

242   BERK ET AL.

Brennan, Timothy
    1987   Classification: An Overview of Selected Methodological issues. In Don M.
             Gottfredson and Michael H. Tonry (eds.), Prediction and Classification:
             Criminal Justice Decision Making. Chicago, IL: University of Chicago
             Press.
    1993   Risk assessment: An evaluation of statistical classification methods. In
             Classification: A tool for Managing Today's Offenders. Laurel, MD:
             American Correctional Association.

Campbell, Donald T., and Julian C. Stanley
    1963   Experimental and Quasi-Experimental Designs for Research. Chicago, IL:
             Rand McNally.

Hardyman, Patricia L. and Terri Adams-Fuller
    2001   National Institute of Corrections Prison Classification Peer Training and
             Strategy Session: What's happening with prison classification systems?
             September 6–7, 2000.

Hardyman, Patricia L., James Austin, and Owan C. Tulloch
    2000   Revalidating External Classification Systems: The Experience of Seven
             States and Model for Classification Reform. Report submitted to the
             National Institute of Corrections. Washington, D.C.: The Institute on
             Crime, Justice and Corrections at The George Washington University.

Kane, Thomas R.
    1986   The validity of prison classification: An introduction to practical consider-
             ations and research issues. In Lawrence A. Bennette (ed.), Crime &
             Delinquency 32, Newbury Park, CA: Sage.

Richard Berk is Professor of Statistics and Sociology at UCLA and Director of the UCLA Statistical Consulting Center. He is an elected fellow of the American Association for the Advancement of Science and the American Statistical Association. Recent research in criminal justice includes the use of new data mining procedures to find prison inmates with unusually high probabilities of engaging in violence in-prison behavior.

Heather Ladd is a statistician at the UCLA/NPI Health services Research Center. Her current interests include health care and education policy research.

Jong-Ho Baek is a graduate student in the UCLA Department of Statistics. He is currently working on methods for recursive partitioning.

Heidi Graziano is a graduate student in the UCLA Department of Statistics. She is currently working on regression methods for spatial data.

[3]

Does Research Design
Affect Study Outcomes
in Criminal Justice?

By DAVID WEISBURD, CYNTHIA M. LUM,
and ANTHONY PETROSINO

ABSTRACT: Does the type of research design used in a crime and justice study influence its conclusions? Scholars agree in theory that randomized experimental studies have higher internal validity than do nonrandomized studies. But there is not consensus regarding the costs of using nonrandomized studies in coming to conclusions regarding criminal justice interventions. To examine these issues, the authors look at the relationship between research design and study outcomes in a broad review of research evidence on crime and justice commissioned by the National Institute of Justice. Their findings suggest that design does have a systematic effect on outcomes in criminal justice studies. The weaker a design, indicated by internal validity, the more likely a study is to report a result in favor of treatment and the less likely it is to report a harmful effect of treatment. Even when comparing randomized studies with strong quasi-experimental research designs, systematic and statistically significant differences are observed.

David Weisburd is a senior research fellow in the Department of Criminology and Criminal Justice at the University of Maryland and a professor of criminology at the Hebrew University Law School in Jerusalem.

Cynthia M. Lum is a doctoral student in the Department of Criminology and Criminal Justice at the University of Maryland.

Anthony Petrosino is a research fellow at the Center for Evaluation, Initiative for Children Program at the American Academy of Arts and Sciences and a research associate at Harvard University. He is also the coordinator of the Campbell Crime and Justice Coordinating Group.

NOTE: We are indebted to a number of colleagues for helpful comments in preparing this article. We especially want to thank Iain Chalmers, John Eck, David Farrington, Denise Gottfredson, Doris MacKenzie, Joan McCord, Lawrence Sherman, Brandon Welsh, Charles Wellford, and David Wilson.

THERE is a growing consensus among scholars, practitioners, and policy makers that crime control practices and policies should be rooted as much as possible in scientific research (Cullen and Gendreau 2000; MacKenzie 2000; Sherman 1998). This is reflected in the steady growth in interest in evaluation of criminal justice programs and practices in the United States and the United Kingdom over the past decade and by large increases in criminal justice funding for research during this period (Visher and Weisburd 1998). Increasing support for research and evaluation in criminal justice may be seen as part of a more general trend toward utilization of scientific research for establishing rational and effective practices and policies. This trend is perhaps most prominent in the health professions, where the idea of evidence-based medicine has gained strong government and professional support (Millenson 1997; Zuger 1997), though the evidence-based paradigm is also developing in other fields (see Nutley and Davies 1999; Davies, Nutley, and Smith 2000).

A central component of the movement toward evidence-based practice and policy is reliance on systematic review of prior research and evaluation (Davies 1999). Such review allows policy makers and practitioners to identify what programs and practices are most effective and in which contexts. The Cochrane Collaboration, for example, seeks to prepare, maintain, and make accessible systematic reviews of research on the effects of health care interventions (see Chalmers and Altman 1995;

www.cochrane.org.) The *Cochrane Library* is now widely recognized as the single best source of evidence on the effectiveness of health care and medical treatments and has played an important part in the advancement of evidence-based medicine (Egger and Smith 1998). More recently, social scientists following the Cochrane model established the Campbell Collaboration for developing systematic reviews of research evidence in the area of social and educational interventions (see Boruch, Petrosino, and Chalmers 1999). In recognition of the growing importance of evidence-based policies in criminal justice, the Campbell Collaboration commissioned a coordinating group to deal with crime and justice issues. This group began with the goal of providing the best evidence on "what works in crime and justice" through the development of "systematic reviews of research" on the effects of crime and justice interventions (Farrington and Petrosino 2001 [this issue]).

In the Cochrane Collaboration, and in medical research in general, clinical trials that randomize participants to treatment and control or comparison groups are considered more reliable than studies that do not employ randomization. And the recognition that experimental designs form the gold standard for drawing conclusions about the effects of treatments or programs is not restricted to medicine. There is broad agreement among social and behavioral scientists that randomized experiments provide the best method for drawing causal inferences between treatments and programs and their outcomes (for example, see Boruch, Snyder, and DeMoya 2000; Campbell and Boruch 1975; Farrington 1983; Feder, Jolin, and Feyerherm 2000). Indeed, a task force convened by the Board of Scientific Affairs of the American Psychological Association to look into statistical methods concluded that "for research involving causal inferences, the assignments of units to levels of the causal variable is critical. Random assignment (not to be confused with random selection) allows for the strongest possible causal inferences free of extraneous assumptions" (Wilkinson and Task Force on Statistical Inference 1999).

While reliance on experimental studies in drawing conclusions about treatment outcomes has become common in the development of evidence-based medicine, the Campbell Collaboration Crime and Justice Coordinating Group has concluded that it is unrealistic at this time to restrict systematic reviews on the effects of interventions relevant to crime and justice to experimental studies. In developing its *Standards for Inclusion of Studies in Systematic Reviews* (Farrington 2000), the group notes that it does not require that reviewers select only randomized experiments:

This might possibly be the case for an intervention where there are many randomized experiments (e.g. cognitive-behavioral skills training). However, randomized experiments to evaluate criminological interventions are relatively uncommon. If reviews were restricted to randomized experiments, they would be relevant to only a small fraction of the key questions for policy and practice in criminology. Where there are few randomized experiments, it is expected that reviewers will select both randomized and non-randomized studies for inclusion in detailed reviews. (3)

In this article we examine a central question relevant both to the Campbell Collaboration crime and justice effort and to the more general emphasis on developing evidence-based practice in criminal justice: Does the type of research design used in a crime and justice study influence the conclusions that are reached? Assuming that experimental designs are the gold standard for evaluating practices and policies, it is important to ask what price we pay in including other types of studies in our reviews of what works in crime and justice. Are we likely to overestimate or underestimate the positive effects of treatment? Or conversely, might we expect that the use of well-designed nonrandomized studies will lead to about the same conclusions as we would gain from randomized experimental evaluations?

To examine these issues, we look at the relationship between research design and study outcomes in a broad review of research evidence on crime and justice commissioned by the National Institute of Justice. Generally referred to as the Maryland Report because it was developed in the Department of Criminology and Criminal Justice at the University of Maryland at College Park, the study was published under the title *Preventing Crime: What Works, What*

Doesn't, What's Promising (Sherman et al. 1997). The Maryland Report provides an unusual opportunity for assessing the impact of study design on study outcomes in crime and justice both because it sought to be comprehensive in identifying available research and because the principal investigators of the study devoted specific attention to the nature of the research designs of the studies included. Below we detail the methods we used to examine how study design affects study outcomes in crime and justice research and report on our main findings. We turn first, however, to a discussion of why randomized experiments as contrasted with quasi-experimental and non-experimental research designs are generally considered a gold standard for making causal inferences. We also examine what prior research suggests regarding the questions we raise.

WHY ARE RANDOMIZED EXPERIMENTS CONSIDERED THE GOLD STANDARD?

The key to understanding the strength of experimental research designs is found in what scholars refer to as the internal validity of a study. A research design in which the effects of treatment or intervention can be clearly distinguished from other effects has high internal validity. A research design in which the effects of treatment are confounded with other factors is one in which there is low internal validity. For example, suppose a researcher seeks to assess the effects of a specific drug treatment program on recidivism. If at the end of the evaluation the researcher can present study results and confidently assert that the effects of treatment have been isolated from other confounding causes, the internal validity of the study is high. But if the researcher has been unable to ensure that other factors such as the seriousness of prior records or the social status of offenders have been disentangled from the influence of treatment, he or she must note that the effects observed for treatment may be due to such confounding causes. In this case internal validity is low.

In randomized experimental studies, internal validity is developed through the process of random allocation of the units of treatment or intervention to experimental and control or comparison groups. This means that the researcher has randomized other factors besides treatment itself, since there is no systematic bias that brings one type of subject into the treatment group and another into the control or comparison group. Although the groups are not necessarily the same on every characteristic—indeed, simply by chance, there are likely to be differences—such differences can be assumed to be distributed randomly and are part and parcel of the stochastic processes taken into account in statistical tests. Random allocation thus allows the researcher to assume that the only systematic differences between the treatment and comparison groups are found in the treatments or interventions that are applied. When the study is complete, the researcher can argue with confidence that if a difference has been observed between treatment and comparison groups, it is likely the result of the treatment itself (since randomization has isolated the treatment effect from other possible causes).

In nonrandomized studies, two methods may be used for isolating treatment or program effects. Quasi-experiments, like randomized experiments, rely on the design of a research study to isolate the effects of treatment. Using matching or other methods in an attempt to establish equivalence between groups, quasi-experiments mimic experimental designs in that they attempt to rule out competing causes by identifying groups that are similar except in the nature of the treatment that they receive in the study. Importantly, however, quasi-experiments do not randomize out the effects of other causes as is the case in randomized experimental designs; rather they seek to maximize the equivalence between the units studied through matching or other methods. Threats to internal validity in quasi-experimental studies derive from the fact that it is seldom possible to find or to create treatment and control groups that are not systematically different in one respect or another.

Nonexperimental studies rely primarily on statistical techniques to distinguish the effects of the intervention or treatment from other confounding causes. In practice, quasi-experimental studies often rely as well on statistical approaches to increase the equivalence of the comparisons made.[1] However, in nonexperimental studies, statistical controls are the primary method applied in attempts to increase the level of a study's internal validity. In this case, multivariate statistical methods are used to isolate the effects of treatment from that of other causes. This demands of course that the researcher clearly identify and measure all other factors that may threaten the internal validity of the study outcomes. Only if all such factors are included in the multivariate models estimated can the researcher be confident that the effects of treatment that have been reported are not confounded with other causes.

In theory, the three methods described here are equally valid for solving the problem of isolating treatment or program effects. Each can ensure high internal validity when applied correctly. In practice, however, as Feder and Boruch (2000) note, "there is little disagreement that experiments provide a superior method for assessing the effectiveness of a given intervention" (292). Randomization, according to Kunz and Oxman (1998), "is the only means of controlling for unknown and unmeasured differences between comparison groups as well as those that are known and measured" (1185). While random allocation itself ensures high internal validity in experimental research, for quasi-experimental and nonexperimental research designs, unknown and unmeasured causes are generally seen as representing significant potential threats to the internal validity of the comparisons made.[2]

INTERNAL VALIDITY
AND STUDY OUTCOMES
IN PRIOR REVIEWS

While there is general agreement that experimental studies are more likely to ensure high internal validity than are quasi-experimental or nonexperimental studies, it is difficult to specify at the outset the effects that this will have on study outcomes. On one hand, it can be assumed that weaker internal validity is likely to lead to biases in assessment of the effects of treatments or interventions. However, the direction of that bias in any particular study is likely to depend on factors related to the specific character of the research that is conducted. For example, if nonrandomized studies do not account for important confounding causes that are positively related to treatment, they may on average overestimate program outcomes. However, if such unmeasured causes are negatively related to treatment, nonrandomized studies would be expected to underestimate program outcomes. Heinsman and Shadish (1996) suggested that whatever the differences in research design, if nonrandomized and randomized studies are equally well designed and implemented (and thus internal validity is maximized in each), there should be little difference in the estimates gained. Much of what is known empirically about these questions is drawn from reviews in such fields as medicine, psychology, economics, and education (for example, see Burtless 1995; Hedges 2000; Kunz and Oxman 1998; Lipsey and Wilson 1993). Following, what one would expect in theory, a general conclusion that can be reached from the literature is that there is not a consistent bias that results from use of nonrandomized research designs. At the same time, a few studies suggest that differences, in whatever direction, will be smallest when nonrandomized studies are well designed and implemented.

Kunz and Oxman (1998), for example, using studies drawn from the Cochrane database, found varying results when analyzing 18 meta-analyses (incorporating 1211 clinical trials) in the field of health care. Of these 18 systematic reviews, 4 found randomized and higher-quality studies[3] to give higher estimates of effects than nonrandomized and lower-quality studies, and 8 reviews found randomized or high-quality studies to produce lower estimates of effect sizes than nonrandomized or lower-quality studies. Five other reviews found little or inconclusive differences between different types of research designs, and in one review, low-quality studies were found to be more likely to report findings of harmful effects of treatments.

Mixed results are also found in systematic reviews in the social sciences. Some reviews suggest that nonrandomized studies will on average underestimate program effects. For example, Heinsman and Shadish (1996) looked at four meta-analyses that focused on interventions in four different areas: drug use, effects of coaching on Scholastic Aptitude Test performance, ability grouping of pupils in secondary schools, and psychosocial interventions for postsurgery outcomes. Included in their analysis were 98 published and unpublished studies. As a whole, randomized experiments were found to yield larger effect sizes than studies where randomization was not used. In contrast, Friedlander and Robins (2001), in a review of social welfare programs, found that non-experimental statistical approaches often yielded estimates larger than those gained in randomized studies (see also Cox, Davidson, and Bynum 1995; LaLonde 1986).

In a large-scale meta-analysis examining the efficacy of psychological, educational, and behavioral treatment, Lipsey and Wilson (1993) suggested that conclusions reached on the basis of nonrandomized studies are not likely to strongly bias conclusions regarding treatment or program effects. Although studies varied greatly in both directions as to whether nonrandomized designs overestimated or underestimated effects as compared with randomized designs, no consistent bias in either direction was detected. Lipsey and Wilson, however, did find a notable difference between studies that employed a control/comparison design and those that used one-group pre and post designs. The latter studies produced consistently higher estimates of treatment effects.

Support for the view that stronger nonrandomized studies are likely to provide results similar to randomized experimental designs is provided by Shadish and Ragsdale (1996). In a review of 100 studies of marital or family psychotherapy, they found overall that randomized experiments yielded significantly larger weighted average effect sizes than nonequivalent control group designs. Nonetheless, the difference

between randomized and nonrandomized studies decreased when confounding variables related to the quality of the design of the study were included.

Works that specifically address the relationship between study design and study outcomes are scarce in criminal justice. In turn, assessment of this relationship is most often not a central focus of the reviews developed, and reviewers generally examine a specific criminal justice area, most often corrections (for example, see Bailey 1966; MacKenzie and Hickman 1998; Whitehead and Lab 1989). Results of these studies provide little guidance for specifying a general relationship between study design and study outcomes for criminal justice research. In an early review of 100 reports of correctional treatment between 1940 and 1960, for example, Bailey (1966) found that research design had little effect on the claimed success of treatment, though he noted a slight positive relationship between the "rigor" of the design and study outcome. Logan (1972), who also reviewed correctional treatment programs, found a slight negative correlation between study design and claimed success.

Recent studies are no more conclusive. Wilson, Gallagher, and MacKenzie (2000), in a meta-analysis of corrections-based education, vocation, and work programs, found that run-of-the-mill quasi-experimental studies produced larger effects than did randomized experiments. However, such studies also produced larger effects than did low-quality designs that clearly lacked comparability among groups. In a review of

165 school-based prevention programs, Whitehead and Lab (1989) found little difference in the size of effects in randomized and non-randomized studies. Interestingly however, they reported that nonrandomized studies were much less likely to report a backfire effect whereby treatment was found to exacerbate rather than ameliorate the problem examined. In contrast, a more recent review by Wilson, Gottfredson, and Najaka (in press) found overall that nonrandomized studies yielded results on average significantly lower than randomized experiments' results, even accounting for a series of other design characteristics (including the overall quality of the implementation of the study). However, it should be noted that many of these studies did not include delinquency measures, and schools rather than individuals were often the unit of random allocation.[4]

THE STUDY

We sought to define the influence of research design on study outcomes across a large group of studies representing the different types of research design as well as a broad array of criminal justice areas. The most comprehensive source we could identify for this purpose has come to be known as the Maryland Report (Sherman et al. 1997). The Maryland Report was commissioned by the National Institute of Justice to identify "what works, what doesn't, and what's promising" in preventing crime. It was conducted at the University of Maryland's Department of Criminology and Criminal Justice over a yearlong period between 1996 and 1997. The report attempted to identify all available research relevant to crime prevention in seven broad areas: communities, families, schools, labor markets, places, policing, and criminal justice (corrections). Studies chosen for inclusion in the Maryland Report met minimal methodological requirements.[5]

Though the Maryland Report did not examine the relationship between study design and study outcomes, it did define the quality of the methods used to evaluate the strength of the evidence provided through a scientific methods scale (SMS). This SMS was coded with numbers 1 through 5, with "5 being the strongest scientific evidence" (Sherman et al. 1997, 2.18). Overall, studies higher on the scale have higher internal validity, and studies with lower scores have lower internal validity. The 5-point scale was broadly defined in the Maryland Report (Sherman et al. 1997) as follows:

1: Correlation between a crime prevention program and a measure of crime or crime risk factors.

2: Temporal sequence between the program and the crime or risk outcome clearly observed, or a comparison group present without the demonstrated comparability to the treatment group.

3: A comparison between two or more units of analysis, one with and one without the program.

4: Comparison between multiple units with and without the program, controlling for other factors, or a non-equivalent comparison group has only minor differences evident.

5: Random assignment and analysis of comparable units to program and comparison groups. (2.18-2.19)

A score of 5 on this scale suggests a randomized experimental design, and a score of 1 a nonexperimental approach. Scores of 3 and 4 may be associated with quasi-experimental designs, with 4 distinguished from 3 by a greater concern with control for threats to internal validity. A score of 2 represents a stronger nonexperimental design or a weaker quasi-experimental approach. However, the overall rating given to a study could be affected by other design criteria such as response rate, attrition, use of statistical tests, and statistical power. It is impossible to tell from the Maryland Report how much influence such factors had on each study's rating. However, correspondence with four of the main study investigators suggests that adjustments based on these other factors were uncommon and generally would result in an SMS decrease or increase of only one level.

Although the Maryland Report included a measure of study design, it did not contain a standardized measure of study outcome. Most prior reviews have relied on standardized effect measures as a criterion for studying the relationship between design type and study findings. Although in some of the area reviews in the Maryland Report, standardized effect sizes were calculated for specific studies, this was not the case for the bulk of the studies

reviewed in the report. Importantly, in many cases it was not possible to code such information because the original study authors did not provide the specific details necessary for calculating standardized effect coefficients. But the approach used by the Maryland investigators also reflected a broader philosophical decision that emphasized the bottom line of what was known about the effects of crime and justice interventions. In criminal justice, the outcome of a study is often considered more important than the effect size noted. This is the case in good part because there are often only a very small number of studies that examine a specific type of treatment or intervention. In addition, policy decisions are made not on the basis of a review of the effect sizes that are reported but rather on whether one or a small group of studies suggests that the treatment or intervention works.

From the data available in the Maryland Report, we developed an overall measure of study outcomes that we call the investigator reported result (IRR). The IRR was created as an ordinal scale with three values: 1, 0, and –1, reflecting whether a study concluded that the treatment or intervention worked, had no detected effect, or led to a backfire effect. It is defined by what is reported in the tables of the Maryland Report and is coded as follows:[6]

1: The program or treatment is reported to have had an intended positive effect for the criminal justice system or society. Outcomes in this case supported the position that interventions or treatments lead to reductions in crime, recidivism, or related measures. [7]

0: The program treatment was reported to have no detected effect, or the effect was reported as not statistically significant.

−1: The program or treatment had an unintended backfire effect for the criminal justice system or society. Outcomes in this case supported the position that interventions or treatments were harmful and lead to increases in crime, recidivism, or related measures.[8]

This scale provides an overall measure of the conclusions reached by investigators in the studies that were reviewed in the Maryland Report. However, we think it is important to note at the outset some specific features of the methodology used that may affect the findings we gain using this approach. Perhaps most significant is the fact that Maryland reviewers generally relied on the reported conclusions of investigators unless there was obvious evidence to the contrary.[9] This approach led us to term the scale the *investigator reported result* and reinforces the fact that we examine the impacts of study design on what investigators report rather than on the actual outcomes of the studies examined.

While the Maryland reviewers examined tests of statistical significance in coming to conclusions about which programs or treatments work,[10] they did not require that statistical tests be reported by investi-

gators to support the specific conclusions reached in each study. In turn, the tables in the Maryland Report often do not note whether specific studies employed statistical tests of significance. Accordingly, in reviewing the Maryland Report studies, we cannot assess whether the presence or absence of such tests influences our conclusions. Later in our article we reexamine our results, taking into account statistical significance in the context of a more recent review in the corrections area that was modeled on the Maryland Report.

Finally, as we noted earlier, most systematic reviews of study outcomes have come to use standardized effect size as a criterion. While we think that the IRR scale is useful for gaining an understanding of the relationship between research design and reported study conclusions, we recognize that a different set of conclusions might have been reached had we focused on standardized effect sizes. Again, we use the corrections review referred to above to assess how our conclusions might have differed if we had focused on standardized effect sizes rather than the IRR scale.

We coded the Scientific Methods Scale and the IRR directly from the tables reported in *Preventing Crime: What Works, What Doesn't, What's Promising* (Sherman et al. 1997). We do not include all of the studies in the Maryland Report in our review. First, given our interest in the area of criminal justice, we excluded studies that did not have a crime or delinquency outcome measure. Second, we excluded studies that did not provide an SMS score (a feature of some

TABLE 1		
STUDIES CATEGORIZED BY SMS		
	Studies	
SMS	n	Percentage
1	10	3
2	94	31
3	130	42
4	28	9
5	46	15
Total	308	100

TABLE 2		
STUDIES CATEGORIZED BY THE IRR		
	Studies	
IRR	n	Percentage
−1	34	11
0	76	25
1	198	64
Total	308	100

tables in the community and family sections of the report). Finally, we excluded the school-based area from review because only selected studies were reported in tables.[11] All other studies reviewed in the Maryland Report were included, which resulted in a sample of 308 studies. Tables 1 and 2 display the breakdown of these studies by SMS and IRR.

As is apparent from Table 1, there is wide variability in the nature of the research methods used in the studies that are reviewed. About 15 percent were coded in the highest SMS category, which demands a randomized experimental design. Only 10 studies included were coded in the lowest SMS category, though almost a third fall in category 2. The largest category is score 3, which required simply a comparison between two units of analysis, one with and one without treatment. About 1 in 10 cases were coded as 4, suggesting a quasi-experimental study with strong attention to creating equivalence between the groups studied.

The most striking observation that is drawn from Table 2 is that almost two-thirds of the crime and justice studies reviewed in the Maryland Report produced a reported result in the direction of success for the treatment or intervention examined. This result is very much at odds with reviews conducted in earlier decades that suggested that most interventions had little effect on crime or related problems (for example, see Lipton, Martinson, and Wilks 1975; Logan 1972; Martinson 1974).[12] At the same time, a number of the studies examined, about 1 in 10, reported a backfire effect for treatment or intervention.

RELATING STUDY DESIGN
AND STUDY OUTCOMES

In Tables 3 and 4 we present our basic findings regarding the relationship between study design and study outcomes in the Maryland Report sample. Table 3 provides mean IRR outcome scores across the five SMS design categories. While the mean IRR scores in this case present a simple method for examining the results, we also provide an overall statistical measure of correlation, Tau-c (and the associated significance level), which is more appropriate for data of this type. In Table 4 we provide the

TABLE 3
**MEAN IRR SCORES
ACROSS SMS CATEGORIES**

SMS	Mean	n	Standard Deviation
1	.80	10	.42
2	.66	94	.63
3	.56	130	.67
4	.39	28	.83
5	.22	46	.70
Total	.53	308	.69

NOTE: Tau-c = –.181. $p < .001$.

cross-tabulation of IRR and SMS scores. This presentation of the results allows us to examine more carefully the nature of the relationship both in terms of outcomes in the expected treatment direction and outcomes that may be classified as backfire effects.

Overall Tables 3 and 4 suggest that there is a linear inverse relationship between the SMS and the IRR. The mean IRR score decreases with each increase in step in the SMS score (see Table 3). While fully nonexperimental designs have a mean IRR score of .80, randomized experiments have a mean of only .22. The run of the mill quasi-experimental designs represented in category 3 have a mean IRR score of .56, while the strongest quasi experiments (category 4) have a mean of .39. The overall correlation between study design and study outcomes is moderate and negative (–.18), and the relationship is statistically significant at the .001 level.

Looking at the cross-tabulation of SMS and IRR scores, our findings are reinforced. The stronger the method

in terms of internal validity as measured by the SMS, the less likely is a study to conclude that the intervention or treatment worked. The weaker the method, the less likely the study is to conclude that the intervention or treatment backfired.

While 8 of the 10 studies in the lowest SMS category and 74 percent of those in category 2 show a treatment impact in the desired direction, this was true for only 37 percent of the randomized experiments in category 5. Only in the case of backfire outcomes in categories 4 and 5 does the table not follow our basic findings, and this departure is small. Overall the relationship observed in the table is statistically significant at the .005 level.

Comparing the highest-quality nonrandomized studies with randomized experiments

As noted earlier, some scholars argue that higher-quality nonrandomized studies are likely to have outcomes similar to outcomes of randomized evaluations. This hypothesis is not supported by our data. In Table 5 we combine quasi-experimental studies in SMS categories 3 and 4 and compare them with randomized experimental studies placed in SMS category 5. Again we find a statistically significant negative relationship ($p < .01$). While 37 percent of the level 5 experimental studies show a treatment effect in the desired direction, this was true for 65 percent of the quasi-experimental studies.

Even if we examine only the highest-quality quasi-experimental studies as represented by category 4 and

TABLE 4
CROSS-TABULATION OF SMS AND IRR

IRR	SMS									
	1		2		3		4		5	
	n	Percentage	n	Percentage	n	Percentage	n	Percentage	n	Percentage
−1	0	0	8	9	13	10	6	21	7	15
0	2	20	16	17	31	24	5	18	22	48
1	8	80	70	74	86	66	17	61	17	37
Total	10	100	94	100	130	100	28	100	46	100

NOTE: Chi-square = 25.487 with 8 *df* ($p < .005$).

TABLE 5
COMPARING QUASI-EXPERIMENTAL
STUDIES (SMS = 3 OR 4) WITH
RANDOMIZED EXPERIMENTS (SMS = 5)

IRR	SMS			
	3 or 4		5	
	n	Percentage	n	Percentage
−1	19	12	7	15
0	36	23	22	48
1	103	65	17	37
Total	158	100	46	100

NOTE: Chi-square = 12.971 with 2 *df* ($p < .01$).

TABLE 6
COMPARING HIGH-QUALITY QUASI-
EXPERIMENTAL DESIGNS (SMS = 4)
WITH RANDOMIZED DESIGNS (SMS = 5)

IRR	SMS			
	4		5	
	n	Percentage	n	Percentage
−1	6	21	7	15
0	5	18	22	48
1	17	61	17	37
Total	28	100	46	100

NOTE: Chi-square = 6.805 with 2 *df* ($p < .05$).

compare these to the randomized studies included in category 5, the relationship between study outcomes and study design remains statistically significant at the .05 level (see Table 6). There is little difference between the two groups in the proportion of backfire outcomes reported; however, there remains a very large gap between the proportion of SMS category 4 and SMS category 5 studies that report an outcome in the direction of treatment effectiveness. While 61 percent of the category 4 SMS studies reported a positive treatment or intervention effect,

this was true for only 37 percent of the randomized studies in category 5. Accordingly, even when comparing those nonrandomized studies with the highest internal validity with randomized experiments, we find significant differences in terms of reported study outcomes.

*Taking into account tests
of statistical significance*

It might be argued that had we used a criterion of statistical significance, the overall findings would not have been consistent with the analyses reported above. While we cannot examine this question in the context of the Maryland Report, since statistical significance is generally not reported in the tables or the text of the report, we can review this concern in the context of a more recent review conducted in the corrections area by one of the Maryland investigators, which uses a similar methodology and reports Maryland SMS (see MacKenzie and Hickman 1998). MacKenzie and Hickman (1998) examined 101 studies in their 1998 review of what works in corrections, of which 68 are reported to have included tests of statistical significance.

Developing the IRR score for each of MacKenzie and Hickman's (1998) studies proved more complex than the coding done for the Maryland Report. MacKenzie and Hickman reported all of the studies' results, sometimes breaking up results by gender, employment, treatment mix, or criminal history, to list a few examples. Rather than count each result as a separate study, we developed two different methods that followed different assumptions for coding the IRR index.

The first simply notes whether any significant findings were found supporting a treatment effect and codes a backfire effect when there are statistically significant negative findings with no positive treatment effects (scale A).[13] The second (scale B) is more complex and gives weight to each result in each study.[14]

Taking this approach, our findings analyzing the MacKenzie and Hickman (1998) data follow those reported when analyzing the Maryland Report. The correlation between

TABLE 7

RELATING SMS AND IRR ONLY FOR STUDIES IN MacKENZIE AND HICKMAN (1998) THAT INCLUDE TESTS OF STATISTICAL SIGNIFICANCE

SMS	Scale A		Scale B	
	Mean	n	Mean	n
1		0		0
2	0.83	24	1.46	24
3	0.62	26	1.04	26
4	0.36	11	0.64	11
5	0.00	7	0.14	7
Total	.59	68	1.03	68

NOTE: Tau-c for scale A = $-.285$ ($p < .005$). Tau-c for scale B = $-.311$ ($p < .005$).

study design and study outcomes is negative and statistically significant ($p < .005$) irrespective of the approach we used to define the IRR outcome scale (see Table 7). Using scale A, the correlation observed is $-.29$, while using scale B, the observed correlation is $-.31$.

Comparing effect size and IRR score results

It might be argued that our overall findings are related to specific characteristics of the IRR scale rather than the underlying relationship between study design and study outcomes. We could not test this question directly using the Maryland Report data because, as noted earlier, standardized effect sizes were not consistently recorded in the report. However, MacKenzie and Hickman (1998) did report standardized effect size coefficients, and thus we are able to reexamine this question in the context of corrections-based criminal justice studies.

Using the average standardized effect size reported for each study reviewed by MacKenzie and Hickman (1998) for the entire sample (including studies where statistical significance is not reported), the results follow those gained from relating IRR and SMS scores using the Maryland Report sample (see Table 8). Again the correlation between SMS and study outcomes is negative; in this case the correlation is about −.30. The observed relationship is also statistically significant at the .005 level. Accordingly, these findings suggest that our observation of a negative relationship between study design and study outcomes in the Maryland Report sample is not an artifact of the particular codings of the IRR scale.

DISCUSSION

Our review of the Maryland Report Studies suggests that in criminal justice, there is a moderate inverse relationship between the quality of a research design, defined in terms of internal validity, and the outcomes reported in a study. This relationship continues to be observed even when comparing the highest-quality nonrandomized studies with randomized experiments. Using a related database concentrating only on the corrections area, we also found that our findings are consistent when taking into account only studies that employed statistical tests of significance. Finally, using the same database, we were able to examine whether our results would have differed had we used standardized effect size measures rather than the

TABLE 8

RELATING AVERAGE EFFECT SIZE AND SMS FOR STUDIES IN MacKENZIE AND HICKMAN (1988)

SMS	Effect Size Available from the Entire Sample	
	Mean	n
1		0
2	.29	39
3	.23	30
4	.19	13
5	.00	7
Total	.23	89
Missing values		12

NOTE: Correlation $(r) = -.296$ $(p < .005)$.

IRR index that was drawn from the Maryland Report. We found our results to be consistent using both methods. Studies that were defined as including designs with higher internal validity were likely to report smaller effect sizes than studies with designs associated with lower internal validity.

Prior reviews of the relationship between study design and study outcomes do not predict our findings. Indeed, as we noted earlier, the main lesson that can be drawn from prior research is that the impact of study design is very much dependant on the characteristics of the particular area or studies that are reviewed. In theory as well, there is no reason to assume that there will be a systematic type of bias in studies with lower internal validity. What can be said simply is that such studies, all else being equal, are likely to provide biased findings as compared with results drawn from randomized experimental designs. Why then do we find in reviewing a broad group of crime and justice studies what appears to be a systematic relationship between study design and study outcomes?

One possible explanation for our findings is that they are simply an artifact of combining a large number of studies drawn from many different areas of criminal justice. Indeed, there are generally very few studies that examine a very specific type of treatment or intervention in the Maryland Report. And it may be that were we able to explore the impacts of study design on study outcomes for specific types of treatments or interventions, we would find patterns different from the aggregate ones reported here. We think it is likely that for specific areas of treatment or specific types of studies in criminal justice, the relationship between study design and study outcomes will differ from those we observe. Nonetheless, review of this question in the context of one specific type of treatment examined by the Campbell Collaboration (where there was a substantial enough number of randomized and nonrandomized studies for comparison) points to the salience of our overall conclusions even within specific treatment areas (see Petrosino, Petrosino, and Buehler 2001). We think this example is particularly important because it suggests the potential confusion that might result from drawing conclusions from nonrandomized studies.

Relying on a systematic review conducted by Petrosino, Petrosino, and Buehler (2001) on Scared Straight and other kids-visit programs, we identified 20 programs that included crime-related outcome measures. Of these, 9 were randomized experiments, 4 were quasi-experimental trials, and 7 were fully nonexperimental studies. Petrosino, Petrosino, and Buehler reported on the randomized experimental trials in their Campbell Collaboration review. They concluded that Scared Straight and related programs do not evidence any benefit in terms of recidivism and actually increase subsequent delinquency. However, a very different picture of the effectiveness of these programs is drawn from our review of the quasi-experimental and nonexperimental studies. Overall, these studies, in contrast to the experimental evaluations, suggest that Scared Straight programs not only are not harmful but are more likely than not to produce a crime prevention benefit.

We believe that our findings, however preliminary, point to the possibility of an overall positive bias in nonrandomized criminal justice studies. This bias may in part reflect a number of other factors that we could not control for in our data, for example, publication bias or differential attrition rates across designs (see Shadish and Ragsdale 1996). However, we think that a more general explanation for our findings is likely to be found in the norms of criminal justice research and practice.

Such norms are particularly important in the development of nonrandomized studies. Randomized experiments provide little freedom to the researcher in defining equivalence between treatment and comparison groups. Equivalence in randomized experiments is defined simply through the process of randomization. However, nonrandomized studies demand much insight and knowledge in the development of comparable groups of subjects. Not only must the researcher understand the factors that influence treatment so that he or she can prevent confounding in the study results, but such factors must be measured and then controlled for through some statistical or practical procedure.

It may be that such manipulation is particularly difficult in criminal justice study. Criminal justice practitioners may not be as strongly socialized to the idea of experimentation as are practitioners in other fields like medicine. And in this context, it may be that a subtle form of creaming in which the cases considered most amenable to intervention are placed in the intervention group is common. In specific areas of criminal justice, such creaming may be exacerbated by self-selection of subjects who are motivated toward rehabilitation. Nonrandomized designs, even in relatively rigorous quasi-experimental studies, may be unable to compensate or control for why a person is considered amenable and placed in the intervention group. Matching on traditional control variables like age and race, in turn, might not identify the subtle components that make individuals amenable to treatment and thus more likely to be placed in intervention or treatment categories.

Of course, we have so far assumed that nonrandomized studies are biased in their overestimation of program effects. Some scholars might argue just the opposite. The inflexibility of randomized experimental designs has sometimes been seen as a barrier to development of effective theory and practice in criminology (for example, see Clarke and Cornish 1972; Eck 2001; Pawson and Tilley, 1997). Here it is argued that in a field in which we still know little about the root causes and processes that underlie phenomena we seek to influence, randomized studies may not allow investigators the freedom to carefully explore how treatments or programs influence their intended subjects. While this argument has merit in specific circumstances, especially in exploratory analyses of problems and treatments, we think our data suggest that it can lead in more developed areas of our field to significant misinterpretation and confusion.

CONCLUSION

We asked at the outset of our article whether the type of research design used in criminal justice influences the conclusions that are reached. Our findings, based on the Maryland Report, suggest that design does matter and that its effect in criminal justice study is systematic. The weaker a design, as indicated by internal validity, the more likely was a study to report a result in favor of treatment and the less likely it was to report a harmful effect of treatment. Even when comparing studies defined as randomized designs in the Maryland Report with strong quasi-experimental research designs, systematic and statistically significant differences were observed. Though our study should bscores e seen only as a preliminary step in understanding how research design affects study outcomes in criminal justice, it suggests that systematic reviews of what works in criminal justice may be strongly biased when including nonrandomized studies. In efforts such as those being developed by the Campbell Collaboration, such potential biases should be taken into account in coming to conclusions about the effects of interventions.

Notes

1. Statistical adjustments for random group differences are sometimes employed in experimental studies as well.

2. We should note that we have assumed so far that external validity (the degree to which it can be inferred that outcomes apply to the populations that are the focus of treatment) is held constant in these comparisons. Some scholars argue that experimental studies are likely to have lower external validity because it is often difficult to identify institutions that are willing to randomize participants. Clearly, where randomized designs have lower external validity, the assumption that they are to be preferred to nonrandomized studies is challenged.

3. Kunz and Oxman (1998) not only compared randomized and nonrandomized studies but also adequately and inadequately concealed randomized trials and high-quality versus low-quality studies. Generally, high-quality randomized studies included adequately concealed allocation, while lower-quality randomized trails were inadequately concealed. In addition, the general terms *high-quality trials* and *low-quality trials* indicate a difference where "the specific effect of randomization or allocation concealment could not be separated from the effect of other methodological manoeuvres such as double blinding" (Kunz and Oxman 1998, 1185).

4. Moreover, it may be that the finding of higher standardized effects sizes for randomized studies in this review was due to school-level as opposed to individual-level assignment. When only those studies that include a delinquency outcome are examined, a larger effect is found when school rather than student is the unit of analysis (Denise Gottfredson, personal communication, 2001).

5. As the following Scientific Methods Scale illustrates, the lowest acceptable type of evaluation for inclusion in the Maryland Report is a simple correlation between a crime prevention program and a measure of crime or crime risk factors. Thus studies that were descriptive or contained only process measures were excluded.

6. There were also (although rarely) studies in the Maryland Report that reported two findings in opposite directions. For instance, in Sherman and colleagues' (1997) section on specific deterrence (8.18-8.19), studies of arrest for domestic violence had positive results for employed offenders and backfire results for nonemployed offenders. In these isolated cases, the study was coded twice with the same scientific methods scores and each of the investigator-reported result scores (of 1 and −1) separately.

7. For studies examining the absence of a program (such as a police strike) where social conditions worsened or crime increased, this would be coded as 1.

8. For studies examining the absence of a program (such as a police strike) where social conditions improved or crime decreased, this would be coded as −1.

9. Only in the school-based area was there a specific criterion for assessing the investigator's conclusions. As noted below, however, the school-based studies are excluded from our review for other reasons.

10. For example, the authors of the Maryland Report noted in discussing criteria for deciding which programs work, "These are programs that we are reasonably certain of preventing crime or reducing risk factors for crime in the kinds of social contexts in which they have been evaluated, and for which the findings should be generalizable to similar settings in other places and times. Programs coded as 'working' by this definition must have at least two level 3 evaluations with statistical

significance tests showing effectiveness and the preponderance of all available evidence supporting the same conclusion" (Sherman et al. 1997, 2-20).

11. It is the case that many of the studies in this area would have been excluded anyway since they often did not have a crime or delinquency outcome measure (but rather examined early risk factors for crime and delinquency).

12. While the Maryland Report is consistent with other recent reviews that also point to greater success in criminal justice interventions during the past 20 years (for example, see Poyner 1993; Visher and Weisburd 1998; Weisburd 1997), we think the very high percentage of studies showing a treatment impact is likely influenced by publication bias. The high rate of positive findings is also likely influenced by the general weaknesses of the study designs employed. This is suggested by our findings reported later: that the weaker a research design in terms of internal validity, the more likely is the study to report a positive treatment outcome.

13. The coding scheme for scale A was as follows. A value of 1 indicates that the study had any statistically significant findings supporting a positive treatment effect, even if findings included results that were not significant or had negative or backfire findings. A value of 0 indicates that the study had only nonsignificant findings. A value of –1 indicates that the study had only statistically significant negative or backfire findings or statistically significant negative findings with other nonsignificant results.

14. Scale B was created according to the following rules. A value of 2 indicates that the study had only or mostly statistically significant findings supporting a treatment effect (more than 50 percent) when including all results, even nonsignificant ones. A value of 1 indicates that the study had some statistically significant findings supporting a treatment effect (50 percent or less, counting both positive significant and nonsignificant results) even if the nonsignificant results outnumbered the positive statistically significant results. A value of 0 indicates that no statistically significant findings were reported. A value of –1 indicates that the study evidenced statistically significant backfire effects (even if non-

significant results were present) but no statistically significant results supporting the effectiveness of treatment.

References

Bailey, Walter C. 1966. Correctional Outcome: An Evaluation of 100 Reports. *Journal of Criminal Law, Criminology and Police Science* 57:153-60.

Boruch, Robert F., Anthony Petrosino, and Iain Chalmers. 1999. The Campbell Collaboration: A Proposal for Systematic, Multi-National, and Continuous Reviews of Evidence. Background paper for the meeting at University College–London, School of Public Policy, July.

Boruch, Robert F., Brook Snyder, and Dorothy DeMoya. 2000. The Importance of Randomized Field Trials. *Crime & Delinquency* 46:156-80.

Burtless, Gary. 1995. The Case for Randomized Field Trials in Economic and Policy Research. *Journal of Economic Perspectives* 9:63-84.

Campbell, Donald P. and Robert F. Boruch. 1975. Making the Case for Randomized Assignment to Treatments by Considering the Alternatives: Six Ways in Which Quasi-Experimental Evaluations in Compensatory Education Tend to Underestimate Effects. In *Evaluation and Experiment: Some Critical Issues in Assessing Social Programs*, ed. Carl Bennett and Arthur Lumsdaine. New York: Academic Press.

Chalmers, Iain and Douglas G. Altman. 1995. *Systematic Reviews*. London: British Medical Journal Press.

Clarke, Ronald V. and Derek B. Cornish. 1972. *The Control Trial in Institutional Research: Paradigm or Pitfall for Penal Evaluators?* London: HMSO.

Cox, Stephen M., William S. Davidson, and Timothy S. Bynum. 1995. A Meta-Analytic Assessment of Delinquency-

Related Outcomes of Alternative Education Programs. *Crime & Delinquency* 41:219-34.

Cullen, Francis T. and Paul Gendreau. 2000. Assessing Correctional Rehabilitation: Policy, Practice, and Prospects. In *Policies, Processes, and Decisions of the Criminal Justice System: Criminal Justice 3*, ed. Julie Horney. Washington, DC: U.S. Department of Justice, National Institute of Justice.

Davies, Huw T. O., Sandra Nutley, and Peter C. Smith. 2000. *What Works: Evidence-Based Policy and Practice in Public Services*. London: Policy Press.

Davies, Philip. 1999. What Is Evidence-Based Education? *British Journal of Educational Studies* 47:108-21.

Eck, John. 2001. Learning from Experience in Problem Oriented Policing and Crime Prevention: The Positive Functions of Weak Evaluations and the Negative Functions of Strong Ones. Unpublished manuscript.

Egger, Matthias and G. Davey Smith. 1998. Bias in Location and Selection of Studies. *British Medical Journal* 316:61-66.

Farrington, David P. 1983. Randomized Experiments in Crime and Justice. In *Crime and Justice: An Annual Review of Research*, ed. Norval Morris and Michael Tonry. Chicago: University of Chicago Press.

———. 2000. Standards for Inclusion of Studies in Systematic Reviews. Discussion paper for the Campbell Collaboration Crime and Justice Coordinating Group.

Farrington, David P. and Anthony Petrosino. 2001. The Campbell Collaboration Crime and Justice Group. *Annals of the American Academy of Political and Social Science* 578:35-49.

Feder, Lynette and Robert F. Boruch. 2000. The Need for Experiments in Criminal Justice Settings. *Crime & Delinquency* 46:291-94.

Feder, Lynette, Annette Jolin, and William Feyerherm. 2000. Lessons from Two Randomized Experiments in Criminal Justice Settings. *Crime & Delinquency* 46:380-400.

Friedlander, Daniel and Philip K. Robins. 2001. Evaluating Program Evaluations: New Evidence on Commonly Used Non-Experimental Methods. *American Economic Review* 85:923-37.

Hedges, Larry V. 2000. Using Converging Evidence in Policy Formation: The Case of Class Size Research. *Evaluation and Research in Education* 14:193-205.

Heinsman, Donna T. and William R. Shadish. 1996. Assignment Methods in Experimentation: When Do Nonrandomized Experiments Approximate Answers from Randomized Experiments? *Psychological Methods* 1:154-69.

Kunz, Regina and Andy Oxman. 1998. The Unpredictability Paradox: Review of Empirical Comparisons of Randomized and Non-Randomized Clinical Trials. *British Medical Journal* 317:1185-90.

LaLonde, Robert J. 1986. Evaluating the Econometric Evaluations of Training Programs with Experimental Data. *American Economic Review* 76:604-20.

Lipsey, Mark W. and David B. Wilson. 1993. The Efficacy of Psychological, Educational, and Behavioral Treatment: Confirmation from Meta-Analysis. *American Psychologist* 48:1181-209.

Lipton, Douglas S., Robert M. Martinson, and Judith Wilks. 1975. *The Effectiveness of Correctional Treatment: A Survey of Treatment Evaluation Studies*. New York: Praeger.

Logan, Charles H. 1972. Evaluation Research in Crime and Delinquency—A Reappraisal. *Journal of Criminal Law, Criminology and Police Science* 63:378-87.

MacKenzie, Doris L. 2000. Evidence-based Corrections: Identifying What Works. *Crime & Delinquency* 46:457-71.

MacKenzie, Doris L. and Laura J. Hickman. 1998. *What Works in Corrections* (Report submitted to the State of Washington Legislature Joint Audit and Review Committee). College Park: University of Maryland.

Martinson, Robert. 1974. What Works? Questions and Answers About Prison Reform. *Public Interest* 35:22-54.

Millenson, Michael L. 1997. *Demanding Medical Excellence: Doctors and Accountability in the Information Age.* Chicago: University of Chicago Press.

Nutley, Sandra and Huw T. O. Davies. 1999. The Fall and Rise of Evidence in Criminal Justice. *Public Money & Management* 19:47-54.

Pawson, Ray and Nick Tilley. 1997. *Realistic Evaluation.* London: Sage.

Petrosino, Anthony, Carolyn Petrosino, and John Buehler. 2001. Pilot Test: The Effects of Scared Straight and Other Juvenile Awareness Programs on Delinquency. Unpublished manuscript.

Poyner, Barry. 1993. What Works in Crime Prevention: An Overview of Evaluations. In *Crime Prevention Studies.* Vol. 1, ed. Ronald V. Clarke. Monsey, NY: Criminal Justice Press.

Shadish, William R. and Kevin Ragsdale. 1996. Random Versus Nonrandom Assignment in Controlled Experiments: Do You Get the Same Answer? *Journal of Consulting and Clinical Psychology* 64:1290-305.

Sherman, Lawrence W. 1998. *Evidence-Based Policing.* In *Ideas in American Policing.* Washington, DC: Police Foundation.

Sherman, Lawrence W., Denise C. Gottfredson, Doris Layton MacKenzie, John E. Eck, Peter Reuter, and Shawn D. Bushway. 1997. *Preventing Crime: What Works, What Doesn't, What's Promising.* Washington, DC: U.S. Department of Justice, National Institute of Justice.

Visher, Christy A. and David Weisburd. 1998. Identifying What Works: Recent Trends in Crime Prevention. *Crime, Law and Social Change* 28:223-42.

Weisburd, David. 1997. *Reorienting Crime Prevention Research and Policy: From the Causes of Criminality to the Context of Crime* (Research Report NIJ 16504). Washington, DC: U.S. Department of Justice, National Institute of Justice.

Whitehead, John T. and Steven P. Lab. 1989. A Meta-Analysis of Juvenile Correctional Treatment. *Journal of Research in Crime and Delinquency* 26:276-95.

Wilkinson, Leland and Task Force on Statistical Inference. 1999. Statistical Methods in Psychology Journals: Guidelines and Explanations. *American Psychologist* 54:594-604.

Wilson, David B., Catherine A. Gallagher, Doris L. MacKenzie. 2000. A Meta-Analysis of Corrections-Based Education, Vocation, and Work Programs for Adult Offenders. *Journal of Research in Crime and Delinquency* 37:347-68.

Wilson, David B., Denise C. Gottfredson, and Stacy S. Najaka. In Press. School-Based Prevention of Problem Behaviors: A Meta-Analysis. *Journal of Quantitative Criminology.*

Zuger, Abigail. 1997. New Way of Doctoring: By the Book. *New York Times,* 16 Dec.

[4]

The Efficacy of Psychological, Educational, and Behavioral Treatment

Confirmation From Meta-Analysis

Mark W. Lipsey and David B. Wilson

Conventional reviews of research on the efficacy of psychological, educational, and behavioral treatments often find considerable variation in outcome among studies and, as a consequence, fail to reach firm conclusions about the overall effectiveness of the interventions in question. In contrast meta-analytic reviews show a strong, dramatic pattern of positive overall effects that cannot readily be explained as artifacts of meta-analytic technique or generalized placebo effects. Moreover, the effects are not so small that they can be dismissed as lacking practical or clinical significance. Although meta-analysis has limitations, there are good reasons to believe that its results are more credible than those of conventional reviews and to conclude that well-developed psychological, educational, and behavioral treatment is generally efficacious.

Systematic knowledge about the efficacy of psychological, educational, and behavioral intervention for individual and social problems is almost entirely dependent on research conducted within the experimental or quasi-experimental framework. In any given treatment area, such research often yields an ambiguous mix of results—decidedly positive, suggestive, convincingly null, and hopelessly inconclusive. Research reviewers must then pick through these results with hopes of finding a preponderance of evidence supporting a conclusion about treatment efficacy. More specifically, they must attempt to sort and choose among studies on the basis of their methods, treatment variants, respondents, and the like to find those situations for which conclusions can be drawn.

It is a distressing observation that, over recent decades, the results of treatment research and reviews of that research have not yielded convincing support for the efficacy of many psychological, educational, and behavioral treatments. The controversial history of assessment of the effects of psychotherapy is representative. Some reviewers were adamant that the research showed no convincing effects (e.g., Eysenck, 1952, 1965), whereas others interpreted the evidence as generalized efficacy (e.g., Luborsky, Singer, & Luborsky, 1975). Similar controversy has characterized intervention in social work, counseling, education, criminal justice, organizational development (Fischer, 1978; Prather & Gibson, 1977), and a host of

related areas. Rossi and Wright (1984) echoed many reviewers in these areas when they described evaluation research as a "parade of close-to-zero effects" (p. 342). Such controversy and pessimism has cast a shadow of doubt over all but a few claims for the efficacy of psychological, educational, and behavioral interventions.

The Advent of Meta-Analysis

A new approach to integrating and interpreting a body of treatment effectiveness research arose in the mid-1970s and has come to fruition in recent years. Dubbed "meta-analysis" by Glass (1976), this approach is quite different from the research integration practices that preceded it. In particular, it is characterized by its framing of research integration as, in large part, a research exercise in its own right. Eligible research studies are viewed as a population to be systematically sampled and surveyed. Individual study results and characteristics are then abstracted, quantified, coded, and assembled into a database that is statistically analyzed much like any other quantitative survey data.

Since Smith and Glass's (1977) pioneering meta-analysis of psychotherapy research, literally hundreds of meta-analyses have been conducted in different treatment research areas. Although much of this work has been rather crude and certainly is not above criticism, there can be no doubt that meta-analysis has become an accepted technique that has rapidly developed in conceptual, methodological, and statistical sophistication (Cook et al., 1992; Durlak & Lipsey, 1991; Glass, McGaw, & Smith, 1981; Hedges & Olkin, 1985; Hunter & Schmidt, 1990; Rosenthal, 1991a).

The purpose of this article is to examine the large body of meta-analyses of psychological, educational, and behavioral treatment research that has cumulated in the last decade and a half. It will perhaps not be surprising that this systematic approach to research integration has resulted in refinements of our understanding of the effects of treatment. What does not seem to be widely recognized,

Mark W. Lipsey, Department of Human Resources, Vanderbilt University; David B. Wilson, Vanderbilt Institute for Public Policy Studies.

Gary VandenBos served as action editor for this article.

Correspondence concerning this article should be addressed to Mark W. Lipsey, Department of Human Resources, Box 90 GPC, Vanderbilt University, Nashville, TN 37203.

however, is that, in contrast to the previous era of conventional research reviews, meta-analysis has yielded stark, dramatic patterns of evidence for the general efficacy of such treatment.

Meta-Analysis of Treatment Research

The quantity and variety of meta-analysis of experimental and quasi-experimental treatment research has been so great that it is necessary to identify the boundaries of this review. Of interest here is meta-analysis of research on the effects of treatments that are based on manipulation of psychological variables and are intended to induce psychological change, whether emotional, attitudinal, cognitive, or behavioral (hereafter referred to as *psychological treatments*). The extensive meta-analysis of clinical trials research in medicine, therefore, falls outside the boundaries. Psychologically based intervention within medical settings (e.g., preoperative counseling), however, is included. Moreover, attention is restricted to those treatments that are directed at practical individual and social problems. Excluded, therefore, are meta-analyses of interventions and manipulations of primarily theoretical interest or those that do not represent currently practiced interventions in "real world" domains of applicability (e.g., teacher expectancy effects).

Also, within the area of psychological treatment it is necessary to consider the level or scope of intervention. At one end of a rough continuum we can distinguish treatment techniques—separable elements of intervention that do not, by themselves, constitute a freestanding treatment (e.g., self-disclosure by therapists or use of advance organizers in a teacher's lesson plan). At the other end of this rough continuum are broad policies or programs that combine many treatments and treatment elements, organizational arrangements, and so forth (e.g., school desegregation or mental health deinstitutionalization). We exclude both ends of this continuum to focus on midrange treatments, those relatively freestanding intervention packages with rather specific purposes that are deliverable at a defined site for a target population. In this category we include such interventions as psychotherapy, parent effectiveness training, medical patient education, smoking-cessation programs, job enrichment, computer-aided instruction, science curricula, and open classrooms (see Table 1 for a fuller list). Although there are gray areas at both ends of this midrange, we found it possible to categorize most interventions subjected to meta-analysis with reasonable confidence.

With the above boundaries in mind, a series of computer and manual searches was made of bibliographies of articles dealing with meta-analysis, various standard social science abstracts (Psychological Abstracts, Sociological Abstracts, etc.), and listings of unpublished materials (Dissertation Abstracts International, ERIC). All reports that appeared eligible on the basis of the title and abstract were retrieved, and 290 of them were found to meet the inclusion criteria. Because some reports presented more than one independent meta-analysis, the total number examined for the present study was 302. The

search and retrieval effort was thorough and, although it doubtless missed some number of eligible reports, we believe that the resulting collection represents a high proportion of the available work of interest to this review.

Treatment Effects: Broad Patterns

Table 1 lists, by broad categories, the meta-analysis studies that were discovered in this search and the treatment areas they cover. As is evident, a number of these meta-analyses are replications, near replications, subsets, or have overlapping studies with others in the list. Thus some studies and some subjects are represented in more than one meta-analysis. We will come back to this matter later but, for now, will ignore the redundancies and make a general examination of the treatment effects found in this collection of meta-analyses.

The right-hand columns of Table 1 report the overall mean treatment effect size found in each meta-analysis and the number of studies on which it was based. The effect size metric used here is the standardized difference between the mean of the treatment group and the mean of the control group for a given outcome measure in a given study.[1] Typically, a mean effect size over all studies and all outcome measures is shown. When the original meta-analysis reported mean effect sizes for quite different categories of treatment or outcome, the highest level of aggregation is presented for the major category or categories under investigation. One exception to this procedure was for educational treatments in which the great preponderance of effects were on achievement measures. In such cases, only the mean achievement effect was recorded.

Given the inconsistent findings reported in conventional research reviews for many of these treatment areas and the high proportion of studies with statistically nonsignificant results identified in both conventional and meta-analytic reviews, one might expect quite a mix of mean treatment effect sizes in Table 1, with many hovering around zero. Moreover, given the wide range of different treatments represented, one might expect some proportion to have negative mean effect sizes (i.e., control groups outperforming treatment groups) and a quite modest proportion to have strongly positive mean effect sizes. After all, we would not expect every treatment to work well.

Figure 1 presents the distribution of mean effect sizes from Table 1. We do this solely for descriptive purposes, as an alternate depiction of the information in Table 1, and with no implication that these are independent data points or that they represent a statistical sample or population (later we will present a more refined distribution with better statistical properties).

The striking feature of Figure 1 is the strong skew toward positive effects. Of 302 meta-analyses, only 6 pro-

(*text continues on page 1192*)

---

[1] Effect size is typically computed as $(M_t - M_c)/s$, where M_t is the treatment group mean, M_c is the control group mean, and s is the pooled standard deviation or, sometimes, the control group standard deviation.

Table 1
Meta-Analysis Studies

Treatment area and reference	M effect size	N
1. Mental Health, Health		
1.1. Psychotherapy, General		
Psychotherapy; all outcomes (Smith, Glass & Miller, 1980)[a]	0.85	475
Psychotherapy with adults; all outcomes (Shapiro & Shapiro, 1982, 1983)	0.93	143
Psychotherapy vs. placebo controls; all outcomes (Prioleau, Murdock, & Brody, 1983)	0.42	32
Psychotherapy (random assignment studies with good controls); all outcomes (Landman & Dawes, 1982)	0.78	42
Psychotherapy; self-concept outcomes (Cook, 1988)[a]	0.37	34
Psychotherapy (individual); all outcomes (Tillitski, 1990).	1.16	9
Psychotherapy (group); all outcomes (Tillitski, 1990)	1.31	9
Psychotherapy with children; all outcomes (Casey & Berman, 1985)[a]	0.71	64
Psychotherapy with children and adolescents; all outcomes (Weisz, Weiss, Alicke, & Klotz, 1987)	0.79	108
Psychotherapy with adult neurotic patients; all outcomes (Nicholson & Berman, 1983)	0.68	67
Psychotherapy for neuroses, phobias & emotional-somatic complaints; all outcomes (G. Andrews & Harvey, 1981)	0.72	81
Psychotherapy for the treatment of depression; all outcomes (L. A. Robinson, Berman, & Neimeyer, 1990)	0.72	58
Psychotherapy for neurotic depression; all outcomes (Prince Henry Hospital, 1983)	0.65	10
Psychotherapy for unipolar depression in adults; all outcomes (Steinbrueck, Maxwell, & Howard, 1983)	1.22	16
Psychotherapy vs. drug therapy for the treatment of bulimia; all outcomes (Laessle, Zoettl, & Pirde, 1987)	0.95	23
Psychotherapy for bulimia; all outcomes (Bryan, 1989)[a]	0.92	31
Client-centered therapy, transactional analysis, and non-directive therapy; all outcomes (Champney & Schulz, 1983)	0.25	18
Mental health specialists vs. general medical practitioners; all outcomes (Balestrieri, Williams, & Wilkinson, 1988)	0.22	11
1.2. Psychotherapy, Cognitive Behavioral/Behavior Modification		
Cognitive behavioral therapies vs. nonspecific factors controls; all outcomes (Barker, Funk, & Houston, 1988)	0.67	17
Cognitive therapy for anxiety disorders; all outcomes (Berman, Miller, & Massman, 1985)	0.73	25
Cognitive therapy, modification of covert self-statements of adult patients; all outcomes (Dush, Hirt, & Schroeder, 1983)[a]	0.66	69
Cognitive therapy with nonpsychotic patients with clinic complaints; all outcomes (Miller & Berman, 1983)	0.77	48
Cognitive behavior therapy with adult populations; all outcomes (Polder, 1986)	0.69	53
Cognitive behavioral therapy; effect on trait anxiety and neuroticism (Jorm, 1989)	0.53	63
Cognitive behavioral therapy (paradoxical interventions); all outcomes (Shoham-Salomon & Rosenthal, 1987)	0.89	10
Cognitive behavioral therapy (paradoxical interventions); all outcomes (Hampton, 1988)[a]	0.15	29
Cognitive behavioral therapy (paradoxical interventions); all outcomes (Hill, 1987)[a]	0.99	15
Cognitive therapy for depression; Beck Depression Inventory outcomes (Dobson, 1989)	0.99	28
Cognitive and behavioral treatments of depression and phobic anxiety; all outcomes (Eifert & Craill, 1989)	0.83	36
Cognitive behavioral therapy with children; modification of self-statements (Dush, Hirt, & Schroeder, 1989)	0.37	48
Cognitive behavioral modification strategies with children; educationally relevant behavioral outcomes (Duzinski, 1987)[a]	0.47	45
Cognitive behavioral therapy with dysfunctional children; all outcomes (Durlak, Fuhrman, & Lampman, 1991)[a]	0.53	64
Cognitive therapy and systematic desensitization for public speaking anxiety; all outcomes (Allen, Hunter, & Donohue, 1989)	0.52	97
Systematic desensitization; all outcomes (Berman, Miller, & Massman, 1985)	0.62	25
Training children in use of verbal self-instructions to control their behavior in non-training situations; all outcomes (Rock, 1986)[a]	0.51	47
Behavior therapy vs. placebo controls; all outcomes (Bowers & Clum, 1988)	0.55	69
Behavioral self-management, social skills training, cognitive-behavioral therapy, and biofeedback/relaxation training with problem children; clinically relevant outcomes (Wyma, 1990)	0.61	43
Behavioral treatment (biofeedback) for Raynaud's disease; all outcomes (Montross, 1990)	1.06	18
Behavioral treatment (progressive relaxation therapy); all outcomes (Paterson, 1988)[a]	0.34	71
Behavioral treatment with spouse involvement in treatment of agoraphobia; effect on symptoms (Dewey & Hunsley, 1990)	0.10	6

(table continues)

Table 1 (*continued*)

Treatment area and reference	M effect size	N
Behavioral therapy and tricyclic medication in the treatment of obsessive–compulsive disorder; all outcomes (Christensen, Hadzi-Pavlovic, Andrews, & Mattick, 1987)	1.02	27

1.3. Couseling, Psycho-Educational Treatment, Special Therapy

1.3.1. Family/marital interventions

Treatment area and reference	M effect size	N
Family therapy; all outcomes (Hazelrigg, Cooper, & Borduin, 1987)	0.36	20
Family therapy (conjoint); all outcomes (Markus, Lange, & Pettigrew, 1990)	0.57	19
Family therapy for child identified problems; all outcomes (Montgomery, 1991)	0.61	43
Family and marital therapies; behavioral outcomes (Shadish, 1992)[a]	0.70	58
Behavioral marital therapy; all outcomes (Hahlweg & Markman, 1988)	0.95	17
Behavioral premarital intervention studies; all outcomes (Hahlweg & Markman, 1988)	0.79	7
Parent effectiveness training; all outcomes (B. Cedar & Levant, 1990; R. B. Cedar, 1986)[a]	0.33	26
Marriage/family enrichment programs for nonclinical couples and families; all outcomes (Giblin, Sprenkle, & Sheehan, 1985)[a]	0.44	85
Minnesota Couple Communication Program (communication skills); immediate outcomes (Wampler, 1983)[a]	0.52	20

1.3.2. Treatment programs for offenders

Treatment area and reference	M effect size	N
Treatment programs for juvenile delinquents; delinquency outcomes (Lipsey, 1992)[a]	0.17	397
Treatment programs for juvenile delinquents; all outcomes (Gottschalk, Davidson, Gensheimer, & Mayer, 1987a)	0.48	91
Treatment programs for adjudicated delinquents in residential/institutional settings; all outcomes (Garrett, 1985a, 1985b)	0.37	111
Treatment programs for juvenile delinquents (random assignment studies); delinquency outcomes (Kaufman, 1985)	0.25	20
Social learning treatment programs for juvenile delinquents; all outcomes (Mayer, Gensheimer, Davidson, & Gottschalk, 1986)	0.77	39
Diversion programs for juvenile delinquents; all outcomes (Gensheimer, Mayer, Gottschalk, & Davidson, 1986)	0.40	44
Behavioral treatment approaches for juvenile delinquents; long-term outcomes (Gottschalk, Davidson, & Mayer, 1987b)	0.40	25
Treatment programs for juvenile offenders; all outcomes (Whitehead & Lab, 1989)	0.27	50
Treatment programs for adult and juvenile offenders; all outcomes (D. A. Andrews et al., 1990)	0.20	80
Correctional treatment with adults; all outcomes (Losel & Koferl, 1989)	0.25	16

1.3.3. Meditation, psychological outcomes

Treatment area and reference	M effect size	N
Meditation and relaxation techniques; effects on trait anxiety (Eppley, Abrams, & Shear, 1989)	0.42	145
Passive individual meditation techniques; psychological affective outcomes (Ferguson, 1981)	0.56	51
Transcendental meditation; effects on self-actualization (Alexander, Rainforth, & Gelderloos, 1991)	0.88	18
Effects of meditation; anxiety outcomes (Edwards, 1991)[a]	0.59	21
Effects of hypnosis; anxiety outcomes (Edwards, 1991)[a]	0.71	54

1.3.4. Other couseling, psycho-educational treatment or special therapy

Treatment area and reference	M effect size	N
Innovative outpatient programs vs. traditional aftercare for mental health patients released from hospitals; all outcomes (Straw, 1982)[a]	0.36	130
Community-based alternatives vs. institutionalization for mental health patients; all outcomes (Straw, 1982)[a]	0.14	30
Deinstitutionalization programs for the chronically mentally ill; all outcomes (L. C. Harris, 1987)	0.36	111
The Primary Mental Health Project (identification and treatment of maladjusted school children); all outcomes (Stein & Polyson, 1984)[a]	0.25	7
Primary prevention program in mental health; all outcomes (Susskind & Bond, 1981)	0.08	13
Treatment by paraprofessionals in mental health, education, law, and social work vs. untreated controls; all outcomes (Truax, 1984)[a]	0.60	57
Companionship treatment (paraprofessionals) with children; all outcomes (Stein, 1987)	0.22	19
Training in interpersonal cognitive problem solving skills for children; effects on interpersonal skills and behavior adjustment (Almeida & Denham, 1984; Denham & Almedia, 1987)[a]	0.66	27
Group assertion training for students and adults; all outcomes (Branwen, 1982)[a]	1.51	40
Assertiveness training; effects on assertiveness and social skills (Shatz, 1984)	0.79	21
Alcohol and drug use prevention programs; behavior, attitudes and knowledge outcomes (Rundall & Bruvold, 1988)	0.27	76
(Bangert-Drowns, 1988)	0.41	33
(Tobler, 1986)[a]	0.30	98
Guidance and counseling programs in the regular school curriculum for high school; effects on psychological maturity (Sprinthall, 1981; see also 3.5.2.)[a]	1.20	6
Career counseling interventions; all outcomes (Oliver & Spokane, 1988; see also 3.5.2.)	0.48	58
Counseling and guidance programs in high school; all outcomes (Nearpass, 1990; see also 3.5.2.)[a]	0.38	77
Career education programs for K–12 students; all outcomes (Baker & Popowicz, 1983, see also 3.5.2.)	0.50	18

Table 1 (continued)

Treatment area and reference	M effect size	N
Primary prevention education programs in schools (e.g., career maturity, coping/communication skills, moral & psychological education, substance abuse, values); all outcomes (Baker, Swisher, Nadenichek, & Popowicz, 1984; see also 3.5.2.)[a]	0.55	41
Vocational programs for persons with mental illness; all outcomes (Bond, 1988)[a]	0.54	18
Mental practice of motor skills; effects on learning (Fletz & Landers, 1983)[a]	0.48	60
Social work interventions for mental illness; all outcomes (Videka-Sherman, 1988)[a]	0.51	30
Social skills training with schizophrenics (Benton & Schroeder, 1990)	0.65	27
Social skills training with children K–12; all outcomes (Hanson, 1989)[a]	0.65	63
Treatment of public speaking anxiety; effect on anxiety (Allen, 1989)	0.43	116
Self-administered psychological treatments for habits, phobias, affective disturbances and skills training; all outcomes (Scogin, Bynum, Stephens, & Calhoun, 1990)	0.34	40

1.4. Health Related Psychological or Educational Treatment

1.4.1. Education/counseling for medical patients

Educational or psychological interventions with adult hospitalized elective surgery patients; effects on patient well-being (Devine, 1984; Devine & Cook, 1983)[a]	0.46	105
Preoperative instruction of adults scheduled for surgery; effects on postoperative outcome (Hathaway, 1985)	0.44	68
Special preoperative preparation of children for surgery vs. routine nursing care; effects on anxiety (Howell, 1985)[a]	0.40	23
Psychological preparation of children for medical procedures; all outcomes (Saile, Burgmeier, & Schmidt, 1988)	0.44	75
Patient education for people with a chronic disease or medical problem; effects on compliance and health (Mazzuca, 1982)[a]	0.52	27
Psychological support for patients facing surgery or recovering from heart attacks; effects on anxiety, cooperation, and recovery (Mumford, Schlesinger, & Glass, 1982)[a]	0.49	34
Programs to increase compliance with medical treatment regimens; all outcomes (Posavac, Sinacore, Brotherton, Helford, & Turpin, 1985)	0.47	58
Patient education about treatment regimens, preventive behavior, self-care, etc.; all outcomes (Posavac, 1980)	0.74	23

1.4.2. Biofeedback/relaxation/medication training for clinical symptoms

Biofeedback and relaxation training for migraine and tension headaches; improvement scores (Blanchard, Andrasik, Ahles, Teders, & O'Keefe, 1980)	0.63	35
Meditation and relaxation techniques; effect on blood pressure (Kuchera, 1987)	0.93	26
Relaxation training for clinical (medical) symptoms; all outcomes (Hyman, Feldman, Harris, Levin, & Malloy, 1989)[a]	0.52	48

1.4.3. Tobacco smoking cessation/reduction programs

Smoking cessation/reduction programs; effects on abstinence (Feehan, 1984)	0.64	97
Smoking cessation/reduction programs (physician delivered); effect on quit rates (Dotson, 1990)[a]	0.34	8
Smoking cessation/reduction programs (worksite); effect on quit rates (Fisher, 1990)[a]	0.21	20

1.4.4. Psychological treatments for pain

Music therapy in medicine to reduce pain; effect on pain reduction (Standley, 1986)[a]	0.98	29
Pain management interventions with children; behavioral, self-report and physiologic outcomes (Broome, Lillis, & Smith, 1989)[a]	0.39	30
Non-medical psychologically based treatment of chronic pain; all outcomes (Malone, Strube, & Scogin, 1989)	1.10	48
Cognitive coping strategies for the treatment of pain; effects on pain perception (Fernandez & Turk, 1989)	0.51	47
Multidisciplinary treatments for chronic back pain; all outcomes (Flor, Fydrich, & Turk, 1992)	1.25	65

1.4.5. Other health related psychological or educational treatment

Psychosocial preventive care for the elderly; all outcomes (Wilson, Simson, & McCaughey, 1983)	0.45	8
Adolescent pregnancy education programs; all outcomes (Iverson & Levy, 1982)	0.35	14
Prenatal childbirth classes for adults; all outcomes (Jones, 1983)[a]	0.34	58
Training of new mothers about sensory/perceptual capabilities of newborns; effects on maternal-infant interaction (Turley, 1984)[a]	0.44	20
Behavioral treatment for obesity; effects on weight loss (O'Flynn, 1983)	1.06	80
Behavioral management of obesity for couples; effects on weight loss (Black, Gleser, & Kooyers, 1990)	0.33	12
The Feingold diet (free of food additives) for children; effects on hyperactivity (Kavale & Forness, 1983)	0.02	23
Treatment for stuttering; all outcomes (G. Andrews, Guitar, & Howie, 1980)	1.30	42
Stress management programs; all outcomes (Nicholson, Duncan, Hawkins, Belcastro, & Gold, 1988)	0.75	18
Stress coping interventions; all outcomes (Cannella, 1988)[a]	0.46	94

(table continues)

Table 1 (continued)

Treatment area and reference	M effect size	N
Psychological treatment of Type A Behavior; effects on risk for coronary heart disease (Nunes, Frank, & Kornfeld, 1987)	0.61	10
Subjective well-being interventions among elderly; subjective well being outcomes (Okun, Olding, & Cohn, 1990)[a]	0.42	31
Exercise interventions for depression; effects on depression (North, 1989)[a]	0.54	77
Educational interventions for diabetic adults; knowledge, metabolic control, self-care and psychological outcomes (Brown, 1990)[a]	0.43	82
Death education; attitude and affective outcomes (Durlak & Riesenberg, 1991)	0.28	47

2. Work Setting or Organizational Interventions

Psychologically based organizational intervention programs; effects on worker productivity (Guzzo, Jette, & Katzell, 1985)	0.44	98
Sociotechnical systems interventions in organizations; all outcomes (Beekun, 1989)	0.41	17
Job enrichment or work redesign; effects on turnover (McEvoy & Cascio, 1985)[a]	0.35	5
Realistic job previews before entering an organization; effect on turnover		
(McEvoy & Cascio, 1985)[a]	0.18	13
(Reilly, Brown, Blood, & Malatesta, 1981)	0.14	11
Training programs for managerial or supervisory personnel; effects on learning, behavior, and results		
(Burke & Day, 1986)	0.42	70
Personal training techniques; sensitivity training (Falcone, 1986)[a]	0.63	106
Managerial human relations training; effects on managerial performance (Brannick, 1987)[a]	0.47	46
Employee training programs; effects on productivity (Leddick, 1987)	0.67	48
Organizational development programs; effects on attitudes (Neuman, Edwards, & Raju, 1989)	0.32	126
Quality circles programs; effects on job satisfaction and job involvement (Eskew, 1989)	0.12	13
Management education in institutional settings; all outcomes (Niemiec, Sikorski, Clark, & Walberg, 1992)	0.85	22

3. Education

3.1. General Education, K–12 and College

3.1.1. Computer aided/based instruction

Computer based instruction; effects on achievement (Gillingham & Guthrie, 1987)	1.05	13
Computer based instruction, K–12; effects on achievement (J. A. Kulik & Kulik, 1987)	0.31	199
Computer based instruction with elementary school students; all outcomes (Niemiec, 1985; Niemiec, Samson, Weinstein, & Walberg, 1987)[a]	0.45	48
Computer assisted instruction with elementary school students; effects on achievement (Ryan, 1991)[a]	0.31	40
Computer assisted vs. conventional instruction for elementary students; effects on achievement (C. C. Kulik, Kulik, & Bangert-Drowns, 1984)	0.48	25
Computer aided instruction vs. conventional methods in secondary school classrooms; effects on achievement (J. A. Kulik, Bangert, & Williams, 1983)[a]	0.32	51
Computer-based education for junior and senior high school students; effect on achievement (Bangert-Drowns, Kulik, & Kulik, 1985)	0.26	42
Computer aided instruction vs. conventional methods for college instruction; effects on achievement (C. C. Kulik, Kulik, & Cohen, 1980)[a]	0.25	59
Computer assisted instruction for exceptional (special education) students, elementary through high school; effects on achievement (Schmidt, Weinstein, Niemiec, & Walberg, 1986; see also 3.5.3.2.)[a]	0.66	18
Computer aided instruction with learning disabled and educable mentally retarded students; effects on achievement (McDermid, 1990; see also 3.5.3.2.)	0.57	15
Computer assisted mathematics instruction vs. traditional instruction, elementary and secondary students; effects on math achievement (Burns, 1982; see also 3.5.1.)	0.35	40
Computer assisted mathematics instruction and computer programming, elementary and secondary students; effects on math achievement (Lee, 1990; see also 3.5.1.)[a]	0.38	72

3.1.2. Programmed or individualized instruction

Individualized instruction; effects on achievement (Hood, 1991)[a]	0.17	70
Individualized systems of instruction for 6–12 grade students; effects on achievement (Bangert, Kulik, & Kulik, 1983)	0.10	51
Individualized instruction in science courses vs. traditional lecture methods, secondary school students; effects on achievement (Aiello & Wolfe, 1980; Aiello, 1981; see also 3.5.1.)[a]	0.35	115
Individualized mathematics instruction for elementary and secondary students; effects on math achievement (Hartley, 1977; see also 3.5.1.)[a]	0.29	153
Self-paced modularized individualized mathematics instruction vs. traditional instructions for elementary and secondary students; effect on achievement (Horak, 1981; see also 3.5.1.)	−0.07	41
Programmed instruction vs. conventional instruction with secondary school students; effects on achievement (C. C. Kulik, Schwalb, & Kulik, 1982)[a]	0.08	48
Programmed instruction vs. conventional instruction for college teaching; effect on achievement (J. A. Kulik, Cohen, & Ebeling, 1980)[a]	0.28	56

Table 1 (continued)

Treatment area and reference	M effect size	N
Keller's personalized system of instruction (PSI) vs. traditional lecture methods for college teaching; effects on achievement (J. A. Kulik, Kulik, & Cohen, 1979a)[a]	0.49	72
Mastery learning with Kellers's Personalized System of Instruction & Bloom's Learning for Mastery with college students; all outcomes (C. C. Kulik, Kulik, & Bangert-Drowns, 1990)[a]	0.52	103
Feedback about correct answers in computerized and programmed instruction with adult learners; effects on learning (Schimmel, 1983)[a]	0.47	15
3.1.3. Audio and visual based instruction		
Visual-based instruction (film, TV, etc.) vs. conventional teaching for college students; effects on achievement (Cohen, Ebeling, & Kulik, 1981)[a]	0.15	65
Postlethwait's audio-tutorial method of instruction vs. traditional lecture methods in college teaching; effects on achievement (J. A. Kulik, Kulik, & Cohen, 1979b)[a]	0.20	47
Visual media instruction for students in nursing education; effects on attitude change (Schermer, 1984)[a]	0.68	12
Interactive video instruction; effects on achievement (McNeil & Nelson, 1990)[a]	0.50	63
Interactive video instruction in defense training, industrial training and higher education; effects on knowledge, performance, retention and instruction completion time (Fletcher, 1990)	0.50	28
3.1.4. Cooperative task structures		
Cooperative vs. uncooperative task structures; effects on achievement and productivity (Johnson, Maruyama, Johnson, Nelson, & Skon, 1981)[a]	0.72	122
Cooperative learning with K–12 students; all outcomes (Hall, 1989)	0.30	37
Cooperative vs. competitive and individualistic instructional approaches in adult education; effects on achievement (Johnson & Johnson, 1987)[a]	0.62	133
Cooperative learning with students with mild disabilities; effects on achievement (Stevens & Slavin, 1991; see also 3.5.3.2.)	0.31	11
Cooperative learning methods with handicapped K–12 students in mainstreamed classrooms; effects on achievement (Carlson, 1987; see also 3.5.3.2.)	0.16	13
Cooperative vs. noncooperative task arrangements for handicapped–nonhandicapped and ethnically different groups; all outcomes (Johnson, Johnson, & Maruyama, 1983; see also 3.5.3.2.)[a]	0.75	98
3.1.5. Student tutoring		
Student tutoring of elementary and secondary students (tutor's experience); effects on achievement (Cohen, Kulik, & Kulik, 1982)[a]	0.33	38
Student tutoring of elementary and secondary students; effects on achievement (Cohen, Kulik, & Kulik, 1982)[a]	0.40	52
Tutoring of special education students by other special education students (tutor's experience); effects on achievement (S. B. Cook, Scruggs, Mastropieri, & Castro, 1986)[a]	0.65	19
Tutoring of special education students by other special education students; effects on achievement (S. B. Cook et al., 1986)[a]	0.59	19
Tutorial methods of training the conservation concept in preoperational children; effects on mastery (Phillips, 1983)[a]	0.98	302
3.1.6. Behavioral objectives, reinforcement, cues, feedback, etc.		
Behavioral objectives for instruction with elementary through adult students; effects on achievement (Asencio, 1984)[a]	0.12	111
Positive reinforcement in the classroom; effects on learning (Lysakowski & Walberg, 1980, 1981)[a]	1.17	39
Instructional cues, student participation, and corrective feedback in the classroom; effects on learning (Lysakowski & Walberg, 1982)	0.97	54
3.1.7. Other general education		
Mastery learning, group based, grades 1–12 and college; all outcomes (Guskey & Pigott, 1988)[a]	0.61	43
Mastery learning, group based, primary and secondary students; effects on achievement (Slavin, 1987b)	0.25	17
Home instruction supported by school-based programs for elementary school children; effects on achievement (Grane, Weinstein, & Walberg, 1983)[a]	0.68	29
Assignment of homework to elementary and secondary students; effects on achievement (Paschal, Weinstein, & Walberg, 1984)[a]	0.30	15
Modality based instruction; effects on achievement (Kavale & Forness, 1987)[a]	0.14	39
Technology based instructional approaches with American and Japanese students; effects on achievement (Shwalb, 1987)[a]	0.41	116
Technology based, non-technology based and combination teaching strategies with the mathematically disadvantaged; all outcomes (Williams, 1990)[a]	0.14	127
Use of simulation games in instruction; effect on achievement (Dekkers & Donatti, 1981)[a]	0.28	93
Instructional simulation games vs. conventional instruction; effects on cognitive learning (Szczurek, 1982)	0.33	33
Enrichment programs for gifted students; cognitive, creativity and affective outcomes (Wallace, 1990)[a]	0.55	20

(table continues)

1187

Table 1 (*continued*)

Treatment area and reference	M effect size	N
Psychological and affective interventions for underprepared learners; grade-point average and persistance outcomes (W. L. Collins, 1987)[a]	0.36	14
3.2. Classroom organization/environment		
3.2.1. Open classroom vs. traditional		
Open classroom vs. traditional plan; effects on achievement		
(Giacomia & Hedges, 1982)[a]	−0.07	153
(Hetzel, Rasher, Butcher, & Walberg, 1980)	−0.03	25
(Madamba, 1981)	0.01	72
(Peterson, 1980)	−0.13	45
3.2.2. Class size		
Small class size vs. large class size, all grade levels; effects on achievement (Hedges & Stock, 1983)[a]	0.20	77
Small class size (under 30) vs. large class size (over 30), all grade levels; effects on achievement (Glass & Smith, 1979)	0.21	77
Small class size (under 30) vs. large class size (over 30); effects on student and teacher attitudes and climate of instruction (Smith & Glass, 1980)	0.53	59
3.2.3. Between and within class ability grouping		
Between and within class ability grouping of secondary school students; effects on achievement (C. C. Kulik & Kulik, 1982a, 1982b)[a]	0.10	52
Between and within class ability grouping of elementary students; effects on achievement (Slavin, 1987a)[a]	0.22	39
Between and within class ability grouping of secondary students; effects on achievement (Slavin, 1990)	−0.03	29
Between class ability grouping of elementary students; effects on achievement (C. C. Kulik & Kulik, 1984)	0.19	31
Between class ability grouping in grades K–12; effects on achievement (Noland, 1985)[a]	0.01	50
Between class ability grouping for gifted students; effects on achievement (Goldring, 1990)[a]	0.32	23
3.2.4. Other classroom organization/environment		
Pull-out programs for gifted students, grades K–9; effects on achievement (Vaughn, Feldhusen, & Asher, 1991)[a]	0.47	9
Full vs. half-day kindergarten; all outcomes (Karweit, 1987)[a]	0.48	11
3.3. Feedback to teachers		
Feedback to teachers about individual academic performance of students, grades K–12; effects on achievement (Fuchs & Fuchs, 1986)[a]	0.70	21
Feedback of student ratings to college instructors during a course; effects on student assessment and outcome (Cohen, 1980)	0.38	17
(L'Hommedieu, Menges, & Brinko, 1990)[a]	0.30	28
Teacher consultation for modifying teacher behavior and attitudes; effects on teacher and student behavior and attitudes (Batts, 1988)[a]	0.66	40
Staff development training procedures for changing teacher's attitudes, knowledge and skill acquisition; effects on attitudes, knowledge and skill acquisition (Bennett, 1988)[a]	1.01	112
3.4. Test Taking		
3.4.1. Coaching programs for test performance		
Coaching programs for achievement test performance, elementary through college; effects on test scores (Bangert-Drowns, Kulik, & Kulik, 1983)[a]	0.25	30
Coaching programs on SAT aptitude tests for college students; effects on test scores (DerSimonian & Laird, 1983)	0.19	22
Coaching programs for SAT and other aptitude tests, elementary through college; effects on tests scores (J. A. Kulik, Bangert-Drowns, & Kulik, 1984)[a]	0.33	35
Coaching for the SAT aptitude tests; effects on test scores (Messick & Jungeblut, 1981)	0.15	12
(Becker, 1990)	0.30	23
Training in test-taking skills for elementary and secondary students; effects on achievement test scores (Samson, 1985)[a]	0.33	24
Training in test-taking skills on standardized achievement tests for elementary students; effects on test scores (Scruggs, Bennion, & White, 1984)	0.21	24
Practice test taking on aptitude and achievement tests, elementary through college; effects on test scores (J. A. Kulik, Kulik, & Bangert, 1984)	0.32	40
3.4.2. Test anxiety		
Therapy for test anxiety; effects on performance (O'Bryan, 1985)	0.36	119
Therapy for test anxiety; effects on anxiety (O'Bryan, 1985)	1.07	119
Therapy for test anxiety; all outcomes (Hembree, 1988)	0.63	125
(Thompson, 1987)[a]	0.57	195
Therapy for test anxiety (college students); all outcomes (Dole, Rockey, & DiTomasso, 1983)	0.80	46
Therapy for test anxiety (college students); effects on anxiety and performance (M. M. Harris, 1988)	0.58	70
3.4.3. Examiner		
Familiar vs. unfamiliar examiner testing children; effects on test performance (D. Fuchs & Fuchs, 1985)[a]	0.35	22

Table 1 (continued)

Treatment area and reference	M effect size	N
3.5. Specific Instructional or Content Areas		
3.5.1. Science and math instruction		
Modern ("new") mathematics curricula vs. traditional instruction; effects on achievement (Athappily, Smidchens, & Kofel, 1983)[a]	0.24	134
Three major activity-based elementary science programs vs. traditional curriculum; effects on achievement (Bredderman, 1983)[a]	0.34	57
New science curriculum vs. traditional curricula with primary and secondary students; effects on achievement (Kyle, 1982; Shymansky, 1984; Shymansky, Kyle, & Alport, 1982, 1983)[a]	0.37	105
(Shymansky, Hedges, & Woodworth, 1990)	0.30	81
Innovative science curricula vs. traditional instruction, grades 6–12; effects on achievement (Weinstein, Boulanger, & Walberg, 1982)	0.47	33
Instructional systems in science education vs. traditional instruction, grades K–12; effects on achievement (Willett, Yamashita, & Anderson, 1983)[a]	0.07	130
Teaching students to control variables in science education, all grades and college; effects on learning (Ross, 1988)[a]	0.73	62
Innovative science teaching techniques vs. traditional techniques, grades 6–12; effect on achievement (Boulanger, 1981)[a]	0.55	51
Innovative approaches to teaching college economics vs. traditional lecture methods; effects on achievement (C. L. Cohn, 1985)[a]	0.20	48
Instruction in problem-solving in science and mathematics vs. conventional instruction for K–12 students; effects on achievement (Curbelo, 1985)[a]	0.54	68
Teaching biology as inquiry vs. traditional methods for high school and college students; effects on achievement (El-Nemr, 1980)[a]	0.16	59
Inductive vs. deductive approaches to science teaching, grades 4–12; effects on achievement (Lott, 1983)	0.06	24
Systematic methods of teaching mathematics problem-solving to elementary and secondary students; effects on problem solving achievement (Marcucci, 1980)[a]	0.13	33
Innovative science teaching techniques vs. traditional techniques, grades 6–college; effects on achievement (Wise & Okey, 1983)[a]	0.35	160
Diagnostic testing and feedback vs. none during science instruction, middle school through college; effects on achievement (Yeany & Miller, 1983)	0.53	21
Treatment of mathematics anxiety; effects on anxiety (Hembree, 1990)[a]	0.37	115
Mathematics instructional method, K–12; effects on attitudes (Bradford, 1991)[a]	0.15	102
Computer assisted mathematics instruction vs. traditional instruction, elementary and secondary students; effects on math achievement (Burns, 1982; see also 3.1.1.)	0.35	40
Computer assisted mathematics instruction and computer programming, elementary and secondary students; effects on math achievement (Lee, 1990; see also 3.1.1.)[a]	0.38	72
Individualized instruction in science courses vs. traditional lecture methods, secondary school students; effects on achievement (Aiello, 1981; Aiello & Wolfle, 1980; see also 3.1.2.)[a]	0.35	115
Individualized mathematics instruction for elementary and secondary students; effects on math achievement (Hartley, 1977; see also 3.1.2.)[a]	0.29	153
Self-paced modularized individualized mathematics instruction vs. traditional instructions for elementary and secondary students; effect on achievement (Horak, 1981; see also 3.1.2.)	−0.07	41
Computer programming instruction; cognitive outcomes (Liao & Bright, 1991)[a]	0.41	65
3.5.2. Special content other than science and math		
Reading instruction strategies for elementary students; effects on achievement (Pflaum, Walberg, Karegianes, & Rasher, 1980)	0.60	31
Reading improvement and/or study skills programs for college students; effects on reading ability, GPA, and study habits (Sanders, 1979)[a]	0.94	28
Whole language and language experience approaches to teaching reading; effects on language achievement (Stahl & Miller, 1989)[a]	0.09	54
Instructional programs for teaching writing composition, elementary through college; effects on writing quality (Hillocks, 1984)[a]	0.28	60
Accelerated instruction for gifted students; effects on achievement (J. A. Kulik & Kulik, 1984)[a]	0.88	13
Creativity training techniques; effects on creative performance and other outcomes (C. M. G. Cohn, 1985)[a]	0.57	106
Creative thinking training programs; effects on Torrance Test of Creative Thinking (Rose & Lin, 1984)	0.47	46
Creative drama with elementary students; effect on achievement (Kardash & Wright, 1987)[a]	0.67	16
Primary prevention education programs in schools (e.g., career maturity, coping/communication skills, moral & psychological education, substance abuse, values); all outcomes (Baker, Swisher, Nadenichek, & Popowicz, 1984; see also 1.3.4.)[a]	0.55	41

(table continues)

1189

Table 1 (continued)

Treatment area and reference	M effect size	N
Programs for training moral judgment, junior high through adults; effects on Defining Issues Test (Schlaefli, Rest, & Thoma, 1985)[a]	0.25	55
Career education programs for K–12 students; all outcomes (Baker & Popowicz, 1983; see also 1.3.4.)	0.50	18
Guidance and counseling programs in the regular school curriculum for high school; effects on psychological maturity (Sprinthall, 1981; see also 1.3.4.)[a]	1.20	6
Career counseling interventions; all outcomes (Oliver & Spokane, 1988; see also 1.3.4.)	0.48	58
Counseling and guidance programs in high schools; all outcomes (Nearpass, 1990; see also 3.5.2.)[a]	0.38	77
Nutrition education programs for school age children; effects on knowledge behavior, and attitudes (Levy, Iverson, & Walberg, 1980)[a]	1.25	6
Vocabulary instruction, elementary through college; effects on learning and comprehension (Stahl & Fairbanks, 1986)[a]	0.90	52
(Klesius & Searls, 1990)[a]	0.32	15
Vocabulary instruction with poor readers, 3rd–12th grades; effects on word knowledge and comprehension (Marmolejo, 1990)	0.47	15

3.5.3. Preschool and special education; developmental disabilities

3.5.3.1. Early intervention for disadvantaged or handicapped

	M effect size	N
Headstart early childhood education programs; cognitive outcomes (Administration for Children, Youth, and Families, 1983)[a]	0.34	71
(R. C. Collins, 1984)	0.33	49
Preschool intervention programs for culturally disadvantaged children; 5–14 year follow-up effects on achievement and cognitive outcomes (Goldring & Presbrey, 1986)[a]	0.24	8
Early intervention programs for environmentally at-risk (disadvantaged) infants; effects on IQ and other variables (Casto & White, 1984; Utah State University Exceptional Child Center, 1983)[a]	0.43	26
Early intervention programs with handicapped preschoolers; all outcomes (Casto & Mastropieri, 1986; Utah State University Exceptional Child Center, 1983)[a]	0.68	74
Intervention programs for kindergarten children; all outcomes (Lewis & Vosburgh, 1988)	0.41	65

3.5.3.2. Special education programs or classrooms

	M effect size	N
Special education classroom placement vs. regular class placement for exceptional children; effects on achievement (Carlberg & Kavale, 1980)	−0.15	50
Early childhood special education; all outcomes (Snyder & Sheehan, 1983)	0.48	8
Mainstreaming vs. segregated special education for disabled K–9 students; effects on achievement (Wang & Baker, 1986)	0.44	11
Direct instruction in special education; effects on achievement, intellectual ability, readiness skills, on-task behavior and affect (White, 1987)[a]	0.84	25
Educational interventions for at-risk populations (students in danger of failing to complete their education), K–12; effects on achievement (Slavin & Madden, 1989)[a]	0.63	28
Computer assisted instruction for exceptional (special education) students, K–12; effects on achievement (Schmidt et al., 1986; see also 3.1.1.)[a]	0.66	18
Computer aided instruction with learning disabled and educable mentally retarded students; effects on achievement (McDermid, 1990; see also 3.1.1.)	0.57	15
Cooperative learning with students with mild disabilities; effects on achievement (Stevens & Slavin, 1991; see also 3.1.4.)	0.31	11
Cooperative learning methods with handicapped K–12 students in mainstreamed classrooms; effects on achievement (Carlson, 1987; see also 3.1.4.)	0.16	13
Cooperative vs. noncooperative task arrangements for handicapped–nonhandicapped and ethnically different groups; all outcomes (Johnson, Johnson, & Maruyama, 1983; see also 3.1.4.)[a]	0.75	98

3.5.3.3. Perceptual-motor and sensory stimulation treatment for developmental disabilities

	M effect size	N
Perceptual–motor training for learning disabled and disadvantaged children; effects on academic, cognitive, and perceptual-motor outcomes (Kavale & Mattson, 1983)	0.08	180
Frostig training for development of visual perception in children with learning problems; effects on perceptual skills and academic achievement (Kavale, 1984)[a]	0.09	59
Sensory integration therapy for patients with developmental disabilities or learning disabilities; effects on academic achievement, motor performance, and language function (Ottenbacher, 1982)	0.79	8
Clinically applied vestibular stimulation as a sensory enrichment therapy for infants at risk and children with developmental delay; effects on cognitive, language, motor, alertness, and physiological outcomes (Ottenbacher & Petersen, 1984)[a]	0.71	14
Tactile stimulation of developmentally delayed and at-risk infants; all outcomes (Ottenbacher et al., 1987)	0.58	19

Table 1 (continued)

Treatment area and reference	M effect size	N
Early intervention and sensory stimulation programs for organically impaired developmentally delayed children; effects on development, motor, cognitive, language, social, and self-help outcomes (Ottenbacher & Petersen, 1985)	0.97	38
3.5.3.4. Remedial language programs and bilingual instruction		
Remedial and developmental language programs for linguistically deficient or disadvantaged preschool and elementary students; outcomes on Illinois Test of Psycholinguistic Ability (Kavale, 1980, 1981, 1982)[a]	0.39	34
Bilingual vs. English instruction in K–12 school programs; effects on achievement (Willig, 1985)[a]	0.12	16
Language therapy/training for language/learning disabled children; effects on language improvement (Nye, Foster, & Seaman, 1987)[a]	1.04	43
Language interventions for preschool children; language and non-language outcomes (Pioner, 1990)[a]	0.50	61
3.5.3.5. Other special education		
Educational treatment programs for emotionally disturbed students; effects on achievement and classroom behavior (Rosenbuam, 1983)	1.02	99
Special classroom or residential treatment for behaviorally disordered students; all outcomes (Skiba & Casey, 1985)	0.93	10
Training for mentally retarded persons on memory and learning tasks; all outcomes (Mattson, 1985)[a]	0.70	96
Special remedial programs for high risk and disadvantaged college students; effects on achievement (C. C. Kulik, Kulik, & Shwalb, 1983)[a]	0.27	60
3.5.4. Teacher training		
3.5.4.1. Inservice training for teachers		
Inservice training for elementary and secondary school teachers; all outcomes (Harrison, 1981)	0.80	47
(Wade, 1984, 1985)	0.52	91
Inservice training for elementary and secondary school teachers; effect on teachers and their students (Joslin, 1981)[a]	0.47	137
Science inservice training for teachers; effects on teachers and their students (Enz, Horak, & Blecha, 1982)[a]	0.84	16
Inservice and preservice training of teachers in the inquiry strategy for teaching science; effects on teachers (Sweitzer & Anderson, 1983)[a]	0.77	68
Human relations training programs for teachers; all outcomes (A. W. Robinson & Hyman, 1984)[a]	0.51	14
Strategy analysis training for science teachers; effects on teachers and their students (Yeany & Porter, 1982)[a]	1.31	12
Classroom management training programs for teachers; effects on student achievement and, teacher and student behavior, attitudes and affect (A. W. Robinson, 1989)[a]	0.47	79
3.5.4.2. Practice or field experience during teacher training		
Practice or beginning teaching; effects on self-concept and attitudes (Colosimo, 1982, 1984)	0.30	7
Classroom field experience for college students in teacher education programs; effects on teachers (M. R. Malone, 1984)[a]	0.12	40
Field experience in instructional settings during teacher training; effects on self-concept and teaching attitudes (Samson, Borger, Weinstein, & Walberg, 1984)	0.23	38
3.6. Miscellaneous Educational Interventions		
Hawthorne effect in educational research; all outcomes (Adair, Sharpe, & Huynh, 1989)[a]	0.20	38
Placebo control group effect in educational research; all outcomes (Adair, Sharpe, & Huynh, 1990)[a]	0.62	57
Continuing medical education for physicians; all outcomes (Beaudry, 1989)[a]	0.60	41
Interventions designed to enhance the communication skills of health-care providers; effects on communication skills (Anderson & Sharpe, 1991)	0.62	25
Continuing education for nurses, test of Cervero Model; effects on nursing practice (Waddell, 1991)	0.73	34
Training programs for graduate level counselors (Microcounseling Approach); all outcomes (Baker, Daniels, & Greeley, 1990)[a]	0.63	23
(Baker & Daniels, 1989)[a]	0.83	79
Training programs for graduate level counselors (Human Resource Training/Development Approach); all outcomes (Baker, Daniels, & Greeley, 1990)[a]	1.07	8
Training programs for graduate level counselors (Interpersonal Process Recall Approach); all outcomes (Baker, Daniels, & Greeley, 1990)[a]	0.20	10
Career development courses for college students; effect on maturity and decidedness (Hardesty, 1991)	0.40	12
Interventions to modify attitudes toward persons with disabilities; effects on attitudes (Shaver, Curtis, Jesunathadas, & Strong, 1989)	0.37	273
Mass media campaigns; effects on automobile occupant restraint behavior (Moore, 1990)[a]	0.14	35

[a] Studies included in refined distribution.

Figure 1
Distribution of Mean Effect Sizes From All Meta-Analyses

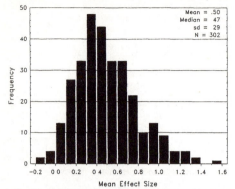

duced negative mean effect sizes (and 3 of these were in the same treatment area), and relatively few mean effect sizes were in the immediate vicinity of zero. More than 90% of the mean effect sizes were 0.10 or larger, and 85% were 0.20 or larger. There is little in conventional reviews and past discussion of these treatment areas, either individually or collectively, that prepares a reviewer for the rather stunning discovery that meta-analysis shows nearly every treatment examined to have positive effects.

Indeed, the effect size distribution in Figure 1 is so overwhelmingly positive that it hardly seems plausible that it presents a valid picture of the efficacy of treatment per se. What seems more likely is that these results reflect some artifact or misrepresentation that makes them look stronger than they actually are. Before drawing any conclusion about the efficacy of psychological treatment, therefore, we must attempt to identify and examine what potential distortions we can in the distribution of meta-analysis treatment effect estimates.

Methodological Quality

One possible explanation for the strong skew toward positive effect sizes in meta-analyses of treatment research is bias resulting from the type of research designs typically used to study treatment effectiveness. Any methodological artifact that caused treatment effects to be overestimated and was also widespread in primary studies would inflate the mean effect sizes found in meta-analyses based on those studies.

It is relatively easy to identify widespread methodological features of treatment effectiveness research that would potentially act to underestimate treatment effect sizes (e.g., unreliable, insensitive, or irrelevant outcome measures and inconsistent or incomplete treatment implementation; Boruch & Gomez, 1977; Hunter & Schmidt, 1990; Lipsey, 1990). Methodological artifacts that would serve to inflate

effect size estimates, however, are not so readily identifiable. The most obvious candidate is selection bias favoring treatment groups in designs that do not use random assignment to treatment conditions. If treatment groups often consist of respondents whose initial, pretreatment status is better than that of the control groups with which they are compared, their posttreatment status is also likely to be better, whether or not they have received effective treatment. Because nonequivalent comparison group and other such quasi-experimental designs are quite common in treatment effectiveness research—indeed, more common than randomized designs in many areas (Lipsey, Crosse, Dunkle, Pollard, & Stobart, 1985)—there is potential for widespread bias.

Fortunately, meta-analysts often consider the possibility that nonrandomized designs will yield different effect size estimates than randomized designs. A number of the meta-analyses listed in Table 1 provided a breakdown of the mean effect size for different design categories, typically random versus nonrandom assignment and, sometimes, one-group pre-and-post designs as well. Others divided primary studies according to some coding of methodological quality in which method of subject assignment was heavily weighted. These various stratifications make it possible to compare the distribution of mean treatment effects found for different design configurations.

Table 2 presents the mean effect sizes for different design and methodological quality categories for the subset of meta-analyses listed in Table 1 that provide such breakdowns. For purposes of Table 2, meta-analyses were selected only if they reported a mean effect size separately for different design categories or quality levels for a body of research studies in the same treatment area. In cases where more than one meta-analysis reported such information for the same treatment domain, the meta-analysis with the most complete information or, if that was equivalent, the one using the largest number of primary studies was selected.

Table 2
Methodological Quality Comparisons for Meta-Analyses Providing Information

	Effect size		
Comparison	M	SD	N
Control/comparison designs			
Random studies	0.46	0.28	74
Nonrandom studies	0.41	0.36	74
Design type			
Control/comparison	0.47	0.29	45
One-group pre–post	0.76	0.40	45
Methodological quality ratings			
High	0.40	0.27	27
Low	0.37	0.29	27

Note. For each comparison, only those meta-analyses that provided a breakout for that comparison were included (e.g., 74 meta-analyses provided a mean effect size for random and nonrandom studies).

The information displayed in Table 2 reveals that the mean effect size for nonrandomized control or comparison group designs is actually slightly smaller than that for randomized designs. If we assume that the same pattern holds for those meta-analyses that did not report this comparison, we must conclude that the mean effect sizes of Figure 1 are not inflated by inclusion of studies with such designs in the respective meta-analyses. Indeed, it would appear that, if anything, inclusion of nonrandomized comparison group designs, on average, slightly suppresses the overall effect size a meta-analysis yields.

By contrast, Table 2 shows a different result when we compare the effect sizes from one-group pre-and-post designs with those from control or comparison group designs (random and nonrandom combined) for those 45 meta-analyses that included and broke out both types. One-group pre-and-post designs yielded effect sizes that averaged 61% larger than those resulting from control or comparison group designs in the same treatment areas. It seems clear, therefore, that one-group pre-and-post designs do have the potential to substantially inflate mean effect sizes if they are included in a meta-analysis (more on this later).[2]

Also included in Table 2 are the results of comparing effect sizes for studies rated high in methodological quality with those rated low among meta-analyses that coded quality and reported a breakdown. Methodological quality is coded many different ways by meta-analysts. Most schemes represent internal validity as a predominant component, especially whether assignment to conditions was randomized. Some schemes, however, include various other factors related to construct, statistical conclusion, or external validity.

As Table 2 indicates, the 27 meta-analyses that compared mean effect sizes for studies rated high and low for methodological quality found little difference. As with the random versus nonrandom comparison studies, the small difference favored higher quality studies. Again, we see that inclusion of lower quality studies in these meta-analyses would, on average, slightly lower the overall mean effect size found, not inflate it.

Further evidence on this point is provided by 23 additional meta-analyses that reported the correlation between study-level effect sizes and the meta-analyst's ratings of the methodological quality of the studies. The mean correlation for those meta-analyses, weighted by the number of studies contributing to each meta-analysis, was −.01. Although the direction of this relationship is for lower quality studies to have higher effect sizes, its magnitude is so close to zero that it represents no inconsistency with the results reported earlier.

It may be useful to emphasize what is and is not implied by the foregoing analysis. These various comparisons do not indicate that it makes no difference to the validity of treatment effect estimates if a primary study uses random versus nonrandom assignment to conditions. Nor do they indicate that methodological quality is not important. What these comparisons do indicate is that there is no strong pattern or bias in the direction of the

difference made by lower quality methods. In a given treatment area, poor design or low methodological quality may result in a treatment estimate quite discrepant from what a better quality design would yield, but it is almost as likely to be an underestimate as an overestimate.

This general point is made more evident if, instead of comparing effect size means for different design types, we difference those means within a given meta-analysis and examine the distribution of differences. Figures 2, 3, and 4 show the distributions of such differences for the three methodological comparisons in Table 2. The differences between effect size estimates based on randomized versus nonrandomized designs, for example, ranges from near −1.00 to over 1.00, even though the mean difference is modest (Figure 2). In some treatment areas, therefore, nonrandom designs (relative to random) tend to strongly underestimate effects, and in others, they tend to strongly overestimate effects. The distribution of differences on methodological quality ratings shows a similar pattern (Figure 4).

The type of control or comparison design and overall methodological quality do matter, therefore, but no consistent pattern emerges in the direction of bias introduced when less valid approaches are used. Quite a different pattern appears, however, with one-group pre-and-post designs, which, as Figure 3 shows, generally overestimate treatment effects.

In all of these cases the results shown here provide no warrant for researchers to neglect the principles of

Figure 2
Distribution of Differences in Mean Effect Sizes for Random Minus Nonrandom Designs

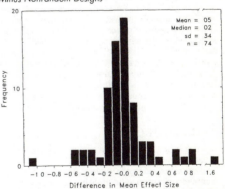

Mean = 05
Median = 02
sd = 34
n = 74

Difference in Mean Effect Size

---

[2] It is an open question why one-group pre-and-post studies yield inflated effect sizes. This may be an artifact of how meta-analysts handle the correlated scores from these studies when computing effect sizes, a confounding of maturational effects with treatment effects, or any of a number of other possibilities.

Figure 3
*Distribution of Differences in Mean Effect Sizes for One-
Group Pre–Post Minus Comparison Group Designs*

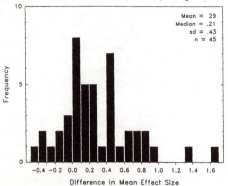

good research design on the grounds that it makes no
difference in the ultimate treatment effect estimate. What
these results do show is that, for the range of treatment
areas represented in available meta-analyses, no substantial skew in the distribution of treatment effect estimates
is apparent because those meta-analyses include studies
with nonrandomized comparison groups or weaker overall methodological quality. These factors, therefore, are
not sufficient to account for the strong positive trend in
mean treatment effect estimates shown in Figure 1.

One-group pre-and-post designs, on the other hand,
clearly are capable of upwardly biasing the mean treatment effect estimates derived from meta-analysis. If many
of the meta-analyses whose results are plotted in Figure
1 included a relatively high proportion of such studies,
that fact might well account for the strong positive results
shown there. As it happens, few of those meta-analyses
did include pre-and-post studies and, for those, they represented a modest proportion of the total. After looking
at some other potential biasing factors, we will refine the
distribution of treatment effects to eliminate this source
of bias.

Availability Bias

Another factor that might inflate the treatment effect estimates found in meta-analysis is a bias in the way meta-
analysts select studies to include in their syntheses. If,
from the whole population of eligible studies, those studies
most readily available to meta-analysts, and thus most
likely to be included, tended to show larger effects, whereas
those not included showed smaller effects, the result would
be a regular overestimation of treatment effects. The eas-
iest studies to identify and locate in a meta-analysis, of
course, are those that are formally published in journals
and books and hence have the highest probability of being

known to and cited by researchers in the field, listed by
the major bibliographic services (e.g., Psychological Abstracts), and found in university libraries.

There is good reason to believe that published studies
of treatment effectiveness research will tend to show higher
effect sizes than unpublished studies (Greenwald, 1975).
Authors may be more likely to attempt to publish a study
that finds large, statistically significant effects (even though
such results can occur solely by chance). Journal editors
and reviewers, in turn, are likely to look more favorably
on such results when they are submitted for publication.
Moreover, there is direct evidence that larger effect sizes
do indeed appear more frequently in the published than
the unpublished research on the same treatment (Smith,
1980).

The question for our assessment of the strongly positive mean effects displayed in Figure 1, therefore, is
whether they can be explained by differential effect sizes
in published versus unpublished research combined with
oversampling of published studies in the typical meta-
analysis. Because many meta-analysts show some awareness of this issue, it is not uncommon for them to stratify
the studies in their synthesis and report mean effect sizes
separately by publication source. This provides a database
we can use to examine the role that availability bias may
have made in the overall distribution of treatment effects.

Separate estimates of the mean treatment effect for
published versus unpublished studies were extracted
whenever possible from each meta-analysis listed in Table
1. If two meta-analyses in the same treatment area yielded
estimates, the one with the larger number of primary
studies was selected. A total of 92 meta-analyses provided
nonredundant comparisons by publication source; the
results are presented in Table 3. As shown, there is clearly
a differential between the mean treatment effect size es-

Figure 4
*Distribution of Differences in Mean Effect Sizes for High
Minus Low Methodological Quality*

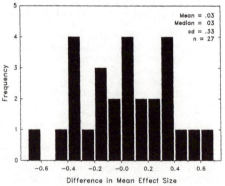

Table 3
Comparison of Effect Sizes Reported in Published Versus Unpublished Studies

Document source	Effect size		
	M	SD	N
Published studies	0.53	0.30	92
Unpublished studies	0.39	0.28	92

Note Only those meta-analyses that provided a breakout for this construct were included

Figure 5
Distributions of Mean Effect Sizes From Published and Unpublished Studies for Meta-Analyses Reporting Both Breakouts

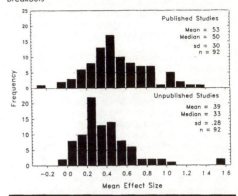

timate derived from published studies and that derived from unpublished studies within the same set of meta-analyses. Published studies yielded mean effect sizes that averaged 0.14 *SDs* larger than unpublished studies. It is evident, therefore, that the treatment effects reported in published studies are indeed generally biased upward, relative to those in unpublished studies.

It is noteworthy, however, that the mean effect size estimates for both published and unpublished studies fall in the positive range; published studies are just more positive than unpublished studies. We would still find positive mean effect sizes in most treatment areas, even if we made the estimate entirely from the results of unpublished studies. This is shown in Figure 5, which plots the distributions for the effect size estimates summarized in Table 3. Even if we look at only the distribution of mean effect size estimates from unpublished studies, we find that nearly 89% are 0.10 or greater and 78% are 0.20 or greater. Moreover, because the true mean effect size for a given treatment across the full population of eligible studies should lie somewhere between the separate estimates from published and unpublished studies, we can be relatively confident that the distribution across treatment areas will be more positive than the estimates derived from unpublished studies alone.

Oversampling of published studies in a meta-analysis, therefore, does indeed upwardly bias treatment effect estimates. The amount of that bias, however, does not appear to be large enough to account for the generally positive findings of the meta-analyses conducted on psychological treatment research. Nonetheless, to get a better assessment of the distribution of the effects of psychological treatment, we should restrict our attention to those meta-analyses that base their estimates on both published and unpublished studies. We will return to this issue after examining additional factors that may be implicated in the positive findings of Figure 1.

Small Sample Bias

Hedges (1981) has demonstrated that the mean of effect sizes based on small subject samples is biased upward as a statistical estimator of the population effect size mean. If a sizeable proportion of the mean effect sizes represented in Figure 1 were based on studies using small sam-

ples, this bias might account for part of the skew toward positive effects.

The magnitude of the small sample bias can be easily calculated and proves to be negligible for effect sizes based on a total sample size of 50 or more (e.g., 25 each in the treatment and control conditions). Indeed, the total sample size must be as small as 10 or less before the bias is appreciable, that is, 10% or more inflation. Table 4 shows the actual mean effect sizes based on different sized samples for the 39 independent meta-analyses from Table 1 that broke out their results by sample size. Another 25 reported the correlation between sample size and effect size. The mean correlation for these meta-analyses, weighted by the number of studies contributing to each meta-analysis, was only −.03.

Table 4 shows that the difference between mean effect sizes based on samples of 50 or less was only 0.06 larger than that based on samples of 51–100. Even if a large

Table 4
Comparison of Effect Sizes Based on Studies With Different Sized Samples

Sample size	Effect size		
	M	SD	N
N less than 50	0.58	0.32	39
N 51 to 100	0.52	0.43	39
N more than 100	0.35	0.30	39

Note Only those meta-analyses that provided a breakout for this construct were included

proportion of the studies represented in the mean effect sizes of Figure 1 was based on small samples, therefore, the upward bias from that source would be modest. In fact, of the 134 meta-analyses that reported sample size information, the mean sample size per primary study was 122. Therefore, the typical effect size contributing to the means represented in Figure 1 does not appear to be based on small enough samples to yield appreciable bias from that source.

It is worth noting that for the 39 meta-analyses contributing to Table 4, effect sizes based on samples of more than 100 were considerably smaller than those for both categories of lesser sample sizes. This difference is not attributable to the statistical bias inherent in small sample estimation of effect sizes, because as noted above, that bias is known to be negligible for samples over about 50. Apparently this pattern represents an empirical finding that perhaps reflects distinctive differences in the nature of studies conducted with larger samples. Such studies may use different treatment variants, less well-implemented treatments, or different measures or methods—any one of which might influence effect size.

Generalized Placebo Effect

Still another possible explanation for the strongly positive effects found in meta-analyses of studies of psychological treatment is that such positive effects are not actually due to the specific efficacy of the treatments provided. This might happen if the superiority of treatment group performance that is reflected in meta-analysis effect sizes resulted from some sort of placebo effect on the treatment group.[3] It may be that those generalized effects of treatment that are not usually present for control groups (e.g., receiving attention and having positive expectations) have fairly universal positive effects that show up in meta-analysis, even though the distinct elements of the treatments provided are ineffectual.

The hypothesis of a generalized placebo effect that yields widespread positive treatment effects is more difficult to appraise and interpret than the factors considered earlier. Two questions need to be addressed. First, is there any evidence that the generally positive effects of treatment meta-analyses could be accounted for by placebo effects alone? Second, even if they could, does that really undermine the claim that psychological treatment is generally efficacious? We will consider each of these in turn.

One line of evidence bearing on the placebo issue can be derived from the meta-analyses listed in Table 1. In some of the treatment areas represented there, placebo control groups are occasionally included in studies of treatment effects. And, in some cases, the meta-analyst coded and reported information on the effect size for the contrast between treatment and placebo controls separately from that between treatment and no treatment controls. Extraction of those separate estimates for 30 independent meta-analyses yielded the results shown in Table 5.

Table 5 shows that treatment effects estimated relative to placebo controls are indeed smaller, on average,

Table 5

Comparison of Effect Sizes Based on Studies With Different Control Conditions

	Effect size		
Control condition	M	SD	N
No treatment control	0.67	0.44	30
Placebo treatment control	0.48	0.26	30

Note Only those meta-analyses that provided a breakout for this construct were included.

than those estimated relative to no-treatment control conditions. Those effects do not reduce to zero, however. The distribution of effects relative to placebo still falls largely in the positive range (90% greater than 0.20) and thus shows evidence of "value added" by treatment beyond that attained with administration of placebos. The data for this comparison is limited, however. Rather few meta-analyses reported separate effect estimates for placebo controls, and the majority of those were in the area of mental health and thus do not necessarily extend to other treatment domains.

Another line of evidence on the generalized placebo hypothesis comes from those treatment research domains in which the customary comparison is not between a treatment condition and a "no-treatment" control condition but, rather, between the treatment of interest to the researcher (usually an innovative or experimental treatment) and "treatment as usual." This situation is often found, for instance, in research on educational interventions. A new curriculum is compared with the old curriculum, an open classroom is compared with a "normal" classroom, and so forth. The question in these studies is not whether the treatment of interest is better than nothing—because nothing is not a realistic option in the relevant settings—but whether it is better than established or traditional treatment.

Positive treatment effect sizes in these domains are analogous to those derived from treatment versus placebo comparisons. To the extent that an experimental treatment shows better results than treatment as usual, it must be adding some useful element above and beyond generalized placebo effects (which presumably would also be represented in treatment as usual).

In Figure 6 the mean effect sizes are plotted for those independent meta-analyses of educational interventions in Table 1 that were based, as nearly as we could tell, on studies in which treatment versus treatment-as-usual comparisons predominated. As can be seen, this distribution also falls largely in the positive effect range and thus provides little indication of treatment effects attributable entirely to generalized placebo effects.

What we can glean from the limited analysis above is that there are quite likely some generalized placebo

---

[3] Thanks to J. D. P. Sinha for this suggestion.

Figure 6
Distribution of Mean Effect Sizes for Educational Studies in Which the Control Group Received an Alternate or Traditional Treatment

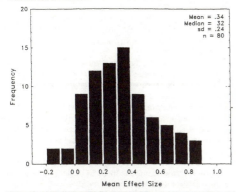

Mean = .34
Median = .32
sd = .24
n = 80

Frequency (y-axis)
Mean Effect Size (x-axis): −0.2, 0.0, 0.2, 0.4, 0.6, 0.8, 1.0

effects that contribute to the overall effects of psychological treatment, but their magnitude does not seem sufficient to fully account for those overall effects.

To the extent that the treatment effects shown in Figure 1 do reflect a boost from a generalized placebo effect, however, it is arguable whether this undermines their validity. In psychological treatment, unlike medical treatment, it is conceptually difficult to distinguish placebo effects from the treatment with which they are associated. In medical treatments a relatively clear separation is possible between the nature of, say, surgical or pharmaceutical intervention and the accompanying patient morale, expectations, social interaction, and the like. Psychological treatment, on the other hand, is often presumed to work through just those mechanisms of social interaction, expectations, and attitude change that likely constitute the key elements of the placebo effect. As Wilkins (1986) has argued, placebo effects may be constituent parts of psychological treatment, not artifacts to be separated out in any assessment of that treatment.

Summary of Identifiable Influences on Observed Effect Sizes

The considerations examined earlier indicate that there are indeed some factors that may upwardly bias the mean effect sizes shown in Table 1 and Figure 1. Two such factors are especially notable. First, one-group pre-and-post designs for assessing treatment effects seem almost universally to overestimate the size of those effects relative to randomized studies of the same treatment. Meta-analyses based in substantial part on such studies, therefore, cannot be accepted as sources of good estimates of the efficacy of treatment.

Second, it seems clear that there is a differential between the effect sizes derived from published studies and those found in unpublished studies of a given treatment. Published studies are more likely to report stronger—that is, larger and more positive—effects than unpublished studies. It follows, therefore, that meta-analyses based only on published studies cannot be expected to yield good estimates of overall treatment effects.

In addition, it seems likely that some portion of the positive results of psychological treatment stems from generalized placebo effects rather than the specific effects of the treatment delivered. The indication from the meta-analyses reviewed here, however, is that positive treatment effect sizes cannot be accounted for entirely by generalized placebo effects; indeed, such effects are rather modest. Moreover, given the inherently psychological nature of psychological treatment, it is arguable whether generalized placebo effects should be excluded from consideration when assessing such treatments.

Because the mean effect size array in Figure 1 includes the results of meta-analyses based, in part, on pre-and-post studies and those restricted to published studies, we must, therefore, ask whether those factors account for the surprisingly positive effects displayed there. It is worth remembering, incidentally, that there are many factors that may reduce observed effect sizes that cannot be examined in the available meta-analysis results. Our concern, however, is to guard against an overly optimistic assessment of treatment efficacy, and we thus emphasize those factors that may produce upward bias in effect sizes.

Refined Examination of the Distribution of Treatment Effects

We are now in a position to make a more refined and probing assessment of the distribution of mean treatment effects reported in the meta-analyses of Table 1 and Figure 1. For this purpose, we make the following selections: (a) We use only treatment effect estimates based on control or comparison group designs and eliminate those based on or mixed with estimates derived from one-group pre-and-post designs; (b) we use only treatment effect estimates based on both published and unpublished studies; and (c) in cases in which two or more meta-analyses cover the same or highly overlapping research literatures, we retain only the treatment estimates from the meta-analysis with the broadest coverage, that is, the largest number of studies.

The result of these refinements is a distribution of mean treatment effect estimates that are relatively independent, that is, do not substantially share studies or respondents, and that eliminate or at least appreciably reduce the biases identified earlier. In particular, this distribution should not seriously overestimate treatment effects because of inclusion of estimates based on one-group pre-and-post studies or because of estimates based entirely on published studies. The studies contributing mean effect sizes to this refined distribution are marked with superscript[a] in Table 1, presented earlier.

This refined distribution, shown in Figure 7, provides a reasonable basis for assessing the general efficacy of psychological, educational, and behavioral treatment.

Figure 7
Refined Distribution of Mean Effect Sizes From Selected Meta-Analyses

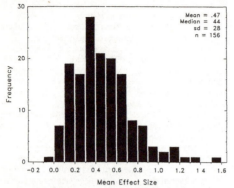

Collectively, the 156 meta-analyses represented there encompass approximately 9,400 individual treatment effectiveness studies ($M = 60$ per meta-analysis) and more than one million individual subjects ($M = 8,055$ per meta-analysis), estimated on the basis of the 59 meta-analyses that reported sample size information.

The grand mean treatment effect in this refined distribution is 0.47 *SD*s. That is, the average treatment group scored 0.47 *SD*s higher on the average outcome measure than did the average control group.[4] Moreover, Figure 7 shows a relatively modest proportion of meta-analyses that yielded mean treatment effect sizes in the zero and negative range. In particular, 83% of the mean effect sizes in the refined distribution were 0.20 or greater. Only one was actually negative. We are left, therefore, with the same observation with which we began—the evidence from meta-analysis indicates that the psychological, educational, and behavioral treatments studied by meta-analysts generally have positive effects. We turn now to the question of whether those positive effects are of meaningful practical magnitude.

Statistical Versus Practical Effects

Treatment effect estimates in standard deviation units have little intuitive meaning. How much of a treatment effect is 0.20 or 0.50 of a standard deviation? Is it possible that, although most of the mean effect sizes in Figure 7 are numerically positive, they represent small effects that are not practically or clinically meaningful in the contexts in which the respective treatments are applied?

The issue of relating statistical differences in measured treatment outcomes to practical significance is a complex and difficult one. The thrust of discussion in the technical literature, however, is recognition that numerically small statistical effects do not necessarily imply

small practical effects (Abelson, 1985; Carver, 1975; Lipsey, 1990; Rosenthal & Rubin, 1982; Sechrest & Yeaton, 1982). One useful demonstration of this point is the translation of such bivariate statistical information as effect sizes into a more intuitively comprehensible form. Rosenthal and Rubin have suggested use of the binomial effect size display (BESD), a depiction of effects in terms of the proportion of treatment versus control subjects above a common success threshold (defined arbitrarily as the overall median).

In BESD terms, the grand mean effect size of 0.47 from the meta-analyses in Figure 7 can be represented as a contrast between a treatment group with a success rate of 62% versus a control group with a success rate of 38%. A 24-percentage-point spread between treatment and control success rates hardly sounds like a negligible difference. Correspondingly, an effect size of 0.20 translates to a 10-percentage-point spread between the treatment and control success rate, 55% versus 45%. Note that a 10% improvement on a 45% (control) baseline represents an increase of more than 20% (10/45)—a value that is hard to declare categorically trivial.

The practical significance of an effect, of course, is very much dependent on the nature of the outcome at issue and its importance to patients or clients. In a life-and-death situation, a mortality decrement of 5% or less may well be clinically significant. Rosenthal (1991b) has observed, for example, that the physicians' study on the effects of aspirin on heart attacks was judged conclusive and prematurely ended when the effect size reached 0.07 (in *SD*s), equivalent on the BESD to less than a 3.5-percentage-point spread between treatment and control groups.

Although psychological treatments rarely deal with life-and-death issues, it is illuminating to compare the range of statistical effects shown in Figure 7 with the effects of medical treatment, a domain of acknowledged (though not universal) efficacy. To accomplish this, we searched for meta-analyses of medical interventions whose results were stated in, or could be converted to, the standard deviation metric so that they could be compared with the results of psychological interventions shown in Figure 7.[5] We did not attempt to be exhaustive and doubtless missed many pertinent reports. For those reports we found, however, we exercised no selectivity other than requiring statistically comparable effect metrics and a summary judgment by the author of the report that the treatment was judged effective. This latter requirement

---

[4] This value is not greatly different from the grand mean effect size of the unrefined distribution (Figure 1), which was 0.50 SDs, nor do the standard deviations of these distributions differ greatly. Inclusion of meta-analyses using one-group pre-and-post studies, selecting only published studies, or overlapping the research base of other meta-analyses thus did not strongly bias the distribution of Figure 1, although the potential was certainly there.

[5] Although a considerable number of meta-analyses have been conducted in the medical field, most report only odds ratios or other effect indicators that cannot generally be converted to the standardized mean difference metric without additional information (e. g., marginals or base rates) that is often unreported.

ensured that we were comparing psychological treatment to successful medical treatment and not to treatment failures.

The results of the meta-analyses of medical treatment that we found by this procedure are presented in Table 6 under three headings. The first listing is for the mean effects of successful medical intervention on mortality. Not surprisingly, given the life-and-death issue involved, treatments yielding numerically small effect sizes were nonetheless judged beneficial. The range of effect sizes for these treatments (0.08 to 0.47) falls below the grand mean effect size for psychological treatment (see Figure 7).

The second section of Table 6 shows the mean effect sizes on medical outcomes other than mortality for various treatments judged beneficial in the meta-analysis reports we located. These effect sizes ranged from 0.24 to 0.80, quite comparable with the range of effect sizes shown in Figure 7 for psychological treatments.

Finally, in the last section of Table 6, we present the results of those meta-analyses we located that estimated the effects of medical interventions on psychological or behavioral outcomes, not unlike many of those represented in Figure 7. These mean effect sizes varied from 0.11 to 0.96, a range that, once again, fell well within that shown in Figure 7 for psychological treatment effects.

The point of these comparisons is not to argue that psychological treatment is as effective as medical treatment. There are too many differences in treatment, respondents, research contexts, and the nature of the outcome variables to make such a simple claim. Furthermore, it may well be that psychological treatment aimed at, say, improvement in employees' job satisfaction needs to achieve much larger statistical effects to have noticeable consequences than a medical treatment for angina. What does seem clear, however, is that in assessing meta-analytic estimates of the effects of psychological, educational, and behavioral treatment, we cannot arbitrarily dismiss statistically modest values (even 0.10 or 0.20 SDs) as obviously trivial. Translated into BESD success rates, they do not seem indisputably negligible and comparable numerical values are judged to represent benefits in the medical domain, even when similar outcome variables are at issue. On balance, therefore, the magnitude of effect size estimates that meta-analysis reveals for psychological treatment seems sufficiently large to support the claim that such treatment is generally efficacious in practical as well as statistical terms.

Discussion

What we conclude from this broad review of meta-analytic evidence is that well-developed psychological, educational, and behavioral treatments generally have meaningful positive effects on the intended outcome variables. The number and scope of effective treatments covered by this conclusion are impressive, and the magnitude of the effects for a substantial portion of those treatments is in a range of practical significance by almost any reasonable criterion.

Table 6
Selected Meta-Analyses of Medical Treatment Judged Effective

Outcome variable	Mean effect size or effect size range
Medical	
Mortality	
Aortocoronary bypass sugery (Lynn & Donovan, 1980)	0.15
AZT for AIDS (Rosenthal, 1991b)	0.47
Cyclosporine in organ transplants (Rosenthal, 1991b)	0.30
Chemotherapy for breast cancer (EBCTCG, 1988)	0.08 to 0.11
Intravenous streptokinase for myocardial infarction (Stampfer, Goldhaber, Yusuf, Peto, & Hennekens, 1983)	0.08
Other outcomes	
By-pass surgery; effects on angina (Lynn & Donovan, 1980)	0.80
Dipyridamole; effects on angina (Sacks, Ancona-Berk, Berrier, Nagalingam, & Chalmers, 1988)	0.24
Drug treatment for arthritis; various outcomes (Felson, Anderson, & Meenan, 1990)	0.45 to 0.77
Cyclosporine; effects on organ rejection (Rosenthal, 1991b)	0.39
Anticoagulants; effects on thromboembolism rates (Chalmers, Matta, Smith, & Kunzler, 1977)	0.30
Psychological	
Drug treatment for behavioral disorders; behavioral and cognitive outcomes (Kavale & Nye, 1984)	0.28 to 0.74
Electroconvulsive therapy; effects on depression (Janick et al., 1985)	0.80
Drug treatment for hyperactivity; cognitive, behavioral and social outcomes (Kavale, 1982; Ottenbacher & Cooper, 1983; Thurber & Walker, 1983)	0.47 to 0.96
Neuroleptic drugs for dementia; effects on agitation (Schneider, Pollock, & Lyness, 1990)	0.37
Hypertensive drug therapy; effects on quality of life (Beto & Bansal, 1992)	0.11 to 0.28

Furthermore, we have found that this broad positive finding cannot be explained away by any simple hypotheses of bias stemming from inclusion of studies using weak research designs, oversampling of published studies, or heavy representation of very small sample studies. Also, whether one views placebo effects as artifacts that inflate treatment results or an inherent constituent of psychological treatment, their magnitude appears to be too modest to account for more than a portion of the generally positive effects of such treatment.

We acknowledge that the information available in the current treatment research meta-analysis literature is too crude to permit a truly probing analysis of the potential biases in estimates of treatment effect sizes. Thus the factors we examined may still create bias in ways too subtle for us to detect, or other artifacts we did not or could not examine may yet account for the broad positive findings. On the other hand, it is worth mentioning once again that most of the factors with potential to bias treatment effect estimates that come readily to mind operate to produce underestimates, not overestimates. If the treatment effect estimates in Figure 7 were corrected for unreliability of measurement, range restriction, incomplete treatment implementation, and variability due to stable individual differences in respondents, they would certainly increase appreciably (see Boruch & Gomez, 1977; Hunter & Schmidt, 1990; Lipsey, 1990). Therefore, although the description presented here may still overestimate treatment effects due to unexamined sources of upward bias, it also almost certainly reflects the influence of substantial downward bias.

We thus believe that a strongly favorable conclusion about the efficacy of well-developed psychological treatment is justified by the results of meta-analytic investigation. We must emphasize, however, the limitation of this conclusion to well-developed treatment approaches and elaborate on what that means. The sweep of the positive findings reported here is so broad as to perhaps suggest that virtually everything works in psychological treatment. That would be a false conclusion. The meta-analytic evidence reviewed here, despite its breadth, falls far short of encompassing the full range of psychological, educational, and behavioral practice. Meta-analysis is only possible for treatment approaches that have generated a corpus of research sufficient in quantity and comparability for systematic analysis within a statistical framework. Such a body of studies, in turn, is only likely to be produced for widely used and well-developed approaches growing out of established theory or practice, or for promising innovations. Thus the treatment approaches represented in meta-analysis and reviewed in this article represent rather mature instances that are sufficiently well developed and credible to attract practitioners and sufficiently promising (or controversial) to attract a critical mass of research. For treatment approaches meeting these criteria, it is perhaps not surprising that a high proportion do prove at least moderately efficacious.

What may be more surprising to those not familiar with the advantages of meta-analysis as a research synthesis technique is the failure of conventional research-reviewing techniques over the decades to identify more decisively the generally positive effects of psychological treatment. Indeed, most of the meta-analyses reviewed here are introduced with commentary on the inconclusiveness or controversy of prior conventional research reviews. If well-developed and well-researched treatments are broadly and robustly skewed toward positive results,

as shown in Figures 1 and 7, why has this not been more readily apparent from conventional reviews of the respective research?

The fault here almost surely lies with the flaws in conventional reviewing practice. This has been discussed extensively elsewhere (e.g., Cook & Leviton, 1980; Hunter & Schmidt, 1990; Schmidt, 1992), but the essence of the problem with conventional research reviews is a naive use of vote-counting assessments of the statistical significance of study outcomes (Hedges & Olkin, 1980). When alpha is set at the usual levels (e.g., .05) to limit Type I error, Type II error will be unrestrained and can range very high (e.g., 50%–90%) unless sample sizes are quite large (Schmidt, 1992). Type II error, recall, is the probability of failing to reject the null hypothesis when, in fact, it is false. Because, as Figures 1 and 7 show, the null hypothesis is generally false in the treatment research reviewed here and, also, sample sizes are modest, high Type II error rates will result in a large proportion of spurious null (statistically nonsignificant) results in treatment research.[6] Conventional reviewers inspecting a body of treatment research in which a sizeable proportion of studies did not yield statistically significant results have generally not recognized the high Type II error rates and have felt that there was little basis for judging the treatment to be broadly efficacious.

Meta-analysis, by comparison, is based on an aggregation of statistical estimates of the magnitude of treatment effects irrespective of whether, individually, they are statistically significant. Statistical tests are then applied to the aggregate results (e.g., the mean and variance of the distribution of study level effect sizes; Hedges & Olkin, 1985; Hunter & Schmidt, 1990). The aggregation of samples inherent in meta-analysis greatly increases statistical power and decreases Type II error. In cases in which the null hypothesis is false (i.e., treatment is effective) and individual studies use modest sample sizes (e.g., under 500), therefore, the conclusions of meta-analysis can diverge markedly from those of conventional reviews. The evidence reviewed here indicates that psychological treatment generally presents such a case.

Although meta-analysis offers significant advantages as a research synthesis technique, especially with regard to statistical issues, it is not without limitations of its own. Most striking in the present situation are the deficiencies in practice, rather than those inherent in the technique itself. In the applications reviewed above, simple checks of the dependence of the effect size estimates on the methodological characteristics of the primary

---

[6] The mean sample size for the studies in those 156 meta-analyses in Figure 7 that reported usable sample size information was 134, or about 67 each in the treatment and comparison groups. The statistical power with that sample size, alpha equal to .05, and a treatment effect of 0.47 (the mean in Figure 7), is 0.76. Thus despite the positive treatment effect in this average case, 24% of the individual studies would be expected to yield statistically nonsignificant results; that is, the Type II error rate equals .24. As the effect size (ES) ranges below the mean of 0.47, or sample size falls below 67 per group, power drops off quite sharply. With ES = 0.20 and n = 50, for example, the Type II error rate jumps to .83.

studies or the extent of the sampling of unpublished studies are far from universal. Moreover, most of these meta-analyses were confined to estimating the mean effect size over the studies of interest with little attention, beyond crude stratifications, to probing the variations in treatments, respondents, and outcomes that would better reveal the circumstances of more and less effective implementations. As a consequence, what is learned about psychological treatment from these hundreds of meta-analyses is well short of the potential inherent in meta-analytic technique.

Moreover, even in its most advanced and differentiated form, meta-analysis is limited by the nature of the primary studies to which it is applied. Those studies too often report only crude comparisons between undifferentiated "black box" treatment packages and control conditions with little attention to potential interactions with client characteristics, the range of outcome variables, or temporal factors (Lipsey, 1988; Lipsey et al., 1985).

The proper agenda for the next generation of treatment effectiveness research, for both primary and meta-analytic studies, is investigation of which treatment variants are most effective, the mediating causal processes through which they work, and the characteristics of recipients, providers, and settings that most influence their results. Such a research agenda is justified by a basic assumption that psychological treatment can be, and generally is, effective, so that the questions of interest are not whether it works but how it works and how it can be made to work better. The present generation of meta-analytic research supports that assumption.

REFERENCES

Abelson, R. P. (1985). A variance explanation paradox: When a little is a lot. *Psychological Bulletin, 97,* 129–133.

Beto, J. A., & Bansal, V. K. (1992). Quality of life in treatment of hypertension: A meta-analysis of clinical trials. *American Journal of Hypertension, 5,* 125–133.

Boruch, R. F., & Gomez, H. (1977). Sensitivity, bias, and theory in impact evaluations. *Professional Psychology, 8,* 411–434.

Carver, R. P. (1975). The Coleman Report: Using inappropriately designed achievement tests. *American Educational Research Journal, 12,* 77–86.

Chalmers, T. C., Matta, R. J., Smith, H., & Kunzler, A. (1977). Evidence favoring the use of anticoagulants in the hospital phase of acute myocardial infarction. *The New England Journal of Medicine, 297,* 1091–1096.

Cook, T. D., Cooper, H., Cordray, D. S., Hartmann, H., Hedges, L. V., Light, R. J., Louis, T. A., & Mosteller, F. (Eds.). (1992). *Meta-analysis for explanation A casebook* New York: Russell Sage Foundation.

Cook, T. D., & Leviton, L. C. (1980). Reviewing the literature: A comparison of traditional methods with meta-analysis. *Journal of Personality, 48,* 449–472.

Durlak, J. A., & Lipsey, M. W. (1991). A practitioner's guide to meta-analysis. *American Journal of Community Psychology, 19,* 291–332.

EBCTCG (Early Breast Cancer Trialists' Collaborative Group). (1988). Effects of adjuvant tamoxifen and of cytotoxic therapy on mortality in early breast cancer. *The New England Journal of Medicine, 319,* 1681–1692.

Eysenck, H. J. (1952). The effects of psychotherapy: An evaluation. *Journal of Consulting Psychology, 16,* 319–324.

Eysenck, H. J. (1965). The effects of psychotherapy. *Journal of Psychology, 1,* 97–118.

Felson, D T., Anderson, J. J., & Meenan, R. F. (1990) The comparative efficacy and toxicity of second-line drugs in rheumatoid arthritis. *Journal of the American College of Rheumatology, 33,* 1449–1461.

Fischer, J. (1978). Does anything work? *Journal of Social Service Research, 1,* 215–243

Glass, G. V. (1976). Primary, secondary, and meta-analysis of research. *Educational Researcher, 5,* 3–8.

Glass, G. V., McGaw, B., & Smith, M. L. (1981). *Meta-analysis in social research* Newbury Park, CA: Sage

Greenwald, A. G. (1975). Consequences of prejudice against the null hypothesis. *Psychological Bulletin, 82,* 1–20.

Hedges, L. V. (1981). Distribution theory for Glass's estimator of effect size and related estimators. *Journal of Educational Statistics, 6,* 107–128.

Hedges, L. V., & Olkin, I. (1980) Vote-counting methods in research synthesis. *Psychological Bulletin, 88,* 359–369.

Hedges, L. V., & Olkin, I. (1985). *Statistical methods for meta-analysis* San Diego, CA: Academic Press.

Hunter, J. E., & Schmidt, F. L. (1990) *Methods of meta-analysis Correcting error and bias in research findings* Newbury Park, CA: Sage.

Janick, P. G., Davis, J. M., Gibbons, R. D., Ericksen, S., Chang, S., & Gallagher, P. (1985). Efficacy of ECT: A meta-analysis. *American Journal of Psychiatry, 142,* 297–302.

Kavale, K. (1982). The efficacy of stimulant drug treatment for hyperactivity: A meta-analysis. *Journal of Learning Disabilities, 15,* 280–289.

Kavale, K. A., & Nye, C. (1984). The effectiveness of drug treatment for severe behavior disorders: A meta-analysis. *Behavioral Disorders, 9,* 117–130.

Lipsey, M. W. (1988). Practice and malpractice in evaluation research. *Evaluation Practice, 9*(4), 5–24.

Lipsey, M. W. (1990). *Design sensitivity Statistical power for experimental research* Newbury Park, CA: Sage.

Lipsey, M. W., Crosse, S., Dunkle, J., Pollard, J., & Stobart, G. (1985). Evaluation: The state of the art and the sorry state of the science. *New Directions for Program Evaluation, 27,* 7–28.

Luborsky, L., Singer, B., & Luborsky, L. (1975). Comparative studies of psychotherapies. *Archives of General Psychiatry, 32,* 995–1008.

Lynn, D. D., & Donovan, J. M. (1980). Medical versus surgical treatment of coronary artery disease. *Evaluation in Education, 4,* 98–99.

Ottenbacher, K. J., & Cooper, H. M. (1983). Drug treatment of hyperactivity in children. *Developmental Medicine and Child Neurology, 25,* 358–366.

Prather, J. E., & Gibson, F. K. (1977). The failure of social programs *Public Administration Review, 37,* 556–564.

Rosenthal, R. (1991a). *Meta-analytic procedures for social research* (Rev. ed.). Newbury Park, CA: Sage.

Rosenthal, R. (1991b). Meta-analysis: A review. *Psychosomatic Medicine, 53,* 247–271.

Rosenthal, R., & Rubin, D. B. (1982). A simple, general purpose display of magnitude of experimental effect. *Journal of Educational Psychology, 74,* 166–169.

Rossi, P. H., & Wright, J. D. (1984). Evaluation research: An assessment. *Annual Review of Sociology, 10,* 331–352.

Sacks, H. S., Ancona-Berk, V. A., Berrier, J., Nagalingam, R., & Chalmers, T. C. (1988). Dipyridamole in the treatment of angina pectoris: A meta-analysis. *Clinical Pharmacologic Therapy, 43,* 610–615.

Sechrest, L., & Yeaton, W. H. (1982). Magnitudes of experimental effects in social science research. *Evaluation Review, 6,* 579–600.

Schmidt, F. L. (1992). What do data really mean? Research findings, meta-analysis, and cumulative knowledge in psychology. *American Psychologist, 47,* 1173–1181.

Schneider, L. S., Pollock, V. E., & Lyness, S. A. (1990). A meta-analysis of controlled trials of neuroleptic treatment in dementia. *Journal of the American Geriatric Society, 38,* 553–563.

Smith, M. L. (1980). Publication bias and meta-analysis. *Evaluation and Education, 4,* 22–24.

Smith, M. L., & Glass, G. V. (1977). Meta-analysis of psychotherapy outcome studies. *American Psychologist, 32,* 752–760.

Stampfer, M. J., Goldhaber, S. Z., Yusuf, S., Peto, R., & Hennekens, C. H. (1983). Effects of intravenous streptokinase on acute myocardial infarction: Pooled results from randomized trials. In R. J. Light (Ed.), *Evaluation studies review annual* (Vol. 8, pp. 494–496). Newbury Park, CA: Sage.

Thurber, S., & Walker, C. E. (1983). Medication and hyperactivity: A meta-analysis. *Journal of General Psychology, 108,* 79–86.

Wilkins, W. (1986). Placebo problems in psychotherapy research: Social-psychological alternatives to chemotherapy concepts. *American Psychologist, 41,* 551–556.

APPENDIX

References for Studies in Table 1

Adair, J. G., Sharpe, D., & Huynh, C.-L. (1989). Hawthorne control procedures in educational experiments: A reconsideration of their use and effectiveness. *Review of Educational Research, 59,* 215–228.

Adair, J. G., Sharpe, D., & Huynh, C. L. (1990). The placebo control group: An analysis of its effectiveness in educational research. *Journal of Experimental Education, 59,* 67–86.

Administration for Children, Youth, and Families (1983). *The effects of the Head Start program on children's cognitive development (Preliminary report): Head Start evaluation, synthesis, and utilization project.* Washington, DC : U.S. Department of Health and Human Services. (ERIC Document Reproduction Service No. ED 248 989)

Aiello, N. C. (1981). A meta-analysis comparing alternative methods of individualized and traditional instruction in science (Doctoral dissertation, Virginia Polytechnic Institute and State University). *Dissertation Abstracts International, 42,* 977A.

Aiello, N. C., & Wolfle, L. M. (1980). *A meta-analysis of individualized instruction in science* (ERIC Document Reproduction Service No. ED 190 404)

Alexander, C. N., Rainforth, M. V., & Gelderloos, P. (1991). Transcendental-meditation, self-actualization, and psychological health—A conceptual overview and statistical metaanalysis. *Journal of Social Behavior and Personality, 6*(5), 189–248.

Allen, M. (1989). A comparison of self-report, observer, and physiological assessments of public speaking anxiety reduction techniques using meta-analysis. *Communication Studies, 40*(2), 127–139.

Allen, M., Hunter, J. E., & Donohue, W. A. (1989). Meta-analysis of self-report data on the effectiveness of public speaking anxiety treatment techniques. *Communication Education, 38*(3), 54–76.

Almeida, M. C., & Denham, S. A. (1984). *Interpersonal cognitive problem-solving: A meta-analysis.* (ERIC Document Reproduction Service No. ED 247 003)

Anderson, L. A., & Sharpe, P. A. (1991). Improving patient and provider communication—A synthesis and review of communication interventions. *Patient Education and Counseling, 17,* 99–134.

Andrews, D. A., Zinger, I., Hoge, R. D., Bonta, J., Gendreau, P., & Cullen, F. T. (1990). Does correctional treatment work—A clinically relevant and psychologically informed metaanalysis. *Criminology, 28,* 369–404.

Andrews, G., Guitar, B., & Howie, P. (1980). Meta-analysis of the effect of stuttering treatment. *Journal of Speech and Hearing Disorders, 45,* 287–307.

Andrews, G., & Harvey, R. (1981). Does psychotherapy benefit neurotic patients? A reanalysis of the Smith, Glass, and Miller data. *Archives of General Psychiatry, 38,* 1203–1208.

Asencio, C. E. (1984). Effects of behavioral objectives on student achievement: A meta-analysis of findings. *Dissertation Abstracts International, 45,* 501A. (University Microfilms No. 84–12499)

Athappilly, K., Smidchens, U., & Kofel, J. W. (1983). A computer-based meta-analysis of the effects of modern mathematics in comparison with traditional mathematics. *Educational Evaluation and Policy Analysis, 5,* 485–493.

Baker, S. B., & Daniels, T. G. (1989). Integrating research on the microcounseling program: A meta-analysis. *Journal of Counseling Psychology, 36,* 213–222.

Baker, S. B., Daniels, T. G., & Greeley, A. T. (1990). Systematic training of graduate-level counselors: Narrative and meta-analytic reviews of three major programs. *Counseling Psychologist, 18,* 355–421.

Baker, S. B., & Popowicz, C. I. (1983). Meta-analysis as a strategy for evaluating effects of career education interventions. *The Vocational Guidance Quarterly, 31,* 178–186.

Baker, S. B., Swisher, J. D., Nadenichek, P. E., & Popowicz, C. L. (1984). Measured effects of primary prevention strategies. *Personnel and Guidance Journal, 62,* 459–464.

Balestrieri, M., Williams, P., & Wilkinson, G. (1988). Specialist mental health treatment in general practice: A meta-analysis. *Psychological Medicine, 18,* 711–717.

Bangert, R. L., Kulik, J. A., & Kulik, C. C. (1983). Individualized systems of instruction in secondary schools. *Review of Educational Research, 53,* 143–158.

Bangert-Drowns, R. L. (1988). The effects of school-based substance abuse education: A meta-analysis. *Journal of Drug Education, 18,* 243–264.

Bangert-Drowns, R. L., Kulik, J. A., & Kulik, C. C. (1983). Effects of coaching programs on achievement test performance. *Review of Educational Research, 53,* 571–585.

Bangert-Drowns, R. L., Kulik, J. A., & Kulik, C. C. (1985). Effectiveness of computer-based education in secondary schools. *Journal of Computer-Based Instruction, 12,* 59–68.

Barker, S. L., Funk, S. C., & Houston, B. K. (1988). Psychological treatment versus nonspecific factors: A meta-analysis of conditions that engender comparable expectations for improvement. *Clinical Psychology Review, 8,* 579–594.

Batts, J. W. (1988). The effects of teacher consultation: A meta-analysis of controlled studies (Doctoral dissertation, University of Kentucky). *Dissertation Abstracts International, 49,* 1404A.

Beaudry, J. S. (1989). The effectiveness of continuing medical education: A quantitative synthesis. *Journal of Continuing Education in the Health Professions, 9,* 285–307.

Becker, B. J. (1990). Coaching for the Scholastic Aptitude Test: Further synthesis and appraisal. *Review of Educational Research, 60,* 373–417.

Beekun, R. I. (1989). Assessing the effectiveness of sociotechnical interventions: Antidote or fad? *Human Relations, 42,* 877–897.

Bennett, B. B. (1988). The effectiveness of staff development training practices: A meta-analysis (Doctoral dissertation, University of Oregon, 1987). *Dissertation Abstracts International, 48,* 1739A.

Benton, M. K., & Schroeder, H. E. (1990). Social skills training with schizophrenics: A meta-analytic evaluation. *Journal of Consulting and Clinical Psychology, 58,* 741–747.

Berman, J. S., Miller, R. C., & Massman, P. J. (1985). Cognitive therapy versus systematic desensitization: Is one treatment superior? *Psychological Bulletin, 97,* 451–461.

Black, D. R., Gleser, L. J., & Kooyers, K. J. (1990). A meta-analytic evaluation of couples weight-loss programs. *Health Psychology, 9,* 330–347.

Blanchard, E. B., Andrasik, F., Ahles, T. I., Teders, S. J., & O'Keefe, D. (1980). Migraine and tension headache: A meta-analytic review. *Behavior Therapy, 11,* 613–631.

Bond, G. R. (1988). *Employment outcomes from psychiatric rehabilitation.* Unpublished manuscript, Indiana University-Purdue University at Indianapolis.

Boulanger, F. D. (1981). Instruction and science learning: A quantitative synthesis. *Journal of Research in Science Teaching, 18,* 311–327.

Bowers, T. G., & Clum, G. A. (1988). Relative contribution of specific and nonspecific treatment effects: Meta-analysis of placebo-controlled behavior therapy research. *Psychological Bulletin, 103,* 315–323.

Bradford. J W. (1991). A meta-analysis of selected research on student attitudes towards mathematics (Doctoral dissertation, University of Iowa, 1990). *Dissertation Abstracts International, 51,* 4049A.

Brannick, J. P. (1987). A meta-analytic study of human relations training research (Doctoral dissertation, Bowling Green State University). *Dissertation Abstracts International, 48,* 3439B.

Branwen, M. F. (1982). Meta-analysis of the effectiveness of assertion training groups (Doctoral dissertation, University of Wisconsin-Madison). *Dissertation Abstracts International, 43,* 1234B. (University Microfilm International No. 82–15931)

Bredderman, T. (1983). Effects of activity-based elementary science on student outcomes: A quantitative synthesis. *Review of Educational Research, 53,* 499–518.

Broome, M. E., Lillis, P. P., & Smith, M. C. (1989). Pain interventions with children—A meta-analysis of research. *Nursing Research, 38,* 154–158.

Brown, S. A. (1990). Studies of educational interventions and outcomes in diabetic adults—A metaanalysis revisited. *Patient Education and Counseling, 16,* 189–215.

Bryan, D. R. (1989). Psychological and psychopharmacological treatment of bulimia: A meta-analytic review (Doctoral dissertation, Kent State University). *Dissertation Abstracts International, 50,* 2615B.

Burke, M. J., & Day, R. R. (1986). A cumulative study of the effectiveness of managerial training. *Journal of Applied Psychology, 71,* 232–245.

Burns, P. K. (1982). A quantitative synthesis of research findings relative to the pedagogical effectiveness of computer-assisted instruction in elementary and secondary schools (Doctoral dissertation, University of Iowa, 1981). *Dissertation Abstracts International, 42,* 2946A.

Cannella, K. A. S. (1988). The effectiveness of stress coping interventions: A meta-analysis with methodological implications (Doctoral dissertation, Georgia State University, College of Education, 1987). *Dissertation Abstracts International, 48,* 1705A.

Carlberg, C., & Kavale, K. (1980). The efficacy of special versus regular class placement for exceptional children: A meta-analysis. *Journal of Special Education, 14,* 295–309.

Carlson, M. (1987). *Social and academic outcomes of cooperative learning in the mainstreamed classroom A meta-analysis* Unpublished manuscript, Claremont Graduate School, Claremont, CA.

Casey, R. J., & Berman, J. S. (1985). The outcome of psychotherapy with children. *Psychological Bulletin, 98,* 388–400.

Casto, G., & Mastropieri, M. A. (1986). The efficacy of early intervention programs: A meta-analysis. *Exceptional Children, 52,* 417–424.

Casto, G., & White, K. (1984). The efficacy of early intervention programs with environmentally at-risk infants. *Journal of Children in Contemporary Society, 17,* 37–50.

Cedar, B., & Levant, R. F. (1990). A metaanalysis of the effects of parent effectiveness training. *American Journal of Family Therapy, 18,* 373–384.

Cedar, R. B. (1986). A meta-analysis of the parent effectiveness training outcome research literature (Doctoral dissertation, Boston University, 1985). *Dissertation Abstracts International, 47,* 420A. (University Microfilm International No. 86–09263)

Champney, T. F., & Schulz, E. M. (1983). *A reassessment of the effects of psychotherapy.* Midwestern Psychological Association. (ERIC Document Reproduction Service No. ED 237 895)

Christensen, H., Hadzi-Pavlovic, D., Andrews, G., & Mattick, R. (1987). Behavior therapy and tricyclic medication in the treatment of obsessive–compulsive disorder: A quantitative review. *Journal of Consulting and Clinical Psychology, 55,* 701–711.

Cohen, P. A. (1980). Effectiveness of student-rating feedback for improving college instruction: A meta-analysis of findings. *Research in Higher Education, 13,* 321–341.

Cohen. P. A., Ebeling, B. J., & Kulik, J. A. (1981). A meta-analysis of outcome studies of visual-based instruction. *Educational Communication and Technology, 29,* 26–36.

Cohen, P. A., Kulik, J. A., & Kulik, C. C. (1982). Educational outcomes of tutoring: A meta-analysis of findings. *American Educational Research Journal, 19,* 237–248.

Cohn. C. L. (1986). A meta-analysis of the effects of teaching innovations on achievement in college economics (Doctoral dissertation, Illinois State University, 1985). *Dissertation Abstracts International, 47,* 594A. (University Microfilms International No. 86–08948)

Cohn, C. M. G. (1985). Creativity training effectiveness: A research synthesis (Doctoral dissertation, Arizona State University, 1984). *Dissertation Abstracts International, 45,* 2501A. (University Microfilm International No. 84–24639)

Collins, R. C. (1984). *Head Start A review of research with implications for practice in early childhood education* American Educational Research Association. (ERIC Document Reproduction Service No. ED 245 833)

Collins, W. L. (1987). Psychological/affective interventions with underprepared adult learners: A meta-analystic and triangulation study (Doctoral dissertation, Union for Experimenting Colleges, University Without Walls and Union Graduate School). *Dissertation Abstracts International, 48,* 1806B.

Colosimo, M. L. (1982). The effect of practice or beginning teaching on the self-concepts and attitudes of teachers: A quantitative synthesis (Doctoral dissertation, University of Chicago, 1981). *Dissertation Abstracts International, 42,* 4272A.

Colosimo, M. L. (1984). Attitude change with initial teaching experience. *College Student Journal, 18,* 119–125.

Cook, P. J. A. (1988). Meta-analysis of studies on self-concept between the years of 1976 and 1986 (Doctoral dissertation, North Texas State University, 1987). *Dissertation Abstracts International, 48,* 1984A.

Cook, S. B., Scruggs, T. E., Mastropieri, M. A., & Casto, G. C. (1986). Handicapped students as tutors. *Journal of Special Education, 19,* 483–492.

Curbelo, J. (1985). Effects of problem-solving instruction on science and mathematics student achievement: A meta-analysis of findings (Doctoral dissertation, Florida State University, 1984). *Dissertation Abstracts International, 46,* 23A.

Dekkers, J., & Donatti, S. (1981). The integration of research studies on the use of simulation as an instructional strategy. *Journal of Educational Research, 74,* 424–427.

Denham, S. A., & Almeida, M. C. (1987). Children's social problem-solving skills, behavioral adjustment, and interventions: A meta-analysis evaluating theory and practice. *Journal of Applied Developmental Psychology, 8,* 391–409.

DerSimonian, R., & Laird, N. M. (1983). Evaluating the effect of coaching on SAT scores: A meta-analysis. *Harvard Educational Review, 53,* 1–15.

Devine, E. C. (1984). Effects of psychoeducational interventions: A meta-analytic review of studies with surgical patients (Doctoral dissertation, University of Illinois at Chicago, 1983). *Dissertation Abstracts International, 44,* 3356B. (University Microfilms International No. 84–04400)

Devine, E. C., & Cook, T. D. (1983). A meta-analytic analysis of effects of psychoeducational interventions on length of postsurgical hospital stay. *Nursing Research, 32,* 267–274.

Dewey, D., & Hunsley, J. (1990). The effects of marital adjustment and spouse involvement on the behavioral treatment of agoraphobia: A meta-analytic review. *Anxiety Research, 2*(2), 69–83.

Dobson, K. S. (1989). A meta-analysis of the efficacy of cognitive therapy for depression. *Journal of Consulting and Clinical Psychology, 57,* 414–419.

Dole, A. A., Rockey, P. B., & DiTomasso, R. (1983). *Meta-analysis of outcome research in reducing test anxiety. Interventions, rigor, and inertia* American Educational Research Association. (ERIC Document Reproduction Service No. ED 231 844)

Dotson, J. H. (1990). Physician-delivered smoking cessation interventions: An information synthesis of the literature (Doctoral dissertation, University of Maryland, 1989). *Dissertation Abstracts International, 50,* 1953A.

Durlak, J. A., Fuhrman, T., & Lampman, C. (1991). *Effectiveness of cognitive behavior therapy for maladapting children A meta-analysis.* Unpublished manuscript, Loyola University, Chicago.

Durlak, J. A., & Riesenberg, L. A. (1991). The impact of death education. *Death Studies, 15*(1), 39–58.

1203

Dush, D. M., Hirt, M. L., & Schroeder, H. (1983). Self-statement mod-ification with adults: A meta-analysis. *Psychological Bulletin, 94,* 408–422.

Dush, D. M., Hirt, M. L., & Schroeder, H. E. (1989). Self-statement modification in the treatment of child-behavior disorders—A meta-analysis. *Psychological Bulletin, 106,* 97–106.

Duzinski, G. A. (1987). The educational utility of cognitive behavior modification strategies with children (Doctoral dissertation, University of Illinois at Chicago). *Dissertation Abstracts International, 48,* 339A.

Edwards, D. L. (1991). A meta-analysis of the effects of meditation and hypnosis on measures of anxiety (Doctoral dissertation, Texas A&M University, 1990). *Dissertation Abstracts International, 52,* 1039B.

Eifert, G. H., & Craill, L. (1989). The relationship between affect, be-haviour, and cognition in behavioural and cognitive treatments of depression and phobic anxiety [Special issue—Depression: Treatment and theory]. *Behaviour Change, 6,* 96–103.

El-Nemr, M. A. (1980). A meta-analysis of the outcomes of teaching biology as inquiry (Doctoral dissertation, University of Colorado, 1979). *Dissertation Abstracts International, 40,* 5813A. (University Microfilms International No. 80–11274)

Enz, J., Horak, W. J., & Blecha, M. K. (1982). *Review and analysis of reports of science inservice projects: Recommendations for the future.* National Science Teachers Association. (ERIC Document Reproduction Service No. ED 216–883)

Eppley, K. R., Abrams, A. I., & Shear, J. (1989). Differential effects of relaxation techniques on trait anxiety—A meta-analysis. *Journal of Clinical Psychology, 45,* 957–974.

Eskew, D. M. (1989). The effect of quality circle participation on job involvement, productivity and satisfaction (Masters thesis, Michigan State University). *Masters Abstracts, 27,* 328.

Falcone, A. J. (1986). Meta-analysis of personnel training techniques for three populations (Doctoral dissertation, Illinois Institute of Tech-nology, 1985). *Dissertation Abstracts International, 47,* 412B. (University Microfilms International No. 86–06497)

Feehan, G. G. (1984). A meta-analysis of psychotherapeutic interventions for the cessation and reduction of smoking (Doctoral dissertation, University of Manitoba). *Dissertation Abstracts International, 45,* 1583B.

Feltz, D. L., & Landers, D. M. (1983). The effects of mental practice on motor skill learning and performance: A meta-analysis. *Journal of Sport Psychology, 5,* 25–57.

Ferguson, P. C. (1981). An integrative meta-analysis of psychological studies investigating the treatment outcomes of meditation techniques (Doctoral dissertation, University of Colorado). *Dissertation Abstracts International, 42,* 1547A. (University Microfilms International No. 81–22282)

Fernandez, E., & Turk, D. C. (1989). The utility of cognitive coping strategies for altering pain perception: A meta-analysis. *Pain, 38,* 123–135.

Fisher, K. J. (1990). Worksite smoking cessation: A meta-analysis of controlled studies (Doctoral dissertation, University of Oregon, 1989). *Dissertation Abstracts International, 50,* 5007B.

Fletcher, J. D. (1990). *Effectiveness and cost of interactive videodisc in-struction in defense training and education* (IDA Report No. R2372). Arlington, VA: Institute for Defense Analysis. (ERIC Document Re-production Service No. ED 326 194)

Flor, H., Fydrich, T., & Turk, D. C. (1992). Efficacy of multidisciplinary pain treatment centers: A meta-analytic review. *Pain, 49,* 221–230.

Fuchs, D., & Fuchs, L. S. (1985). *The importance of context in testing: A meta-analysis.* American Educational Research Association. (ERIC Document Reproduction Service No. ED 255 559)

Fuchs, L. S., & Fuchs, D. (1986). Effects of systematic formative eval-uation: A meta-analysis. *Exceptional Children, 53,* 199–208.

Garrett, C. J. (1985a). Effects of residential treatment on adjudicated delinquents: A meta-analysis. *Journal of Research in Crime and De-linquency, 22,* 287–308.

Garrett, C. J. (1985b). Meta-analysis of the effects of institutional and community residential treatment on adjudicated delinquents (Doctoral dissertation, University of Colorado, 1984). *Dissertation Abstracts In-ternational, 45,* 2264A. (University Microfilms International No. 84–22608)

Gensheimer, L. K., Mayer, J. P., Gottschalk, R. Davidson, W. S., II. (1986). Diverting youth from the juvenile justice system—A meta-analysis of intervention efficacy. In S. J. Apter & A. P. Goldstein (Eds.), *Youth violence* (pp. 39–57). New York: Pergamon Press.

Giacomia, R. M., & Hedges, L. V. (1982). Identifying features of effective open education. *Review of Educational Research, 52,* 579–602.

Giblin, P., Sprenkle, D. H., & Sheehan, R. (1985). Enrichment outcome research: A meta-analysis of premarital, marital, and family inter-ventions. *Journal of Marital and Family Therapy, 11,* 257–271.

Gillingham, M. G., & Guthrie, J. T. (1987). Relationships between CBI and research on teaching. *Contemporary Educational Psychology, 12,* 189–199.

Glass, G. V., & Smith, M. L. (1979). Meta-analysis of research on class size and achievement. *Educational Evaluation and Policy Analysis, 1,* 2–16.

Goldring, E. B. (1990). Assessing the status of information on classroom organizational frameworks for gifted students. *Journal of Educational Research, 83,* 313–326.

Goldring, E. B., & Presbrey, L. S. (1986). Evaluating preschool programs: A meta-analytic approach. *Educational Evaluation and Policy Anal-ysis, 8,* 179–188.

Gottschalk, R., Davidson, W. S., II, Gensheimer, L. K., & Mayer, J. P. (1987a). Community-based interventions. In H. C. Quay (Ed.), *Handbook of juvenile delinquency* (pp. 266–289). New York: Wiley.

Gottschalk, R., Davidson, W. S., II, Mayer, J., & Gensheimer, R. (1987b). Behavioral approaches with juvenile offenders: A meta-analysis of long-term treatment efficacy. In E. K. Morris & C. J. Braukmann (Eds.), *Behavioral approaches to crime and delinquency: A handbook of ap-plication, research, and concepts* (pp. 399–422). New York: Plenum Press.

Grane, M. E., Weinstein, T., & Walberg, H. J. (1983). School-based home instruction and learning: A quantitative synthesis. *Journal of Educational Research, 76,* 351–360.

Guskey, T. R., & Pigott, T. D. (1988). Research on group-based mastery learning programs: A meta-analysis. *Journal of Educational Research, 81,* 197–216.

Guzzo, R. A., Jette, R. D., & Katzell, R. A. (1985). The effects of psy-chologically based intervention programs on worker productivity: A meta-analysis. *Personnel Psychology, 38,* 275–291.

Hahlweg, K., & Markman, H. J. (1988). Effectiveness of behavioral mar-ital therapy: Empirical status of behavioral techniques in preventing and alleviating marital distress. *Journal of Consulting and Clinical Psychology, 56,* 440–447.

Hall, L. E. (1989). The effects of cooperative learning on achievement: A meta-analysis (Doctoral dissertation, University of Georgia, 1988). *Dissertation Abstracts International, 50,* 343A.

Hampton, B. R. (1988). The efficacy of paradoxical interventions: A quantitative review of the research evidence (Doctoral dissertation, University of Texas at Austin). *Dissertation Abstracts International, 49,* 2378B.

Hanson, R. E. (1989). Social skill training: A critical meta-analytic review (Doctoral dissertation, Texas Women's University, 1988). *Dissertation Abstracts International, 50,* 903A.

Hardesty, P. H. (1991). Undergraduate career courses for credit—A re-view and metaanalysis. *Journal of College Student Development, 32,* 184–185.

Harris, L. C. (1987). Deinstitutionalization via community-linked pro-grams: A meta-analysis (Doctoral dissertation, University of Texas at Austin, 1986). *Dissertation Abstracts International, 47,* 3956B.

Harris, M. M. (1988). Meta-analyses of test anxiety among college stu-dents (Doctoral dissertation, Ohio State University, 1987). *Dissertation Abstracts International, 49,* 543B.

Hathaway, D. K. (1985). A meta-analysis of studies which examine the effect preoperative instruction of adults has on postoperative outcomes (Doctoral dissertation, University of Texas, Austin, 1984). *Dissertation Abstracts International, 46,* 475B. (University Microfilms International No. 85–08277)

Hazelrigg, M. D., Cooper, H. M., & Borduin, C. M. (1987). Evaluating the effectiveness of family therapies: An integrative review and analysis. *Psychological Bulletin, 101,* 428–442.

Hedges, L. V., & Stock, W. (1983). The effects of class size: An examination of rival hypotheses. *American Educational Research Journal, 20,* 63–85.

Hembree, R. (1988). Correlates, causes, effects, and treatment of test anxiety. *Review of Educational Research, 58*(1), 47–77.

Hembree, R. (1990). The nature, effects, and relief of mathematics anxiety. *Journal for Research in Mathematics Education, 21*(2), 33–46.

Hetzel, D. C., Rasher, S. P., Butcher, L., & Walberg, H. J. (1980). *A quantitative synthesis of the effects of open education* American Educational Research Association. (ERIC Document Reproduction Service No. ED 191 902)

Hill, K. A. (1987). Meta-analysis of paradoxical interventions. *Psychotherapy, 24,* 266–270.

Hillocks, G. (1984). What works in teaching composition: A meta-analysis of experimental treatment studies. *American Journal of Education, 93,* 133–170.

Hood, D. F. (1991). Using meta-analysis for input evaluation (Doctoral dissertation, Florida State University, 1990). *Dissertation Abstracts International, 51,* 4099A.

Horak, V. M. (1981). A meta-analysis of research findings on individualized instruction in mathematics. *Journal of Educational Research, 74,* 249–253.

Howell, J. K. (1985). Effects of preoperative preparation of children having minor surgery: A literary synthesis with meta-analysis (Doctoral dissertation, University of Texas, Austin, 1984). *Dissertation Abstracts International, 46,* 1116B. (University Microfilms International No. 85–13231)

Hyman, R. B., Feldman, H. R., Harris, R. B., Levin, R. F., & Malloy, G. B. (1989). The effects of relaxation training on clinical symptoms—A meta-analysis. *Nursing Research, 38,* 216–220.

Iverson, B. K., & Levy, S. R. (1982). Using meta-analysis in health education research. *The Journal of School Health, 52,* 234–239.

Johnson, D. W., & Johnson, R. T. (1987). Research shows the benefits of adult cooperation. *Educational Leadership, 45*(3), 27–30.

Johnson, D. W., Johnson, R. T., & Maruyama, G. (1983). Interdependence and interpersonal attraction among heterogeneous and homogeneous individuals: A theoretical formulation and a meta-analysis of the research. *Review of Education Research, 53,* 5–54.

Johnson, D. W., Maruyama, G., Johnson, R., Nelson, D., & Skon, L. (1981). Effects of cooperative, competitive, and individualistic goal structures on achievement: A meta-analysis. *Psychological Bulletin, 89,* 47–62.

Jones, L. C. (1983). A meta-analytic study of the effects of childbirth education research from 1960 to 1981 (Doctoral dissertation, Texas A&M University). *Dissertation Abstracts International, 44,* 1663A. (University Microfilms International No. 83–23680)

Jorm, A. F. (1989). Modifiability of trait anxiety and neuroticism—A meta-analysis of the literature. *Australian and New Zealand Journal of Psychiatry, 23,* 21–29.

Joslin, P. A. (1981). Inservice teacher education: A meta-analysis of the research (Doctoral dissertation, University of Minnesota, 1980). *Dissertation Abstracts International, 41,* 3058A. (University Microfilms International No. 81–02055)

Kardash, C. A. M., & Wright, L. (1987). Does creative drama benefit elementary school students? A meta-analysis. *Youth Theatre Journal, 1*(3), 11–18.

Karweit, N. L. (1987). *Full or half-day kindergarten—Does it matter?* (Report No. II). Baltimore, MD: John Hopkins University, Center for Research on Elementary and Middle Schools. (ERIC Document Reproduction Service No. ED 287 597)

Kaufman, P. (1985). *Meta-analysis of juvenile delinquency prevention programs* Unpublished manuscript, Claremont Graduate School.

Kavale, K. (1980). Psycholinguistic training. *Evaluation in Education, 4,* 88–90.

Kavale, K. (1981). Functions of the Illinois Test of Psycholinguistic Abilities (ITPA): Are they trainable? *Exceptional Children, 47,* 496–510.

Kavale, K. (1982). Psycholinguistic training programs: Are there differential treatment effects? *Exceptional Child, 29,* 21–30.

Kavale, K., & Mattson, P. D. (1983). One jumped off the balance beam: Meta-analysis of perceptual-motor training. *Journal of Learning Disabilities, 16,* 165–173.

Kavale, K. A. (1984). A meta-analytic evaluation of the Frostig test and training program. *Exceptional Child, 31,* 134–141.

Kavale, K. A., & Forness, S. R. (1983). Hyperactivity and diet treatment: A meta-analysis of the Feingold hypothesis. *Journal of Learning Disabilities, 16,* 324–330.

Kavale, K. A., & Forness, S. R. (1987). Substance over style: Assessing the efficacy of modality testing and teaching. *Exceptional Children, 54,* 228–239.

Klesius, J. P., & Searls, E. F. (1990). A meta-analysis of recent research in meaning vocabulary instruction. *Journal of Research and Development in Education, 23,* 226–235.

Kuchera, M. M. (1987). The effectiveness of meditation techniques to reduce blood pressure levels: A meta-analysis (Doctoral dissertation, Loyola University of Chicago). *Dissertation Abstracts International, 47,* 4639B.

Kulik, C. C., & Kulik, J. A. (1982a). Effects of ability grouping on secondary school students: A meta-analysis of evaluation findings. *American Education Research Jouranl, 19,* 415–428.

Kulik, C. C., & Kulik, J. A. (1982b). Research synthesis on ability grouping. *Educational Leadership, 39,* 619–621.

Kulik, C. C., & Kulik, J. A. (1984). *Effects of ability grouping on elementary school pupils. A meta-analysis.* Washington, DC: American Psychological Association. (ERIC Document Reproduction Service No. ED 255 329)

Kulik, C. C., Kulik, J. A., & Bangert-Drowns, R. L. (1984). *Effects of computer-based education on elementary school pupils.* American Educational Research Association. (ERIC Document Reproduction Service No. ED 244 616)

Kulik, C.-L. C., Kulik, J. A., & Bangert-Drowns, R. L. (1990). Effectiveness of mastery learning programs: A meta-analysis. *Review of Educational Research, 60,* 265–299.

Kulik, C. C., Kulik, J. A., & Cohen, P. A. (1980). Effectiveness of computer-based college teaching: A meta-analysis of findings. *Review of Educational Research, 50,* 525–544.

Kulik, C. C., Kulik, J. A., & Shwalb, B. J. (1983). College programs for high-risk and disadvantaged students: A meta-analysis of findings. *Review of Educational Research, 53,* 397–414.

Kulik, C. C., Schwalb, B. J., & Kulik, J. A. (1982). Programmed instruction in secondary education: A meta-analysis of evaluation findings. *Journal of Educational Research, 75,* 133–138.

Kulik, J. A., Bangert, R. L., & Williams, G. W. (1983). Effects of computer-based teaching on secondary school students. *Journal of Educational Psychology, 75,* 19–26.

Kulik, J. A., Bangert-Drowns, R. L., & Kulik, C. C. (1984). Effectiveness of coaching for aptitude tests. *Psychological Bulletin, 95,* 179–188.

Kulik, J. A., Cohen, P. A., & Ebeling, B. J. (1980). Effectiveness of programmed instruction in higher education: A meta-analysis of findings. *Educational Evaluation and Policy Analysis, 2,* 51–63.

Kulik, J. A., & Kulik, C. C. (1984). Effects of accelerated instruction on students. *Review of Educational Research, 54,* 409–425.

Kulik, J. A., Kulik, C. C., & Bangert, R. L. (1984). Effects of practice on aptitude and achievement test scores. *American Educational Research Journal, 21,* 435–447.

Kulik, J. A., Kulik, C. C., & Cohen, P. A. (1979a). A meta-analysis of outcome studies of Keller's personalized system of instruction. *American Psychologist, 34,* 307–318.

Kulik, J. A., Kulik, C. C., & Cohen, P. A. (1979b). Research on audiotutorial instruction: A meta-analysis of comparative studies. *Research in Higher Education, 11,* 321–341.

Kulik, J. A., & Kulik, C.-L. C. (1987). Review of recent research literature on computer-based instruction. *Contemporary Educational Psychology, 12,* 222–230.

Kyle, W. C. (1982). A meta-analysis of the effects on student performance of new curricular programs developed in science education since 1955 (Doctoral dissertation, University of Iowa). *Dissertation Abstracts International, 43,* 1104A. (University Microfilms International No. 82–22249)

L'Hommedieu, R., Menges, R. J., & Brinko, K. T. (1990). Methodological explanations for the modest effects of feedback from student ratings. *Journal of Educational Psychology; 82,* 232–241.

Laessle, R. G., Zoettl, C., & Pirde, K.-M. (1987). Metaanalysis of treatment studies for bulimia. *International Journal of Eating Disorders, 6*, 647–653.

Landman, J. T., & Dawes, R. M. (1982). Psychotherapy outcome: Smith and Glass's conclusions stand up under scrutiny. *American Psychologist, 37*, 504–516.

Leddick, A. S. (1987). Effects of training on measures of productivity: A meta-analysis of the findings of forty-eight experiments (Doctoral dissertation, Western Michigan University). *Dissertation Abstracts International, 48*, 910A.

Lee, W.-C. (1990). The effectiveness of computer-assisted instruction and computer programming in elementary and secondary mathematics: A meta-analysis (Doctoral dissertation, University of Massachusetts). *Dissertation Abstracts International, 51*, 775A.

Levy, S. R., Iverson, B. K., & Walberg, H. J. (1980). Nutrition-education research: An interdisciplinary evaluation and review. *Health Education Quarterly, 7*, 107–126.

Lewis, R. J., & Vosburgh, W. T. (1988). Effectiveness of kindergarten intervention programs: A meta-analysis. *School Psychology International, 9*, 265–275.

Liao, Y.-K. C., & Bright, G. W. (1991). Effects of computer-assisted instruction and computer programming on cognitive outcomes: A meta-analysis. *Journal of Educational Computing Research, 7*, 251–268.

Lipsey, M. W. (1992). Juvenile delinquency treatment: A meta-analytic inquiry into the variability of effects. In T. D. Cook, H. Cooper, D. S. Cordray, H. Hartmann, L. V. Hedges, R. J. Light, T. A. Louis, & F. Mosteller, (Eds.), *Meta-analysis for explanation* (pp. 83–127). New York: Russell Sage Foundation.

Losel, F., & Koferl, P. (1989). Evaluation research on correctional treatment in West Germany: A meta-analysis. In H. Wegener, F. Losel, & J. Haisch (Eds.), *Criminal behavior and the justice system: Psychological perspectives* (pp. 334–355). New York: Springer.

Lott, G. W. (1983). The effect of inquiry teaching and advance organizers upon student outcomes in science education. *Journal of Research in Science Teaching, 20*, 437–451.

Lysakowski, R. S., & Walberg, H. J. (1980). Classroom reinforcement. *Evaluation in Education, 4*, 115–116.

Lysakowski, R. S., & Walberg, H. J. (1981). Classroom reinforcement and learning: A quantitative synthesis. *Journal of Educational Research, 75*, 69–77.

Lysakowski, R. S., & Walberg, H. J. (1982). Instructional effects of cues, participation, and corrective feedback: A quantitative synthesis. *American Educational Research Journal, 19*, 559–578.

Madamba, S. R. (1981). Meta-analysis on the effects of open and traditional schooling on the teaching–learning of reading (Doctoral dissertation, University of California, Los Angeles, 1980). *Dissertation Abstracts International, 41*, 3508A. (University Microfilms International No. 81–02856)

Malone, M. D., Strube, M. J., & Scogin, F. R. (1989). Meta-analysis of non-medical treatments for chronic pain: Corrigendum. *Pain, 37*(1), 128.

Malone, M. R. (1984). *Project MAFEX. Report on preservice field experiences in science education.* National Association for Research in Science Teaching. (ERIC Document Reproduction Service No. ED 244 928).

Marcucci, R. G. (1980). A meta-analysis of research on methods of teaching mathematical problem-solving (Doctoral dissertation, University of Iowa). *Dissertation Abstracts International, 41*, 2485A. (University Microfilms International No. 80–28278)

Markus, E., Lange, A., & Pettigrew, T. F. (1990). Effectiveness of family-therapy—A metaanalysis. *Journal of Family Therapy, 12*, 205–221.

Marmolejo, A. (1990). The effects of vocabulary instruction with poor readers: A meta-analysis (Doctoral dissertation, Columbia University). *Dissertation Abstracts International, 51*(3), 807A.

Mattson, P. D. (1985). A meta-analysis of learning and memory in mental retardation (Doctoral dissertation, University of California, Riverside, 1985). *Dissertation Abstracts International, 46*, 1879A. (University Microfilms International No. 85–20636)

Mayer, J. P., Gensheimer, L. K., Davidson, W. S., II, & Gottschalk, R. (1986). Social learning treatment within juvenile justice—A meta-analysis of impact in the natural environment. In S. J. Apter & A. P.

Goldstein (Eds.), *Youth violence* (pp. 24–39). New York: Pergamon Press.

Mazzuca, S. A. (1982). Does patient education in chronic disease have therapeutic value? *Journal of Chronic Disease, 35*, 521–529.

McDermid, R. D. (1990). A quantitative analysis of the literature on computer-assisted instruction with the learning-disabled and educable mentally retarded (Doctoral dissertation, University of Kansas, 1989). *Dissertation Abstracts International, 51*, 1196A.

McEvoy, G. M., & Cascio, W. F. (1985). Strategies for reducing employee turnover: A meta-analysis. *Journal of Applied Psychology, 70*, 342–353.

McNeil, B. J., & Nelson, K. R. (1990). *Meta-analysis of interactive video instruction: A 10-year review of achievement effects.* (ERIC Document Reproduction Service No. ED 321 761)

Messick, S., & Jungeblut, A. (1981). Time and method in coaching for the SAT. *Psychological Bulletin, 89*, 191–216.

Miller, R. C., & Berman, J. S. (1983). The efficacy of cognitive behavior therapies: A quantitative review of the research evidence. *Psychological Bulletin, 94*, 39–53.

Montgomery, L. M. (1991). The effects of family therapy for treatment of child identified problems: A meta-analysis (Doctoral dissertation, Memphis State University, 1990). *Dissertation Abstracts International, 51*, 6115B.

Montross, J. F. (1990). Meta-analysis of treatment efficacy in Raynaud's phenomenon (Doctoral dissertation, Texas A&M University, 1989). *Dissertation Abstracts International, 50*, 4811B.

Moore, S. D. (1990). A meta-analysite review of mass media compaigns designed to change automobile occupant restraint behavior (Doctoral dissertation, University of Illinois at Urbana-Champaign, 1989). *Dissertation Abstracts International, 50*, 1840A.

Mumford, E., Schlesinger, H. J., & Glass, G. V. (1982). The effects of psychological intervention on recovery from surgery and heart attacks: An analysis of the literature. *American Journal of Public Health, 72*, 141–151.

Nearpass, G. L. (1990). Counseling and guidance effectiveness in North American High Schools: A meta-analysis of the research findings (Doctoral dissertation, University of Colorado at Boulder, 1989). *Dissertation Abstracts International, 50*, 1948A.

Neuman, G. A., Edwards, J. E., & Raju, N. S. (1989). Organizational development interventions: A meta-analysis of their effects on satisfaction and other attitudes. *Personnel Psychology, 42*, 461–489.

Nicholson, R. A., & Berman, J. S. (1983). Is follow-up necessary in evaluating psychotherapy? *Psychological Bulletin, 93*, 261–278.

Nicholson, T., Duncan, D. F., Hawkins, W., Belcastro, P. A., & Gold, R. (1988). Stress treatment: Two aspirins, fluids, and one more workshop. *Professional Psychology: Research and Practice, 19*, 637–641.

Niemiec, R. P. (1985). The meta-analysis of computer assisted instruction at the elementary school level (Doctoral dissertation, University of Illinois at Chicago, 1984). *Dissertation Abstracts International, 45*, 3330A. (University Microfilms International No. 85–01250)

Niemiec, R. P., Sikorski, M. F., Clark, G., & Walberg, H. J. (1992). Effects of management education: A quantitative synthesis. *Evaluation and Program Planning, 15*, 297–302.

Niemiec, R., Samson, G., Weinstein, T., & Walberg, H. J. (1987). The effects of computer based instruction in elementary schools: A quantitative synthesis. *Journal of Research in Computing in Education, 20*, 85–103.

Noland, T. K. (1985). The effects of ability grouping: A meta-analysis of research findings (Doctoral dissertation, University of Colorado, 1985). *Dissertation Abstracts International, 46*, 2909A. (University Microfilms International No. 85–28511)

North, T. C. (1989). The effect of exercise on depression: A meta-analysis (Doctoral dissertation, University of Colorado at Boulder, 1988). *Dissertation Abstracts International, 49*, 5027B.

Nunes, E. V., Frank, K. A., & Kornfeld, D. S. (1987). Psychologic treatment for the Type A behavior pattern and for coronary heart disease: A meta-analysis of the literature. *Psychosomatic Medicine, 49*, 159–173.

Nye, C., Foster, S. H., & Seaman, D. (1987). Effectiveness of language intervention with the language/learning disabled. *Journal of Speech and Hearing Disorders, 52*, 348–357.

O'Bryan, V. L. (1985). The treatment of test anxiety: A meta-analytic review (Doctoral dissertation, Ohio University, 1985). *Dissertation Abstracts International, 46*, 2818B. (University Microfilms International No. 85–23654)

O'Flynn, A. I. (1983). Meta-analysis of behavioral intervention effects on weight loss in the obese (Doctoral dissertation, University of Connecticut, 1982). *Dissertation Abstracts International, 43*, 2502B. (University Microfilms International No. 83–02083)

Okun, M. A., Olding, R. W., & Cohn, C. M. G. (1990). A metaanalysis of subjective well-being interventions among elders. *Psychological Bulletin, 108*, 257–266.

Oliver, L. W., & Spokane, A. R. (1988). Career-intervention outcome: What contributes to client gain? *Journal of Counseling Psychology, 35*, 447–462.

Ottenbacher, K. (1982). Sensory integration therapy: Affect or effect. *American Journal of Occupational Therapy, 36*, 571–578.

Ottenbacher, K. J., Muller, L., Brandt, D., Heintzelman, A., Hojem, P., & Sharpe, P. (1987). The effectiveness of tactile stimulation as a form of early intervention: A quantitative evaluation. *Journal of Developmental and Behavioral Pediatrics, 8*, 68–76.

Ottenbacher, K., & Petersen, P. (1985). The efficacy of early intervention programs for children with organic impairment: A quantitative review. *Evaluation and Program Planning, 8*, 135–146.

Ottenbacher, K. J., & Petersen, P. (1984). The efficacy of vestibular stimulation as a form of specific sensory enrichment. *Clinical Pediatrics, 23*, 428–433.

Paschal, R. A., Weinstein, T., & Walberg, H. J. (1984). The effects of homework on learning: A quantitative synthesis. *Journal of Educational Research, 78*, 97–104.

Paterson, C. E. (1988). Progressive relaxation: A meta-analysis (Doctoral dissertation, Ohio State University, 1987). *Dissertation Abstracts International, 48*, 2790B.

Peterson, P. L. (1980). Open versus traditional classrooms. *Evaluation in Education, 4*, 58–60.

Pflaum, S. W., Walberg, H. J., Karegianes, M. L., & Rasher, S. P. (1980). Reading instruction: A quantitative synthesis. *Educational Researcher, 9*, 12–18.

Phillips, G. W. (1983). Learning the conservation concept: A meta-analysis (Doctoral dissertation, University of Kentucky). *Dissertation Abstracts International, 44*, 1990B. (University Microfilms International No. 83–22983)

Piorier, B. M. (1990). The effectiveness of language intervention with preschool handicapped children: An integrative review (Doctoral dissertation, Utah State University, 1989). *Dissertation Abstracts International, 51*, 137A.

Polder, S. K. (1986). A meta-analysis of cognitive behavior therapy (Doctoral dissertation, University of Wisconsin-Madison). *Dissertation Abstracts International, 47*, 1736B.

Posavac, E. J. (1980). Evaluations of patient education programs: A meta-analysis. *Evaluation and the Health Professions, 3*, 47–62.

Posavac, E. J., Sinacore, J. M., Brotherton, S. E., Helford, M. C., & Turpin, R. S. (1985). Increasing compliance to medical treatment regimens: A meta-analysis of program evaluation. *Evaluation and the Health Professions, 8*, 7–22.

Prince Henry Hospital. (1983). A treatment outline for depressive disorders: The quality assurance project. *Australian and New Zealand Journal of Psychiatry, 17*, 129–146.

Prioleau, L., Murdock, M., & Brody, N. (1983). An analysis of psychotherapy versus placebo studies. *The Behavioral and Brain Sciences, 6*, 275–310.

Reilly, R. R., Brown, B., Blood, M. R., & Malatesta, C. Z. (1981). The effects of realistic previews: A study and discussion of the literature. *Personnel Psychology, 34*, 823–834.

Robinson, A. W. (1989). A meta-analysis of the efficacy of classroom management training programs for teachers (Doctoral dissertation, Temple University). *Dissertation Abstracts International, 50*, 1634A

Robinson, A. W., & Hyman, I. A. (1984). *A meta-analysis of human relations teacher training programs* National Association of School Psychologists. (ERIC Document Reproduction Service No. ED 253 521)

Robinson, L. A., Berman, J. S., & Neimeyer, R. A. (1990). Psychotherapy for the treatment of depression: A comprehensive review of controlled outcome research. *Psychological Bulletin, 108*, 30–49.

Rock, S. L. (1986). A meta-analysis of self-instructional training research (Doctoral dissertation, University of Illinois, 1985). *Dissertation Abstracts International, 46*, 3322A. (University Microfilms International No. 86–00295)

Rose, L. H., & Lin, H. T. (1984). A meta-analysis of long-term creativity training programs. *Journal of Creative Behavior, 18*, 11–22.

Rosenbuam, C. M. (1983). A meta-analysis of the effectiveness of educational treatment programs for emotionally disturbed students (Doctoral dissertation, The College of William and Mary). *Dissertation Abstracts International, 44*, 730A. (University Microfilms International No. 83–17068)

Ross, J. A. (1988). Controlling variables: A meta-analysis of training studies. *Review of Educational Research, 58*, 405–437.

Rundall, T. G., & Bruvold, W. H. (1988). A meta-analysis of school-based smoking and alcohol-use prevention programs. *Health Education Quarterly, 15*, 317–334.

Ryan, A. W. (1991). Metaanalysis of achievement effects of microcomputer applications in elementary schools. *Educational Administration Quarterly, 27*, 161–184.

Saile, H., Burgmeier, R., & Schmidt, L. R. (1988). A meta-analysis of studies on psychological preparation of children facing medical procedures. *Psychology and Health, 2*, 107–132.

Samson, G. E. (1985). Effects of training in test-taking skills on achievement test performance: A quantitative synthesis. *Journal of Educational Research, 78*, 261–266.

Samson, G. E., Borger, J. B., Weinstein, T., & Walberg, H. J. (1984). Pre-teaching experiences and attitudes: A quantitative synthesis. *Journal of Research and Development in Education, 17*, 52–56.

Sanders, V. H. (1979). A meta-analysis: The relationship of program content and operation factors to measured effectiveness of college reading-study programs (Doctoral dissertation, University of the Pacific). *Dissertation Abstracts International, 40*, 2507A. (University Microfilms International No. 79–23975)

Schermer, J. D. (1984). Visual media and attitude formation and attitude change in nursing education (Doctoral dissertation, Wayne State University, 1983). *Dissertation Abstracts International, 44*, 3581A. (University Microfilms International No. 84–06022)

Schimmel, B. J. (1983, April). *A meta-analysis of feedback to learners in computerized and programmed instruction* Paper presented at the annual meeting of the American Educational Research Association, Montreal, Canada. (ERIC Document Reproduction Service No. ED 233 708)

Schlaefli, A., Rest, J. R., & Thoma, S. J. (1985). Does moral education improve moral judgment? A meta-analysis of intervention studies using the defining issues test. *Review of Educational Research, 55*, 319–352.

Schmidt, M., Weinstein, T., Niemiec, R., & Walberg, H. J. (1986). Computer-assisted instruction with exceptional children. *Journal of Special Education, 19*, 493–502.

Scogin, F., Bynum, J., Stephens, G., & Calhoon, S. (1990). Efficacy of self-administered treatment programs: Meta-analytic review. *Professional Psychology Research and Practice, 21*, 42–47.

Scruggs, T. E., Bennion, K., & White, K. (1984). *Teaching test-taking skills to elementary grade students A meta-analysis* Salt Lake City: Utah University, Developmental Center for the Handicapped. (ERIC Document Reproduction Service No. ED 256 082)

Shadish, W. R., Jr. (1992). Do family and marital psychotherapies change what people do? A meta-analysis of behavioral outcomes. In T. D. Cook, H. Cooper, D. S. Cordray, H. Hartmann, L. V. Hedges, R. J. Light, T. A. Louis, & F. Mosteller (Eds.), *Meta-analysis for explanation* (pp. 129–208). New York: Russell Sage Foundation.

Shapiro, D. A., & Shapiro, D. (1982). Meta-analysis of comparative therapy outcome studies: A replication and refinement. *Psychological Bulletin, 92*, 581–604.

Shapiro, D. A., & Shapiro, D. (1983). Comparative therapy outcome research: Methodological implications of meta-analysis. *Journal of Consulting and Clinical Psychology, 51*, 42–53.

Shatz, M. A. (1984). Assertiveness training: A meta-analysis of the research findings (Doctoral dissertation, University of Florida, 1983).

Dissertation Abstracts International, 44, 2047A. (University Microfilms International No. 83–25006)

Shaver, J. P., Curtis, C. K., Jesunathadas, J., & Strong, C. J. (1989). The modification of attitudes toward persons with disabilities: Is there a best way? *International Journal of Special Education, 4*(4), 33–57.

Shoham-Salomon, V., & Rosenthal, R. (1987). Paradoxical interventions: A meta-analysis. *Journal of Consulting and Clinical Psychology, 55*, 22–28.

Shwalb, B. J. (1987). Instructional technology in American and Japenese schools: A meta-analysis of achievement findings (Doctoral dissertation, University of Michigan). *Dissertation Abstracts International, 48*, 370A.

Shymansky, J. (1984). BSCS programs: Just how effective were they? *American Biology Teacher, 46*, 54–57.

Shymansky, J. A., Hedges, L. V., & Woodworth, G. (1990). A reassessment of the effects of inquiry-based science curricula of the 60's on student performance. *Journal of Research in Science Teaching, 27*, 127–144.

Shymansky, J. A., Kyle, W. C., & Alport, J. (1982). Research synthesis on the science curriculum projects of the sixties. *Educational Leadership, 40*, 63–66.

Shymansky, J. A., Kyle, W. C., & Alport, J. M. (1983). The effects of new science curricula on student performance. *Journal of Research in Science Teaching, 20*, 387–404.

Skiba, R., & Casey, A. (1985). Interventions for behaviorally disordered students: A quantitative review and methodological critique. *Behavioral Disorders, 10*, 239–252.

Slavin, R. E. (1987a). Ability grouping and student achievement in elementary schools: A best evidence synthesis. *Review of Educational Research, 57*, 293–236.

Slavin, R. E. (1987b). Mastery learning reconsidered. *Review of Educational Research, 57*, 175–213.

Slavin, R. E. (1990). Achievement effects of ability grouping in secondary schools: A best-evidence synthesis. *Review of Educational Research, 60*, 471–499.

Slavin, R. E., & Madden, N. A. (1989). What works for students at risk: A research synthesis. *Educational Leadership, 46*(4), 4–13.

Smith, M. L., & Glass, G. V. (1980). Meta-analysis of research on class size and its relationship to attitudes and instruction. *American Educational Research Journal, 17*, 419–433.

Smith, M. L., Glass, G. V., & Miller, T. I. (1980). *The benefits of psychotherapy*. Baltimore: John Hopkins University Press.

Snyder, S., & Sheehan, R. (1983). Integrating research in early childhood special education: The use of meta-analysis. *Diagnostique, 9*, 12–25.

Sprinthall, N. A. (1981). A new model for research in the service of guidance and counseling. *Personnel and Guidance Journal, 59*, 487–494.

Stahl, S. A., & Fairbanks, M. M. (1986). The effects of vocabulary instruction: A model-based meta-analysis. *Review of Educational Research, 56*, 72–110.

Stahl, S. A., & Miller, P. D. (1989). Whole language and language experience approaches for beginning reading: A quantitative research synthesis. *Review of Educational Research, 59*(5), 87–116.

Standley, J. M. (1986). Music research in medical–dental treatment—Meta-analysis and clinical applications. *Journal of Music Therapy, 23*(2), 56–122.

Stein, D. M. (1987). Companionship factors and treatment effects in children. *Journal of Clinical Child Psychology, 16*, 141–146.

Stein, D. M., & Polyson, J. (1984). The Primary Mental Health Project reconsidered. *Journal of Consulting and Clinical Psychology, 52*, 940–945.

Steinbrueck, S. M., Maxwell, S. E., & Howard, G. S. (1983). A meta-analysis of psychotherapy and drug therapy in the treatment of unipolar depression with adults. *Journal of Consulting and Clinical Psychology, 51*, 856–863.

Stevens, R. J., & Slavin, R. E. (1991). When cooperative learning improves the achievement of students with mild disabilities: A response to Tateyama-Sniezek. *Exceptional Children, 57*, 276–280.

Straw, R. B. (1982). Meta-analysis of deinstitutionalization in mental health (Doctoral dissertation, Northwestern University, 1982). *Dissertation Abstracts International, 43*, 2006B. (University Microfilms International No. 82–26026)

Susskind, E. C., & Bond, R. N. (1981). *The potency of primary prevention A meta-analysis of effect size.* Eastern Psychological Association. (ERIC Document Reproduction Service No. ED 214 067)

Sweitzer, G. L., & Anderson, R. D. (1983). A meta-analysis of research on science teacher education practices associated with inquiry strategy. *Journal of Research in Science Teaching, 20*, 453–466.

Szczurek, M. (1982). Meta-analysis of simulation games effectiveness for cognitive learning (Doctoral dissertation, Indiana University). *Dissertation Abstracts International, 43*, 1031A. (University Microfilms International No. 82–20735)

Thompson, J. M. (1987). A meta-analysis of test anxiety therapy outcome studies (Doctoral dissertation, Texas Christian University, 1986). *Dissertation Abstracts International, 47*, 3570B.

Tillitski, C. J. (1990). A meta-analysis of estimated effect sizes for group versus individual versus control treatments. *International Journal of Group Psychotherapy, 40*, 215–224.

Tobler, N. S. (1986). Meta-analysis of 143 adolescent drug prevention programs—Quantitative outcome results of program participants compared to a control or comparison group. *Journal of Drug Issues, 16*, 537–567.

Truax, M. E. (1984). A meta-analytic review of studies evaluating paraprofessional effectiveness in mental health, education, law, and social work (Doctoral dissertation, University of Kansas, 1983). *Dissertation Abstracts International, 44*, 4A. (University Microfilms International No. 84–03625)

Turley, M. A. (1984). A meta-analysis of informing mothers concerning the sensory and perceptual capabilities of their infants (Doctoral dissertation, University of Texas, Austin, 1983). *Dissertation Abstracts International, 45*, 1B. (University Microfilms International No. 84–14461)

Utah State University Exceptional Child Center. (1983). *Early intervention research institute: Final report, 1982—83 work scope.* Logan: Utah State University. (ERIC Document Reproduction Service No. ED 250 845)

Vaughn, V. L., Feldhusen, J. F., & Asher, J. W. (1991). Meta-analyses and review of research on pull-out programs in gifted education. *Gifted Child Quarterly, 35*, 92–98.

Videka-Sherman, L. (1988). Meta-analysis of research on social work practice in mental health. *Social Work, 33*, -338.

Waddell, D. L. (1991). The effects of continuing education on nursing practice: A meta-analysis (Doctoral dissertation, University of Georgia, 1990). *Dissertation Abstracts International, 51*, 8A.

Wade, R. K. (1984). What makes a difference in inservice teacher education: A meta-analysis of the research (Doctoral dissertation, University of Massachusetts). *Dissertation Abstracts International, 45*, A. (University Microfilms International No. 84–10341)

Wade, R. K. (1985). What makes a difference in inservice teacher education? A meta-analysis of research. *Educational Leadership, 42*, 54.

Wallace, T. A. (1990). The effects of enrichment on gifted students: A quantitative synthesis (Doctoral dissertation, University of Illinois at Chicago, 1989). *Dissertation Abstracts International, 50*, 1A.

Wampler, K. S. (1983). Bringing the review of literature into the age of quantification: Meta-analysis as a strategy for integrating research findings in family studies. *Journal of Marriage and the Family, 44*, 9–1023.

Wang, M. C., & Baker, E. T. (1986). Mainstreaming programs: Design features and effects. *Journal of Special Education, 19*, 503–523.

Weinstein, T., Boulanger, F. D., & Walberg, H. J. (1982). Science curriculum effects in high school: A quantitative synthesis. *Journal of Research in Science Teaching, 19*, 511–522.

Weisz, J. R., Weiss, B., Alicke, M. D., & Klotz, M. L. (1987). Effectiveness of psychotherapy with children and adolescents: A meta-analysis for clinicians. *Journal of Consulting and Clinical Psychology, 55*, 542–549.

White, W. A. T. (1987). The effects of direct instruction in special education: A meta-analysis (Doctoral dissertation, University of Oregon, 1986). *Dissertation Abstracts International, 47*, 1A.

Whitehead, J. T., & Lab, S. P. (1989). A meta-analysis of juvenile correctional treatment. *Journal of Research in Crime and Delinquency, 26*, 276–295.

Willett, J B., Yamashita, J. M., & Anderson, R. D. (1983). A meta-analysis of instructional systems applied in science teaching. *Journal of Research in Science Teaching, 20,* 405–417.

Williams, W. V. L. (1990). A meta-analysis of the effects of instructional strategies delivered to the mathematically disadvantaged (Doctoral dissertation, George Peabody College for Teachers of Vanderbilt University, 1989). *Dissertation Abstracts International, 51,* A.

Willig, A. C. (1985). A meta-analysis of selected studies on the effectiveness of bilingual education. *Review of Educational Research, 55,* 269–317.

Wilson, L. B., Simson, S., & McCaughey, K. (1983). The status of preventive care for the aged: A meta-analysis. *Prevention in Human Services, 3,* 38.

Wise, K. C., & Okey, J. R. (1983). A meta-analysis of the effects of various science teaching strategies on achievement. *Journal of Research in Science Teaching, 20,* 419–435.

Wyma, R. J. (1990). Involving children as active agents of their own treatment: A meta-analysis of self-management training (Doctoral dissertation, Fuller Theological Seminary, School of Psychology). *Dissertation Abstracts International, 51,* 0B.

Yeany, R. H., & Miller, P. A. (1983). Effects of diagnostic/remedial instruction on science learning: A meta-analysis. *Journal of Research in Science Teaching, 20,* 26.

Yeany, R. H., & Porter, C. F. (1982). *The effects of strategy analysis on science teacher behaviors: A meta-analysis.* National Association for Research in Science Teaching. (ERIC Document Reproduction Services No. ED 216 858)

Part II
Quantitative Issues in Sampling

[5]

Missing Data Problems in Criminological Research: Two Case Studies

Robert Brame[1,3] and Raymond Paternoster[2]

This paper considers the problem of missing data in two circumstances commonly confronted by criminologists. In the first circumstance, there is missing data due to subject attrition—some cases drop out of a study. In this context, analysts are frequently interested in examining the association between an independent variable measured at time $t(x_t)$ and an outcome variable that is measured at time $t + 1(y_t + 1)$; the problem is that the outcome variable is only observed for those cases which do not drop out of the study. In the second circumstance there is missing data on an independent variable of interest for typical reasons (i.e., the respondent did not wish to answer a question or could not be located). In this case, researchers are interested in estimating the association between the independent variable with missing data and an outcome variable that is fully observed. Criminologists often handle these two missing data problems by conducting analyses on the subsample of observations with complete data. In this paper, we explore this problem with two case studies and we then illustrate the use of methods that directly address the uncertainty produced by missing data.

KEY WORDS: missing data; sensitivity analysis; identification problems.

1. INTRODUCTION

In this paper, we address the problem of missing data in criminological research. Criminological researchers confront missing data problems in practically every analysis they perform. Despite the frequency with which the problem occurs, however, there are not many tools available to researchers who wish to carefully explore the implications of missing data for their results. This is a sufficiently large problem that it is not going to be resolved in any single work. Nevertheless, we believe that an incremental

[1]Department of Criminology and Criminal Justice, University of South Carolina, Columbia, SC 29208.
[2]Department of Criminology and Criminal Justice, 2220 Samuel J. LeFrak Hall, University of Maryland, College Park, Maryland 20742.
[3]To whom correspondence should be addressed. E-mail: bramer@gwm.sc.edu

approach of illustrating the application of missing data methods by way of actual analysis results with criminological data can make a useful contribution to the eventual development of missing data tools and greater awareness of missing data problems in our field.

Our reading of the literature suggests that criminologists often respond to missing data problems by performing an analysis on those observations where complete data are available (i.e., complete-case analysis).[4] In some circumstances, this approach will yield valid inferences but in other circumstances it will not. Our vehicle for discussing this issue is the consideration of two specific examples or case studies that typify problems commonly encountered in criminological research. In the first case study, we consider the problem of missing data due to a loss of observations in a longitudinal research project. More specifically, we are interested in estimating the association between an independent variable measured at one time and an outcome variable measured at a later time. The problem is that we are not able to observe the outcome variable for all individuals because some cases drop out of the study between the two time points. In the second case study, we consider the problem created when the objective is to estimate the association between an independent variable and an outcome variable when some of the observations have missing data on the independent variable. This type of situation often arises when data on the outcome variable are easy to collect (i.e., information in official government records) and data on the independent variable are more difficult to collect (i.e., interview information). The methods we use in this analysis are based on likelihood functions and models that have been described in previous work by Little and Rubin (1987), Little and Schenker (1995), Vach (1994), and Wainer (1986).

---

[4]Actually, criminologists employ a number of different strategies for addressing various missing data problems and complete-case analysis is only one of those strategies. For example, when the analysis involves investigation of a matrix of pairwise correlations researchers will sometimes calculate each of the correlations using all available data on the two variables being correlated. This leads to a situation where various correlations in the correlation matrix are calculated with different numbers of observations. Researchers refer to this practice as "pairwise deletion of missing data." Another approach involves imputation of the mean score (calculated on observed cases) on the missing variable. Occasionally, researchers will use multiple imputation methods such as those described by Little and Rubin (1987), Rubin (1987), and Schafer (1997) or weighting methods to adjust for the probability of nonresponse (see, e.g., Thompson, 1997:161). In some circumstances, these methods will produce parameter estimates that are more reasonable than those obtained from a complete case analysis. However, these methods must also be applied with a great deal of care because, as Little and Rubin (1987) and Allison (2000) have shown, they can lead to biased estimates that are worse than those obtained from complete-case analysis when applied incorrectly. Our paper focuses primarily on issues associated with complete-case analysis since this strategy is used more frequently in the criminological literature than the other methods described above.

2. OVERVIEW OF MISSING DATA PROBLEMS AND TERMINOLOGY

In this section, we briefly describe some of the different types of missing data problems typically encountered in criminological research. This typological framework is consistent with material set forth in Little and Rubin (1987) and Little and Schenker (1995). To fix ideas, we let y be a variable about which we are interested in developing an inference. We also define two groups of individuals. In the first group, y is missing (an event we denote by the letter, m) and, in the second group y is observed (which is simply the complement of m). In addition, we let x be a vector of variables that is observed for all individuals. Below, we describe three general categories of missing data problems: (1) data on y are missing completely at random; (2) data on y are missing at random; (3) data on y are nonrandomly missing.

Category #1: Missing Completely at Random (MCAR): When the probability distribution of m is independent of x and y, we say that the data on y are missing completely at random:

$$p(m) = p(m|x, y)$$

In this context, complete-case analysis typically presents no serious inferential problems because the probability distribution of the variable of interest (y) is independent of the missing data (m) distribution.

Category #2: Missing at Random (MAR): When the probability distribution of m is not independent of x but is independent of y, we say that the data on y are missing at random:

$$p(m|x) = p(m|x, y)$$

but, of course, there is the remaining issue that

$$p(m) \neq p(m|x)$$

Complete-case analysis can lead to some difficulties in this situation. For example, if one wishes to develop an inference about some aspect of the distribution of y and there is an important association between x and y, then reliance on complete-case analysis without adjusting for information provided by x would result in misleading inferences. How might this operate in practice? Consider a simple regression model with a single independent variable and a single outcome variable. Some of the observations have missing data on the independent variable but all individuals have valid data for the outcome variable. If the missing data mechanism is associated with the outcome variable and we analyze only those individuals with valid data on both the independent and outcome variables are inferences will be biased and inconsistent.

Category #3: Nonrandomly Missing Data: When the probability distribution of m is not independent of y, then we say that the data on y are nonrandomly missing. Formally, we have:

$$p(m) \neq p(m|y)$$

or, alternatively, even after conditioning the missing data distribution on x, there might be residual dependence between m and y which would result in the following inequality:

$$p(m|x) \neq p(m|x, y)$$

This is the most difficult type of missing data problem because it is impossible to develop a valid inference about the distribution of y if there is some important dependence between y and our ability to observe variation in y.[5] Statistical models of the form outlined in categories 1 and 2 above are often called ignorable models because it is possible to use the available data to develop a valid inference about the distribution of y. Statistical models of the form described in this third category, on the other hand, are generally referred to as nonignorable models because they are underidentified (Little and Rubin, 1987; Manski, 1995). The only way to make progress toward developing an inference about the distribution of y in this situation is to formulate identification restrictions that will just-identify the model. These sorts of models must be designed to fit the features of particular studies and are, consequently, more difficult to implement.[6]

In practice, a researcher cannot usually be sure about the form of the missing data mechanism. The main problem is that we only have the opportunity to observe the distribution of y among individuals with valid, observed data on y. We often have an underdeveloped intuition about what the distribution of y looks like among individuals who are not observed. This problem is a central theme of both of the case studies discussed below.

[5]One implication of this inequality is that the practice of comparing a group of individuals with valid data on y to a group of individuals with missing data on y along a range of factors, x, that are observed for everyone is of limited relevance for this problem. When researchers conduct these comparisons and then find that there are no or few differences in x between the groups it is reassuring insofar as we can establish that the groups don't differ on the variables that we can see for both groups. What this exercise cannot establish, however, is whether the groups differ in ways that cannot be observed.

[6]An anonymous reviewer of this manuscript suggested that one of the most pervasive examples of this problem involves survey questions about one's income or other sensitive matters such as involvement in criminal behavior. In these settings, it seems quite implausible that nonresponse is independent of the underlying distributions on the variables researchers are attempting to study.

3. CASE STUDIES

3.1. Overview

In this section, we describe the methodology and results of our two case studies. Although these studies are both confronted by a significant quantity of missing data, the missing data problem manifests itself in somewhat different ways in each case. In both cases, we show that a complete-case analysis model which assumes the data are MCAR is an inadequate specification. We also explore various alternative specifications that lead to conclusions that differ from those obtained under the identifying assumption that the data are MCAR.

3.2. Case Study #1: Attrition in a Longitudinal Study

Although longitudinal data are often quite useful for addressing various criminological problems, it is difficult to retain all of the individuals for each wave of data collection. Some individuals drop out of the study because they do not wish to continue participating, others are difficult to locate, and some may die or become inaccessible for other reasons. This subsection is divided into three parts. The first part explains the substantive problem addressed by this analysis and it describes the data set we use for this particular case study. In the second part, we apply both the complete-case estimator and a more general estimator to the data. Finally, the third part illustrates the implications of a model that is estimated under the assumption that the data are MAR but not MCAR. This model is interesting because it makes some strong assumptions but those assumptions are still less demanding than those required for identifying the complete-case estimates.

3.2.1. Overview of Substantive Problem and Data

In this analysis, we address the following substantive question: Is residence in a household that receives public assistance during adolescence associated with involvement in criminal activity during early adulthood? To address this question, we use data from waves 1 and 5 of the National Youth Survey. This sample was designed to be representative of all youth in the United States between the ages of 11 and 17 in 1977 (Elliott, Huizinga, and Menard, 1989). Our sample is comprised of 659 (96.5%) of the 683 individuals who were between the ages of 15 and 17 at the first wave of data collection and 19 and 21 at the fifth wave of data collection. We deleted a small number of individuals ($n = 34$; 3.5%) who did not have complete data at the first wave of the study. This is not the source of missing data that is most problematic, however. Instead, the more problematic issue is that

Table I. Joint Distribution of Adolescent Public Assistance and
Early Adult Criminal Activity

Criminal activity during early adulthood	Recepit of public assistance in adolescence		
	No	Yes	Total
No reported criminal activity	420	76	496
At least one reported act	47	13	60
Number lost to attrition	84	19	103
Total number of cases	551	108	659
$p(y = 1\|x, m = 0)$	0.101	0.146	
$p(m = 1\|x)$	0.153	0.176	

Note: Our measure of criminal activity includes the following acts:
(1) aggravated assault; (2) sexual assault; (3) gang fight involvement; (4) motor vehicle theft; (5) robbery; (6) breaking and
entering; and (7) larceny of property valued in excess of $50.

15.6% of the sample has been lost to attrition by the fifth wave of data
collection. Table I presents a summary of the data used in this analysis.[7]

Our substantive attention here is focused on the conditional distribution of the binary outcome variable, y_i (involvement in criminal activity
during early adulthood collected at the fifth wave: coded 1 if yes, 0 if no),
given the binary independent variable, x_i (household receives public assistance collected at the first wave: coded 1 if yes, 0 if no). We also note that a
missing data indicator variable, m_i, is coded 1 if individual i is missing at
wave 5 and 0 if individual i is observed at wave 5. The likelihood function
for the joint distribution of the outcome and the missing data indicator
conditional on the independent variable is given by:

$$L(\theta, \gamma) = \prod_{i=1}^{N} \left[p(y_i|x_i; \theta) \times p(m_i|y_i, x_i; \gamma) \right]$$

[7]We note that there are a number of different kinds of attrition problems that can hamper
inferences in longitudinal studies and our analysis example deals with one of the simplest possible
cases of this problem. In fact, our analysis is actually an example of a bivariate analysis where
there is valid data on the independent variable and missing data on the outcome variable. The
MAR model that we implement later in this section does exploit an important feature of the
longitudinal nature of the data set but this is still a simple example. A more complicated example
would be a case where interest centers on estimating the effect of a time-varying predictor variable on a time-varying outcome variable when individuals drop out of the study as it progresses.
Little (1995) provides a full discussion of attrition problems in longitudinal studies including
both ignorable and nonignorable models with a variety of different kinds of dropout processes.

where θ and γ are parameter vectors estimated by the method of maximum likelihood. The problem in our case is that $y_i|m_i = 1$ is not observed. In the special case where the missing data indicator and the outcome variable are independent of each other, the above likelihood function simplifies to:

$$L(\theta, \gamma) = \prod_{i=1}^{N} \left[p(y_i|x_i; \theta) \times p(m_i|x_i; \gamma) \right] \tag{1}$$

and the two probabilities in the likelihood function are now independent and can be estimated completely separately. This is an important simplification because it implies that we do not need to have information on all individuals to develop a valid inference about the conditional distribution of y_i given x_i. We also noted above that when the missing data indicator, m, is associated with fully observable variables like x, it is necessary to adjust for that dependence to develop valid inferences about the distribution of y because the data are MAR instead of MCAR. It turns out in this particular case that the adjustment is quite simple. Specifically, all that is necessary in this situation is to simply condition the distribution of y on x for those cases where y is observed (see e.g., Little and Rubin, 1987). The reason for this is that Eq. (1) factors into independent parts so that our inference about θ does not depend on whether we estimate γ. In short, we have:

$$L(\theta) = \prod_{i=1}^{N} [p(y_i|x_i; \theta)]$$

and our inference about θ in this case will be identical to the inference about θ based on the likelihood function in Eq. (1). This is exactly what we assume when we conduct a complete-case analysis. While this simplifies matters considerably, it will often be more realistic to relax the constraint that these two probabilities are independent. To do this, we allow individuals to contribute to the likelihood function in different ways depending upon whether they have missing information. For those individuals with valid data, we write the likelihood function as:

$$L(\theta, \gamma) = \prod_{i \in (m_i=0)} \left[p(y_i|x_i; \theta) \times p(m_i = 0| y_i, x_i; \gamma) \right]$$

while, for individuals with missing data, we write the likelihood function as:

$$L(\theta, \gamma) = \prod_{i \in (m_i=1)} \left[\int p(y_i|x_i; \theta) \times p(m_i = 1| y_i, x_i; \gamma) \underline{d} y_i \right]$$

and this equation turns out to be relatively simple to implement since both y and m are binary variables:

$$L(\theta, \gamma) = \prod_{i \in (m_i=1)} \left[\sum_{y_i=(0,1)} p(y_i|x_i\,;\,\theta) \times p(m_i = 1 \big| y_i, x_i\,;\,\gamma) \right]$$

where we parameterize the probability distribution for y by:

$$\log\left(\frac{p(y_i = 1|x_i\,;\,\theta)}{1 - p(y_i = 1|x_i\,;\,\theta)} \right) = \theta_0 + \theta_x\, x_i$$

and $\exp(\theta_x)$ gives the odds ratio summarizing the association between x and y. For the missing data indicator variable, m, we have:

$$\log\left(\frac{p(m_i = 1 \big| y_i, x_i\,;\,\gamma)}{1 - p(m_i = 1 \big| y_i, x_i\,;\,\gamma)} \right) = \gamma_0 + \gamma_x\, x_i + \gamma_y\, y_i + \gamma_{xy}\, x_i\, y_i$$

where γ_y and γ_{xy} are not identified from the data because y is only observed for individuals with valid data. If we impose constraints on the values of these two unidentified parameters, however, then the remaining parameter estimates are identified (for similar approaches see Vach, 1994; Nordheim, 1984). Using the missing data terminology defined above, this is a non-ignorable specification for data that are not MCAR or MAR.

For our first analysis, we estimate the association between adolescent receipt of public assistance and adult involvement in criminal activity. We begin by reporting the results of a traditional complete-case analysis including only those individuals with observed data at both Waves 1 and 5. The estimated logistic regression coefficient for the effect of public assistance during adolescence on early adult offending is $+0.424$, the odds ratio associated with this coefficient is 1.528, and Yule's $Q = +0.209$, indicating that those who received public assistance were more likely than those who did not to self-report involvement in criminal activity during early adult-hood.[8] Construction of a 95% CI around our estimate of θ_x reveals that it is not significantly different from zero. From this evidence, we would conclude that public assistance received during one's adolescence has no effect on

---

[8]Although odds ratios are often reported in the literature, they are somewhat difficult to interpret. The most common application of an odds ratio is its use as a measure of association for a 2×2 contingency table. In this setting, the odds ratio is directly related to another well-known measure of association called Yule's Q. Q is a proportional reduction in error (PRE) based measure for a 2×2 contingency table and it ranges from -1 (perfect negative association) to 0 (independence) to $+1$ (perfect positive association). The relationship is given by $Q = \left(\frac{\exp(\theta_x)-1}{\exp(\theta_x)+1} \right)$ where θ_x is the logistic regression coefficient estimating the association between the independent variable and the outcome variable (Agresti, 1996:258).

young adult criminal activity in the population from which this sample was drawn.

3.2.2. Sensitivity Analysis

Deletion of cases with missing data as we did in this analysis is equivalent to assuming that the outcome variable is independent of the dropout process (Little and Rubin, 1987; Little and Schenker, 1995). We now examine the relationship between our independent variable (public assistance during adolescence) and the outcome variable (young adult offending) under different assumptions about the process by which individuals drop out of the study. More specifically, we vary the two unidentified parameters discussed above: (1) γ_y which measures the relationship between the outcome variable and the probability of missing data when the independent variable is equal to zero; and (2) γ_{xy}, which measures an adjustment to γ_y depending on the level of the independent variable (i.e., an interaction term). In the complete case analysis reported in Table II both γ_y and γ_{xy} are both implicitly constrained to be equal to zero. In short, our sensitivity analysis allows us to see the implications of relaxing this constraint.

Table III presents the results of this sensitivity analysis and these results are presented in graphical form in the Appendix. What this analysis indicates is that when the two unidentified parameters are varied across the interval (−0.75 to +0.75), the magnitude of the estimated association between the independent variable and the outcome variable changes substantially.[9] Across the range of constraints considered in this sensitivity analysis, our estimates of Q range from +0.139 to +0.309. Moreover, some of these estimates are statistically significant while others are not. Based on the evidence from this sensitivity analysis, it appears that our conclusion about the magnitude of the association between public assistance and young adult involvement in criminal behavior depends on strong yet untestable assumptions about the missing data mechanism.

3.2.3. An Alternative Specification Using Supplementary Information

While the investigation in Section 3.2.2 reveals wide variation in our conclusions about the magnitude of the association between the indepen-

---

[9]Our choice of the (−0.75 to +0.75) interval is arbitrary but a logistic regression coefficient of 0.75 corresponds to a Yule's Q value of +0.358. Thus, the main effect of the outcome variable on the missing data indicator is constrained to have a Q value in the range (−0.358 to +0.358). Allowing for the possibility of interaction between the independent variable and the outcome variable on the probability of missing data the total effect, $Q_{max} = [(\exp(2\gamma_y) - 1]/[\exp(2\gamma_y) + 1)]$ is constrained to have a Q value in the range (−0.635 to +0.635). This interval seems reasonable to us because it covers a variety of possibilities ranging from weak to moderate associations between the outcome variable and the missing data indicator.

Table II. Logistic Regression of Early Adult Criminal Activity on Adolescent Public Assistance Among Individuals With Complete Data ($N = 556$)

Parameter	Estimate	Std. Error	$|z|$-ratio
θ_0	-2.190	0.154	14.24
θ_x	0.424	0.337	1.26
Log-likelihood	-189.481		

Note: x_i is coded 1.0 if adolescent's parent(s) report receiving public assistance within the previous year (data collected at wave 1) and 0.0, otherwise. The positive estimate of θ_x implies that individuals who received public assistance during adolescence were more likely than individuals who did not to self-report offending in early adulthood. We cannot reject the null hypothesis that the association is equal to zero in the population from which the sample was drawn, however. The odds ratio is $\exp(\theta_x) = \exp(0.424) = 1.528$ (where odds ratio of 1.0 implies independence). This corresponds to a Yule's Q estimate of $+0.209$.

dent and outcome variables, it is sometimes possible to achieve identification under assumptions that are less demanding than those required for a conventional complete-case analysis (Carroll *et al.*, 1995:235–236). This approach does, however, require the incorporation of supplementary information that is observed for all individuals. Because of this constraint, the model is an ignorable specification based on the missing at random (MAR) assumption. To specify this model, we assume that there is a variable, z, which is observed for all individuals and that can be viewed as a proxy measure of the outcome variable, y. This supplementary information model depends on two key assumptions: (1) that the joint conditional distribution of y and z given x is independent of whether an individual drops out of the study (i.e., $p(y, z|x, m) = p(y, z|x)$); and (2) the probability of an individual dropping out of the study is independent of y after conditioning on both x and z (i.e., $p(m|x, z, y) = p(m|x, z)$). Although this is a restrictive estimator and does not have the desirable properties of ML estimators unless these assumptions are strictly met, the assumptions it makes are still less demanding than those required by a complete-case estimator which does not allow any supplementary information at all to contribute to the analysis and thereby assumes that the missing data mechanism is independent of y after conditioning on x. In light of this increased generality, the supplementary information analysis should be a useful complement to the complete-case estimator. In this model, individuals once again make different contributions to the likelihood function depending upon whether they have

Missing Data Problems in Criminological Research 65

Table III. Sensitivity of Relationship Between Adolescent Public Assistance and Early Adult Involvement in Criminal Activity to Different Sets of Assumptions About Missing Data Mechanism ($N = 659$)

Missing data parameters		Results of conditional maximim likelihood estimation			
γ_{xy}	γ_y	θ_x	$|z|(\theta_x)$	$\exp(\theta_x)$	Q
−0.750	−0.750	0.349	1.04	1.417	0.173
	−0.375	0.336	1.00	1.399	0.166
	0.000	0.320	0.95	1.377	0.159
	0.375	0.301	0.89	1.351	0.149
	0.750	0.280	0.83	1.323	0.139
−0.375	−0.750	0.374	1.11	1.453	0.185
	−0.375	0.370	1.10	1.448	0.183
	0.000	0.365	1.08	1.441	0.181
	0.375	0.360	1.07	1.433	0.178
	0.750	0.353	1.05	1.423	0.175
0.000	−0.750	0.408	1.21	1.504	0.201
	−0.375	0.416	1.23	1.515	0.205
	0.000	0.424	1.26	1.529	0.209
	0.375	0.433	1.29	1.542	0.213
	0.750	0.440	1.31	1.552	0.216
0.375	−0.750	0.453	1.35	1.574	0.223
	−0.375	0.475	1.41	1.607	0.233
	0.000	0.497	1.48	1.645	0.244
	0.375	0.519	1.55	1.681	0.254
	0.750	0.537	1.63	1.710	0.262
0.750	−0.750	0.512	1.52	1.669	0.251
	−0.375	0.548	1.63	1.729	0.267
	0.000	0.584	1.74	1.793	0.284
	0.375	0.616	1.86	1.852	0.299
	0.750	0.639	1.97	1.894	0.309

missing or valid outcome data. For individuals who remain in the study, the likelihood function is given by:

$$L(\theta, \delta, \gamma) = \prod_{i \in (m_i = 0)} \left[p(y_i|x_i; \theta) \times p(z_i|y_i, x_i; \delta) \times p(m_i = 0|z_i, x_i; \gamma) \right]$$

and since m and y are conditionally independent, the likelihood function factors into two components leaving:

$$L(\theta, \delta) = \prod_{i \in (m_i = 0)} \left[p(y_i|x_i; \theta) \times p(z_i|y_i, x_i; \delta) \right]$$

In addition, for individuals with missing data on y, the likelihood function will take the following form:

$$L(\theta) = \prod_{i \in (m_i = 1)} \left[\int p(y_i | x_i; \theta) \times p(z_i | y_i, x_i; \delta) \underline{d} y_i \right]$$

and since y and z are binary variables, here, the integral is a sum yielding:

$$L(\theta) = \prod_{i \in (m_i = 1)} \left[\sum_{y_i = (0,1)} p(y_i | x_i; \theta) \times p(z_i | y_i, x_i; \delta) \right]$$

and we use the logistic parameterization for the conditional distribution of z which is given by:

$$\log \left(\frac{p(z_i = 1 | y_i, x_i; \delta)}{1 - p(z_i = 1 | y_i, x_i; \delta)} \right) = \delta_0 + \delta_x x_i + \delta_y y_i + \delta_{xy} x_i y_i$$

In our example, we have been examining the association between public assistance at the first wave of the study and early adult criminal offending measured at the fifth wave. For purposes of this supplementary information analysis, we decided to exploit the longitudinal nature of the study by using the first wave measurement of the dependent variable (self-reported criminal offending at wave 1) as a proxy measure of the early adult self-reported criminal offending variable measured at wave 5. As Table IV suggests, this variable appears to meet the conditions we described above since it is observed for virtually all subjects who were studied at the first wave and it appears to be associated with wave 5 self-reported criminal activity (at least within the subsample of individuals who stay in the study).

Table 5 presents the results of our supplementary information analysis. The parameter of interest in this analysis is θ_x which is the association between receipt of public assistance in adolescence (wave 1) and young adult criminal offending (wave 5).[10] The estimate for $\theta_x = 0.603$ and the odds ratio is 1.828. This transforms to $Q = +0.293$ which is at the upper end of the range of values considered in our earlier sensitivity analysis. This estimate suggests that those youths whose families received public assistance when they were adolescents were more likely to self-report criminal

---

[10]The other parameters of interest in this model are δ_y and δ_{xy}. The parameter δ_y measures the relationship between the proxy outcome variable (self-reported offending at wave 1) and the partially observed outcome variable (self-reported offending at wave 5). As expected this association is moderately strong and positive. The parameter δ_{xy} is an interaction term measuring the adjustment to the association between offending activity at the two time periods at different levels of the independent variable (receipt of public assistance during adolescence).

Table IV. Joint Distribution of Adolescent and Early Adult Criminal Activity

Criminal activity during early adulthood (wave 5)	Criminal activity during adolescence (wave 1)		
	No	Yes	Total
No reported criminal activity	408	88	496
At least one reported act	28	32	60
Number lost to attrition	74	29	103
Total number of cases	510	149	659
$p(y = 1|z, m = 0)$	0.064	0.267	
$p(m = 1|z)$	0.145	0.195	

Note: Our measure of criminal activity includes the following acts: (1) aggravated assault; (2) sexual assault; (3) gang fight involvement; (4) motor vehicle theft; (5) robbery; (6) breaking and entering; and (7) larceny of property valued in excess of $50

offending as young adults than those whose families did not receive public assistance. Moreover, the estimated effect is significantly different from zero. This would also tend to imply that the attrition existing in these data are nonrandom with respect to this particular research question. We wish to point out, however, that this is only true to the extent that our assumptions underlying this model are correct and there is no way to conclusively test those assumptions. Nevertheless, we believe that there is a reasonable argument that this estimator is at least as plausible as the complete-case estimator. In sum, unlike the complete-case analysis reported in Table 2, this supplementary information model suggests that there is a statistically significant association between receipt of public assistance in adolescence and involvement in criminal activity during early adulthood.

3.3. Case Study #2: Missing Data on the Independent Variable

3.3.1. Overview of Substantive Problem and Data

Our second case study emphasizes estimation of the association between an outcome variable, y that is observed for all individuals and an independent variable x that is only observed for some individuals. For this case study, we will use data from the Charlotte Spouse Assault Replication Project conducted by Hirschel and his colleagues (1992). The original objective of this study was to estimate the effect of different types of police responses to misdemeanor spouse assault incidents on the occurrence of future offenses against the same victim. The outcome variable indicates whether or not the offender was arrested for another victimization against

Table V. Logistic Regression Analysis of Adolescent Public
Support Receipt and Early Adult Criminal Activity: Missing
Data Model Based on Auxiliary Information ($N = 659$)

Parameter	Estimate	Std. Error	$|z|$-ratio
θ_0	−2.190	0.154	14.22
θ_x	0.424	0.331	1.82
δ_0	−1.506	0.119	12.64
δ_x	0.125	0.312	0.40
δ_y	1.382	0.320	4.32
δ_{xy}	1.496	0.800	1.87
Log-likelihood	−521.08		

Note: x_i is coded 1.0 if adolescent's parent(s) report receiving
public assistance within the previous year (data collected at
wave 1) and 0.0, otherwise. The positive estimate of θ_x implies
that individuals who received public assistance during adolescence were more likely than individuals who did not to self-
report offending in early adulthood. The z-ratio for the ML
estimate of θ_x also exceeds the one-tailed critical value
($\alpha = 0.05$), so we reject the null hypothesis that $\theta_x = 0$ in the
population from which the sample was drawn. The odds ratio is
$\exp(\theta_x) = \exp(0.603) = 1.828$ (where odds ratio of 1.0 implies
independence). This corresponds to a Yule's Q estimate of
+0.293.

the same victim within six months of the original incident. This information
was secured from official records and was available for all individuals in the
study. We assigned all victims who experienced a subsequent revictimization
a code of $y_i = 1$ and victims who did not experience a revictimization during
the follow-up period were assigned a code of $y_i = 0$. The independent
variable is the victim's age as reported in an interview with the victim that
occurred approximately one month after the original incident. We assigned
victims who were 35 years of age or older a code of $x_i = 1$ on this variable,
while victims who were 34 years of age or younger were assigned a code of
$x_i = 0$.

Our substantive interest is in estimating the association between the
victim's age and the probability that her attacker is rearrested for future
attacks against her within the six month follow-up period. Ordinarily,
obtaining an estimate of the association between victim age and revictimization (as measured by rearrest) would be a relatively straightforward task.
In the example at hand, however, our analysis is more complicated because
223 of the 626 victims in the study (36%) were not interviewed. This is not
necessarily problematic because a selection rule that depends only on the
independent variable does not induce bias. As King (1989:208) notes, the

critical issue is whether the selection is correlated with the dependent variable or whether there is some interaction between the independent and dependent variable in determining whether observations have missing data (i.e., perhaps younger victims who have been revictimized are reluctant to participate in an interview). The methods we use in this section will allow us to adjust for this possibility.

An interesting feature of the Charlotte study is that additional data were collected from the police department's service call database, and age of the victim was included in that file. In this particular study, then, we have outside information that will allow us to compare the results we would have obtained from a complete case analysis with the answer that we would have obtained from the complete data set. Descriptive information on the victim's age and the revictimization outcomes for both interviewed and non-interviewed cases are displayed in Table VI.[11]

3.3.2. Complete Case Analysis

A typical approach to estimating the association between the two variables in our study might involve deletion of observations with missing age information and conducting a complete case analysis on the remaining observations. The likelihood function using this approach is:

$$L(\theta) = \prod_{i \in (m_i = 0)} p(y_i | x_i ; \theta)$$

where $m_i = 0$ denotes the event that individual i has valid data on x and this likelihood function is based on the logistic specification which is given by:

$$\log\left(\frac{p(y_i = 1 | x_i ; \theta)}{1 - p(y_i = 1 | x_i ; \theta)}\right) = \theta_0 + \theta_x x_i$$

where x denotes the independent variable (i.e., victim age) and y denotes the dependent variable (i.e., future victimization). Table VII presents the results of the complete-case analysis of these data. The maximum likelihood estimate of the logistic regression coefficient, θ_x is -0.540 which corresponds to an odds ratio of $\exp(\theta_x) = 0.583$ and $Q = -0.264$ which implies a moderate negative association between victim age and risk of future victimization.

---

[11]The original analysis by Hirschel and his colleagues (1992) focused on a sample of 650 cases whereas our sample is based on 626 cases. Our analysis differs from theirs because we exclude a small number of cases where the age information does not appear in the police service call database. Within our sample of 626 cases, we encounter six discrepancies on our age classification variable (34 years old or younger vs. 35 years old or older) between the initial interview and police service call databases. In these cases, we set the age classification variable equal to the value obtained by the interviewers rather than the police.

Table VI. Descriptive Overview of Data from Charlotte Spouse Assault Experiment

Category	Number of observations	Percent of total
Interviewed cases with no rearrest		
Victim 35 years old or younger	236	37.7
Victim 36 years old or older	90	14.3
Interviewed cases with rearrest		
Victim 35 years old or younger	63	10.1
Victim 36 years old or older	14	2.2
Non-interviewed cases with no rearrest		
Victim 35 years old or younger	151	24.1
Victim 36 years old or older	46	7.3
Non-interviewed cases with rearrest		
Victim 35 years old or younger	19	3.0
Victim 36 years old or older	7	1.1
Total	626	100.0

Table VII. Logistic Regression of Future Victimization (Measured by Rearrest) on Age at Time of Entry into Experiment among Individuals with Complete Data ($N = 403$)

Parameter	Estimate	Std. error	$|z|$-ratio
θ_0	−1.321	0.142	9.30
θ_x	−0.540	0.320	1.69
Log-likelihood	−195.04		

Note: x_i is coded 1.0 if victim is 36 years old or older at the time of entry into experiment and 0.0 if victim is 35 years old or younger. The negative estimate of θ_x implies that younger victims were more likely to be victimized than older victims. Using a one-tailed, 95% confidence level, we reject the null hypothesis that the association is equal to zero in the population. The odds ratio is $\exp(\theta_x) = \exp(-0.540) = 0.583$ (where odds ratio of 1.0 implies independence). This corresponds to a Yule's Q estimate of −0.264.

Under a one-tailed significance test, this result is statistically significant at the 95% confidence level. Substantively this result implies that victims who are at least 35 years of age are at reduced risk of future victimization than their counterparts who are 34 years of age or younger. In addition, this result is consistent with more general findings in the victimization literature showing that risk of violent victimization is a declining function of age (see e.g., Zawitz *et al.*, 1993:18).

3.3.3 Sensitivity Analysis

In contrast to the complete case analysis presented in Table VII, a model that takes the uncertainty created by the missing data into account requires evaluation of the trivariate distribution of the independent variable, x, the outcome variable, y, and the missing data indicator variable, m (coded 1 if x is missing; 0 if x is observed) (Vach, 1994; Little and Schenker, 1995). Each individual's contribution to the likelihood function depends on the information that individual has available. For cases where age is obtained from victim surveys, the likelihood function is:

$$L(\theta, \gamma, \delta) = \prod_{i\in(m_i=0)} \left[p(y_i|x_i;\theta) \times p(m_i|y_i, x_i;\gamma) \times p(x_i|\delta) \right]$$

while for cases where age is not available from victim interviews, the likelihood function is given by:

$$L(\theta, \gamma, \delta) = \prod_{i\in(m_i=1)} \left[\int p(y_i|x_i;\theta) \times p(m_i|y_i, x_i;\gamma) \times p(x_i|\delta)\underline{d}x_i \right]$$

and, since both x and m are binary variables, the integral becomes a sum which yields:

$$L(\theta, \gamma, \delta) = \prod_{i\in(m_i=1)} \left[\sum_{x_i=(0,1)} p(y_i|x_i;\theta) \times p(m_i|y_i, x_i;\gamma) \times p(x_i|\delta) \right]$$

The probabilities for the missing data and independent variable components of this likelihood function are calculated using the logistic specification. For the missing data component, we have:

$$\log\left(\frac{p(m_i=1|y_i, x_i;\gamma)}{1-p(m_i=1|y_i, x_i;\gamma)} \right) = \gamma_0 + \gamma_x x_i + \gamma_y y_i + \gamma_{xy} x_i y_i$$

and, for the independent variable (i.e., victim age), the parameterization is given by:

$$\log\left(\frac{p(x_i=1|\delta)}{1-p(x_i=1|\delta)} \right) = \delta$$

Because x is not observed for all individuals, this model is underidentified. By this, we mean that the likelihood surface is completely flat for any choice of values for γ_x and γ_x. If we fix the values of these parameters, however, the model is just identified and the parameter estimates associated with that model will be conditionally valid given that the constraints are valid. In the special case where $\gamma_x = \gamma_{xy} = 0$ then the missing data are missing at random (because γ_y is not necessarily equal to zero) and a consistent parameter estimate for θ_x can be obtained by complete-case analysis. In most practical situations, we will not be able to determine whether a particular choice of constraints is valid. However, it will usually be possible to examine the sensitivity of our conclusions to different choices of constraints. In this particular situation, we actually have access to supplementary data on the independent variable and we can use this information to estimate the association between victim age and future victimization with all observations. This will allow us to verify the validity of our conditional inference when we impose an appropriate set of constraints on γ_x and γ_{xy}.

Table VIII presents the results of our sensitivity analysis where we allow the two unidentified parameters, γ_x and γ_{xy} to jointly vary across the range (-0.75 to $+0.75$) and these results are graphically displayed in the Appendix. This again implies that our sensitivity analysis is confined to modest departures from the assumptions upon which a complete-case analysis is based. Based on the results in Table 8 this appears to be a situation in which different sets of assumptions about these unidentified quantities produces wide variation in our estimate of the age effect (i.e., θ_x).

This table (and the graph in the Appendix) contains two special cases worth noting. The first is the case where both θ_x and θ_{xy} are fixed to zero. In this situation, our estimate of θ_x corresponds exactly to that produced by the complete-case estimator based on the $N = 403$ case data set. The second is the case where γ_x and $\gamma_x y$ are fixed to the values obtained from the complete data (i.e., $N = 626$ instead of $N = 403$). For this application, we can simply use the full $N = 626$ data set to regress m on x, y, and the product of x and y. We then rely on the results of this auxiliary regression to impose the appropriate set of constraints on $_x$ and γ_{xy}. Our footnote to Table VIII indicates that the maximum likelihood estimate of $\gamma_x = -0.225$ and the maximum likelihood estimate of $\gamma_{xy} = +0.730$. We can use this information in conjunction with the data in Table VII to assess who is most likely to have missing age data in this analysis. Among younger individuals who were not revictimized, the probability of missing data are $151/(236 + 151) = 0.390$ while for older individuals who were not revictimized the probability of missing data are $46/(90 + 46) = 0.338$. For older individuals who were revictimized, the probability of missing data are $7/(14 + 7) = 0.333$ and among younger individuals who were revictimized the probability of missing

Table VIII. Sensitivity of Relationship Between Age at Time of Victimization and Probability of Future Victimization to Different Sets of Assumptions about Missing Data Mechanism ($N = 403$)

Missing data parameters		Results of conditional Maximim likelihood estimation			
γ_{xy}	γ_y	θ_x	$|z|(\theta_x)$	$\exp(\theta_x)$	Q
−0.750	−0.750	−0.541	1.71	0.582	−0.264
	−0.375	−0.615	1.94	0.541	−0.298
	0.000	−0.695	2.18	0.499	−0.334
	0.375	−0.774	2.42	0.461	−0.369
	0.750	−0.842	2.64	0.431	−0.398
−0.375	−0.750	−0.501	1.58	0.606	−0.246
	−0.375	−0.562	1.76	0.570	−0.274
	0.000	−0.626	1.96	0.535	−0.303
	0.375	−0.688	2.15	0.503	−0.331
	0.750	−0.740	2.32	0.477	−0.354
0.000	−0.750	−0.448	1.41	0.639	−0.220
	−0.375	−0.493	1.54	0.611	−0.242
	0.000	−0.540	1.69	0.583	−0.264
	0.375	−0.585	1.83	0.557	−0.284
	0.750	−0.623	1.98	0.536	−0.302
0.375	−0.750	−0.379	1.19	0.684	−0.187
	−0.375	−0.407	1.27	0.666	−0.201
	0.000	−0.437	1.37	0.646	−0.215
	0.375	−0.469	1.48	0.626	−0.230
	0.750	−0.499	1.61	0.607	−0.245
0.750	−0.750	−0.293	0.92	0.746	−0.146
	−0.375	−0.304	0.95	0.738	−0.151
	0.000	−0.321	1.01	0.725	−0.159
	0.375	−0.344	1.11	0.709	−0.171
	0.740	−0.374	1.24	0.688	−0.185

Note: Because we have access to both observed and unobserved cases, we have valid estimates of γ_x (−0.225) and γ_{xy} (0.730). After conditioning on this information, our valid estimate of θ_x is −0.316 with a $|z|$-ratio of 1.20, an odds ratio of 0.730 and Yule's Q of −0.157. This estimate of θ_x is not significantly different from zero at the 95% confidence level.

data are somewhat lower $19/(63 + 19) = 0.232$. This pattern of probabilities reveals the reason for the positive interaction effect: age conditions the relationship between the outcome variable and the probability of missing data. Specifically, among younger victims, those who were revictimized were less likely to have missing data while, among older victims there was essentially no association at all between revictimization and the probability of missing data.

If we use the missing data model that we employed for our sensitivity analysis after imposing the appropriate restrictions on γ_x and γ_{xy}, we obtain an estimate of θ_x that is substantially lower than what is obtained from our analysis with the missing cases omitted $\theta_x = -0.320$; $|z|$-ratio $= 1.01$; $p > 0.05$; Yule's $Q = -0.159$). This estimate is virtually identical to the estimate of θ_x that we obtain when we regress revictimization on age using all 626 cases ($\theta_x = -0.316$; $|z|$-ratio $= 1.20$; $p > 0.05$; Yule's $Q = -0.157$). It is important to note that the $|z|$-ratio for the estimate from the missing data model is smaller than the $|z|$-ratio of 1.20 that we obtain by estimating a logistic regression among all of the cases. The reason for this is that the missing data estimator takes the uncertainty associated with the missing survey data into account and adjusts the standard errors of the parameter estimates accordingly. As a practical matter, use of this missing data estimator results in an appropriately less precise estimate of θ_x. Our final conclusion is that younger and older victims exhibit similar probabilities of official revictimization. This conclusion is at odds with what we would have concluded from a complete-case analysis after deleting observations with missing age information.

4. CONCLUSIONS

Criminologists are frequently confronted with missing data in their analyses. While some tools to address this problem are available they tend to be complicated to implement and not widely used. The most typical response to missing data problems within criminology is to delete missing observations from the analysis. This probably is not a major problem in studies where the proportion of cases with missing data are small. In such situations, the departures from complete case analysis assumptions would often have to be quite large for them to have a meaningful impact on one's results.

On the other hand, when the proportion of cases with missing data are substantial, complete case analysis may produce misleading results. Using two very simple problems from actual criminological data sets, we tried to illustrate the potential consequences of complete-case analysis using simple models with a single independent variable and a single dependent variable.[12] Our analyses are further simplified by the fact that they could ordinarily be conducted using only a 2×2 contingency table if missing data were not a

---

[12]We note here that our analysis does not address any previously published research on these topics with these data. We used these data sets because they were convenient and typical of data often analyzed by criminological researchers.

problem. Even in this very simple setting, the results of our complete case analyses did not stand up to the scrutiny of a basic sensitivity analysis that critically evaluated the assumptions upon which the complete-case model was based.

This paper leaves a number of issues unresolved. First, since the problems addressed in this paper are among the simpler types of analyses that criminologists ever conduct, it stands to reason that missing data specifications become more complicated when basic statistical models become more complicated. Second, some researchers will take comfort in the fact that new software programs are being made available to implement multiple imputation strategies such as those described by Schafer (1997) and Rubin (1987) and many contemporary surveys utilize sophisticated methodologies that allow researchers to use weights to adjust for nonresponse (see e.g., Thompson, 1997; Little and Schenker, 1995). While we think these are positive developments, we also believe they are not panaceas. As noted earlier, Allison (2000) has recently shown that multiple imputation models that are specified incorrectly can actually produce inferences that exhibit more bias than those obtained by a standard complete-case analysis.

We suggested earlier in this paper that complete-case analysis can actually be a good choice in some situations where data are not missing completely at random. For example, if one has missing data on an outcome variable and one is also willing to assume that the probability of missing data are independent of the outcome variable after conditioning on the independent variables, complete-case analysis should produce valid inferences (see e.g., Little, 1992:1227). In a regression framework, selection on an independent variable does not ordinarily create a problem so long as the selection rule is not correlated with the outcome variable (King, Keohane, and Verba, 1994:137–138). It follows that in these cases the use of complete case analysis will yield valid results and more complicated methods would not be warranted.

On the other hand, as Little and Schenker (1995) have noted, strategies based on ignorable missing data mechanisms are all based on strong assumptions which cannot be tested easily. A corollary to this position is that complete case analysis after comparing complete cases and missing cases on characteristics that are observed for everyone does not substitute for a sensitivity analysis or a critical appraisal of the uncertainties created by incomplete data. The possibility of nonignorable missing data always lurks behind the scenes of such analyses. In particular, whenever, the distribution of the variable about which we wish to develop inferences differs between cases with and without missing data on that variable, the missing data problem is nonignorable. Each case needs to be evaluated separately to determine the likely costs and consequences of missing data in that particular context.

In sum, we believe our research has two useful implications for criminological work. First, it suggests that there is some value in the development of methods that will allow researchers to investigate the robustness of their conclusions to different assumptions about missing data mechanisms. As Rubin (1987) and Little and Rubin (1987) have shown, multiple imputation strategies can be adapted to meet this need but these strategies are more complicated than multiple imputation models based on ignorability assumptions. In the end, if researchers have reason to believe that their inferences critically depend on the assumptions that justify a complete-case analysis, then it seems sensible to investigate the sensitivity of our inferences to changes in those assumptions. Such efforts will help our field to systematically address the uncertainty created by missing data and make it a central feature of its analytic efforts.

Second, and perhaps most important, is the fact that missing data can inject considerable ambiguity into criminological research. With two very simple problems, we have seen how this ambiguity can significantly impact what at first appear to be straightforward conclusions. The solutions we have devised, however, are back-end in nature; in other words, we have explored methods for addressing a problem that emerges after data collection is complete. Clearly, the very best solution to the missing data problem is a front-end solution—to minimize the amount of missing data. While, in some ways, this is an obvious point it is also true that much primary criminological research emphasizes the collection of many hundreds of variables on individual units (i.e., survey respondents, city characteristics, etc.). The demands of collecting such detailed data sets, however, often means that compromises in tracking units or securing basic information from all units must be made. The choice of collecting rich, detailed data sets that result in substantial proportions of cases with missing information or collecting basic information but successfully locating and securing information from all respondents is not a happy one. Each option imposes serious costs on criminological research. Nonetheless, we believe that the costs of missing information are quite high and that such costs should be given great weight in the design and implementation of criminological research efforts.

APPENDIX

Sensitivity of Yule's Q to different assumptions about the missing data mechanism

Case Study #1: Adolescent Public Assistance & Adult Offending

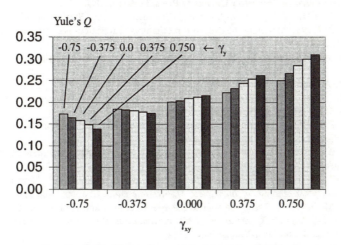

Case Study #2: Victim Age and Six-Month Revictimization

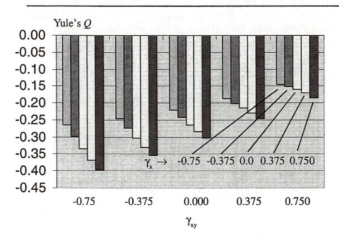

REFERENCES

Agresti, A. (1996). *An Introduction to Categorical Data Analysis*. Wiley, New York.

Allison, P. D. (2000). Multiple imputation for missing data: a cautionary tale. *Sociol. Methods Res.* 28: 301–309.

Carroll, R. J., Ruppert, D., and Stefanski, L. A. (1995). *Measurement Error in Nonlinear Models*. Chapman and Hall, London.

Elliott, D. S., Huizinga, D., and Menard, S. (1989). *Multiple Problem Youth: Delinquency, Substance Use, and Mental Health Problems*. Springer-Verlag, New York.

Hirschel, J. D., Hutchison, I. W., and Dean, C. W. (1992). The failure of arrest to deter spouse assault. *J. Res. Crime Delinq.* 29: 7–33.

King, G. (1989). *Unifying Political Methodology: the Likelihood Theory of Statistical Inference*. Cambridge University Press, New York.

King, G., Keohane, R. O., and Verba, S. (1994). *Designing Social Inquiry: Scientific Inference in Qualitative Research*. Princeton University Press, Princeton, NJ.

Little, R. J. A. (1992). Regression with missing x's: a review. *J. Am. Stat. Assoc.* 87: 1227–1236.

Little, R. J. A. (1995). Modeling the drop-out mechanism in repeated-measures studies. *J. Am. Stat. Assoc.* 90: 1112–1121.

Little, R. J. A., and Rubin, D. B. (1987). *Statistical analysis with missing data*. Wiley, New York.

Little, R. J. A., and Schenker, N. (1995). *Missing Data*. In Arminger, G., Clogg, C. C. and Sobel, M. E. (eds.), Handbook of statistical modeling for the social and behavioral sciences, pp. 39–75. Plenum Press, New York.

Manski, C. F. (1995). *Identification Problems in the Social Sciences*. Harvard University Press, Cambridge, MA.

Nordheim, E. V. (1984). Inference from nonrandomly missing categorical data: An example from a genetic study on Turner's Syndrome. *J. Am. Stat. Assoc.* 79: 772–780.

Rubin, D. B. (1987). *Multiple Imputation for Nonresponse in Surveys*. Wiley, New York.

Schafer, J. L. (1997). *Analysis of Incomplete Multivariate Data*. Chapman and Hall, London.

Thompson, M. E. (1997). *Theory of Sample Surveys*. Chapman and Hall, London.

Vach, W. (1994). *Logistic Regression with Missing Values in the Covariates*. Lecture notes in statistics, vol. 48. Springer-Verlag, New York.

Wainer, H. (1986). *Drawing Inferences from Self-Selected Samples*. Springer-Verlag, New York.

Zawitz, M. W., Klaus, P. A., Bachman, R., Bastian, L. D., DeBerry, M. M., Rand, M. R., *et al.* (1993). *Highlights from 20 Years of Surveying Crime Victims: The National Crime Victimization Survey, 1973–1992*. Bureau of Justice Statistics, Washington, DC.

[6]

David Weisburd
with Anthony Petrosino and Gail Mason

Design Sensitivity in Criminal Justice Experiments

ABSTRACT

Interest in randomized experiments with criminal justice subjects has grown, in recognition that experiments are much better suited for identifying and isolating program effects than are quasi-experimental or nonexperimental research designs. Relatively little attention, however, has been paid to methodological issues. Using the statistical concept of power—the likelihood that a test will lead to the rejection of a hypothesis of no effect, a survey examines the design sensitivity of experiments on sanctions. Contrary to conventional wisdom advocating large sample designs, little relationship is found in practice between sample size and statistical power. Difficulty in maintaining the integrity of treatments and the homogeneity of samples or treatments employed offsets the design advantages of larger investigations.

Only experimental designs allow researchers to make an unambiguous link between effects and their causes. Random assignment of subjects into treatment and "control" groups—the defining feature of experimental research—provides a statistical basis for making the assumption that the outcomes observed in an experiment result from the interven-

David Weisburd is associate professor of criminal justice at Rutgers—The State University. Anthony Petrosino is research specialist, New Jersey Division of Criminal Justice. Gail Mason is a tutor in the Department of Legal Studies, La Trobe University. Research for this essay was supported by the National Institute of Justice (grant 88IJCX-0007) and by the School of Criminal Justice, Rutgers—The State University. We wish to thank Christopher Maxwell, Ana Lopes, and Martha J. Smith for their assistance. Helpful comments were provided by Ronald Clarke, Joseph Naus, Albert J. Reiss, Jr., Lawrence Sherman, Michael Tonry, Joel Garner, Lorraine Green, and Simcha Landau.

tions that are studied.[1] In contrast, correlational or quasi-experimental designs are always plagued by the possibility that some important confounding factor has not been taken into account by researchers. Randomized experiments thus have a distinct design advantage over nonexperimental studies. Nonetheless, the ethical and bureaucratic problems associated with random allocation of subjects in real-life criminal justice settings have generally led criminologists to other less controversial and more easily developed research methods.

Support for experimental methods in crime and justice has been growing over the last decade (e.g., see Farrington, Ohlin, and Wilson 1986) as has the number of important experimental studies (Garner and Visher 1988). Interest in experimentation, however, has been accompanied by a concern with the adequacy of experimental methods in criminal justice. Petersilia, for example, argues that little attention has been paid to the special difficulties of designing and managing field experiments in the justice system, or the potential strategies that might be used to overcome such problems (Petersilia 1989; see also Dennis 1988; Weisburd and Garner 1992). That most experimental studies in criminal justice have not led to statistically significant research findings adds support to such concerns (e.g., see Farrington 1983; Weisburd, Sherman, and Petrosino 1990), though the link between experimental design and study outcomes has not been explicitly tested. In this essay we examine this question in the context of a review of experimental studies in criminal justice sanctions conducted by Weisburd, Sherman, and Petrosino (1990). Focusing on the problem of statistical power, we challenge traditional assumptions about the relationship between research design and experimental results.

Statistical power provides the most direct measure of whether a study has been designed to allow a fair test of its research hypothesis. When a study is underpowered it is unlikely to yield a statistically significant result even when a relatively large program or intervention effect is found. For example, in the Kansas City Preventive Patrol Experiment (Kelling et al. 1974) inadequate statistical power biased the study toward the null hypothesis of no difference between the experimental and control conditions (see Feinberg, Larntz, and Reiss 1976). Had a more powerful study design been used, the study's major finding—that preventive patrol does not affect crime—might have

---

[1] In criminal justice experiments there is seldom a group that receives no treatment. More commonly, as is illustrated later, offenders are given different types of treatments—for example, intensive versus traditional probation.

been reversed for specific offenses (Sherman and Weisburd 1992). In the Kansas City experiment, as in much empirical study in the social sciences (see Chase and Chase 1976; Orme and Tolman 1986), research designs employed by investigators often make it very difficult for a study to obtain statistical support for the research hypothesis. In lay terms, such studies may be seen as "designed for failure," not because of inadequacies in the theories or programs evaluated, but because of the methods employed by investigators.

It is commonly assumed that increasing the size of a sample provides the most straightforward method for increasing the statistical power of a research design and thus avoiding the possibility that an investigation is biased toward a finding of no difference or no effect (e.g., see Kraemer and Thiemann 1987; Kolata 1990). Larger studies, all else being equal, are more powerful than smaller ones, which naturally leads researchers to the conclusion that bigger is better when it comes to experimental research. Our review of criminal justice experiments in sanctions suggests a much more cautious conclusion for researchers that takes into account the special difficulties that larger investigations present to those who have to manage, implement, and evaluate them.

The design benefits of larger studies are often offset by the implementation and management difficulties they present. Using sample estimates as a guide, the very largest investigations are no more powerful than the very smallest. Indeed, we find little relationship in practice between sample size and statistical power. While this conclusion is very, much at odds with common assumptions in experimental research, it is consistent with our knowledge of the challenges that experimenters face in developing large-scale projects. In studies with larger samples it is often much more difficult to ensure that treatments are delivered consistently or effectively. Such studies are also more likely to include a wider diversity of subjects than are smaller investigations. Accordingly, all else is not equal in larger and smaller studies. Problems of implementation and the heterogeneity of larger studies make such investigations less likely to yield strong and consistent effects. Together they serve to constrain the design benefits that should derive from larger samples.

We begin our discussion of design sensitivity in randomized criminal justice studies with a general introduction to statistical power in Section I. Section II presents a brief description of the experimental studies examined, and Section III looks at general methodological characteristics of those experiments. In Section IV we examine the

relationship between sample size and the actual outcomes of experiments. Our finding in that section, that larger studies should lead to
more powerful research designs but do not, is discussed in Section V
in terms of various components of the design and management of field
experiments. In Section VI we suggest ways of overcoming the weaknesses of large sample designs and present some concluding comments
on the implications of our findings for future experimental research.

I. Statistical Power

There are two types of errors that can be made when deciding whether
to reject or accept the null hypothesis (the hypothesis that an intervention will have no effect, or "null effect") in an empirical study. The
most commonly discussed is type I error, which assesses the likelihood
of falsely rejecting the null hypothesis based on findings in a sample
when there is no difference between the groups under study in the
population. This error is what is referred to when reporting the statistical significance of a study. Type II error, which is the central feature
of statistical power, takes account of precisely the opposite type of
risk. Its concern is with the possibility of falsely accepting the null
hypothesis when there is a difference in the population characteristics
of the groups examined.

In contrast to statistical significance—which identifies for the researcher the risk of stating that factors are related when they are not—
statistical power provides an estimate of how often one would fail to
identify a relationship that in fact existed. In statistical terms, power
is defined as "1 − type II error," or one minus the probability of
accepting the null hypothesis when it is false. Type II error occurs in
an experiment when the researcher finds no difference in outcomes
between treatment and control groups studied, but such differences
do exist in the population from which they are drawn. Its relationship
to the proposition that many experiments are designed for failure is
straightforward. If examined at the outset, statistical power can identify when a research enterprise is likely to fail to provide support for
the existence of an effect that is present in the population.

The importance of statistical power is often not fully understood by
researchers, who are generally much more concerned with the concept
of statistical significance. While little, if any, attention is paid to statistical power in the design of criminal justice studies (Brown 1989),
researchers carefully set significance levels at the outset of an experi-

ment in order to avoid accusations of bias later on. It has become virtually impossible to present research findings without attention to the statistical significance of research results, and norms concerning significance criteria are strongly established. Generally, a .05 level of significance is set. In other words, it is assumed that taking a risk of rejecting the null hypothesis five in 100 times, when it is in reality correct, is acceptable. Such clear standards for significance thresholds have allowed researchers to guard against the problem of biasing results to the research hypothesis.[2]

The notion that researchers may be biasing results against the research hypothesis (or for a finding of "no effect") has appeared less troubling to criminal justice scholars. Especially in experimental studies, which are often developed to test the effectiveness of expensive government interventions, the possibility that a study would be designed in a way that made it difficult to identify program success has appeared unlikely. Nonetheless, evidence from primarily nonexperimental criminological research (Brown 1989) suggests that criminal justice studies are often severely underpowered. This means that research is often designed in such a way that even if the effect the researcher posits is present in the population it is unlikely to be detected in the sample under study.

At this point it may be useful if we discuss a concrete example. Suppose a researcher wanted to examine the effects of methadone treatment on the six-month recidivism rate of drug addicts. Following the experimental method, addicts would be randomly allocated into control and treatment groups. The statistical power of this experiment is the probability that the statistical test employed would lead to a significant finding. Clearly, the researcher would not want to design a study that would make it highly unlikely to establish a relationship between methadone treatment and reduced recidivism if one existed. But, importantly, if a test is not statistically powerful, then the risk of such an error (a type II error) is very high. How then can one design a powerful study? More simply, what are the components that make up statistical power?

In understanding the factors that contribute to the power of an experimental study, four matters warrant consideration and are discussed

---

[2] When significance thresholds that make it easier to reject the null hypothesis (e.g., $p < .10$) are used, the researcher is generally expected to carefully explain his or her departure from established convention.

below.[3] First is the significance criterion employed in a statistical test. This is the threshold for rejection of the null hypothesis that an investigator sets at the outset of an experiment. Second is directionality, or the choice between employing a "one-tailed" or "two-tailed" test of significance. The third component of statistical power is what statisticians define as "effect size." Finally, and most commonly associated with the power of an experimental study, is the size of the sample examined by an investigator.

Clearly, the simplest way to decrease the likelihood of failing to reject the null hypothesis is to adjust the test statistic used as a threshold for statistical significance. One way to do this is to change the risk of type I error (the likelihood of rejecting the null hypothesis when it is in fact true) employed in an experiment. Because statistical power and statistical significance are directly related, when a less stringent level of significance is chosen (e.g., .10 as opposed to .05) it makes it easier to reject the null hypothesis and achieve statistical significance, and thus the experiment becomes more powerful. While this method for increasing statistical power is direct, it is usually not a practical suggestion since, as already discussed, norms concerning levels of significance are fairly well established.

A more practical method for changing the value of the test statistic needed to reject the null hypothesis is to limit the direction of the research hypothesis. A "one-tailed test" provides greater power than a "two-tailed test" for the same reason that a less stringent level of significance provides more power than a more stringent one. By choosing a one-tailed test of significance the researcher reduces the value of the test statistic needed to reject the null hypothesis. This occurs because the critical region (the part of a sampling distribution that defines the area of rejection of the null hypothesis) is shifted to test only one of the two potential outcomes in an experiment. For example, in the methadone experiment discussed above, the researcher could rule out the possibility at the outset that treatment might backfire and increase drug use. While there are many cases in which a directional research hypothesis is appropriate, once a one-directional test is posited, a sur-

---

[3] Though not discussed at length in the following paragraphs, the type of statistical test (e.g., chi-square or analysis of variance) used in an experiment can also affect its statistical power. Some tests are more appropriate in particular situations and provide more powerful tests of research hypotheses. Nonetheless, the differences between the power of different tests (equally appropriate to the problem at hand) is usually relatively small.

prising finding in the opposite direction cannot be touted as a major result.[4]

"Effect size" measures the influence of the intervention that is being assessed by taking the ratio of the magnitude of the differences between treatment and control groups to the standard deviation of those differences (see Cohen 1988).[5] Effect, as it is discussed here, is thus dependent on the size of the impact of a treatment, taking into account how much individuals in the sample vary in the outcomes measured. Statistinians do not simply examine the observed differences between the groups because they want to standardize the effects found in an experiment. Such standardization brings into perspective the differences between the groups and allows comparison of the size of an effect between studies that use different types of measures.

The relationship between statistical power and effect size is a straightforward one. When an effect in a population is larger it is harder to miss in any particular sample. Since statistical power asks what the likelihood is of detecting a particular effect (i.e., achieving statistical significance) in a given sample, when effect size is larger the experiment is more powerful. Where effects are hypothesized to be relatively small, other aspects of design must be maximized in order to achieve an acceptable level of statistical power.

Effect size is generally seen as the characteristic of statistical power that is most difficult to manipulate. A test is ordinarily conducted in order to determine the influence of an intervention on subjects. In experimental field research the intervention itself is usually arrived at through a complex series of negotiations between researchers and practitioners. Though, as we discuss later, effect size can be manipulated in ways that do not adversely affect the theoretical or practical goals of an experiment, there has been relatively little consideration of effect size in efforts to increase the power of experimental designs.[6]

The final component of statistical power, and the one most often used to manipulate power in social science research, is sample size (Kraemer and Thiemann 1987). Larger samples, all else being equal, provide more stable and reliable results than do smaller samples. The

---

[4] This is a case where you cannot have your cake and eat it too. If the advantage of a one-tailed test is sought, the researcher must sacrifice any finding in a direction opposite to that originally predicted. To do otherwise brings into question the integrity of the researcher's statistical design.

[5] We say more about the computation of effect size coefficients in Section IV below.

[6] For an important exception, see Lipsey (1990).

statistical logic is not complex. Larger samples are more "trustworthy" than smaller ones. For example, one would not be surprised to get two or three heads in a row from tosses of an honest coin. However, if the coin produced only heads in a sample of twenty-five tosses, we would be much more suspicious. Getting 100 heads in 100 coin tosses would lead even the most trusting person to doubt the fairness of the coin. In this same sense, larger samples are more powerful since they are more likely to be able to identify an effect, if it exists in a population, than are smaller studies. Conversely, as Kraemer and Thiemann note, "the smaller the sample size the smaller the power" (1987, p. 27). Because sample size provides a method for increasing statistical power that is straightforward and does not involve manipulations in either the significance levels employed or the treatments administered, it has played a central role in power analyses in the social sciences.

Returning to the methadone example, the researcher would, as David Farrington has suggested, "assess the size of effect (e.g., percentage difference) that would have practical significance and then calculate the sample size that would be needed to obtain statistical significance with this size of effect" (1983, p. 286). Put differently, the researcher's central problem is to identify the sample size needed to provide a powerful experiment based on the significance criteria and the effect size hypothesized. At a minimum, it is generally recommended that a statistical test have a power level greater than .50—indicating that the test is more likely to show a significant result than not (e.g., see Gelber and Zelen 1985, p. 413). But it is generally accepted that the most powerful experiments seek a power level of .80 or above (e.g., see Cohen 1973; Gelber and Zelen 1985). Such experiments are, given the researcher's assumptions about significance and effect size, highly likely to evidence a significant finding. The problem for our methadone researcher, simply stated, is to collect enough cases to achieve this threshold of power.

This is the process generally followed in developing powerful research designs. It is on its face a way of ensuring that a particular study is not designed for failure. While it makes assumptions about significance and effect size, it is primarily reliant on sample size to achieve a desired level of statistical power. It is based on the assumption that all else being equal, larger samples provide for a more powerful research design. But as we discuss below, the simple assumption that effect size is fixed, staying basically constant across samples of different sizes, is a flawed assumption.

II. The Sample: Experiments in Sanctions

Our analysis of experimental design is drawn from a review carried out by Weisburd, Sherman, and Petrosino (1990). They attempted to identify all randomized studies reported in English that were conducted in criminal justice settings and used coercive "treatment" or "control" conditions. Five specific criteria were used for inclusion of studies: (1) that individuals were used as the primary unit of analysis, (2) that those individuals were randomly allocated into multiple treatment groups or treatment and control groups,[7] (3) that at least one outcome variable (whether self-report or drawn from a criminal justice agency) measured crime-related activities, (4) that the intervention or treatment (or the control condition) be coercively applied by a criminal justice agency in response to or in anticipation of a criminal act, and (5) that there be a minimum of fifteen cases included in at least two of the groups examined.[8] Weisburd, Sherman, and Petrosino identified seventy-six experiments that fit their criteria after a search of both computerized and noncomputerized criminal justice and general social science bibliographic indexes (see the Appendix).[9] Once identified,

[7] In seven cases, studies were included that randomized according to alternative allocation schedules. For example, in the Denver Drunk Driving Experiment (Ross and Blumenthal 1974, 1975) investigators allocated subjects based on alternative months. In the Hamilton Juvenile Services Project Experiment (Byles and Maurice 1979) and the California Juvenile Behavior Modification and Transactional Analysis Experiment (Jesness et al. 1972; Jesness 1975), the investigators used an odd/even system for placing offenders in treatment and control groups. In the Police Foundation Shoplifting Arrest Experiment, investigators noted that offenders were "alternatively assigned to an arrest or release category" (Williams, Forst, and Hamilton 1987). Such allocation procedures are random in the sense that there were not systematic biases in the choice of subjects who would be placed in each of the allocation sequences. However, because such studies might be seen as violating components of a classical experimental design, we replicated our basic analyses without them. The results do not differ substantially from those reported here.

[8] Farrington, Ohlin, and Wilson (1986, p. 66) argue that a "randomized experiment can control for all extraneous variables . . . only if a reasonably large number of people (at least fifty) are assigned to each condition." We could find no statistical reason for using this particular threshold, and Farrington, Ohlin, and Wilson do not detail their thinking on this question. The relatively low threshold used by Weisburd, Sherman, and Petrosino (1990) reflects their desire to include as broad a sample as possible.

[9] The search for studies began with a review of Farrington (1983) and Farrington, Ohlin, and Wilson (1986). From the references and studies included there, additional references and studies were reviewed, including bibliographies, qualitative works on the topic of randomized field experiments, and elaborations of studies already included in the sample. A search of the *Criminal Justice Abstracts* data base was also conducted. At the same time, additional narrative review articles on experimentation, deterrence, rehabilitation, sentencing, and corrections were examined. A search of the National Criminal Justice Reference System was completed in June 1989 for 1973–88 using the following key words: (*a*) randomization, (*b*) controlled study, (*c*) random assignment, (*d*) randomly assigned, (*e*) random allocation, (*f*) field experiment, (*g*) randomized experi-

346   David Weisburd

each experiment was described in a registry and included in a computerized data base that detailed specifics of subjects, sanctions, methods,
and outcomes.

Some mention should be made at the outset of the limitations created
by identifying a sample of experiments through published studies and
reports. A sample of what is reported is not the same as the universe
of all studies. We might expect, for example, that studies that show a
significant effect for criminal justice interventions would be more likely
to be disseminated and published than studies showing no effect. Accordingly, there may be a bias to "successes" in this review as in others
(see Coleman 1989). Studies conducted in criminal justice settings by
agency researchers, as compared with studies supervised by university
researchers, are also more likely to escape inclusion in a review of
published materials. No doubt there are other biases that relate to the
dissemination of research findings. Nevertheless, we do not want to
over-emphasize such limitations. Most of the studies found did not
report any statistically significant results, and many were conducted
without any substantial university (or research institute) involvement.[10]

The criteria employed by Weisburd, Sherman, and Petrosino cast a
fairly wide net for the identification of experimental criminal justice
studies. There is, for example, tremendous diversity in the sanctions
evaluated by researchers. While such penalties as probation, parole,
and imprisonment occur most often in the studies examined, there
are also studies evaluating police interventions, such as arrests (e.g.,
Sherman and Berk 1984*a;* Williams, Forst, and Hamilton 1987); prison
tours, like the Scared Straight experiment in New Jersey (Finckenauer
1982); and restitution (e.g., Schneider and Schneider 1983; Schneider
1986).

Most often the experiments tested the influence of alternative criminal justice sanctions or the application of differing dosages of a particular sanction. For example, Ross and Blumenthal (1974, 1975) randomly
assigned drunk drivers to three groups: a group that received a fine,
one that received regular probation, or one that received therapeutic
probation. In the Sacramento 601 Diversion Project (Baron, Feeney,
and Thornton 1972, 1973), one of thirteen diversion studies in the
review, juvenile delinquents were randomly assigned to an experimen-

---

ment, and (*b*) controlled trial. Almost 70 percent of the experiments were reported
in scholarly journals or books. Twenty-eight percent were discussed in government
publications, and 3 percent were identified only in nongovernmental research reports.

[10] In seven out of ten studies no significant differences were found between groups
included in the experiment. Thirty-seven of the experiments were conducted without
major support from a university or research institute.

tal group receiving family and individual counseling or to a control condition that went before the juvenile court. A number of parole studies varied the intensity of caseloads or supervision services. This was the case, for example, in the California Special Intensive Parole Experiment (Reimer and Warren 1957) conducted in the early 1950s. In one unusual probation study, Illinois parolees were randomly assigned to regular probation supervision or probation supervision carried out by volunteer lawyers (Berman 1975, 1978).

There are relatively few experiments where the experimental or control group was able to avoid criminal justice intervention altogether, though some of these are particularly well known.[11] For example, in the Minneapolis Domestic Violence Experiment (Sherman and Berk 1984a, 1984b; Berk and Sherman 1985, 1988) suspects were randomly allocated either to an arrest group, or to a group that received discretionary mediation, or to one in which suspects were ordered to stay away from home for eight hours. In the Police Foundation Shoplifting Arrest Experiment (Glick, Hamilton, and Forst 1986; Sherman and Gartin 1986; Williams, Forst, and Hamilton 1987) those in the experimental group were arrested after being identified as shoplifters. Members of the control group were released. While a few prison experiments contrasted continued incarceration with some type of work release or halfway house supervision (e.g., Lamb and Goertzel 1974a, 1974b), only one contrasted imprisonment with release. In the California Reduced Prison Sentence Experiment (Berecochea, Jaman, and Jones 1973; Berecochea and Jaman 1981), inmates were randomly assigned to six-month early release or a group that finished out their full sentences.

Eight of the studies tested the effects of group assignment to different institutional "wards," "regimes," or "communities." For example, in the Fricot Ranch Experiment (Jesness 1965, 1971a), male delinquents were randomly assigned to an experimental twenty-bed dormitory or to a more traditional fifty-bed unit. In the English Borstal Allocation Experiment (Williams 1970, 1975) youths were assigned to three types of borstal institutions: one that emphasized therapeutic treatment, one that included group counseling, or one that emphasized hard work and paternalistic control.

More than a quarter of the experiments involved treatments that are added onto traditional criminal justice sanctions, often in the context

---

[11] It could be argued that the diversion experiments did this as well. But when offenders were diverted from traditional criminal justice processing they usually received a fairly intrusive regimen of counseling or supervision.

of a prison or jail stay. Many of these studies would not have been seen by the original investigators as sanctioning experiments but rather as attempts at arriving at effective rehabilitative treatments. For example, in the Copenhagen Short Term Offender Experiment (Berntsen and Christiansen 1965), adult male prisoners were randomly assigned to an experimental group receiving psychological examination, interviews with social workers, or some form of individualized treatment geared toward resocialization. Members of the control group received services available through routine custody. In the California Juvenile Probation and Group Counseling Experiment (Adams 1965), juvenile male probationers were randomly assigned to an experimental group that received counseling sessions each week over six months or a control group that received normal probation services. Such experiments were included by Weisburd, Sherman, and Petrosino when inmates were coerced into participating. In cases where participation in the experiment was voluntary, the study was excluded (e.g., see Annis 1979).

The experiments reviewed included a substantial degree of diversity in the types of offenders examined. Nonetheless, most of the studies had predominantly male samples, and a majority of the subjects in most of the experiments were white. Half of the studies reviewed were conducted only with juveniles and most included offenders prosecuted for relatively minor offenses. Indeed, a number of the experiments specifically excluded high-risk offenders. Though, as already discussed, there are difficulties in making inferences from a sample of published materials, we suspect that the controversy surrounding random allocation of criminal justice interventions makes it more difficult to include offenders convicted of serious crimes and perhaps easier to conduct studies with juveniles. Still, half the experiments included some adult offenders and a few randomly allocated persons convicted of more serious crimes.[12]

The sample includes experiments from eighteen states as well as the District of Columbia. Fifteen studies were conducted outside the United States, with eleven carried out in England. Perhaps it is not surprising, given the tradition of support for empirical research in California, that more than 40 percent of the studies came from that state. Overall, most of the studies were carried out across institutions within a state or local jurisdiction. Nonetheless, two studies were car-

---

[12] For example, see the North Carolina Butner Correctional Facility Experiment (Love, Allgood, and Samples 1986) and the English Prison Intensive Social Work Experiment (Shaw 1974).

ried out across institutions in the federal justice system. Nineteen of the experiments were carried out in only one institution.

Weisburd, Sherman, and Petrosino thus identify a broad spectrum of experimental studies. Nonetheless, their inclusion criteria led them to exclude a number of better-known experiments in criminal justice. For example, the Kansas City Preventive Patrol Experiment (Kelling et al. 1974), which claimed to allocate varying amounts of police patrol randomly, was excluded because it involved random allocation of geographic areas (beats) rather than people.[13] Similarly, Tornudd's (1968) study of the effects of differential prosecutions on drunkenness randomly allocated towns rather than offenders.

The sanctioning criteria employed by Weisburd, Sherman, and Petrosino also led to the exclusion of a number of well-known studies. For example, the Living Insurance for Ex-Prisoners (LIFE) and the Transitional Aid Research Project (Tarp) experiments, both often thought of as criminal justice studies, were excluded from the sample (see Berk, Lenihan, and Rossi 1980; Rossi, Berk, and Lenihan 1980). These experiments randomly assigned subjects released from prison to groups that received weekly stipends or to a control group that did not. The study did not meet the requirements for inclusion in the sample because payments were not administered by criminal justice agents. The classic Cambridge-Somerville Youth Study (Powers and Witmer 1951) was excluded for similar reasons. It involved a social work response that could be refused by the subjects or their families.

The criterion that the experiment include crime-related outcome measures meant that studies like the Manhattan Bail Project (Ares, Rankin, and Sturz 1963), an often-cited experiment, also do not appear in this sample. There it was the success of pretrial recommendations for release or bail rather than the influence of sanctions on recidivism that was assessed. Similarly, Taylor's (1967) study of the effects of psychotherapy on Borstal girls was excluded because only psychological outcome measures were examined.

III. Experiments in Sanctions: Methodological Characteristics

Comparatively few experimental studies in criminal justice provide very much detail about the methods employed in designing and carrying out research (Lipsey 1990). This is due, in part, to the norms of

---

[13] Had the Kansas City study met this criterion it might have been excluded as a result of questions raised concerning the randomization procedures used by investigators (see Feinberg, Larntz, and Reiss 1976; Farrington 1983).

report writing. There is just not the same demand for discussion of methodological details of research as there is for elaboration about outcomes or theoretical perspectives. Nonetheless, it is possible to examine in a general way a number of characteristics of the experimental research reviewed by Weisburd, Sherman, and Petrosino (1990). Before turning specifically to the relationship between effect size and sample size, we examine below a series of other design issues that are related to the power of experimental studies.

As described earlier, the size of a sample is directly related to the statistical power of an experiment. All else being equal, larger experiments are more powerful, and for this reason sample size has become the primary design characteristic manipulated by experimental researchers in order to increase the power of their research. Interestingly, while focusing on larger samples, few researchers have taken advantage of the fact that studies in which the sizes of the groups examined are relatively similar are more powerful than those in which the sizes of the groups are markedly different. While the benefit here is usually small, it can be large when the number of cases included in different groups examined in a study differ widely. And this is the case for a number of the experimental studies examined by Weisburd, Sherman, and Petrosino (1990).

The problem is illustrated by a formula for standardizing sample size in experimentation used by Cohen (1988, p. 42) in developing statistical power computations:

$$\frac{2(N_1)(N_2)}{N_1 + N_2}. \tag{1}$$

For example, if there is a total of 500 subjects in a study, but 400 in one group and 100 in another, the weighted or standardized sample size (N) per group used in power (and significance) calculations is only 160, while the N for a two-group study equally divided between experimental and control groups is 250. Though the overall size of both studies is the same, the design of the latter is more powerful.

Often it is impossible to identify why the sizes of experimental and control groups are unequal.[14] We suspect that the reason is usually linked to randomization itself. Many studies randomly allocated subjects in ways that limited their control over the number of individuals

---

[14] It should be noted that four in ten of the studies reviewed did not describe how randomization was carried out.

TABLE 1

Statistical Power under Assumptions of Small, Moderate,
and Large Effect Size

Standardized Sample Size	N*	Assumed Effect Size		
		Small	Moderate	Large
15–50	12	.12	.49	.82
51–100	25	.26	.87	.99
101–200	21	.37	.98	.99
201–400	5	.60	.99	.99
Over 400	11	.91	.99	.99

*See note 25.

that fell in each group. For example, in the Sacramento Juvenile 601
Diversion Experiment (Baron, Feeney, and Thornton 1972, 1973), offenders were allocated to treatment and control groups based on randomly chosen days. Five of the experiments used a toss of a coin or a
die to randomly allocate subjects. In eighteen of the forty-four experiments that described randomization procedures, researchers reported
the use of random numbers tables. Though one might expect relatively
equal groups using this technique, this was not always true.

Table 1 illustrates the direct relationship between statistical power
and sample size. The experiments are divided into five categories based
on the standardized number of cases per group in each study: "15–50,"
"51–100," "101–200," "201–400," and "over 400." Across the table are
the average power coefficients for the experiments in each group given
assumptions of "small," "moderate," and "large" effects (see Cohen
1988).[15]

Looking at table 1 it is clear that there is substantial diversity in the
number of cases found in the samples examined by Weisburd, Sherman, and Petrosino (1990). For example, twelve of the studies include
fifty or fewer standardized cases per group, and eleven include more
than 400 standardized cases per group. As is to be expected, as the
average sample size gets larger, the power levels associated with each

[15] Cohen's estimates are commonly used, but like other conventions are fairly arbitrary. As he notes in his widely cited text on statistical power: "Although arbitrary, the
proposed conventions will be found to be reasonable by reasonable people. An effort
was made in selecting these operational criteria to use levels of ES (effect size) that
accord with a subjective average of effect sizes such as are encountered in behavioral
science" (1988, p. 13).

352   David Weisburd

TABLE 2

Statistical Power in Various Fields (under Assumptions of Small, Moderate, and Large Effect Size)

Field	Effect Size		
	Small	Moderate	Large
Criminal justice experiments in sanctions (Weisburd, Sherman, and Petrosino 1990)	.39	.86	.96
Gerontology (Levernson 1980)	.37	.88	.96
Social work (Orme and Combs-Orme 1986)	.35	.76	.91
Applied psychology research (Chase and Chase 1976)	.25	.67	.86
Abnormal and social psychology (Sedlmeier and Gigerenzer 1989)	.21	.50	.84
Education, general (Brewer and Owen 1973)	.28	.79	.91
Speech pathology (Kroll and Chase 1975)	.16	.44	.73

hypothesized effect size also increase. For the smallest experiments, a very large effect would be needed for the researcher to be confident of identifying a statistically significant outcome. For the very largest experiments, however, even a small effect in the population would be very likely (power > .90) to lead to a statistically significant finding.

The experiments overall do not support the notion that randomized criminal justice studies are designed for failure, at least in terms of the number of cases examined by investigators. On average, experiments we examine allow a very high likelihood of detecting a moderate effect and are almost certain to detect a large effect (see table 2). While the power level achieved for a small effect is less than .40, here criminal justice experiments in sanctions are not very much different from research in other social sciences. When we compare experiments in sanctions with other reviews of statistical power in other disciplines, we find that criminal justice experiments are, on average, using these standardized criteria, fairly powerful (see table 2). In most areas where power has been assessed, studies have not been designed for detection of small effects, and in this regard criminal justice experiments in sanctions are more powerful than research in areas such as social work, applied and abnormal psychology, education, and speech pathology.

When experimenters are unable to ensure the integrity of the randomization process, the power of experimental research is also affected. Breakdowns in randomization bring into question the computed significance levels reported by investigators. Such levels are dependent on certain assumptions, fair randomization being one of them. While slight violations of this assumption, like others, are unlikely to bias study results seriously, in a number of cases randomization break-downs were serious. For example, in the Denver Drunk Driving Sentencing Experiment (Ross and Blumenthal 1974, 1975), judges circumvented the randomization process in more than half the cases, mostly in response to defense attorney pleas to have their clients receive fines rather than the probation conditions. In sixteen of the studies reviewed by Weisburd, Sherman, and Petrosino (1990), randomization failures were reported by investigators.[16]

"Randomization overrides," where investigators allow practitioners to disregard randomization criteria because of institutional or public safety considerations, present similar problems, though when they are planned investigators can more carefully measure their influence on experimental results. For example, in the Minneapolis Domestic Violence Experiment (Sherman and Berk 1984*a*, 1984*b*, 1985; Berk and Sherman 1985, 1988), overrides were allowed if the offender attempted to assault the police, the victim demanded an arrest, a restraining order was violated, or offenders would not leave the premises when ordered to do so by the police. Though such overrides occurred in 18 percent of the cases, the investigators had carefully documented overrides and were able to analyze their occurrence and their influence on the experimental results. In eleven of the experiments, researchers reported that practitioners were allowed to override the randomization process.[17]

Treatment breakdowns have a direct impact on the statistical outcomes of experiments. When the investigator cannot ensure that a "treatment" or "control" condition has been administered, or that it has been administered in the dosage planned, the statistical power of a study is usually reduced.[18] This happens because the "effect" of an

---

[16] We suspect that such failures are underreported in published studies.

[17] A somewhat similar problem is evidenced in eight studies in which offenders were allowed to opt out of the less punitive sanction condition. For example, in the Ellsworth House Study (Lamb and Goertzel 1974*a*, 1974*b*), offenders could choose to remain in prison rather than be assigned to a halfway house. Breakdowns in assignment, like those reported in the Ellsworth House Experiment, were generally small because offenders were likely to want to take advantage of the more lenient randomized condition.

[18] Treatment integrity is usually discussed only in terms of the experimental condition. However, as noted earlier, most criminal justice studies compare alternative types of sanctions, and thus "control" groups may be better described as "comparison" groups. In such cases, there is also a "treatment" (often traditional criminal justice processing) that must be monitored and maintained. In the case of experiments with a more traditional "control" group, it is still the case that the experimenter must maintain the integrity of the "no sanction" condition.

experiment is directly related to the differences in treatment found between the experimental and control conditions. For example, in the California Special Intensive Parole Experiment (Reimer and Warren 1957), parole officers in the control group increased their contacts with parolees and thus simulated the treatments found in the experimental condition. Reimer and Warren (1957) offer this as one potential explanation for the small and insignificant differences found between the treatment and control groups studied in the second year of their study. Similarly, in the California Parole Research Project Experiment (Johnson 1962a, 1962b) control subjects often received more contact with their officers than did those in the experimental group, a factor that Johnson argues led to a finding of no difference between the experimental and control groups. In this case a nonexperimental reanalysis of the study showed that when supervision was classified by actual intensity (rather than experimental allocation), a strong relationship existed between parole success and increased contact (Johnson 1962b).

IV. Statistical Power and Sample Size: A Reevaluation of Common Assumptions

Sample size is generally viewed as the most straightforward method for affecting the power of experiments.[19] All else being equal, the power of a study grows with each increment in the number of cases included. This fact was illustrated in table 1, where we estimated the expected power of the Weisburd, Sherman, and Petrosino (1990) experiments under assumptions of small, moderate, and large "effects." If we assumed a small effect, the average power of the studies grew from .12 for those with fifty or fewer standardized cases per group to over .90 for those with over four hundred cases. While the expected design benefits of larger samples decrease as assumed effect size grows (see Lipsey 1990), we still found an average difference of .50 in estimated power for the largest and smallest experiments under assumptions of moderate effects and a .17 difference if large effects were assumed.

These results help explain why researchers concerned with statistical power try to gather as many cases for inclusion in their samples as possible. In criminological research, which often tackles very serious public policy problems that are very difficult to affect, the benefits of

---

[19] Though Lipsey argues that affecting change in "effect size" is more cost-effective (1990, p. 169).

larger samples are particularly attractive. For example, it might not be expected that a particular prison program would have a very large influence on subsequent violence by offenders. Nonetheless, even if a relatively small group were deterred from committing future murders or rapes, the benefits for the community would be great. It is precisely in such studies, where researchers seek to design a test sensitive to even relatively small changes, that sample size has its largest influence on statistical power.

But the benefits associated with larger samples are based on the assumption that there is little relationship between the number of cases in a study and the effect of treatments on the subjects examined.[20] If, for example, we assumed that the effect of a study declined the larger it became, the gain in statistical power associated with larger samples would be offset by the smaller effect coefficients found in such studies. Given the reliance on sample size as a means of increasing statistical power, we set out to examine this relationship directly.[21]

---

[20] It also assumes that there is little relationship between sample size and significance criteria on the type of statistical tests employed. But in the case of these characteristics of power, an assumption of no relationship is not troublesome. The size of a study does not alter the substance of significance criteria, nor does it influence the basic characteristics of a statistical test—except to the extent that it affects the choices made by researchers.

[21] This can be illustrated by turning to measures of statistical significance and their relationship to the standardized effect coefficients and sample size estimates used in statistical power. Generally, significance tests in experimental research are derived by taking the ratio of the size of the differences between an experimental and control group to the standard error associated with those differences:

$$\frac{\text{size of difference}}{\text{standard error}} \qquad (2)$$

The size of the difference between the two samples is simply the magnitude of the difference in the dependent measures employed (usually means or percentages). The standard error associated with these estimates, the denominator of the equation, is a function of the pooled standard deviation of the outcomes observed and the number of cases included in the study. Taking a commonly used test, the t-test, we can see why larger studies are more powerful than smaller ones:

$$t = \frac{\overline{X}_1 - \overline{X}_2}{\hat{\sigma}\sqrt{\dfrac{N_1 + N_2}{N_1 N_2}}} \qquad (3)$$

As the number of cases grows, the standard error (the denominator of the t-test) will get smaller. This leads to a larger test statistic and thus a higher likelihood of rejecting the null hypothesis and achieving a statistically significant finding. The t-test also illustrates why tests with larger "effects" are, all else being equal, more powerful. In power analysis, effect size is generally computed by taking the ratio of the difference between sample estimates to the standard deviation of those estimates (see Cohen 1988; Lipsey 1990). In eq. (3), effect size would be expressed as d (Cohen 1988, p. 20), which includes the ratio of the difference of means to the pooled within-group standard deviation of

356   David Weisburd

Our primary empirical problem was to develop estimates of effect
size for each of the experiments examined. We were aided in this
process by the fact that many of the experiments included only one
outcome measure, usually assessed at only one time period. Nonetheless, about six in ten of the studies reviewed included either multiple
outcome measures or multiple follow-up periods or both. Our problem
was to decide which of these estimates, or which combination of them,
to use for identifying the "observed" effect size for each particular study.

One solution used by others who have reviewed effect size across
studies (e.g., Chase and Chase 1976; Levernson 1980) is to take the
mean of all of the outcome measures included by investigators. This
solution has the benefit of not focusing on a "deviant" effect in a study.
Because we wanted some degree of consistency across the experiments
reviewed, we developed an "average effect size" (AES) measure by
taking the mean of all the effect coefficients at the follow-up period
closest to one year.[22] While "average effect size" provides one overall
view of the influence of the studies on their subjects, it does not take
into account that investigators often thought of their studies as tests
of a series of research hypotheses, often linked to different outcome
measures. In order to allow some sensitivity to this problem we developed an additional measure—maximum effect size (MES)—that provides an upper range of effect for the experiments.[23] "Maximum effect
size" identifies the largest effect evidenced in each study for the twelve-
month (or closest) follow-up period.[24]

Assessing effect size from these measures, our first conclusion relates
not to the relationship between sample size and effect size but to the
magnitude of the effects found in criminal justice experiments con-

---

those means (i.e., $\overline{X}_1 - \overline{X}_2/\hat{\sigma}$). As d grows in size—either through a growth in the
absolute difference in the means ($\overline{X}_1 - \overline{X}_2$) or a decline in the amount of variability of
the estimates ($\hat{\sigma}$)—the t-statistic gets larger, and rejection of the null hypothesis is more
likely. Returning to our earlier concern, if effect size were to get smaller as the number
of cases in a study increased, then the benefits of a larger sample might be offset.

[22] Thirty-six of the studies used a one-year follow-up period; most of the others had
a follow-up period somewhere between six and eighteen months. For experiments with
more than one outcome measure, we took the mean of the effect size for each outcome
measure. In experiments where the subjects were divided into more than two groups,
the effect size was calculated by taking the difference between each of the groups and
then calculating the mean of those differences.

[23] To calculate "maximum effect size" we also took the follow-up period closest to
twelve months for each experiment. For experiments with more than one outcome measure, we took the measure with the largest effect size. If an experiment had only one
outcome measure, the effect size for that measure was used.

[24] We also developed another measure that examines the largest standardized effect
size for any outcome measure at any follow-up period. The results using this measure
were similar to those reported in tables 3 and 4.

TABLE 3

Effect Size and Sample Size

Average				Maximum			
Effect Size	N	Percent	Mean Standard N	Effect Size	N	Percent	Mean Standard N
.00–.20	45	61	235	.00–0.20	37	50	253
.21–.40	20	27	118	.21–.40	22	30	136
.41–.60	3	4	37	.41–.60	5	7	56
.61–.80	5	7	51	.61–.80	9	12	66
.81–1.00	1	1	32	.81–1.00	1	1	32

cerned with sanctions (see table 3). Of the seventy-four studies in which effect size estimates could be computed, less than four in ten have standardized effects above .20 using our average effect size measure.[25] Even using the less conservative maximum effect size estimates, only half of the studies have effects of this magnitude. This means that most of the studies did not achieve what is generally defined as the threshold for a small effect (see Cohen 1988). Only one experiment evidences what Cohen describes as a large effect (a standardized effect coefficient above .80) using either measure of effect size.

Following these results, we might conclude that adjustments in sample size are likely to have a large yield in criminal justice studies. As we noted earlier, it is precisely in the case where the investigator desires to detect small effects that the influence of the number of cases on statistical power is greatest. But this conclusion does not seem to hold when we turn to the relationship between sample size and effect size. If we look at the standardized number of cases (per group) for studies that fall in each of the effect size categories reviewed in table 3, we can see that there is a generally inverse relationship between sample size and effect size.[26] Indeed, the mean number of cases per group for the studies with the largest effects (.61–1.00) is between one-quarter and one-fifth of that for the studies with the smallest effects (0–.20), whether we use the maximum or average effect size measures. Only in the case of the comparison between studies with effects of .41–.60 and .61–.80 does the number of standardized cases increase, and here the change is relatively small.

[25] In two of the seventy-six cases insufficient information was provided by investigators to develop effect size coefficients. These cases are also excluded from analyses presented in tables 1 and 2.

[26] In experiments with more than one outcome measure, the standardized N was calculated by taking the mean of the standardized N's for each outcome measure.

358   David Weisburd

TABLE 4

Average Effect Size and Statistical Power (by Sample Size)

Standardized Sample Size	N	Mean Effect	Mean Power*
15–50	12	.42	.46
51–100	25	.23	.29
101–200	21	.17	.33
201–400	5	.18	.45
Over 400	11	.08	.35

* Power estimates are derived by taking the mean power of all outcome measures examined.

What this means substantively is that estimates of statistical power arrived at by manipulating sample size, while assuming a constant effect size, are misleading. Although there is clearly a gain to be had from increasing the size of a sample, the negative relationship between sample size and effect size offsets, at least in part, the design benefits of increasing the number of cases studied.[27] How much of a loss is illustrated in table 4. Here we calculate the statistical power of the experiments based on average effect size coefficients evidenced in the samples studied.[28]

Quite surprisingly, given the general trend of using sample size as

[27] One anonymous reviewer suggested that this finding might result from investigators who "stop when they are winning." In other words, if a large and significant effect is achieved with a small number of subjects the investigator would stop the experiment and publish the results. If he or she gets a weak effect the experiment would be continued until the effect either is found to be significant or is viewed as unlikely to ever reach that threshold. Our own reading of the cases indicates that investigators usually define the randomization process at the outset of experiment and seldom analyze results early enough to substantively alter the basic design of a study. A second alternative explanation for these findings is that smaller studies are much less likely to be published if they do not achieve a significant result. While we cannot assess this speculation directly, we suspect that the rarity of experimental research in criminal justice leads to more unsuccessful studies being reported than is the case with nonexperimental designs. Among the larger studies this is particularly likely, and our basic finding holds for the largest sample size groupings. It is important to note that in some studies a finding of no difference (e.g., between prison and early release) would be taken by investigators as a program "success" since it indicates that a less expensive and less intrusive criminal justice intervention is as effective as the more punitive and costly sanction condition.

[28] While statistical power relates to the population characteristics of a study, we use these measures as a "best guess" of the true parameters under the assumptions made by investigators.

a method to increase statistical power, we do not find that larger studies have a power advantage. Indeed, the largest studies (those with more than 400 standardized cases per group) are less powerful under these assumptions than the smallest ones. They are also less powerful than studies with between 201 and 400 standardized cases and only marginally more powerful than those with 51–200 standardized cases per group. There is a slight increase in power between the second (51–100) and third (101–200) sample size categories and an increase in average power of .12 between the third and fourth (201–400) sample size groupings. However, the group that on average provides the most powerful investigations includes the smallest studies examined.

In the face of a result so at odds with conventional assumptions about statistical power, we were concerned that specific characteristics of our sample, rather than a more general process inherent to experimentation in criminal justice sanctions, might be responsible for our results. If, for example, a particular type of experimental research was more likely to include fewer subjects and such experiments were also more effective, this would explain in part our basic finding. Our efforts to examine this problem were hampered by the fact that the experiments varied so greatly. But we were able to look at the basic relationship between sample size and a series of specific characteristics that cut broadly across the studies. In the case of type of outcome measure (e.g., percent arrested or percent violating parole), type of investigator (practitioner vs. university researcher), type of sanction (e.g., parole or probation), and gender of subjects, we found little evidence that would lead us to challenge our conclusion that larger studies, regardless of their type, yielded generally smaller effects. However, we did find that the smallest studies were more likely to include only juvenile offenders or to involve treatments added onto conventional sanctions.[29]

Those experiments that were conducted primarily with juveniles are much more likely than others to fall into the smallest sample size categories (see table 5). Indeed, the larger the study, the less likely it is to involve primarily juvenile offenders. Nine of twelve of the studies including less than fifty standardized cases per group concentrated on

[29] We also found that studies with a six-month follow-up period or shorter were more likely to include fewer cases. We do not include this question in our discussion because the number of studies involved here is small (only eleven overall, with five in the fifteen to fifty sample size category) and makes a substantive analysis suspect. However, when we do examine the AES (average effect size) estimates across sample size categories for these eleven experiments, we find a similar pattern to that evidenced in our overall analysis.

360   David Weisburd

TABLE 5

Average Effect Size for Experiments
Including Only Juveniles

Standardized Sample Size	N	Mean Effect
15–50	9	.52
51–100	16	.22
101–200	7	.21
201–400	2	.28
Over 400	3	.09

these younger subjects. This was true for only three of the eleven studies in the largest sample-size grouping. Nonetheless, when we examine the relationship between sample size and effect size within the experiments including only juveniles, our results are generally consistent with the earlier findings (see table 5).

Experiments that involve treatments added onto conventional sanctions (e.g., coercive group counseling programs in a prison) accounted for less than one in three of the studies reviewed by Weisburd, Sherman, and Petrosino (1990). But they make up half of the experiments in the smallest sample grouping and none in the two largest categories. Accordingly, it might be argued that our basic finding reflects the relationship between sample size and experiment type. While it is the case that treatment experiments overall have larger effects than other experiments we reviewed, the relationship of sample size and effect size for treatment experiments follows the general pattern of our results (see table 6). There is a very large drop in effect size between the smallest studies and those with 51–200 standardized cases.

V. Why Larger Studies Are Not More Powerful

The simple assumption that statistical power can be increased merely by adding cases to a study is not supported by our data. The largest studies are not necessarily more powerful than smaller ones; indeed, using sample estimates as a guide, the very largest investigations are no more likely to lead to rejection of the null hypothesis than are the very smallest. This challenges conventional wisdom in experimental research (e.g., see Kolata 1990). Nonetheless, we believe this result is consistent with the experiences of those who have approached the very

TABLE 6

Average Effect Size for "Treatment"
Experiments

Standardized Sample Size	N	Mean Effect
15–50	6	.59
51–100	11	.19
101–200	4	.18
201–400	. . .	. . .
Over 400	. . .	. . .

difficult task of designing and implementing randomized experiments in the real world of criminal justice.

It is generally easier to keep track of 100 or 200 subjects than 800 or 1,000. Similarly, three or four administrators are easier to monitor than twenty-five or fifty. As the scale of experimental research grows, so do the difficulties of implementation and management. But, even when criminal justice researchers set out with an awareness of the potential problems that large field studies entail, they are often surprised by the special difficulties they encounter. For example, Joan Petersilia, in describing her experience as an evaluator of a large Bureau of Justice Assistance probation study, provides a good example of how even experienced researchers are likely to underestimate the complexities of large-scale experimental research:

> The author anticipated that monitoring a field experiment of these dimensions would require tremendous effort. However, the extra burdens imposed by high turnover and loss of motivation among the projects' staff and administrators was not anticipated. Nor did we realize how difficult it would be to get adequate data from the sites, which were responsible for collecting and forwarding the data to RAND. [Petersilia 1989, p. 452]

That larger studies are more difficult to monitor and control than smaller ones has two important implications for the statistical power of experimental research in sanctions. First, the management and monitoring problems associated with larger studies often lead to treatments being administered less effectively or less consistently than contem-

362   David Weisburd

plated. Second, the need to gather large numbers of cases for study often leads to a great deal of heterogeneity in the nature of the samples studied. Because these characteristics of larger studies influence the magnitude of differences between groups in an experiment (the numerator of the effect size coefficient) and the variability of those differences (the denominator of effect size), they also influence the statistical power of experimental studies.

Problems in administering treatments in larger studies are illustrated in a number of the experiments we examined. In some cases, treatment failures result from the difficulty of keeping track of a very large number of subjects. For example, in the California Reduced Prison Experiment (Berecochea, Jaman, and Jones 1973; Berecochea and Jaman 1981), which included more than one thousand inmates, the experimental subjects, who were supposed to serve longer prison terms, sometimes served less prison time than the control group. But the difficulties in managing large numbers of criminal justice practitioners also led to treatments not being administered in the dosages proposed by experimenters. In the Vera Institute Pretrial Adult Felony Offender Diversion Experiment (Baker and Sadd 1979, 1981; Baker and Rodriguez 1979), for example, almost 40 percent of the diversion group (N = 410) never received the experimental treatment.[30]

These cases illustrate how an inability to ensure the implementation of treatments can have an impact on the outcomes of experiments by minimizing the differences between the experiences of treatment and control group members. But breakdowns in treatment integrity may also affect the variability of outcome measures. In the Memphis Juvenile Diversion Experiment, for example, the principal investigators note that the 785 youths in the experimental group received somewhere between 11 percent and 140 percent of their projected treatments

---

[30] We believe that treatment failures are more likely to occur in larger studies, and, when they do occur, are likely to be more serious. Nonetheless, using evidence of any treatment breakdowns as described by investigators, we do not find a clear linear relationship between sample size and treatment failure. There is comparatively little difference between the smallest studies and the sample groupings ranging up to 400 standardized cases per group. Among studies that fall into these categories, treatment failures noted by investigators average between 15 and 20 percent. The largest studies have a somewhat higher rate of failure, about a third, though the absolute difference here in the number of cases that have treatment failures (as contrasted with the smallest studies) is not large. These results reflect not only difficulties in administering treatment but also the attention paid by investigators to reporting such failures. We suspect it is likely that the greater attention given to detail in the smaller studies also led to more careful identification and reporting of problems encountered.

(Whitaker and Severy 1984). Because different offenders received different treatments, we would expect that the overall effects of the study would vary tremendously from subject to subject. While heterogeneity in the administration of treatment is common in both large and small experiments, our readings of the cases suggest that such variability is likely to be much greater in larger studies.

Variability is also increased by the heterogeneity of subjects studied in larger experiments. In planning such investigations it is often necessary to establish very broad eligibility requirements in order to gain the number of cases that investigators desire. For example, in the California Special Intensive Parole Experiment (Reimer and Warren 1957) described earlier, some 80 percent of the prison population qualified for inclusion in the study.[31]

Many times investigators in larger studies are forced to relax eligibility requirements once the project is ongoing. In the English Intensive Probation Experiments (Folkard et al. 1974; Folkard, Smith, and Smith 1976), for example, the original design, which called for high-risk male probationers, was changed when researchers saw that they were unable to fulfill project quotas. In the RAND study described by Petersilia, overestimation of the number of eligible offenders also led the sites involved to relax eligibility requirements in the midst of the experiment. Indeed, Petersilia argues that it eventually became "unclear who was participating" (1989, p. 450).

The effects of this heterogeneity in the subjects examined on the statistical power of experiments is illustrated in two studies that analyzed subgroups of offenders separately after the original project design had failed to yield significant results. The Police Foundation Shoplifting Arrest Experiment (Williams, Forst, and Hamilton 1987) examined shoplifters six years of age and older. Looking at the entire sample, no significant deterrent effects of arrest were noted. But when subjects were categorized into those under seventeen years of age, and those seventeen years of age and older, significant results were found for the juvenile group. In the Memphis Juvenile Diversion Experiment (Severy and Whitaker 1982, 1984; Whitaker and Severy 1984; Whitaker, Severy, and Morton 1984), investigators also found no significant differences when the entire sample was examined. But within

[31] Interestingly, even though the eligibility requirements were so broad, in the second phase of this project it was necessary to include subjects who were not eligible in the first phase.

the experimental group those youths needing social adjustment or education assistance were more likely to have a successful experience when
compared to those needing family or individual counseling.

Though in both these cases the statistical design of the experiments
was violated by a post facto division of the experimental and control
groups, they follow a developing consensus among criminologists that
different types of offenders will respond differently to different types
of sanctions (see Farrington, Ohlin, and Wilson 1986). Where an experiment includes a heterogeneous population, effects of sanctions on one
subgroup of offenders may be hidden by a different effect on another,
as appears to be the case, for example, in the Police Foundation Shoplifting Arrest Experiment. Where there is less systematic variation in
the study, but still great diversity in the types of subjects included,
the variability of the estimates gained will grow, again leading to a
smaller effect coefficient and thus a less powerful study.

Our observations on the relationship between sample size and problems of implementing and monitoring experimental research are based
on a relatively small group of studies. Nonetheless, they are consistent
with findings that develop out of a very large review of correctional
treatment programs conducted by Lipton, Martinson, and Wilks
(1975). Although they did not look specifically at the relationship between sample size and the quality of the 231 studies they examined,
they did rate the studies in terms of the strength of the overall research
design and the success of investigators in carrying out the studies.[32] In
a reanalysis of these data, Palmer found "a strong inverse relationship
between both quality and strength [of the studies], on the one hand,
and sample size, on the other" (1978, p. 160). Among the better designed and implemented studies ("A" studies), the average sample size
was 459. Among lower-quality studies ("B" studies), the average sam-

---

[32] Studies were selected for inclusion in the survey on the basis of the following
criteria: the study must represent an evaluation of a treatment method applied to criminal
offenders; it must have been completed after January 1, 1945; it must include empirical
data resulting from comparison of treatment and control groups; and these data must
be measures of improvement in performance on some relevant dependent variables.
Studies specifically excluded were after-only studies without comparison groups, prediction studies, studies that only describe and subjectively evaluate treatment programs,
and clinical speculations about feasible treatment methods. Following assessment by a
professional researcher, each study was reviewed by a committee and allocated to one
of three categories: "A" studies, acceptable for the survey with no more than minimal
research shortcomings; "B" studies, acceptable for the survey with research shortcomings
that place reservations on interpretation of the findings; and "Other Studies." Under
"Other Studies" were reports and articles excluded because two or more of a possible
eleven conditions existed. See Lipton, Martinson, and Wilks (1975, pp. 6–7) for a list
of these conditions.

ple size was 900. While Palmer relegated these findings to an appendix, they suggest to us that our observations concerning the difficulties of developing and managing larger studies are not limited to our sample of criminal justice experiments in sanctions.

VI. Implications and Conclusions

Our examination of the statistical power of experiments in sanctions leads to an ironic conclusion about the relationship between experimental design and study outcomes. Had more attention been paid to statistical power in developing sanctioning studies in criminal justice, the power of the studies themselves would probably not have increased significantly. The naive assumption behind much power analysis, that sample size is unrelated to effect size, is not consistent with our findings. Investigators of larger studies are likely to encounter more serious problems in implementing treatments than smaller studies. They are often forced as well to draw more heterogeneous samples. Both these factors influence the outcomes of experiments, and thus the power advantages of larger samples are often offset.

Our results suggest that larger studies are not to be preferred over smaller investigations. Nonetheless, there are significant difficulties in generalizing from small and restricted samples, and the design advantages they seem to offer do not offset the power disadvantages inherent to studies of such a small size. Using sample estimates as a guide, we found that the very smallest studies examined were more powerful than the very largest. Yet such studies did not offer even an equal chance of finding a statistically significant difference between treatment and control groups. Just as the small effects of large investigations offset the advantages of increasing the number of cases examined, the small samples in smaller investigations offset the advantages gained from larger effects. The task accordingly is to focus not on smaller studies but rather on strategies that will allow researchers to increase sample size while maintaining the integrity of treatments and minimizing variability.

Petersilia (1989) provides one lesson in this regard from the RAND Intensive Supervision Demonstration Project. Experimenters cannot allow practitioners to control the implementation of important aspects of study design, even though this is often one way of conserving much-needed research funds. As is the case for many other large-scale investigations, economic and practical constraints forced RAND to rely on practitioners to carry out many research tasks that would have been

366   David Weisburd

more directly controlled by researchers had the investigation been smaller. For RAND these decisions did not turn out to be cost-effective in the long run. They created both greater variability in treatments and in the pool of offenders examined than had been proposed in the original project design (Petersilia and Turner 1990; Turner 1991). More generally, the RAND experience illustrates the importance of maintaining researcher control over each stage of an experiment's design and implementation.

One example of a method for monitoring the implementation of treatments when they are controlled by practitioners is provided by the Minneapolis Hot Spots Patrol Experiment (Sherman and Weisburd 1992). Sherman and Weisburd randomly allocated increased police patrol to fifty-five of 110 high-crime locations, called "hot spots." While the number of cases in that study was relatively small, the number of practitioners involved was very large. Indeed, the entire patrol force in Minneapolis was used in increasing the patrol dosage in the experimental locations. In trying to avoid a problem encountered in the earlier Kansas City Preventive Patrol Experiment (Kelling et al. 1974), in which there was some doubt as to whether the treatments were successfully administered, Sherman and Weisburd conducted 6,500 hours of random observations of the experimental and control sites. While the observations were intended primarily as a means of documenting dosage, they also were seen by investigators as a method for keeping practitioners "honest."

Variability in the larger studies we examined often developed from overestimation of the number of cases that fit the original eligibility requirements of investigators. This problem has become widely recognized in recent experimental research (see Petersilia 1989) and has led a number of investigators to conduct what have been termed "case flow" studies. In the National Institute of Justice's Domestic Violence Replication Program, for example, researchers in each of the five sites involved in the program conducted a careful analysis before the study began of the potential universe of cases available for randomization (Uchida 1991). This process allowed investigators to avoid midstream changes in eligibility requirements. More generally, case flow studies provide an effective method for preventing the "watering down" of the experimental pool in order to achieve quotas set in the original research design.

Even when following the original project design, investigators often include a great deal of diversity in the types of subjects examined. As we observed earlier, larger studies are likely to be more variable than smaller ones, which explains in part the reduction in effect size that is found in the largest investigations. Statisticians offer one solution to this problem—randomization within blocks (e.g., see Lipsey 1990)—that has generally been ignored by criminal justice researchers. Block designs, which randomly allocate subjects within groups, minimize the effects of variability in an experiment by making sure that like subjects will be compared one to another. A commonly used method randomly allocates subjects within pairs, for example by random allocation of twins in psychological studies. While randomization of matched pairs is unlikely to be practical in criminological field experiments, blocking within larger groups does provide an effective method for minimizing the effects of variability in a study. Sherman and Weisburd (1989), for example, randomly allocated police patrol within five independent blocks based on prior crime activity. While blocking demands more complex statistical analyses than traditional experimental designs, it provides a relatively inexpensive method for dealing with the diversity of subjects found in most large studies.

These examples provide some evidence of recent attempts to manage the design difficulties that are likely to be encountered in large experiments. But such efforts have not been joined systematically, nor linked directly to the issues we have raised. The nature of the problems criminal justice researchers examine demand that they design for relatively large studies. Our findings suggest that there will be few gains from increasing sample size until the design difficulties that larger samples pose are directly addressed. For the future, this demands much greater attention to problems of method and design in experimentation than has been evident to date. For the present, it suggests that commonly used approximations of statistical power that do not take into account the relationship between sample size and effect size provide a very misleading view of the design advantages of larger studies.

APPENDIX

Studies Selected by Weisburd, Sherman, and Petrosino (1990)

Name of Experiment	Source of Experiment
California Crofton House Experiment	Kirby 1969
California Early Parole Discharge Experiment	Jackson 1978, 1983

368   David Weisburd

California Ellsworth House Experiment	Lamb and Goertzel 1974*a*, 1974*b*
California Fremont Program Experiment	Seckel 1967
California Group Counseling Prison Experiment	Kassebaum, Ward, and Wilner 1971
California Juvenile Behavior Modification and Transactional Analysis Experiment	Jesness, DeRisi, McCormick, and Wedge 1972; Jesness 1975
California Juvenile CTP Phase I Experiment—Sacramento/Stockton	Stark 1963; Warren 1967; Palmer 1971, 1974
California Juvenile CTP Phase I Experiment—San Francisco	Stark 1963; Warren 1967; Palmer 1971, 1974
California Juvenile Probation and Group Counseling Experiment	Adams 1965
California Parole Research Project Experiment	Johnson 1962*a*, 1962*b*
California Parole Work Unit Experiment	Burkhart 1969
California Paso Robles Experiment	Seckel 1965
California Pico Experiment	Adams 1970
California Preston School Typology Experiment	Jesness 1971*b*
California Reduced Prison Sentence Experiment	Berecochea, Jaman, and Jones 1973; Berecochea and Jaman 1981
California Short-Term Psychiatric Treatment Experiment—Preston	Guttman 1963
California Short-Term Psychiatric Treatment Experiment—Nelles	Guttman 1963
California Special Intensive Parole Experiment: Phase I	Reimer and Warren 1957
California Special Intensive Parole Experiment: Phase II	Reimer and Warren 1958
California Summary Parole Experiment	Star 1978
California Unofficial Probation Experiment	Venezia 1972
California Youth Training Center Experiment	Seckel 1965
Canadian I-Level Maturity Probation Experiment	Barkwell 1976
Clark County (Washington) Status Offender Deinstitutionalization Experiment	Schneider 1980

Design Sensitivity 369

Copenhagen Short-Term Offender Experiment	Berntsen and Christiansen 1965
Denver Drunk Driving Sentencing Experiment	Ross and Blumenthal 1974, 1975
English Borstal Allocation Experiment	Williams 1970, 1975
English Intensive Probation Experiment—Sheffield	Folkard, Fowles, McWilliams, Smith, Smith, and Walmsley 1974; Folkard, Smith, and Smith 1976
English Intensive Probation Experiment—Dorset	Folkard, Fowles, McWilliams, Smith, Smith, and Walmsley 1974; Folkard, Smith, and Smith 1976
English Intensive Probation Experiment—London	Folkard, Fowles, McWilliams, Smith, Smith, and Walmsley 1974; Folkard, Smith, and Smith 1976
English Intensive Probation Experiment—Staffordshire	Folkard, Fowles, McWilliams, Smith, Smith, and Walmsley 1974; Folkard, Smith, and Smith 1976
English Intensive Welfare Experiment	Fowles 1978
English Juvenile Therapeutic Community Experiment	Clarke and Cornish 1972; Cornish and Clarke 1975; Cornish 1987
English Police Cautioning Experiment	Rose and Hamilton 1970
English Prison Intensive Social Work Experiment	Shaw 1974
English Psychopathic Delinquent Experiment	Craft, Stephenson, and Granger 1964
Fairfield School for Boys Experiment	Persons 1966, 1967
Florida Inmate Work Release Experiment	Waldo and Chiricos 1977
Florida Project Crest Experiment	Lee and Haynes 1978, 1980
Fricot Ranch Delinquent Dormitory Experiment	Jesness 1965, 1971a
Hamilton (Canada) Juvenile Services Project Experiment	Byles and Maurice 1979
Illinois Juvenile Tours Experiment	Greater Egypt Regional Planning and Development Commission 1979
Illinois Volunteer Lawyer Parole Supervision Experiment	Berman 1975, 1978

370   David Weisburd

Juvenile Diversion and Labeling Paradigm Experiment	Klein 1986; Lincoln, Klein, Teilmann, and Labin (n.d.)
Kentucky Village Psychotherapy Experiment	Truax, Wargo, and Silber 1966
Leeds (United Kingdom) Truancy Experiment	Berg, Consterdine, Hullin, McGuire, and Tyrer 1978; Berg, Hullin, McGuire, and Tyrer 1978; Berg, Hullin, and McGuire 1979
Los Angeles Community Delinquency Control Project Experiment	Pond 1970
Los Angeles Silverlake Experiment	Empey and Lubeck 1971
Memphis Drunk Driving Sanctioning Experiments—Social Drinkers	Holden, Stewart, Rice, and Manker 1981; Holden 1982, 1983
Memphis Drunk Driving Sanctioning Experiments—Problem Drinkers	Holden, Stewart, Rice, and Manker 1981; Holden 1982, 1983
Memphis Juvenile Diversion Experiment	Severy and Whitaker 1982, 1984; Whitaker and Severy 1984; Whitaker, Severy, and Morton 1984
Michigan Juvenile Offenders Learn Truth (JOLT) Experiment	Yarborough 1979
Minneapolis Domestic Violence Experiment	Sherman and Berk 1984*a*, 1984*b*, 1985; Berk and Sherman 1985, 1988
Minneapolis Informal Parole Experiment	Hudson 1973; Hudson and Hollister 1976
National Restitution Experiment— Boise	Schneider and Schneider 1983; Schneider 1986
National Restitution Experiment— Washington, D.C.	Schneider and Schneider 1983; Schneider 1986
National Restitution Experiment— Clayton County, Georgia	Schneider and Schneider 1983; Schneider 1986
National Restitution Experiment— Oklahoma County, Oklahoma	Schneider and Schneider 1983; Schneider 1986

Design Sensitivity   371

New Jersey Juvenile Awareness Program (Scared Straight) Experiment	Finckenauer 1982
North Carolina Butner Correctional Facility Experiment	Love, Allgood, and Samples 1986
Ohio Juvenile Probationer Behavior Modification Experiment	Ostrom, Steele, Rosenblood, and Mirels 1971
Ontario (Canada) Social Interaction Training Experiment	Shivrattan 1988
Pinellas County (Florida) Juvenile Services Program Experiment	Quay and Love 1977
Police Foundation Shoplifting Arrest Experiment	Glick, Hamilton, and Forst 1986; Sherman and Gartin 1986; Williams, Forst, and Hamilton 1987
Ramsey County (Minnesota) Community Assistance Program Experiment	Owen and Mattessich 1987
Sacramento (California) Juvenile 601 Diversion Experiment	Baron, Feeney, and Thornton 1972, 1973
Sacramento (California) Juvenile 602 Diversion Experiment	Baron and Feeney 1976
San Diego (California) Chronic Drunk Offender Experiment	Ditman, Crawford, Forgy, Moskowitz, and Macandrew 1967
San Fernando (California) Juvenile Crisis Intervention Experiment	Stratton 1975
San Pablo (California) Adult Diversion Experiment	Austin 1980
San Quentin (California) Squires Program Experiment	Lewis 1979, 1981, 1983
Tacoma Juvenile Inmate Modeling and Group Discussion Experiment	Sarason and Ganzer 1973; Sarason 1978
Utah Provo Experiment	Empey and Rabow 1961; Empey and Erickson 1972
Vera Institute (New York) Pretrial Adult Felony Offender Diversion Experiment	Baker and Rodriguez 1979; Baker and Sadd 1979, 1981
Washington, D.C., Pretrial Supervision Experiment	Welsh 1978
Wayne County (Michigan) Project Start Experiment	Lichtman and Smock 1981

372   David Weisburd

REFERENCES

Adams, S. 1965: "An Experimental Assessment of Group Counseling with Juvenile Probationers." *Journal of the California Probation, Parole and Correctional Association* 2:19–25.

———. 1970. "The Pico Project." In *The Sociology of Punishment and Correction*, edited by N. B. Johnston, L. Savitz, and M. E. Wolfgang. New York: Wiley.

Annis, H. M. 1979. "Group Treatment of Incarcerated Offenders with Alcohol and Drug Problems: A Controlled Evaluation." *Canadian Journal of Criminology* 21:3–15.

Ares, C. E., A. Rankin, and H. Sturz. 1963. "The Manhattan Bail Project: An Interim Report on the Use of Pre-trial Parole." *New York University Law Review* 38:67–93.

Austin, J. F. 1980. "Instead of Justice: Diversion." Doctoral dissertation, University of California, Department of Sociology. Ann Arbor, Mich.: University Microfilms International.

Baker, S. H., and O. Rodriguez. 1979. "Random Time Quota Selection: An Alternative to Random Selection in Experimental Evaluation." In *Evaluation Studies Review Annual*, vol. 4, edited by L. Sechrest. Beverly Hills, Calif.: Sage.

Baker, S. H., and S. Sadd. 1979. *Court Employment Project: Evaluation.* Final report. New York: Vera Institute of Justice.

———. 1981. *Diversion of Felony Arrests; An Experiment in Pretrial Intervention: Evaluation of the Court Employment Project.* Summary report. Washington, D.C.: National Institute of Justice.

Barkwell, L. J. 1976. "Differential Treatment of Juveniles on Probation: An Evaluative Study." *Canadian Journal of Criminology and Corrections* 18:363–78.

Baron, R., and F. Feeney. 1976. *Juvenile Diversion through Family Counseling: A Program for the Diversion of Status Offenders in Sacramento County, California.* Washington, D.C.: National Institute of Law Enforcement and Criminal Justice.

Baron, R., F. Feeney, and W. E. Thornton. 1972. *Preventing Delinquency through Diversion: The Sacramento County Probation Department 601 Diversion Project, A First Year Report.* Sacramento, Calif.: Sacramento County Probation Department.

———. 1973. "Preventing Delinquency through Diversion." *Federal Probation* 37:13–18.

Berecochea, J. E., and D. R. Jaman. 1981. *Time Served in Prison and Parole Outcome: An Experimental Study.* Report no. 2. Sacramento: California Department of Corrections Research Division.

Berecochea, J. E., D. R. Jaman, and W. A. Jones. 1973. *Time Served in Prison and Parole Outcome: An Experimental Study.* Report no. 1. Sacramento: California Department of Corrections Research Division.

Berg, I., M. Consterdine, R. Hullin, R. McGuire, and S. Tyrer. 1978. "The Effect of Two Randomly Allocated Court Procedures on Truancy." *British Journal of Criminology* 18:232–44.

Berg, I., R. Hullin, and R. McGuire. 1979. "A Randomly Controlled Trial of Two Court Procedures in Truancy." In *Psychology, Law and Legal Processes*, edited by D. P. Farrington, K. Hawkins, and S. M. Lloyd-Bostock. Atlantic Highlands, N.J.: Humanities Press.

Berg, I., R. Hullin, R. McGuire, and S. Tyrer. 1978. "Truancy and the Courts: Research Note." *Journal of Child Psychiatry and Psychology* 18:359–65.

Berk, R. A., K. J. Lenihan, and P. H. Rossi. 1980. "Crime and Poverty: Some Experimental Evidence from Ex-offenders." *American Sociological Review* 45:766–86.

Berk, R. A., and L. W. Sherman. 1985. "Data Collection Strategies in the Minneapolis Domestic Assault Experiment." In *Collecting Evaluation Data: Problems and Solutions*, edited by L. Burstein, H. E. Freeman, and P. H. Rossi. Beverly Hills, Calif.: Sage.

————. 1988. "Police Responses to Family Violence Incidents: An Analysis of an Experimental Design with Incomplete Randomization." *Journal of the American Statistical Association* 83:70–76.

Berman, J. J. 1975. "The Volunteer in Parole Program." *Criminology* 13:111–13.

————. 1978. "An Experiment in Parole Supervision." *Evaluation Quarterly* 2:71–90.

Berntsen, K., and K. O. Christiansen. 1965. "A Resocialization Experiment with Short-Term Offenders." In *Scandinavian Studies in Criminology*, vol. 1, edited by K. O. Christiansen. London: Tavistock.

Brewer, J. K., and P. W. Owen. 1973. "A Note on the Power of Statistical Tests." *Journal of Educational Measurement* 10:71–74.

Brown, S. E. 1989. "Statistical Power and Criminal Justice Research." *Journal of Criminal Justice* 17:115–22.

Burkhart, W. 1969. "The Parole Work Unit Programme: An Evaluation." *British Journal of Criminology* 9:125–47.

Byles, J. A., and A. Maurice. 1979. "The Juvenile Services Project: An Experiment in Delinquency Control." *Canadian Journal of Criminology* 21:155–65.

Chase, L. J., and R. B. Chase. 1976. "A Statistical Power Analysis of Applied Psychological Research." *Journal of Applied Psychology* 61:234–37.

Clarke, R. V. G., and D. B. Cornish. 1972. *The Controlled Trial in Institutional Research—Paradigm or Pitfall for Penal Evaluators?* London: H.M. Stationery Office.

Cohen, J. 1973. "Statistical Power Analysis and Research Results." *American Educational Research Journal* 10:225–30.

————. 1988. *Statistical Power Analysis for the Behavioral Sciences*, 2d ed. Hillsdale, N.J.: Erlbaum.

Coleman, D. 1989. "Charge Dropped on Bogus Work." *New York Times* (April 4).

Cornish, D. B. 1987. "Evaluating Residential Treatments for Delinquents: A Cautionary Tale." In *Social Intervention: Potential and Constraints*, edited by K. Hurrelmann, F. Kaufmann, and F. Losel. Berlin: de Gruyter.

374   David Weisburd

Cornish, D. B., and R. V. G. Clarke. 1975. *Residential Treatment and Its Effects on Delinquency*. London: H.M. Stationery Office.

Craft, M., G. Stephenson, and C. Granger. 1964. "A Controlled Trial of Authoritarian and Self-governing Regimes with Adolescent Psychopaths." *American Journal of Orthopsychiatry* 34:543–54.

Dennis, M. L. 1988. "Implementing Randomized Field Experiments: An Analysis of Criminal and Civil Justice Research." Doctoral dissertation, Northwestern University, Department of Psychology.

Ditman, K. S., G. G. Crawford, E. W. Forgy, H. Moskowitz, and C. Macandrew. 1967. "A Controlled Experiment on the Use of Court Probation for Drunk Arrests." *American Journal of Orthopsychiatry* 124:160–63.

Empey, L. T., and M. L. Erickson. 1972. *The Provo Experiment*. Lexington, Mass.: Heath.

Empey, L. T., and S. G. Lubeck. 1971. *The Silverlake Experiment*. Chicago: Aldine.

Empey, L. T., and J. Rabow. 1961. "The Provo Experiment in Delinquency Rehabilitation." *American Sociological Review* 26:679–96.

Farrington, D. P. 1983. "Randomized Experiments on Crime and Justice." In *Crime and Justice: An Annual Review of Research*, vol. 4, edited by M. Tonry and N. Morris. Chicago: University of Chicago Press.

Farrington, D. P., L. E. Ohlin, and J. Q. Wilson. 1986. *Understanding and Controlling Crime*. New York: Springer-Verlag.

Feinberg, S., K. Larntz, and A. J. Reiss, Jr. 1976. "Redesigning the Kansas City Preventive Patrol Experiment." *Evaluation* 3:124–31.

Finckenauer, J. O. 1982. *Scared Straight*. Englewood Cliffs, N.J.: Prentice-Hall.

Folkard, M. S., A. J. Fowles, B. C. McWilliams, D. D. Smith, D. E. Smith, and G. R. Walmsley. 1974. *IMPACT: Intensive Matched Probation and After-Care Treatment*. Vol. 1, *The Design of the Probation Experiment and an Interim Evaluation*. London: H.M. Stationery Office.

Folkard, M. S., D. E. Smith, and D. D. Smith. 1976. *IMPACT: Intensive Matched Probation and After-Care Treatment*. Vol. 2, *The Results of the Experiment*. London: H.M. Stationery Office.

Fowles, A. J. 1978. *Prison Welfare*. London: H.M. Stationery Office.

Garner, J., and C. A. Visher. 1988. "Experiments Help Shape New Policies." *NIJ Reports*, no. 211 (September/October).

Gelber, R. D., and M. Zelen. 1985. "Planning and Reporting Clinical Trials." In *Basic Principles and Clinical Management of Cancer*, edited by P. Calabrese, P. S. Schein, and S. A. Rosenberg. New York: Macmillan.

Glick, B., E. Hamilton, and B. Forst. 1986. "Shoplifting: An Experiment in Lesser Crimes and Punishments." Draft final report. Washington, D.C.: Police Foundation.

Greater Egypt Regional Planning and Development Commission. 1979. *Menard Correctional Center Juvenile Tours Impact Study*. Carbondale, Ill.: Greater Egypt Regional Planning and Development Commission.

Guttman, E. 1963. "Effects of Short-Term Psychiatric Treatment on Boys in Two California Youth Authority Institutions." Research Report no. 36. Sacramento: California Youth Authority.

Hays, W. L. 1981. *Statistics.* 3d ed. New York: Holt, Rinehart & Winston.

Holden, R. T. 1982. "Legal Reactions to Drunk Driving." Doctoral Dissertation, Vanderbilt University, Department of Sociology. Ann Arbor, Mich.: University Microfilms International.

———. 1983. "Rehabilitative Sanctions for Drunk Driving: An Experimental Evaluation." *Journal of Research in Crime and Delinquency* 20:55–72.

Holden, R. T., L. T. Stewart, J. N. Rice, and E. Manker. 1981. *Tennessee DUI Probation Follow-up Demonstration Project.* Final report. Springfield, Va.: Department of Transportation.

Hudson, C. H. 1973. *An Experimental Study of the Differential Effects of Parole Supervision for a Group of Adolescent Boys and Girls.* Summary report. Minneapolis: Minnesota Department of Corrections.

Hudson, J., and C. D. Hollister. 1976. "An Experimental Study of Parole Supervision of Juveniles and Social Service Utilization." *Iowa Journal of Social Work* 4:80–89.

Jackson, P. C. 1978. *The Bay Area Parole Study.* Sacramento: California Youth Authority.

———. 1983. "Some Effects of Parole Supervision on Recidivism." *British Journal of Criminology* 23:17–34.

Jesness, C. F. 1965. *The Fricot Ranch Study.* Sacramento: California Youth Authority.

———. 1971a. "Comparative Effectiveness of Two Institutional Treatment Programs for Delinquents." *Child Care Quarterly* 1:119–30.

———. 1971b. "The Preston Typology Study." *Journal of Research in Crime and Delinquency* 8:38–52.

———. 1975. "Comparative Effectiveness of Behavior Modification Transactional Analysis Programs for Delinquents." *Journal of Consulting and Clinical Psychology* 43:758–79.

Jesness, C. F., W. J. DeRisi, P. M. McCormick, and R. F. Wedge. 1972. *The Youth Center Research Project.* Sacramento: California Youth Authority.

Johnson, B. M. 1962a. *Parole Performance of the First Year's Releases: Parole Research Project: Evaluation of Reduced Caseloads.* Research Report no. 27. Sacramento: California Youth Authority.

———. 1962b. *An Analysis of Predictions of Parole Performance and of Judgments of Supervision in the Parole Research Project.* Research Report no. 32. Sacramento: California Youth Authority.

Kassebaum, G., D. Ward, and D. Wilner. 1971. *Prison Treatment and Parole Survival.* New York: Wiley.

Kelling, G. L., T. Pate, D. Dieckman, and C. E. Brown. 1974. *The Kansas City Patrol Experiment: A Technical Report.* Washington, D.C.: Police Foundation.

Kirby, B. C. 1969. "Crofton House: An Experiment with a County Halfway House." *Federal Probation* 33:53–58.

Klein, M. W. 1986. "Labeling Theory and Delinquency Policy: An Experimental Test." *Criminal Justice and Behavior* 13:47–79.

Kolata, G. 1990. "In Clinical Trials, Some Contend, Big is Beautiful." *New York Times* (April 15).

Kraemer, H. C., and S. Thiemann. 1987. *How Many Subjects? Statistical Power Analysis in Research.* Newbury Park, Calif.: Sage.

376   David Weisburd

Kroll, R. M., and L. J. Chase. 1975. "Community Disorders: A Power Analytic Assessment of Recent Research." *Journal of Communication Disorders* 8:237–47.

Lamb, H. R., and V. Goertzel. 1974*a*. "Ellsworth House: A Community Alternative to Jail." *American Journal of Psychiatry* 131:64–68.

———. 1974*b*. "A Community Alternative to County Jail: The Hopes and the Realities." *Federal Probation* 38:33–39.

Lee, R., and N. M. Haynes. 1978. "Counseling Juvenile Offenders: An Experimental Evaluation of Project Crest." *Community Mental Health Journal* 14:267–71.

———. 1980. "Project Crest and the Dual-Treatment Approach to Delinquency: Methods and Research Summarized." In *Effective Correctional Treatment*, edited by R. R. Ross and P. Gendreau. Toronto: Butterworths.

Levernson, R. L., Jr. 1980. "Statistical Power Analysis: Implications for Researchers, Planners and Practitioners in Gerontology." *Gerontologist* 20:494–98.

Lewis, R. V. 1979. *The Squires of San Quentin: Preliminary Findings on an Experimental Study of Juvenile Visitation at San Quentin Prison*. Sacramento: California Youth Authority, Division of Research.

———. 1981. *The Squires of San Quentin: An Evaluation of a Juvenile Awareness Program*. Sacramento: California Youth Authority, Division of Research.

———. 1983. "Scared Straight—California Style." *Criminal Justice and Behavior* 10:209–26.

Lichtman, G. M., and S. M. Smock. 1981. "The Effects of Social Services on Probational Recidivism." *Journal of Research in Crime and Delinquency* 18:81–100.

Lincoln, C. M., M. W. Klein, K. S. Teilmann, and S. Labin. N.d. "Control Organizations and Labeling Theory: Official versus Self-reported Delinquency." Unpublished manuscript. Los Angeles: University of Southern California.

Lipsey, M. W. 1990. *Design Sensitivity: Statistical Power for Experimental Research*. Newbury, Calif.: Sage.

Lipton, D., R. Martinson, and J. Wilks. 1975. *The Effectiveness of Correctional Treatment*. New York: Praeger.

Love, C. T., J. G. Allgood, and F. P. S. Samples. 1986. "The Butner Research Projects." *Federal Probation* 50:32–39.

Orme, J. G., and T. D. Combs-Orme. 1986. "Statistical Power and Type II Errors in Social Work." *Social Research and Abstracts* 22:3–10.

Orme, J. G., and R. M. Tolman. 1986. "The Statistical Power of a Decade of Social Work Education Research." *Social Service Review* 60:619–32.

Ostrom, T. M., C. M. Steele, L. K. Rosenblood, and H. L. Mirels. 1971. "Modification of Delinquent Behavior." *Journal of Applied Social Psychology* 1:118–36.

Owen, G., and P. W. Mattessich. 1987. *Community Assistance Program: Results of a Control Study of the Effects of Non-residential Corrections on Adult Offenders in Ramsey County*. St. Paul, Minn.: Wilder Foundation.

Palmer, T. B. 1971. "California's Community Treatment Program for Delinquent Adolescents." *Journal of Research in Crime and Delinquency* 8:74–92.

———. 1974. "The Youth Authority's Community Treatment Project." *Federal Probation* 38:3–14.

———. 1978. *Correctional Intervention and Research*. Toronto: Lexington Books.

Persons, R. W. 1966. "Psychological and Behavioral Change in Delinquents Following Psychotherapy." *Journal of Clinical Psychology* 22:337–40.

———. 1967. "Relationship between Psychotherapy with Institutionalized Boys and Subsequent Community Adjustment." *Journal of Consulting Psychology* 31:137–41.

Petersilia, J. 1989. "Implementing Randomized Experiments: Lessons from BJA's Intensive Supervision Project." *Evaluation Review* 13:435–58.

Petersilia, J., and S. Turner. 1990. *Intensive Supervision for High-Risk Probationers: Findings from Three California Experiments*. Santa Monica, Calif.: RAND.

Pond, E. M. 1970. *The Los Angeles Community Delinquency Control Project: An Experiment in the Rehabilitation of Delinquents in an Urban Community*. Sacramento: California Youth Authority.

Powers, E., and H. Witmer. 1951. *An Experiment in the Prevention of Delinquency: The Cambridge-Somerville Youth Study*. New York: Columbia University Press.

Quay, H. C., and C. T. Love. 1977. "The Effects of a Juvenile Diversion Program on Rearrests." *Criminal Justice and Behavior* 4:377–96.

Reimer, E., and M. Warren. 1957. "Special Intensive Parole Unit: Relationship between Violation Rate and Initially Small Caseload." *National Probation and Parole Association Journal* 3:222–29.

———. 1958. *Special Intensive Parole Unit, Phase II: Thirty-Man Caseload Study*. Sacramento: California Department of Corrections.

Rose, G., and R. A. Hamilton. 1970. "Effects of a Juvenile Liaison Scheme." *British Journal of Criminology* 10:2–20.

Ross, H. L., and M. Blumenthal. 1974. "Sanctions for the Drinking Driver: An Experimental Study." *Journal of Legal Studies* 3:53–61.

———. 1975. "Some Problems in Experimentation in a Legal Setting." *American Sociologist* 10:150–55.

Rossi, P. H., R. A. Berk, and K. J. Lenihan. 1980. *Money, Work and Crime*. New York: Academic Press.

Sarason, I. G. 1978. "A Cognitive Social Learning Approach to Juvenile Delinquency." In *Psychopathic Behavior: Approaches to Research*, edited by R. D. Hare and D. Schalling. Chichester: Wiley.

Sarason, I. G., and V. J. Ganzer. 1973. "Modeling and Group Discussion in the Rehabilitation of Juvenile Delinquents." *Journal of Counseling Psychology* 20:442–49.

Schneider, A. L. 1980. "Effects of Status Offender Deinstitutionalization: A Case Study." In *Evaluation and Criminal Justice Policy*, edited by R. Roesch and R. R. Corrado. Beverly Hills, Calif.: Sage.

———. 1986. "Restitution and Recidivism Rates of Juvenile Offenders: Results from Four Experimental Studies." *Criminology* 24:533–52.

Schneider, P. R., and A. L. Schneider. 1983. *An Analysis of Recidivism Rates in Six Federally-funded Restitution Projects in Juvenile Courts: A Statistical Summary*. Washington, D.C.: National Institute of Justice.

Seckel, J. P. 1965. *Experiments in Group Counseling at Youth Authority Institutions.* Sacramento: California Youth Authority, Division of Research.

———. 1967. *The Fremont Experiment: Assessment of Residential Treatment at a Youth Authority Reception Center*. Sacramento: California Youth Authority, Division of Research.

Sedlmeier, P., and G. Gigerenzer. 1989. "Do Studies of Statistical Power Have an Effect on the Power of Studies?" *Psychological Bulletin* 105:309–16.

Severy, L. J., and J. M. Whitaker. 1982. "Juvenile Diversion: An Experimental Analysis of Effectiveness." *Evaluation Review* 6:753–74.

———. 1984. "Memphis-Metro Youth Diversion Project: Final Report." *Child Welfare* 63:269–77.

Shaw, M. 1974. *Social Work in Prison.* London: H.M. Stationery Office.

Sherman, L. W., and R. A. Berk. 1984a. "The Deterrent Effects of Arrest for Domestic Assault." *American Sociological Review* 49:261–72.

———. 1984b. *The Minneapolis Domestic Violence Experiment*. Washington, D.C.: Police Foundation.

———. 1985. "The Randomization of Arrest." In *Randomization and Field Experimentation: New Directions for Program Evaluation, Number 28*, edited by R. F. Boruch and W. Wothke. San Francisco: Jossey-Bass.

Sherman, L. W., and P. R. Gartin. 1986. "Differential Recidivism: A Field Experiment of the Specific Sanction Effects of Arrest for Shoplifting." Paper presented at the American Society of Criminology annual meeting, Atlanta, November.

Sherman, L. W., and D. Weisburd. 1989. *Policing the Hotspots of Crime: A Redesign of the Kansas City Preventive Patrol Experiment*. Washington, D.C.: Crime Control Institute.

———. 1992. "Does Patrol Prevent Crime: The Minneapolis Hot Spots Experiment." Paper presented at the Forty-seventh International Society of Criminology Course on Urban Crime Prevention, Tokyo, April.

Shivrattan, J. L. 1988. "Social Interactional Training and Incarcerated Juvenile Delinquents." *Canadian Journal of Criminology* 30:145–63.

Star, D. 1978. *Summary Parole: A Six and Twelve Month Follow-up*. Research Report no. 60. Sacramento: California Department of Corrections.

Stark, H. G. 1963. "A Substitute for Institutionalization of Serious Delinquents: A California Youth Study Experiment." *Crime and Delinquency* 9:242–48.

Stratton, J. G. 1975. "Effects of Crisis Intervention Counseling on Predelinquent and Misdemeanor Juvenile Offenders." *Juvenile Justice* 26:7–18.

Taylor, A. J. W. 1967. "An Evaluation of Group Psychotherapy in a Girl's Borstal." *International Journal of Group Psychotherapy* 17:168–77.

Tornudd, P. 1968. "The Preventive Effect of Fines for Drunkenness: A Controlled Experiment." *Scandinavian Studies in Criminology* 2:109–24.

Truax, C. B., D. G. Wargo, and L. D. Silber. 1966. "Effects of Group Psychotherapy with High Accurate Empathy and Non-possessive Warmth upon Female Institutionalized Delinquents." *Journal of Abnormal Psychology* 71:267–74.

Turner, Susan. 1991. Personal communication with author, February.

Uchida, Craig. 1991. Personal communication with author, February.

Venezia, P. S. 1972. "Unofficial Probation: An Evaluation of Its Effectiveness." *Journal of Research in Crime and Delinquency* 9:149–70.

Waldo, G. P., and T. G. Chiricos. 1977. "Work Release and Recidivism: An Empirical Evaluation of a Social Policy." *Evaluation Quarterly* 1:87–108.

Warren, M. Q. 1967. "The Community Treatment Project: History and Prospects." In *Law Enforcement Science and Technology*, edited by S. A. Yefsky. Washington, D.C.: Thompson.

Weisburd, D., and J. Garner. 1992. "Experimentation in Criminal Justice: Editor's Introduction." *Journal of Research in Crime and Delinquency* 29(1):3–6.

Weisburd, D., L. W. Sherman, and A. J. Petrosino. 1990. *Registry of Randomized Criminal Justice Experiments in Sanctions.* Sponsored by Rutgers—The State University and Crime Control Institute. Los Altos, Calif.: Sociometric Corporation, Data Resources Program of the National Institute of Justice.

Welsh, J. D. 1978. "Is Pretrial Performance Affected by Supervision?" In *Pretrial Services Annual Journal: 1978*, edited by D. A. Henry. Washington, D.C.: Pretrial Services Resource Center.

Whitaker, J. M., and L. J. Severy. 1984. "Service Accountability and Recidivism for Diverted Youth."*Criminal Justice and Behavior* 11:47–73.

Whitaker, J. M., L. J. Severy, and D. S. Morton. 1984. "A Comprehensive Community-based Youth Diversion Program." *Child Welfare* 63:175–81.

Williams, H., B. Forst, and E. E. Hamilton. 1987. "Stop! Should You Arrest That Person?" *Security Management* 31:52–58.

Williams, M. 1970. *A Study of Some Aspects of Borstal Allocation.* London: Home Office Prison Department, Office of the Chief Psychologist.

———. 1975. "Aspects of the Psychology of Imprisonment." In *The Use of Imprisonment: Essays in the Changing State of English Penal Policy*, edited by S. McConville. London: Routledge.

Yarborough, J. C. 1979. *Evaluation of JOLT as a Deterrence Program.* Lansing: Michigan Department of Corrections.

[7]

FORMAL PROCESSING AND FUTURE DELINQUENCY: DEVIANCE AMPLIFICATION AS SELECTION ARTIFACT

DOUGLAS A. SMITH

RAYMOND PATERNOSTER

Does referring a case to juvenile court or diverting it affect a person's future delinquent/criminal behavior? Labeling theory suggests that it does, arguing that formal processing by the juvenile justice system is part of a deviance amplification process that ultimately results in increased criminal/delinquent activity. But critics point out that a higher rate of future offending among those referred to court, often interpreted as evidence supporting the deviance amplification argument, could be nothing more than a selection artifact. Specifically, those referred to juvenile court may have more attributes that are related to future offending than do those who are diverted from the system. Under this scenario, differences between these groups in later offending could simply reflect preexisting differences in criminal propensity. This article discusses approaches for testing the deviance amplification argument against the alternative hypothesis of a selection artifact.

INTRODUCTION

Labeling theorists (Lemert, 1951; Becker, 1963) contend that social reactions to initial or primary deviance may restrict one's ability to maintain a conventional lifestyle. Limitations arise because being labeled may create barriers to legitimate employment or lead to social censure from conventional others. This process, described by Tannenbaum (1938: 19–20) as the "dramatization of evil," increases the likelihood that the labeled person will become more involved in and committed to a deviant line of activity than he or she was before the labeling experience. While considerable debate exists regarding the specific intervening mechanisms that lead from being labeled to secondary deviance (see Paternoster and Iovanni, 1989), a fundamental empirical prediction of labeling theory is that being sanctioned or negatively labeled will *increase*

We thank Dan Nagin for helpful comments during the evolution of this article. We also thank Charles Tittle and Debbie Curran for providing the data used in this article and the Computer Science Center at the University of Maryland for providing computer support for this research.

1110   FUTURE DELINQUENCY

one's involvement in future deviant conduct—a deviance amplification effect.[1]

The possibility that more severe sanctioning of youthful offenders may increase their future delinquent activity has been a rallying point for certain policy approaches in juvenile justice. Proponents of the labeling perspective have long argued that responsible social policy regarding the problem of juvenile misconduct should be based on "a refusal to dramatize the evil" (Tannenbaum, 1938: 20). If attempts by the juvenile justice system to solve the problem of delinquency/crime appear only to solidify a commitment to additional rule breaking, it is best to do as little as possible (see Klein, 1986). This "doing best by doing nothing" ideology in juvenile justice has been expressed at various times as a policy of "radical nonintervention" (Schur, 1973), "decarceration" (Scull, 1977), and "diversion" (Klein, 1975, 1979).

Assessing the deviance amplification hypothesis involves a deceptively simple question: All else being equal, does the degree of formal processing of juvenile offenders increase their future criminal activity? While there is no shortage of research on this question, there is little agreement regarding what the research shows. A persistent point of uncertainty in evaluating the empirical evidence involves whether variables that impact future offending are in fact equal across groups who are handled differently by the juvenile justice system (see critiques of labeling theory by Hirschi, 1975; Tittle, 1975; Wellford, 1975).

To frame ideas, consider the following equation:

$$R = \theta_1 X_1 + \alpha T + u_1, \tag{1}$$

where R is a measure of recividism, X_1 is a vector of variables that are thought to be associated with recidivism, θ_1 is a conformable coefficient vector, T is a dummy variable coded 1 if the individual is referred to court and 0 if not referred, α is the effect of being referred to court on future offending, and u_1 contains both a random component and unmeasured correlates of recidivism. Our substantive interest in this model is the sign and magnitude of the estimate of the coefficient α. Regardless of the functional form of this equation, if T is uncorrelated with u_1, α will be a consistent estimate of the effect of being referred to court on future offending. Under the hypothesis of deviance amplification this coefficient should be positive.

---

[1] Deterrence theorists are equally concerned with the importance of social reactions to delinquent behavior. However, those working from a deterrence perspective predict that punishment will *reduce* the sanctioned person's involvement in subsequent delinquency—a specific deterrent effect. Because our focus here is on whether previous evidence supporting the secondary deviance component of labeling theory may be the result of a selection artifact, we will not pursue the specific deterrence argument.

SMITH AND PATERNOSTER   1111

But a positive and statistically significant estimate of α can arise for two very distinct reasons. First, referral to court could cause an increase in future offending—a deviance amplification effect. Second, a statistically significant positive coefficient could emerge because of a positive correlation between the variable indicating whether one is referred to court and the disturbance term in the recidivism equation—a selection artifact. In this second case the dummy variable for referral acts as a proxy for correlates of recidivism that are not included as independent variables in the recidivism equation. The important point is that if the variable indicating whether one is referred to juvenile court is correlated with the disturbance term in equation (1), the estimated effect of being referred to court on future offending will be biased and inconsistent.[2]

Such bias is potentially widespread in the empirical literature. For example, early research in this area often took the form of simple comparisons of the extent of recidivism between groups of persons who were handled differently by the juvenile justice system (see Wilkens, 1969, and Lipton *et al.*, 1975, for a review of this research). But it soon became apparent that comparing differences in measures of future offending across groups who received different court dispositions was an inadequate test of whether more severe juvenile court interventions had any effect on subsequent delinquent behavior. The basic problem is that assignment to treatment groups (diversion vs. referred to juvenile court, for example) is the result of a nonrandom process in which high-risk youth are more likely to receive more severe dispositions. Thus,

---

[2] To see this bias in the case of an ordinary least squares regression equation, let recidivism be a function only of whether one is referred to court or not.

$$R = \alpha T + u_1.$$

The least squares solution is α is:

$$\hat{\alpha} = (T'T)^{-1}T'R.$$

Substituting the equation for recidivism into this equation yields

$$\hat{\alpha} = \alpha + (T'T)^{-1}T'u_1,$$

so that the expected value for α̂ is

$$E(\hat{\alpha}) = \alpha + E[(T'T)^{-1}T'u_1].$$

If the covariance between the variable measuring whether one is referred to court (T) and the disturbance term (u_1) is not zero, the second term on the right-hand side of the last equation is not equal to zero and thus the estimated value of α is not equal to its true value. Note also that if the covariance between T and u_1 is positive, $\hat{\alpha} > \alpha$.

1112   FUTURE DELINQUENCY

those individuals assigned more severe sanctions would be more likely to commit new offenses whether or not any relationship existed between juvenile court dispositions and future offending. It is not surprising that research in this tradition often found that the more severe the sanction, the greater the likelihood of future offending—a finding often interpreted as showing support for labeling theory.

Recognizing these potential problems, researchers sought other approaches to assess the effects of juvenile justice interventions on future criminal activity. One strategy was to use a matching design. As an example of this approach, Gold and Williams (1969) examined the effect of police contacts on the subsequent behavior of apprehended youths and a control group matched on sex, race, age, prior offenses, and recency of last offense. They reported that in twenty of thirty-five matched pairs the apprehended youth committed more subsequent offenses (a deviance amplification effect), in ten pairs the apprehended youth committed fewer offenses (a specific deterrent effect), and in five pairs there was no difference. Testifying to the difficulty of matching groups based on several criteria, however, Gold and Williams were only able to match thirty-five of seventy-four youths in their study who had been apprehended.

One way overcome the difficulty of adequate matching in assuring the comparability of treatment groups is to use random assignment of subjects into these groups. In theory, and in large samples, random assignment of subjects can ensure that different treatment groups will be comparable in terms of extraneous variables which may be related to the dependent variable under investigation—subsequent involvement in delinquency. Note that in relation to equation (1), random assignment to referral or diverted status would imply that T is uncorrelated with u_1, and thus the estimate of α will be a consistent estimate of the true impact of being referred to court on future offending.

Unfortunately, it is not always possible to randomly assign subjects to control and experimental conditions, and there are relatively few published reports of randomized experiments on the relationship between juvenile justice interventions and future delinquency (see the review by Farrington, 1983). In addition, there is often a considerable difference between the design of a randomized experiment and the resulting implementation of the experiment (cf. Empey and Erickson, 1972; Sherman and Berk, 1984).

If matching techniques control for too few relevant variables and randomization strategies are either impractical or fall short in practice, an alternative strategy used in much recent research is to obtain statistical control over extraneous variables by using multivariate statistical models. In this approach, the effects of juvenile justice processing on future criminal activity are estimated while other variables that are hypothesized to influence future offending are controlled for.

Some recent examples of research within this tradition are reported by Horwitz and Wasserman (1979), Rausch (1983), Shannon (1980, 1988), and Wooldredge (1988). Horwitz and Wasserman, for example, examine the relationship between severity of juvenile court disposition and the number of subsequent arrests and report that the severity of juvenile court disposition has a marginal labeling effect, leading to a greater number of subsequent arrests. Shannon's research, also based on bivariate and multivariate models, shows that more severe juvenile court sanctions are significantly associated with an increase in individual's future criminal activity. On the other hand, Wooldredge finds mixed results in his study of the relationship between severity of juvenile court dispositions and future offending.

But while these studies do control for some correlates of future offending when estimating the association between juvenile court sanctions and subsequent delinquency, they may overlook others. Thus, the estimated association between juvenile court status and future delinquency could still be capturing the influence of other variables not included in the analysis but nonetheless correlated with both referral status and criminal propensity. Later in this article we discuss several approaches to this issue that use information about the nonrandom nature of referral decisions when estimating the effect of referral to court on future offending. We also show that failure to consider this information can have profound consequences for the conclusions drawn regarding the relationship between sanctions and future offending.

DATA AND VARIABLES

Data used in this analysis are a subset of cases referred in 1979 to the juvenile justice intake division of the Florida Department of Health and Rehabilitative Services (HRS). Since all juvenile complaints in Florida are processed through the intake division of HRS, the data set contains information on initial decisions to refer youth for formal processing or to handle cases in a variety of informal or nonjudicial ways (see Bishop and Frazier, 1988).

Case data were collected from the central planning and research division of HRS for thirty-one counties in the state. Within each county a random sample of about two hundred cases was selected from all cases referred to juvenile justice intake during 1979. In counties where fewer than two hundred cases were referred, all cases were selected for analysis (see Tittle and Curran, 1988). The number of cases by county range from 82 for Madison County to 214 for Dade County and totaled 5,669 for the entire sample. The following analysis restricts itself to only black and

1114   FUTURE DELINQUENCY

Table 1. Means of Variables Used in Analysis

Variable	Referred to Court (N=1,544)	Not Referred (N=1,636)
Independent variables		
No. of charges	1.22	1.03
Black youth (1=black, 0=white)	0.31	0.22
Male youth (1=male, 0=female)	0.84	0.76
No. of priors	1.94	0.66
Age	15.06	14.40
Currently under supervision[a]	0.15	0.05
In School[a]	0.76	0.83
Lives with biological parents[a]	0.35	0.45
Lives in single parent household[a]	0.38	0.31
Felony[a]	0.58	0.21
Natural log of intake caseload	5.30	5.35
No. alternative/diversion programs	8.03	9.28
Natural log of county crime rate per 100,000	8.63	8.66
Percentage of county population in urban areas	60.65%	61.47%
Outcome measures based on cases with at least one year of follow-up data (N=2,716)		
Any subsequent referral to intake[a]	0.36	0.23
No. of subsequent referrals to intake[b]	1.07	0.54

[a] 1 = yes, 0 = no.
[b] For the pooled sample the mean number of subsequent referrals is .77 with a standard deviation of 2.0.

white youth referred to HRS for felonies or misdemeanors. This reduces the sample to 3,180 cases.[3]

Table 1 lists the variables used in this analysis. Means of the independent variables are presented separately for the samples of referred and diverted cases. The independent variables include individual and case attributes as well as a few measures of county or jurisdictional characteristics. The sample is 80 percent male and 27 percent black and has an average age of 14.7 years. Other individual level variables in the data include number of charges in the current referral, number of prior referrals, and a series of dummy variables indicating whether the youth is currently under juvenile court supervision, in school, and whether the current referral is for a felony or misdemeanor. Two additional dummy variables identify whether the child resides with both biological parents or lives in a single-parent household. The reference category for these two variables is such other family arrangements as one biological and one step-parent.

In addition to these individual variables, aggregate data are available to measure the caseload of each intake unit (defined as

---

[3] In Florida HRS processes all juvenile complaints, including those not involving any criminal behavior by the youth such as dependency and neglect cases, truancy, and runaways. These cases, as well as such traffic infractions such as DUI and driving without a license, are excluded from the current analysis.

the number of cases referred to each intake office in 1979 divided by the number of intake officers) and the number of alternative diversion programs available to intake officers when deciding whether to refer a case for formal court processing. Additionally, we include information on county crime rates per 100,000 population and the degree of urbanization for each of the thirty-one counties.[4]

Two indicators are used to measure future criminal activity. One is a binary measure of whether a youth has any subsequent referrals to juvenile justice intake for a felony or misdemeanor offense. However, as Farrington (1987) and others have argued, whether a youth commits an additional offense or not is only one measure of the impact of juvenile justice intervention. Thus, the following analysis will also examine the *number* of referrals to juvenile justice intake for felonies and misdemeanors during the follow-up period.

Since cases were sampled from those brought to the intake division during 1979 and because the data on subsequent referrals were collected by county from November 1980 until March 1981, persons are in the follow-up period for different amounts of time. To address this heterogeneity in exposure risk, we include a variable measuring the number of months from the time of the instant referral until the date on which data on subsequent referrals were collected. On average youths were in the follow-up period for 19.9 months.[5] All else being equal, we expect the probability of any subsequent criminal behavior and the frequency of such behavior to increase with the length of the follow-up period.

Finally, it is worth noting that our data are closely related to the data Bishop and Frazier (1988) used in their analysis of racial disparity in juvenile justice processing. Their data contain 54,266 felony and misdemeanor cases referred to juvenile justice intake in Florida from 1979 to 1981. They report (1988: 250) that for this time period 49.4 percent of youth referred to intake for misdemeanors or felonies are recommended for formal processing. For our much smaller sample of 3,180 cases from 1979 the comparable figure is 49 percent. There are other similarities between the two data sets in the demographics of the samples. In their data 28 percent of youth referred to intake are black, 78 percent are male, with an average age of 15 years. The comparable figures for the data used here are 27 percent black, 80 percent male, with an average age of 14.7 years. Thus, while the data used here contain only a small percentage of the cases processed by HRS in 1979, they ap-

---

[4] The data on crime rates and the percentage of persons residing in urban areas are from 1979 county census data. See Tittle and Curran (1988) for additional details.

[5] If a youth turned 18 before the end of the data collection period, his/her time in the follow-up period is the number of months from the instant referral until his/her 18th birthday.

1116   FUTURE DELINQUENCY

pear representative of the larger population of youths referred to
juvenile justice intake in Florida in 1979.

MODELS AND FINDINGS

We first report results from a series of equations for future offending that do not use information about the process by which
cases are selected for referral to juvenile court. These results are
compatible with equation (1) discussed above. In these models a
dummy variable indicating whether intake recommends referral to
court is included as an independent variable along with several
other variables that are thought to be related to recidivism. Results from four equations are reported in Table 2. The first column lists results from a probit model in which the dependent variable is coded as 1 if the youth has any future referrals for a felony
or misdemeanor and 0 otherwise. The dependent variable for the
remaining three models—ordinary least squares, tobit, and negative binomial regression—is the actual number of subsequent referrals to juvenile court.[6]

Results of these models show that black, male, and older
youth have higher recidivism rates. Subsequent offending is also
greater for persons with more prior offenses and for those with
more charges against them in the instant offense. Recidivism also
varies directly with the crime rate of the county in which the individual resides and with the length of time in the follow-up period.
But most central to our concern is the finding that while controlling for these and several other variables, those recommended by
intake for formal juvenile court processing are significantly more
delinquent during the follow-up period.[7] This finding is consistent
whether future criminality is measured as a yes/no variable or examined in terms of the number of future referrals.

Such results have often been interpreted as showing support
for the labeling position that formal processing by the juvenile justice system leads to increased future criminal conduct (Horwitz
and Wasserman, 1979; Meade, 1974; Shannon, 1988; Thornberry,
1971). But this inference depends on the validity of the assumption that the dummy variable indicating whether one is referred to

---

[6] Since about 70 percent of persons have no future referrals to intake
during the follow-up period, the linearity assumption of OLS is problematic.
Thus, we estimate two additional models for future offending. The tobit
model is a censored regression model and is discussed in Amemiya (1985). The
negative binomial regression model is appropriate when the dependent variable is a count of event such as future offenses. We estimate the version of this
model discussed in Cameron and Trivedi (1986) as NEGBIN II. This model is
an extension of the Poisson regression model and is appropriate when the
mean of the dependent variable is not equal to its variance. In these data the
mean number of future referrals is .77 with a variance of 4.0.

[7] In our analysis of future offending, to ensure that each person in the
sample was followed for at least one year after the instant offense, we excluded those who were 17 years of age or older. This left us with a sample of
2,716.

Table 2. Models of the Association Between Independent Variables and Subsequent Offending, Ignoring Selection (N = 2,716)

Independent Variable	Probit I		OLS II		Tobit III		Negative Binomial Regression[a] IV	
No. of charges	0.335[b]	(5.83)[c]	0.402	(4.98)	1.142	(5.54)	0.408	(3.65)
Black	0.126	(2.00)	0.178	(2.07)	0.548	(2.19)	0.197	(1.94)
Male	0.399	(5.56)	0.510	(5.63)	2.010	(6.66)	0.990	(8.55)
No. of priors	0.137	(10.51)	0.195	(11.59)	0.462	(10.67)	0.189	(7.88)
Age	0.058	(3.36)	0.021	(1.13)	0.202	(3.36)	0.068	(2.90)
Under supervision	0.111	(1.05)	0.057	(0.38)	0.378	(0.94)	-0.013	(-0.08)
In school	-0.028	(-0.40)	-0.084	(-0.86)	-0.125	(-0.44)	-0.047	(-0.43)
Felony	-0.029	(-0.49)	-0.013	(-0.16)	-0.141	(-0.58)	-0.065	(-0.74)
Biological parents	-0.105	(-1.51)	0.022	(0.23)	-0.313	(-1.12)	-0.122	(-1.16)
Single parent	0.053	(0.76)	0.151	(1.58)	0.312	(1.11)	0.137	(1.26)
County crime rate	0.247	(2.88)	0.345	(3.06)	1.246	(3.56)	0.659	(4.65)
Urbanization	-0.001	(-0.06)	0.001	(0.34)	-0.001	(-0.06)	-0.001	(-0.74)
Months in follow-up[d]	0.025	(3.32)	0.040	(4.06)	0.121	(4.04)	0.916	(4.20)
Intake recommendation	0.148	(2.45)	0.175	(2.13)	0.722	(2.95)	0.245	(2.82)
Constant	-4.953		-4.53		-22.58		-11.45	
Sigma/Alpha[e]					4.344		2.902	(17.48)
Log likelihood	-1,441.50		-5,565.51		-3,040.62		-2,802.4	

[a] This model is described in Cameron and Trivedi (1986) as NEGBIN II.
[b] Coefficients are maximum likelihood estimates except for ordinary least squares which are metric coefficients.
[c] Asymptotic t-ratio.
[d] The natural log of months is used for the negative binomial regression model.
[e] The coefficient in this row for the tobit model is the maximum likelihood estimator of sigma; for the negative binomial regression model this coefficient is the variance parameter alpha defined in Cameron and Trivedi (1986).

1118   FUTURE DELINQUENCY

juvenile court is independent of the residual term in the equation for future offending. We think that in most empirical research on this topic, this inference is problematic.

Suppose, for example, that a youth's future criminal involvement is associated with some variables that are not measured in the data—say, parental or sibling criminality. Further assume that intake officers are sometimes aware of the criminal histories of other family members and that this knowledge increases the chances that intake will recommend referral to juvenile court. Under this or a number of other plausible scenarios, the treatment status of individuals (referred or diverted) is related to unmeasured characteristics (parental or sibling criminality) that in turn influence the dependent variable of interest (future offending). Thus, the variable measuring whether a case is referred to juvenile court is potentially confounded with unmeasured variables that influence future offending.

Viewed from this perspective, bias in estimating the effect of referral to court on future offending results from common omitted variables that influence both the probability of being referred to court and likelihood of future offending. One way to compensate for such bias is to utilize information about the process by which cases are selected for referral to juvenile court. Let this process be represented by the equation

$$T = \theta_2 X_2 + u_2, \tag{2}$$

where T is a dummy variable coded as 1 if the person is referred to court and 0 otherwise, X_2 is a vector of measured variables that influence the probability of referral, θ_2 is a coefficient vector, and u_2 contains both a random component and unmeasured variables associated with the probability of being referred to court.

Introducing an equation for the process by which persons are selected for referral to court makes explicit the fact that referral status itself is an endogenous variable, potentially influenced by both observed (X_2) and unmeasured (u_2) variables. Estimating equation (2) provides additional information that can be used to correct for the bias in estimating the effect of referral to court on future offending that arises from common omitted variables in the referral and recidivism equations. One way to use this additional information involves estimating the equation for referral and recidivism simultaneously and allowing the disturbance terms between these equation to correlate. A second approach involves using the predicted values from the referral equation as an instrumental variable in the recidivism equation. A third approach involves estimating the residuals from the referral equation, conditional on the independent variables in that equation and whether the person is in fact referred to court or diverted. These condi-

SMITH AND PATERNOSTER 1119

Table 3. Probit Models of Intake Recommendation for Formal Processing

Independent Variable	I		II	
No. of charges	.525[a]	(7.62)[b]	0.584	(8.17)
Black	.261	(4.59)	0.235	(3.99)
Male	.093	(1.53)	0.119	(1.88)
No. of priors	.070	(6.51)	0.075	(6.31)
Age	.073	(6.26)	0.062	(5.07)
Under supervision	.480	(5.08)	0.516	(5.23)
In school	−.110	(−1.75)	−0.182	(−2.80)
Felony	.956	(18.69)	1.000	(18.69)
Biological parents	−.045	(−0.73)	−0.042	(−0.64)
Single parent	.185	(2.89)	0.147	(2.21)
County crime rate	−.242	(−3.26)	−0.395	(−4.17)
Urbanization	.006	(4.07)	0.011	(6.73)
Intake caseload	−.265	(−3.97)	−0.571	(−6.75)
Alternative programs	−.011	(−3.95)	−0.018	(−6.18)
County 1			1.550	(8.40)
County 2			0.897	(4.44)
County 3			1.289	(7.47)
County 4			1.384	(4.66)
County 5			−0.901	(−4.28)
County 6			0.845	(5.62)
County 7			−1.097	(−4.38)
Constant	0.952		3.695	
Log L	−1,788.57		−1647.04	
Percentage correct	72.0%		74.6%	
RIOC	.476		.534	

[a] Maximum likelihood probit coefficient.
[b] Asymptotic t-ratio.

tional residuals are then entered as an independent variable in the recidivism equation.

A Model for the Decision to Refer a Case to Juvenile Court

Since the cornerstone of each of these approaches is a model for the process by which cases are selected for referral to juvenile court, we estimate a series of probit equations for the intake officers' decisions to recommend referral to juvenile court. Results from two equations are presented in Table 3.

The first equation reported in Table 3 (I) shows that decisions to recommend formal processing are related to attributes of individual cases as well as characteristics of counties and intake offices. The probability that intake will recommend referral to juvenile court varies directly with the gravity of the offense (felony or misdemeanor), the number of prior offenses, and whether the youth is currently under court supervision. In addition, black and older youth as well as those living in single-parent households are significantly more likely to be referred to court. Intake recommendations for formal processing also vary with the size of intake caseloads and the number of alternative treatment programs in the jurisdiction. Larger caseloads and more alternative programs decrease the probability that a case will be recommended for refer-

1120   FUTURE DELINQUENCY

ral to juvenile court. Finally, referral decisions vary with two
county characteristics. Cases brought to intake in more urban
counties are more likely to be referred to court, while those in
higher crime rate counties are less likely to be referred to court.[8]

Since our data are drawn from thirty-one countries, the
county in which a case is processed may have an independent effect on the probability that intake will recommend referral to juvenile court. To assess this possibility, we examined the proportion of between-county variance in the residuals from equation I in
Table 3. Using an analysis of variance model, we found that 12.4
percent of the variance in these residuals was between counties.
This procedure also identified seven counties in which the observed proportion of referrals differed significantly from the proportion that would be expected based on the results on the first
equation in this table. Thus, we estimated the equation again adding seven dummy variables to represent these counties. These results are shown as equation II in Table 3.

These results show that the probability of being referred to juvenile court can vary significantly from one county to the next. In
five of these counties, for example, youth brought to intake are
significantly more likely to be referred to juvenile court, while in
two others they are much less likely to be referred to court. Moreover, these differences are independent of the other fourteen variables in the equation. Adding these seven county dummy variables
also improves the fit of the model. The likelihood of equation 3.II
is significantly larger than for the equation that does not include
these seven variables, and the percentage of variance in the residuals from this equation that lies between counties is reduced from
12.4 to 2.3. Moreover, this model correctly classifies 74.6 percent of
cases with respect to these decisions and reduces classification errors relative to predictions based on chance (RIOC) by 53.4 percent
(see Loeber and Dishion 1983).

This model not only offers a better statistical fit to the data; in
addition, the specification of equation 3.II is more congenial with
the realities of juvenile justice decisionmaking. It is likely that intake offices develop a set of decision rules that shape their decisionmaking and that some intake offices will see referral to juvenile court as a solution while others may see it as part of the
problem (Cicourel, 1968; Emerson, 1969). Put simply, the collective beliefs of juvenile intake offices may vary from one intake office to the next regarding the utility of referring cases for formal
court processing (Cohen and Kluegel, 1978; Cohen, 1975; Bailey
and Peterson, 1981). While we do not know why these differences

---

[8] Because more urban counties tend to have higher crime rates, we estimated this equation deleting the crime-rate variable. When the crime-rate variable is removed, the coefficient on urbanization remains positive and significant. Moreover, when urbanization is removed from the model, the coefficient
on the crime-rate variable remains negative and significant.

emerge, it is clear from these data that such differences exist and should be included when modeling the process by which cases are selected for referral to juvenile court. Thus, equation II in Table 3 is used to represent the process by which cases are selected for referral to juvenile court.

A Bivariate Probit Model

One way to utilize information from the process by which persons are selected for referral to court involves simultaneously estimating two probit equations: one for referral and one for recidivism (see Heckman, 1976, 1978; Meng and Schmidt, 1985).[9] This approach loses some information on future offending by creating a dummy variable for recidivism. If we assume that the disturbance terms in these two equations are normally distributed and that their joint distribution is bivariate normal, we can estimate these two probit equations simultaneously using maximum likelihood methods.[10] Results from the recidivism portion of this model are presented in the first column of Table 4.

These results are generally consistent with those from the univariate probit model shown earlier in Table 2. Persons with more charges in the instant offense and who are black, male, or older have a significantly higher probability of subsequent offending. Also, the probability of recidivism is higher for those with prior records and among those who live in counties with higher crime rates. But there is also one major difference between the results from the univariate and bivariate probit models. In the univariate model, the coefficient for whether intake recommends formal processing is .148 with a *t*-ratio of 2.45, which implies that being referred to juvenile court is positively and significantly associated with recidivism. But in the bivariate probit model, whether intake recommends referral to court is not significantly associated with recidivism. Moreover, the estimated coefficient for this variable is negative in sign ($-.134$).

The difference between these results is consistent with the argument that a selection artifact operates to create the mistaken impression that being referred to juvenile court is criminogenic. Under the hypothesis of a selection artifact, the variable indicating

---

[9] We thank an anonymous reviewer of an earlier version of this manuscript for suggesting this approach.

[10] It should be noted that in the probit model the dependent variable is an observed realization of a continuous unobserved variable. In the recidivism equation, for example, this unobserved variable might be called individual criminal propensity. We only observe whether a person's criminal propensity is sufficiently great to manifest itself in any criminal behavior. A point to note is that the disturbance term in the probit model is also assumed to be a continuous variable that is not directly observable. Thus, the assumption of bivariate normality applies to the joint distribution of unobservable continuous variables. The same logic can be applied to a model involving the observed number of future offenses by invoking several thresholds along the latent variable rather than a single threshold as in the probit model.

Table 4. Models of the Association Between Independent Variables and Subsequent Offending Utilizing Information on the Selection Process (N = 2,716)

Independent Variable	Bivariate Probit I		BCG/Heckman II		Instrumental Variable Approach					
					NLTSLS III		Tobit IV		Negative Binomial Regression[a] V	
No. of charges	.371[b]	(6.43)[c]	.470	(5.37)	.453	(5.26)	1.244	(5.59)	.461	(3.83)
Black	.147	(2.29)	.224	(2.52)	.215	(2.42)	.625	(2.42)	.240	(2.32)
Male	.406	(5.61)	.525	(5.76)	.452	(5.26)	2.038	(6.71)	1.004	(8.46)
No. of priors	.143	(13.79)	.206	(11.64)	.204	(11.56)	.477	(10.32)	.201	(8.18)
Age	.065	(4.01)	.032	(1.68)	.034	(1.72)	.228	(3.56)	.079	(3.31)
Under supervision	.134	(1.29)	.142	(0.91)	.092	(0.61)	.436	(1.06)	.008	(0.05)
In school	-.042	(-0.57)	-.110	(-1.12)	-.109	(-1.13)	-.195	(-0.68)	-.093	(-0.81)
Felony	.067	(0.76)	.159	(1.37)	.128	(1.12)	.151	(0.44)	.079	(0.54)
Biological parents	-.112	(-1.60)	.017	(0.19)	.016	(0.17)	-.331	(-1.18)	-.132	(-1.24)
Single parent	.070	(1.00)	.185	(1.89)	.181	(1.86)	.383	(1.34)	.164	(1.47)
County crime rate	.231	(2.67)	.315	(2.76)	.317	(2.77)	1.174	(3.28)	.606	(4.37)
Urbanization	.001	(0.08)	.001	(0.53)	.001	(0.45)	.001	(0.06)	-.001	(-0.47)
Months in follow-up[d]	.025	(3.38)	.041	(4.13)	.048	(4.41)	.138	(4.22)	1.077	(4.37)
Intake recommendation	-.134	(-0.70)	-.323	(-1.27)	-.254	(-0.97)	-.156	(-0.20)	-.189	(-0.53)
Constant	-4.887		-4.414		-4.597		-22.591		-11.576	
Cov (u_1, u_2)[e] Sigma/Alpha[f]	.185	(1.55)	.327	(2.08)			4.353		2.925	(17.45)
Log likelihood	-2,886.5		-5,563.3				-3,044.9		-2,804.5	

[a] This model is described in Cameron and Trivedi (1986) as NEGBIN II.
[b] Coefficients for the bivariate probit, tobit, and negative binomial regression models are maximum likelihood estimates. Metric coefficients are reported for the BCG/Heckman and the nonlinear two-stage least squares models.
[c] Asymptotic t-ratio.
[d] The natural log of months is used for the negative binomial regression model.
[e] For the bivariate probit model the coefficient is the estimated correlation between the disturbance terms in the referral and recidivism equations. For the BCG/Heckman model the coefficient is the estimated covariance between these two terms.
[f] The coefficient in this row for the tobit model is the rule of sigma, for the negative binomial regression model this coefficient is the variance parameter alpha defined in Cameron and Trivedi (1986).

whether one is referred to court acts as a proxy for other variables that correlate with both the probability of being referred to court and future offending. If the omitted variables in the referral and recidivism equation are positively correlated as they are in these data (.185), the estimated effect of being referred to court on future offending will be biased upward in favor of the deviance amplification hypothesis. The fact that the estimated coefficient on the referral variable declines from .148 to −.134 when the disturbance terms between the referral and recidivism equations are allowed to correlate is consistent with this expectation.

The Instrumental Variable Approach

Another approach to purge the referral variable of its correlation with unmeasured causes of recidivism is to use an instrumental variable in place of the referral variable in the recidivism equation. Using the instrumental variable approach does not require any assumptions about the joint distribution of the disturbance terms in the referral and recidivism equation (see Heckman and Robb, 1985). All that is required is information on at least one variable which influences the probability of being referred to juvenile court that is also not a predictor of recidivism. An examination of results from the probit model for whether one is referred to juvenile court (Table 3) reveals several such variables. Specifically, the size of the intake office's caseload and the number of alternative diversion programs in the county significantly reduce the probability that intake will recommend referral to court. These variables have no obvious theoretical relationship to whether an individual commits future offenses and are thus useful instrumental variables. Additionally, whether the instant offense is a felony or misdemeanor has a strong effect on the probability of referral to court but no apparent relationship to the number of future offenses. Finally, results from the probit model reveal that the probability of being referred to court varies with the intake office which handles the case. We speculated that these effects reflect the collective attitudes and beliefs of intake officers regarding the utility of referring a case to juvenile court, and see no compelling theoretical reason to think that these variables have a direct causal effect on individual recidivism.

Following arguments in Hausman (1983) and Barnow *et al.* (1980), we form an instrumental variable for whether one is referred to court in the following way. Using the results from the second probit equation reported in Table 3, we calculate the predicted probability that an individual will be referred to juvenile court $[p(T=1|X_2]$. Then, we regress the dummy variable indicating whether one is referred to court on the predicted probability that they will be referred and all of the independent variables in the recidivism equation. The predicted values from this regression

1124   FUTURE DELINQUENCY

equation are, by construction, independent of the disturbance term
in the recidivism equation and are used as an instrumental variable for referral when estimating the equations for recidivism.

Results from three instrumental variable models are shown in
Table 4. The results under the third column (NLTSLS, for nonlinear two-stage least squares) use a least squares regression model
for the second-stage recidivism equation.[11] Results in the fourth
and fifth columns use the instrumental variable described above as
an independent variable in a tobit and negative binomial regression model for recidivism.

Results from each of these three instrumental variable models
show that referral for the current offense has no significant independent effect on recidivism, and in each of these models the
point estimate for this effect is negative. This is consistent with
the results from the bivariate probit analysis. Thus, when an instrumental variable is used to purge the referral variable of its association with unmeasured correlates of recidivism, the apparent
labeling effect reported in Table 2 disappears.

The Model of Barnow, Cain, and Goldberger

Another approach that utilizes information on how cases are
selected for referral to court when estimating the effect of being
referred to court on future offending is discussed in Barnow *et al.*
(1980) and Heckman and Robb (1985). This approach is motivated
by the following equation:

$$R = \alpha T + C^* + \epsilon, \tag{3}$$

in which C^* represents true individual criminal propensity, and T
is defined again as a dummy variable indicating whether one is referred to court and R is a measure of recidivism.

If it were possible to measure a person's criminal propensity,
we could estimate equation (3) and obtain an unbiased estimate of
the effect of being referred to juvenile court on future offending.
But in practice, this equation cannot be estimated because true
criminal propensity is an unobserved variable. Instead, researchers use variables that are related to true criminal propensity to approximate the model represented by equation (3). If we reconsider
equation (1):

$$R = \alpha T + \theta_1 X_1 + u_1,$$

we see that the term $\theta_1 X_1$ is a proxy for true criminal propensity
in equation (3). If true criminal propensity were completely captured by the independent variables in this equation (X_1), then esti-

---

[11] The standard errors of coefficients in the second-stage equation are
corrected using the method outlined in Green (1990).

mating this model would produce an unbiased estimate of the effect of being referred to court on future offending. But these control variables are related to true criminal propensity (C^*) by

$$C^* = \theta_1 X_1 + u_3, \tag{4}$$

where u_3 contains both a random component and unmeasured correlates of criminal propensity. Thus, in practice, equation (1) becomes, by substitution,

$$R = \alpha T + \theta_1 X_1 + u_1, \tag{5}$$

where $u_1 = u_3 + \epsilon$. This is just another way of saying that the disturbance term in the recidivism equation may contain unmeasured correlates of criminal propensity. To repeat a central theme of this article, if any of these omitted correlates of criminal propensity (such as parental or sibling criminality) are also related to the selection of cases for referral to juvenile court, then the variable measuring whether a person is referred to juvenile court (T) will be correlated with the disturbance term in equation (5). Under these conditions the estimated coefficient on the variable identifying whether a case is referred to juvenile court will be biased. This is essentially an omitted variable bias.

Barnow and his associates (1980) and Heckman (1978) and colleagues (Heckman and Robb, 1985; Heckman and Hotz, 1989) discuss a two-part model that, under certain assumptions, can be used to correct for this type of selectivity bias in estimating the effect of being referred to juvenile court on future offending.[12] The first step in using this approach is to estimate a probit model for the process by which cases are selected for referral to court, as was done in Table 3. The next step is to calculate the expected value of the residual in this equation for each person in the sample, conditional on that person's scores on the independent variables in the referral equation (X_2) and whether they are referred to juvenile court or not [i.e., $E(u_2|X_2, T)$].[13] These conditional residuals provide information on each youth's score on *unmeasured* variables

---

[12] A primary assumption in using this approach is that the disturbance terms in the recidivism and referral equations have a bivariate normal distribution. The papers by Heckman and Robb (1985) and Heckman and Hotz (1989) are published with discussions that focus on assumptions in these models, and interested readers may find these exchanges of value. We believe that a critical point in using these models is that there is no one generic cure for selectivity bias and that applications of these models must make substantive sense in the context of specific applications. For that reason we will discuss why we believe this model is appropriate in the context of estimating the effect of being referred to juvenile court on future offending.

[13] These conditional residuals are calculated as follows (see Barnow *et al.*, 1980: 54; Heckman, 1978: 938). Let the predicted value for each case in the probit equation for referral to court be $\hat{T}$. If the case is referred to court (i.e., $T = 1$) then the $E(u_2|X^2, T = 1)$ is equal to $\phi(\hat{T})|\Phi(\hat{T})$, where ϕ and Φ represent respectively the standard normal density and distribution functions. If the

that influence referral decisions. To clarify this, consider two hypothetical cases whose predicted scores from the referral equation are .7, and −.7. Since these are predicted values in a probit equation, higher values are associated with a higher predicted probability that the case will be referred to juvenile court (for these two scores the corresponding probabilities of being referred to juvenile court are .76, and .24, respectively). What can we infer about these cases if both are referred to juvenile court despite their very different predicted probabilities of being referred?

It is important to note that the predicted probability of whether intake will recommend referral to juvenile is based on variables that are available in the data set. But referral decisions may also be influenced by variables, such as parental criminality, that are not contained in the data set and thus cannot be included in the referral equation. It seems reasonable that, over a large number of cases, those whose predicted probability of being referred to court is only .24 but who are in fact referred to court have more of these *unmeasured* variables that increase the probability of referral than persons whose predicted probability of being referred to court is .76. Thus, among cases referred to juvenile court, those with *lower* predicted probabilities of being referred will have larger (i.e., more positive) residuals. Specifically, the $E(u_2|X_2, T=1)$ equals 1.29 for the case whose predicted probability of being referred to court is .24. For the case whose predicted probability of being referred to court is .76, the $E(u_2|X_2, T=1)$ equals .41. Thus, individuals with larger conditional expected values of the residuals from the probit (selection) equation will, on average, rank higher on unmeasured variables that increase the probability of being referred to juvenile court.[14]

In sum, values of the conditional residuals from the selection equation are intended to capture the heterogeneity among persons in the sample on unmeasured variables that influence the probability of being referred to juvenile court. This heterogeneity, by itself, will not bias the estimate of the effect of being referred to juvenile court on future offending. But bias will exist if some of the unmeasured variables that influence referral decisions are also correlated with recidivism.

---

case is not referred to juvenile court (i.e., $T=0$) then $E(u_2|X_2, T=0)$ is equal to $-\phi(\hat{T})[1 - \Phi(\hat{T})]$.

[14] The same result holds if we consider cases not referred to juvenile court (i.e., $T=0$). For example, the $E(u_2|X_2, T=0)$ is equal to -1.29 for the case whose predicted probability of being referred to court is .76. For the person whose predicted probability of being referred to court is .24, the $E(u_2|X_2, T=0)$ is equal to $-.441$. The smaller of these two values (-1.29) corresponds to the case that had a higher predicted probability of being referred to court but was in fact not referred to court. Thus, this case probably had fewer unmeasured variables that would increase the probability of being referred to court. Hence, among cases not referred to court, larger residual values correspond to cases that rank higher on unmeasured variables associated with more severe intake recommendations.

Thus, the second part of this model involves estimating an equation for future offending which includes the conditional residuals from the referral equation as an independent variable. The equation for recidivism now becomes:

$$R = \alpha T + \theta_1 X_1 + \sigma_{23}[E(u_2|X_2, T)] + \epsilon, \qquad (5)$$

where σ_{23} is the estimated covariance between the disturbance terms in the referral and recidivism equations and ϵ is a random error component.[15] A test of the null hypothesis of no selectivity bias is a test of whether σ_{23} is equal to zero. Estimating equation 5 provides a direct test of this and produces a consistent estimate of the effect of being referred to juvenile court on future offending (see Heckman, 1978).[16]

Results from estimating this model are shown in Table 4 in the second column. Two points are worth noting. First, the estimated covariance between the disturbance terms in the referral and recidivism equations is positive (.327) and significant ($t = 2.08$), which is consistent with the position that unmeasured variables which increase the probability of being referred to court are significantly associated with a greater likelihood of committing future offenses. Second, when this potential source of bias is taken into account, the estimated effect of intake's recommendation for formal processing on future offending is not significant and is also negative in sign ($-.327$). This finding is consistent with results from the bivariate probit and instrumental variable models and suggests that, in these data, evidence supporting the deviance amplification thesis is artifactual.

---

[15] An area of some concern and controversy involves the identification of the parameter σ_{23}. If all of the variables in the referral equation are also included as independent variables in the recidivism equation, the parameters in the recidivism equation are only identified by the assumption that the joint distribution of the disturbance terms in the referral and recidivism equation error terms is bivariate normal. This is weak identification and rests on an assumption that is not readily testable. A recent discussion of preliminary work on estimators that are more robust to violations of distributional assumptions in selection models can be found in Duncan (1983, 1986). In the current application, the parameters in the recidivism equation are identified by exclusion restrictions; variables in the referral equation that are not in the recidivism equation. This form of identification is stronger to the degree that the exclusion restrictions are valid (see Olsen, 1980, and Heckman and Robb, 1985, for additional discussion on this point). As we noted earlier, there are variables that influence the probability of being referred to court that have no obvious theoretical relationship to recidivism.

[16] While the parameter estimates from equation (5) are consistent, they may be biased in small samples. Some simulation evidence of this is provided by Stoltzenberg and Relles (1990) when the second-stage regression model is based on samples of fifty cases. But since the bias and variance of a consistent estimator decreases as the sample size increases, our sample size of 2,716 cases is worth noting. Additionally, the estimated standard errors for applying OLS to equation (5) are incorrect and are adjusted using the method discussed by Green (1981).

1128   FUTURE DELINQUENCY

SUMMARY AND DISCUSSION

We have examined the claim that more formal processing by juvenile justice agencies is part of a deviance amplification process that increases future criminal activity. We have outlined an alternative argument suggesting that the positive association between being referred to court and future offending arises because of a selection artifact. This alternative hypothesis reflects the realities of the process by which persons are selected for further court processing and the limitations inherent in nonexperimental data. When youth are brought to juvenile intake, the staff of these agencies makes distinctions between high- and low-risk youth. To some extent these are subjective judgments based on a set of decisions rules formed from experience. Moreover, intake officers are more likely to refer higher-risk youth to juvenile court. The result is that the sample of persons referred to court will contain more high-risk youth who possess a greater likelihood of future delinquent activity. Since we may never be able to fully measure the factors on which youth are selected for referral to juvenile court, there will be heterogeneity between the samples of referred and diverted cases on factors used by intake officers to make referral decisions.

Selectivity bias arise if this heterogeneity is also related to youths' future offending. If intake officers are able to differentiate high-risk from low-risk youth with some degree of accuracy, decisions to refer cases to juvenile court will be positively correlated with unmeasured variables that also increase future offending. Under this scenario, the variable measuring whether a case is referred to court is confounded with unmeasured variables that are themselves causes of future criminal activity. To the extent such confounding exists, models that ignore this type of selection bias will overestimate the true effect of being referred to court on future offending.

Consistent with this expectation, results from a variety of models which assume that selection bias does not exist (Table 2) show that referral to court has a significant positive effect on recidivism. But further analyses which recognize the potential heterogeneity in risk factors between referred and diverted cases (Table 4) reveal that this apparent labeling effect of court referral can instead be attributed to a selection artifact.

Where does this leave us? We think the results reported here raise issues which future tests of deviance amplification should confront. One of these is that serious consideration be given to the possibility that a selection artifact may be responsible for the association between sanctions and future offending in previous analyses of nonexperimental data. Increased attention to this possibility is necessary to make strong inferences about the effects of sanctions on future behavior. In examining whether formal processing by the juvenile justice system increases future offending, the most appropriate null hypothesis is that juvenile justice processing has no causal effect on future offending. This does not mean that we believe this hypothesis is true. It does mean that the burden of proof rests with those who claim that a causal effect exists. Such claims are strengthened to the degree that rival explanations, such as selection bias, can be ruled out. The literature testing the deviance amplification hypothesis has been deficient on this point. We hope that results reported here stimulate future empirical work to correct this weakness.

We also hope that increased attention to possible selection bias in empirical tests of the deviance amplification hypothesis will lead to more conclusive evidence regarding the effects of sanctions on future criminal activity. Progress in this area requires more careful consideration of the assumptions underlying empirical tests. Each of the models we estimated to correct for selectivity bias invoke different assumptions which are either not testable or are matters for theory to resolve. Some of these models depend on distributional assumptions, others on the validity of specific exclusion restrictions. While we think that the specific exclusion restrictions used in the models we estimated make theoretical sense, these exclusion restrictions can never be proven to be true. Thus, results from our analyses remain subject to some degree of uncertainty. And while the results from alternative models to correct for selection bias are quite consistent in showing that referral to court does not lead to increased future offending, additional replications are essential to enhance confidence in this conclusion.

But it cannot be overlooked that models that ignore possible selectivity bias also make strong assumptions. The most critical of these is the assumption that there are no common unmeasured or omitted variables that influence both the probability of referral and the likelihood of future offending. We think our results cast considerable doubt on the validity of this assumption. Moreover, maintaining this assumption when it is not true can lead to substantial bias in the estimated effect of being referred to court on future offending.

In sum, determining whether the positive association between formal processing and future delinquent activity is the result of deviance amplification or a selection artifact is important for both theoretical reasons and from a public policy perspective. This article has focused on some issues in testing these alternative positions and finds no empirical support for the deviance amplification hypothesis. We hope that increased attention to the issues we have discussed and additional research will being us closer to resolving ongoing debates in theory and public policy regarding the effect of sanctions on future offending.

1130   FUTURE DELINQUENCY

REFERENCES

AMEMIYA, Takeshi (1985) *Advanced Econometrics*. Cambridge, MA: Harvard University Press.

BAILEY, William C., and Ruth D. PETERSON (1981) "Legal Versus Extralegal Determinants of Juvenile Court Dispositions," 32 *Juvenile and Family Court Journal* 41.

BARNOW, B.S., G. CAIN, and A. GOLDBERGER (1980) "Issues in the Analysis of Selectivity Bias," in E. Stromsdorfer and G. Farkas (eds.), 5 *Evaluation Studies*. San Francisco: Sage Publications.

BECKER, Howard (1963) *Outsiders*. New York: Free Press.

BISHOP, Donna, and Charles FRAZIER (1988) "The Influence of Race in Juvenile Justice Processing," 25 *Journal of Research in Crime and Delinquency* 242.

CAMERON, A. Colin, And P.K. TRIVEDI (1986) "Econometric Models Based on Count Data: Comparison and Applications of Some Estimators and Tests," 1 *Journal of Applied Econometrics* 29.

CICOUREL, Aaron V. (1968) *The Social Organization of Juvenile Justice*. New York: Wiley.

COHEN, Lawrence E. (1975) "Delinquency Dispositions: An Empirical Analysis of Processing Decisions in Three Juvenile Courts." Washington DC: U.S. Department of Justice.

COHEN, Lawrence E., and James KLUGEL (1978) "Determinants of Juvenile Court Dispositions: Ascriptive and Achieved Factors in Two Metropolitan Courts," 43 *American Sociological Review* 162.

DUNCAN, Gregory (1983) "Sample Selection as a Proxy Variable Problem: On the Use and Misuse of Gaussian Selectivity Corrections," *Research in Labor Economics*, Suppl. 2.

―――― (1986) "Continuous/Discrete Econometric Models with Unspecified Error Distribution," 32 *Journal of Econometrics* 1.

EMERSON, Robert (1969) *Judging Delinquents: Context and Process in Juvenile Court*. Chicago: Aldine.

EMPEY, Lemar T., and Maynard Erickson (1972) *The Provo Experiment*. Lexington, MA: D. C. Heath.

FARRINGTON, David P. (1983) "Randomized Experiments on Crime and Justice," in M. Tonry and N. Norris (eds.), 4 *Crime and Justice: An Annual Review of Research*. Chicago: University of Chicago Press.

―――― (1987) "Predicting Individual Crime Rates," in D. Gottfredson and M. Tonry (eds.), 9 *Crime and Justice: An Annual Review of Research*. Chicago: University of Chicago Press.

GOLD, Martin, and Jay R. WILLIAMS (1969) "A National Survey of the Aftermath of Apprehension," 3 *Prospectus* 3.

GREEN, William (1981) "Sample Selection Bias as a Specification Error: Comment," 49 *Econometrica* 795.

―――― (1990) *Econometric Analysis*. New York: MacMillan.

HECKMAN, James J. (1976) "Simultaneous Equation Models with Continuous and Discrete Endogenous Variables and Structural Shifts," in S. Goldfeld and R. Quandt (eds.), *Studies in Non-Linear Estimation*. Cambridge, MA: Ballinger.

―――― (1978) "Dummy Endogenous Variables in a Simultaneous Equation System," 46 *Econometrica* 931.

HECKMAN, James J., and V.J. HOTZ (1989) "Choosing Among Alternative Nonexperimental Methods for Estimating the Impact of Social Programs: The Case of Manpower Training," 84 *Journal of the American Statistical Association* 862.

HECKMAN, James J., and R. ROBB (1985) "Alternative Methods for Evaluating the Impact of Interventions," in J. Heckman and B. Singer (eds.), *Longitudinal Analysis of Labor Market Data*. New York: Cambridge University Press.

HIRSCHI, Travis (1975) "Labeling Theory and Juvenile Delinquency: An Assessment of the Evidence," in W. Gove (ed.), *The Labelling of Deviance: Evaluating a Perspective*. New York: Halstead Press.

HORWITZ, Allan, and Michael WASSERMAN (1979) "The Effect of Social

Control on Delinquent Behavior: A Longitudinal Test," 12 *Sociological Focus* 52.

KLEIN, Malcolm (1975) "Alternative Dispositions for Juvenile Offenders." Unpublished manuscript.

———— (1979) "Deinstitutionalization and Diversion of Juvenile Offenders: A Litany of Impediments," *in* N. Morris and M. Tonry (eds.), 1 *Crime and Justice: An Annual Review of Research*. Chicago: University of Chicago Press.

———— (1986) "Labeling Theory and Delinquency Policy," 13 *Criminal Justice and Behavior* 47.

LEMERT, Edwin M. (1951) *Social Pathology*. New York: McGraw Hill.

LIPTON, Douglas, Robert MARTINSON, and Judith WILKS (1975) *The Effectiveness of Correctional Treatment: A Survey of Treatment Evaluation Studies*. New York: Praeger.

LOEBER, Rolf, and Thomas DISHION (1983) "Early Predictors of Male Delinquency: A Review," 94 *Psychological Bulletin* 68.

Maddala, G. (1983) *Limited-dependent and Qualitative Variables in Econometrics*. New York: Cambridge University Press.

MEADE, Anthony C. (1974) "The Labeling Approach to Delinquency: State of the Theory as a Function of Method," 53 *Social Forces* 83.

MENG, Chun-Lo, and Peter SCHMIDT (1985) "On the Cost of Partial Observability in the Bivariate Probit Model," 26 *International Economic Review* 71.

OLSEN, R.J. (1980) "A Least Squares Correction for Selectivity Bias," 48 *Econometrica* 1815.

PATERNOSTER, Raymond, and Leeann IOVANNI (1989) "The Labeling Perspective and Delinquency: An Elaboration of the Theory and an Assessment of the Evidence," 6 *Justice Quarterly* 359.

RAUSCH, Sharla (1983) "Court Processing Versus Diversion of Status Offenders: A Test of Deterrence and Labeling Theories," 20 *Journal of Research in Crime and Delinquency* 39.

SCHUR, Edwin M. (1973) *Radical Non-intervention: Rethinking the Delinquency Problem*. Englewood Cliffs, NJ: Prentice-Hall.

SCULL, Andrew T. (1977) *Decarceration, Community Treatment and the Deviant: A Radical View*. Englewood Cliffs, NJ: Prentice-Hall.

SHANNON, Lyle W. (1980) "Assessing the Relationship of Adult Criminal Careers to Juvenile Careers," *in* C. Abt (ed.), *Problems in American Social Policy Research*. Cambridge: Abt.

———— (1988) *Criminal Career Continuity*. New York: Human Sciences Press.

SHERMAN, Lawrence W., and Richard A. BERK (1984) "The Specific Deterrent Effects of Arrest for Domestic Assault," 49 *American Sociological Review* 261.

STOLTZENBERG, Ross M., and D. A. RELLES (1990) "Theory Testing in a World of Constrained Research Design: The Significance of Heckman's Censored Sampling Bias Correction for Nonexperimental Research," 18 *Sociological Methods and Research* 395.

TANNENBAUM, Frank (1938) *Crime and the Community*. Boston: Ginn.

THORNBERRY, Terence P. (1971) "Punishment and Crime: The Effect of Legal Dispositions on Subsequent Criminal Behavior." Ph.D. Thesis, University of Pennsylvania.

TITTLE, Charles R. (1975) "Deterrents or Labeling," 53 *Social Forces* 399.

TITTLE, Charles R., and D. A. CURRAN (1988) "Contingencies for Dispositional Disparities in Juvenile Justice," 67 *Social Forces* 23.

WELLFORD, Charles F. (1975) "Labeling Theory and Crime: An Assessment," 22 *Social Problems* 332.

WILKINS, Leslie T. (1969) *Evaluation of Penal Measures*. New York: Random House.

WOOLDREDGE, John (1988) "Differentiating the Effects of Juvenile Court Sentences on Eliminating Recidivism," 25 *Journal of Research in Crime and Delinquency* 264.

Part III
Issues in Measurement

[8]

A NOTE ON THE USES OF OFFICIAL STATISTICS[1]

JOHN I. KITSUSE
Northwestern University
and
AARON V. CICOUREL
University of California, Riverside

Current theoretical and research formulations in the sociology of deviance are cast within the general framework of social and cultural differentiation, deviance, and social control. In contrast to the earlier moralistic conceptions of the "pathologies," the focus of description and analysis has shifted from the vagaries of morbid behavior to the patterning effects of the social-cultural environment on forms of deviant conduct. These forms of deviation are conceived as social products of the organization of groups, social structures, and institutions.

Three major lines of inquiry have developed within this general framework. One development has been the problem of explaining the rates of various forms of deviation among various segments of the population. The research devoted to this problem has produced a large body of literature in which individual, group, and areal (e.g., census tracts, regions, states, etc.) characteristics are correlated with rates of deviation. Durkheim's pioneer study of suicide is a classic example of this sociological interest. Merton's more general theory of social structure and anomie[2] may be cited as the most widely circulated statement of this problem.

The second line of investigation has been directed to the question of how individuals come to engage in various types of deviant behavior. From the theoretical standpoint, this question has been posed by the fact that although an aggregate of individuals may be exposed to the "same" sociogenic factors associated with deviant behavior, some individuals become deviant while others do not. Research into this problem has led some sociologists into the field of actuarial statistics and others to social and depth psychology to investigate differences in individual "adaptation" to the social-cultural environment. The search for the etiology of deviant behavior in individual differences has re-introduced the notion of "pathology," in the garb of "emotionally disturbed," "psychopathic personality," "weak ego-structure," and other psychological concepts, which has created an hiatus between sociological and social psychological

[1] We wish to acknowledge the support of the Youth Development Program of the Ford Foundation in facilitating the preparation of this paper.

[2] Robert K. Merton, *Social Theory and Social Structure*. revised, Glencoe: The Free Press, 1957, Chapter 4.

132   SOCIAL PROBLEMS

approaches. Sutherland's differential association theory[3] represents a counter-formulation which attempts to account for the etiology of deviant behavior within the general framework of "normal" learning processes.

A third line of inquiry has been concerned with the developmental processes of "behavior systems." Theory and research on this aspect of deviant behavior focuses on the relation between the social differentiation of the deviant, the organization of deviant activity, and the individual's conception of himself as deviant. Studies of the professional thief, convicts, prostitutes, alcoholics, hoboes, drug addicts, carnival men, and others describe and analyze the deviant sub-culture and its patterning effects on the interaction between deviant and others. The work of Lemert[4] presents a systematic theoretical and empirical integration of this interest in the sociology of deviance.

Although the three lines of investigation share a common interest in the organizational "sources" of deviant behavior, a theoretical integration between them has not been achieved. This is particularly apparent in the theoretical and methodological difficulties posed by the problem of relating the rates of deviant behavior to the distribution of "sociogenic" factors within the social structure. These difficulties may be stated in the form of two questions: (1) How is "deviant behavior" to be defined sociologically, and (2) what are the relevant rates of deviant behavior which constitute the "facts to be explained"? We shall propose that these difficulties arise as a consequence of the failure to distinguish between the social conduct which

produces a *unit* of behavior (the behavior-producing processes) and organizational activity which produces a unit in the rate of *deviant* behavior (the rate-producing processes.)[5] The failure to make this distinction has led sociologists to direct their theoretical and empirical investigations to the behavior-producing processes on the implicit assumption that the rates of deviant behavior may be explained by them. We shall discuss some of the consequences of this distinction for theory and research in the sociology of deviance by examining the problems of the "appropriateness" and "reliability" of official statistics.[6]

I

The following statement by Merton is a pertinent and instructive point of departure for a discussion of the questions raised above:

"Our primary aim is to discover how some *social structures exert a definite pressure upon certain persons in the society to engage in non-conforming rather than conforming conduct.* If we can locate groups peculiarly subject to such pressures, we would expect to find fairly high rates of deviant behavior in those groups, not because the human beings comprising them are compounded of distinctive biological tendencies but because they are responding normally to the social situation in which they find themselves. Our perspective is sociologi-

[3] Edwin H. Sutherland and Donald R. Cressey, *Principles of Criminology*, fifth edition, New York: Macmillan, 1956, Chapter 4.

[4] Edwin M. Lemert, *Social Pathology*, New York: McGraw-Hill, 1951, esp. Chapters 1-4. See also, Sutherland and Cressey, *op. cit.*, Chapters 12-13.

[5] The conception of the "rate-producing" processes as socially organized activities is taken from work by Harold Garfinkel, and is primarily an application of what he has termed the "praxeological rule." See Harold Garfinkel, "Some Sociological Concepts and Methods for Psychiatrists," *Psychiatric Research Reports*, 6 (October, 1956), pp. 181-195; Harold Garfinkel and Harry Brickman, "A Study of the Composition of the Clinic Patient Population of the Outpatient Department of the U.C.L.A. Neuropsychiatric Institute," unpublished manuscript.

[6] For a discussion of these problems, see Sophia M. Robison, *Can Delinquency Be Measured?*, New York: Columbia University Press, 1936. See also Sutherland and Cressey, *op. cit.*, Chapter 2.

A Note on the Uses of Official Statistics 133

cal. We look at variations in the *rates* of deviant behavior, not at its incidence."[7]

The central hypothesis that Merton derives from his theory is that "aberrant behavior may be regarded as a symptom of dissociation between culturally prescribed aspirations and socially structured avenues for realizing these aspirations."[8] The test of this general hypothesis, he suggests, would be to compare the variations in the rates of aberrant behavior among populations occupying different positions within the social structure. The question arises: What are the units of behavior which are to be tabulated to compile these rates of aberrant behavior?

Merton answers this question by discussing the kinds of rates which are "inappropriate," but he is less explicit about what may be considered "appropriate" data for sociological research. Discussing the relevance of his theory for research on juvenile delinquency, Merton presents two arguments against the use of "official" rates of deviant behavior. He asks:

". . . to what extent and for which purposes is it feasible to make use of existing data in the study of deviant behavior? By existing data I mean the data which the machinery of society makes available—census data, delinquency rates as recorded in official or unofficial sources, data on the income distribution of an area, on the state of housing in an area, and the like . . .

"There is little in the history of how statistical series on the incidence of juvenile delinquency came to be collected that shows them to be the result of efforts to identify either the sources or the contexts of juvenile delinquency. These are social bookkeeping data. And it would be a happy coincidence if some of them turned out to be in a form relevant for research.

"From the sociological standpoint, 'juvenile delinquency' and what it encompasses is a form of deviant behavior for which the epidemiological data, as it were, may not be at hand. You may have to go out and collect your own appropriately organized data rather than to take those which are ready-made by governmental agencies."[9]

Our interpretation of this statement is that for the purposes of sociological research, official statistics may use categories which are unsuitable for the classification of deviant behavior. At best such statistics classify the "same" forms of deviant behavior in different categories and "different" forms in the same categories. Thus, the "sources or the contexts" of the behavior are obscured.

Merton also argues against the use of official statistics on quite different grounds. He states that such data are "unreliable" because "successive layers of error intervene between the actual event and the recorded event, between the actual rates of deviant behavior and the records of deviant behavior."[10] In this statement, the argument is that the statistics are unreliable because some individuals who manifest deviant behavior are apprehended, classified and duly recorded while others are not. It is assumed that if the acts of all such individuals were called to the attention of the official agencies they would be defined as deviant and so classified and recorded. In referring to the "unreliability" of the statistics in this sense, however, Merton appears to suspend his "sociologically relevant" definition of deviant behavior and im-

---

[7] Robert K. Merton, *op. cit.*, p. 147. Merton's comments on the theory of social structure and anomie may be found in Chapter 5 of that volume, and in "Social Conformity, Deviation, and Opportunity Structures: A Comment on the Contributions of Dubin and Cloward," *American Sociological Review*, 24 (April, 1959), pp. 177-189; See also his remarks in *New Perspectives for Research on Juvenile Delinquency*. H. Witmer and R. Kotinsky, editors, U. S. Government Printing Office, 1956.
[8] *Social Theory and Social Structure, op. cit.*, p. 134.

[9] *New Perspectives for Research on Juvenile Delinquency, op. cit.*, p. 32.
[10] *Ibid.*, p. 31.

plicitly invokes the definitions applied by the agencies which have compiled the statistics. That is, the "unreliability" is viewed as a technical and organizational problem, not a matter of differences concerning the definition of deviant behavior.

Thus, Merton argues against the use of official statistics on two separate grounds. On the one hand, official statistics are not appropriately organized for sociological research because they are not collected by the application of a "sociologically relevant" definition of deviant behavior. On the other hand, he implies that official statistics *could* be used if "successive layers of error" did not make them "unreliable." But if the statistics are inappropriate for sociological research on the first ground, would they not be inappropriate regardless of their "unreliability"?

It is evident, however, that "inappropriate" or not, sociologists, including Merton himself,[11] do make use of the official statistics after a few conventional words of caution concerning the "unreliability" of such statistics. The "social bookkeeping data" are, after all, considered to bear some, if unknown, relation to the "actual" rates of deviant behavior that interest sociologists. But granted that there are practical reasons for the use of official statistics, are there any theoretical

grounds which justify their use, or is this large body of data useless for research in the sociology of deviance? This question directs us to examine more closely the theoretical and methodological bases of the two arguments against their use.

II

The objection to the official statistics because they are "inappropriate" is, as indicated above, on definitional grounds. The argument is that insofar as the definitions of deviant behavior incorporated in the official statistics are not "sociologically relevant," such statistics are *in principle* "inappropriate" for sociological research. What then is a sociologically relevant definition of deviant behavior and what are to be considered "appropriately organized data" for sociological research?[12]

We suggest that the question of the theoretical significance of the official statistics can be re-phrased by shifting the focus of investigation from the processes by which *certain forms of behavior* are socially and culturally generated to the processes by which *rates*

---

[11] For example, ". . . crude (and not necessarily reliable) crime statistics suggest . . ." etc., *Social Theory and Social Structure*, op. cit., p. 147. In a more extensive comment on the limitations imposed on research by the use of official statistics, Merton states: "Its decisive limitation derives from a circumstance which regularly confronts sociologists seeking to devise measures of theoretical concepts by drawing upon an array of social data which *happen* to be recorded in the statistical series established by agencies of the society —namely, the circumstance that these data of social bookkeeping which happen to be on hand are not necessarily the data which best measure the concept. . . . Pragmatic considerations of this sort are of course no suitable alternative to theoretically derived indicators of the concept." p. 165.

[12] Merton proposes to define deviant behavior in terms of the "acceptance" or "rejection" of cultural goals and/or institutionalized means. Interpreting the two terms literally, a given form of behavior (adaptation) is to be considered deviant if it is oriented by some cultural goals (to be specified by the sociologists) and/or the institutionalized means (also to be specified) which govern conduct with respect to those goals. By this definition, appropriately organized data would require that behaviors be classified in the typology of "modes of individual adaptation." But what are the operational criteria by which "acceptance" or "rejection" of cultural goals and institutionalized means are to be inferred from observed behavior? How, for example, is the sociologist to distinguish between behavior which indicates "conformity" from "over-conformity" (which presumably would be classified as "ritualism"), or "retreatism" from "innovation"? Unless a set of rules for the classification of behavior as deviant can be derived from the theory, rates of deviant behavior cannot be constructed to test its validity.

of deviant behavior are produced. Merton states that his primary aim is to explain the former processes, and he proposes to look at variations in the rates of deviant behavior as indices of the processes. Implicit in this proposal is the assumption that an explanation of the behavior-producing processes is also an explanation of the rate-producing processes. This assumption leads Merton to consider the correspondence between the forms of behavior which his theory is designed to explain and their distribution in the social structure as reflected in some set of statistics, including those commonly used official statistics "which are ready-made by governmental agencies."

Let us propose, however, the following: Our primary aim is to explain the *rates of deviant behavior*. So stated, the question which orients the investigation is not how individuals are motivated to engage in behavior defined by the sociologist as "deviant." Rather, the definition and content of deviant behavior are viewed as problematic, and the focus of inquiry shifts from the forms of behavior (modes of individual adaptation in Merton's terminology) to the "societal reactions" which define various forms of behavior as deviant.[13] In contrast to Merton's formulation which focuses on forms of behavior as dependent variables (with structural pressures conceived to be the independent variables), we propose here to view the rates of deviant behavior as dependent variables. Thus, the explanation of rates of deviant behavior would be concerned specifically with the processes of rate construction.

The problem of the definition of "deviant behavior" is directly related to the shift in focus proposed here. The theoretical conception which guides us is that the *rates of deviant behavior* are produced by *the actions* taken by persons in the social system which define, classify and record certain behaviors as deviant.[14] If a given form of behavior is not interpreted as deviant by such persons it would not appear as a unit in whatever set of rates we may attempt to explain (e.g., the statistics of local social welfare agencies, "crimes known to the police," Uniform Crime Reports, court records, etc.). The persons who define and activate the rate-producing processes may range from the neighborhood "busybody" to officials of law enforcement agencies.[15] From this point of view, *deviant behavior* is behavior which is organizationally defined, processed, and treated as "strange," "abnormal," "theft," "delinquent," etc., by the personnel in the social system which has produced the rate. By these definitions, a sociological theory of deviance would focus on three interrelated problems of explanation: (1) How different forms of behavior come to be defined as deviant by various groups or organizations in the society, (2) how individuals manifesting such behaviors are organizationally processed to produce rates of deviant behavior among various segments of the population, and (3) how acts which are officially or unofficially defined as deviant are generated by such conditions as family organization, role inconsistencies or situational "pressures."

---

[13] For a discussion of the concept of "societal reaction" see Edwin M. Lemert, *op. cit.*, Chapter 4.

[14] For a preliminary research application of this formulation, see John I. Kitsuse, "Societal Reaction to Deviant Behavior: Problems of Theory and Method," *Social Problems*, 9 (Winter, 1962), pp. 247-56.

[15] We recognize, of course, that many individuals may be labeled "strange," "crooks," "crazy," etc., and ostracized by members of a community, yet be unknown to the police or any other official agency. Insofar as such individuals are labeled and treated as deviants, they constitute a population which must be explained in any theory of deviance. In this paper, however, we are primarily concerned with the theoretical relevance of official statistics for the study of deviance.

What are the consequences of these definitions for the question regarding the relevance of official statistics for sociological research? First, the focus on the processes by which rates are produced allows us to consider any set of statistics, "official" as well as "unofficial," to be relevant. The question of whether or not the statistics are "appropriately organized" is not one which is determined by reference to the correspondence between the sociologist's definition of deviant behavior and the organizational criteria used to compile the statistics. Rather the categories which organize a given set of statistics are taken as given—the "cultural definitions," to use Merton's term, of deviant behavior are *par excellence* the relevant definitions for research. The specification of the definitions explicitly or implicitly stated in the statistical categories is viewed as an empirical problem. Thus, the question to be asked is not about the "appropriateness" of the statistics, but about the definitions incorporated in the categories applied by the personnel of the rate-producing social system to identify, classify, and record behavior as deviant.

Second, a unit in a given rate of deviant behavior is not defined in terms of a given form of behavior or a "syndrome" of behavior. The behaviors which result in the classification of individuals in a given deviant category are *not necessarily* similar, i.e., the "objective" manifestation of the "same" forms of behavior may result in the classification of some individuals as deviant but not others. For example, with reference to the rates of delinquency reported by the police department, we would ask: What are the criteria that the police personnel use to identify and process a youth as "incorrigible," "sex offender," "vandal," etc.? The criteria of such categories are vague enough to include a wide range of behaviors which in turn may be produced by various "sources and contexts" within the social structure.[16]

Third, the definition of deviant behavior as behavior which is organizationally processed as deviant provides a different perspective on the problem of the "unreliability" of the official statistics. Insofar as we are primarily concerned with explaining rates rather than the forms of deviant behavior, such statistics may be accepted as a record of the number of those who have been differentiated as variously deviant at different levels of social control and treatment. The "successive layers of error" which may result from the failure of control agencies to record all instances of certain forms of behavior, or from the exclusion of cases from one set of statistics that are included in another, do not render such statistics "unreliable," unless they are assigned self-evident status. By the definition of deviance proposed here, such cases are not among those processed as deviant by the organizations which have produced the statistics and thus are not officially deviant. To reject these statistics as "unreliable" because they fail to record the "actual" rate of deviant behavior assumes that certain behavior is always deviant independent of social actions which define it as deviant.

Forth, the conception of rates of deviant behavior as the product of the socially organized activities of social structures provides a method of specifying the "relevant structure" to be investigated. The rates are constructed from the statistics compiled by specifiable organizations, and those rates must be explained in terms of the deviant-

---

[16] In any empirical investigation of such criteria, it is necessary to distinguish between the formal (official) interpretive rules (as defined by a manual of procedures, constitution, and the like) which are to be employed by the personnel of the organizations in question, and the unofficial rules used by the personnel in their deviant-processing activities, e.g., differential treatment on the basis of social class, race, ethnicity, or varying conceptions of "deviant" behavior.

processing activities of those organizations. Thus, rates can be viewed as indices of organizational processes rather than as indices of the incidence of certain forms of behavior. For example, variations in the rates of deviant behavior among a given group (e.g., Negroes) as reflected in the statistics of different organizations may be a product of the differing definitions of deviant behavior used by those organizations, differences in the processing of deviant behavior, differences in the ideological, political, and other organizational conditions which affect the rate-making processes.

III

We wish now to discuss briefly some recent work[17] concerning adult and juvenile criminal acts which lends support to the thesis presented above. Let us assume that an ideal system of law-enforcement would lead to the apprehension of all persons who have committed criminal acts as defined by the statutes, and adjudicated in the manner prescribed by those statutes. In the ideal case, there would be little room for administrative interpretation and discretion. The adjudication process would proceed on the basis of evidence deemed legally admissible and the use of the adversary system to convict those who are guilty and exonerate those against whom there is insufficient evidence.[18] Criminologists have long recognized that the practiced and

enforced system of criminal law, at all levels of the process, does not fulfill this ideal conception of criminal justice strictly governed by the definitions and prescriptions of statutes. Therefore, criminal statistics clearly cannot be assumed to reflect a system of criminal justice functioning as ideally conceived, and "labels assigned convicted defendants" are not to be viewed as "the statutory equivalents of their actual conduct."[19]

What such statistics do reflect, however, are the specifically organizational contingencies which condition the application of specific statutes to actual conduct through the interpretations, decisions and actions of law enforcement personnel. The decisions and discretionary actions of persons who administer criminal justice have been documented by the American Bar Foundation study cited above. That study and other research[20] indicates the following:

1. There is considerable ambiguity in defining the nature of criminal conduct within the limits defined by the statutes. Categories of criminal conduct are the product of actual practices within these limits, and the decisions which must be made to provide the basis for choosing the laws which will receive the greatest attention.
2. The discretion allowed within the administration of criminal justice means that admissible evidence may give way to the prosecutor's power to determine whether or not to proceed, even in cases where there is adequate evidence to prosecute. The judge, as well as the police or the victim, also has discretion (e.g., sentencing), and some discretion is also extended to correctional institutions.
3. Most persons charged with criminal conduct plead guilty (from 80 to 90 per cent, according to the references cited by Newman) and jury trials are rare. Thus, the adversary aspect of the law is not always practiced because many of the lower income of-

---

[17] The material in this section is taken from an unpublished paper by Cicourel entitled "Social Class, Family Structure and the Administration of Juvenile Justice," and is based on a study of the social organization of juvenile justice in two Southern California communities with populations of approximately 100,000 each.
[18] See Donald J. Newman, "The Effects of Accommodations in Justice Administration on Criminal Statistics," *Sociology and Social Research,* 46 (Jan., 1962), pp. 144-155; *Administration of Criminal Justice,* Chicago: American Bar Foundation, 1955, unpublished.

[19] Newman, "The Effects of Accommodations. . . ," *op. cit.,* pp. 145-146.
[20] See *ibid.,* pp. 146-151, and the references cited.

fenders cannot afford lawyers and often distrust public defenders. Criminal justice depends upon a large number of guilty pleas. Many of these cases would be acquitted if there were more trials.

4. Statistics are affected by such "accommodations in the conviction process." Some offenders are excluded because they are not processed even though known to be guilty (e.g. drug addicts, prostitutes and gamblers are often hired by the police or coerced by them to help apprehend other offenders), and the practice of re-labeling offenses and reducing sentences because of insufficient evidence, "deals," and tricks (e.g., telling the defendant or his lawyer that because the offender "seems like a decent person" the charge will be reduced from a felony to a misdemeanor, when in fact the prosecution finds there is insufficient evidence for either charge.) These accommodations may occur at the time of arrest, or during prior or subsequent investigation of crimes, filing of complaints, adjudication, sentencing and post-sentencing relations with authorities, and so on.

The significance of the American Bar Foundation study goes beyond the documentation of the usual complaints about inadequate recording, inflated recording, and the like. More importantly, it underlines the way criminal statistics fail to reflect the decisions made and discretion used by law-enforcement personnel and administrators, and the general accommodations that can and do occur. An offender's record, then, may never reflect the ambiguous decisions, administrative discretions, or accommodations of law enforcement personnel; a statistical account may thus seriously distort an offender's past activities.

. The administration of justice vis-a-vis juveniles is even more discretionary than for adults due to the philosophy of the juvenile court law. The juvenile offender is not officially viewed as a criminal, but rather as an adolescent who is "mis-directed," "disturbed," from a "poor environment," and the like. The legal concept of an adversary system is notably absent. The philoso-

phy, however, is differentially interpreted, with police more likely to view juveniles as adult criminals, while probation officers and some judges view the offender within the intended meaning of the law. The early work of Paul Tappan on juvenile court practices[21] shows how a juvenile court judge, on the counsel of a social worker or other "treatment oriented" personnel, may dispose of a case in a manner which negates all previous characterizations of the offender by police, probation officer, school officials, and the like. The report of the more recent California Special Study Commission on Juvenile Justice[22] alludes vaguely to and in some passages flatly states that many variations of organizational procedures and interpretations by personnel differentially influence the administration of juvenile justice in California. The use of existing stereotypes and imputations of social characteristics to juvenile defendants by law enforcement personnel routinely introduce nonlegal criteria and actions into the organizational procedures of the legal process and significantly influences the realization of judicial objectives."[23]

We wish to state explicitly that the interpretation of official statistics proposed here *does not* imply that the forms of behavior which the sociolo-

---

[21] *Juvenile Delinquency*, New York: McGraw-Hill, 1949.

[22] Report of the *Governor's Special Study Commission on Juvenile Justice*, Parts I and II, Sacramento: California State Printing Office, 1960.

[23] To illustrate how organizational procedures and imputations can affect official statistics, we refer to a preliminary finding by Cicourel (cited in footnote 17) which shows that one of two communities studied (Community A) has both a slightly larger population and a higher adult crime rate. Yet this community had (as of November, 1962) 3200 current cases of juveniles suspected or confirmed to be offenders. Community B, on the other hand, had approximately 8000 current suspected or confirmed juvenile cases. Community A has two juvenile officers on its staff, while Community B has five juvenile officers.

gist might define and categorize as deviant (e.g., Merton's modes of adaptation) have no factual basis or theoretical importance. Nor do we wish to imply that the question of how behaviors so defined are produced by the social structure is not a sociologically relevant question. The implication of our interpretation is rather that *with respect to the problem of rates of deviant behavior* the theoretical question is: what forms of behavior are organizationally defined as deviant, and how are they classified, recorded and treated by persons in the society?

In our discussion, we have taken the view that official statistics, reflecting as they do the variety of organizational contingencies in the process by which deviants are differentiated from nondeviants, are sociologically relevant data. An individual who is processed as "convicted," for example, is sociologically differentiable from one who is "known to the police" as criminal— the former may legally be incarcerated, incapacitated and socially ostracized, while the latter remains "free." The fact that both may have "objectively" committed the same crime is of theoretical and empirical significance, but it does not alter the sociological difference between them. The *pattern* of such "errors" is among the facts that a sociological theory of deviance must explain, for they are indications of the organizationally defined processes by which individuals are differentiated as deviant.

Indeed, in modern societies where bureaucratically organized agencies are increasingly invested with social control functions, the activities of such agencies are centrally important "sources and contexts" which generate as well as maintain definitions of deviance and produce populations of deviants. Thus, rates of deviance constructed by the use of statistics routinely issued by these agencies are social facts *par excellence*. A further implication of this view is that if the sociologist is interested in how forms of *deviant* behavior are produced by social structures, the forms that must be explained are those which not only are defined as deviant by members of such structures but those which also activate the unofficial and/or "official" processes of social control. By directing attention to such processes, the behavior-producing and rate-producing processes may be investigated and compared within a single framework.

[9]

On Exploring the "Dark Figure" of Crime*

By Albert D. Biderman and Albert J. Reiss, Jr.

ABSTRACT: The history of criminal statistics bears testimony to a search for a measure of "criminality" present among a population, a search that led increasingly to a concern about the "dark figure" of crime—that is, about occurrences that by some criteria are called crime yet that are not registered in the statistics of whatever agency was the source of the data being used. Contending arguments arose about the dark figure between the "realists" who emphasized the virtues of completeness with which data represent the "real crime" that takes place and the "institutionalists" who emphasize that crime can have valid meaning only in terms of organized, legitimate social responses to it. This paper examines these arguments in the context of police and survey statistics as measures of crime in a population. It concludes that in exploring the dark figure of crime, the primary question is not how much of it becomes revealed but rather what will be the selective properties of any particular innovation for its illumination. Any set of crime statistics, including those of survey research, involve some evaluative, institutional processing of people's reports. Concepts, definitions, quantitative models, and theories must be adjusted to the fact that the data are not some objectively observable universe of "criminal acts," but rather those events defined, captured, and processed as such by some institutional mechanism.

Albert D. Biderman, Ph.D., Washington, D.C., is Senior Research Associate, Bureau of Social Science Research, Inc., Washington, D.C. He explored uses of crime statistics as social indicators in a recent monograph on Social Indicators and Goals (1966).

Albert J. Reiss, Jr., Ph.D., Ann Arbor, Michigan, is Professor and Chairman, Department of Sociology, and Director, Center for Research on Social Organization, University of Michigan. He is the author of some thirty articles and studies on crime, juvenile delinquency, and law enforcement.

* The support of the Russell Sage Foundation is gratefully acknowledged.

STATISTICAL criminology began with the development of *moral statistics*.[1] No subject has dominated the field of criminal statistics more since its inception than the search for the key moral statistic—a measure of the "criminality" present among a population. This search led increasingly to a concern about the "dark figure" of crime—that is, about occurrences that by some criteria are called crime yet that are not registered in the statistics of whatever agency was the source of the data being used.[2]

The history of criminal statistics testifies to continuing contention between those who sought to bring more of the dark figure to statistical light and those who deplored elements of invalidity in each such attempt. The major object of this contention for over a century was police statistics. Both official and scholarly comprehensions of the incidence of crime were almost exclusively based on statistics of indictments or adjudications. There were those who sought the development of police sta-

tistics to supplement, if not supplant, them. The contending arguments were fundamentally between what we can loosely term "realist" as opposed to "institutionalist" emphases.[3] The former emphasized the virtues of completeness with which data represented the "real crime that takes place." The institutionalist perspective emphasized that crime could have valid meaning only in terms of organized, legitimate social responses to it.

The ultimate juristic view is that a given crime is not validly known to have taken place until a court finds someone guilty of that offense. Only at that point in the process has there been an irrevocable decision as to the evidence regarding the objective facts in relation to their legal significance. Outside the United States, there was little resistance to utilizing data from earlier stages in the adjudicatory process, such as prosecution, indictment, arraignment, or even investigation, particularly in legal

[1] The French are generally credited with the early development of moral statistics. Especially noteworthy is the work of A. M. Guerry, *Essai sur la statistique morale de la France* (Paris, 1833). Guerry calculated rates of crimes against persons and property for 86 departments of France and age-sex specific crime rates for seventeen crimes against the person and seventeen against property. The rates were presented in tabular, graphic, and cartographic forms.

[2] The earliest published discussion of the dark-figure problem that we have been able to find is that of Bulwer. In his two-volume treatise on France, published in 1836, Bulwer devoted an entire chapter to crime in France, based primarily on A. M. Guerry's major work. Bulwer (pp. 174–175) discusses the problem of using either offenses known or of the accused as measures of crime and concludes that, despite their limitations, they are more accurate than calculations based on convictions. See Henry Lytton Bulwer, *France, Social, Literary, Political,* Vol. I, Book I: *Crime* (London: Richard Bentley, 1836), pp. 169–210.

[3] William Douglas Morrison stated the distinction rather well in a paper before the Royal Statistical Society in 1897: "If . . . we are anxious to know how the criminal law is being administered, we shall analyse and classify the contents of the statistics from that point of view. If on the other hand we desire to know the movement of crime, the criminal conditions of the community, and the relative value of the several methods by which these methods are to be ascertained, we shall adopt a somewhat different method of classifying the contents of criminal statistics. I have ventured to classify criminal statistics into police statistics, judicial statistics, and prison statistics because I desire, at least in the first place, to point out the amount of weight to be attached to each of these methods of recording the nature and proportions of crime." —"The Interpretation of Criminal Statistics," *Journal of the Royal Statistical Society,* Vol. LX, Part I (March 1897), pp. 1–24, at pp. 1–2. Also: "But it would be a mistake to suppose that the number of crimes known to the police is a complete index of the total yearly volume of crime. The actual number of offenses annually committed is always largely in excess of the number of officially recorded crimes" (*Ibid.,* p. 4).

systems where there are police magistrates.[4] In all countries, however, most criminologists were less ready to credit the competence of the police to make determinations of the objective facts and to classify them validly—police competence being judged in terms of legitimacy, skill, and the adequacy of information available to the police. Presumably, the lower social status of the police than of the bench—and, correlatively, the greater political power of the judiciary—together with the loose fashion in which police systems were for long grafted on the legal-institutional systems, has much to do with these views.[5]

There has been a long contest to gain institutional acceptance for police statistics over opposition from legalistic traditionalism. In England, a plan was worked out for the collection of police statistics on a uniform and national basis in 1856, and they have been a regular part of the annual report of criminal statistics since 1857. While from the outset, police statistics were logically placed prior to judicial statistics in the published volumes, in 1893

they were placed after court statistics with the statement:

The tables of the results of judicial proceedings, which are at once the most important, the most definite, and the most accurate of all criminal statistics, occupy the first place. The tables as to police action . . . are of less statistical value, and follow in a subordinate position.[6]

Not until 1923 did the argument over their merit abate sufficiently in England so that they were accepted as a valid basis for estimating crime.[7] Even today, in England, police statistics are considered less reliable than judicial statistics.

An additional difficulty inhered in the localistic nature of police organization in the United States. Not only did this make for dubiousness about the judgment and record-keeping capabilities of police in all but the larger jurisdictions, but producing national series also posed formidable problems of standardization and compilation of data from a multitude of jurisdictions having a myriad of laws, definitions, and practices. The present voluntary system of national crime reporting in the United States owed its form and many of its limitations to the fact that the national government cannot (at least not readily) compel local governments to report on their operations.[8]

As police statistics were legitimated, statistics on arrests generally gained acceptance earlier than those based on

[4] In France, for example, early statistical compilations of crime provided information on *accusations, accusés, acquités,* and *condamnés.* See *Recherches statistiques sur la ville de Paris et le department de la Seine* (A Paris de l'Imprimerie Royale, 1821–1830). See also Guerry, *op. cit.*

[5] The *Report on Criminal Statistics,* U.S. National Commission on Law Observance and Enforcement (Washington, D.C.: U.S. Government Printing Office, 1931) stated contemporary views in the United States: "If it took the highly centralized English Government 66 years to get its famous and highly efficient police to report correctly crimes known to the police, it is evident that it will be many years before our decentralized and nonprofessional police forces can be induced to make trustworthy reports of crimes known to the police" (p. 55). After more than a third of a century, patience is still being counseled: see Peter P. Lejins, "Uniform Crime Reports," *Michigan Law Review,* 64 (April 1966), pp. 1011–1030.

[6] Great Britain, *Judicial Statistics, England and Wales,* 1893, Part I: *Criminal Statistics,* p. 14.

[7] *Ibid.,* 1923, p. 5.

[8] For a good history and discussion of the problems of uniform crime reporting in the United States during the formative period, see U.S., Department of Justice, *Ten Years of Uniform Crime Reporting, 1930–1939: A Report by the Federal Bureau of Investigation* (Washington, D.C.: U.S. Government Printing Office, 1939), esp. chap. v.

citizen complaints or reports of offenses known to the police. Arrests involve the legal authority system, while the status of a citizen complaint is moot. Eventually, however, realist perspectives prevailed, and the Uniform Crime Reports (UCR's) from the outset gathered information on all offenses reported or known to the police. Nonetheless, there is a strong disposition to count as offenses only those that are substantiated by police investigation—a process of "unfounding" citizen complaints. Published reports of UCR count only the number of "actual offenses" that survive police "unfounding" procedures.

To a considerable degree, precisely what the institutional view regarded as the vices of police statistics, the realist one regarded as sources of virtue. This was the absence of any "institutional processing" of the data—the selecting, defining, and winnowing of records of events by legitimate organizations of the legal system in accordance with legally established evidentiary and evaluative criteria and procedures. The classical statement for American police statistics by Sellin sums up why police statistics of "offenses known" provide the "best index" of crime:

In general, it may be said that the value of a crime rate for index purposes is in inverse ratio to the procedural distance between the commission of the crime and the recording of it as a statistical unit. An index based on crimes reported to or known to the police is superior to others, and an index based on statistics of penal treatment, particularly prison statistics, is the poorest.[9]

Each remove from the crime, in terms of official procedures, leaves more of the actual crime taking place in a community submerged in the dark figure. Each procedural step, furthermore, is so selective that the "visible tip of the

iceberg of crime" looks progressively different from the huge submerged mass.

The classically realist view in the use of police statistics as an index of criminality attaches greatest emphasis to those police data which are least dependent on agency action. Arrests, which vary with the extent, skill, and discretion of police activity, thus are regarded as a less satisfactory basis for an index of criminality than complaints, reports, and directly observed ("police on-view") "crimes." The realist view, at the same time, held that even police statistics distort the "real crime problem." An "index" of "crime," therefore, was devised that would provide a measure of the "crime problem" least subject to effects of jurisdiction. The UCR annual report states the case:

Not all crimes come readily to the attention of the police; not all crimes are of sufficient importance to be significant in an index; and not all important crimes occur with enough regularity to be meaningful in an index.[10]

Among all offenses known to the police, those were selected for index purposes for which, in theory at least, the police function most nearly as passive recorders and nondiscretionary classifiers of events that take place. Index crimes are, in each case, offenses which largely come to the attention of the police by complaints from those victimized by the event. Violations which do not involve specific victims, or which largely or wholly come to be registered only as a result of police action, such as disorderly conduct, assaulting an officer, and receiving stolen property, are excluded from the measure. Of-

[9] *Encyclopedia of the Social Sciences*, Vol. 4, p. 565.

[10] U.S., Department of Justice, Federal Bureau of Investigation, *Crime in the United States: Uniform Crime Reports* (Washington, D.C.: U.S. Government Printing Office, 1930—— [annually]). The above quotation is taken from the annual report for 1964, p. 48.

fenses also deemed unsuitable for an index are those unlikely to be reported to the police either because they involve only persons disinclined toward police action, as is usually the case for gambling, prostitution, and other illegal services, or because the offenses are frequently too trivial to be "worth the bother" of reporting, such as petty larcenies and acts of malicious mischief. An additional criterion of the realist position was that the criminal act should be uniformly classifiable, independently of the varying local laws and practices. Miscegenation, until recently, afforded a clear example of an offense unsuitable for an index.

Realist views in the United States became predominant, first in criminological theory and then in practice, with the establishment in 1929 of the compilation of a national crime statistics series by the Federal Bureau of Investigation from voluntary reports by police agencies. The UCR index of crime that resulted from the application of these "realist" criteria consists of counts of offenses known to the police falling in seven predatory, common-law classifications: homicide, forcible rape, robbery, aggravated assault, burglary, larceny ($50 and over), and automobile theft.

Although police statistics gained acceptance largely as a result of realists' efforts to achieve more comprehensive and less selective indexes than were provided by institutional data, the victory of police statistics had barely begun to be consolidated before some realists attacked these statistics on the same grounds. Police statistics were challenged as not reflecting "the real crime picture." The criticism, as had been the case with older dissatisfactions with court and prison statistics, concentrated on the "real crime" that *escaped* the police data rather than on *invalid* classification of events as crimes. Critics

pointed out that police statistics reflected only an unknown and selective portion of "all crime" and that they distorted in many ways the kinds of crime they did reflect. Interestingly, defenses of police statistics have come to rest increasingly on institutionalist arguments, rather than the realist ones to which they largely owe their acceptance. In rebutting criticisms of UCR, for example, Lejins writes:

The existence of serious offenses not reported in the police statistics should not be accorded exaggerated meaning in the sense of detracting from the significance of the criminal activity that *is* reflected in the *Reports*, since the latter do encompass the bulk of the conventional, serious behavior to which society chooses to react through its public law enforcement agencies.[11]

It is beyond the scope of this essay to recapitulate the many criticisms and defenses that have been made of police statistics, generally, and the Crime Index, in particular.[12] It is important here, however, to formulate the thrust of these criticisms with respect to the misleading social implications that were seen in police statistics.

Because of the partial and selective nature of the police data, comparisons based on them of variations in "actual

---

[11] Lejins, *op. cit.*, p. 1010.

[12] For recent criticisms, see Daniel Glaser, "National Goals and Indicators for the Reduction of Crime and Delinquency," *Social Goals and Indicators for American Society*, Vol. I, The Annals, Vol. 371 (May 1967), pp. 104–126; Stanton Wheeler, "Criminal Statistics: A Reformulation of the Problem," *Journal of Criminal Law and Criminology*, Vol. 58 (September 1967); Marvin E. Wolfgang, "Uniform Crime Reports: A Critical Appraisal," *University of Pennsylvania Law Review*, Vol. 111 (April 1963), pp. 708–738. For a defense, see Lejins, *op. cit.*, pp. 1011–1130. See also Albert D. Biderman, "Social Indicators and Goals," in Raymond A. Bauer (ed.), *Social Indicators* (Cambridge, Mass: The M.I.T. Press, 1966).

crime" over time, between places, and among components of the population, are all held to be grossly invalid. Furthermore, because of the fundamental subordination of police statistics to the particular normative perspectives and workings of this institution, it is contended, there are limitations and distortions inherent in the significance drawn from them for social policy.

Barely masked in these contentions regarding statistics have been more fundamental ideological cleavages.[13] It is useful to make explicit that much of the argument over appropriate indexes of criminality tends to array on one side those who regard a person's social status as largely a product of his own vices and virtues, and on the other, those who interpret status, as well as vices and virtues, as largely a product of socially conferred advantages and disadvantages. With regard to measures for dealing with crime, the cleavages are, for example, between deterrence and social amelioration, or between punishment and therapy.

Ideological cleavage had clear expression in Sutherland's denunciation of the failure of conventional crime statistics to reflect "white-collar crime." In prevalence and in economic and social effects, Sutherland sought to show, law violations by a person of "the upper socioeconomic class in the course of his occupational activities" were more consequential than the typically lower-class crimes that comprised the index. Something of the same thrust was inherent in the innovation of self-reporting studies. The high proportions of middle-class persons who admit having committed serious delicts indicated both that the dark figure of crime must be of vast proportions and, at the very least, that "criminal" behavior was not nearly as exclusively a lower-class

[13] Lejins, *op. cit.*, pp. 1029–1030.

property as suggested by arrest and juvenile delinquency statistics.[14]

Despite the great effort devoted to developing and operating a uniform reporting system, the use of the police data for interarea comparisons has also been subject to vigorous criticism on a variety of grounds. One form of criticism pointed to the many instances in which abrupt and vast increases of crime figures for cities occurred when police reforms curtailed the practice of "killing crime on the books." Police departments and political administrations controlling them, it is often alleged, frequently have too great a stake in the effects of their crime figures on their "image" to be trusted to report fully and honestly. Beyond these qualms regarding "statistical conflicts of interest," there was evidence that police departments with effective and centralized controls over the reporting by individual officers and divisions reflected more of "true crime" in their communities than did less tightly organized departments.[15]

In recent years, the strongest complaint against police statistics has suggested that much of the rapid and extreme reported increases in the extent of criminality are spurious, being but a surfacing of what has heretofore been

[14] For a recent summary, see Harwin L. Voss, "Socioeconomic Status and Reported Delinquent Behavior," *Social Problems,* 13 (Winter 1966), pp. 314–324. See also Albert J. Reiss, Jr. and Albert Lewis Rhodes, "The Distribution of Juvenile Delinquency in the Social Class Structure," *American Sociological Review,* 26 (October 1961), pp. 720–732.

[15] In U.S., President's Commission on Law Enforcement and Administration of Justice, *The Challenge of Crime in a Free Society,* hereinafter referred to as General Report (Washington, D.C.: U.S. Government Printing Office, 1967), of the two recommendations concerning the measurement of crime, one was that each city adopt centralized procedures for handling crime reports from cities (pp. 27, 293).

in the dark figure. The most general argument takes the form that crime *statistics* are as much (and perhaps more) a product of modern urban social organization as are the so-called urban forms of criminal behavior.[16] For example, it is suggested that the professionalization and bureaucratization of police forces with centralized command and control leads to improved record-keeping and greater use of formal, as opposed to informal, police procedures, with consequent increases in figures of offenses and arrests. And it is maintained that as larger proportions of the population become integrated into the dominant society and come to share its normative conceptions, more people mobilize the police to enforce middle-class norms regarding property, violence, and public deportment. At the same time, these public agencies become less disposed toward a tolerant view and informal processing of deviance.[17]

That improvements in law enforcement frequently have the effect of decreasing the dark figure, and consequently inflating statistics used to judge the magnitude of the crime problem, can be disconcerting for those planning innovational reforms. The President's Commission on Law Enforcement and Administration of Justice (hereinafter referred to as the National Crime Commission), for example, produced a table illustrating reporting-system changes in a dozen major cities that resulted in Crime Index increases of from 27 per cent to more than 200 per cent over the immediately preceding report.[18] The nation's two largest cities,

it went on to say, in this way, "have several times produced large paper increases in crime." [19] Current attempts at improving police-community relations conceivably could produce sharp "paper increases" in some classes of crime were they to result in a greater disposition of citizens to report offenses.[20]

But no basis exists for forming proportionate estimates of what kinds of criminal behavior are reported to the police. Primarily with this problem in mind, the National Crime Commission undertook exploration of the use of cross-sectional survey methods.[21] A central idea was that one could discover crimes not known to the police by screening random samples of the population to find the victims of these crimes.

Sample Surveys and the Dark Figure

Given the growth of what is literally a vast citizen-interviewing industry in the United States, it perhaps is surprising that the sample survey had not hitherto been applied to systematic examination of the crime problem.[22] Perhaps, the very availability of the captive populations in correctional institutions (if we include educational institutions as such), and of the neatly

[16] For a discussion, see Albert D. Biderman, "Social Indicators and Goals," in Bauer (ed.), *op. cit.*, pp. 124–125.

[17] John Kitsuse and Aaron Cicourel, "A Note on the Use of Official Statistics," *Social Problems*, 11 (Fall 1963), pp. 131–139.

[18] U.S., President's Commission on Law Enforcement and Administration of Justice, General Report, *op. cit.*, p. 25.

[19] *Ibid.*, p. 26.

[20] Neil Rackham, "The Crime-Cut Campaign," *New Society*, 238 (April 1967), pp. 563–564.

[21] Albert D. Biderman, "Surveys of Population Samples for Estimating Crime Incidence," in this issue of The Annals, pp. 16–33. Subsequently, a similar survey was undertaken by the Government Social Survey of Great Britain. The results of this work were not available at the time of writing. (Personal communication from Louis Moss, Director, Great Britain Government Social Survey, July 18, 1967.)

[22] A search of the Roper Public Opinion Research Center poll repository disclosed that, until 1964, public opinion surveys had given little attention to crime, except for polling sentiments regarding capital punishment and juvenile delinquency.

compiled agency statistics, diverted attention from such possibilities.

Neglect of the interview survey represents some discontinuity in the history of social research on crime, however. In the nineteenth century, a far more prominent place was accorded surveys of populations for knowledge. Henry Mayhew and Charles Booth, who often are credited with having set the path for the survey movement, were, for example, very conscious that the significance of crime for the poor of the city resided as much in their being its victims as in their being its contributors.[23] Booth's systematic survey sought to investigate "the numerical relation which poverty, misery, and depravity bear to the regular earnings and comparative comfort, and to describe the general conditions under which each class lives." [24]

Although there has been an occasional specific suggestion of using "Gallup Poll" methods[25] as a specific check on official statistics, the current turning to the cross-sectional survey method probably has received greater impetus from recent comments that criminology has been neglecting the victim in its concentration on the criminal. These writings argue that attention in criminology has been misdirected by the usual tendency to regard the victim of crimes as a purely passive and accidental target of the criminal act. A science of "victimology" is proposed to explain social, psychological, and behavioral characteristics that predispose some individuals to victimization, including factors considerably more subtle than such commonly recognized contributing acts as negligence and provocation by which some persons precipitate criminal acts toward themselves.[26]

Attention to the victim has also been urged from a quite different evaluative standpoint. In prefacing the 1963 volume of *Crime in the United States: Uniform Crime Reports,* the Director of the Federal Bureau of Investigation wrote:

Statistics herein are published in terms of the number of crimes reported and persons arrested. At the same time, they also represent a count of millions of victims. While some of these victims may have been "merely inconvenienced," the vast majority suffered property losses they could ill afford and many lost their physical or mental health while others lost their lives. Nevertheless, many impassioned and articulate pleas are being made today on behalf of the offender tending to ignore the victim and obscuring the right of a free society to equal protection under the law.[27]

In the 123 pages of "general United States crime statistics" in the 1963 *Uniform Crime Reports,* however, the equivalent of only two pages provides any information on the victims of crime —and this only if we include categories of property as "victims." But two tables dealt with persons as victims: one on "Murder Victims [by age]— Weapons Used" and one on "Murder Victims by Age, Sex and Race."

In sponsoring cross-sectional interviewing surveys, the National Crime Commission hoped to be able to develop

[23] Henry Mayhew, *London Labour and the London Poor: Cyclopedia of the Conditions and Earnings of Those That Will Not Work* (London: Charles Griffin, 1861); Charles Booth, *Labour and Life of the People* (London: Williams and Norgate, 1891).

[24] Booth, *op. cit.,* Vol. 1, p. 6.

[25] Inkera Anttila, "The Criminological Significance of Unregistered Criminality," *Excerpta Criminologica,* Vol. 4 (1964), pp. 411–414.

[26] See selected bibliography in B. Mendelsohn, "The Origin of the Doctrine of Victimology," *Excerpta Criminologica,* Vol. 3 (May–June, 1963).

[27] U.S., Department of Justice, Federal Bureau of Investigation, *Crime in the United States: Uniform Crime Reports, op. cit.,* 1963, p. vii.

data on the characteristics of victims that would go considerably beyond the scant information available from police sources. Since the same surveys were directed toward developing data on citizens' behavior and attitudes toward the crime problem and toward law enforcement, it would also be possible to relate such attitudes to actual experience with crime as contrasted with secondary influences such as the mass media.

HOW MUCH CRIME IS THERE?

It should be apparent that the answer to the question of how much crime there is depends to a great extent upon whether one phrases the question from an institutionalist or a realist position. The choice of indicators and their labels, to a great extent, bears marks of these positions. The hallmarks of the realists are the prevalence of criminals and their acts of crime; more recently, of victims. The hallmarks of the institutionalists are the prevalence of only such of these as survive institutional validation.

But there are no rates without some organized intelligence system, whether that of the scientist, the police, or the jurist. The sample survey, the citizen's mobilization of the police, and the pretrial and trial proceedings are all organized intelligence systems that process events and people to determine their crime status. The criteria of knowing, defining, and processing lie in organization.

Given the diversity of sources and types of information on crimes, the procedures that one develops for determining whether an event has occurred and who was involved in it must vary. It is doubtful, therefore, whether, logically, any currently organized way of knowing makes possible the computation of a measure of crime that can serve equally all purposes and perspectives.

Kitsuse and Cicourel state the purposes and perspectives of a sociologistic institutionalist:

Indeed in modern societies where bureaucratically organized agencies are increasingly invested with social control functions, the activities of such agencies are centrally important sources and contexts which generate as well as maintain definitions of deviance which produce populations of deviants. Thus, rates of deviance constructed by the use of statistics routinely issued by these agencies are social facts *par excellence*.[28]

This quotation discriminates the use of agency data from the perspective of the institutional processing of observations from that of the realist. Realists use agencies as a tool for observations of realities external to them.

The ideal mechanism for a realist would be a universal surveillance of time and space by recording mechanisms completely sensitive to all pertinent phenomena. Yet any organization confronts technical limitations to observation. Inherent in any observational system are errors from sampling probability, faulty observation and measurement, imperfections in operational translation of observational categories, and impedance to flow and feedback in communication.

Organizations such as the police have their own surveillance purposes. For processors inside the organization, an ideal surveillance mechanism is not an alien concept. However, action and observational mechanisms are inextricably linked one to the other.

From a realist point of view, this linkage makes the organization serve observational purposes poorly. For example, operational organizations such as the police or courts choose not to observe more than they can process with given resources, and they selectively screen observations to fit organizational goals, strategy, and tactics. Further-

[28] Kitsuse and Cicourel, *op. cit.*, p. 139.

more, organizations suffer from their own form of deviance, the subversion of organizational goals by their members. Three strategies are open to realists in overcoming these organizational barriers to information. First, they can insulate the surveillance apparatus from operations, as, for example, through the creation of central communications, intelligence, and records divisions.[29] Second, they can undertake independent surveillance of the operating system, by monitoring through outside observers either the operations or records of the organization.[30] Third, they can develop surveillance completely independent of the organization. The sample survey of the public is one of a variety of such devices.[31] A separate intelligence organization is another.

The deviance of members of the system from system norms, with respect to reporting as well as technical limitations to observation that are errors from a realist point of view, negates the social-choice interpretations of organizational data made by institutionalists. From a radical institutionalist point of view, these errors are treated, in part, as irrelevant, in that the differential sensitivity of surveillance reflects, to a substantial degree, social choices of what

it is important to observe. Nonetheless, technical limitations as well as social choice reflect what is responded to. Indeed, realism itself is a system norm for members of organizations.

From the standpoint of a scientific criminology, a defect of the institutionalist point of view is that it uses concepts and data derived exclusively from those employed by formal organizations of the law-enforcement and legal systems. There is more to social life than its formally organized aspects. For scientific purposes, independently organized observations employing appropriate concepts and tools of measurement are necessary.

Thus, attacking the institutionalist point of view, Glaser points out that:

> Variation in the public definition of most predatory crimes is not appreciable, especially outside of so-called "white-collar crimes." The categories of predatory crimes most commonly distinguished in the law—for example, murder, robbery, burglary, theft, fraud, and rape—have almost everywhere and always been employed to denote essentially the same types of behavior as criminal. In almost all societies, they comprise the majority of acts for which severe negative sanctions are imposed.[32]

But, clearly, a large proportion of these "crimes" are "processed," if at all, only by informal mechanisms. "The criminal offense" itself is an important social transaction, quite apart from social transactions that ensue thereafter. It should be evident that police data, whether on offenses or arrests, exaggerate the incidence of those kinds of offenses for which an identifiable person is suspect, in that these are more likely to be reported to the police and processed by the department through investigation.

The neglect of victims in processing

---

[29] For a discussion of this strategy by police chiefs, see David J. Bordua and Albert J. Reiss, Jr., "Command, Control, and Charisma: Reflections on Police Bureaucracy," *American Journal of Sociology*, Vol. 72 (July 1966), pp. 68–76.

[30] For an organized observational study of the police, see Donald J. Black and Albert J. Reiss, Jr., "Patterns of Behavior in Police and Citizen Transactions," in Albert J. Reiss (ed.), *Studies in Crime and Law Enforcement in Major Metropolitan Areas*, U.S. President's Commission on Law Enforcement and Administration of Justice Field Survey III (Washington, D.C.: U.S. Government Printing Office, 1967).

[31] See Albert D. Biderman, "Surveys of Population Samples for Estimating Crime Incidence," in this issue of THE ANNALS, pp. 16–33.

[32] Glaser, *op. cit.*, p. 107.

by law-enforcement, legal, and correctional agencies is another case in point. Offense rates, today, are based on data from the police; victim rates, on data from independently organized means.

Offense Rates and Victimization Rates

Any simple incidence rate consists of but two elements, a population that is exposed to the occurrence of some event (the denominator) and a count of the events (the numerator). Both of these events are measured for a given point or period of time. An offense rate states the probability of occurrence of an offense for a given population while a victimization rate states the probability of being a victim of some offense.

There is no simple relationship between offense and victimization rates, however. Consider an event occurring that is to be defined as a crime or a criminal offense. A single social encounter may involve more than one offense leading to multiple indictments of an offender or offenders in the event. This is the case, for example, when one is charged with larceny of an auto and larceny from an auto or when one is charged with armed robbery and simple assault. A single encounter may involve one or more persons as victims or it may involve no persons as victims. An offense against public order or decency may be observed only by a police officer, while the robbery of patrons in an establishment may involve large numbers of victims. Similarly, the number of offenders may vary, and indeed there may be mutual victimization and offending, as is the case in assaults that give rise to cross-complaints. Furthermore, for a given period of time over which the rate is calculated, any person may be a victim of one or more crime events—one's house may be burglarized on several occasions, for instance.

Given the fact that a single event may produce multiple victimization and multiple offenses and that, over time, there is repeated victimization, it is difficult to calculate *a priori* the relationship between offense and victimization rates. For some types of crimes, the number of crime victims exceeds the number of offenses, particularly if one makes rather simple assumptions that "collective property" *ipso facto* defines "collective victimization." Thus, if one defines all members of a household as victims of a burglary, a single breaking and entering of a household involves all of its members as victims. Indeed, it may involve more than members of the household. A breaking and entering, for example, that does damage to property, may involve a landlord as victim of a breaking and tenants as victims of burglary. On the other hand, repeated victimization of a person by offenses over time and multiple offenses against a victim in a single event lead to conditions where the number of offenses exceeds the number of victims.

While, in the aggregate of all crime events, it would appear that the victimization rate should be higher than the offense rate, assuming that the number of crime victims exceeds the number of offenses, it is by no means clear what the magnitude of the difference is. Indeed, much depends upon how one counts the offenses and victims in a situation and upon the time interval over which one is calculating the event. The problem may not be unlike that for morbidity, where, in a relatively short time interval, the number of visits to a physician exceeds the number of persons who are ill.

Salience of Events and Their Recall

Applying the sample-survey method to the realist's objective of illuminating the dark figure of crime assumes that events are salient to persons as real experiences and that what appear to be socially salient events, such as crimes, will be readily recalled and recounted. The organized processes of the mind are regarded as providing more valid and reliable information than the organized processes of organizations, the armament of the institutionalists.

Yet, recent research on recall of events assumed to be salient and significant to persons clearly indicates that, even in the very short time interval, there is a selective recall of events. There is a significant amount of underreporting noted in studies of hospitalization and visits to doctors, for example.[33] These studies and others where the sample survey is used to recall events that organizations record as having taken place lead to several generalizations. First, underreporting increases with

length of time between the event and the interview. Second, the degree of social threat or embarrassment is negatively related to rate of reporting. Third, the greater the involvement in institutional processing, the more likely it is to be recalled. Episodes that involve surgical treatment and long stays are more likely to be recalled, for example.[34] Fourth, respondents report their own experiences better than those of others. Fifth, the more events to which one has been subject, the more likely one is to report a known event.

Perhaps the crucial matter is that underreporting is selective among classes of persons and events, and by time. For analysis, then, the problem of separating truth from differences in reporting rates is confronted precisely as in any other organizationally processed data. Survey interviewing, in fact, has become an institutionalized device, with its own meanings for the population. Consequently, rates of mentions of events can be subject to institutional interpretation. One such interpretation might be the salience of a type of experience to different classes of respondents.

The study of crime events makes apparent each of these conditions affecting recall. Indeed, it is likely that institutional processing of an event is an important factor in recall; yet it clearly is not a sufficient condition, as events where institutional processing occurs—calling the police, for example—prove to be insufficient conditions for recall. What does seem obvious is that, provided individuals can be brought to report events to organizations, organi-

[33] A study of visits to doctors for the National Health Survey showed that 30 per cent of the known visits to doctors during a two-week period prior to the week of interviewing were *not* reported in response to a standard National Health Survey question; 23 per cent remained unreported after three special probe questions had been asked. The study also shows that underreporting was greater for less recent visits, that women reported better than men, and that persons with more serious health conditions and more visits during the two-week period were more likely to report. See Charles F. Cannell and Floyd J. Fowler, "A Study of the Reporting of Visits to Doctors in the National Health Survey," Survey Research Center, University of Michigan, October 1963, p. 8.

The study of hospitalization of persons showed that hospitalized persons in the sample underreported for themselves by 7 per cent, while the rate for both proxy adults and children was twice as high. The underreporting rate was lowest for women reporting the birth of a child, being but 2 per cent. See U.S., National Center for Health Statistics, *Comparison of Hospitalization Reporting in the Health Interview Survey*, U.S. Department of Health, Education, and Welfare Series 2, No. 6 (Washington, D.C.: U.S. Government Printing Office, July 1965), p. 8.

[34] U.S., National Center for Health Statistics, *Comparison of Hospitalization Reporting in Three Survey Procedures*, U.S. Department of Health, Education, and Welfare Series 2, No. 8 (Washington, D.C.: U.S. Government Printing Office, July 1965), p. 7

zational intelligence is superior to recall. The weight of the argument, in that sense, lies with the institutionalists.

Comparability of Police and Survey Statistics

Many of the limitations of police statistics, for which the survey has been claimed as a corrective, are not inherent in the theoretical capabilities of law enforcement as a system. Indeed, police agencies today collect far more information than they process statistically or publish. They collect, but rarely publish, information, for example, on victims, multiple offenders and offenses, suspects, the nature of criminal transactions, and the time and place of their occurrence. It is primarily the failure to process information, rather than inherent limitations in collection, that renders comparison between survey and police data difficult.

The survey is generally designed to gain data on victimization, while the police report data on complaints and observed violations, reporting them as offenses known to the police. Even when one sets the denominator in an incidence rate—the exposed population —common to both, it is no simple matter to render the two sets comparable.

To gain some comparability of victimization rates with police offense rates, it is necessary to adjust survey data for victimization occurring outside the jurisdiction sampled (a trivial problem for a national sample); victimization of more than one person in given incidents; and "false" or "baseless" reports. Furthermore, if one is interested in comparing survey estimates of offenses with police estimates of them, the survey estimates should take account of whether or not the respondent reported the event to the police.

At the same time, police data must be rendered comparable with that from survey sources. Since police data are collected by place of occurrence rather than by place of residence of the victim, for less than national units, they must be adjusted for place of residence. Furthermore, police data include offenses against businesses and other organizations; household samples may not. Finally, if only the adult population is sampled and there is no reporting for others in the household, offenses involving persons not included in the sample must be eliminated.

The fact that the two series are not altogether comparable should make clear that institutionalist and realist perspectives are built into the data for reasons that derive from these very perspectives. Consider the fact that police statistics are for offenses by place of occurrence of the event. It should be obvious that a law-enforcement system based on a strategy and tactics of deployment of technology and manpower is interested in the location of events—events that dictate proactive and reactive strategies. Such an interest is not incompatible with exploration of the dark figure *per se*, but it is incompatible with the realist ideology of how much crime there is.

Validity of Survey Data on Crime

The crux of the traditional realist-versus-institutionalist controversy involves questions of validity rather than reliability. The cross-section sample survey may represent an extreme pole in the movement from "institutionalist" to "realist" approaches to crime statistics, in its complete dependence on the unsupported verbal testimony of a non-official character.

This logical possibility should not obscure the fact that formal organizational processing systems similarly rely primarily on unsupported oral testimony—the complaints of citizens or officers as witnesses, without other evidence. Indeed, most adjudicatory processes, such as the pretrial hearing or the decision to prosecute, rely heavily on unsupported testimony. Nonetheless, these formal systems, unlike the survey, rest on both the potential of investigation and formal sanctions to reduce fabrication. Technically, the survey might employ many of the same techniques available to the police; but these are alien to its basic premises, and the survey organization lacks formal sanctions.

The survey method, rather, tries to exploit the advantage that no material consequences ensue from testimony. The guarantee of anonymity, the relative absence of sanctions for providing information, and the general absence of consequences in giving information avoid some conditions that give rise to nonreporting to the police and other formal agencies. Such an advantage is of no little consequence in exploring the dark figure of crime.

In exploring the dark figure of crime, the survey generally has several other advantages over other organizationally processed statistics. First, it provides a form of organization that can transcend local practices by providing uniform operational definitions. Second, the survey taps the definitions of victims, independent of organizational processing, and it can compare these with those of formal processing organizations. Third, the survey can identify and compare what is institutionally labeled as crime with that consensually labeled as crime.

Although the data cannot be adduced here, problems of evidence rather than of inference probably predominate statistically in exploring the dark figure. Determining the objective character of events seems more problematic than inferring the motivation and competence that make acts *legally* criminal.

CONCLUSION

Statistical criminology, from its outset, has searched for the key moral statistic, a measure of the "criminality" present among a population. Both "institutionalists" and "realists" have pursued this search. The foregoing discussion has not made explicit our key premise, that is, the question of whether this search has been a scientific one. If pragmatic objectives of criminal statistics are posed, there are no data *par excellence*, nor is there a theory *par excellence*.

Although a neat polar distinction has been employed that pits institutionalist against realist perspective, in practice, neither camp has been comfortable in, and hence rarely consistent with, its position. The neglect of the role of organization in the production of knowledge has led both camps astray. On the one hand, the realists neglect the shaping of objective reality by whatever the organizational mode of registering knowledge. On the other, the institutionalists confuse the observational efficacy of organizations with their normative functioning. Realist objectives are best served by special organizational structures for observing and recording events. Institutionalist goals would be best served by special organizational structures for developing and scientific processing of operational organizational activity. Concepts and operational definitions will differ depending upon formally organized or informal social processes, whether those of science, of operations, or of social policy are the primary objective.

In exploring the dark figure of crime, the primary question is not how much of it becomes revealed but rather what will be the selective properties of any

On Exploring the "Dark Figure" of Crime 15

particular innovation for its illumination. As in many other problems of scientific observation, the use of approaches and apparatuses with different properties of error has been a means of approaching truer approximations of phenomena that are difficult to measure.

Any set of crime statistics, including those of the survey, involves some evaluative, institutional processing of people's reports. Concepts, definitions, quantitative models, and theories must be adjusted to the fact that the data are not some objectively observable universe of "criminal acts," but rather those events defined, captured, and processed as such by some institutional mechanism.

[10]

Rap Sheets in Criminological Research: Considerations and Caveats

Michael R. Geerken[1]

The types of errors found in official criminal history records are not completely understood by many researchers, and this lack of understanding can lead to serious misinterpretations. Analyses of a recently developed database of New Orleans offenders indicate that the use of rap sheets with a limited catchment area can lead to gross distortions of the effects of variables related to geographic mobility, such as race and age. Evidence from a number of sources indicates that false-negative error is a serious problem, particularly in fingerprint-based record systems. In addition, arrest records lend themselves to a variety of common misinterpretations by researchers in the coding process, including failing to identify multievent arrests, misclassifying arrests, and treating arrest or custody process events as crimes indicating criminal activity of the individual while free. Solutions to some of these problems are suggested.

KEY WORDS: rap sheet; criminal history; arrest record; false-negative error.

1. INTRODUCTION

Official records of individuals' arrests, convictions, and custody have always held and will continue to hold an important place in criminological research. These records are traditionally used in research on recidivism and, most recently, among researchers developing the "criminal career" model. Though many researchers have wrestled with the methodological issues involved in assembling and interpreting rap sheets, the problems have never been systematically addressed in the published literature. Substantial attention has been paid by criminologists to Uniform Crime Reports data and the construction of criminal statistics by officials. Studies focus on the determinants of citizen reporting of crimes to police and on police recording or nonrecording of these alleged offenses. The records of arrests found in individual criminal histories maintained by local and state agencies and the

[1]Orleans Parish Criminal Sheriff and Department of Sociology, Tulane University, New Orleans, Louisiana 70118.

FBI, however, are generated by very different processes involving a different set of issues. The errors common in these records, which are the result primarily of processes within and among criminal justice agencies where citizen reporting is not an issue, have not been systematically explored in terms of their potential effect on research results.

Rap sheets are sometimes accepted at face value by researchers. Indeed, with rare exceptions (see, e.g., Widom, 1989), the source and scope of rap sheet data (FBI database, state fingerprint depository, or local rap sheet) are not clearly identified. Even when the source is clearly identified, the only problems recognized are (1) missing rap sheets, (2) conflicts between rap sheets from different sources, and (3) the absence of final disposition or incarceration data.

The most pernicious forms of error found in rap sheet data arise from local police department booking and fingerprint procedures and state and FBI criminal history system policies and actual procedures. Detailed knowledge of such matters is limited to a small group of criminal justice professionals directly involved in maintaining these databases or in policy-making in certain narrow areas, such as the SEARCH Group.[2] They are familiar with many problems that have important implications for criminological research but are not primarily concerned with their implications for such research.

This paper outlines the methodological problems that rap sheet data present to criminologists, with a primary focus on the adequacy of official criminal history data for estimating an offender's criminal activity. This study should help to sensitize both researchers who use rap sheets and consumers of this research to biases that might, at the least, suggest alternative explanations of findings. A criminal history database recently assembled for the New Orleans Offender Study is used to test the effects of rap sheet source and scope on research results and to develop preliminary estimates of the nature, extent, and importance of some sources of rap sheet error for criminological research.

2. CRIMINAL HISTORY DATABASES IN THE UNITED STATES

There are well over 200 million criminal history records in the United States, 45 million maintained by state governments [Bureau of Justice Statistics (BJS), 1991], about 27 million of which are automated, 25 million by the FBI, and an estimated 135 million by local law enforcement agencies (Laudon, 1986, p. 11). Forty-two states have computerized at least part of

---

[2]This is an offshoot of the LEAA, which is now a private consulting group for state and federal criminal justice agencies.

their criminal history records and about 12.5 million of the criminal finger-print files maintained by the FBI have been placed on computer. There is no estimate available of the extent to which local law enforcement agencies have automated their ciminal records, although most large metropolitan jurisdiction do have computerized criminal history systems.

In some ways rap sheet problems are simply the result of the severely decentralized nature of the American criminal justice system. Most law enforcement, including the arrest and booking of offenders, takes place at the local level, and state governments often do a poor job of regulating and systematizing the record keeping of these arrests. The history of the development of computerized criminal record systems shows not only that the states are often unwilling to conform to federal guidelines, but also that Washington cannot formulate a consistent approach of its own.

A history of the development of a criminal records policy in the United States is outside the scope of this paper (see Marchand, 1980; Laudon, 1986), but certain consistent themes in that history have important implications for problems in offenders' rap sheets. Since the mid-1960's, it has been recognized that there are vast deficiencies in the completeness, consistency, and accuracy of criminal justice data and that modern computer technology has the potential for remedying these deficiencies (President's Commission on Law Enforcement and the Administration of Justice, 1967). Through Title I of the Omnibus Crime Control and Safe Streets Act of 1968, Congress created a federal agency, the Law Enforcement Assistance Administration (LEAA), responsible for funding reform and modernization of the criminal justice system. Through its power to fund the development of state computerized criminal justice information systems,[3] the LEAA during the decade of the 1970s fostered a tremendous expansion of state systems. From the beginning, however, this program was intended to promote a decentralized, federated system, an example of President Nixon's "New Federalism."

The early 1970s saw a struggle among the LEAA, the FBI, and Congress both to define the nature of a national computerized criminal history system (CCH) and to control it. The FBI's early plans to develop a national, computerized criminal history database was gradually modified into the current system, in which the FBI maintains criminal history records for 26 states but only an identification system for the others. The 24 states that participate in the Interstate Identification Index (III) maintain their own criminal history databases: arrests in these states are not submitted to the FBI database. Instead, the FBI maintains an offender index for these states. Inquiries on

---

[3]From 1972 to 1978, the LEAA spent more than $68 million through the CDS program to fund the development of state criminal justice information systems. This does not include LEAA block fund expenditures for the development of these systems (Marchand, 1980, p. 73).

an offender result in a request for information sent by the FBI to that state
if the FBI's index indicates that the offender has an arrest there. The state
can then respond with its information over one of two communications
networks (NCIC or NLETS). Eventually, all states are expected to participate in the III. The FBI will then maintain arrest histories only on federal
offenders.

This decentralized, state-based approach to the maintenance of criminal history systems has important implications for research. Even when
working properly, the system is designed for one-at-a-time inquiries by
a law enforcement agency about an individual offender. If the offender
has been active in many states, the inquiry will generate separate responses
from each state, which the agency must then collate and interpret. Even
if a researcher were to obtain access to the system to make inquiries,
the assembly of a comprehensive national database of a large number of
offenders using such an approach would be extremely and, in most cases,
prohibitively expensive. This will force most researchers to rely on one
local or state database for rap sheets. As we shall see, this limitation
can have important ramifications.

3. RAP SHEET SCOPE

The difficulty involved in getting access to and assembling rap sheets
leads many researchers to rely on local or single state information systems,
with the implicit assumption that arrests from other jurisdictions are
randomly distributed over variables of interest. This is not, however,
necessarily the case. To determine if the jurisdictional scope or arrest
catchment area of the rap sheet can affect research results, the criminal-
history database recently assembled for the New Orleans Offender Study
(NOOS) was used.

The NOOS database is a data set created by merging five criminal
justice databases. This analysis focuses on two arrest history databases; the
New Orleans Police Department's arrest history system (MOTION), years
1973–1986, and the Louisiana criminal history system (FINDEX) maintained by the Louisiana Department of Public Safety, years 1974–1986. The
FINDEX database includes all arrests submitted on fingerprint cards and
accepted by the Louisiana State Police. FINDEX also includes arrests outside Louisiana maintained by the FBI. FBI-maintained arrests are added
when fingerprint cards on arrestees are submitted either by the State Police
or by local jurisdictions to the FBI. FBI rap sheets are then forwarded to
the State Police and added to FINDEX. The NOOS database, then, includes

Table I. Percentage of New Orleans Burglary and Armed Robbery Offenders Born Out of State by Race and Age in 1985

Age in 1985	Race					
	Black	(N)	White	(N)	All	(N)
<17	5.7	(1,513)	26.7	(140)	7.5	(1,653)
17–25	8.9	(6,713)	36.1	(1,095)	12.7	(7,808)
26–35	14.3	(6,424)	51.5	(1,174)	20.0	(7,598)
36+	20.7	(2,105)	67.8	(323)	27.0	(2,428)
All	12.2	(16,755)	46.0	(2,732)	16.9	(19,487)

arrests maintained by the local information system, by the state, and by the FBI.[4]

The criminal histories developed in the NOOS were the result of extensive matching procedures on a variety of identifiers that searched for all arrest records for an individual (for a description of the process, see Geerken *et al.*, 1993). The NOOS focuses on the effect of the criminal justice system on the crimes of burglary and armed robbery committed in New Orleans and, specifically, on the incapacitative effect of incarceration. The study population is all offenders arrested at least once for burglary or armed robbery in New Orleans during the 14-year period 1973–1986.

The scope of rap sheet data will affect research results to the extent that geographic mobility is correlated with race, sex, age, employment, and other demographic factors. In particular, the correlation of arrest-based measures with these demographic variables will not be accurately estimated if the rap sheet is limited in geographic scope.

Table I shows the potential distortion geographic mobility can introduce into race and age comparisons. There are large racial differences in the mobility of both burglars and armed robbers, and these differences persist within age categories. Whites and older offenders who commit crime in New Orleans are much more likely to have moved there from outside Louisiana. This suggests that a larger percentage of their arrests would be available to researchers only from other state or FBI rap sheets. Comparisons in number of arrests based on local data only, then, might seriously exaggerate the criminality of blacks relative to whites and younger offenders relative to older offenders.

These conclusions are supported by arrest data from the NOOS official record database. To assess directly the effect rap sheet scope has on research,

[4]Since FBI rap sheets are forwarded to the State Police only when a Louisiana fingerprint card is received, non-Louisiana arrests are included in the NOOS database only prior to the last recorded Louisiana arrest. Therefore the following analysis focuses on periods prior to a Louisiana arrest or as early in the 1974–1986 measurement period as possible.

Table II. Race Effects by Rap Sheet Type

	Race		
Rap sheet type	Black	White	Ratio
	Prior index arrests[a]		
New Orleans only	3.04	1.62	1.89
MOTION system	3.08	2.44	1.26
Louisiana	3.46	2.92	1.18
All arrests	3.73	3.52	1.06
(N)	(1,565)	(339)	
	Index rearrest rate[b]		
New Orleans only	2.09	0.91	2.30
MOTION system	2.18	1.19	1.83
Louisiana	2.26	1.28	1.77
All arrests	2.34	1.50	1.56
(N)	(2,118)	(616)	

[a]For criterion arrest (burglary or armed robbery) in 1985.
[b]Years 1974–1979 after criterion arrest in 1974.

two samples were selected from the NOOS database: those with criterion (burglary or armed robbery) arrests in 1985 and those with criterion arrests in 1974. For the 1985 sample, the number of prior index arrests was calculated by rap sheet source and type. For the 1974 sample, the number of index arrests for the subsequent 5-year period was calculated, again by rap sheet source and type.[5]

Prior index arrests and post arrest 5-year rates were separately calculated for (1) New Orleans arrests only (any database), (2) the local arrest history system (MOTION) only, which includes New Orleans and a number of surrounding parishes, (3) Louisiana arrests only (MOTION and FINDEX databases), and (4) all arrests.

Table II shows the dependence of race–crime effects on rap sheet scope. It is clear that a large racial effect appears for both arrests and postarrest 5-year rate when only local arrests are considered. Rates for blacks are about twice those for whites. When all arrests are considered, however, the racial effect is substantially reduced and, in the case of prior index arrest rate, virtually eliminated.

[5]The samples were selected in this way for the following two reasons: (a) Prior arrest and post arrest years are marked only from years when criterion arrests occurred to simulate typical research analyses, where prior arrests are used to predict the disposition of a current arrest or conviction (pretrial release, sentence, etc) and post arrests are used to measure recidivism after some criminal justice contact; and (b) 1985 is chosen as the prior arrest criterion year and 1974 as the post arrest year to ensure that as much time as possible in the measurement period is covered by all the study databases.

Table III. Age Effects by Rap Sheet Type

Rap sheet type	Age			
	<17	17–25	26–35	36+
	Prior index arrests[a]			
New Orleans only	1.01	2.56	3.59	4.09
MOTION system	1.09	2.89	3.91	3.13
Louisiana	1.09	3.00	4.45	5.38
All arrests	1.09	3.08	4.93	7.22
(N)	(277)	(994)	(501)	(169)
	Index rearrest rate[b]			
New Orleans only	3.38	1.46	1.03	0.91
MOTION system	3.44	1.63	1.16	0.93
Louisiana	3.50	1.74	1.23	0.99
All arrests	3.53	1.86	1.41	1.15
(N)	(678)	(1,401)	(492)	(165)

[a]For criterion arrest (burglary or armed robbery) in 1985.
[b]Years 1974–1979 after criterion arrest in 1974.

Rap sheet scope has a significant effect on the age–crime relationship as well (see Table III). In this case the local rap sheet presents an exaggerated estimate of the age–crime relationship for the postarrest index rate and an underestimate for the prior arrest measure.

These distortions will not be consistent from city to city, as patterns of geographic mobility by race and age will differ from one area to another. In some cities, for example, more blacks might be recent migrants or have their residences outside county limits, so that local rap sheets would underestimate their arrests relative to whites. Other variables that may be correlated with geographic mobility, including employment, occupation, education, nationality, and military service, will have their relationship to rap sheet-based criminality indicators distorted by the use of local rap sheets. The nature of the distortion will vary from area to area for these variables as well. Similar distortions are likely in studies that use reconvictions or new charges in a single court system to measure recividivism.

Even rap sheets drawn from statewide systems will lead to distortion related to geographic mobility if the state has a relatively large proportion of interstate migrants and if these migration patterns vary by demographic variables of interest.

The distortions and the unpredictability of the distortion effects lead to the conclusion that local rap sheets alone should never be used in criminological research and that statewide rap sheets should be used with great caution and sensitivity to the geographic mobility issue.

4. SOURCES OF RAP SHEET ERROR

4.1. Lack of Dispositions

In state, federal, and most local record systems, rap sheets are designed to be records of arrests and the disposition of those arrests (conviction and sentence or dismissal). Sometimes incarceration records (date of entry and release) are also linked to the arrest.

Even if the researcher is able to assemble a rap sheet from a number of nonlocal sources, he/she is still faced with error in the state and FBI fingerprint-based systems. It is widely known that many of these arrest records are, in fact, "incomplete" in the sense that court dispositions and incarceration records are often not available in the same database. Blumstein and Cohen (1979) found, in a sample of Washington, DC, offenders for whom the FBI supplied rap sheets, that there was no recorded disposition beyond arrest in 59% of the cases. Data on the time served by offenders were even less complete. In a more recent study of FBI and state criminal history systems by Laudon (1986, p. 140) FBI arrest records were very conservatively estimated to be from 28.5 to 43.2% incomplete, and state records from 29 to 70% incomplete. A recent survey of state criminal history systems indicates that half of the states willing to respond report that 50% or less of final arrest dispositions are recorded (BJS, 1991).

Even if recorded, dispositions are sometimes difficult to connect reliably with arrests. Since the disposition is a separate entry and may indicate a charge different from that on the original arrest, it may be impossible to connect with the original arrest entry if the two are intertwined with other arrests and dispositions. Finally, some disposition abbreviations are so cryptic as to be indecipherable outside the local jurisdiction.

4.2. False–Negative Error in Arrest Records

"Completeness," as the term is used by both researchers and criminal justice professionals responsible for maintaining these databases, usually refers to the presence of final disposition data. The term is almost never used to refer to the comprehensiveness of the list of arrests. This focus on dispositions is a symptom of a bias toward eliminating false–positive error common among criminal justice officials and elected policymakers. The entire weight of legal process and statutory mandates seek to ensure that an individual is not tagged with an arrest or conviction that is not properly his. The consequences of false–positive error include the setting aside of arrests or searches, the setting aside of sentences, money relief under Section 1983 of the Civil Rights Act, and relief under tort law theories. [see Belair (1984, pp. 31–57) for a discussion of legal remedies.] There are, however, no negative legal consequences of false-negative error. From a human rights perspective, such an emphasis is understandable and necessary. From a research perspective, however, lack of attention to false-negative error—the failure to record all arrests—can lead to serious underestimates of an offender's criminal justice system contacts.

False-negative error on rap sheets is caused primarily by the misidentification of offenders and by the failure of local agencies to submit usable reports of arrests (generally, fingerprint cards) to state repositories and the FBI. Identification of an offender is made by a local law enforcement agency at the time of booking through verbal responses of the arrestee to questions and through documents (driver's license, etc.) carried by the arrestee. In the largest agencies, the offender's prints will be checked against a local fingerprint file as well. This check sometimes reveals deception on the part of the arrestee. For example, of 111,879 individuals in custody on state statute charges in New Orleans during the period 1985–1991, 1284, or about 1.1%, lied about their names at booking and were discovered during a local fingerprint check. The deception was caught only in cases in which the individual had been previously arrested and fingerprinted in New Orleans and the fingerprint clerk was sufficiently diligent in searching for matches.[6] Deception is much more likely to succeed for the highly mobile offender. In general, most jurisdictions rely on state and FBI repositories to confirm the identity of arrestees, but this confirmation is usually received long after the offender has been released. When misidentifications are discovered, and the offender is still in custody, the original records of arrest are changed. However, a long chain of paperwork in prosecutor's and court files, which carry the original name, will no longer match the booking or arrest record. Since these records are not within the booking agency's control, they may not be altered to match the corrected booking record. Some larger jurisdictions have computerized record-keeping systems which can keep track of multiple names (aliases) of offenders, but many small local jurisdictions do not. Even when multiple names or aliases can be properly associated in local arrest history systems, court systems in the same jurisdictions often cannot make the same associations.

At the most basic level, it is generally impossible for a booking agency to determine an individual's "real name." Since they have no easy and routine access to birth records and no time to research identities beyond a fingerprint check, the offender's "real name" is simply the first name under which he was arrested. Experience in the New Orleans system indicates that

---

[6] This search is now performed by an Automated Fingerprint Identification System (AFIS), a computer especially developed for this function. The database, however, is still limited to persons previously arrested in New Orleans.

Table IV. Percentage of New Orleans Offenders with Known Aliases by Race and Age in 1985

Age in 1985	Race					
	Black	(*N*)	White	(*N*)	All	(*N*)
<17	8.2	(1,513)	6.3	(140)	8.0	(1,653)
17–25	20.9	(6,713)	18.0	(1,095)	20.5	(7,808)
26–35	33.4	(6,424)	30.5	(1,174)	33.0	(7,598)
36+	40.5	(2,105)	43.9	(323)	41.0	(2,428)
All	27.0	(16,755)	25.8	(2,732)	26.8	(19,487)

a "new" individual is often created in a criminal history records system not only because of deception but because of an inadequate search for a match on the part of the booking officer. An individual may reappear in the system as another person because of a misspelled first or last name, a different race (Hispanics may be coded as black or white), or some other discrepancy.

As an offender ages and remains active, the odds that identification problems will fragment the offender's history into multiple identities increases. The NOOS included a vigorous effort to combine the records of offenders under all known aliases. Table IV demonstrates that the age of the offender is, in fact, strongly correlated with the number of aliases. This leads not only to underestimates of the criminal careers of older offenders but also to distortions of the age–crime relationship.[7]

Another serious source of false–negative error in state and national fingerprint depositories is the local agencies' failure to submit fingerprint cards or failure to submit usable cards. An Office of Technology Assessment (OTA) (1982) report found that in 1982, 18% of local arrests were not reported to state central depositories. Also, arrests reported to central repositories may not be reported to the FBI. An 8-week audit of arrests reported to the Illinois repository found that 26% of arrests had not been reported by local agencies to the FBI (Belair, 1985, p. 26). Even when cards are submitted, they may be rejected by the FBI and the arrests not recorded if one or more prints are not usable. The FBI rejects 11% of cards submitted for this reason (Belair, 1985). Rejection rates vary greatly. The BJS (1991) survey of state agencies indicates that 13 states reject 10% or more of the prints submitted.

Therefore, if we take the more conservative OTA estimate (18% of arrests not reported) and assume that, on the average, states reject prints at the 11% FBI rate, we can estimate that 27% of arrests will not find their way onto fingerprint-based systems for these reasons alone.

---

[7] In addition, some older offenders have rap sheets in manual criminal history systems that have never been converted to computer. These "missing" arrests will also lead to underestimation of the older offender's arrests relative to the younger offender's.

The extent of false–negative error in rap sheets can be estimated by comparing local, state, and FBI rap sheets on a group of offenders to determine the distribution and overlap of criminal records. Such an analysis has been performed by Widom (1989) for the adult records of 908 victims of child abuse and 667 members of a control group found in the metropolitan area of midwestern state. She reports a very vigorous identification effort, using Bureau of Motor Vehicle records to obtain Social Security numbers and marriage license records to obtain maiden names for females. Subjects were also searched in the local state, and FBI databases under all known aliases. Even after this effort, she finds that each of the three databases lack many of the individuals' arrests. Only 28.4% of the arrests are found in all three databases, and 43.6% are found in only one of the three databases. Further, it is clear that even with her careful efforts, this researcher has failed to count many arrests.[8]

Certainly, false–negative error will lead to underestimates of the number of arrests and therefore underestimates of recidivism and seriousness of prior history. The extent to which this missing arrest data leads to distortion of relationships between demographic variables and criminal behavior is not easily measurable. If we assume that fingerprint cards from metropolitan areas are more likely to be consistently submitted to state and federal repositories than those from small law enforcement agencies, offenders who spend much of their time in rural areas would tend to have less complete rap sheets. In any criminological study, if offenders being compared come from different jurisdictions, and jurisdiction of residence is correlated with, for example, race or employment status, differences between jurisdictions in the quality and reliability of fingerprint submissions will distort the effects of race and employment status on criminal behavior.

5. INTERPRETATION OF RAP SHEET DATA

5.1. Charges, Arrests, and Incidents: Definitional Problems

The bulk of all arrests is made by local law enforcement agencies, usually a police agency or a county sheriff, who generally maintains some

---

[8] Only two-thirds of the arrest records in the local database of Widom's (1989) metropolitan area appear in the state or FBI records. On the assumption that the same slippage occurs in other local jurisdictions, it can be estimated that the 20% of the arrests that occur outside the metropolitan area represent, at best, only two-thirds of the arrests that actually occurred outside the area. Even this two-thirds is probably inflated, since arrests outside large cities are even less likely to find their way into state or FBI records than are urban arrests. Thus it is likely that the total number of arrests for the sample of offenders has been underestimated by at least 10%.

record of these arrests. A person is arrested for one or more offenses related to one or more criminal incidents. An arrest may be made on a warrant requested from a court by the arresting agency or some other local or state criminal justice agency, it may be made without a warrant on probable cause, or an arrest may be made at the direction of a court for some offense related to the court process such as failure to pay a fine or to appear in court. Finally, an individual may be arrested because a warrant for his arrest has been issued by some other jurisdiction.

An "arrest" is technically the seizure of a suspected offender to answer for a crime. However, the definition of an arrest within a law enforcement record system may vary. A single "seizure" for multiple criminal incidents may in fact be recorded as multiple arrests all occurring on the same date or as a single arrest. Charges listed under an arrest date in a local criminal history system may be associated with an "incident identifier" that corresponds to a written incident report and/or a call for assistance logged in a computer-aided dispatch system. Some systems record a separate arrest for each incident, and thus multiple "arrests" may be recorded during a single continuous booking session. This is rarely the case, however, outside large urban police jurisdictions. In short, an "arrest" may or may not have a one-to-one correspondence with a criminal incident, and therefore, charges listed under an arrest identifier may refer to one or more than one incident. This mixing of criminal events within an arrest occurs both in state fingerprint-based record systems and within the FBI system. Such mixing is not detectable because event identifiers are not part of the systems. This is the case because arrests in these systems are identified by an arrest date, so that all charges recorded during a booking event are necessarily combined under that date.

Table V gives the distribution of the charges recorded at booking in New Orleans for 22,404 offenders arrested at least once for burglary or armed robbery in New Orleans. Only those arrests that contained an event identifier are included. These offenders were arrested 177,549 times in New Orleans. On the average, each arrest consisted of 1.76 charges and about 39% of all arrests consisted of more than one charge. If all charges other than index charges (FBI Part 1 Crimes) are removed from the analysis, about 18.4% of index arrests (arrests where at least one charge was for an index crime) include more than one index charge. Clearly, the characterization of the multiple charge arrest is not a trivial problem.

The typical method of handling a multicharge arrest is to treat it as a single crime on the basis of the "most serious" charge. This approach has at least three flaws: (1) The arrest may actually refer to more than one criminal incident, (2) the proper seriousness ranking for crimes is

Table V. Distribution of Charges Among Arrests

All charges			Index only		
Number of arrests	Number of charges	Percentage	Number of arrests	Number of charges	Percentage
108,190	1	60.9	58,909	1	82
40,154	2	22.6	9,265	2	13
15,101	3	8.5	2,046	3	3
6,951	4	3.9	781	4	2
2,997	5	1.7	357	5	0
4,156	6+	2.3	640	6+	1
177,549			71,998		
Total number of charges	312,130			95,648	
Average number charges/arrest	1.76			1.33	
Charges NOT counted if arrests are reduced to a single charge	43%			33%	

problematic, and (3) the approach may be inappropriate to the research questions asked.

The extent to which the multievent arrest might represent a measurement problem can be estimated by analyzing a database that contains an event identifier. Such information is available for some arrest records in the population drawn for the New Orleans Offender Study. In addition to the date of arrest and other descriptive information about the charge, most New Orleans charge records also include an event identifier known as an "item number." An item number is the number assigned to a criminal event by the police department's dispatching system. If an individual is arrested (booked) at the same time for three burglaries, each burglary will have a different item number. If he is booked for two charges related to the same criminal incident (for example, burglary and possession of the stolen property taken during the burglary or rape and murder of the same victim), the charges will carry the same item number. If two individuals are arrested for committing a crime together, the charges for each individual will carry the same item number.

Table VI indicates that the multievent arrest presents a significant problem. A multievent arrest is defined as multicharge arrest generated from a booking session during which an offender is booked for criminal acts committed in more than one incident, i.e., for criminal acts that occurred on at least two separate occasions. Such booking sessions result in the production

Table VI. Distribution of Criminal Events Among Multicharge Arrests

All charges			Index only		
Number of arrests	Number of events	Percentage	Number of arrests	Number of events	Percentage
54,780	1	79.0	8,307	1	63.5
10,980	2	15.8	3,209	2	24.5
2,038	3	2.9	744	3	5.7
626	4	0.9	287	4	2.2
312	5	0.5	169	5	1.3
623	6+	0.9	373	6+	2.9
69,359			13,089		
Total number of events	92,091			22,887	
Average number events/arrest	1.33			1.75	
Events NOT counted if arrests are reduced to a single charge[a]	12%			12%	
Persons with at least one multievent arrest	9,082	(41%)		3,947	(18%)

[a]Includes single-charge arrests.

of a single fingerprint card covering more than one criminal event. This booking will appear as a single multicharge arrest on the offender's state or national rap sheet. Multievent arrests were identified for this analysis by the use of item number event identifiers. Had this identifier not been available, *12%* of index criminal events would have been missed. Since event identifiers do not exist in state and FBI databases, it is likely that the multievent arrest is an important source of error in these databases. These errors are not confined to a few high-frequency offenders. If only Part I index charges are considered, about 37% of all multicharge arrests include charges from more than one event. About 18% of all offenders in the study had at least one multievent arrest among their index arrests. Almost 43% of offenders with long arrest records (10 arrests) have at least one multievent arrest. Since only New Orleans arrests could be checked for multievent arrests, and only portions of the criminal careers of some offenders are included in the study period, it is certain that the actual percentage of offenders with multievent arrests is significantly higher than the results presented here.

5.2. Arrests vs Charges

Even when all charges are related to a single event, it is generally considered necessary for purposes of analysis to "characterize" that arrest as to type. One charge is selected to characterize the criminal event, and the criteria for selection are almost always some measure of "seriousness." Selecting among charges on the basis of seriousness is widely known to be a very problematic enterprise.

Yet it is difficult to find more than a few examples of research that uses arrests as a measure of criminal activity that describe how multicharge arrests are coded. Most researchers who fail to describe their ranking method probably used the FBI hierarchy method or simply chose the first listed charge. But even those conscientious researchers who attempt to use empirically based seriousness measures still face the problem of scoring gross UCR or state statute categories.

In general, "collapsing" arrests to a single charge using some seriousness criterion will result in undercounting of less serious offenses relative to more serious offenses. This distortion, coupled with the problematic aspect of the ranking process itself, implies that collapsing arrests should be done only when there is no other alternative. In fact, in practice, the coding of arrest by most serious charge, a practice that affects 39% of all arrests, is often done too early (at the data coding stage), is often unnecessary for the analysis, and is almost always done without adequate discussion or justification. If the number of arrests is used as an indicator of criminal activity, the way the multicharge arrest is to be coded should depend on the precise question asked. If we wish to compare offenders in a general way, such as on the basis of total index arrests, we simply count arrests where at least one charge is an index offense—seriousness ranking is unnecessary. Most prior arrest variables are coded this way. If, however, we wish to estimate the level of a particular type of activity—burglary, for example—we need to count the number of burglary charges, not the number of arrests where burglary is the most serious charge. If we wish to count "prior property arrests," we count the number of arrests that include at least one property charge, not the number of arrests where a property charge was the most serious.

5.3. Process Crimes

An additional problem in interpreting rap sheet data involves the treatment of charges referring not to offenses committed while free but to acts related to arrest, court processing, custody, or supervision procedures: "process" crimes. Arrest process charges include "resisting arrest," "flight to elude," and, usually, "battery on a police officer." A researcher interested in arrest charges as indicators of offenses committed while free should ignore such charges. But this is not possible when a battery on a police officer is recorded simply as "assault and battery," which might then be coded by the researcher as the index crime "aggravated assault." Law enforcement agency records do not distinguish "seizure process" crimes from other crimes.

Detention and correctional agencies record their own set of "process" offenses as arrests, even when a seizure has not actually been made because the offender is already in custody when he commits the crime. While some of these crimes can by definition be committed only by the incarcerated (contraband offenses and escape), virtually the full range of street crimes, from murder to theft, can also be committed while incarcerated. The extent to which these offenses result in official arrests is a function of their seriousness and the policy of the correctional agency. An incarceration crime can be identified as such by the researcher only if the correctional institution is recorded as the arresting agency. But this is not always the case. Most state penitentiary system officers are not commissioned law enforcement officers. The local sheriff or the state police generally serve as arresting agents for serious crimes in penitentiaries. In jails, detention officers are sometimes commissioned officers, but they cannot be distinguished from patrol officers from the same department in arrest records. One solution to this problem might involve treating a charge filed during a offender's known term of incarceration as an incarceration process crime. Unfortunately, individuals incarcerated may also be charged with crimes committed before their incarceration when their connection to an earlier crime is established in the course of a criminal investigation.

An additional problem created by correctional agency fingerprint submissions is the tendency for prints submitted for identification purpose to appear as arrests on rap sheets. Correctional agencies, especially penitentiaries and probation or parole agencies, often submit a sentenced offender's fingerprints to its state fingerprint repository and to the FBI as a means of verifying identification. These submissions may be indistinguishable from arrests with the conviction charge appearing as an arrest charge with a final disposition, except that the submitting agency is a correctional institution. Such records duplicate arrest records generated by the original arresting agency for these crimes. It is often not possible to identify instances of such duplications, however, since original charges are often modified during the court process. It is therefore important that arrest records submitted by correctional agencies not be counted as separate criminal incidents.

6. DISCUSSION

A careful consideration of the problems of "rap sheet" data leads to certain general conclusions.

(1) The use of rap sheets only from local sources should be avoided because of the distortions it introduces into relationships between criminal behavior and demographic variables, such as age and race, that are associated with geographic mobility.

(2) The methods by which official criminal histories are built and maintained are likely to produce a predominance of false-negative error over false-positive error. On the average, offenders' arrests will be undercounted in any official criminal history, particularly if the records system relies on fingerprint submissions of other agencies.

The problem of false-negative error stems primarily from two sources: the problem of identification and the problem of nonsubmission/rejection of fingerprint cards. The problem of identification can be addressed in part by actively searching for duplications—the same individual treated as more than one individual—in all databases. Judgments will have to be made about goodness of fit: Are two individuals with the same last names and places and dates of birth, but with differently spelled first names, really the same individual? Or are they twin brothers? Inevitably, the researcher will begin to generate some false-positive error in making such judgments.

The problem of incompleteness in the list of arrests because of nonsubmission/rejection can be addressed only by combining databases from different sources. Whenever possible, multiple official databases should be merged and their inconsistencies carefully resolved.

(3) Rap sheets are deficient in final disposition and incarceration information. The disposition data that exist are frequently confusing and sometimes completely useless.

This problem can be addressed only by merging court and corrections databases with arrest databases. Terms of incarceration and supervision are best measured directly from correctional databases rather than deduced from sentences. Most states follow complex rules for calculation of normal release date, with good time, work or education credits, and a variety of other factors that are applied differentially based on criminal history or conviction charge. Of greater importance are parole, which is typically awarded after one-third of a sentence has been served, and pardon, which can be awarded at any time. Furlough and work release involve unsupervised street time and further complicate the picture.

(4) About 18% of arrests for index crimes in our sample include more than one index charge. The reduction of a multicharge arrest to a single charge for purposes of analysis should be done only when the analysis absolutely requires it. The coding of the multicharge arrest should be based on the intended use of the arrest variable in the analysis. About 37% of multicharge index arrests include index charges for more than one criminal event. A multievent arrest, however, can be identified only from those arrest

records that include an event identifier, and there is no way to make such an identification in most fingerprint-based systems. The multicharge and multievent analyses reported here suggest that it is almost always better to use charges rather than arrests as the unit of analysis.

(5) Certain charges recorded on rap sheets refer not to criminal acts committed while free, but to arrest or correctional process behaviour, or are duplications of charges already submitted by the original arresting agency. All of these must be ignored if charges are to be used as a proxy for offense rate while free. It is not always possible, however, to distinguish process crimes from street crimes.

The best course in coding possible correctional crimes is a compromise between counting all possible correctional process charges and counting none. If a charge is submitted by a correctional institution or is an arrest or correctional process type of offense (battery on a police or correctional officer, contraband offenses, escape), it should be removed from the analysis; however, other charges that occur during a period of incarceration should be assumed to apply to an offense prior to that incarceration term.

ACKNOWLEDGMENTS

This research was supported by National Institute of Justice, United States Department of Justice, Grants 86-IJ-CX-0021 and 90-IJ-CX-0019. The contents of this document do not necessarily reflect the views or policies of the National Institute of Justice or the U.S. Department of Justice.

I would like to thank Sheriff Charles C. Foti, Jr., for his support of this project and Dr. Al Miranne, Dr. Dwayne Smith, Hennessey Hayes, Mary Baldwin Kennedy, and the anonymous reviewers for their comments on early drafts of this paper. I am also grateful to Gary Lagarde for his help in researching unpublished information on rap sheet databases.

REFERENCES

Belair, R. (1984). Legal rules and policy initiatives in the use of criminal justice information. In *Information Policy and Crime Control Strategies. Proceedings of a BJS/SEARCH Conference*, SEARCH Group, Inc., Sacramento CA.

Belair, R. (1985). *Data Quality of Criminal History Records*, U.S. Department of Justice, Bureau of Justice Statistics, Washington, DC.

Blumstein, A., and Cohen, J. (1979). Estimation of individual crime rates from arrest records. *J. Crim. Law and Criminol.* 70: 561–585.

Bureau of Justice Statistics (1991). *Survey of Criminal History Information Systems*, NCJ-125620.

Geerken, M., Miranne, A., and Kennedy, M. B. (1993). *The New Orleans Offender Study: Development of Official Record Databases*, Report to the National Institute of Justice.

Laudon, K. C. (1986). *Dossier Society: Value Choices in the Design of National Information Systems*, Columbia University Press, New York.

Marchand, D. A. (1980). *The Politics of Privacy, Computers, and Criminal Justice Records*, Information Resources Press, Arlington, VA.

Office of Technology Assessment (1982). *An Assessment of Alternatives for a National Computerized Criminal History System*, OTA, Washington, DC.

President's Commission on Law Enforcement and the Administration of Justice (1967). *The Challenge of Crime in a Free Society*, U.S. Government Printing Office, Washington, DC.

Widom, C. (1989). Child abuse, neglect, and violent criminal behavior. *Criminology* 27: 251–271.

[11]

AN EXPERIMENTAL COMPARISON OF TWO SELF-REPORT METHODS FOR MEASURING LAMBDA

JULIE HORNEY

INEKE HAEN MARSHALL

Criticisms of the RAND Second Inmate Survey have implied that missing and ambiguous responses and problems related to trying to measure self-reported crime rates over extended periods of time may have led to inflated estimates of λ. In the present study, the authors randomly assigned prison inmates to two groups, one to be interviewed using the RAND method for measuring crime rates, and one to be interviewed using the authors' modified month-by-month reporting method. The authors expected that their month-by-month method would produce lower estimates of λ. They found that the two distributions of λ did not differ significantly from each other, suggesting that the RAND results are very robust.

One focus of criminal careers research has been on the measurement of individual offending frequency, or lambda (λ) (Blumstein, Cohen, Roth and Visher 1986). Because actual rates of committing crimes are poorly represented by official statistics, the development by RAND Corporation researchers of a self-report methodology for estimating λ in adult offenders (Peterson and Braiker 1980; Rolph, Chaiken, and Houchens 1981; Chaiken and Chaiken 1982; Greenwood and Abrahamse 1982, Peterson, Chaiken,

This article is based on work supported by grant no. 89-IJ-CX-0030 from the National Institute of Justice, Office of Justice Programs, U.S. Department of Justice and by a grant from the Urban Conditions Program of the College of Public Affairs and Community Service at the University of Nebraska at Omaha. The authors are grateful to Winifred L. Reed, NIJ Project Monitor, and to the participants in the NIJ Crime Control Conferences for their encouragement and feedback; to the administration and staff of the Diagnostic and Evaluation Unit of the Nebraska Department of Corrections for facilitating the interviews; and to Carol Marshall, Kit Lemon, Mickey Coffey, Tara Ingram, Mike Mead, Lisa Lannin, Kelly Green, and Allison Brown-Corzine for their valuable research assistance. We would also like to acknowledge Wayne Osgood's suggestion on statistical analysis and the helpful comments of one anonymous reviewer on an earlier version of this article. Points of view or opinions in this document are those of the authors and do not necessarily represent the official position or policies of the U.S. Department of Justice.

Ebener and Honig 1982) represents a major criminological contribution. In the study now referred to as the RAND Second Inmate Survey, Chaiken and Chaiken (1982) presented data on nearly 2,200 inmates of prisons and jails in three states which indicated that the distribution of λ is highly skewed. Most of the inmates in that study reported committing only five or fewer crimes per year, but a small number of offenders indicated that they committed crimes at very high rates—hundreds or thousands per year, depending on the crime.

The RAND Corporation self-report research has generated much interest and controversy. Many were surprised by the extremely high rates of offending estimated for some respondents. Interest in the precise estimates has been especially stimulated by the application of RAND λs to policy questions, as in Zedlewski's (1987) projections of cost savings to be gained through incarceration. Zedlewski used the RAND study's estimate of mean annual crime rate to project that incarcerating 1,000 more offenders would prevent 187,000 felonies through incapacitation alone.

In an earlier study (Horney and Marshall 1991) we reported on our development of a modified version of the RAND self-report instrument that used month-by-month reporting of crimes in order to take into account intraindividual variability in offending rates. Using individual interviews rather than self-administered questionnaires and a more detailed calendar to facilitate recall, we used that instrument to survey incarcerated felons in Nebraska. Our findings in that study suggested that the use of the month-by-month reporting method for determining offending rates might produce lower estimates of λ than the RAND method.

There are, of course, numerous problems in trying to compare our results to those of Chaiken and Chaiken (1982). The fact that we used individual interviews rather than self-administered questionnaires, or the fact that we used a more detailed calendar as a reference point for reporting of offending may have produced different estimates of λ. Differences might also be related to the nearly 10 years that separated the two studies. Overall changes in offending during that time might have produced different distributions of λ. Probably most important, the RAND study was conducted with inmates in California, Texas, and Michigan; our respondents were incarcerated in Nebraska. The considerable variability among estimates of λ for RAND's three groups indicates that we should be very cautious in comparing inmates from different correctional systems. Not only may the characteristics of offender populations differ across geographic locations, but distributions of λ may also reflect differences in correctional policies across states. Thus it has been suggested that the lower estimates of λ Chaiken and Chaiken (1982) obtained in Texas may have resulted because thresholds for incarceration in Texas are lower than in California and Michigan. In other words, a wider net for incarcerating individuals would result in a prison population with a larger percentage of low-rate offenders.

Because of these problems with trying to compare our results to those of Chaiken and Chaiken (1982), this earlier study did not allow us to directly address the question of whether our method would produce lower estimates of λ than the RAND method. In order to answer that question, we conducted a follow-up study, using a randomized experimental design. Although most experiments in the field of criminal justice attempt to test the effectiveness of innovative programs (Farrington 1983), the present article reports on a somewhat different use of experimentation. In our study, random assignment was used not to determine whether a new treatment or policy had any effect, but to compare two different survey methods. Although different in focus, our experiment builds on the research conducted by Hindelang, Hirschi, and Weis (1981), who employed a quasi-experiment to assess the impact of method of administration (questionnaire or interview) on the amount of delinquency reported by respondents and on the validity and reliability of such reports. In the present study, we randomly assigned prison inmates to two groups, one to be interviewed using the RAND method for measuring crime rates, and one to be interviewed using our modified month-by-month reporting method. The dependent variable was the magnitude of self-reported offending frequency. The use of an experimental design let us assume that the underlying distributions of λ for the two groups would be essentially equal, and therefore conclude that any differences in the estimates of λ must be due to the methods employed to measure offending. In this article we explain the reasons for expecting differences between the experimental group and control group, and then we present the results of our experiment.

Were RAND Lambdas Too High?

Most criticisms of the RAND data have implied that methodological problems may have led to estimates of λ that were too high. Critics have focused on specific problems that RAND researchers faced because of missing and ambiguous responses in their data set and on general problems related to trying to measure response rates over extended periods of time.

MISSING DATA PROBLEMS

The RAND self-report instrument is long and complicated with many skip patterns and questions repeated with varying formats. In the Second Inmate

Survey, the questionnaire was self-administered, with instructions given to groups of 15 to 32 inmates at a time. As a result, RAND researchers had to deal with the problem of many missing or ambiguous responses to questions critical to the computation of λ. They adopted a set of strategies that led to computing minimum and maximum estimates of λ. Visher (1986) suggested that the RAND strategies may have led to overestimating λ. Using more conservative strategies for handling the missing and ambiguous responses, she reanalyzed the data for inmates who reported committing robbery and burglary and obtained single estimates of λ that were very close to the RAND minimum estimates and quite different from their maximum estimates.

MEASUREMENT OVER EXTENDED TIME PERIODS

Trying to obtain estimates of rates of activity over extended time periods is difficult, and results can vary greatly depending on how the questions are asked. In fact RAND researchers obtained widely discrepant results with two different versions of the self-report instrument.

Chaiken and Chaiken (1982) obtained estimates of λ by asking respondents who reported committing a particular crime 10 or fewer times in the reference period to give the exact number of offenses committed. Respondents who reported committing more than 10 offenses were asked to give the number of street months in which they were active in committing that crime and the number of offenses per day, week, or month they were *usually* doing while active. In an earlier RAND study (Peterson and Braiker 1980), all respondents were simply asked to indicate the total number of times they had committed an offense during the reference period. The estimates of λ obtained with the more detailed questions were much higher.

Although it seems that the more detailed questions should produce more valid estimates of offending rates, there are still potential problems that may have led to inflated estimates of λ. Asking about the "usual" rates of offending implies either an assumption that offenders commit crimes at constant rates or that they are able to mentally compute an average rate from rates that may vary considerably over time. It is likely that neither assumption is justified. Rolph, Chaiken, and Houchens (1981), in fact, found evidence in additional analyses of RAND data that offenders commit crimes in "spurts" rather than at constant rates. As for the mental averaging, Cohen (1986) suggested that rather than averaging across periods of high and low activity to arrive at a typical rate, offenders are more likely to refer to high-rate periods in reporting typical rates because those high rates of offending have greater saliency. Visher (1986) suggested that another salient period to which offenders might refer in reporting "typical" rates is the recent period just before arrest. If that tends to be a period in which offenses are committed at a high rate, referring to those rates in describing "typical" rates would also lead to overestimating λ.

Month-by-Month Method

Concerns about the accuracy of the estimates of λ obtained in the RAND study led us to develop a refined approach to measuring λ through self-reports (Horney and Marshall 1991). We used individual interviews to avoid problems of missing and ambiguous responses, we developed a more detailed calendar system to facilitate recall of criminal activity, and we asked respondents to describe their criminal activity month-by-month in terms of four different levels of activity. In our pilot study testing this method, we found evidence of considerable variability of offending rates within individuals and found that patterns of variability differed across crime types. We found, for example, that rates of committing burglary were the most variable during offenders' active periods; drug dealing offenses, in contrast, were much more likely to be committed throughout an offender's entire reference period and were also more likely to be committed at a constant rate during active periods.

Because our method asked offenders to define their "high," "medium," and "low" rates of offending, we were able to simulate the λs that might have been obtained using the RAND method if respondents had referred to their high rates or recent rates in estimating their typical active rates. We found that if *high* rates were used, the RAND method could lead to estimates of λ being inflated by from 2% to 120%, depending on the crime category, with the greatest overestimation for crimes with the largest variability in offending frequencies.

We were surprised to find that *recent* rates (offending rates in the 3 months preceding arrest) were not necessarily higher than overall rates. If our respondents had referred to these recent rates in describing typical rates, estimates based on the RAND method would be less discrepant than if they referred to their high rates. In some cases the use of recent rates in calculating λ led to lower estimates than use of all the month-by-month data.

Like Chaiken and Chaiken (1982), as well as others who have replicated the RAND study with various modifications (Mande and English 1987; Miranne and Geerken 1991), we found highly skewed distributions of offending, with most people committing one or two offenses but with a small number of people committing offenses at very high rates. Our simulated results, using high-rate estimates to calculate λ, suggested, however, that our method of month-by-month reporting might produce lower overall estimates of λ than the RAND method. Because differences in populations, general survey methods, and time periods precluded meaningful comparisons of our results with those of Chaiken and Chaiken (1982), we designed the present study to directly test the two methods for estimating λ in a controlled experiment.

METHODOLOGY

Respondents

Our respondents were 700 convicted male offenders sentenced to the Nebraska Department of Corrections. We attempted to interview all men admitted to the Diagnostic and Evaluation Unit for new offenses until we had our required sample size. We chose to use an actual intake cohort for three reasons. First, an intake cohort gives us a representative sample of convicted offenders. A sample of prison residents, in contrast, is biased by length of stay in the institution because more people with long sentences are included.[1] Second, using an intake cohort makes the reference period we ask about (a period just preceding the current conviction) a similarly recent period for all respondents.[2] Finally, there is evidence that higher response rates may be achieved with an intake cohort.[3] Mande and English (1987) attributed their high response rate on a similar survey to the fact that their sample was housed in the Diagnostic Unit of the Department of Corrections and that inmates were not yet involved in work projects or treatment programs that could cause scheduling problems.

Our respondents represent 90% of all males admitted to the Nebraska Department of Corrections during a 9-month period. Some admissions were missed because they were transferred out of the Diagnostic and Evaluation Unit before we could interview them. Six people could not be interviewed because they did not speak English, and we were not allowed to interview one person because of his mental instability and violence. Our interviewers met with a total of 746 inmates to explain the study and invite participation; 94% of that group completed the interviews.

Procedures

Usually within one week of the time inmates were admitted to the Diagnostic and Evaluation Unit, they were brought to a private visiting room to meet with an interviewer to have the study explained. The interviewer gave a brief explanation of the study and then read aloud an informed consent form, after which the inmate could either sign the form and proceed with the interview or return to his unit or other activity.

The interviewers read all the questions and wrote down the respondents' answers. They answered any questions their respondents asked and attempted to make sure that respondents understood the survey questions adequately. If respondents' answers were ambiguous or inappropriate to the question, interviewers asked the question again and tried to make it clear to the respondent. For critical aspects of the survey such as crime definitions, they did not go beyond the descriptions written in the instrument. Each interview took from 45 to 90 minutes.

ASSIGNMENT TO CONDITIONS

We randomly assigned respondents to the experimental and control conditions. Those in the experimental condition were asked about offending rates with the more detailed calendars and month-by-month recording. Those in the control condition were questioned with the RAND questions about typical rates. Before the interviews began, all survey instruments—350 with RAND questions and 350 with the modified questions—were placed in unmarked envelopes. We then generated by computer a listing of the numbers 1 to 700 in random sequence. Following that list of randomly ordered numbers, we placed a number on each of the 700 envelopes. After numbering the envelopes, we rearranged them in numerical order. Interviews were conducted strictly following the sequence; that is, the interviewer had to conduct the interview numbered 001 before 002, and so on. The interviewers thus did not know which interview method would be used for any given interview. They also had no knowledge about an inmate before the interview, except the person's name. Because the instruments were randomly assigned to interviews, it also meant that the random assignment applied to inmates who actually participated in the study rather than to the list of potential participants.

Survey Instrument

The basic instrument we used is based on that used in the RAND Corporation's Second Inmate Survey (Chaiken and Chaiken 1982). In addition to the questions that are the focus of this article, the survey also asks about criminal history, substance abuse, attitudes and beliefs about crime and the criminal justice system, predictions of future criminal behavior, and basic demographic variables.

In the critical section of the interview we asked respondents to consider a reference period[4] immediately preceding the arrest for the offense from which their current incarceration followed. For that period we asked them about the frequency of criminal activity for nine different crimes (defined according to Chaiken and Chaiken 1982): burglary, business robbery, personal robbery, assault, theft, auto theft, forgery, fraud, and drug dealing.[5]

Crime Rate Questions

The key difference between the experimental and the control group was in the questions used for determining crime rates. The questions used for the control group were the same ones used by Chaiken and Chaiken (1982) in the RAND study. For the experimental group we used our month-by-month method with more detailed calendars for facilitating recall and recording responses.

CONTROL CONDITION

For the control condition (RAND method), respondents were shown a 24-month calendar to establish the reference period. We asked the respondent to identify the month in which he had been arrested for his current offense(s); we then crossed out all the months after that one. We then asked if he had been locked up for a month or more during any of the earlier months on the calendar; if so those months were also crossed out. The remaining months were designated as the "street months." We then asked the respondent whether during any of the street months he had been: in the service, in the hospital, going to school, working, living with a wife, living with a girlfriend, drinking heavily, or using drugs. If the respondent answered affirmatively, we asked him to specify during how many of the street months that category had been applicable. We also asked how many times during the street months the respondent had moved from one city to another.

Next, the interviewer asked, for each target crime, whether during the street months the respondent had done any of various offenses (burglaries, for example). If the answer was "no," the interviewer skipped to the next target crime. If "yes," we then asked the respondent to indicate whether he had done 1 to 10 or 11 or more. If he answered "1 to 10," he specified how many. If he answered 11 or more he was then asked to indicate how often he usually did the crime, using the following categories:

1. Every day or almost every day. (If yes, then how many per day and how many days a week usually?)

2. Several times a week. (If yes, then how many per week?)
3. Every week or almost every week. (If yes, then how many per month?)
4. Less than every week. (If yes, then how many per month?)

EXPERIMENTAL CONDITION

For respondents in the experimental condition we used two different calendars—an "event calendar," and a "crime calendar," to establish the reference period and also to record detailed information. We first determined the "street months" for each respondent with the 36-month event calendar (see Horney and Marshall 1991, Figure 2), using the same procedures as in the control condition.

We then asked the respondent whether during any of the street months he had been: in the service, in the hospital, going to school, working, living with a wife, living with a girlfriend, drinking heavily, or using drugs. For each positive answer we asked the respondent to identify the specific months when the activity was occurring. The interviewer then placed a check beside the appropriate items for those months. The respondent also indicated whether he had moved from city to city during the street months; each move was recorded also on the calendar.

Next, we showed the respondent the crime calendar (see Figure 1). The interviewer marked out all but the street months as recorded on the event calendar and then asked, for each target crime, whether during the street months the respondent had done any of various offenses (burglaries, for example). If the answer was "no," the interviewer skipped to the next target crime. If "yes," then we asked the respondent to indicate whether he had done 1 to 10 or 11 or more. If he answered "1 to 10," he specified how many, and then indicated on the "crime calendar" during which months he did those burglaries. The interviewer placed a check next to "burglary" for those months.

If the respondent reported having committed 11 or more burglaries during the reference period, the interview proceeded in a different manner. The interviewer showed him the crime calendar and first asked him to point to the months during which he did *no burglaries*. The interviewer then entered a "0" in the space beside "burglary" for those months. Next the interviewer asked the respondent to think about months when he was doing burglaries at low, medium, or high rates, and told him to define those rates with any numbers he wanted. First the respondent was asked to indicate the months when he was doing burglaries at a "low" rate; the interviewer entered a "1" in the space next to "burglary" for those months. At that point the respondent's definition of low rate was established by asking him how often he usually did burglaries during those low-rate months. He was given choices that led to specifying how many burglaries per day, week, or month he committed (the same alternatives described above for the control condition).

The interviewer then proceeded in the same manner to have the respondent identify months with "medium" and "high" rates of committing burglaries. Respondents were not forced to use all levels of responding, but they were asked to specify either zero or a low, medium, or high rate for every month. The same procedure was then used for each of the other offense categories.[6]

RESULTS

Estimates of Lambda

For the control (RAND) group, λ was calculated in the manner described by Chaiken and Chaiken (1982, p. 42). If a respondent with a 22-month measurement period (from beginning of the 2-year calendar period until the arrest that led to the present incarceration) spent 6 of those months in jail, he would have a total of 16 street months—the time during which he had opportunities for committing crimes. If he reported committing a total of 6 burglaries during that time his annualized crime rate would be:

$$\lambda = \text{total burglaries} \times (12 \text{ months/year})/\text{street months}$$
$$= 6 \times (12/16)$$
$$= 4.5 \text{ burglaries/year}$$

If that respondent had reported committing 11 or more target crimes, a "typical" monthly rate would be calculated, based on his answers to the questions described earlier. That rate is then multiplied by the number of months he said he was doing burglaries to determine the total committed. If, for example, a respondent indicated that he did 11 or more burglaries, that he usually committed about 2 burglaries a day, and usually did them 4 days a week during the 10 months he was doing burglaries, his typical rate would be 34.4 per month (2/day × 4 days/week × 4.3 weeks). His total burglaries during the reference period would be 344 (34.4 burglaries/month × 10 months active in burglary). His annualized offending rate would be:

$$\lambda = \text{total burglaries} \times (12 \text{ months/year})/\text{street months}$$
$$= 344 \times 12/16$$
$$= 258 \text{ burglaries per year}$$

Year: _____

Jan.	Feb.	March	April	May	June
Burglary __	Burglary __	Burglary __	Burglary __	Burglary __	Burglary __
Rob-Bus. __	Rob-Bus. __	Rob-Bus. __	Rob-Bus. __	Rob-Bus. __	Rob-Bus. __
Rob-Per. __	Rob-Per. __	Rob-Per. __	Rob-Per. __	Rob-Per. __	Rob-Per. __
Assault __	Assault __	Assault __	Assault __	Assault __	Assault __
Theft __	Theft __	Theft __	Theft __	Theft __	Theft __
Car Theft__	Car Theft__	Car Theft__	Car Theft__	Car Theft__	Car Theft__
Forgery __	Forgery __	Forgery __	Forgery __	Forgery __	Forgery __
Fraud __	Fraud __	Fraud __	Fraud __	Fraud __	Fraud __
Drugs __	Drugs __	Drugs __	Drugs __	Drugs __	Drugs __
Rape __	Rape __	Rape __	Rape __	Rape __	Rape __

Year: _____

Jan.	Feb.	March	April	May	June
Burglary 0	Burglary 0	Burglary 2	Burglary 2	Burglary __	Burglary __
Rob-Bus. __	Rob-Bus. __	Rob-Bus. __	Rob-Bus. __	Rob-Bus. __	Rob-Bus. __
Rob-Per. __	Rob-Per. __	Rob-Per. __	Rob-Per. __	Rob-Per. __	Rob-Per. __
Assault __	Assault __	Assault __	Assault __	Assault __	Assault __
Theft __	Theft __	Theft __	Theft __	Theft __	Theft __
Car Theft__	Car Theft__	Car Theft__	Car Theft__	Car Theft__	Car Theft__
Forgery __	Forgery __	Forgery __	Forgery __	Forgery __	Forgery __
Fraud __	Fraud __	Fraud __	Fraud __	Fraud __	Fraud __
Drugs __	Drugs __	Drugs __	Drugs __	Drugs __	Drugs __
Rape __	Rape __	Rape __	Rape __	Rape __	Rape __

Year Arrested:

Jan.	Feb.	March	April	May	June
Burglary 0	Burglary 0	Burglary 1	Burglary 1	Burglary 1	Burglary 2
Rob-Bus. __	Rob-Bus. __	Rob-Bus. __	Rob-Bus. __	Rob-Bus. __	Rob-Bus. __
Rob-Per. __	Rob-Per. __	Rob-Per. __	Rob-Per. __	Rob-Per. __	Rob-Per. __
Assault __	Assault __	Assault __	Assault __	Assault __	Assault __
Theft __	Theft __	Theft __	Theft __	Theft __	Theft __
Car Theft__	Car Theft__	Car Theft__	Car Theft__	Car Theft__	Car Theft__
Forgery __	Forgery __	Forgery __	Forgery __	Forgery __	Forgery __
Fraud __	Fraud __	Fraud __	Fraud __	Fraud __	Fraud __
Drugs __	Drugs __	Drugs __	Drugs __	Drugs __	Drugs __
Rape __	Rape __	Rape __	Rape __	Rape __	Rape __

For the experimental group we compute λ in the RAND manner for those who reported committing 1 to 10 offenses. For those who reported committing 11 or more crimes, the computation becomes more complex. Let us take an example of a respondent who also has a 22-month measurement period, of which 6 months were spent in jail, giving him 16 street months (refer to the last 2 years of the calendar in Figure 1). Of those 16 months, he identified 6 months during which he did no burglaries, 3 as months during which he did burglaries at a low rate, 5 as medium-rate months, and 2 as months during

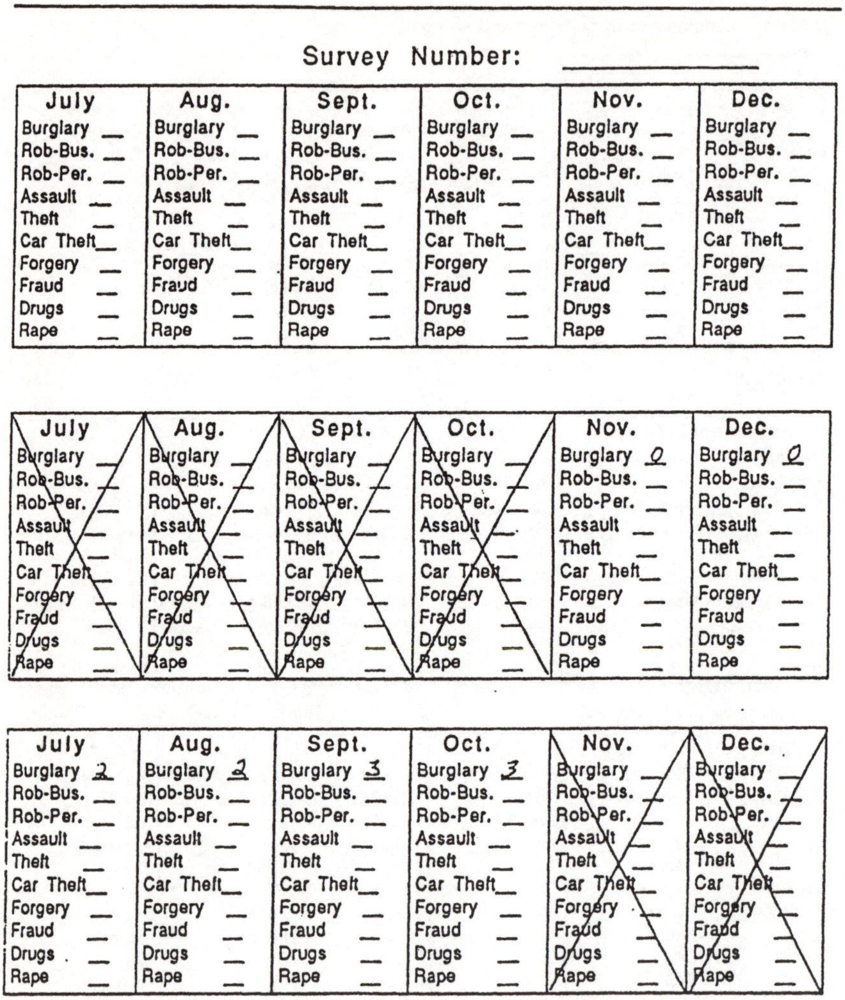

Survey Number: _____

Figure 1: Crime Calendar

which he did burglaries at a high rate. In the follow-up questions, we determined that, to him, doing burglaries at a low rate meant 2 per month, a medium rate meant 1 per week, and a high rate meant 2 per day and usually 4 days per week. Thus we will calculate his low rate as 2 per month, his medium rate as 4.3 per month (1/week × 4.3 weeks), and his high rate at 34.4 per month (2/day × 4 days/week × 4.3 weeks). We can then calculate his annualized burglary rate as:

TABLE 1:   Estimates of Lambda by Crime Category

			For Actives			
	Percentage Active	χ^2 Signifi- cance Level	Median	90th Percentile	Mean	Mann- Whitney U Significance Level
Burglary						
Experimental	22	.7848	1.70	49.35	29.86	.1075
Control	23		2.18	154.80	67.32	
Robbery						
Experimental	7	.4825	2.09	20.91	12.18	.7098
Control	9		1.30	140.52	31.06	
Theft						
Experimental	20	.4590	4.94	770.54	296.02	.5736
Control	22		4.71	247.21	125.10	
Auto theft						
Experimental	11	1.00	1.26	19.20	67.92	.3102
Control	11		1.50	36.00	9.51	
Forgery						
Experimental	13	.2876	3.53	300.46	85.14	.4028
Control	10		2.11	268.16	96.97	
Fraud						
Experimental	5	.1984	4.67	553.80	137.17	.2734
Control	3		1.57	1365.52	180.29	
Assault						
Experimental	30	.7394	1.82	50.16	43.83	.1713
Control	29		2.49	36.00	135.89	
Drug deals						
Experimental	41	.8782	361.20	7,799.49	2,438.05	.7170
Control	42		166.71	13,141.98	3,918.56	
Total crime						
(No Drug)						
Experimental	60	.2832	4.00	285.56	175.07	.5559
Control	56		4.42	341.55	180.82	

$$\lambda = \text{total burglaries} \times (12 \text{ months/year})/\text{street months}$$
$$= ((6 \times 0) + (3 \times 2) + (5 \times 4.3) + (2 \times 34.4)) \times 12/16$$
$$= 96.3 \times 12/16$$
$$= 72.23 \text{ burglaries/year}$$

Table 1 presents the summary data for our comparisons of the experimental and control (RAND) groups (for these analyses, we combined business robbery and personal robbery into a single measure of total robbery). The

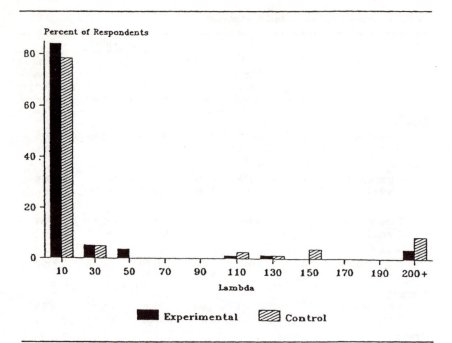

Figure 2: Distribution of Annualized Burglary Rates
NOTE: Lambda values represent midpoints.

presentation of λs for groups of inmates is complicated by the highly skewed nature of the resulting distributions. Figures 2, 3, and 4, which plot distributions for burglary, drug dealing, and total crimes except for drug dealing, illustrate this problem. As Chaiken and Chaiken (1982) and others have noted, the mean is not an adequate measure because it is so sensitive to the extreme values of the highest-rate offenders. The median is also not completely satisfactory because it conveys so little information about those high-rate individuals. In Table 1 we thus present the mean, median and 90th percentile, as well as percent active in each crime category.

The percentage of respondents active in each crime category is the percentage who reported committing at least one of that offense during the reference period we asked them to consider. The mean, median and 90th percentile then refer to the λs calculated for that active group. Because the distributions clearly do not meet the necessary assumption of normality, a test of difference in means is not appropriate for comparing the two groups. Instead we used the Mann-Whitney U test to see if the methods of asking about offense rates produced any significant differences in the calculated λs.

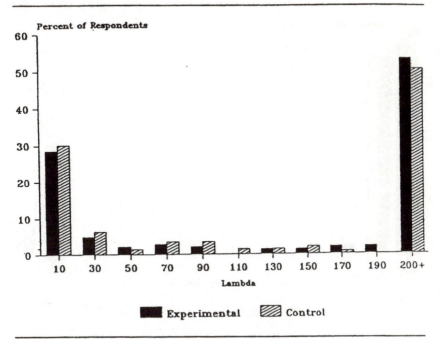

Figure 3: Distribution of Annualized Drug Dealing Rates
NOTE: Lambda values represent midpoints.

In addition we used the chi-square test to compare the percentage of respondents who are active in each crime category for the two groups. As Table 1 indicates, there were no significant differences between the two groups, either in the percentage active, or in the crime commission rates.[7]

The experimental method of asking about crime rates only differed from the control method when a respondent reported committing more than 10 offenses within a crime type during the reference period. Differences produced by the two methods thus may have been obscured by the large number of respondents who reported committing between 1 and 10 offenses during that period. In order to check this possibility, we compared the distributions of those who reported more than 10 offenses, again using the Mann-Whitney test. Table 2 shows the percentage who committed more than 10 offenses in each group and the test results. We do not present results for robbery, auto theft, forgery, or fraud because the numbers of respondents who reported committing more than 10 offenses were so small. For the remaining offenses, there were again no significant differences, although differences for those active in burglary approached significance at the .05 level.

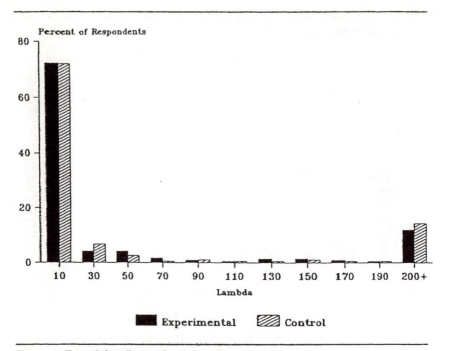

Figure 4: Total Crime Rates (Excluding Drug Dealing)
NOTE: Lambda values represent midpoints.

DISCUSSION

The measurement of individual offending frequency (λ), or the number of crimes committed per year by an active offender, is a central focus of criminal careers research. Reliance on official statistics severely limits the study of offending at the individual level; thus the self-report methodology pioneered by the RAND Corporation (Peterson and Braiker 1980; Rolph, Chaiken, and Houchens 1981; Chaiken and Chaiken 1982; Greenwood and Abrahamse 1982; Peterson, Chaiken, Ebener, and Honig 1982) represented a major contribution to this area of criminological research. The importance of the RAND research is highlighted by the fact that it stimulated both secondary analysis of the data (Visher 1991) and several replications with modifications (Mande and English 1987; Miranne and Geerken 1991; Horney and Marshall 1991). In our earlier study we reported on our attempts to refine that methodology to obtain even more precise estimates of λ. Our month-by-month reporting method took into account intraindividual variability in offending rates and avoided asking respondents to mentally average different

TABLE 2:   Estimates of Lambda by Crime Category for Respondents Reporting More than Ten Offenses

	Percentage Active Over 10	For Actives Over 10			
		Median	90th Percentile	Mean	Mann-Whitney U Significance Level
Burglary					
Experimental	4	48.00	712.08	157.21	.0541
Control	5	154.80	939.12	302.29	
Theft					
Experimental	8	142.90	1,806.00	710.06	.5966
Control	7	154.80	1,517.04	382.47	
Assault					
Experimental	5	59.81	1,553.16	272.92	.9650
Control	4	54.32	6,852.48	1,014.87	
Drug deals					
Experimental	31	903.00	9,752.40	3,242.31	.8849
Control	30	1,057.80	21,672.00	5,432.99	

rates over extended periods of time. In the present study we experimentally compared the month-by-month method with the original RAND method for obtaining self-reports to see if they produced different estimates of λ. More specifically, because of suggestions that the RAND estimates had been too high, we wanted to find out if the month-by-month method produced lower estimates of λ.

Even though data produced by the month-by-month method indicate that respondents do commit crimes at varying rates during their active periods (Horney and Marshall 1991), we found that the two methods produced distributions of λ that did not differ significantly from each other. Our experiment, especially in light of other replications of the RAND study (Mande and English 1987; Miranne and Geerken 1991), in fact suggests that the RAND results are very robust. These replications have been very consistent in finding heavily skewed distributions, with most respondents committing a relatively small number of offenses a year and a very few respondents reporting extremely high rates of offending. The finding of different patterns across crime categories has also been replicated, with crimes such as robbery and auto theft committed at relatively low rates and crimes like theft at much higher rates. We also found, as have the other studies, that drug dealing is reported to occur at astoundingly high rates.

We believe that our findings suggest that the self-report methodology is a valid tool for the study of criminal careers. Because the RAND instrument is so long and complicated, and because it was self-administered in the original study, questions have been raised as to whether a population of prison inmates, with limited verbal skills, were capable of producing valid data with this method. The fact that RAND researchers had to develop a set of assumptions and strategies for handling missing and ambiguous responses further clouded interpretation of their results. In the present study we used individual interviews in order to avoid these problems. Our calculations of λ were straightforward; we did not have to interpret responses, substitute mean values, or use minimum and maximum estimates for any of the components. With these advantages, we still obtained results that are overall quite comparable to the original RAND results.[8]

Our month-by-month reporting method has indicated that there is considerable variability in offending rates within individuals over relatively short time periods (Horney and Marshall 1991). We thus speculated that methods for determining λ that involve assumptions of constant rates would produce invalid estimates. The results of our experiment, however, indicate that the month-by-month method, even though it takes intraindividual variability into account, produces overall estimates of lambda that do not differ from those produced by the RAND method. One interpretation of the lack of significant differences is that when respondents are asked about their "typical" rates of responding they do a fairly good job of averaging over their different rates. Because the longest reference period being considered by any respondent was 24 months, and the reference period was much shorter for most respondents, it is possible that people are better at averaging than we expected.

The month-by-month method may fail to produce significantly different results because it focuses on the offenders who committed more than 10 offenses in a category, as does the detailed rate questioning of the RAND method. Thus the differences in the two methods are aimed at fairly small groups of respondents, albeit perhaps the most important respondents—the high-rate offenders. Detection of differences between the methods may be hampered by the problems inherent in the highly skewed distributions with extreme values—which can either be considered "outliers" or the most important values in the samples—producing very unstable means. There is no totally satisfactory way for handling these extreme values. We chose a fairly conservative strategy of using nonparametric tests to compare the distributions, and we believe that is the most reasonable strategy.

Although the month-by-month method does not change overall estimates of λ, we believe it has other important advantages for the study of criminal

120   JOURNAL OF RESEARCH IN CRIME AND DELINQUENCY

careers. Using this method, we have already learned a considerable amount about differences in activity patterns. Our data have raised questions of whether the activity patterns associated with different crimes reflect the nature of specific offenses or differences in lifestyles associated with particular offenses. We also believe that the variability in offending rates within individuals may have important implications for understanding criminal behavior and developing intervention strategies. Our method will allow us to identify the situational correlates of these different offending rates within individuals, which may be as important as identifying the correlates of participation in crime.

NOTES

1. The RAND researchers conducted their surveys with a resident population, but because of this bias, they drew a sample designed to simulate a cohort of incoming prisoners. There were several differences, however, between their samples and actual incoming cohorts in the three states; for example, younger offenders were underrepresented.

2. In the RAND study, because they sampled resident populations, respondents were asked to consider a window period separated from the interview by whatever time they had already been incarcerated. Visher (1986, Table 5) indicates that 26% of the respondents had served at least 2 years at the time of the survey. These respondents were thus being asked to think about events 4 years and more in the past. Because respondents are being asked to recall detailed information, we believe there is considerable advantage to having a recent recall period.

3. Concern has been expressed about the response rate in the RAND survey (Visher 1986); response rates in California and Michigan prisons were 49.4% and 49%, and a response rate of 82.2% was obtained in Texas prisons.

4. The RAND study used a 2-year period. In the RAND method, the date of arrest established the second calendar year; inmates were instructed to consider the portion of that year up to and including the month of arrest plus the preceding calendar year. The measurement period thus varied from 13 months (for inmates arrested in January of the second calendar year) to 24 months (for inmates arrested in December of the second calendar year). If an inmate who started with a measurement period of only 13 months had spent any of that time locked up, the possible active period could be very short.

Because we were also interested in studying the variability in individual offending over time, it was important to have relatively long street times for measuring offense rates. We thus used the year of arrest (the months up to and including the month of arrest) and the two calendar years preceding the year of arrest in the experimental condition. The measurement period for each inmate then varied from 25 months to 36 months. The longer window period we used should not cause greater recall problems than occurred in the Rand study because we used an actual intake cohort and interviewed them immediately after their admission to the Department of Corrections. Respondents were thus considering a 3-year period very close to the interview time. For our comparisons of the two methods in this article, we calculate λ based only on the 2-year period before arrest for the experimental condition.

5. We added the crime of rape to our survey. Some respondents reported multiple rapes, but the overall number of respondents who admitted to committing rapes was so small, that the results are not presented here.

6. We also asked the more detailed rate questions for assaults; the original RAND study only asked for total number of assaults.

7. We also used chi-square tests of differences in distributions with cut points used by Chaiken and Chaiken (1982, p. 49) as well as with cut points creating fewer categories. None reached a .05 significance level.

8. We still cannot say, of course, with any certainty that the original RAND estimates were not inflated because of problems with the self-administered questionnaires. Our results should perhaps be more appropriately compared to estimates provided by the Visher (1986) reanalysis.

REFERENCES

Blumstein, Alfred, Jacqueline Cohen, Jeffrey A. Roth, and Christy Visher, eds. 1986. *Criminal Careers and "Career Criminals,"* 2 vols. Washington, DC: National Academy Press.

Chaiken, Jan M. and Marcia Chaiken. 1982. *Varieties of Criminal Behavior.* Santa Monica, CA: RAND.

Cohen, Jacqueline. 1986. "Research on Criminal Careers: Individual Frequency Rates and Offense Seriousness." In *Criminal Careers and "Career Criminals,"* Vol. 1, edited by Alfred Blumstein, Jacqueline Cohen, Jeffrey A. Roth, and Christy Visher. Washington DC: National Academy Press.

Farrington, David P. 1983. "Randomized Experiments on Crime and Justice." In *Crime and Justice,* Vol. 4, edited by Michael Tonry and Norval Morris. Chicago: University of Chicago Press.

Greenwood, Peter and Allan Abrahamse. 1982. *Selective Incapacitation.* Santa Monica, CA: RAND.

Hindelang, Michael J., Travis Hirschi, and Joseph G. Weis. 1981. *Measuring Delinquency.* Beverly Hills, CA: Sage.

Horney, Julie and Ineke Haen Marshall. 1991. "Measuring Lambda Through Self-Reports." *Criminology* 29:471-95.

Mande, Mary J. and Kim English. 1987. *Individual Crime Rates of Colorado Prisoners.* Denver: Colorado Department of Public Safety, Division of Criminal Justice.

Miranne, Alfred C. and Michael R. Geerken. 1991. "The New Orleans Inmate Survey: A Test of Greenwood's Predictive Scale." *Criminology* 29:497-518.

Peterson, Mark A. and Harriet B. Braiker. 1980. *Doing Crime: A Survey of California Prison Inmates.* Santa Monica, CA: RAND.

Peterson, Mark A., Jan Chaiken, Patricia Ebener, and Paul Honig. 1982. *Survey of Prison and Jail Inmates: Background and Method.* Santa Monica, CA: RAND.

Rolph, John E., Jan M. Chaiken, and Robert L. Houchens. 1981. *Methods for Estimating Crime Rates of Individuals.* Santa Monica, CA: RAND.

Visher, Christy A. 1986. "The RAND Inmate Survey: A Reanalysis." In *Criminal Careers and "Career Criminals,"* Vol. 2, edited by Alfred Blumstein, Jacqueline Cohen, Jeffrey Roth, and Christy Visher. Washington DC: National Academy Press.

Zedlewski, Edwin F. 1987. *Research in Brief: Making Confinement Decisions.* Washington, DC: U.S. Department of Justice, National Institute of Justice.

[12]

The Age-Crime Debate: Assessing the Limits of Longitudinal Self-Report Data*

JANET L. LAURITSEN, *University of Missouri-St. Louis*

Abstract

Research presented in this article addresses some of the competing claims about the value of prospective longitudinal self-report data for studying the relationship between age and crime. More specifically, the debate over the magnitude of potential testing effects in longitudinal data is assessed by analyzing involvement in delinquency, serious offending, and victimization using self-report data from the first five waves of the National Youth Survey. The results of growth curve analyses suggest that panel and maturation effects warrant serious concern in longitudinal studies that rely on self-report information. The analyses show that regardless of the subject's age at the start of data collection, average self-reported involvement in crime declined substantially over time. Data from external sources suggest that period effects are not responsible for this decline. Furthermore, while traditional measures of delinquency are reliable for studying between-individual differences in crime, these same measures may lack the reliability necessary for studying between-individual differences in changes in crime over time.

Few substantive issues in criminology have been more contentious than those raised by the study of age and crime. While most social scientists agree that the aggregate age-crime curve reaches a peak during late adolescence and declines rapidly thereafter, there are ongoing debates about the theoretical meaning of this "brute fact" (e.g., Blumstein, Cohen & Farrington 1988; Farrington 1986; Gottfredson & Hirschi 1986, 1987, 1988; Hirschi & Gottfredson 1983). In order to resolve some

I am grateful to Wayne Osgood, Rob Sampson, and an anonymous reviewer for helpful comments on an earlier draft. The National Youth Survey data were obtained from the Inter-University Consortium for Political and Social Research at Ann Arbor, Michigan. Direct all correspondence to the author at Department of Criminology and Criminal Justice, University of Missouri-St. Louis, 8001 Natural Bridge Road, St. Louis, MO 63121.

128 / Social Forces 77:1, September 1998

of these disagreements, several researchers have promoted the collection of prospective longitudinal self-report data. Advocates of these designs argue that such data are best suited for determining whether the age-crime curve is a function of the use of aggregated official arrest records (and hence police activity), or the failure of arrest data to distinguish prevalence of offending from frequency of involvement.

Research presented in this article addresses some of the competing claims about the value of longitudinally gathered self-report data for studying the relationship between age and crime. Self-report data from the first five waves of the National Youth Survey (NYS) are used to construct age-crime curves in order to determine the form of the relationship between age and self-reported involvement in crime from ages 11 through 21, and the extent to which individuals vary in their involvement in crime over this period of the life course. By taking advantage of recent developments in the modeling of multi-age-cohort longitudinal data, these analyses have the potential to shed light on some of the competing methodological and substantive debates. Without a better understanding of the methodological challenges unique to longitudinal self-report data, assessments of general theory models (e.g., Gottfredson & Hirschi 1990) versus developmental models (e.g., Moffitt 1993) of crime and deviance over the life course are incomplete. In addition, the methodological issues raised here are relevant to the use of other self-report longitudinal data increasingly available to social scientists.

Like all nonexperimental research designs, the value of longitudinal self-report data for studying age and crime depends on our understanding of the method's strengths and weaknesses. One of the primary threats to internal validity in analyses based on longitudinal self-report data is the possibility of testing effects (Cook & Campbell 1979). Both sides of the criminological debate agree that testing effects from repeated interviews with the same respondents are potential problems in longitudinally gathered self-report data. However, disagreements exist over the expected magnitude of this threat. Gottfredson and Hirschi (1987) contend that testing effects may be substantial, while Blumstein, Cohen, and Farrington (1988) disagree and counter that there is no solid empirical research supporting this position. Both positions are correct in that there has been little research on this topic. Prior analyses of the National Crime (Victimization) Survey have found some evidence of testing effects in self-report victimization data (e.g., Woltman & Bushery 1984), and examinations of prevalence data from adjacent panels of the NYS have raised concerns about possible testing effects in self-report delinquency measures (e.g., Thornberry 1989; Osgood et al. 1989). Yet apart from the analyses noted above, little research has examined whether testing effects may affect self-reports of crime and delinquency.

A second potential threat to research based on longitudinal self-report data has received even less attention — changing content validity related to the age of the respondent. Since most longitudinal self-report data on crime and delinquency focuses on the experiences of adolescents and young adults undergoing substantial developmental changes, such threats also must be given serious consideration. If subjects' interpretations of self-report items tend to change as they mature, then observed changes in crime and delinquency scores over time may reflect changes in the meaning or content validity of the questions rather than actual changes in behavior. The potential role of such effects in the study of age and crime is also discussed in this research.

Examination of the relationship between age and self-reported crime begins by addressing four basic questions: (1) What is the general form of the age-crime curve in the NYS self-report data? (2) Is the age-crime curve a function of how crime is operationalized? (3) Is there significant variation in age-crime curves (or trajectories) across subjects? and (4) Can the NYS age cohort data be linked to reveal a typical trajectory of self-reported involvement in crime across adolescence? The answers to these questions will be provided through the use of growth curve analysis in the context of hierarchical linear modeling. The results of these analyses also permit an assessment of some of the methodological vulnerabilities of longitudinal self-report data.

Age and Crime in Accelerated Longitudinal Designs

Recent applications of hierarchical linear modeling (HLM) have shown how variation in individual development across a variety of attitudinal and behavioral domains can be studied in a sophisticated yet accessible way (Bryk & Raudenbush 1992; Raudenbush & Chan 1992; Horney, Osgood & Marshall 1995). In a recent article Raudenbush and Chan (1992) demonstrated how HLM techniques permit the evaluation of age, period, and cohort effects on attitudes toward deviance using panel data from the NYS. By linking five years of panel data from 11- and 14-year-old age cohorts, they were able to describe the development of deviant attitudes from ages 11 through 18. While their analysis was restricted to attitudinal data, they clearly illustrated how the age-crime curve can be investigated by treating the NYS panel data as an accelerated longitudinal design with multiple age cohorts.

Multiple age-cohort accelerated longitudinal designs are those studies in which randomly selected subjects of varying ages are followed over time. These designs are preferred over single age cohort panel designs because the latter may confound age and period effects. As discussed by Raudenbush and Chan (1992), panel studies such as the NYS do not confound age and period influences because they contain multiple observations of youths of a given age at various points in time. For instance, the present analyses will investigate changes in criminal involvement over time among four youth cohorts — those who were either 11, 13, 15, or 17 years old at the first wave of data collection (in 1976). Since data were collected annually over a consecutive five-year period, multiple age-specific estimates of crime are available for comparison across cohorts. Inferences about age-crime developmental patterns

130 / *Social Forces* **77:1, September 1998**

can be made by comparing average crime levels and rates of change of the various cohorts at points of overlap. If estimates of crime involvement and change are not significantly different from one another in the cohort comparisons, then it is logical to infer that a single developmental trajectory describes average involvement in crime from ages 11 to 21. The age-crime curve can thus be described by linking age-cohort time trends.

In their analysis of the 11- and 14-year-old cohorts from the NYS, Raudenbush and Chan (1992) found that attitudes toward deviance and rates of change in those attitudes during adolescence were very similar at the points where the cohort data overlapped. Moreover, they found that attitudes toward deviance were related to age in ways analogous to the aggregate (arrest) age-crime curve. That is, prodeviant attitudes increased during early adolescence and peaked around the ages of 16 and 17. Finally, they also demonstrated that there was significant individual variation in the age-deviant attitudes curves, and that gender was related to some of the parameters of the trajectory.

In order to link information about crime from multiple age cohorts, it is necessary to first estimate growth curves for each subject in an age cohort. Growth curve analysis represents an efficient way for researchers to organize and test hypotheses about individual change over time, but these analyses must be guided by theoretical insight and a strong understanding of the outcome variable. As Bryk and Raudenbush (1992) note, the investigation of hypotheses about growth curves and variations in these trajectories present a unique set of conceptual, design, and measurement challenges.

Conceptual issues center around the development of a general growth model to guide preliminary analyses. In the case of age and crime, criminologists can begin by examining a model in which offense involvement is characterized by a curve that increases during early adolescence, peaks in late adolescence, and declines thereafter. Exactly what the best fitting growth curve looks like is determined by a series of model estimations, beginning with the simplest linear model and progressing to more complex nonlinear models. Design issues include determining the number of time periods necessary for an adequate assessment of individual change. In the case of the NYS data used here, the complexity of the curves that can be fitted are limited by the fact that five data points are available for each subject. Also important are the number and size of the age cohorts in the sample since these factors affect the model's ability to separate age and cohort effects and to signal significant patterns and variations in the growth curve or trajectory. Finally, measurement issues unique to longitudinal analyses are a concern because most outcome measures have been developed to study between-individual differences rather than individual change over time. The modeling of stability and change in offending requires that the outcome measure retains the same meaning across all time points, and that the measure remains valid and reliable over time as well (see Bryk & Raudenbush 1987; Willett & Sayer 1994). The relevance of these conceptual, design, and measurement issues for studying the relationship between age and crime is discussed in more detail as they arise in the analyses.

Before turning to the analyses, a brief overview of the logic of growth curve analysis via hierarchical linear modeling is provided so that those unfamiliar with the technique can follow the statistical analyses presented here. For much greater detail on hierarchical linear modeling, readers are referred to Raudenbush and Chan (1992) and Bryk and Raudenbush (1992). The main advantage of using HLM techniques for studying age and crime is the flexibility of the models for describing and decomposing between- and within-individual variations in offense involvement, and the ability to separate age and period effects. The fact that the technique is understandable to persons familiar with standard OLS regression techniques is also valuable.

Briefly stated, the relationship between age and crime can be examined by using a two-level hierarchical linear model in which data from the first level is used to describe each individual's pattern of crime involvement over time, while data from the second level is used to examine how person-level characteristics (e.g., gender) are related to these age (or time) patterns. Through these analyses, the average crime trajectory (or growth curve) across all persons of a given age cohort is described and the question of whether or not this curve varies systematically according to some individual characteristic can be assessed. The information derived from growth curve analyses can thus be used to address some of the basic substantive debates about the relationship between age and crime.

The first step in such a process is to estimate a level-1 model which provides the longitudinal profile parameters for the crime trajectories for each person in a sample. The parameters of these trajectories (e.g., the intercept and slope of the trend lines) describe the relationship between offending and age for each person in a given age cohort. The level-1 equation used to estimate the involvement in crime of a particular person at a given age is examined as a function of a systematic trajectory associated with age, plus random error:

$$Y_{it} = \pi_{0i} + \pi_{1i}(age_{it}) + e_{it} \tag{1}$$

where Y_{it} is the observed offending for person i (for $i = 1, \ldots, n$ persons) at time t (for $t = 1, \ldots, 5$); π_{0i} and π_{1i} represent the intercept and slope parameters, respectively, for the individual trajectories, and e_{it} is the random within-subject error in prediction for person i at time t.[1] For each of the cohort analyses presented here, age is coded $-2, -1, 0, 1, 2$, so that π_{0i} indicates the intercept of person i when the subject is in the third panel of data collection.[2] Ordinary least-squares regression procedures provide the estimates for these parameters.

The parameters obtained from the level-1 analyses can be used as outcome variables in a level-2 model investigating systematic variation in offending patterns across individuals. To estimate the amount of variation in levels and rates of change in individuals' crime curves, the simplest level-2 model is specified; that is, one

132 / *Social Forces* **77:1, September 1998**

containing no covariates for between-individual differences. Such analyses produce useful information about the total variation in each of the parameters describing the curve. The corresponding equations for this model can be represented as follows:

$$\pi_{0i} = \beta_{00} + \mu_{0i}$$
$$\pi_{1i} = \beta_{10} + \mu_{1i}$$

(2)

where β_{00} is the grand mean involvement in crime score (when $age = 0$), β_{10} is the grand mean rate of change in involvement in crime, and μ_{0i} and μ_{1i} represent the random effect of person i on the crime score and the rate of change in the crime score when $age = 0$. When the level-1 and level-2 equations are combined, the following equation results:

$$Y_{it} = \beta_{00} + \beta_{10}(age) + e_{it}$$

(3)

Ordinary least-squares regression is inappropriate for estimating this equation because the errors are correlated over time for each subject and are heteroscedastic due to their dependence on time. HLM software estimates these parameters using a restricted maximum-likelihood procedure for variance component estimation and a generalized least-squares approach for effect coefficients (see Bryk & Raudenbush 1992; Raudenbush & Chan 1992). The analyses discussed below will describe the form of the NYS age-crime curves by estimating the above equations for each of the four age cohorts.

Data and Measures

As noted earlier, data from the first five waves of the NYS are used to model the age-crime curve (Elliott 1985). The NYS is a well-known prospective longitudinal study designed to provide information on the incidence and prevalence of various types of delinquency events (see Elliott & Ageton 1985). Personal interviews were conducted with adolescents living in randomly selected households beginning in 1977, and the next four interviews were conducted on an annual basis. At the time of the first wave youths' ages ranged from 11 to 17; thus by the fifth wave subjects were 15 to 21 years old. Consequently, these data can be used to estimate the age-crime curve for the 11- to 21-year age period of the life course. To simplify the presentation of results, the analyses are restricted to four of the seven available age cohorts (11-, 13-, 15-, and 17-year-olds in wave 1).[3]

In order to assess whether the general form of the age-crime curve is a function of how crime is measured, several outcome variables are considered at various levels of measurement. The outcome variables include scales of general delinquency, serious offending, and victimization. The items composing these scales are found in the appendix. General delinquency is a summary measure of the number of times in the prior year the youth reported engaging in minor and serious assault, minor and serious theft, and robbery. With NYS data, one can construct the general delinquency and serious offending scales by either summing the original raw frequency counts of the number of self-reported incidents, or the nine-point ordinal scales provided for each item.[4] The raw frequency counts are heavily influenced by a handful of respondents who reported extensive involvement (e.g., more than 100 incidents) in particular behaviors. Since errors in self-reporting made by low frequency offenders are likely to be less than those made by high frequency offenders, the use of the ordinal responses rather than raw frequencies increases the general reliability of the scale (see Huizinga & Elliott 1986). The present analyses emphasize the scales summarizing the ordinal responses; however, it should be noted that parallel analyses were conducted on the raw frequency count data and the conclusions were substantively similar (results not shown).

The serious offending measure is a subset of the general delinquency scale. This measure was given separate consideration as an outcome variable since it has been found in test-retest experiments of the NYS data that scales of less frequent, but more serious offenses have the highest precision (i.e., the smallest difference in frequencies reported over a four-week retest period) (Huizinga & Elliott 1986). The serious offending scale consists of self-reports of serious assault, serious theft, and robbery. Minor theft and assault items have been found to have lower reliability and face validity since subjects are more likely to include trivial events in these self-reports (Huizinga & Elliott 1986).

The victimization measure sums the number of times subjects experienced any of four types of incidents in the prior year — assault (or attempted assault), robbery (or attempted robbery), larceny, and vandalism. Only raw frequency counts of victimization incidents are available in the data. However, there is much less variation in the victimization measures than in the offending measures as these data do not contain as many extreme values.

The general delinquency, serious offending, and victimization summary scales are somewhat skewed in their distributions. Therefore a decision must be made whether to analyze the variables in their current metric or as a nonlinear transformation. Fortunately, HLM software permits analyses of outcome variables that are skewed, so these variables were examined in event count models and as logarithmically transformed. Because these results were substantively the same for both sets of measures, and because the reliability coefficients were found to be higher for the logarithmically transformed variables, the results presented here are for the transformed variables. Measures with higher reliability are preferred in growth curve analyses because they are more likely to generate systematic patterns in the data.

Finally, it should be noted that each scale was also recoded and reanalyzed as a prevalence measure (0 = no incidents in the prior year, 1 = one or more incidents) to determine how the relationship between age and prevalence of crime compares to the relationship between age and frequency of crime. In preliminary binary outcome analyses, the relationship between age and prevalence was found to be substantively the same as the relationship between age and the logarithmic measures. Given the similarity in the prevalence and incidence findings, the more reliable logarithmically transformed measures were again preferred.

Results

COHORT SPECIFIC ANALYSES OF GENERAL DELINQUENCY

The results describing the general delinquency trajectories for the 11-, 13-, 15-, and 17-year-old age cohorts are presented in Table 1. For each age cohort, estimates of the intercept and slope coefficients, variation in these coefficients, and the reliability of the coefficients are shown. These results show that, with the exception of the 11-year-old cohort, the average rate of change in general delinquency over time is significantly *negative* (see β_{10} estimates). That is, regardless of whether the respondent was 13, 15, or 17 years old at the start of data collection, the average subject reported *decreasing* involvement in general delinquency in the subsequent four panels. Among the 11-year-old cohort, the coefficient is also negative, but not statistically significant. In other words, 11-year-old subjects reported no significant changes in their general delinquency involvement through age 15. The average delinquency trajectories for each of the four cohorts are graphically displayed in Figure 1.

Clearly these descriptive results are contrary to what one might expect based on general knowledge of the aggregate age-crime curve. Self-reported delinquency was expected to have exhibited growth (i.e., significant positive coefficients) among the 11- and 13-year-old cohorts, and decline among the age 17 cohort. Since the peak age of offending is likely to come before age 17, the 15-year-old cohort should have exhibited a significant nonlinear pattern. In order to examine this possibility and to determine whether the negative slopes for the other cohorts are a function of the linear specification of the model, tests for nonlinear relationships were conducted (results not shown). In the first of these tests, a quadratic term was added to equation (1) to see if the delinquency trajectories had a tendency to accelerate or decelerate over time. The results of these analyses for each of the four cohorts found there to be no significant tendency for the growth curve to decelerate or accelerate. A linear trajectory provided a better description of the cohorts' average growth curves than did this nonlinear specification.[5]

A second test for nonlinearity was conducted in order to determine whether the negative slopes might be related to the inclusion of follow-up questions at later waves of data collection. In the first three waves of the NYS, delinquency questions were asked without follow-up questions. Beginning in wave 4, follow-up questions were added to collect additional information about specific delinquency events. If respondents learned that positive responses could lead to additional questions that

TABLE 1: Results of Hierarchical Linear Model for Age 11, 13, 15, and 17 Cohorts

	General Delinquency							
	Age 11		Age 13		Age 15		Age 17	
Fixed Effects								
Predictor	Coeff. (S.E.)	t-ratio	Coeff. (S.E.)	t-ratio	Coeff. (S.E.)	t-ratio	Coeff. (S.E.)	t-ratio
For base rate, π_{0i}								
Intercept, β_{00}	.51* (.04)	14.34	.61* (.04)	15.21	.62* (.04)	14.34	.39* (.03)	12.25
For linear change, π_{1i}								
Intercept, β_{10}	−.02 (.01)	−1.36	−.07* (.01)	−5.18	−.14* (.01)	−10.76	−.13* (.01)	−9.63

Variance Components

Parameter	Est.	Chi-square[a]	Est.	Chi-square[b]	Est.	Chi-square[c]	Est.	Chi-square[d]
$Var(\pi_{0i}) = \tau_{00}$	.23*	1,466.99	.34*	2,268.61	.37*	1,985.09	.15*	771.43
$Var(\pi_{1i}) = \tau_{11}$	.02*	395.54	.02*	509.84	.02*	384.92	.01*	293.81
$Var(e_{it}) = \sigma^2$	.19		.18		.21		.21	

Reliability

For base rate, π_{0i}	.84		.88		.87		.74	
For linear change, π_{1i}	.44		.53		.41		.34	

[a] df = 219 for variance components analyses.
[b] df = 237 for variance components analyses.
[c] df = 226 for variance components analyses.
[d] df = 185 for variance components analyses.

* p ≤ .01

were perceived to be burdensome, then deliberate under-reporting in waves four and five may be large enough to account for a general negative trend among the cohorts.

To examine this change in instrumentation hypothesis, a "piece-wise" time trajectory was estimated in place of the original time coding.[6] The logic of this test is to determine whether the slope describing waves 1 through 3 is significantly different from the slope describing waves 4 to 5. If so, and if the slope was increasingly negative from wave 4 to 5, this would be evidence that the addition of follow up questions may have influenced self-reporting. These piecewise trajectories were examined for each of the four cohorts and for each of the three outcome variables. In all but one instance, the differences in the direction and magnitudes of the slopes were not significant.[7] Therefore the hypothesis that changes in

136 / *Social Forces* 77:1, September 1998

FIGURE 1: Age-Cohort General Delinquency Trajectories

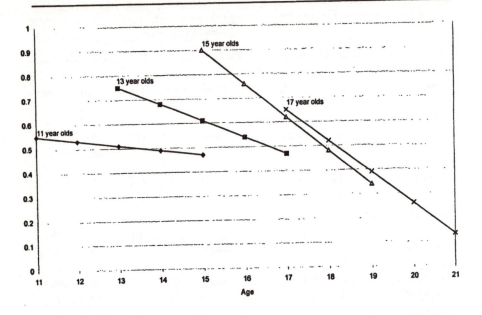

instrumentation led to increased burden on the respondents and subsequent underreporting was not supported.

One might also hypothesize that the negative slopes are due to selective sample attrition in the outcome variables. Two pieces of evidence speak against this interpretation. First, the HLM analytic method does not eliminate subjects who are missing data at level one. If a subject is missing outcome data at any of the waves, the software estimates the best fitting trajectory based upon the available data points. Second, in preliminary analyses (not shown) sample attrition was not significantly related to the outcome or level-2 variables used here.

In sum, the growth curves for the age cohorts taken as a whole do not approximate the expected age-crime curve, regardless of whether prevalence or frequency measures are used. The exception to this general pattern is the negative trajectory observed for the 17-year-old cohort (and perhaps the 15-year-old cohort) whose delinquency was expected to have declined over the subsequent five years. Even though similar analyses have shown that the NYS data measuring attitudes toward deviance parallel the expected age-crime curve (Raudenbush & Chan 1992), this pattern is not observed for involvement in general delinquency.

The variance components shown in Table 1 reveal the amount of variation attributable to each of the parameters estimated in the fixed effects analyses. The variance in π_{0i} (τ_{00}) represents the amount of between-person variation in general delinquency status (at wave 3), while the amount of between-person variation in the slope is indicated by the variance of π_{1i} (τ_{1i}). Residual within-person variance over time is indicated by σ^2. The chi-square tests for the variance components indicate that both the intercepts and slopes of the trajectories do vary significantly across individuals.

A more general issue can also be assessed by examining the variance components estimates — that is, the amount of overall variance in an outcome variable attributable to within-person change versus between-person differences. This is done by estimating the model examined above without the age parameter specification at level-1. In analyses (not shown) of the three outcome measures for each of the four cohorts, it was found that approximately half (40% to 60%) of the total outcome variance was due to between-individual differences and half to within-individual changes over time (see Bryk & Raudenbush 1992).

The reliabilities of the intercept and slope parameters are also provided for each of the cohort analyses (see Bryk & Raudenbush 1992). These estimates are useful for determining how much of the variability in the intercept and slope estimates is due to error versus parameter variance. The reliability coefficients shown here suggest that the reliability of the base rate estimate is good (range = .74 to .88), but the reliability of the data for estimating changes over time is not nearly so strong (range = .34 to .53). That is, the outcome measure is reliable enough to support analyses of between-individual differences in status, but may not be sufficient for detecting between-individual differences in patterns of change over time.

To examine the issue of how the age-crime trajectories might vary systematically across subject, a simple investigation of race and gender differences in slopes and intercepts was conducted for each of the outcome variables and each of the age cohorts. These variables were chosen because prior research has shown that the general reliability and validity of self-reports of offending among adolescents is related to race and gender (Hindelang, Hirschi & Weis 1981). These analyses require a respecification of the level-2 model:

$$\pi_{0i} = \beta_{00} + \beta_{01}X_i + \mu_{0i}$$
$$\pi_{1i} = \beta_{10} + \beta_{11}X_i + \mu_{1i}$$

where $X_i = 1$ if male, 0 if female (or $X_i = 1$ if black, 0 if white).[8] With this specification it can be determined whether males (or blacks) scored differently from females (or whites) in average status or slope. These analyses (not shown) found race to be unrelated to either average status or rate of change in general delinquency, serious offending, or victimization. Black and white youth exhibited the same

138 / *Social Forces* **77:1, September 1998**

average intercepts and slopes. On the other hand, gender was found to be related to average status among all age cohorts (and for all outcome measures) with males scoring significantly higher on the general delinquency scale than females. The effect of gender on changes over time is significant in three of the twelve trajectories examined.[9] In these instances, males' slopes were steeper — that is, males self-reported faster declines in crime involvement over time.

As noted earlier, the reliability of the slope estimates is related to the model's ability to find systematic relationships between person-level characteristics and changes over time. As Bryk and Raudenbush (1992) caution, under such conditions it should not necessarily be concluded that the person-level characteristics are unrelated to the slope coefficients. Instead, null relationships may reflect the fact that self-report measures traditionally used to examine between-individual differences are not adequate for detecting systematic differences in changes over time. However, before drawing this conclusion, alternative hypotheses also must be considered. We return to this issue after the results for the other outcome variables are described.

COHORT SPECIFIC ANALYSES OF SERIOUS OFFENDING AND VICTIMIZATION

The results describing the serious offending and victimization trajectories for the 11-, 13-, 15-, and 17-year-old age cohorts are presented in Tables 2 and 3 and displayed in Figures 2 and 3. Generally speaking, both sets of results parallel the findings based on the general delinquency scale. For serious offending, the slopes are significantly negative for the 13-, 15-, and 17-year-old age cohorts, while the slope is null for the 11-year-old cohort. The variance components analyses illustrate significant variation in the slope and intercept parameters for youth in each age cohort, and that much of the between-individual variation is attributed to differences in status, not slope. Here as well, the reliability coefficients are lower for the slope estimates. This low reliability is somewhat more surprising given that previous assessments of the test-retest reliability of these measures show that serious offending items are more accurately reported (i.e., they exhibit greater precision in frequency recall) than less serious offending (Huizinga & Elliott 1986).

The victimization results are also substantively similar to the serious offending and general delinquency results; however, in this instance the 11-year-olds' slope is also statistically significant and negative. Variance components and reliability estimates continue to suggest that much of the between-individual variation in victimization trajectories is due to differences in status rather than slope, and that these self-report measures also may lack sufficient reliability for detecting significant between-individual differences in changes in victimization over time.

In sum, the general form of the cohort-specific age-crime curves in the NYS data is not as expected. The crime trajectories found here do not parallel the NYS deviant attitude curves reported by Raudenbush and Chan (1992). Instead,

TABLE 2: Results of Hierarchical Linear Model for Age 11, 13, 15, and 17 Cohorts

				Serious Offending				
		Age 11		Age 13		Age 15		Age 17
Fixed Effects								
Predictor	Coeff. (S.E.)	t-ratio	Coeff. (S.E.)	t-ratio	Coeff. (S.E.)	t-ratio	Coeff. (S.E.)	t-ratio
For base rate, π_{0i}								
Intercept, β_{00}	.15* (.02)	7.68	.19* (.02)	8.22	.26* (.03)	9.36	.17* (.02)	8.29
For linear change, π_{1i}								
Intercept, β_{10}	.00 (.01)	.45	−.03* (.01)	−3.12	−.04* (.01)	−4.19	−.04* (.01)	−5.23

				Variance Components				
Parameter	Est.	Chi-square[a]	Est.	Chi-square[b]	Est.	Chi-square[c]	Est.	Chi-square[d]
$Var(\pi_{0i}) = \tau_{00}$	.06*	1,059.67	.11*	1,617.21	.15*	1,484.33	.06*	751.20
$Var(\pi_{1i}) = \tau_{11}$	.01*	425.62	.01*	385.20	.01*	371.91	.01*	270.90
$Var(e_{it}) = \sigma^2$	.08		.09		.13		.10	

		Reliability		
For base rate, π_{0i}	.79	.84	.83	.72
For linear change, π_{1i}	.48	.38	.37	.20

[a] df = 219 for variance components analyses.
[b] df = 237 for variance components analyses.
[c] df = 226 for variance components analyses.
[d] df = 185 for variance components analyses.

* p ≤ .01

regardless of whether the respondent was 13, 15, or 17 years old at the start of data collection, the average subject reported decreasing involvement in general delinquency, serious offending, and victimization in the subsequent four panels. Subjects from the 11-year-old cohort reported decreasing victimization on average in the subsequent panels, and exhibit no change in serious offending or general delinquency over time. On the whole, these findings describing the longitudinal age-crime trajectories are not sensitive to the content of the outcome measure or the level of measurement used in the analyses.

Statistically significant variation in the age-crime trajectories across subjects also was found. A search for covariates of these between-individual differences showed that there were significant gender differences in status, but not in most of the slope coefficients. No significant race differences in status or slope estimates

140 / *Social Forces* 77:1, September 1998

TABLE 3:   Results of Hierarchical Linear Model for Age 11, 13, 15, and 17
           Cohorts

	Victimization							
	Age 11		Age 13		Age 15		Age 17	
Fixed Effects								
Predictor	Coeff. (S.E.)	t-ratio	Coeff. (S.E.)	t-ratio	Coeff. (S.E.)	t-ratio	Coeff. (S.E.)	t-ratio
For base rate, π_{0i}								
Intercept, β_{00}	.69* (.04)	18.06	.83* (.04)	20.61	.77* (.05)	17.06	.76* (.05)	16.39
For linear change, π_{1i}								
Intercept, β_{10}	−.09* (.01)	−5.98	−.12* (.02)	−7.39	−.15* (.02)	−9.10	−.11* (.02)	−5.86

Variance Components								
Parameter	Est.	Chi-square[a]	Est.	Chi-square[b]	Est.	Chi-square[c]	Est.	Chi-square[d]
$Var(\pi_{0i}) = \tau_{00}$	.25*	1,084.52	.30*	1,086.31	.38*	1,387.00	.31*	840.61
$Var(\pi_{1i}) = \tau_{11}$	.01*	309.52	.02*	360.82	.02*	374.55	.02*	263.24
$Var(e_{it}) = \sigma^2$	.30		.38		.35		.38	

Reliability								
For base rate, π_{0i}	.78		.77		.81		.77	
For linear change, π_{1i}	.28		.35		.36		.31	

[a] df = 219 for variance components analyses.
[b] df = 237 for variance components analyses.
[c] df = 226 for variance components analyses.
[d] df = 185 for variance components analyses.

* $p \leq .01$

were found. Again, the model's inability to detect significant relationships between person-level characteristics and changes over time may be a function of the low reliability of the slope parameters.

PERIOD EFFECTS OR TESTING EFFECTS?

While the negative trajectories found among the 17-year-olds are consistent with expectations about the age-crime curve, the trajectories for the 11-, 13-, and 15-year-olds are not as expected. Two rival hypotheses may account for these unexpected negative slopes — testing (or panel) effects or period effects. Testing effects are those influences associated with the repeated administration of a survey instrument. Such effects may be due to a variety of factors including memory, survey design, or generalized fatigue, and have been found in other repeated panel

FIGURE 2: Age-Cohort Serious Offending Trajectories

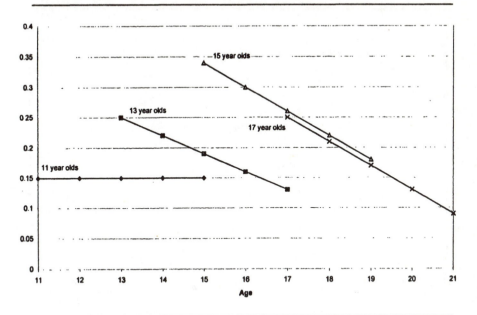

designs. For instance, in the NC(V)S analyses reported earlier (Woltman & Bushery 1984), total personal crime rates reported by subjects interviewed for the fifth time average about 13% lower than those reported by subjects interviewed for the second time (during the same reference period). In other words, number of prior interviews influenced self-reporting when period effects were controlled (see also Lehnen & Reiss 1978). Crude estimates of the magnitude of the decline in the NYS self-reports can be calculated by examining the expected values of the trajectories over time. The NYS estimates (which do not control for possible period changes) are larger; for general delinquency, serious offending, and victimization, the drop in incidence averages approximately 51%, 42%, and 59% respectively, from panels one through five.[10]

The possibility that panel effects may exist in the NYS has been suggested in previous research (Thornberry 1989; Osgood et al. 1989). Thornberry examined the aggregated age-specific prevalence rates for various offenses by wave of data collection and noted a general downward trend in self-reported offending across panels. By comparing prevalence levels in adjacent waves of NYS data, he found that declines in delinquency characterized approximately two-thirds of the year-to-year contrasts. The findings reported here show that downward reporting patterns exist when *individual* growth trajectories are the object of study and that the declines occur similarly across each of the age cohorts examined. Furthermore, the present

142 / *Social Forces* 77:1, September 1998

FIGURE 3: Age-Cohort Victimization Trajectories

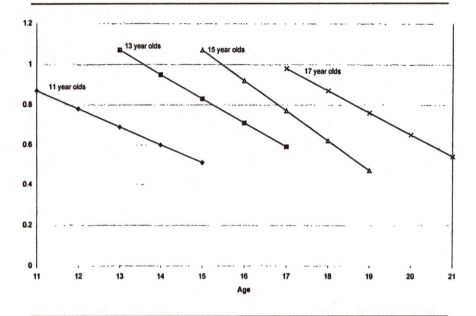

analyses show that the declines are not a function of sample attrition, levels of measurement, or the use of single items as opposed to more stable scales of crime. The piecewise trajectory analyses reported earlier confirms Thornberry's suspicion that the downward declines in self-reporting are unlikely to reflect a simple testing effect due to changes in instrumentation. Instead, these results are more consistent with a generalized testing effect (e.g., panel fatigue) or a maturation process (i.e., changing content validity) explanation.

The alternative hypothesis that a period decline accounts for the decreasing prevalence rate across waves of the NYS was suggested by Menard (1987). He reported that offense prevalence among 16- and 17-year-olds in the NYS decreased from 1976 to 1980; however, he interpreted this decline as evidence of a period trend rather than a panel effect. By comparing trends in the NYS reports to UCR (16- and 17-year-olds') arrest data and general NC(V)S trends, Menard concluded that the NYS data were detecting trends that the other data sources were incapable of uncovering. A similar strategy of comparing the NYS age-specific crime estimates to outside data sources is used here to evaluate the likelihood of a period effect. However, additional data not previously compared are examined. If period changes are small or non-negative during this time period, then methodological explanations must be given greater weight.

Evidence on period trends in juvenile crime for these years is available from previous analyses of official and self-report data including the UCR, the NC(V)S, and the Monitoring the Future (MTF) studies. Cook and Laub (1986) examined Uniform Crime Report data for 13- to 17-year-olds' offense involvement and reported that the total arrest rate and the serious crime arrest rates among juveniles fluctuated from 1976 to 1980, with no clear observable trend. Serious (index) crime rates among juveniles increased 1% from 1976 to 1980, while total arrests decreased 1% over this same time period. Research describing crime-specific annual arrest rates for 17-year-olds showed increasing rates of assault, robbery, larceny, and vandalism from 1976 to 1980 (Osgood et al. 1989). Thus according to arrest data, trends in adolescent offending rates were generally flat over this five-year period.

The National Crime (Victimization) Survey also has been used to examine period trends in adolescent *offending* (Laub 1983). Respondents who were victims of a personal crime (i.e., rape, robbery, assault, or personal larceny) were asked to report the perceived age of the offender in lone-offender incidents or the perceived age of the oldest offender in multiple-offender incidents. Laub (1983) reports the annual rates of offending for 12- to 17-year-olds and for 18- to 20-year-olds for the period encompassing 1976 to 1980. When rates of offending for these two groups are combined, little change is found in personal crime offending by adolescents (+1%). Thus, according to victims, adolescent offending rates changed little from 1976 to 1980.

NC(V)S data on juvenile *victimization* trends also have been studied. Parker et al. (1991) report that 12- to 19-year-olds' assault, robbery, and larceny victimization rates remained fairly flat or slightly increased from 1974 to 1982. More specific comparisons of violence and theft victimization data for 12- to 15-year-olds and for 16- to 19-year-olds show stable or slightly increasing rates from 1976 to 1979, but decreases for both crime types from 1979 to 1980 (U.S. Department of Justice 1991). Overall victimization rates among juveniles changed relatively little over these five years, with the exception of a downward turn during the final year of the series.[12]

Finally, other self-report data more similar in instrumentation to the NYS have been examined for period trends. Osgood et al. (1989) compared MTF data from 1975 to 1985 with age-specific arrest data from the same years in order to separate time trends from age effects. They report that the MTF self-report data concur with arrest data in that both indicate an age decline in offending from ages 17 through 23. As noted earlier, their analyses of age-specific time trends in arrests showed no clear decreases in age-controlled assault, robbery, larceny, auto theft, arson, or vandalism rates. The MTF trend data agree with arrest data showing increases in assault, and no trends in vandalism; however, the MTF data disagree with arrest trends for theft (arrests increased while self-reports indicated a decline). For other

144 / *Social Forces* 77:1, September 1998

crime types it was more difficult to compare arrest and self-report data, since these offenses occurred at lower rates and exhibited no clear period trends.

Thus, the MTF trend data do not reveal significant declines in 17-year-olds' offending rates from 1976 to 1980. Since these data conflict with the trends found in the NYS, Osgood et al. (1989) suggest that the NYS patterns probably reflect the methodological vulnerabilities of panel designs. They state, "We have greater confidence in our results than Menard's due to our use of much larger annual samples, each comparably and independently selected. We suspect that the apparent trend observed by Menard reflects differential attrition or effects of repeated testing" (412).

In sum, data from several major sources other than the NYS fail to show similar age-specific period trends in adolescent offending or victimization. Period trends are not likely to be responsible for the negative trajectories observed here. This difference alone might not be sufficient to warrant serious methodological concerns over longitudinal self-report data. However, when considered in conjunction with the findings noted earlier (i.e., low reliability coefficients and other known panel effects) it appears that methodological weaknesses due to repeated testing or changing content validity are a likely occurrence with the NYS self-report data. A precise estimate of the magnitude of these effects cannot be calculated with currently available data. Nonetheless, these findings raise concerns about whether traditionally used crime and delinquency measures found in longitudinal self-report studies are well suited for studying individual pathways of delinquency or victimization over time.

LINKING COHORTS

Given the methodological weaknesses noted above, is there still enough patterning in the data to permit linking of the NYS cohort data? Despite the suggestion that panel and/or maturation effects appear to be confounded with age in some of these crime trajectories, the growth curves for 17-year-olds were in general accordance with substantive expectations. Here it is examined whether it is possible to link any of the cohort trajectories in such a way as to permit inferences about age-crime developmental patterns. Inferences about crime development can be made by comparing the average crime levels and the rates of change of the various cohorts at points of overlap. If estimates of crime involvement and change are not significantly different from one another in each of the cohort comparisons, then it is logical to infer that a single developmental trajectory describes involvement in crime from ages 11 to 21.

Visual examination of Figures 1, 2, and 3 illustrates that we are unlikely to be able to infer an overall age-crime curve by linking these cohorts, but we may be able to link some of the cohort trajectories for some of the outcome measures. For example, in Figure 1 it is apparent that the estimates of delinquency status for the

TABLE 4: Results of Hierarchical Linear Model Linking Age 11 and Age 13 Cohorts

	General Delinquency			Serious Offending			Victimization		
Fixed Effects									
Predictor	Coeff.	S.E.	t-ratio	Coeff.	S.E.	t-ratio	Coeff.	S.E.	t-ratio
For base rate, π_{0i}									
Intercept, β_{00}	.68*	.04	17.36	.22*	.02	9.75	.95*	.04	23.52
Cohort, β_{01}	−.19*	.06	−3.36	−.07*	.03	−2.17	−.35*	.06	−5.99
For linear change, π_{1i}									
Intercept, β_{10}	−.07*	.01	−5.72	−.03*	.01	−3.52	−.12*	.02	−8.12
Cohort, β_{11}	.05*	.02	2.97	.03*	.01	2.80	.04	.02	1.62
Variance Components									
Parameter	Estimate	Chi-square[a]		Estimate	Chi-square		Estimate	Chi-square	
$Var(\pi_{0i}) = \tau_{00}$	.31*	3,046.96		.10*	2,357.88		.28*	1,678.42	
$Var(\pi_{1i}) = \tau_{11}$	.01*	864.18		.01*	751.34		.02*	665.88	
$Var(e_{it}) = \sigma^2$	.19			.09			.35		
Reliability									
For base rate, π_{0i}	.82			.76			.71		
For linear change, π_{1i}	.40			.29			.29		

[a] df = 456 for variance components analyses.

* p ≤ .01

17-year-old cohort at ages 17, 18, and 19 are comparable to the estimates of delinquency status provided by the 15-year-old cohort when they were 17, 18, and 19 years of age. Moreover, the slopes of these two trajectories also appear alike. A similar pattern for these two cohorts can be observed in the serious offending trajectories presented in Figure 2.

In order to test whether two adjacent cohorts share the same expected crime status and slope, data from the two cohorts are pooled and the level-1 equation becomes

$$Y_{it} = \pi_{0i} + \pi_{1i}(LIN) + e_{it}$$

where *LIN* is a linear contrast coefficient corresponding to the subject's age at time *t* (see Raudenbush & Chan 1992). When comparing the 15-year-old cohort's trajectory to that of the 17-year-old cohort, *LIN* ranges from −3 to +3 and corresponds to ages 15 through 21. Here, π_{0i} is the expected outcome at age 18 (the midpoint of the age overlap between the two cohorts), and π_{1i} is the expected rate of change at age 18.

Next a variable indicating cohort is included in the level-2 equation:

$$\pi_{0i} = \beta_{00} + \beta_{01}X_i + \mu_{0i}$$

146 / *Social Forces* 77:1, September 1998

TABLE 5: Results of Hierarchical Linear Model Linking Age 13 and Age 15
         Cohorts

	General Delinquency			Serious Offending			Victimization		
Fixed Effects									
Predictor	Coeff.	S.E.	t-ratio	Coeff.	S.E.	t-ratio	Coeff.	S.E.	t-ratio
For base rate, π_{0i}									
Intercept, β_{00}	.76*	.04	17.45	.30*	.03	11.05	.92*	.04	20.43
Cohort, β_{01}	−.22*	.06	−3.60	−.13*	.04	−3.46	−.21*	.06	−3.29
For linear change, π_{1i}									
Intercept, β_{10}	−.14*	.01	−10.92	−.04*	.01	−4.47	−.15*	.02	−9.29
Cohort, β_{11}	.07*	.02	4.07	.01	.01	1.11	.03	.02	1.34
Variance Components									
Parameter	Estimate	Chi-square[a]		Estimate	Chi-square		Estimate	Chi-square	
$Var(\pi_{0i}) = \tau_{00}$	.37*	3,302.00		.14*	2,442.90		.34*	1,885.75	
$Var(\pi_{1i}) = \tau_{11}$	.02*	863.08		.01*	773.67		.02*	716.30	
$Var(e_{it}) = \sigma^2$	.20			.11			.38		
Reliability									
For base rate, π_{0i}	.84			.79			.73		
For linear change, π_{1i}	.41			.35			.29		

[a] df = 463 for variance components analyses.

* p ≤ .01

$$\pi_{1i} = \beta_{10} + \beta_{11}X_i + \mu_{1i}$$

where $X_i = 1$ if in the 15-year-old cohort, and 0 if in the 17-year-old cohort. By
estimating the combined level-1 and level-2 equations, we can determine whether
there are statistically significant differences in intercept and slope parameters
between the two cohorts. Separate pooled data files are constructed for these analyses
and similar comparisons analyses are made across the other adjacent cohorts (i.e.,
13- versus 15-year-olds, and 11- versus 13-year-olds).

The results of these cohort comparisons are presented in Tables 4, 5, and 6.
Table 4 displays the findings when the 11-year-olds' trajectories are compared with
those from the 13-year-old cohort. In five of the six tests (see β_{01} and β_{11}), the
cohort variable is statistically significant indicating that the slopes and intercepts
of these two cohorts are different from one another at the midpoint of the trajectory
overlap. The slopes (but not the status) of the two cohorts' victimization trajectories
were not found to be significantly different from one another. While it is impossible
to be certain with these data, this could indicate that panel or maturation effects
have similar impacts on reporting for these cohorts and this outcome measure. As
expected from the visual examination of the growth curves, it is *not* possible to

TABLE 6: Results of Hierarchical Linear Model Linking Age 15 and Age 17 Cohorts

	General Delinquency			Serious Offending			Victimization		
Fixed Effects									
Predictor	Coeff.	S.E.	t-ratio	Coeff.	S.E.	t-ratio	Coeff.	S.E.	t-ratio
For base rate, π_{0i}									
Intercept, β_{00}	.53*	.04	12.72	.22*	.03	8.16	.87*	.05	17.46
Cohort, β_{01}	−.05	.06	−.93	−.01	.04	−.02	−.25*	.07	−3.72
For linear change, π_{1i}									
Intercept, β_{10}	−.13*	.01	−9.45	−.05*	.01	−4.66	−.11*	.02	−6.04
Cohort, β_{11}	−.01	.02	-.66	.00	.01	.36	−.04	.02	−1.77
Variance Components									
Parameter	Estimate	Chi-square[a]		Estimate	Chi-square		Estimate	Chi-square	
$\mathrm{Var}(\pi_{0i}) = \tau_{00}$	.25*	1,943.85		.10*	1,589.85		.34*	1,657.35	
$\mathrm{Var}(\pi_{1i}) = \tau_{11}$	.01*	653.48		.01*	644.59		.02*	621.57	
$\mathrm{Var}(e_{it}) = \sigma^2$	.22			.11			.37		
Reliability									
For base rate, π_{0i}	.75			.71			.71		
For linear change, π_{1i}	.32			.27			.28		

[a] df = 411 for variance components analyses.

* p ≤ .01

link the 11- and 13-year-olds' self-reports to infer a general developmental pattern over time.

Table 5 displays the comparisons between the 13- and 15-year-old cohorts. Similar to the previous results, the status coefficients for delinquency, serious offending, and victimization are significantly different across the two cohorts. However, the slopes of the serious offending and victimization trajectories are not significantly different. The data from these two cohorts also fail to permit inferences about the development of crime involvement from ages 13 through 19.

Finally, Table 6 shows the results when the 15-year-olds' trajectories are compared to those for the 17-year-old cohort. Here there are no significant cohort differences in status for general delinquency or serious offending; however, victimization status does differ significantly across the two cohorts. In addition, the slope coefficients at the points of overlap for the two groups differ very little. In other words, unlike the younger age cohorts, it appears that a general decline in self-reported involvement in crime from ages 15 through 21 can be inferred from linking the 15- and 17-year-olds' responses. This suggests that the methodological problems discussed earlier are likely to be most pronounced among the younger subjects. However, recall that the linear change reliability coefficients for the older cohorts also are low. While this low reliability does not appear to hinder linking

148 / *Social Forces* 77:1, September 1998

the older cohorts, it will continue to make it difficult to detect systematic differences in changes in crime over time.

Summary

Four major questions were investigated in order to address competing methodological claims about the limitations of prospective longitudinal self-report data on crime. First, the general form of three age-crime curves (i.e., general delinquency, serious offending, and victimization) was examined for four age cohorts followed over a five-year period. These results showed that regardless of subjects' age at the time of the first interview, self-reported involvement in crime declined significantly over the subsequent four-year period. An exception occurred in the analyses of the 11-year-old cohort whose declines in delinquency and serious offending were not statistically significant. Numerous other sources of data on adolescent offending and victimization fail to support the hypothesis that these declines are a function of period declines in juvenile crime. Second, the data showed that these declines were not sensitive to how crime was operationalized. That is, the results for prevalence were substantively the same as those for incidence operationalized in various ways. Third, the variance components estimates indicated that of the total variation in the outcome variables, approximately half is attributable to between-individual differences and half to within-individual change over time. However, most of the between-individual variation was due to differences in status rather than to differences in slope. The reliability coefficients suggested that while the self-report data were good for analyzing relative status, these same measures may not be reliable enough for studying changes in behavior over time. Fourth, attempts were made to link the NYS cohort data in order to determine whether inferences about age-crime developmental patterns were possible. Inferences about declining involvement in crime could be drawn by linking the 15- and 17-year-old cohorts, but no inferences could be drawn about earlier involvement, that is, the "onset" of offending. Thus it was difficult to use these self-report data in an accelerated longitudinal design format for purposes of studying the correlates of change.

Advocates of prospective longitudinal research designs have argued that such data are best suited for resolving many of the substantive debates surrounding the relationship between age and crime. Self-report data from cohorts of adolescents followed forward in time should make it possible to determine whether the "brute fact" of the age-crime curve reflects more than official arrest practices and whether the curve better describes prevalence or frequency patterns in offending. Such data also should permit the study of systematic changes in offending over time and between-individual differences in these trajectories. Analyses of the NYS longitudinal data reveal that there are in fact methodological difficulties in studying self-reported patterns of crime involvement over time among adolescents. These problems appear to be due primarily to the difficulty of developing an outcome measure that is theoretically informed yet not subject to testing effects or changes in content validity associated with the age of the respondent.

The study of systematic differences in changes in behavior over time requires an outcome measure that retains high reliability over time. Most outcome measures, including those used in delinquency research, have been developed to study between-individual differences rather than individual change over time. In order to develop a more reliable self-report measure several areas of research are needed.

First, the relationship between age and the reliability and validity of items and scales requires a thorough assessment. It is likely that answers to questions such as "How many times in the last year have you hit (or threatened to hit) other students?" has a different meaning to a subject when s/he is 12 years of age compared to 17 years of age. It seems reasonable to expect that the content validity of this kind of question (or the domain of behavior subjects consider relevant to the question) may change over time, particularly among younger respondents. This notion of changing content validity is consistent with the fact that the 15- and 17-year-old cohort trajectory data could be linked, while the 11-, 13-, and 15-year-old's trajectories could not. While the influence of gender and race on reliability and validity has received extensive investigation, little is known about whether measurement error in self-reports of delinquency and victimization varies with age. Experimental methods similar to those found in Hindelang, Hirschi, and Weis (1981) can provide a good way to begin assessing this issue. At a minimum, it is necessary to determine whether the correlations between self-reports and other external sources of data such as that provided by parents, teachers, and the criminal justice system vary significantly with age. The results of these investigations could shed light on the extent to which maturation (or changing content validity) is a source of error in longitudinal analyses, and appears particularly warranted for those studies in which childhood and adolescent activities are a primary concern.

Second, the relationship between number of previous interviews and self-reported behaviors also is in need of investigation. Because time is perfectly correlated with number of previous interviews in the NYS and other prospective longitudinal studies, the effects of repeated testing cannot be separated from potential developmental processes. The fact that the slopes of each of the crime trajectories were negative and not of strong reliability for each of the age cohorts

150 / *Social Forces* **77:1, September 1998**

suggests that the data do contain some form of testing (or panel) effects. Subjects may learn through repeated testing to report the kinds of events that interviewers are "really" interested in. The magnitude of these effects cannot be determined with currently available data. They can however, be estimated by the use of experiments similar to those conducted for the NC(V)S. Experiments in which age and period are held constant, but number of prior interviews is manipulated, can help determine the magnitude of panel effects on self-reported outcomes.

The results presented here signal a warning that longitudinal analysis of prospective self-report data does have significant methodological challenges and weaknesses. One way to minimize these weaknesses is to include measures of behavior from sources outside the subject. However, until more is known about these limitations, substantive issues surrounding the age-crime debate will remain unresolved.

Notes

1. The equations for estimating these crime trajectories can also include higher order polynomials if the slope is expected to be nonlinear. In the present analyses, nonlinear specifications were considered but found to be unnecessary (see results below).

2. The coding of age determines how the coefficients are interpreted. For instance, in analyses of the 11-year-old cohort, when age is coded 0, the subject is 13 years old. The intercept indicates the expected value of person i at this age.

3. It is also the case that responses to some of the crime questions were not available for the eliminated age cohorts due to a split sample design which resulted in somewhat different sets of items for some respondents at some panels. The four age cohorts examined here were asked the same sets of questions across all five panels.

4. The ordinal responses consist of nine-point scales ranging from "never" having engaged in the activity (in the last year) to engaging in the activity about "two or three times per day."

5. The mean levels of delinquency for each cohort at each age also were compared to the trajectories reported here and no significant departures were apparent.

6. To check whether the two slopes were significantly different, the following combined equation was estimated: $Y_{it} = \beta_{00} + \beta_{10}(\text{slope1}) + \beta_{20}(\text{slope2}) + e_{it}$, where "slope1" was coded 0, 1, 2, 2, 2, and "slope2" was coded 0, 0, 0, 1, 2. See Bryk and Raudenbush (1992:148-51) for more information.

7. Of the 12 models examined, general delinquency among the 15-year-old cohort showed a significant nonlinear pattern. This slope for this cohort was slightly more negative from waves 4 to 5 than from waves 1 to 3.

8. The analyses were done using race and gender separately at level-2 and with both measures simultaneously in the level-2 model. Conclusions from both sets of analyses were the same.

9. Of the twelve trajectories examined (3 outcome measures times 4 age-cohorts), significant differences in slopes were found in general delinquency among the 15- and 17-year-old cohorts and in victimization among the 11-year-old cohort.

10. The average declines were calculated by returning the expected values back to their original (nonlogarithmic) metric, estimating the percent changes over the five-year time period for each of the four cohorts, then summing the percent changes and dividing by four. Since the general delinquency and serious offending slopes for the 11-year-old cohort were nonsignificant, the percent change over time was set to zero in order to calculate these estimates. Because these scales rely on ordinal variables rather than raw frequency counts, the actual decline in frequency would be higher than the crude percentages reported here.

11. Single offense trajectories such as assault and larceny victimization and assault and larceny offending also were examined. Again, the slopes were negative and significant.

12. For violent victimization there was no overall change in rates from 1976 to 1980, while for theft the five-year change indicates an 18% decline.

152 / *Social Forces* 77:1, September 1998

APPENDIX

General delinquency includes the following items:

How many times in the prior year have you

1. stolen (or tried to steal) things worth $5 or less?
2. stolen (or tried to steal) things worth between $5 and $50?
*3. stolen (or tried to steal) a motor vehicle, such as a car or motorcycle?
*4. broken into a building or vehicle (or tried to break in) to steal something or just to look around?
*5. stolen (or tried to steal) something worth more than $50?
*6. knowingly bought, sold, or held stolen goods (or tried to do any of these things)?
*7. used force (strong-arm methods) to get money or things from other students?
*8. used force (strong-arm methods) to get money or things from a teacher or other adult at school?
*9. used force (strong-arm methods) to get money or things from other people (not students or teachers)?
*10. attacked someone with the idea of seriously hurting or killing him/her?
*11. been involved in gang fights?
*12. had (or tried to have) sexual relations with someone against their will?
13. hit (or threatened to hit) a teacher or other adult at school?
14. hit (or threatened to hit) one of your parents?
15. hit (or threatened to hit) other students?

Serious offending items are indicated above by asterisks.

Victimization includes the following items:

1. Has your car, motorcycle, or bicycle been stolen (or such an attempt been made)?
2. Have things been taken from your car, motorcycle, or bike such as hubcaps, books or packages, or bike locks?
3. Have some of your things, such as your jacket, notebooks, or sports equipment, been stolen from a public place such as a school cafeteria, restaurant, or bowling alley?
4. Have you been beaten up (or threatened with being beaten up) by someone other than your mother or father?
5. Have you been attacked with a weapon, such as a gun, knife, bottle, or chair, by someone other than your mother or father?
6. Have any of your things been damaged on purpose, such as car/bike tires slashed or books and clothing ripped up?
7. Has something been taken directly from you (or such an attempt been made) by force or by threatening to hurt you?

References

Blumstein, Alfred, Jacqueline Cohen, and David Farrington. 1988. "Criminal Career Research: Its Value for Criminology." *Criminology* 26:1-36.

Bryk, Anthony, and Stephen Raudenbush. 1987. "Application of Hierarchical Linear Models to Assessing Change." *Psychological Bulletin* 101:147-58.

————. 1992. *Hierarchical Linear Models: Applications and Data Analysis Methods*. Sage.

Cook, Phillip, and John Laub. 1986. "The (Surprising) Stability of Youth Crime Rates." *Journal of Quantitative Criminology* 2:265-77.

Elliott, Delbert. 1985. *National Youth Survey 1976-1980: Wave I-V.*. Behavioral Research Institute. Ann Arbor, Mich.: Inter-University Consortium for Political and Social Research.

Elliott, Delbert, David Huizinga, and Suzanne Ageton. 1985. *Explaining Delinquency and Drug Use*. Sage.

Farrington, David. 1986. "Age and Crime." Pp. 189-250 in *Crime and Justice: An Annual Review of Research*, vol. 7, edited by Michael Tonry and Norval Morris. University of Chicago Press.

Gottfredson, Michael, and Travis Hirschi. 1986. "The True Value of Lambda Would Appear to Be Zero: An Essay on Career Criminals, Criminal Careers, Selective Incapacitation, Cohort Studies, and Related Topics." *Criminology* 24:213-34.

————. 1987. "The Methodological Adequacy of Longitudinal Research on Crime." *Criminology* 25:581-614.

————. 1988. "Science, Public Policy, and the Career Paradigm." *Criminology* 26:37-56.

————. 1990. *A General Theory of Crime*. Stanford University Press.

Hindelang, Michael J., Travis Hirschi, and Joseph G. Weis. 1981. *Measuring Delinquency*. Sage.

Hirschi, Travis, and Michael Gottfredson. 1983. "Age and the Explanation of Crime." *American Journal of Sociology* 89:552-84.

Horney, Julie, D. Wayne Osgood, and Ineke H. Marshall. 1995. "Criminal Careers in the Short Term: Intra-individual Variability in Crime and Its Relation to Local Life Circumstances." *American Sociological Review* 60:655-73.

Huizinga, David, and Delbert Elliott. 1986. "Reassessing the Reliability and Validity of Self-Report Delinquency Measures." *Journal of Quantitative Criminology* 2:293-327.

Laub, John. 1983. *Trends in Juvenile Criminal Behavior in the United States: 1973-1981*. Hindelang Criminal Justice Center, SUNY, Albany.

Lehnen, Robert, and Albert J. Reiss. 1978. "Response Effects in the National Crime Survey." *Victimology: An International Journal* 3:110-24.

Menard, Scott. 1987. "Short-Term Trends in Crime and Delinquency: A Comparison of UCR, NCS, and Self-Report Data." *Justice Quarterly* 4:455-74.

Moffitt, Terrie. 1993. "Adolescent-Limited and Life-Course-Persistent Antisocial Behavior: A Developmental Taxonomy." *Psychological Bulletin* 100:674-701.

Osgood, D. Wayne, Patrick O'Malley, Jerald Bachman, and Lloyd Johnston. 1989. "Time Trends and Age Trends in Arrests and Self-Reported Illegal Behavior." *Criminology* 27:389-418.

Parker, Robert Nash, William Smith, D. Randall Smith, and Jackson Toby. 1991. "Trends in Victimization in Schools and Elsewhere, 1974-1981." *Journal of Quantitative Criminology* 7:3-17.

154 / *Social Forces* 77:1, September 1998

Raudenbush, Stephen, and Wing-Shing Chan. 1992. "Growth Curve Analysis in Accelerated Longitudinal Designs." *Journal of Research in Crime and Delinquency* 29:387-411.

Sampson, Robert, and John Laub. 1993. *Crime in the Making: Pathways and Turning Points through Life.* Harvard University Press.

Sudman, Seymour, Norman Bradburn, and Norbert Schwarz. 1996. *Thinking about Answers: The Application of Cognitive Processes to Survey Methodology.* Jossey-Bass.

Thornberry, Terrence. 1989. "Panel Effects and the Use of Self-Reported Measures of Delinquency in Longitudinal Studies." Pp. 347-69 in *Cross-National Research in Self-Reported Crime and Delinquency*, edited by Malcolm Klein. Kluwer Academic.

U.S. Department of Justice. 1991. *Criminal Victimization in the United States: 1973-88 Trends.* Government Printing Office.

Willett, John, and Aline Sayer. 1994. "Using Covariance Structure Analysis to Detect Correlates and Predictors of Individual Change over Time." *Psychological Bulletin* 116:363-81.

Woltman, Henry, and John Bushery. 1984. "Summary of Results from the National Crime Survey Panel Bias Study." Pp. 98-101 in *The National Crime Survey Working Papers*, vol. 2, *Methodological Studies*, edited by Robert Lehnen and Wesley Skogan. U.S. Government Printing Office.

[13]

SELF-REPORTED DELINQUENCY AND A COMBINED DELINQUENCY SERIOUSNESS SCALE BASED ON BOYS, MOTHERS, AND TEACHERS: CONCURRENT AND PREDICTIVE VALIDITY FOR AFRICAN-AMERICANS AND CAUCASIANS*

DAVID P. FARRINGTON
  University of Cambridge

ROLF LOEBER
MAGDA STOUTHAMER-LOEBER
WELMOET B. VAN KAMMEN
LAURA SCHMIDT
  University of Pittsburgh

The Pittsburgh Youth Study is a prospective longitudinal survey of three samples of Pittsburgh boys (each containing about 500 boys) initially studied in first, fourth, and seventh grades. The first two data collection waves yielded self-reported delinquency and combined delinquency seriousness scores (the combined scores based on information from boy, mother, and teacher) for the middle sample (up to an average age of 10.7 years) and oldest sample (up to an average age of 13.9 years). These scores were compared with records of petitions to the Allegheny County Juvenile Court for delinquency offenses before and up to six years after the assessments. The area under the ROC curve was used as a measure of validity. Concurrent validity was higher than predictive validity. The combined scale had similar concurrent validity but greater predictive validity than the self-report scale, and the combined scale also identified a greater number of boys as serious delinquents. Concurrent validity for admitting offenses was higher for Caucasians, but concurrent validity for admitting arrests was higher for African-Americans. There were no consistent ethnic differences in predictive validity. There was an increase in predictive validity, for both African-Americans and Caucasians, by combining self-report data with information from other sources. After controlling for delinquency measures, African-Americans were more likely than Caucasians to be petitioned in the future, but not in the past. In this research, ethnic

---

* For helpful comments on an earlier draft of this article, we are very grateful to David Fergusson, Martin Gold, Marianne Junger, Marc LeBlanc, and Simon Singer.

494   FARRINGTON ET AL.

*differences in official delinquency were partly attributable to ethnic dif-
ferences in delinquent behavior and were not attributable to differential
ethnic attrition or differential ethnic validity of measures of delinquent
behavior.*

The main aim of this article is to investigate the concurrent and predictive validity of a self-reported delinquency seriousness scale and a combined delinquency seriousness scale (combining information from a boy,
his parent, and his teacher) developed in the Pittsburgh Youth Study. This
project is a prospective longitudinal survey of three samples of Pittsburgh
boys (each containing about 500 boys) initially studied in first, fourth, and
seventh grades (Loeber et al., 1991). This article assesses validity by comparing delinquency seriousness scales derived from the first two waves of
data collection with information about offenses committed by the boys
before and up to six years after these waves and leading to petitions in the
Allegheny County (Pittsburgh) Juvenile Court.

Most delinquency researchers rely on self-reports or official records of
arrests or convictions for their measurement of the key dependent variable
of delinquency. Hence, the validity of self-reports and official records as
measures of delinquent behavior is a key question in criminology. Historically, most delinquency research prior to the 1960s was based on official
records, which generally showed that delinquency was more common in
males than in females, in African-Americans than in Caucasians, and in
lower-class compared with higher-class youths. However, the influential
research of Short and Nye (1957, 1958) triggered the widespread use of
self-reported delinquency scales in the 1960s. Researchers reported that
most youths committed delinquent acts, and argued that groups such as
lower-class, African-American males were disproportionately arrested and
convicted because the police and the courts were biased against them or,
possibly, because of their hostile demeanor (e.g., Chambliss and
Nagasawa, 1969).

More recently, the careful methodological review by Hindelang et al.
(1981) essentially concluded that, with one important exception, the correlates of official and self-reported delinquency are the same. While it may
be true that "everyone does it," it is also true that everyone does not do it
equally frequently or equally seriously. Relationships seen in official
records were attenuated in self-reports for a variety of reasons, including
the overrepresentation of trivial acts in self-report questionnaires and the
focus on prevalence as opposed to frequency in self-report studies. When
like was compared with like, only one major difference remained: "Race is
the only major correlate . . . for which the methodological adjustments
proposed by Hindelang et al. (1979), particularly the controls for type and
seriousness of offense (especially violence), do not make the official and

DELINQUENCY SERIOUSNESS 495

self-report relations consistent in the way they do for sex, social class, and other correlates of crime" (Weis, 1986:8).

Up to the present day, it has commonly been found that African-Americans are more likely than Caucasians to be officially delinquent, but not significantly worse than Caucasians in their prevalence or frequency of self-reported offending (Tracy, 1987). The most common reasons put forward to explain this discrepancy between official records and self-reports are that the police and courts are biased against African-Americans, that delinquent African-Americans are especially likely to be missing from surveyed samples (Weis, 1986), and that the validity of self-reports of delinquency is lower for African-Americans than for Caucasians. Another aim of this article is to investigate the last hypothesis of differential ethnic validity of self-reports.

In summary, the main questions addressed in this article are as follows:

1. What is the concurrent validity of a self-reported delinquency seriousness scale? Is this different for African-Americans and Caucasians?

2. What is the predictive validity of a self-reported delinquency seriousness scale? Is this different for African-Americans and Caucasians?

3. What is the concurrent validity of a combined delinquency seriousness scale? Is this different for African-Americans and Caucasians? Is this greater than for the self-reported delinquency seriousness scale?

4. What is the predictive validity of a combined delinquency seriousness scale? Is this different for African-Americans and Caucasians? Is this greater than for the self-reported delinquency seriousness scale?

CONCURRENT AND PREDICTIVE VALIDITY OF SELF-REPORTED DELINQUENCY

VALIDITY

Unfortunately, as Huizinga (1991:55) pointed out, although the self-report method has been used for several decades, methodological studies are rare. Perhaps rather surprisingly, fewer have been carried out since the important review of Hindelang et al. (1981) than before it. Reiss (1975) castigated self-reported delinquency researchers for paying insufficient attention to psychometric issues, such as reliability, validity, and the standardization of instruments. Farrington (1973) was the first researcher to evaluate self-reported delinquency questionnaires on standard psychometric criteria, such as questionnaire construction, administration procedure, objective scoring, norms for various populations, internal consistency, retest stability, and concurrent and predictive validity. This article focuses on validity issues.

Validity refers to the accuracy with which an instrument measures the construct that it purports to measure. For example, how accurately do self-reports of delinquency measure the prevalence, frequency, and seriousness of actual delinquent behavior? Various types of validity have been identified, including content and construct validity (e.g., Huizinga and Elliott, 1986), but the most important is criterion validity, in which a measure is compared with an external criterion of the same construct (here, delinquent behavior). This comparison can be concurrent (measure and criterion at the same time) or predictive (measure taken before criterion). Notwithstanding the fact that self-reports were intended to overcome some of the perceived deficiencies of official records, self-reported delinquency is usually validated against the external criterion of official delinquency, although other criteria have occasionally been used (e.g., peer reports by Gold, 1966; teacher ratings by Hackler and Lautt, 1969).

In validating self-reports against this external criterion, concurrent validity is assessed by comparing the number of acts admitted by officially recorded versus unrecorded juveniles, or by measuring the probability that recorded juveniles admit the acts for which they were arrested or convicted. Predictive validity depends on how far self-reported delinquency scores predict future arrests or convictions of currently unrecorded youths, and on whether unrecorded youths who admit a particular act on a self-report questionnaire are subsequently recorded for the same act.

Perfect correspondence between official records and self-reports would not be expected. Many delinquent acts go unrecorded, and youths may exaggerate, conceal, or forget their acts. Some officially recorded youths may not define themselves as delinquents (Gould, 1969). There may be problems with self-reports (e.g., insufficiently detailed wording of items) or official records (e.g., plea bargaining, misleading legal categories) that make it difficult to match them exactly. A proportion of self-reported acts may be too trivial to be charged: one-fifth in the research of Gold and Reimer (1975) and one-third of "serious violent offenses" according to Elliott and Huizinga (1989). The worst offenders may be disproportionally missing from self-report survey samples (e.g., Cernkovich et al., 1985; Elliott, 1982). There may also be statistical problems in comparing numbers of self-reported and official acts because of highly skewed distributions; for example, product-moment correlations may be misleading.

CONCURRENT VALIDITY OF SELF-REPORTED DELINQUENCY

Correlations between official records and self-reports are generally positive and statistically significant (e.g., Elliott and Voss, 1974; Hindelang et al., 1981; Hirschi, 1969; Kulik et al., 1968). They tend to be higher for Caucasians than for African-Americans (e.g., Hackler and Lautt, 1969). However, it is more meaningful to demonstrate that the probability of arrest (e.g., Dunford and Elliott, 1984) or conviction (e.g., Le Blanc and Fréchette, 1989) increases with the intensity (e.g., frequency or seriousness) of self-reported delinquency, or that the average self-report scores of official offenders are significantly higher than the average self-report scores of unrecorded youths (e.g., Farrington, 1973; Voss, 1963).

A more direct test of concurrent validity is to study the extent to which officially recorded offenders admit their recorded offenses. For example, Gibson et al. (1970) found that convicted British boys at age 14 admitted almost all of the acts leading to their convictions on a self-report questionnaire, and similarly high percentages have been reported in U.S. research (e.g., Elliott and Voss, 1974; Voss, 1963). However, Hindelang et al. (1981) and Huizinga and Elliott (1986) found that officially recorded African-American boys were less likely to report their offenses than officially recorded Caucasian boys.

CONCURRENT VALIDITY OF SELF-REPORTS OF ARRESTS OR CONVICTIONS

The concurrent validity of self-reports can also be assessed by asking people if they have been officially arrested or convicted and comparing their answers with official records of arrests or convictions. For example, West and Farrington (1977) found that, at age 18, almost all convicted delinquents admitted that they had been convicted, while hardly any unconvicted boys claimed to have been convicted.

The probability of arrested or convicted delinquents admitting their arrests or convictions is also high in other studies (e.g., Erickson and Empey, 1963; Hardt and Peterson-Hardt, 1977). However, there are again indications of differential validity by ethnicity in self-reports of arrests or convictions. For example, Hindelang et al. (1981) found that 76% of Caucasian male official delinquents reported that they had been picked up by the police, compared with 52% of Caucasian females, 50% of African-American males, and only 30% of African-American females.

PREDICTIVE VALIDITY OF SELF-REPORTED DELINQUENCY

Predictive validity is more impressive than concurrent validity, because being officially processed may itself lead to an increase in the probability of admitting delinquent acts (Farrington, 1977), perhaps because the youth assumes that the researcher will know about the record anyway and hence concealment is futile. It is only to be expected that current self-reported delinquency (of past acts) will predict future official delinquency, because many current self-reported delinquents are also official delinquents, and because past official delinquency is likely to be the best predictor of future official delinquency. A better test of the predictive validity of self-

498   FARRINGTON ET AL.

reported delinquency is to investigate how far it predicts future arrests or convictions among *currently unrecorded youths*.

Only two studies of predictive validity among unrecorded youths appear to have been carried out, both in England. Farrington (1973) showed that, for unconvicted boys, a measure of self-reported variety of offending at age 14 significantly predicted convictions in the following three years. Farrington (1989) later repeated this demonstration for specific types of offenses. For example, for boys not convicted of burglary up to age 18, significantly more of those who self-reported burglary up to age 18 were subsequently convicted of burglary up to age 32, in comparison with boys who denied committing burglary up to age 18. Similar results were obtained for theft of vehicles, theft from vehicles, assault, vandalism, and drug use, but not for shoplifting. Both analyses indicate that self-reports of offending have predictive validity.

It appears that there are no existing studies of the predictive validity of self-reported delinquency in the United States, or among African-Americans compared with Caucasians.

THE CURRENT RESEARCH

THE PITTSBURGH YOUTH STUDY

The Pittsburgh Youth Study is a prospective longitudinal survey of the development of offending, antisocial behavior, and mental health problems in three samples of Pittsburgh boys. Of about 1,000 boys in the first, fourth, and seventh grades of Pittsburgh public schools selected for a screening assessment, about 850 boys were actually assessed (Table 1). Importantly, participants did not differ significantly from the comparable male student population in their reading achievement scores on the California Achievement Test (CAT) or in their ethnic composition (African-American or Caucasian; there are very few other minorities in Pittsburgh). Hence, there was no differential attrition of African-American and Caucasian boys.

The boy was interviewed face-to-face in private, while his main caretaker (defined as the person who had most to do with him) completed a questionnaire. For ease of exposition, the main caretaker is referred to as the mother, since this was true in over 90% of cases. The overall 85% participation rate reported in Table 1 refers to data collection from both the boy and the mother, since either could refuse. The boy's teacher also completed a questionnaire for 95% of interviewed boys. The methods used in gaining cooperation are described in Stouthamer-Loeber et al. (1992) and Stouthamer-Loeber and Van Kammen (1995).

Based on screening information from the boy, mother, and teacher, each boy was given a "risk" score according to the number of antisocial

DELINQUENCY SERIOUSNESS 499

Table 1. Pittsburgh Youth Study Samples

	Youngest	Middle	Oldest
City of Pittsburgh			
% African-American	56.5	54.0	54.6
CAT Reading > 50th Percentile	56.5	40.9	36.7
Screening Sample (S)			
N	849	868	856
% Participating	84.6	86.3	83.5
Average Age	6.9	10.2	13.2
% African-American	56.4	54.1	55.8
CAT Reading > 50th Percentile	54.5	40.7	37.9
Follow-up Sample (A)			
High Risk	256	259	257
Low Risk	247	249	249
N	503	508	506
% Participating	95.2	96.1	92.5
Average Age	7.4	10.7	13.9
% African-American	57.3	55.8	57.5
CAT Reading > 50th Percentile	55.2	37.6	36.5

acts (out of 21) that he had ever committed. In order to maximize the eventual yield of serious chronic offenders while still permitting prevalence estimates for the whole population, it was decided to follow up all "high-risk" boys (about 250 in each grade) and an equally sized random sample of "low-risk" boys. Table 1 shows that about 500 boys in each grade were followed up. The first follow-up assessment (A) occurred six months after the screening assessment (S); 95% of selected boys were interviewed and their mothers completed questionnaires, while their teachers completed questionnaires in 92% of cases. The percentages who were African-American were slightly higher in the follow-up sample than in the screening sample, while the percentages with high CAT reading attainment scores were slightly lower.

Because of our concern about the reading and comprehension skills of some boys, and in view of previous research showing numerous missing responses to self-report items (Hindelang et al., 1981), all boys were interviewed face-to-face and all instruments were administered verbally by the interviewer. The oldest sample completed a Self-Reported Delinquency (SRD) questionnaire developed in the National Youth Survey (Elliott et al., 1985) and the Youth Self-Report (Achenbach and Edelbrock, 1987) at screening (S) and follow-up (A).

The SRD questionnaire was judged to be too difficult for the youngest sample, and also some of the acts were age-inappropriate or would have had a very low base rate among first-grade boys (e.g., committing rape,

500   FARRINGTON ET AL.

being drunk in a public place). Consequently, a new Self-Reported Antisocial Behavior (SRA) questionnaire was developed for young children
(Loeber et al., 1989) that included easily understandable items. This was
given to the youngest sample at S and A. The middle sample was given
the SRA at S and the SRD at A. Information about the boy's antisocial
behavior was also obtained from the mother, who completed an extended
Child Behavior Checklist (Achenbach and Edelbrock, 1983) at S and A,
and from the teacher, who completed an extended Teacher Report Form
(Edelbrock and Achenbach, 1984) at S and A.

JUVENILE COURT PETITIONS FOR DELINQUENCY

Allegheny County Juvenile Court records (paper files) were searched in
the summer of 1994 for records of offenses committed by each boy
between his 10th and 18th birthdays. The City of Pittsburgh is included in
and surrounded by Allegheny County, which had a population of about
1,336,000 in 1990 (Hoffman, 1991). Only cases petitioned to the juvenile
court have been counted in this analysis. This means that our recorded
juvenile offenders are relatively serious cases for which there is convincing
evidence of guilt.

The first date of occurrence of each offense type was coded, and it was
classified as occurring before or after the date of assessment A. Offense
types were categorized according to the Federal Bureau of Investigation's
Uniform Crime Report system.[1] Table 2 shows the prevalence of juvenile
court petitions for each offense type in the middle and oldest samples.
The youngest sample was not included in these analyses because of the
low prevalence of petitions (only 26 boys) up to 1994. The average age of
the oldest sample at A was 13.9 years, and hence, they were at risk of
juvenile court petitions for an average of 4.1 years up to the 18th birthday
(which they had all passed). The average age of the middle sample at A
was 10.7 years, and they were at risk for an average of 5.9 years up to the
date of the 1994 search of juvenile court petitions.

---

1. Index violence includes homicide, forcible rape, robbery, and aggravated
assault. Index property includes burglary, larceny, motor vehicle theft, and arson.
Together, index violence and index property comprise index offenses. Nonindex delinquency includes simple assault, forgery, fraud, embezzlement, receiving stolen property,
weapons offenses, vandalism, sex offenses such as prostitution and statutory rape, drug
offenses, malicious mischief, disorderly conduct, criminal conspiracy, threats and endan-
gering, involuntary deviate sexual intercourse (homosexual rape), indecent assault,
indecent exposure, and spousal sexual assault. Index offenses and nonindex delinquency were combined into a "criminal delinquency" category. Other offenses include
liquor law violations, drunkenness, traffic offenses, violations of ordinances (e.g., cru-
elty to animals, vagrancy), and status offenses. Index offenses, nonindex delinquency,
and other offenses together comprise "any delinquency."

DELINQUENCY SERIOUSNESS 501

Table 2. Prevalence of Juvenile Court Petitions for Delinquency

	Ever (%)	Before A (%)	After A (%)
Middle Sample (*N*)	(495)	(501)	(485)
Any Delinquency	29.9	2.0	28.5
Criminal Delinquency	29.7	2.0	28.2
Index Offense	22.2	1.2	21.4
Index Violence	11.9	0.4	11.8
Index Property	18.2	1.2	17.3
Drugs	6.1	0.0	6.2
Oldest Sample (*N*)	(457)	(468)	(396)
Any Delinquency	45.1	13.0	36.6
Criminal Delinquency	44.6	12.8	36.4
Index Offense	34.1	10.5	27.0
Index Violence	14.7	3.2	13.2
Index Property	28.1	8.5	22.2
Drugs	8.2	0.0	9.4

NOTES: Ever = up to May 1994 for the middle sample (average age 16.6 years) and up to the 18th birthday for the oldest sample. A = assessment A, which is the first follow-up assessment after screening (S). Boys with no consent forms or incomplete records (7 in the middle sample and 38 in the oldest sample) were excluded from "Before A." Additionally, boys with no juvenile court petition who lived outside Allegheny County for the majority of the time between assessment A and assessment E two years later (6 in the middle sample and 11 in the oldest sample) were excluded from the numbers "Ever." Additionally, boys who were petitioned before A (10 in the middle sample and 61 in the oldest sample) were excluded from the numbers "After A."

Table 2 shows that, up to A, only 2% of the middle sample had a juvenile court petition for any delinquent offense, compared with 13% of the oldest sample. Virtually all petitioned juveniles had been petitioned for an index or nonindex offense; hardly any were only petitioned for other offenses, such as traffic, status, or drunkenness. Up to an average age of 16.6 years for the middle sample, 30% had a juvenile court petition for any delinquent offense, and 22% for an index offense. Up to the 18th birthday for the oldest sample, 45% had a juvenile court petition for any delinquent offense, and 34% for an index offense.[2]

---

2. The prevalence figures in Table 2 are higher than for all boys in public schools in the City of Pittsburgh because of the oversampling of high-risk boys in the follow-up sample for assessment A. It is easy to reweight the A sample to derive estimates for the City of Pittsburgh public school population. When this was done, the cumulative prevalence of juvenile court petitions for any delinquency came to 26% for the middle sample (up to an average age of 16.6 years) and to 39% for the oldest sample (up to the 18th birthday). The weighted cumulative prevalence of juvenile court petitions for index offenses came to 19% for the middle sample and 28% for the oldest sample.

502   FARRINGTON ET AL.

RESULTS

CONCURRENT AND PREDICTIVE VALIDITY OF SELF-REPORTED DELINQUENCY SERIOUSNESS SCALE

Each boy was classified into one of four categories of seriousness of self-reported delinquency, according to the most serious offense he had ever committed. The seriousness classification was based on ratings published by Wolfgang et al. (1985). The categories were as follows: No delinquency (including minor theft or vandalism in the home); minor delinquency (e.g., stealing an item worth less than $5 or vandalism outside the home, shoplifting, minor fraud such as not paying for a bus ride); moderate delinquency (e.g., stealing an item worth $5 or more, joyriding, carrying a weapon, gang fighting); and serious delinquency (e.g., breaking and entering, stealing a car, strongarming, attacking to seriously hurt or kill someone, selling drugs, forcing sex).[3]

As explained in the appendix, validity was assessed using three measures: χ^2, the odds ratio (OR), and the area between the ROC curve and the diagonal (AROC). The OR measures the strength of a relationship in a 2 x 2 table: Here, the increased risk of a petition associated with being in the serious delinquency category. The familiar χ^2 statistic measures deviation from chance expectation in the full 4 x 2 table, but not strength of relationship. The AROC measures strength of relationship in a 4 x 2 table, on a scale from 0 = chance to 1 = perfect discrimination. *Significant* refers to $p < .05$ on a two-tailed test.

Table 3 shows that the self-reported delinquency seriousness scale had substantial and significant concurrent validity in relation to past delinquency petitions (up to A). The OR and AROC were highest for index violence and lowest for criminal delinquency. The OR for index violence (5.9) indicates impressive discrimination between petitioned and nonpetitioned boys; 8.1% of serious delinquents were petitioned, compared with only 1.5% of the remainder.

The self-report scale also had significant predictive validity in relation to future juvenile court petitions (after A). In the middle sample, the OR

Generally, weighted and unweighted data produce different prevalence estimates but similar correlations between variables. Because our interest is in studying the validity of delinquency seriousness scales rather than in reporting the prevalence of juvenile court petitions, and in the interests of simplicity, we report unweighted data here.

3. We thought that it was more meaningful to develop a simple seriousness scale, with each category indicating the commission of specific types of offenses, rather than some kind of variety, frequency, or seriousness score. Generally, variety, frequency, and seriousness scores are highly intercorrelated (Farrington, 1973). For example, in the oldest sample, the four-category seriousness scale (ever) correlated .73 with a seven-category variety scale (ever) and .62 with a five-category frequency scale (in the past year).

DELINQUENCY SERIOUSNESS 503

Table 3. Self-Reported Delinquency as a Predictor of Court Petitions

| | Self-Reported Delinquency Seriousness | | | | | | |
	None (%)	Minor (%)	Moderate (%)	Serious (%)	χ^2	OR	AROC
Middle Sample							
Predictive (N)	(104)	(218)	(125)	(38)			
Criminal Delinquency	14.4	21.1	44.8	52.6	43.3*	3.1*	.372*
Index Offense	8.7	16.1	34.4	44.7	38.6*	3.3*	.395*
Index Violence	6.7	8.7	16.0	28.9	17.5*	3.6*	.302*
Index Property	5.8	14.2	25.6	39.5	30.2*	3.6*	.388*
Drugs	2.9	6.4	5.6	15.8	8.1*	3.3*	.239*
Oldest Sample							
Concurrent (N)	(115)	(93)	(136)	(124)			
Criminal Delinquency	7.8	4.3	12.5	24.2	23.0*	3.3*	.366*
Index Offense	4.3	2.2	10.3	22.6	30.9*	4.5*	.478*
Index Violence	0.0	0.0	3.7	8.1	16.4*	5.9*	.568+
Index Property	4.3	2.2	7.4	18.5	23.6*	4.4*	.449*
Predictive (N)	(102)	(88)	(116)	(90)			
Criminal Delinquency	18.6	33.0	40.5	54.4	27.9*	2.7*	.332*
Index Offense	11.8	26.1	32.8	37.8	19.3*	1.9*	.288*
Index Violence	4.9	10.3	15.7	22.2	13.7*	2.4*	.331*
Index Property	9.8	21.6	26.7	31.1	14.6*	1.9*	.268*
Drugs	6.9	4.6	11.3	14.4	6.3	2.0	.222*

NOTES: A = assessment A. OR = odds ratio, comparing serious category with remainder. AROC varies from 0 = chance to 1 = perfect discrimination. Predictive = petitions after A. Concurrent = petititions up to A.
* $p < .05$, two-tailed.
+ significance test not possible.

ranged from 3.1 for the prediction of criminal delinquency to 3.6 for the prediction of index violence and index property offenses. The AROC was highest for the prediction of index offenses and lowest for the prediction of drug offenses. (Previously petitioned boys were excluded from tests of predictive validity.) In the oldest sample, the OR ranged from 1.9 for the prediction of index offenses and index property offenses to 2.7 for the prediction of criminal delinquency. The AROC was highest for criminal delinquency and index violence and lowest for the prediction of drug offenses.

Concurrent validity was clearly higher than predictive validity for this self-report scale. All four ORs were higher for concurrent validity in Table 3, as were all four AROCs and three of the four χ^2 values. The OR for index offenses before A was significantly higher than the OR for index

504   FARRINGTON ET AL.

offenses after A ($t = 2.08$), while the AROC for index offenses before A was almost significantly higher than the AROC for index offenses after A ($t = 1.81$). As mentioned, this may be because a past juvenile court petition increases the willingness of boys to admit their delinquent acts.

COMPARING AFRICAN-AMERICANS AND CAUCASIANS

According to self-reports, African-Americans committed more serious delinquent acts than Caucasians. In the oldest sample, 33% of African-Americans were serious delinquents at A, 25% were moderate, 22% were minor, and 20% were nondelinquents. The comparable figures for Caucasians were 18% serious, 33% moderate, 18% minor, and 31% nondelinquents ($\chi^2 = 19.2$, 3 d.f., $p < .05$). In the middle sample, 10% of African-Americans were serious delinquents at A, 31% were moderate, 41% were minor, and 18% were nondelinquents. The comparable figures for Caucasians were 7% serious, 20% moderate, 47% minor, and 27% nondelinquents ($\chi^2 = 12.8$, 3 d.f., $p < .05$).

Table 4 shows that the self-reported delinquency seriousness scale had significant concurrent and predictive validity for both Caucasians and African-Americans, with only one exception: predictive validity for index violence of Caucasians in the oldest sample, where the numbers were small. Concurrent validity was higher for Caucasians on all measures. The OR for criminal delinquency was almost significantly higher for Caucasians ($t = 1.68$). However, predictive validity was not consistently higher for Caucasians or African-Americans.

Logistic regression analyses showed that ethnicity predicted the probability of future petitions independently of self-reported delinquency (cf. Fergusson et al., 1993). For example, the likelihood ratio χ^2 for ethnicity in the prediction of criminal delinquency was 24.9 ($p < .05$) in the middle sample and 11.8 ($p < .05$) in the oldest sample. However, ethnicity was not significantly related to past petitions independently of self-reported delinquency.

CONCURRENT VALIDITY OF SELF-REPORTS OF ARRESTS

At S and A, the boys in the Pittsburgh Youth Study were not asked if they had appeared in the juvenile court, but they were asked if they had ever been arrested or picked up by the police; 21% of the oldest boys said that they had been apprehended, compared with 4% of the middle sample. Table 5 shows, of those in the oldest sample with juvenile court petitions up to A, the proportion who said that they had been arrested or picked up.

In all cases, African-Americans were more likely to admit apprehension than Caucasians. For example, 65% of African-Americans with juvenile court petitions for index offenses said that they had been apprehended,

DELINQUENCY SERIOUSNESS 505

Table 4. Self-Reported Delinquency as a Predictor of Court Petitions, Controlling for Ethnicity

| | | Delinquency Seriousness | | | | | | |
		None (%)	Minor (%)	Moderate (%)	Serious (%)	χ^2	OR	AROC
Middle Sample								
Predictive								
Criminal Delinquency	(C)	10.5	11.5	25.6	35.7	10.0*	3.4*	.283*
	(AA)	19.1	29.8	54.9	62.5	26.2*	2.9*	.375*
Index Violence	(C)	0.0	1.0	2.3	7.1	NV	7.8	.613*
	(AA)	14.9	15.8	23.2	41.7	9.5*	3.2*	.231*
Index Property	(C)	3.5	7.7	18.6	35.7	16.2*	5.7*	.460*
	(AA)	8.5	20.2	29.3	41.7	12.7*	2.7*	.315*
Oldest Sample								
Concurrent								
Criminal Delinquency	(C)	8.3	0.0	5.9	27.0	18.0*	6.3*	.345
	(AA)	7.3	6.9	19.1	23.0	10.6*	2.3*	.311*
Index Offense	(C)	5.0	0.0	4.4	24.3	19.4*	8.4*	.475*
	(AA)	3.6	3.4	16.2	21.8	15.9*	3.1*	.414*
Predictive								
Criminal Delinquency	(C)	11.5	29.4	27.9	44.4	10.8*	2.8*	.324*
	(AA)	26.0	35.2	54.5	58.7	16.2*	2.2*	.313*
Index Violence	(C)	1.9	9.1	6.6	7.4	2.3	1.4	.204
	(AA)	8.0	11.1	25.9	28.6	11.5*	2.2*	.325*
Index Property	(C)	5.8	17.6	21.3	22.2	6.1	1.6	.286*
	(AA)	14.0	24.1	32.7	34.9	7.4	1.7	.233*

NOTES: C = caucasian; AA = African-American. OR = odds ratio, comparing serious category with remainder. NV = not valid. Predictive = petitions after A. Concurrent = petitions up to A.
* $p < .05$, two-tailed.

compared with 53% of Caucasians. None of these differences was statistically significant, but (contrary to the results of Hindelang et al., 1981), they do not suggest that African-Americans tend to underreport police apprehension compared with Caucasians.

CONCURRENT AND PREDICTIVE VALIDITY OF COMBINED DELINQUENCY SERIOUSNESS SCALE

In general, measures based on multiple data sources are likely to be more valid than measures based on a single data source. To some extent, errors may cancel out, or behaviors observed in multiple settings may be more representative than those observed in only one setting. A combined scale may also overcome some of the problems of self-reports, such as concealment and forgetting. This was tested by constructing a combined

506   FARRINGTON ET AL.

Table 5. Percentage of Petitioned Boys who Self-Reported
          Apprehension by the Police

Oldest Sample/Concurrent	All		Caucasian		African-American	
	%	N	%	N	%	N
Criminal Delinquency	56.7	(60)	52.6	(19)	58.5	(41)
Index Offense	61.2	(49)	53.3	(15)	64.7	(34)
Index Violence	73.3	(15)	66.7	(3)	75.0	(12)
Index Property	60.0	(40)	50.0	(12)	64.3	(28)

NOTE: Concurrent = petitions up to A.

delinquency seriousness scale based on information from the boy, the
mother, and the teacher. We are not aware of any other study that has
compared the validity of self-reported delinquency with the validity of a
combined delinquency scale based on several different informants.

Table 6 shows that the combined delinquency seriousness scale had significant concurrent validity in relation to past juvenile court petitions.
Comparing OR and AROC values in Table 6 and Table 3, concurrent
validity was no higher for the combined scale than for the self-report scale.

The combined scale also had significant predictive validity in relation to
Juvenile Court petitions. Comparing OR and AROC values in Table 6
and Table 3, predictive validity was higher for the combined scale than for
the self-report scale. In the middle sample, the highest OR for the self-
report scale was lower than the lowest OR for the combined scale, and the
highest AROC for the self-report scale was lower than the lowest AROC
for the combined scale. The AROC for criminal delinquency was significantly higher for the combined scale ($t = 1.96$), and so was the AROC for
drug offenses ($t = 2.60$). In the oldest sample, the highest AROC for the
self-report scale was lower than the lowest AROC for the combined scale.

It might be expected that concurrent validity would be higher than predictive validity. Indeed, where comparisons could be made directly in
Table 6, three of the four ORs and three of the four AROCs were higher
for concurrent validity (all except criminal delinquency). The χ^2 values
were higher for predictive validity, but this is probably because the prevalence of petitions was higher after assessment A than before it.

COMPARING AFRICAN-AMERICANS AND CAUCASIANS

According to the combined scale, African-Americans committed more
serious delinquent acts than Caucasians. In the oldest sample, 44% of
African-Americans were serious delinquents at A, 23% were moderate,
19% were minor, and 14% were nondelinquents. The comparable figures
for Caucasians were 26% serious, 31% moderate, 21% minor, and 23%

Table 6. Combined Delinquency Scale as a Predictor of Court Petitions

	Delinquency Seriousness						
	None (%)	Minor (%)	Moderate (%)	Serious (%)	χ^2	OR	AROC
Middle Sample							
Predictive (*N*)	(100)	(147)	(108)	(130)			
Criminal Delinquency	10.0	12.2	36.1	53.8	80.3*	5.0*	.521*
Index Offense	8.0	8.8	27.8	40.8	56.0*	4.1*	.475*
Index Violence	5.0	4.8	12.0	24.6	32.1*	4.3*	.459*
Index Property	6.0	6.8	23.1	33.1	45.4*	3.8*	.462*
Drugs	1.0	3.4	1.9	16.9	35.9*	8.8*	.630*
Oldest Sample							
Concurrent (*N*)	(80)	(90)	(126)	(172)			
Criminal Delinquency	6.3	3.3	12.7	20.9	20.5*	3.0*	.382*
Index Offense	3.8	2.2	8.7	19.2	24.7*	4.2*	.477*
Index Violence	0.0	0.0	4.0	5.8	9.6*	3.6*	.434+
Index Property	3.8	2.2	5.6	16.3	21.6*	4.6*	.504*
Predictive (*N*)	(73)	(84)	(107)	(132)			
Criminal Delinquency	15.1	23.8	35.5	56.8	43.9*	3.7*	.425*
Index Offense	8.2	16.7	29.9	41.7	32.5*	2.9*	.385*
Index Violence	2.7	8.4	12.3	22.7	19.2*	3.2*	.397*
Index Property	6.8	13.1	26.2	33.3	24.4*	2.5*	.346*
Drugs	4.1	6.0	5.7	17.4	15.2*	3.7*	.416*

NOTES: A = assessment A. OR = odds ratio, comparing serious category with remainder. Predictive = petitions after A. Concurrent = petitions up to A.
* $p < .05$, two-tailed.
+ significance test not possible.

nondelinquents ($\chi^2 = 19.8$, 3 d.f., $p < .05$). In the middle sample, 35% of African-Americans were serious delinquents at A, 22% were moderate, 29% were minor, and 14% were nondelinquents. The comparable figures for Caucasians were 18% serious, 22% moderate, 32% minor, and 28% nondelinquents ($\chi^2 = 26.9$, 3 d.f., $p < .05$).

Comparisons with the numbers for the self-report scale show that the relation between ethnicity and delinquency was far stronger for the combined scale in the middle sample, but not in the oldest sample. The majority of serious delinquents in the oldest sample (74% of African-Americans and 70% of Caucasians) on the combined scale were also identified by self-reports. In the middle sample, only a minority of serious delinquents (28% of African-Americans and 38% of Caucasians) on the combined scale were also identified by self-reports. Hence, for both African-Americans and Caucasians, the extra informants in the middle sample were crucial in identifying serious delinquents.

Table 7 shows that the combined delinquency seriousness scale had significant concurrent and predictive validity for both Caucasians and African-Americans. Concurrent validity was higher for Caucasians. Comparing Table 7 with Table 4, concurrent validity was lower for the combined scale than for the self-report scale for African-Americans. Concurrent validity was higher with the combined scale for Caucasians according to the AROC values, but lower according to the OR values.

Table 7.   Combined Delinquency Scale as a Predictor of Court Petitions, Controlling for Ethnicity

		None (%)	Minor (%)	Moderate (%)	Serious (%)	χ^2	OR	AROC
		Delinquency Seriousness						
Middle Sample								
Predictive								
Criminal Delinquency	(C)	4.8	8.8	24.0	34.2	20.5*	3.9*	.478*
	(AA)	18.4	15.2	46.6	62.0	47.5*	4.6*	.500*
Index Violence	(C)	0.0	1.5	0.0	5.3	NV	9.9	.518+
	(AA)	13.2	7.6	22.4	32.6	17.9*	3.0*	.375*
Index Property	(C)	3.2	4.4	16.0	26.3	17.8*	4.6*	.507*
	(AA)	10.5	8.9	29.3	35.9	22.3*	2.9*	.391*
Oldest Sample								
Concurrent								
Criminal Delinquency	(C)	4.7	2.5	6.3	22.6	14.9*	5.9*	.513*
	(AA)	8.1	4.0	19.4	20.2	9.4*	2.0	.254
Index Offense	(C)	2.3	2.5	4.7	28.9	13.7*	6.6*	.566*
	(AA)	5.4	2.0	12.9	19.3	11.7*	3.0*	.384*
Predictive								
Criminal Delinquency	(C)	10.3	18.9	26.3	46.3	14.9*	3.6*	.397*
	(AA)	20.6	27.7	46.0	61.5	24.0*	3.3*	.406*
Index Violence	(C)	0.0	5.6	5.3	12.2	5.5	3.5	.401*
	(AA)	5.9	10.6	20.4	27.5	10.2*	2.5*	.325*
Index Property	(C)	2.6	10.8	21.1	26.8	10.6*	2.5*	.391*
	(AA)	11.8	14.9	32.0	36.3	12.1*	2.2*	.293*

NOTES: C = Caucasian; AA = African-American. OR = odds ratio, comparing serious category with remainder. NV = not valid. Predictive = petitions after A. Concurrent = petitions up to A.
* $p < .05$, two-tailed.
+ significance test not possible.

Predictive validity was substantial and significant for both African-Americans and Caucasians. In the middle and oldest samples, for index violence and index property offenses, the OR and AROC values were

DELINQUENCY SERIOUSNESS 509

higher for Caucasians, while χ^2 was higher for African-Americans. However, for criminal delinquency, measures of predictive validity were usually higher for African-Americans. In almost all cases, the OR and AROC values were higher in Table 7 than in Table 4, showing that the combined scale had higher predictive validity than the self-report scale for both Caucasians and African-Americans.

Logistic regression analyses showed that ethnicity predicted the probability of future petitions independently of the combined delinquency scale. For example, the likelihood ratio χ^2 for ethnicity in the prediction of criminal delinquency was 19.5 ($p < .05$) in the middle sample and 9.2 ($p < .05$) in the oldest sample. However, in all cases ethnicity was less important independently of the combined scale than independently of the self-report scale. Ethnicity was not significantly related to past petitions independently of the combined delinquency scale.

CONCLUSIONS

In the Pittsburgh Youth Study, a self-reported delinquency seriousness scale had concurrent and predictive validity in relation to juvenile court petitions. Concurrent validity was higher than predictive validity, possibly because juvenile court petitions increased the willingness of boys to report their delinquent acts. A combined delinquency seriousness scale (based on information from the boy, his mother, and his teacher) had similar concurrent validity but greater predictive validity than the self-reported delinquency seriousness scale.

The self-reported delinquency seriousness scale had concurrent and predictive validity for both African-Americans and Caucasians. Concurrent validity for admitting offenses was higher for Caucasians, but concurrent validity for admitting arrests was higher for African-Americans. There were no consistent ethnic differences in predictive validity. The combined delinquency seriousness scale also had concurrent and predictive validity for both African-Americans and Caucasians, although concurrent validity was again higher for Caucasians. Predictive validity was higher with the combined scale than with the self-report scale for both African-Americans and Caucasians, and there were no consistent ethnic differences in predictive validity. Future research might address why there are ethnic differences in concurrent validity but not in predictive validity.

It seems clear that there is a gain in predictive validity, which is a very important feature of any scale, by combining self-report data with information from other sources (mothers and teachers). In the middle sample, the extra informants yielded a large increase in the proportion of boys identified as serious delinquents. African-American boys were more serious delinquents than Caucasian boys according to both self-report and

510   FARRINGTON ET AL.

combined scales, but the differences between them were greater with the combined scale than with the self-report scale in the middle sample. Interestingly, the extra informants were especially valuable with the middle sample; these 10-year-olds were generally predelinquents in regard to official records.

Within each category of delinquency seriousness, African-American boys were always more likely to be petitioned in the future, but not more likely to have been petitioned in the past. The largest differences in past petitions were found in the "moderate seriousness" category; more African-Americans than Caucasians in this category were petitioned. These differences might be caused by biases in police or court processing, by differences in police patrolling in African-American versus Caucasian areas, by differences in demeanor between African-American and Caucasian boys when apprehended by the police, or by other variables correlated with ethnicity and petitions. However, these kinds of explanations would all predict ethnic differences in past petitions, which were not found. Another possible explanation is that the developmental course of delinquency is quicker or more intense for African-Americans than for Caucasians. In other words, while Caucasians and African-Americans in the same delinquency seriousness category at A may be equivalent, the delinquency of African-Americans may quickly become more frequent and more serious. This hypothesis might be investigated in future research. Interestingly, in the National Youth Survey Elliott (1994) found that African-Americans were more likely than Caucasians to persist in violent offending.

In light of the importance of maximizing the validity of measures of the key dependent variable of delinquency, more methodological research on this topic is clearly needed. This should explore several different data sources (self-reports, official records, parents, teachers, peers, observation, and so on) and should focus especially on predictive validity. In the interests of comparing results from different studies, all researchers should report comparable measures of predictive efficiency (e.g., AROC). It is important to establish when predictive validity is high and when it is low: with which types of people, in which types of contexts, with which data collection methods, and so on. To the extent that measures have low validity, findings about correlates and predictors of delinquency will be of limited use in formulating and testing theories of delinquency. More attention should be given to findings obtained in research using measures of delinquency with proven high validity.

Compared with Hindelang et al. (1981), it may be that we did not find consistent ethnic differences in predictive validity because our self-report data were collected in the context of a nonanonymous, face-to-face interview, which may maximize validity compared with anonymous self-completed questionnaires. Also, our attrition was relatively low. We conclude that, in the Pittsburgh Youth Study, ethnic differences in official delinquency were partly attributable to ethnic differences in delinquent behavior and were not attributable to differential ethnic attrition or differential ethnic validity of measures of delinquent behavior.

REFERENCES

Achenbach, Thomas M. and Craig S. Edelbrock
  1983   Manual of the Child Behavior Checklist and Revised Child Behavior Profile. Burlington: University of Vermont.
  1987   Manual for the Youth Self-Report and Profile. Burlington: University of Vermont.

Cernkovich, Stephen, Peggy Giordano, and Meredith Pugh
  1985   Chronic offenders: The missing cases in self-report delinquency research. Journal of Criminal Law & Criminology 76:705-732.

Chambliss, William J. and Richard H. Nagasawa
  1969   On the validity of official statistics: A comparative study of white, black, and Japanese high school boys. Journal of Research in Crime and Delinquency 6:71-77.

Duncan, O. Dudley, Lloyd E. Ohlin, Albert J. Reiss, Jr., and Howard R. Stanton
  1953   Formal devices for making selection decisions. American Journal of Sociology 58:573-584.

Dunford, Franklyn W. and Delbert S. Elliott
  1984   Identifying career offenders using self-reported data. Journal of Research in Crime and Delinquency 21:57-86.

Edelbrock, Craig S. and Thomas M. Achenbach
  1984   The teacher version of the Child Behavior Profile: I. Boys aged six through eleven. Journal of Consulting and Clinical Psychology 22:207-217.

Elliott, Delbert S.
  1982   Review of "Measuring Delinquency." Criminology 20:527-537.
  1994   Serious violent offenders: Onset, developmental course, and termination. Criminology 32:1-22.

Elliott, Delbert S. and David Huizinga
  1989   Improving self-reported measures of delinquency. In Malcolm W. Klein (ed.), Cross-National Research in Self-Reported Crime and Delinquency. Dordrecht, Netherlands: Kluwer.

Elliott, Delbert S. and Harwin L. Voss
  1974   Delinquency and Dropout. Lexington, Mass.: D.C. Heath.

Elliott, Delbert S., David Huizinga, and Suzanne S. Ageton
  1985   Explaining Delinquency and Drug Use. Beverly Hills, Calif.: Sage.

Erickson, Maynard L. and Lamar T. Empey
  1963   Court records, undetected delinquency and decision-making. Journal of Criminal Law, Criminology and Police Science 54:456-469.

512 FARRINGTON ET AL.

Farrington, David P.
 1973 Self-reports of deviant behavior: Predictive and stable? Journal of
       Criminal Law & Criminology 64:99-110.
 1977 The effects of public labelling. British Journal of Criminology 17:112-125.
 1989 Self-reported and official offending from adolescence to adulthood. In
       Malcolm W. Klein (ed.), Cross-National Research in Self-Reported Crime
       and Delinquency. Dordrecht, Netherlands: Kluwer.

Fergusson, David M., J. K. Fifield, and S. W. Slater
 1977 Signal detectability theory and the evaluation of prediction tables.
       Journal of Research in Crime and Delinquency 14:237-246.

Fergusson, David M., L. John Horwood, and Michael T. Lynskey
 1993 Ethnicity and bias in police statistics. Australian and New Zealand
       Journal of Criminology 26:193-206.

Gibson, Hamilton B., Sylvia Morrison, and Donald J. West
 1970 The confession of known offenses in response to a self-reported
       delinquency schedule. British Journal of Criminology 10:277-280.

Gold, Martin
 1966 Undetected delinquent behavior. Journal of Research in Crime and
       Delinquency 3:27-46.

Gold, Martin and David J. Reimer
 1975 Changing patterns of delinquent behavior among Americans 13 through
       16 years old: 1967-72. Crime and Delinquency Literature 7:483-517.

Gould, Leroy C.
 1969 Who defines delinquency: A comparison of self-reported and officially-
       reported indices of delinquency for three racial groups. Social Problems
       16:325-336.

Hackler, James C. and Melanie Lautt
 1969 Systematic bias in measuring self-reported delinquency. Canadian Review
       of Sociology and Anthropology 6:92-106.

Hardt, Robert H. and Sandra Peterson-Hardt
 1977 On determining the quality of the delinquency self-report method.
       Journal of Research in Crime and Delinquency 14:247-261.

Hindelang, Michael J., Travis Hirschi, and Joseph G. Weis
 1979 Correlates of delinquency: The illusion of discrepancy between self-report
       and official measures. American Sociological Review 44:995-1014.
 1981 Measuring Delinquency. Beverly Hills, Calif.: Sage.

Hirschi, Travis
 1969 Causes of Delinquency. Berkeley: University of California Press.

Hoffman, Martin S. (ed.)
 1991 The World Almanac and Book of Facts, 1990. New York: Pharos.

Huizinga, David
 1991 Assessing violent behavior with self-reports. In J. S. Milner (ed.),
       Neuropsychology of Aggression. Boston: Kluwer.

Huizinga, David and Delbert S. Elliott
 1986 Reassessing the reliability and validity of self-report measures. Journal of
       Quantitative Criminology 2:293-327.

DELINQUENCY SERIOUSNESS 513

Kulik, James A., Kenneth B. Stein, and Theodore R. Sarbin
  1968   Disclosure of delinquent behavior under conditions of anonymity and
          nonanonymity. Journal of Consulting and Clinical Psychology 32:506-509.

Le Blanc, Marc and Marcel Fréchette
  1989   Male Criminal Activity from Childhood through Youth. New York:
          Springer-Verlag.

Loeber, Rolf, Magda Stouthamer-Loeber, Welmoet B. Van Kammen, and David P.
  Farrington
  1989   Development of a new measure of self-reported antisocial behavior for
          young children: Prevalence and reliability. In Malcolm W. Klein (ed.),
          Cross-National Research in Self-Reported Crime and Delinquency.
          Dordrecht, Netherlands: Kluwer.
  1991   Initiation, escalation and desistance in juvenile offending and their
          correlates. Journal of Criminal Law & Criminology 82:36-82.

Mossman, Douglas
  1994   Assessing predictors of violence: Being accurate about accuracy. Journal
          of Consulting and Clinical Psychology 62:783-792.

Reiss, Albert J., Jr.
  1975   Inappropriate theories and inadequate methods as policy plagues: Self-
          reported delinquency and the law. In Norman J. Demerath, Otto Larsen,
          and Karl F. Schuessler (eds.), Social Policy and Sociology. New York:
          Academic Press.

Short, James F. and F. Ivan Nye
  1957   Reported behavior as a criterion of deviant behavior. Social Problems
          5:207-213.
  1958   Extent of unrecorded juvenile delinquency: Tentative conclusions. Journal
          of Criminal Law & Criminology 49:296-302.

Stouthamer-Loeber, Magda and Welmoet B. Van Kammen
  1995   Data Collection and Management: A Practical Guide. Thousand Oaks,
          Calif.: Sage.

Stouthamer-Loeber, Magda, Welmoet B. Van Kammen, and Rolf Loeber
  1992   The nuts and bolts of running a large longitudinal study. Violence and
          Victims 7:63-78.

Swets, John A.
  1986   Indices of discrimination or diagnostic accuracy: Their ROCs and implied
          models. Psychological Bulletin 99:100-117.

Tracy, Paul E.
  1987   Race and class differences in official and self-reported delinquency. In
          Marvin E. Wolfgang, Terence P. Thornberry, and Robert M. Figlio, From
          Boy to Man, from Delinquency to Crime. Chicago: University of Chicago
          Press.

Voss, Harwin L.
  1963   Ethnic differentials in delinquency in Honolulu. Journal of Criminal Law,
          Criminology and Police Science 54:322-327.

514   FARRINGTON ET AL.

Weis, Joseph G.
    1986   Issues in the measurement of criminal careers. In Alfred Blumstein,
              Jacqueline Cohen, Jeffrey A. Roth, and Christy A. Visher (eds.), Criminal
              Careers and "Career Criminals." Vol. 2. Washington, D.C.: National
              Academy Press.

West, Donald J. and David P. Farrington
    1977   The Delinquent Way of Life. London: Heinemann.

Wolfgang, Marvin E., Robert M. Figlio, Paul E. Tracy, and Simon I. Singer
    1985   The National Survey of Crime Severity. Washington, D.C.: U.S. Govern-
              ment Printing Office.

   David P. Farrington, Ph.D. is Professor of Psychological Criminology at Cambridge
University. His main interest is in longitudinal research on the development of
offending.

   Rolf Loeber, Ph.D. is Professor of Psychiatry, Psychology and Epidemiology at the
University of Pittsburgh. His interests lie in the development of delinquency, substance
use, and mental health problems, and the application of developmental findings to
interventions.

   Magda Stouthamer-Loeber, Ph.D. is Associate Professor of Psychiatry and Psychology at the University of Pittsburgh. Her interests are in the implementation of longitudinal studies, the analysis of risk and protective factors for delinquency, and juveniles'
use of services for mental health needs.

   Welmoet B. Van Kammen, Ph.D. is Project Director of the Pittsburgh Youth Study.
Her interests are in the implementation of longitudinal studies and questions pertaining
to substance abuse and drug dealing in juveniles.

   Laura C. Schmidt, M.S. is data analyst on the Pittsburgh Youth Study. Her interests
include psychometrics and longitudinal analyses. She is writing her dissertation on the
influence of social motives on mentoring satisfaction.

APPENDIX
MEASURING CONCURRENT AND PREDICTIVE VALIDITY

How can validity be measured in 4 x 2 contingency tables? For concurrent validity of the self-reported delinquency seriousness scale in relation to past Juvenile Court petitions, Table 3 shows that, in the oldest sample, 24% of those in the serious delinquent category had a petition for criminal delinquency (basically, delinquency excluding traffic, status, and drunkenness offenses) compared with 13% of moderate delinquents, 4% of minor delinquents, and 8% of nondelinquents. An obvious measure of validity is χ^2. In this example, $\chi^2 = 23.0$, 3 d.f., $p < .05$. However, while χ^2 measures statistical significance, it does not measure the strength of a relationship. Also, it depends on sample size and row and column totals (e.g., the prevalence of petitions). Most seriously, it is insensitive to the ordering of the percentages and hence is not a good measure of a linear trend: In this example, the percentage petitioned for criminal delinquency was higher in the none category than in the minor category.

A simple and meaningful index of validity is obtained by contrasting the percentage of those in the serious delinquent category who were petitioned (here, 24%) and of the remainder (here, 9%). The OR is a good measure of strength of relationship in a 2 x 2 table, which is not affected by changes in sample size or in row and column totals. In this example, the OR was 3.3. Basically, knowing that someone was a serious delinquent increased the odds (risk) of his being concurrently petitioned by 3.3 times. Since the 95% confidence interval for this OR (1.9-5.8) did not include the chance value of 1.0, this OR was statistically significant.

There is no widely accepted strength of relationship measure of validity in 4 x 2 tables. However, such a measure can be derived from the area under the ROC (receiver operating characteristic) curve (Swets, 1986). The ROC curve plots the probability of a "hit" (e.g., the percentage of delinquents identified at any selection criterion) versus the probability of a "false positive" (e.g., the percentage of nondelinquents identified at this selection criterion). The area under the ROC curve was used by Mossman (1994) in a meta-analysis of the prediction of violence as a "succinct and commonly used method for summarizing overall discriminating power" (p. 785). The ROC curve was first used in a criminological prediction study nearly 20 years ago by Fergusson et al. (1977), who recommended the use of the area under the curve and showed that it was mathematically related to the Mean Cost Rating of Duncan et al. (1953). The area under the ROC curve, like the odds ratio, is a measure of strength of relationship unaffected by changes in sample size and row and column totals (e.g., prevalence). The area under the ROC curve has a simple and meaningful interpretation (Fergusson et al., 1977): It is equivalent to the proportion of correct predictions in a 2 x 2 table (where chance = .50 and perfect discrimination = 1.0).

Figure 1 shows the best-fitting ROC curve for the probability of past criminal delinquency petitions at different levels of self-reported delinquency seriousness in the oldest sample. The 4 x 2 table on which this curve is based is shown at the bottom of the figure. For example, if only serious delinquents are identified, 30 out of 60 petitioned boys are identified (prob. hit = .5) and 94 out of 408 nonpetitioned boys are identified (prob. false positive = .23). Hence, this criterion corresponds to the point (x = .23, y = .5) in Figure 1, indicated by an asterisk. If serious and moderate delinquents are identified, 47 out of 60 petitioned boys are identified (prob. hit = .78) and 213 out of 408 nonpetitioned boys are identified (prob. false positive = .52). Hence, this criterion corresponds to the point (.52, .78). Similarly, the third point is at (.74, .85). The origin (0, 0) corresponds to where no boys are identified, and the top right-hand corner (1,1) corresponds to where all boys are identified.

The best-fitting ROC curve was calculated by maximum likelihood techniques, assuming underlying normal distributions, using the ROCFIT software of Charles E. Metz. The area under this curve was .683, with a standard deviation of .043. Hence, this area was significantly greater than the chance expectation of 0.5. The exact area under the four segments defined by (0, 0), (.23, .5), (.52, .78), (.74, .85), and (1, 1) was .663. Generally, the area under the best-fitting curve was slightly greater than the area under the segmented "curve." Conclusions about predictive power (based on relative sizes of areas under the ROC curves) are not substantially affected by using either the fitted or the segmented curve, but the best-fitting curve has the advantage of permitting tests of statistical significance (because of the associated standard deviation). However, for tables including two zeros, such as the concurrent relationship with index violence in the oldest sample (Table 3), the best-fitting curve could not be calculated, and in this case the area under the segmented curve is given.

If accuracy was no better than chance, all the points in Figure 1 would fall on the diagonal from (0, 0) to (1, 1), so that area = .5. With perfect discrimination between petitioned and nonpetitioned cases, the points would all fall on the lines from (0, 0) to (0, 1) and from (0, 1) to (1, 1), so that area = 1.0. Hence, the shaded area between the ROC curve and the diagonal, expressed as a fraction of the total area above the diagonal, is a measure of strength of relationship in a 4 x 2 table that varies between 0 (chance) and 1 (perfect). We have termed this the "AROC." In Figure 1, the AROC is .366.

DELINQUENCY SERIOUSNESS   517

Figure 1.   ROC Curve for Past Criminal Delinquency
              Petitions

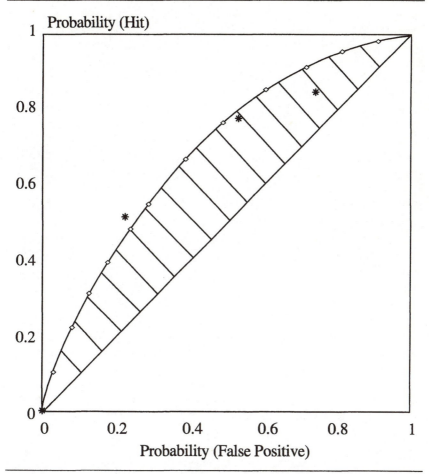

NOTES: Area under ROC curve = .683 (S.D. = .043). AROC = .683-.5/.5=.366.

	None	Minor	Moderate	Serious	Total
Petitioned	9	4	17	30	60
Not Petitioned	106	89	119	94	408
% Petitioned	7.8	4.3	12.5	24.2	12.8

Part IV
Descriptive Analysis of Quantitative Data

[14]

Visualizing Homicide: A Research Note[1]

Michael D. Maltz[2]

This paper provides some examples of the utility of graphical methods in analyzing data. While such methods are not expected to supplant standard statistical
techniques, they can help the researcher in understanding characteristics of the
process in ways that cannot be replicated using the standard methods.

KEY WORDS: hypothesis tests; graphical methods; homicide; Supplementary
Homicide Reports.

Over the past few years the limitations of the statistical methods used
to analyze data in criminal justice and criminology have become more and
more apparent. And not just in these fields; the American Psychological
Association has established a committee to make recommendations about
the utility of statistical tests based on the null hypothesis. In particular, in
developmental psychopathology there are concerns about viewing the world
through a distorted lens of inadequate analytic methods (Richters, 1997). A
symposium on this topic was held by NIMH in December 1997.[3]

My own concerns about this situation were expressed in an article
(Maltz, 1994) that described some of the problems with the current reper-
toire of analytic tools and methods. In it I suggested other techniques that
might be used, including new methods of handling longitudinal data (see
Maltz, 1996), multimodal analyses such as cluster analysis, and graphical
methods of analysis.[4] In this note I focus on the last-mentioned method,
and show how it can be used, not just to *display data*, but as an *analytic*

---

[1]This note was completed while I was a Visiting Fellow at the Bureau of Justice Statistics. The
opinions expressed herein, however, are my own and do not reflect the policies of the U.S.
Department of Justice. I thank Ray Paternoster and David Weisburd for their comments on
an early draft.
[2]Department of Criminal Justice, University of Illinois at Chicago, 1007 W. Harrison Street,
Chicago, Illinois 60607-7140.
[3]The transcript can be found at http://weber.u.washington.edu/~gloftus/Paradigm.html.
[4]For an innovative graphical approach based on Lexis plots, see
http://www.cas.lancs.ac.uk80/alcd/visual/.

tool that can be used to generate hypotheses as well. This is a follow-up to my editorial comment in this journal (Maltz, 1997) about the benefits of graphing data, of getting a picture of potential patterns before committing to a specific line of analysis. It is in keeping with Wild's (1994, p. 168) statement that, in the future, "the primary language for promoting the human understanding of data will be sophisticated computer graphics rather than mathematics."

My concern is hastened by the realization that we will soon be awash in data. The trickle of numbers generated by the FBI's Uniform Crime Reporting (**UCR**) Program[5] will soon become a fire hose of data, when the FBI's National Incident-Based Reporting System (**NIBRS**) for reporting criminal incidents comes up to speed in the near future. [When a police department submits data for the UCR, each record or line of data represents a *separate type of crime*, the datum giving the number of that type of crime that occurred during the reporting period. When a police department submits data in the NIBRS program, each record or line of data represents a *separate crime*, and the characteristics of the crime are given in detail: characteristics of the crime, the location, the victim and (if known) the offender. Analysis of NIBRS data, then, will provide us with a wealth of information about individual events that was unavailable before, but we need to develop methods to deal with this rich information.]

Thus, in the not too distant future we will be facing what Ian Hacking (1990, p. 45) has called "an avalanche of numbers." Sample-based statistical tests will be absolutely meaningless when we have Ns of 200,000! What this means is that we need to develop and use new tools that will provide us with the ability to analyze data, and perform analyses in such a way that we get insights into social processes, not just significance levels.

It is instructive to see what the father of hypothesis testing says about the statistical analysis of large data sets. R. A. Fisher (1922) attempted to define "the task [to] which the statistician sets himself: briefly, and in its most concrete form, the object of statistical methods is the reduction of data. A quantity of data, *which usually by its mere bulk is incapable of entering the mind*, is to be replaced by relatively few quantities which shall adequately represent the whole, or which, in other words, shall contain as much as possible, ideally the whole, of the relevant information contained in the original data" [italics added]. These quantities, usually parameters of a statistical model, provide insights into some of the relationships inherent in the data.

[5]When an acronym is first defined it is set in bold-face type.

At the time when Fisher wrote this, of course, there were no automated ways of handling data in large quantities. Since then, however, the armamentarium of statisticians has grown from the level of slingshots to nuclear weaponry.[6] Software can now handle large data sets with ease; but there still are limits on the extent to which "relevant information contained in the original data" can be extracted from the data using standard statistical software. In this note I provide an example of how graphical methods can be used for this purpose.

One of the techniques I have been using in my own research, most recently in my work as a Visiting Fellow at the Bureau of Justice Statistics, is the application of graphical methods of analyzing data that in essence "let the data speak for themselves" instead of first having them filtered through a statistical algorithm in a software package like SAS or SPSS. They are based on precepts described generally by Tufte (1983, 1990, 1997), and operationalized in a form more useful for data analysis by Cleveland (1993, 1994). The fundamental idea is to develop methods of displaying data that permit the viewer to *see* relationships within the data.

Although software packages like SPSS and SAS provide graphical output, they are used primarily for conducting statistical analyses and generating tables; the graphical output they provide is primarily a means of displaying the results of analyses and not displaying the raw data themselves.[7] Moreover, the approach taken in most analyses that are performed is predominantly a "black box" approach, one in which the data are not inspected (or are inspected only cursorily) and only the results of the analytic methods are displayed. One problem with this approach is that mistakes in the data (which can often be readily detected when the raw data are depicted) cannot be distinguished. A telling example of this is detailed in Cleveland (1993, p. 328): a data set used in an example of analysis of variance by Fisher in 1934, *and in textbooks by many others over the subsequent 40 years*, was found to be in error when the raw data were finally graphed.

Graphs are useful as a first step, to spot data entry errors, as well as to provide some directions for further exploration and investigation.

---

[6]This has not been entirely beneficial; as Barnett (1982) has noted, "The widespread availability of statistical computer packages has put mathematical bazookas in the hands of some people who would be dangerous with an abacus."

[7]However, the software environment is changing. SYSTAT, now published by SPSS, provides greater graphical capabilities as well as a full complement of statistical algorithms. SigmaPlot, also recently purchased by SPSS, is a sophisticated graphical package that incorporates standard statistical routines in its companion package SigmaStat. And S-Plus, published by MathSoft, incorporates both sophisticated graphics capabilities and sophisticated statistical routines.

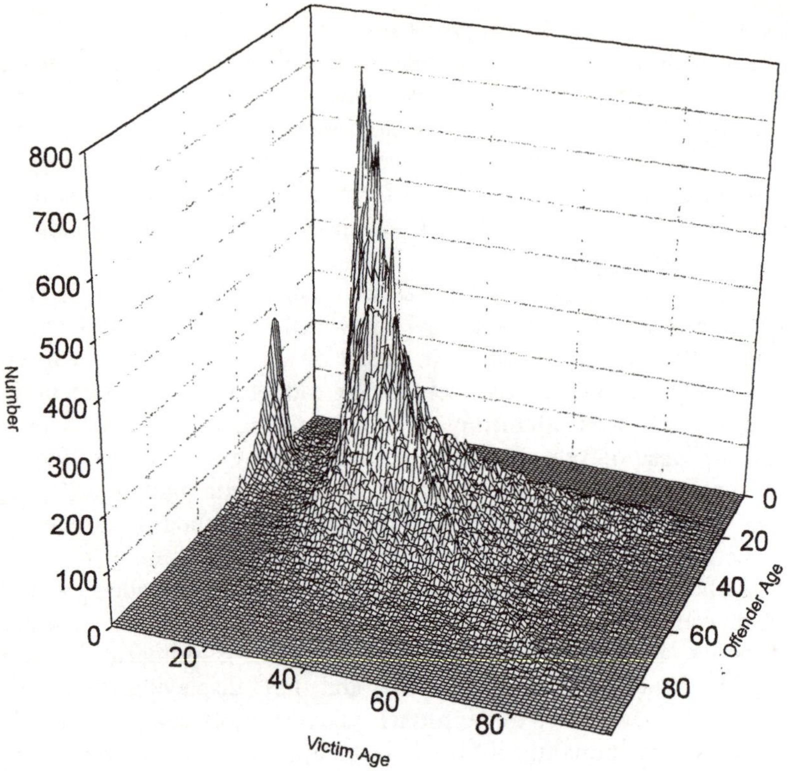

Fig. 1. Number of one-on-one homicides, by age of victim and age of offender, raw data.

Combining graphical methods with standard statistical methods not only provides the analyst with additional tools, it also can provide him/her with additional insight into the relationships, relationships that may not be incorporated in the assumptions of the statistical methods. When shown in a graph, the data are displayed without assumptions.[8]

The best way to explain this approach is to provide examples; after all, a picture is worth a thousand words [or, as Loftus, 1993, noted, a thousand *p*-values]. Figure 1 is a three-dimensional plot of number of homicides (vertical dimension) vs age of victim and age of offender.[9] The figure

---

[8]This is not entirely true; some assumptions are always implicit in the choice of data to collect. For example, Lombrosians would attempt to explain criminality by including such variables as cranium size, color of eyes, height and weight, while now we ordinarily don't include these characteristics.

[9]This plot is three-dimensional because there are three dimensions to the data: victim age, offender age, and number. In too many of the 3-D plots used in research papers the third dimension is gratuitous (a thick bar, for example), exemplary of what Tufte (1983) calls "chartjunk."

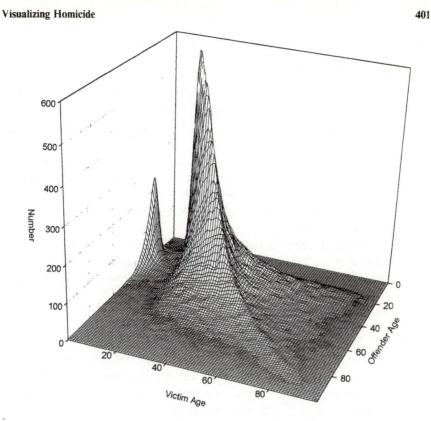

Fig. 2. Number of one-on-one homicides, by age of victim and age of offender, smoothed data.

represents the 222,211 one-on-one (one victim, one offender) homicides in the United States between 1976 and 1996 in which both victims' and offenders' ages are known. Ages 98 and above are included in age category 98. The data are from the FBI-collected Supplementary Homicide Reports (**SHR**) and were obtained from Fox (1998).[10] It did not require sophisticated methods to generate; it is merely a graphical representation of a crosstab of the two variables: age of victim and age of offender. The data are somewhat jagged, so Fig. 2 shows them slightly smoothed (the Appendix explains the smoothing method used), which makes the features of the data easier to discern.

The primary peak is approximately (but not entirely) symmetrical, showing what everyone knows: most offenders are teenagers and young

[10]By the time this article is published, this data set (containing data from 1976 to 1996) is expected to be available for downloading from http://www.icpsr.umich.edu/nacjd/. An earlier version (containing 1976–1994 data) is currently available at this site.

adults, and so are their victims. There are four other features that can be discerned from this figure.

- There is a separate smaller peak off to the "west," showing that many children (aged 0–5) are killed by offenders between 15 and 40, presumably by their "caregivers." This appears to be an "infanticide" peak.
- There seems to be a halcyon period between the two peaks, i.e., between ages 5 and 12, during which very few deaths occur; apparently at those ages youths are beyond danger from their caregivers and not yet endangered by their peers; I call this "the valley of the shadow of death."
- There is a discernible pattern in which young offenders (around 20 years old) kill victims of all ages (the "east"-running ridge).
- There is a diagonal ("northwest-southeast") ridge at older years, showing that offenders aged 40 and above tend to have victims about the same age as themselves.

The diagonal ridge becomes more prominent in Fig. 3, which shows the breakdown of homicides by sex of victim and offender: note that there are prominent ridges for male-on-female and female-on-male homicides but not for the others, strongly suggesting that they may be due to domestic violence. Moreover, the infancitide peaks for the four cases are approximately the same size; this implies that:

- Babies of both sexes have about the same risk of being killed. This is in sharp contrast to other societies (and at other times), when female babies have had a much higher likelihood of being killed (e.g., Aird, 1990, p. 28).
- The offenders are as likely to be male or female. This is in sharp contrast to other types of homicide, where offenders are much more likely to be male (as is seen in the dominant peak).
- One of the most dangerous years of a female's life, in terms of risk of death due to homicide, is her first year of life. Actually, it *is* the most dangerous year, when non-recorded homicides, such as those wrongly attributed to sudden infant death syndrome, are included in the count (Maltz *et al.*, forthcoming).

And the "east"-running ridge (young offenders and victims of all ages) is prominent in the two top graphs (male offenders) but not in the lower graphs, underscoring the lethality of young males, perhaps due in part to their involvement in felonies.

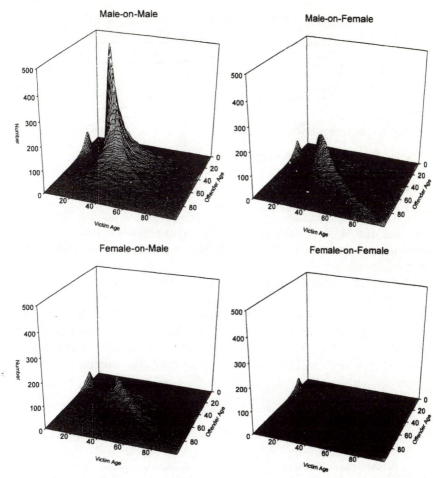

Fig. 3. Number of one-on-one homicides by age of victim and age of offender, by victum and offender, smoothed data.

These figures strongly suggest that many different phemomena are represented in the SHR data set.[11] Another way of stating this is to consider homicide to be not only a crime itself but to be the fatal outcome of another crime. At a minimum the "homicide syndromes" (Block, 1992) apparent from these figures include

- peer homicide among males,
- infanticide and child homicide,
- domestic homicide, and
- felony homicide,

[11]Allen and Buckner (1997) display a two-dimensional plot of the same kind of data. It is the added dimension, however, that provides these insights.

Table I. Number of Homicides of Children Aged 0–
5 by Sex of Victim and Offender

Offender sex	Male	Female
Male	3016	2249
Female	1680	1565

with the respective non-fatal crimes of

- gang crimes and aggravated assault,
- child abuse,
- intimate partner violence, and
- armed robbery and other felonies.

Note that one of the advantages of graphical analysis is that more than one phenomenon can be inferred from the data, which computational methods ordinarily cannot do.

Moreover, sometimes a computational method can be misleading; or at the very least, unhelpful. For example, the numbers of victims aged 0–5 in Fig. 3 are given in Table I.[12] A chi-square test (of independence of sex of victim and offender) results in $p \ll 0.01$, i.e., the sex of victum is not independent of sex of offender. Yet I would submit that the visual analyses (see also Fig. 4) provide more insight than this "scientific" finding.

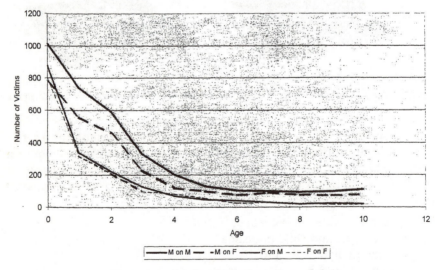

Fig. 4. Age of victim of offender and sex of victim.

[12]The raw (unsmoothed) SHR data were used in compiling this table.

Undoubtedly, not all graphical representations of data will present such clear indications of different phenomena. Moreover, many of these phenomena can be (and have been) noted by other researchers using non-graphical methods; I do not claim that these methods will replace all others. But there are other techniques and methods of presentation (see Cleveland, 1993, 1994) that show how patterns can be extracted from data in ways that would not be possible using computational methods.

What these figures do show is that one can use graphical methods as *investigative* tools, to *find patterns in data* (which to my mind is the essence of statistics, if not all science), and not just to display patterns that are found using standard techniques. Although these techniques do not utilize standardized tests, the fact is they do convey patterns that are of great utility; they are extremely useful in what I consider the more important task of research, hypothesis *generation*, not hypothesis *testing*.

As with any set of methods, there are limitations to graphical methods as well. For example, how much above the general pattern does the "domestic homicide" ridge have to be before it qualifies as a feature? How would you quantify the ridge so that it could be incorporated into an automated means of determining the extent of domestic homicide in, say, the 50 states? Showing (or even creating 50 graphs) could be time-consuming, but a table or numbers could summarize them.

Moreover, one can't look at a lot of variables at once. Sample-based analyses are meaningless with large Ns, true, but one can consider more variables at once. So there are no clear-cut advantages of one set of methods over another.

In addition, color is a necessity in graphs when trying to show more than one or two relationships in the data, and few journals can afford to include color graphics. The authors or journals can, however, store the graphics on a web page or the authors can furnish them either virtually (by e-mail) or by regular mail to interested readers.

The purpose of this note is to encourage research using such "unsophisticated" methods as graphical analysis. As more and more graphical data analysis programs become available, it is my hope that they will be used increasingly to depict data. The *Journal of Quantitative Criminology* stands ready to publish the best of such research, keeping in mind the epigram inscribed in Richard Hamming's (1987) book, "The purpose of computing is insight, not numbers."

APPENDIX: SMOOTHING AND PLOTTING THE HOMICIDE DATA

The methods used in producing these figures are quite simple conceptually, but entail the use of three different software packages: a statistical data base program (I used SPSS, but SAS and others can be used as well), a spreadsheet (I have used Quattro Pro, Excel, and Lotus 1-2-3 for this task), and plotting software (for this paper I used SigmaPlot, but I have also used S-Plus and DeltaGraph effectively for final output).

Because these procedures are graphical, they may take a long time to print. Over 20,000 line segments have to be drawn, which can take over 5 min on a computer with a 266-MHz microprocessor and 80 MB of RAM. As computers and printers increase in speed and capacity, these limitations will disappear.

There are two data files associated with the Supplementary Homicide Reports (SHR), a victim-based file (each record is associated with a victim, regardless of the number of victims or offenders in the incident) and an offender-based file (with one record per offender, regardless of the number of victims or offenders in the incident). I used the victim-based file, and selected all cases in which there is one victim and one offender, and in which the ages of both victim and offender are known. I then generated a crosstab of victim age vs offender age and copied it into the spreadsheet. In the description that follows I assume that the row variable is victim age and the column variable is offender age.

The SHR age data are given from 0 to 99. Age 0 includes all children killed before their first birthday; age 98 includes all people 98 and over; and age 99 represents those for whom the age is unknown (and these cases are therefore excluded). So the data run from 0 to 98 for both offender and victim.

The crosstab generated by SPSS is not complete for plotting purposes. In order to plot the data as shown, *all* victim and offender ages must be represented, not just those for which data exist. Since there are no offenders aged 0–5, there are no data rows for those ages. [Actually, there are one or two isolated cases with offenders of those ages, apparently data entry mistakes that got through the FBI's SHR screening process.] So the appropriate rows have to be added manually to the spreadsheet.[13]

Plotting this crosstab in a spreadsheet as a 3-D plot (called a "surface plot" in Excel) results in a figure much like Fig. 1, except that the "mountain" is banded in different colors, depending on the height. Although there is probably some way to fool the spreadsheet software into producing a single-color figure, I don't know it—and the only alternative to this type of 3-D plot is one that shows all lines (i.e., making the "mountain" transparent), which is too confusing. For this reason I decided to transfer the

---

[13]Columns (offender ages) may also have to be added if any disaggregation of the data occurs that results in a data set with no offenders of a certain age. For example, the data for 1992 include no offenders of age 97, so when looking at data for that year this column must be added.

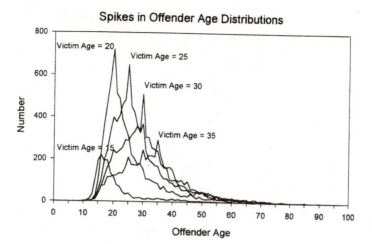

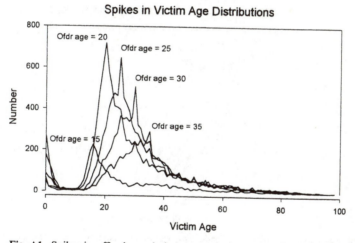

Fig. A1. Spikes in offender and victim age distributions, 5-year intervals.

spreadsheet to SigmaPlot 3.0, a software package that specializes in journal-quality graphics, and provides the user with more control of line weights, colors, headings, and scaling. The result is shown in Fig. 1.

The "spikiness" of this figure looked somewhat suspicious, so I plotted a few cross-sections of the data, shown in Figs. A1 and A2. Note that the spikes occur for the most part when the ages of victim and offender are identical. This may come about when police make guesses about the age of one or the other and for convenience's sake assume that the ages are identical (or in filling out the form they may inadvertently put down the same

Close-up of Spikes in Offender Age Distributions

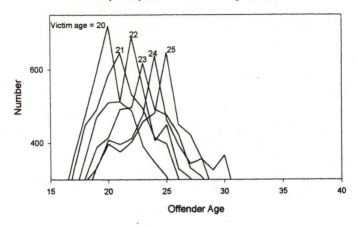

Close-up of Spikes in Victim Age Distributions

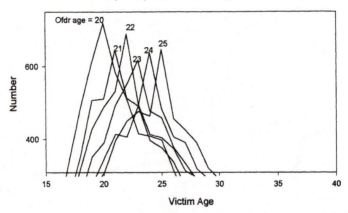

Fig. A2. Close-up spikes in offender and victim age distributions, 1-year intervals.

age). Note also that the spikes are more prominent for ages divisible by 5. This is doubtless due to "age-heaping, the tendency...for ages to be rounded off" (Vaupel *et al.*, 1998, p. 85). To compensate for this situation, I smoothed the data by averaging the number of victims over three years of offender ages. That is, the number of homicides of 25-year-olds committed by 18-year-olds was calculated by adding the number of 25-year-olds killed by 17-, 18-, and 19-year-olds and dividing by 3:

$$\tilde{N}(k, v) = [N(k - 1, v) + N(k, v) + N(k + 1, v)]/3$$

where $N(k, v)$ is the number of victims of age v killed by offenders of age k, and $\tilde{N}(k, v)$ is the estimated number of victims of age v killed by offenders of age k.

This formula cannot be used for offenders of age 98 (or age 0, which is included for the sake of completeness, if not reality), since there are no data for offenders of age $k + 1$, that is, age 99 (or, at the other extreme, of age $k - 1$, that is, age −1). But note that for the "interior ages" (between 1 and 97 inclusive) each datum is used three times: once for the correct age and once each for the previous and next years; since the formulas include division by 3, each datum is used completely.

Although the same formula cannot be used for the "boundary" age of 98, we can still ensure that everything adds up correctly by seeing to it that the data for age 98 be used completely. Since the datum for age 98 is used for the adjacent year (age 97), but weighted by 1/3, in order to use the entire age 98 datum it is weighted by 2/3 for its own year (age 98); and data for the boundary age of 0 are handled similarly. This insures that the sum total of victims is the same for the raw and the smoothed data. For these ages, therefore, we use the following formulas:

$$\tilde{N}(98, v) = [N(97, v) + 2N(98, v)]/3$$

and

$$\tilde{N}(0, v) = [2N(0, v) + N(1, v)]/3$$

Use of these formulas for the boundary ages ensures that total sum of estimated homicides remains equal to the total sum of reported homicides. Although handling the boundary ages in this manner makes little difference when averaging over offender ages—there are virtually no offenders aged 0 or 98—it does make a difference when averaging over victim ages, since there are certainly victims aged 0 and 98.

These formulas are simple to implement in a spreadsheet. The same smoothing procedure is used for victim ages. Application of this smoothing formulas to the data depicted in Fig. 1 results in Fig. 2.

REFERENCES

Aird, J. S. (1990). *Slaughter of the Innocents: Coercive Birth Control in China*, American Enterprise Institute, Washington, DC.

Allen, T. and Buckner, G. (1997). A graphical approach to analyzing relationships between offenders and victims using Supplementary Homicide Reports. *Homicide Stud.* 1(2): 129–140.

Barnett, A. I. (1982). Misapplication reviews. *Interfaces*, September–October.

Block, R., and Block, C. R. (1992). Homicide syndromes and vulnerability: Violence in Chicago community areas over 25 years. *Stud. Crime–Crime Prev.* 1: 61–87.

Cleveland, W. S. (1993). *Visualizing Data*, Hobart Press, Summit, NJ.

Cleveland, W. S. (1994). *The Elements of Graphing Data*, Hobart Press, Summit, NJ.

Fisher, R. A. (1992). On the mathematical foundations of theoretical statistics. Reprinted in Kotz, S., and Johnson, N. L. (eds.), *Breakthroughs in Statistics, Vol. I. Foundations and Basic Theory*, Springer-Verlag, New York.

Fox, J. A. (1998). *Uniform Crime Reports [United States]: Supplementary Homicide Reports 1976–1996* [Computer file], ICPSR version. Northeastern University, College of Criminal Justice [producer], Boston, MA. Inter-university Consortium for Political and Social Research [distributor], Ann Arbor, MI.

Hacking, I. (1990). *The Taming of Chance*, Cambridge University Press, Cambridge.

Hamming, R. W. (1987). *Numerical Methods for Scientists and Engineers*, Dover, New York.

Loftus, G. (1993). A picture is worth a thousand *p*-values: On the irrelevance of hypothesis testing in the computer age. *Behav. Res. Methods Instrum. Comput.* 25: 250–256.

Maltz, M. D. (1994). Deviating from the mean: The declining significance of significance. *J. Res. Crime Delinq.* 31: 434–463.

Maltz, M. D. (1996). Criminality in space and time: Life course analysis and the micro-ecology of crime. In Eck, J., and Weisburd, D. (eds.), *Crime and Place*, Criminal Justice Press, Monsey, New York.

Maltz, M. D., Barrett, R., and O'Keefe, J. (forthcoming). Infanticide in the United States (in preparation).

Richters, J. (1997). The Hubble hypothesis and the developmentalists' dilemma. *Dev. Psychopathol.* 9: 193–229.

Tufte, E. R. (1983). *The Visual Display of Quantitative Information*, Graphics Press, Cheshire, CT.

Tufte, E. R. (1990). *Envisioning Information*, Graphics Press, Cheshire, CT.

Tufte, E. R. (1997). *Graphical Explanations*, Graphics Press, Cheshire, CT.

Vaupel, J. W., Zhenglian, W., Andreev, K. F., and Yashin, A. I. (1998). *Population Data at a Glance: Shaded Contour Maps of Demographic Surfaces over Age and Time*, Odense University Press, Odense, Denmark.

Wild, C. J. (1994). Embracing the "wider view" of statistics. *Am. Stat.* 48: 163–171.

[15]

THE (UN)KNOWN UNIVERSE: MAPPING GANGS AND GANG VIOLENCE IN BOSTON

by

David M. Kennedy
Anthony A. Braga
Anne M. Piehl
Harvard University

Abstract: *The experience, observations, local knowledge, and historical perspective of working police officers and others with routine contact with offenders, communities, and criminal organizations may represent an important underutilized resource for describing, understanding, and crafting interventions aimed at crime problems. Mapping and other information-collecting and -ordering techniques, usually aimed at formal police data, can also be used to good effect to capture and organize these experiential assets. This chapter describes one such exercise carried out as part of a project to apply problem-solving techniques to youth gun violence and gun markets in Boston. A working group comprised of Harvard University researchers, police officers from the Boston Police Department's Youth Violence Strike Force, probation officers covering high-risk neighborhoods, and city-employed gang-mediation "street workers": estimated the number and size of the city's gangs; mapped their turf; mapped their antagonisms and alliances; and classified five years of youth victimization events according to their connection (or lack thereof) to this gang geography. The products of these exercises provide: a "snapshot" of Boston's gang turf; an estimate of gang involvement in high-risk neighborhoods; a sociogram of gang relationships; and an estimate of Boston gangs' direct contribution to youth homicide victimization.*

Address correspondence to: David M. Kennedy, Program in Criminal Justice Policy and Management, John F. Kennedy School of Government, Harvard University, 79 John F. Kennedy Street, Cambridge, MA 02138 (e-mail: David Kennedy@harvard.edu).

INTRODUCTION

The experience, observations, local knowledge, and historical perspective of working police officers and others with routine contact with offenders, communities, and criminal organizations may represent an important underutilized resource for describing, understanding, and crafting interventions aimed at crime problems. Mapping and other information-collecting and -ordering techniques that are usually aimed at formal police data can also be used to good effect to capture and organize these experiential assets. These possibilities include, but are not limited to, "hot-spot" mapping and place-focused intervention. In particular, the identification and analysis of networks hold promise. This paper describes one such exercise carried out as part of a U.S. National Institute of Justice (NIJ)-funded project to apply problem-solving techniques to youth gun violence in Boston.[1] A working group comprised of Harvard University researchers, police officers from the Boston Police Department's Youth Violence Strike Force, probation officers covering high-risk neighborhoods, and city-employed gang-mediation "street workers": estimated the number and size of the city's gangs; mapped their turf; mapped their antagonisms and alliances; and classified five years of youth homicide victimization events according to their connection (or lack thereof) to gangs. The products of these exercises provide: a "snapshot" of Boston's gang turf; an estimate of gang involvement in high-risk neighborhoods; a sociogram of gang relationships; and an estimate of Boston gangs' direct contribution to youth homicide victimization. These products can be combined powerfully with more traditional mapping and network analysis tools and approaches. Such "knowledge-based mapping" is arguably an important contribution to understanding and intervening in crime and public safety problems.

The Current State of Mapping in Police Departments

Crime mapping and spatial analyses have existed in police departments since the beginning of modern policing (Durbak and Rengert, 1993). Manual pin maps of crime and traffic accidents have a very long history. Automated or computerized mapping has developed over the past 25 years in police agencies. In the last few years it has expanded substantially due to: the growing movement toward a more analytic "problem-solving" style of policing; academic interest in hot spots of geographically concentrated crime; the support of the federal government; and significant advances in microcomputer technology (McEwen and Taxman, 1995). A recent poll by the International Association of Chiefs of Police revealed that 30% of 280 police departments in its Law Enforcement Management Information Section regularly use mapping software (Rich, 1995).

Academics have been instrumental in the proliferation of crime mapping and spatial analysis within police departments, as researchers have formed partnerships with police agencies to use mapping to better understand and respond to urban crime problems. Toward this end, the NIJ has funded partnerships between researchers and police departments to implement and assess map-based crime analysis systems such as the Microcomputer-Assisted Police Analysis and Deployment System in Chicago (Maltz et al., 1991), and the five-site Drug Market Analysis Program (DMAP) in Jersey City, NJ, San Diego, Pittsburgh, Kansas City, and Hartford (U.S. National Institute of Justice, 1989; Maltz, 1993).

Applications of mapping and spatial analyses to decision making within police agencies vary depending upon the role of the user. Planners and administrators use maps to inform decisions on deployment, such as determining the number of officers or patrol cars to assign to a certain district or a particular shift (Durbak and Rengert, 1993). Detectives and police investigators use mapping techniques to analyze crime location patterns and to solve complex serial crimes (see Rossmo, 1995). As police departments move toward a problem-solving model of policing, patrol officers can use maps to good effect in identifying trouble spots on their beats and the times of the day these locations are likely to be most active. The Chicago Police Department's Information Collection for Automated Mapping (ICAM) program is an important part of the department's community policing program known as the Chicago Alternative Policing Strategy program. ICAM displays current crime and community conditions, and allows police officers to design custom crime maps and obtain lists of the top crime problems within a specific beat (Rich, 1995).

MAPPING TECHNIQUES AND THE IDENTIFICATION OF URBAN PROBLEMS: A FOCUS ON PLACES, AND PLACE-FOCUSED INTERVENTIONS

Computerized mapping is valued by practitioners and scholars as a powerful tool for identifying crime problems and developing crime control and prevention programs. To date, mapping has been utilized almost entirely in support of place-focused diagnoses and interventions. Maps' innate geographic character have combined with the recent academic interest in hot spots to generate this result. Research on the distribution of crime across city landscapes has revealed that crime does not occur evenly; rather, it is concentrated in relatively small places or hot spots that generate more than half of crime events (Pierce et al., 1988; Sherman et al., 1989; Weisburd et al., 1992). Place-focused interventions based on this insight have demonstrated impressive crime-control results. As part of the Jersey City DMAP a randomized experimental evaluation of a place-oriented drug enforcement strategy found significant reductions in disorder-related calls for service in the target areas, with little evidence of displacement (Weisburd and Green, 1994). The Minneapolis Hot Spots Patrol Experiment revealed that 250% more police presence in the treatment locations produced a 13% overall reduction in reported crime, and a 50% reduction in researcher observations of disorder when compared to control locations (Sherman and Weisburd, 1995).

Geographic mapping applications, particularly when linked to other law enforcement databases, and their associated statistical tools can identify hot-spot locations and generate a wealth of valuable information on their temporal variations, offender characteristics, and victim characteristics. Early geographic analyses of offense locations organized street addresses by the frequency of activity, such as calls for service (see Pierce et al., 1988; Sherman, 1987), and distinguished hot spots by identifying those addresses that produced the highest number of events. Although such analyses were appropriate for certain types of interventions, they did not define hot-spot areas, as a single address may or may not be located within a high-density crime area (Block, 1993). Further, address-level analyses are sensitive to coding errors and short movements of offenders around a specific area (Weisburd and Green, 1995). Crime analysts and researchers sought more sophisticated ways of analyzing their data.

The development of such mapping techniques has progressed immensely over the past ten years. Since the mapping of a large number of data points typically results in a cluttered, uninterpretable map (Maltz et al., 1991), different methods of distinguishing clusters of crime events have developed. Data-driven techniques to identify hot spots of crime range from thematic mapping to very complex point-pattern analyses. Thematic mapping, also known as areal analysis, identifies the density of crime events within arbitrary boundaries such as police reporting areas or Census tracts (Block, 1993). Although policy makers can distinguish areas that experience disproportionate numbers of crimes and target these areas for interventions, areal maps suffer from interpretation problems such as aggregation bias (see Brantingham and Brantingham, 1984). The crime within a "hot" arbitrary areal unit can be concentrated within a very small area, such as a street block. Alternatively, the actual dense area can be divided by boundary lines, diluting the magnitude of the crime problem across areas. These limitations can cause interventions to be mistakenly applied to whole neighborhoods when, in fact, the reality of crime clustering would suggest a much more geographically focused application. Conversely, the limitations can cause actual hot spots to be diluted and therefore missed entirely.

In an effort to better find and describe hot-spot areas, the Illinois Criminal Justice Information Authority developed a software package called Spatial and Temporal Analysis of Crime (STAC). Regardless of artificial boundaries, this program provides a quick way to summarize point data, via complex algorithms, into ellipses drawn around the densest clusters of crime on the map (Block and Block, 1993). STAC is currently being used by at least 69 police departments and continues to be developed (Rich, 1995).

Whatever the means used to identify hot spots, the resulting intervention strategies have almost invariably been place-focused. This is sufficiently true that place-focused strategies have been treated both in practice and in the literature as the only ones feasible. According to Spelman (1995), much of the concentration of crime — for instance, youth crime — at specific places is due to random and temporary fluctuations; police can therefore control about 50% of crime at a particular place through focused problem-solving interventions. "[O]perational personnel need specific objectives that can be reasonably achieved, and at least a rough idea of when to quit. For example, if problem-solving can realistically reduce crime by, say, 40% in some locations, then line officers and neighborhood organizations err if they quit after a 10% reduction — there are many gains left on the table. They also err if they persist after a 38% reduction — there is little left to accomplish, and they could probably achieve more if they took on a different problem" (Spelman, 1995:135-137).

This logic, particularly the last statement, makes sense only as long as the problem-solving strategies in question are focused on the characteristics of the particular places in question. A problem-solving strategy with a different frame of reference could have a much more profound impact (or, of course, one much less profound). An effective youth strategy combining, for example, recreation programs with a curfew might reduce all youth misbehavior, and would therefore necessarily reduce youth misbehavior in hot spots, perhaps beyond what could be achieved through place-focused strategies. At the same time, hot-spot analysis, including mapping, could be an important input into the design and implementation of such strategies.[2] It is important to remember, therefore, that there is no logical reason why hot-spot problems should necessarily be addressed through place-focused interventions.

Neither is there any logical reason that mapping applications should be limited to geographic phenomena, hot-spot analysis, or hot spot/place-focused intervention strategies. For example, many cities have problems with delinquent groups, particularly youth violence fueled by conflicts between gangs (Curry et al., 1994). The resulting crime and disorder problems often exhibit geographic concentration, and mapping can identify hot spots of youth violence. However, such analyses reveal nothing of the violent youth groups, or their conflict networks, that exist across the city. Identifying gangs and understanding the nature of their conflicts could be instrumental in preventing or responding to flare-ups of violence. Interventions focused on serious offenders, violent groups, patterns of conflict, and weapons all hold promise and could reduce violence, including violence concentrated in hot spots.

Criminal network maps and analyses are obvious alternative applications of mapping technology in the problem-solving process. Criminal networks can range from local youth gangs to narcotics organizations to terrorist groups; all represent significant challenges to federal, state, and local law enforcement agencies. A variety of analytic tools and concepts — Anacapa charting systems, computerized link analyses, template matching, event flow charts, and telephone toll analyses — are currently used to examine criminal organizations (Sparrow, 1991). These techniques can be potent tools for combating criminal groups, but are currently utilized primarily by federal law enforcement agencies with respect to more or less traditional organized crime and narcotics trafficking problems. They are underutilized by police agencies with regard to other crime problems. Further, the current state of the art is relatively unsophisticated. Criminal intelligence analysis can be improved by the developing field of structural network analysis, and computerized network analysis programs hold much promise in identifying vulnerabilities, such as central players and weak links, within criminal networks (see Sparrow, 1991).

Other possibilities include the use of mapping to monitor parolees, probationers, and repeat sex offenders (see Rich, 1995) and victims and victim locations (Farrell, 1995). Police agencies have creatively used mapping to solve specific, and often uncommon, problems such as serial murder and rape (Rossmo, 1995; LeBeau, 1992), but rarely use such applications systematically to track potential or more routine existing problems. Mapping can provide an opportunity for technological support for these other problem frames, but the problem-solving frameworks and supporting computer applications both need additional development.

DATA AND INFORMATION RESOURCES

Along with the focus on hot spots and place-focused interventions, mapping has to date relied largely on formal police data. For example, the designers of the Repeat Call Address Policing experiment in Minneapolis avoided using police officers to identify persistent problem addresses for three reasons: "(1) the potential criticism as discriminatory law enforcement; (2) its susceptibility to police officers' pet peeves to the exclusion of major consumers of police resources or major sources of bloodshed; (3) the potential for selection bias in evaluations, resulting from the picking of easier to solve problems" (Buerger, 1994: footnote 3). The result of approaches such as these has been that mapping techniques have been almost totally reliant on official police data. However, such data are known to have important shortcomings. Arrest and investigation data are subject to both underreporting and enforcement bias (Black, 1970). While citizen calls for service are not as affected by police discretion, these data are also subject to both underreporting and overreporting (Pierce et al., 1988; Sherman et al., 1989). No currently available routine reporting systems are good sources of information on disorder and fear (Kennedy and Moore, 1995). Therefore, mapping techniques that rely exclusively on the analysis of official data have their own inherent biases and limits. They also run, to some extent, against the tide of community and problem-solving policing, which seek to manage officer discretion rather than deny it and to promote and benefit from line officers' creativity and problem-solving capacity (Goldstein, 1990; Sparrow et al., 1990; Kennedy and Moore, 1995).

There has been some expansion of mapping analyses to include data from non-police sources. The Illinois Criminal Justice Information Authority developed an extensive geographic database of both community and law enforcement data known as the GeoArchive. The Authority suggests that when combined with a community/problem-solving policing program, a GeoArchive can become "an information foundation for community policing" (Block and Green, 1994:1). A variety of data are collected: street map data; official crime data (calls for service, arrests, offender characteristics, victim characteristics); corrections data (the addresses of persons released on probation or parole); landmark data (parks, schools, public transportation); and population information (Block and Green, 1994). The Chicago Police Department's ICAM system is connected to the city's mainframe computer and provides police officers with the locations of abandoned buildings, businesses, and liquor stores (Rich, 1995). Several multi-agency task forces, such as Denver's PACT (Pulling America's Communities Together) program, have integrated and mapped data to identify risk factors for delinquency in crafting broad, multi-disciplinary solutions to reduce violence (Rich, 1995). These types of information-gathering efforts can be invaluable to police officers and others analyzing urban crime problems and developing appropriate interventions at the local, district, or citywide level.

Even these efforts rely almost entirely on official data collected by public agencies. There have been some exceptions to this rule. For example, in Jersey City, the police department's Planning and Research Bureau and Rutgers University researchers "counted," or assigned, official data to street segments or intersection areas, rather than at specific addresses or larger "areal" units such as police reporting areas. Once the initial counting was complete and the top crime intersection areas were established, these researchers consulted other data sources in determining the groupings of these units into the boundaries of high-activity crime places. In the DMAP, community survey responses and phoned-in citizen tips on narcotics trafficking were used to supplement official data in the identification of drug markets (Weisburd and Green, 1994). Jersey City's pilot problem-oriented policing program to control high-activity violent crime places made use of the observations of Rutgers researchers and the Jersey City Police Department's Violent Crimes Unit officers to identify place boundaries. A wide array of intersection area-level data were considered in defining high-activity crime places, including officers' perceptions of violent crime problems, community perceptions of violent crime problems, physical characteristics, and social characteristics (Braga et al., 1995).

However, some of the richest information for describing public safety problems and driving problem-solving efforts simply is not available from any official data systems. The "experiential assets" of practitioners and community members can make potentially powerful contributions to identifying and understanding crime problems. In particular, qualitative methods such as ethnography, interviews, focus groups, and survey research can supply valuable information.

For communities suffering from violence involving delinquent groups, for example, intelligence on the social networks within groups and the antagonisms between rival groups is important for addressing violent crime in affected neighborhoods. Qualitative methods are appropriate and desirable techniques to collect the relational data on contacts, ties, connections of groups, and group attachments of individuals within networks (Scott, 1991).

Particularly closely linked to crime mapping and hot-spot approaches is cognitive mapping. Cognitive maps represent perceptions of spatial reality (see Smith and Patterson, 1980; Gould and White, 1974) by individuals on such dimensions as street gang territories, drug market areas, and other geographic phenomena. Criminologists have advocated the use of cognitive maps based on the perceptions of law enforcement personnel and community members to enhance community problem-solving efforts within neighborhoods and specific places (see Block and Green, 1994). A key notion in cognitive mapping is that it is the perception of an individual (or the perceptions of individuals) that is being mapped; the resulting construct may or may not have anything meaningful to say about reality. New knowledge, however, can sometimes be gained from the mapping exercise itself, and also from important consistencies and discrepancies between qualitative and official data (Rosenbaum and Lavrakas, 1995). These concepts have been sparsely used in support of crime control and problem-solving exercises; some notable exceptions include the mapping of gang turf based on police officer perceptions in Chicago (Block and Block, 1993), and the identification of problem locations within buildings and common areas by housing project residents in Jersey City (Terrill and Green, 1995).

Both academics and police practitioners have been reluctant to incorporate these methods into easily used mapping approaches and computer applications. Some argue that the subjective assessments of practitioners are not accurate; for example, psychiatrists' ability to predict "dangerous" persons has been found to be minimal (Monahan, 1981; Ennis and Litwack, 1974). Mainstream police administration, and many academic approaches to police and public safety research, have long discounted the views of line police officers as partial, biased, and of no great utility (Goldstein, 1990; Sparrow et al., 1990; Braga et al., 1994). At the same time, many police officers feel that their knowledge and expertise are essentially ineffable — that, in the words of James Fyfe, "It's just something you learn over time, is all" (as quoted in Toch and Grant, 1991:41). Neither attitude — that police officers know nothing, and that police knowledge is irredeema-

bly particular and uncommunicable — lends itself to collecting, testing, and analyzing practitioner knowledge.

However, others feel that practitioners, particularly police officers,
develop rich pictures of their environment and can provide accurate
and valid assessments of area characteristics, crime problems, and
criminal activity (Bittner, 1970; Braga et al., 1994). In Egon Bittner's
classic phrase, some officers know "the shops, stores, warehouses,
restaurants, hotels, schools, playgrounds, and other public places in
such a way that they can recognize at a glance whether what is going
on within them is within the range of normalcy" (1970: 90). These
perceptions sharpen and improve as police mature in their careers
and gain experience (Rubinstein, 1973; Muir, 1977). A rigorous examination of the assessments of experienced narcotics officers relative to other, more formal, measures of drug activity found that the
officers were highly capable of identifying street drug activity based
on quite brief exposures (Braga et al., 1994). To date, though, most
mapping exercises, geographic/hot-spot focused or otherwise, do not
rely heavily on the systematic gathering, analysis, and application of
information from practitioner or community sources. This is an important, but largely unexplored, frontier (Toch and Grant, 1991).

THE BOSTON GUN PROJECT

The authors have been exploring ways to capture the experiential
assets of practitioners, and to incorporate them in the design and
implementation of problem-solving interventions, as part of the Boston Gun Project. The Boston Gun Project is a problem-solving exercise aimed at preventing youth violence in Boston by: convening an
interagency working group; performing original research into Boston's youth violence problem and illicit gun markets; crafting a city-
wide, interagency problem-solving strategy; implementing that strategy; and evaluating the strategy's impact. Key participants in the
project have included gang officers from the Boston Police Department, probation officers whose jurisdictions incorporate those Boston
neighborhoods at high risk for youth gun violence, and city-employed
"streetworkers" — outreach specialists focused on preventing and
mediating gang disputes and diverting youths from gangs.

It was evident from the beginning of the project that these practitioners knew a great deal about kids, gangs, and youth violence in
Boston. In ride-alongs with probation officers through high-risk
neighborhoods, for example, the officers could point out gang turf
with great specificity, describe how turf and turf patterns had

changed over time, trace the history of specific gangs and gang members, describe the criminal activities of particular gangs, and trace the emergence and decline of particular gang-related activities such as wearing particular colors and marking turf with sneakers. Boston Police Department gang officers had a vivid sense of current and historical patterns of gang criminality and conflict, and of gangs' responses to particular police strategies. Streetworkers had insight into all these matters, plus perspective on how gang members and other youths experienced life in their neighborhoods. This included gang members' experience of the threat of other gangs, and how they regarded police and other authorities.

These different groups of practitioners were focused on the same basic issue — in essence, serious youth offending and serious youth offenders — and had a certain amount of experience working with one other. Therefore, their sources of information overlapped to some degree. However, the groups worked from bases of experience that were meaningfully different. Probation officers worked with the courts and convicted offenders, and to some extent with offenders' families, employers, and other community contacts. The probation officers we worked with had also recently begun to "patrol" certain communities at night in conjunction with Boston Police Department gang officers in an effort to control the behavior of high-risk youth offenders in the community. Police gang officers primarily worked the streets, primarily in an adversarial relationship with youth offenders, and had access to police department information. Streetworkers worked closely with individual youths and groups of youths, both in the street and through city-sponsored diversion and recreation programs.

As the project progressed, several key questions emerged regarding the role of gangs and gang conflict in Boston's youth homicide problem. Practitioners felt strongly that several things were true. They believed that Boston had youth gangs, which had identifiable turf and were violent. They believed that the youth homicide problem was almost entirely a gang problem, that essentially all youth homicide offenders were gang members and that essentially all youth homicide victims — excluding innocent bystanders — were gang members. They believed that the basic dynamic that produced gang violence was a vendetta-like "beef" between gangs that was sometimes but not always initiated by drug trafficking or some other instrumental issue, but that once initiated took on a life of its own and could continue indefinitely and even intergenerationally. The authors, in response to this, framed the following essential questions. What was the contribution of gangs to youth homicides in the city? How many gangs and gang-involved youths were there in Boston? Where were gangs' turfs? What were the patterns of conflict and alliance among gangs?

We worked with our practitioner partners to answer these questions in a structured way that would both bring rigor to the analysis and be of utility in designing and implementing a problem-solving response. The following sections describe some of the methods used and the results obtained. We present our various research activities in their proper order of *logical* precedence; the actual research was a bundle of overlapping and simultaneous tasks conducted over roughly the summer of 1995.

Did Boston Have a Gang-Related Youth Homicide Problem?

The central matter was clearly whether youth gangs were important contributors to the city's youth homicide problem. We began, therefore, by addressing this question.

It is noteworthy that this was a question that simply could not have been answered by examining official police records. The Homicide Bureau of the Boston Police Department records as little as possible about the motive in the cases it investigates in order to prevent creating documentation that would be discoverable and of potential use to the defense at trial. The Homicide Bureau has, quite recently, begun issuing annual reports of how many of the previous year's homicides were gang-related, drug-related, domestic, and the like. It does not identify which particular cases belong in these categories, however, and it compiles the reports by polling homicide investigation teams about their previous year's caseload. The bureau's reports, in other words, are themselves based on qualitative methods.

We assessed the contribution of gangs to Boston's youth homicide problem by assembling a group comprised of Boston Police Department gang officers; probation officers; and streetworkers. This group met in three sessions of approximately four hours each.[3] Those participating changed somewhat from session to session, with constant participation by four police officers, one streetworker, and two probation officers, and episodic participation by approximately half a dozen police officers, two streetworkers, and one probation officer.

The authors provided documentary support and kept records of the proceedings.[4] Documentary support consisted of an annualized, alphabetized list of 155 gun and knife homicide victims (that is, each calendar year's victims arranged in alphabetical order) age 21 and under for the years 1990-1994.[5] The list included the names of associated cleared offenders where those names were available; a separate list featured incident locations arranged by victims' names in alphabetical order. Both lists were prepared by the authors using information furnished by the Planning and Research Office of the Boston Police Department. Each participant was provided with this package of documents.

The group examined and discussed each incident of victimization, beginning with the 1994 list and proceeding backward in time. The discussion ranged quite freely but was structured by the authors. For each victimization, the following questions were addressed in roughly the following order. Do you (the group) know what happened in this homicide? Was the victim a gang member? Was the perpetrator (or perpetrators) a gang member (or members)? What was the killing about, and was it gang-related?

As these questions suggest, it took more than gang involvement on either the victim's or perpetrator's part for the incident to "count" as gang-related. The authors did not provide, or press, any particular definition of "gang-related" on the group, though they did sometimes make the formal disposition based on the group discussion. For the most part, however, the practitioners participating had a strong and shared, though often not previously articulated, sense of what it meant for an incident to be gang-related, and this sense was allowed to emerge inductively through the process.

Gang-related, as the group understood it, meant in practice that the incident was either the product of gang behavior such as drug dealing, turf protection, or a continuing "beef" with a rival gang or gangs, or a product of activity that was narrowly and directly connected with gang membership such as a struggle for power within a particular gang. Not all homicide involvement by gang members counted under this definition. A homicide committed by a gang member in the course of an armed robbery of a store, with no other indication of gang-relatedness, would not have been classified as gang-related. The homicide victimization of a gang member, for instance during a street robbery, with no other indication of gang-relatedness, would also not have been classified as gang-related.[6]

The authors also did not provide, or press, a definition of gang on the group.[7] It was clear that violent behavior was central to the conception the practitioners in fact used; during the gang-mapping process, described below, much the same set of participants not infrequently made remarks such as "[group in question] isn't a gang any more, they just sell drugs." In practice, all practitioners used a definition that could be reduced to "self-identified group of kids who act corporately (at least sometimes) and violently (at least sometimes)." "Gang" has much the same place, therefore, in this process that "crime report" has in more traditional mapping operations: though the extent of the connection between the referent and reality is difficult to determine, all participants agree that it has meaning and what that meaning is.

It is worth dwelling on this point. Our process was not intended to, and could not, answer the question "Does Boston have a gang problem?" To do so would have required coming up with a workable definition of gang; ascertaining whether Boston had, by this definition, gangs; and then determining whether Boston's gangs were a problem, with "problem" defined in some way that was independent of the existence of gangs as such. This last step is particularly difficult conceptually; since criminal and violent activity is generally part of the definition of a gang (see, e.g., Miller, 1975), it is hard even in principle to sort out how to differentiate description from diagnosis when discussing "gang violence."

This was not the subject of our inquiry. Though the definition of gang actually used by practitioners is well within the bounds of standard police and academic practice, it is here used essentially as a placeholder conveying no additional information about the nature of gangs in Boston. Our main question could be reframed equally well as "Does Boston have a homicide problem connected to [this youth group phenomenon we have agreed to call gangs]?" We were interested in whether Boston's gangs — gangs as defined by those who worked with them — were an important contributor to the city's youth homicide problem.

Of the 155 victimizations, 107, or 69%, were "known": that is, practitioners could provide an account of what happened. Ninety incidents, or 58% of the total 155 victimizations, were classified by the group as gang-related. All "unknown" incidents were classified as non-gang-related. Seventeen, or 11%, were known but not classified as gang-related. Thus, nearly three-quarters of the incidents classified as non-gang-related were so classified because they were unknown, suggesting that our estimate of the incidence of gang-related homicide is a conservative one.

Certain aspects of this process were noteworthy and shed some light on the validity of the outcomes. There was nearly total consensus across the various practitioner participants concerning what should be classified as known and unknown. There was also nearly total consensus as to what had actually happened in known incidents. These broad agreements could be construed as an unhappy, and falsifying, unwillingness to disagree. We are inclined to construe it otherwise. First, the process itself ran counter in important ways to representations practitioners had already made. They had argued that virtually all youth homicides were gang-related, and that they were familiar with the background of virtually all youth homicides. When the process showed neither proposition to be entirely accurate, the practitioners neither fought it nor indulged in obvious opportunities to "game" the process, for instance, by misclassifying incidents. We are therefore inclined to believe that the various practitioners did in fact know what they said they knew about particular incidents; that there was a genuinely high degree of agreement among members of different agencies, who relied to some extent on different sources of information; and that the results of the process are reasonably reliable.

This exercise therefore produced an assessment that at least 60% of Boston's gun and knife youth homicides over five years were gang-related. In our view, that was sufficient to constitute a gang-related youth homicide problem.

Mapping Gangs and Gang Turf, Estimating Membership, and Identifying Antagonisms and Alliances

Next, we wanted to know how many gangs there were in Boston; what their names, sizes, and turfs were; and what antagonisms and alliances they had. We worked with much the same set of practitioners to answer these questions.

This exercise took three sessions, totaling some ten hours. The first session included only police officers; the second two also included probation officers and streetworkers. The process was extremely straightforward. The practitioners were assembled around a 4'x 8' street map of Boston and asked to identify the territories of individual gangs. As each gang territory was identified, practitioners would draw the territory's boundaries on the map, and one of the authors would number it and record the name of the gang on a separate document.[8] When the territory had been defined, the practitioners were asked to estimate the number of members belonging to the gang. Last, a circle enclosing the numerical gang identifier was drawn on a sheet of flip-chart paper, and the practitioners were asked to name any gangs with whom the instant gang had antagonisms or alliances. These "vectors" were drawn on the flip chart paper, with

one color representing antagonisms and another alliances. Antagonisms that were at the time particularly active were so designated.

There was strong agreement among practitioners about what
gangs were active in the city. There was a considerable amount of
discussion, sparked by examination of the map and the desire to
identify enemies and allies, about whether particular gangs that had
been historically active were still so. These discussions invariably
were resolved in a consensus. There was strong agreement among the
practitioners about both turf boundaries and antagonisms/alliances.
Police officers and probation officers tended to agree on size estimates, with streetworkers offering marginally higher estimates.

The results produced a geographic territory map for the 61 gangs
identified (Figure 1); estimates of membership size; and sociograms of
antagonisms and alliances. Membership estimates totaled between
1,100 and 1,300 youths, only about 3% of those in the affected
neighborhoods.[9] Only a few gangs reached the 60-100 range, with
membership of less than ten not uncommon (see Table 1). The conflict and alliance data were digitized and presented in network form
using KrackPlot 1.7 (Krackhardt et al.,1993); this program facilitates
the drawing of a network's nodes and lines, and creates a corresponding data matrix of relationships. (The data matrix can then be
imported into network analysis software packages such as GRADAP,
STRUCTURE, and UCINET for further analyses, as will be treated
below.) On quick inspection, there appear to be several noteworthy
features of the resulting networks (see Figures 2, 3, and 4). Conflicts
outnumber alliances; certain particularly significant "nodes" (Castlegate, Academy) seem evident; and more or less pervasive, but (at any
given time) quiescent, rivalries outnumber "live" and active rivalries.

Network Analysis and Computer-Based Network Analysis Applications

The nature of this gang network, and the network as a focus of
interventions to reduce serious youth violence, became a central concern as the Boston Gun Project progressed. The research described
above, plus other research that showed both homicide victimization
and offending to be concentrated among high-rate criminal offenders

Figure 1: Boston Gang Areas

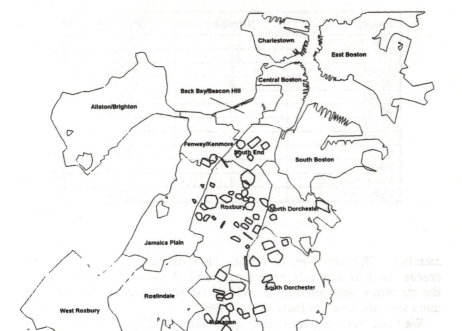

(see Kennedy et al., 1996) made the design of an intervention to reduce gang violence and gang conflict a top priority. Two key ideas emerged: to "tax" gangs for violent activity through focused attention to all their criminal activity, probation and parole conditions, and the like; and to enhance the deterrent impact of this intervention by explicitly communicating the new "rules" in the city to gangs and gang

Table 1: Distribution of Estimated Gang Membership

Range	Number	Percent
Less than 10	11	18.0%
10-19	21	34.4%
20-29	7	11.5%
30-39	8	13.1%
40-49	1	1.6%
50-59	2	3.3%
60-69	2	3.3%
70-79	0	0.0%
80-89	0	0.0%
90-99	1	1.6%
More than 100	1	1.6%
Unknown	7	11.5%

members. The aim was to reduce violence in the community; decrease the fear the kids experience; and throw a "firebreak" across the currently self-sustaining cycle of violence, gun acquisition, and more violence (see Kennedy et al., 1996).

We thus faced two important questions: (1) Which gangs would be the most efficient to target if police agencies wanted to disrupt key sources of conflict? (2) How could we best diffuse the deterrent message across Boston's gang landscape? These are network analysis questions (Sparrow, 1991). We approached them utilizing UCINET IV network analysis software (Borgatti, Everett and Freeman, 1992).

The theoretical concept of "centrality" is clearly important for identifying those gangs that are somehow pivotal or key in the conflict network.[10] "Central" gangs are strategic to target for intervention because their removal will reduce more conflict than targeting peripheral groups. The simplest and most straightforward way to measure centrality is to determine the "degree" of the various nodes in the network. The degree of a point is defined as the number of other points to which it is directly linked (Scott, 1991).

Figure 2: Boston Gang Conflict Network

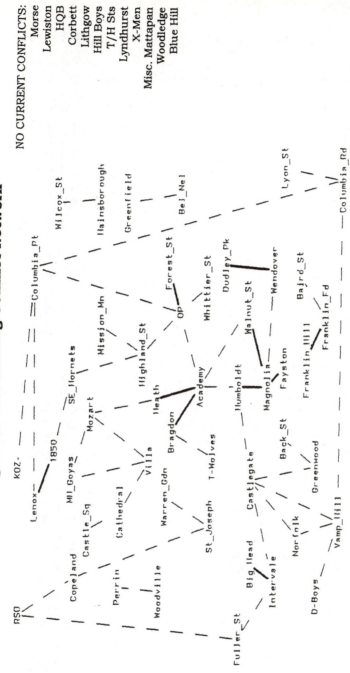

NO CURRENT CONFLICTS:
Morse
Lewiston
HQB
Corbett
Lithgow
Hill Boys
T/H Sts
Lyndhurst
X-Men
Misc. Mattapan
Woodledge
Blue Hill

Key: _ _ _ = conflict
_____ = intense conflict

237

Figure 3: Boston Gang Alliance Network

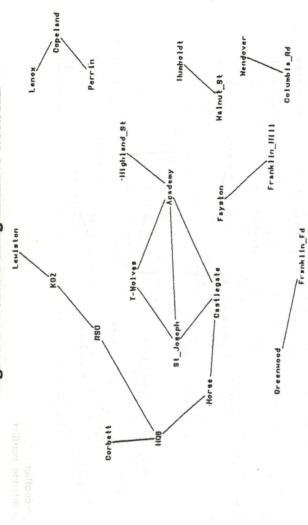

No Current Alliances: Warren Gdn., Woodville, Dudley Park, Lyon St., Back St., D-Boys, Baird St., Wilcox St., Hainsborough, Greenfield, Bel Nel, Lithgow, Mission Main, Hill Boys, T/8 Sts., Lyndhurst, X-Men, Misc Mattapan, Woodledge, Blue Hill, Mozart, Vills, MH Goyas, Heath, Cathedral, Castle Sq., 1 RSO, SE Hornets, Columbia Point, OP, Forest St., Whittier St., Bragdon, Magnolia, Intervale, Fuller St., Big Head, Norfolk, Vamp Hill

Figure 4: Boston Gang Conflict and Alliance Network

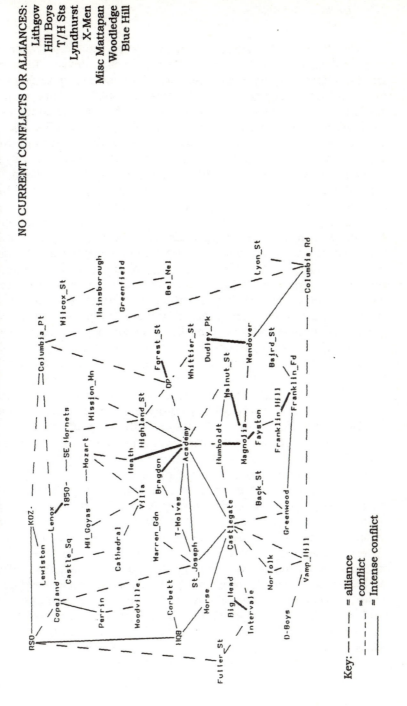

NO CURRENT CONFLICTS OR ALLIANCES:
Lithgow
Hill Boys
T/H Sts
Lyndhurst
X-Men
Misc Mattapan
Woodledge
Blue Hill

Key: ------ = alliance
- - - - = conflict
_____ = Intense conflict

UCINET and other such programs provide the capacity for quick, easy analysis of such questions. We made some simple judgments in analyzing our gang network. The conflict lines were valued according to the intensity of the conflict (values assigned: intense conflict=2, conflict=1). This allowed the weighting of more violent conflicts to be considered in the identification of central gangs. Conflict lines were also represented as non-directional, as the conflicts were not directed (in other words, a conflict between Heath and Academy is a symmetric negative association). UCINET analysis showed Magnolia, Academy, Orchard Park, and Castlegate as the gangs with the highest centrality in Boston's conflict network (see Table 2).

Degrees are measures of "local centrality": the relative importance of a node within its social neighborhood. A more sophisticated assessment of the importance of a particular gang within the conflict would take into account the centrality of the points to which it is connected (Bonacich, 1972).[11] In other words, certain gangs may be more central or pivotal ("in the thick of things") to youth violence across Boston than other gangs that have the same degree of connections.[12] Network theory uses the concept of "eigenvector centrality" to capture this quality of "centrality of centrality."[13] UCINET analysis of eigenvector centralities reveals Magnolia, Academy, Humboldt, Walnut Street, Fayston Street, Heath, Bragdon Street, Orchard Park, Wendover, and Castlegate to be key players in the conflict network (see Table 3). Probably not coincidentally, these are gangs that consistently come up in conversation with our practitioner partners as the most significant and troublesome. Reducing their violence, and their "beefs" with other gangs, would make sensible first steps in an intervention focused on Boston's gang landscape.

We also used structural network analysis in pursuit of support for an effective communications strategy. Here, UCINET was employed to identify naturally existing subgroups, or "cliques," such that "talking" to one member would effectively be talking to all members.[14] Network theory defines cliques as groups of mutually connected individuals or as pockets of dense connections (Knoke and Kuklinski, 1982). If Magnolia, for example, were subjected to an intensive enforcement effort, or was otherwise communicated with — for instance, through probation officers or formal meetings between gang members and authorities — which other gangs could be expected to be aware of the message being sent by law enforcement agencies?

Table 2: Degree Centrality [a]

Gang	Degree	Normalized Degree[b]
Magnolia	7.00	11.67
Academy	7.00	11.67
Orchard Park	6.00	10.00
Castlegate	5.00	8.33
Intervale Posse	4.00	6.67
Humboldt	4.00	6.67
Columbia Point Dogs	4.00	6.67
Vamp Hill Kings	4.00	6.67
Mozart	3.00	5.00
1850 Building Boys	3.00	5.00
Lenox Hill Smokers	3.00	5.00
Villa Victoria	3.00	5.00
Heath	3.00	5.00
Wendover Falcons	3.00	5.00
Highland Street	3.00	5.00
Walnut Street	3.00	5.00
Columbia Road	3.00	5.00
Bragdon Street	3.00	5.00
Franklin Field	3.00	5.00
Big Head Boys	2.00	3.33
Dudley Park	2.00	3.33
Norfolk Kings	2.00	3.33
Franklin Hill Giants	2.00	3.33
Fuller Street	2.00	3.33
RSO	2.00	3.33
Fayston Street	2.00	3.33
Greenwood Street	2.00	3.33
St. Joseph	2.00	3.33
Forest Street Dodgers	2.00	3.33
South End Hornets	2.00	3.33
Copeland	2.00	3.33
Mission Hill Goyas	2.00	3.33
Cathedral	2.00	3.33
KOZ	1.00	1.67
D-Boys	1.00	1.67
Baird Street	1.00	1.67
Wilcox Street	1.00	1.67
Hainsborough	1.00	1.67
Greenfield	1.00	1.67
Bel Nel	1.00	1.67
Mission Main	1.00	1.67
Back Street Boys	1.00	1.67
Warren Gardens	1.00	1.67
Timberwolves	1.00	1.67

242 — *David M. Kennedy et al.*

Gang	Degree	Normalized Degree[b]
Whittier Street	1.00	1.67
Perrin Street	1.00	1.67
Woodville	1.00	1.67
Lyon Street	1.00	1.67
Castle Square	1.00	1.67

(a) The links between nodes were coded as follows: one=conflict; two=intense conflict.

(b) The normalized degree centrality of each gang is the degree divided by the maximum possible degree (number of connections within the sociogram) expressed as a percentage (Borgatti et al. 1992).

Many different theoretical models exist for identifying subgroups within networks.[15] We explored the n-clan technique for identifying cliques, as it is acknowledged as yielding "the most useful and powerful sociological generalization" of cohesive subgroupings[16] (Scott, 1991:120). The n-clan method is regarded as desirable because it limits the diameter (the path between its most distant members) to be no greater than the value of n which defined the clique. In other words, it ensures relatively close linkages by eliminating outsiders as intermediaries. Two was selected, by convention, as the value of n. Path lengths greater than two risk involving more distant and weak links. As Scott (1991) argues, "Values greater than two can be difficult to interpret sociologically. Distance two relations can be straightforwardly interpreted as those which involve a common neighbor who, for example, may act as an intermediary or a broker" (p.119).

We restricted the algorithm, for convenience, to identify clans that had at least five members; the analysis identified 13 subgroups, with several groupings sharing common members (see Table 4). Each of these cliques would make a useful target for communication strategies since a message to one group would effectively reach at least five groups. Gangs that are common to several cliques, such as Academy, would make particularly useful targets.

Table 3: Bonacich Centrality[a]

Gang	Eigenvector	Normalized Eigenvector
Magnolia	0.509	71.957
Academy	0.437	61.856
Humboldt	0.383	54.117
Walnut Street	0.350	49.512
Fayston Street	0.245	34.629
Heath	0.226	31.969
Bragdon Street	0.223	31.597
Orchard Park	0.186	26.309
Wendover	0.159	22.533
Castlegate	0.135	19.137
Forest Street Dodgers	0.090	12.661
Dudley Park	0.077	10.844
Mozart	0.065	9.148
Columbia Point Dogs	0.060	8.540
Timberwolves	0.054	7.603
Vamp Hill Kings	0.054	7.581
Highland Street	0.052	7.289
Intervale	0.046	6.516
Norfolk Kings	0.045	6.429
Whittier Street	0.045	6.330
Greenwood Street	0.035	4.888
Columbia Road	0.029	4.117
Big Head Boys	0.022	3.136
Villa Victoria	0.022	3.101
Lenox Street Smokers	0.021	3.011
Mission Hill Goyas	0.021	2.947
South End Hornets	0.016	2.232
KOZ	0.015	2.055
1850 Building Boys	0.014	1.986
D-Boys	0.013	1.824
Mission Main	0.012	1.754
Fuller Street	0.012	1.671
Back Street	0.008	1.176
Lyon Street	0.007	0.991
Cathedral	0.006	0.792
RSO	0.003	0.428
Castle Square	0.001	0.191
Copeland	0.001	0.110
St. Joseph	0.000	0.028
Warren Garden	0.000	0.007

(a) The normalized eigenvector is the "scaled eigenvector centrality divided by the maximum difference possible expressed as a percentage" (Borgatti et al., 1992). For more discussion on eigenvector centrality, see Bonacich (1972).

Table 4: N-Clans Cliques

Clique	Gangs
1	Heath, Academy, Orchard Park, Highland St., Walnut St., Bragdon St., St. Joseph, Castlegate, Timberwolves, Humboldt
2	Academy, St. Joseph, Castlegate, Humboldt, Intervale, Norfolk Kings, Vamp Hill Kings, Greenwood, Morse
3	Academy, Copeland, St. Joseph, Castlegate, Timberwolves, Warren Garden
4	Academy, Walnut Street, Castlegate, Magnolia, Humboldt
5	Castlegate, Norfolk Kings, Vamp Hill, Columbia Rd., D-Boys
6	Lenox St., Columbia Point, Orchard Park, Columbia Rod., KOZ
7	Lenox St., Columbia Point, Copeland, RSO, KOZ
8	Lenox St., Copeland, St. Joseph, RSO, Perrin St.
9	Academy, South End Hornets, Orchard Park, Forest St., Highland St., Mission Main
10	Academy, Columbia Point, Orchard Park, Forest St., Highland St., Whittier St.
11	Columbia Point, Vamp Hill Kings, Wendover, Columbia Road, Lyon St.
12	Walnut St., Magnolia, Humboldt, Fayston, Wendover
13	Copeland, Fuller St., RSO, KOZ, HQB

Combining Qualitative and Quantitative Mapping[17]

Having produced the qualitatively-derived map of gang territories, some interesting applications of more traditional mapping techniques became possible. The gang territories were hand-digitized using MAPINFO for Windows. MAPINFO sub-routines allowed us to determine that a relatively small portion of the city of Boston is covered by the 61 gang areas: the sum total geographic expanse of the 61 areas is 1.7 square miles, only 3.6% of Boston's 47.47 square miles. Gang turf makes up only 8.1% of the area of even those Boston neighborhoods — Roxbury, Dorchester, Mattapan, Jamaica Plain, Hyde Park, and the South End — with gangs.

We geocoded 1994 Boston police department data on dimensions that might reasonably be expected to be gang-related: gun assault, weapons offenses, drug offenses, armed robbery, youth homicide and calls for service regarding "shots fired." We then examined what proportion of these reported crimes and calls occurred within and outside gang turf. Gang turf areas experience more than 12% of the city's armed robberies and roughly a quarter of all other categories (see Table 5). Armed robberies are overrepresented in gang areas by a factor of nearly 4:1 relative to the rest of the city as a whole; other categories, by a factor of around 8:1 or more. Relative to the high-crime neighborhoods in which they are found, gang areas experience greater criminal activity in ratios of from nearly 3:1 to nearly 7:1 (see Table 6).[18] Interestingly, drug offenses, which are most open to police discretion and enforcement bias, are only somewhat more overrepresented than serious violent crimes.

Several caveats should be considered in reviewing the findings. We do not take this analysis to suggest that any or all of the gang areas identified are Boston's top crime hot spots; we did not set out to identify crime hot spots in the city. Instead, we identified, for other reasons, areas with youth gangs, and examined certain aspects of those areas. Likewise, we have to date only examined the selected reported crimes noted and cannot speak to other important crimes such as sexual assault.

Nor can it be concluded from this analysis that gangs cause crime and are responsible for the high crime rates in gang areas. While this is likely true in some instances, in others it could well not be. If, for instance, a particular housing project has a high crime rate caused primarily by adults and/or outsiders and a youth gang, it would be a mistake to conclude that the youth gang alone was responsible. More work will need to be done to establish these relationships in particular places.

Nor do our crime data for the most part allow us to distinguish between incidents involving juveniles and those involving adults. This cuts two ways. To the extent that our crime data include offenses committed by adults, any link between youth gangs and crime is *overstated*: controlling gang behavior would not much affect crimes committed by adults. However, if youth gangs are responsible for a disproportionate amount of youth crime committed in the city, and if much of this youth crime is committed in gang areas, then our analysis will *understate* both the importance of gang areas and the potential utility of controlling gang behavior, since gang areas would

Table 5: Selected Crime Incidents and "Shots Fired" Calls in Gang Areas

Incident Type	Gang Areas Total	Percent of City Total	Percent of Neighborhood Total
Gun assault	216	24.1%	28.7%
Weapons offense	121	25.7%	31.1%
Drug offense	1,187	26.0%	36.7%
Armed robbery	292	12.7%	19.6%
Youth homicide*	42	27.1%	28.9%
"Shots fired" calls	789	22.0%	28.0%

*Firearm and knife homicide victims, ages 21 and under, between 1990 and 1994

Table 6: Overrepresentation Ratios of Selected Crime Incidents and "Shots Fired" Calls in Gang Areas

Incident Type	City Ratio	Neighborhood Ratio
Gun assault	8.52:1	4.58:1
Weapons offense	9.28:1	5.13:1
Drug offense	9.40:1	6.58:1
Armed robbery	3.91:1	2.76:1
Youth homicide*	10:1	4.67:1
"Shots fired" calls	7.57:1	4.36:1

*Firearm and knife homicide victims, ages 21 and under, between 1990 and 1994

then represent even more youth crime than our calculated ratios would suggest. In that case, doing something about youth gangs in gang areas would have an even greater impact on *youth* crime. Finally, of course, our data do not allow us to measure neighborhood and community fear, which may well be connected to gang areas (see Katz, 1988).

All that said, there is certainly something going on in and/or around the gang territories we have identified. Whatever it is should get some problem-solving attention, and the mix of qualitatively driven mapping and formal-data-driven mapping is a provocative and potentially useful one.

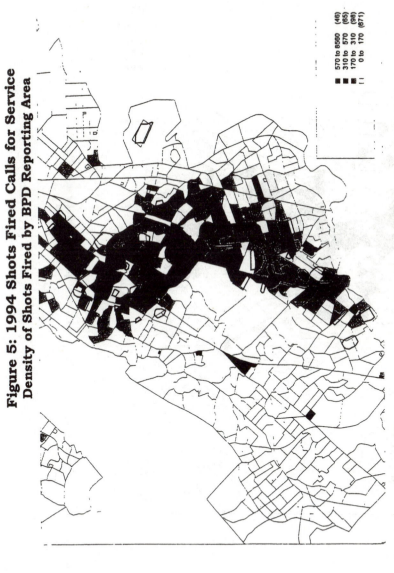

Figure 5: 1994 Shots Fired Calls for Service
Density of Shots Fired by BPD Reporting Area

■	570 to 8560	(46)
■	310 to 570	(55)
■	170 to 310	(98)
□	0 to 170	(671)

Note: Numbers are standardized; Density = Number of shots fired calls by RA Area (Sq. Mi.)

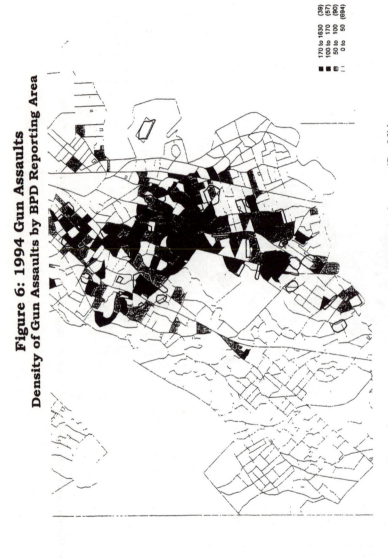

Figure 6: 1994 Gun Assaults
Density of Gun Assaults by BPD Reporting Area

	170 to 1630	(39)
	100 to 170	(57)
	50 to 100	(90)
	0 to 50	(694)

Note: Numbers are standardized; Density = Number of gun assaults by area (Sq. Mi.)

Finally, 1994 shots-fired calls for service and gun assault incidents were matched to the Boston Police Department reporting areas (RAs) from which they originated. Since RAs are of varying geographic size, we adjusted the weighting of the RAs by the RA land area in square miles.[19] This process yielded thematic maps of Boston's RAs with the densest concentration of shot-fired calls and gun assault incidents. A comparison of shots fired calls and gun assault incidents to gang areas yields an arc of high-density shots fired areas that appears to correspond almost exactly to the curve of the gang areas, with "hotter" shots-fired areas tending to cluster around gang areas and groups of gang areas (see Figures 5 and 6).[20] As an alternative method of examining the distribution of crime around the gang areas, we used the Illinois Criminal Justice Information Authority's STAC software to identify gun assault incident and shots-fired hot-spot areas.[21] The densest clusters of gun assaults and shots fired fall entirely within the arc of gang territories defined through our qualitative methods (see Figure 7). Recognizing, as always, that correlation is not causation, this is a striking result deserving further attention to assess the role of gangs and consider the possibility of both gang-focused and hot spot-focused interventions.

VALIDITY

The question remains, of course, of the validity of our qualitative methods and the resulting maps and analyses. Two main issues pertain here. One is, *how accurate is the information practitioners provided as inputs to the processes?* Another is, *what distortions might the processes themselves have imposed on the practitioner information, and thus on the products of these processes?*

On these questions, it should be noted first that mapping exercises are not themselves configured as tests of, and cannot in fact answer questions regarding, the validity of the data used as inputs or of the mapping processes themselves. A traditional police data-driven mapping exercise aimed at identifying hot spots of armed robbery is not a test of, and cannot say much regarding, the (for instance) police incident report and call-for-service data used to drive the mapping process. For this, we must turn to other considerations, such as the large body of existing literature on crime reporting and calls for service. This literature says, as we have noted, that these data have strengths and weaknesses that must be attended to in interpreting the results of mapping and other analytic exercises that employ them. But unless the mapping exercise reveals hitherto unknown

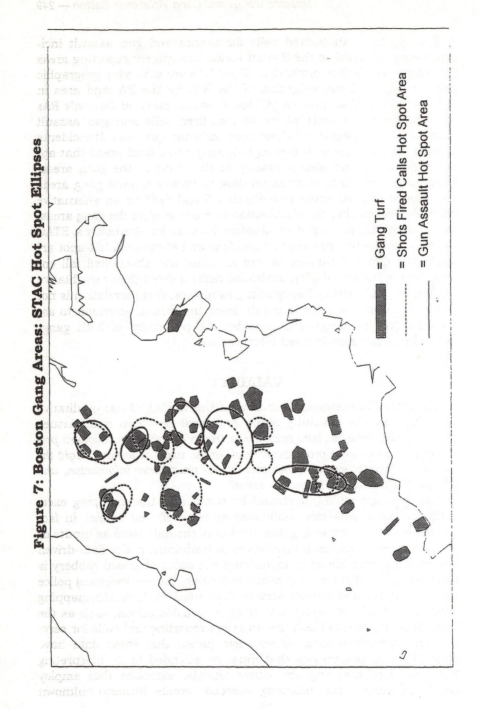

Figure 7: Boston Gang Areas: STAC Hot Spot Ellipses

= Gang Turf

= Shots Fired Calls Hot Spot Area

= Gun Assault Hot Spot Area

problems with a particular official-data data set, such as a gross lack of reported crime and calls in an area known for other reasons to have a high crime rate, it can neither add to nor detract from our understanding of the validity of the data used as inputs.

The same is true with our qualitative methods. The structured information-gathering and mapping exercises we employed cannot in and of themselves tell us very much about the validity of the practitioner information that they employed. And since we lack a literature on police practitioner information, knowledge, and perception equivalent to that on reported crime and calls for service, we have considerably less outside theory and analysis to bring to bear on interpreting our results. Nor do we have a literature on the impact various qualitative methods have on the conclusions drawn from practitioner information, knowledge, and perception. It seems to us, in fact, that these are literatures that badly need creating.

There are still some things we can say about these questions. Our results, it seems to us, have face validity. They do not show, for instance, that Boston's youth gangs are responsible for all youth homicide (or no youth homicide); that vast (or tiny) areas of the city are claimed by youth gangs; or that gangs are active in areas with no youth homicide problems (or that there are areas with serious youth homicide and other youth crime problems but no youth gangs). None of the results fall outside the bounds of what one could reasonably expect.

The findings also have a rather high degree of concurrent validity. Inputs to the processes came from, as we have noted, different agencies with different sources of information, organizational cultures, and operational experiences; the results of the processes were credible to both participants from and policy makers in these agencies. Our findings, also as noted herein, fit nicely with official Boston Police Department data on selected reported crimes and calls for service. In addition, they fit nicely with the results of other research on gang size and offending. Further, the findings fit nicely with other research we have done on the criminal histories of youth homicide victims and offenders in Boston.[22] Finally, they were credible to local practitioners not involved in the process who had their own sources of information and knowledge on the dimensions we examined.[23]

None of this, of course, makes our findings true: practitioners could have a shared, but inaccurate, view of reality, and the match between this and other research does not mean that gang realities in Boston in fact resemble those found elsewhere. To actually test the truth of our findings, we need pertinent and independent sources of information. The trouble is that that information is not available from existing official sources, nor from any other readily utilizable sources. We can work with homicide case files and investigators to construct alternative accounts of the incidents we examined, and we are in fact pursuing this avenue. But homicide investigators do not routinely concern themselves with the key gang/non-gang distinction we are addressing. Thus, they do not address this question in each of their cases, nor do they have definitions of gang and gang-related that are consistent and commensurate with those we used. We can work with gang members and community members to address the issues of gang size, gang relationships, and gang connection to homicide events, but the results of these methods, while interesting and informative, would themselves be subject to questions of validity. As with the results of mapping and other similar exercises based on official quantitative data, the rigorous testing of our results lies on the murky border between difficult and impossible.

Happily, for the purposes for which our exercises were designed, this doesn't matter very much. Our answers are good enough to make policy. They tell us with acceptable reliability whether Boston has a youth gang homicide problem — it does; how productive an effective intervention aimed at that problem could be in the context of youth homicide in the city — it could reach more than half and probably not more than 80% of such victimization; and provide some guidance as to how and where to apply group-, hot spot-, and network-focused interventions. Like more traditional official data-driven mapping tools, the answers are intended to help move the problem-solving process along, and this they do.

CONCLUSION

The exercises described in this article — assessing the contribution of Boston's youth gangs to its youth homicide problem; identifying gang territories; estimating gang memberships; identifying patterns of conflict and alliance among gangs; and analyzing the resulting products to help understand and intervene in a serious local crime problem — rely on the structured gathering of information from practitioners. These approaches represent potentially powerful additions to mapping crime and public safety problems, and to supporting the design and implementation of strategies to address those problems. Our findings indicate that alternative sources of information can be used to good effect in diagnosing and responding to crime and public safety problems. These sources include qualitative methods to structure practitioner knowledge, and alternative mapping concepts and applications such as criminal network maps and computer network analysis. These techniques reveal a rich understanding of the social processes underlying the spatial representations of criminal activity. Without the robust qualitative mapping exercises, traditional mapping techniques and the geographic manifestation of youth firearms violence likely would have steered us toward place-focused interventions. Our expanded problem-solving framework has the potential to produce a more refined and possibly more effective intervention.

The mapping applications utilized in this problem-solving exercise also underscore the value of capturing practitioners' extensive experience and knowledge in understanding crime and public safety problems. The considerable expertise and creative potential of line personnel are important, and currently underutilized, assets. The community and problem-solving policing movement seeks to benefit from the creativity and capacity of line officers to respond to crime problems. Structured qualitative information-gathering and mapping exercises incorporating police officers and other practitioners can be an effective tool in collecting and ordering these experiential assets, and, thus, expanding the potential of police departments and other agencies.

Police departments adopting community and problem-solving policing must also foster enthusiasm and promote creativity among line officers and supervisors, in order to develop their organizational capacity to respond to seemingly intractable crime problems such as youth firearms violence or drug markets. "Knowledge-based" mapping can provide an effective vehicle to generate interest and rally support. The products of our mapping exercises were striking to both our practitioner partners and policy-level officials; they recognized that the description and analysis of Boston's gang landscape, the contribution of gangs to the city's youth homicide problem, and the presentation of gang conflict and alliance networks provided tangible starting points to craft appropriate problem-solving responses. At the same time, many participants were surprised by the various findings and maps, indicating that the structured processes added value to the practitioner knowledge used as inputs, and that the exercise of representing, refining, and structuring such knowledge can be useful even to those from whom knowledge is being drawn. The active participation of practitioners in the data-collection process helped bridge the commonplace and stifling "academic-practitioner gap," generated considerable enthusiasm, and lent greater credibility to the research findings among Boston's law enforcement community. This high level of acceptance and interest proved to be a valuable asset in the implementation of an innovative problem-solving approach aimed at controlling serious youth violence in Boston.

Acknowledgments: This project, "Firearms and Violence: Juveniles, Illicit Markets, and Fear," was supported under award #94-IJ-CX-0056 from the National Institute of Justice, Office of Justice Programs, U.S. Department of Justice. Points of view in this document are those of the authors and do not necessarily represent the official position of the U.S. Department of Justice.

NOTES

1. For more on the Boston Gun Project, see Kennedy et al.,1996.

2. One operation fitting this pattern was Tampa PD's QUAD street drug market disruption, which used police officers and community sources to identify and track street drug-dealing hot spots and then used that information as a key input in a strategy aimed at the entire Tampa street market (see Kennedy, 1993.)

3. The authors would like to thank Amy Solomon for her valuable assistance in coordinating these meetings.

4. These records were in the form of written notes only. The possibility of recording the proceedings was taken up, and soundly rejected, by the practitioners involved.

5. This list of victims is the same one being used for other parts of the Boston Gun Project, such as assessing demographic profiles and criminal histories of victims and offenders, and analyzing weapon utilization (see Kennedy et al., 1996). This sample excluded four obviously non-"street" crimes that otherwise fit this profile (one accident, one suicide, and two fetal homicides). Between 1990 and 1994, these 159 youth victims accounted for 30% of the total number of homicides (524) and 37% of all gun and knife homicides (435) in Boston.

6. Law enforcement agencies in different cities use different definitions for "gang-related" crime, and this impacts the amount of gang-related crimes reported. For example, Los Angeles defines crime as gang-related when gang members participate, regardless of motive; Chicago uses a

more restrictive definition, classifying homicides as "gang-related" only if there is a gang motive evident (Maxson and Klein, 1990).

7. Defining "gang" is a core problem in analyzing and understanding gang- and group-related youth crime and violence (see Begall and Curry, 1995). The character of criminal and disorderly juvenile gangs and groups varies widely both within and across cities (see, e.g., Curry et al., 1994).

8. This approach to mapping gang turfs has similarities, but is not identical, to that used in Carolyn and Richard Block's well-known study of gang homicide in Chicago (Block and Block, 1993). The map of gang territories used in that research was provided by the commander of the centralized gang unit of the Chicago Police Department and later digitized by Richard Block. Although the broad turf geographies of the largest Chicago gangs were extremely illuminating for research purposes, the maps, in practice, were not regarded as useful for decision making by Chicago police officers. Apparently, the broad maps lacked the detail necessary to analyze and respond to conflicts between factions of the largest gangs. Further, the maps needed to be updated regularly to reflect the dynamic changes in gang territories and disputes over time, which was not routinely done. Additional research is being pursued by the authors of the original Chicago study to detail these factions, and to include the perceptions of other important stakeholders such as the narcotics unit and community members (Carolyn Block, personal communication).

9. This figure was calculated by dividing the practitioners' estimate of gang members by the total population aged 14-21 in neighborhoods that had gangs (South End, Roxbury, Jamaica Plain, Mattapan, Hyde Park, North Dorchester, and South Dorchester). The small proportion of Boston's youths involved in gangs is consistent with estimates of youth participation in gangs from other cities (see Klein, 1995; Esbensen and Huizinga, 1993).

10. For a discussion of centrality and other key concepts in network theory, see Sparrow, 1991.

11. As Scott (1991) summarizes, "Bonacich holds that the centrality of a particular point cannot be assessed in isolation from the centrality of all other points to which it is connected...that is to say, the centrality of I equals the sum of its connections to other points, weighted by the centrality of each of these other points" (p.91). Degree and Bonacich centrality are two approaches to identifying central points within a network. Theoretically, these measures were most appropriate to answer our questions; however, other measures exist that researchers may want to consider, including: betweenness, closeness, Euclidean centrality after

multidimensional scaling, point strength, and business (see Sparrow, 1991, for a discussion).

12. Our application of a Bonacich centrality is a departure from convention; this measure of centrality is based on a notion of "transmission" or "transmission of influence" between more central players. In most cases, the transmission mechanism is an association or an alliance. In this study, the mechanisms are antagonisms and recurring violence; the Bonacich measure was used to identify gangs that are central to conflict with other very active "beefing" gangs. We are positing that a law enforcement focus on a central gang will disrupt more antagonisms and efficiently reduce the transmission of violence. These gangs are also efficient to target if practitioners are interested in sending a deterrent message to other active gangs; this is discussed further below.

13. Larger eigenvector coefficients indicate increased importance of a node in the network. The Bonacich centrality routine calculates all possible eigenvalues of the relationship matrix (via factor analysis), but only gives the eigenvector corresponding to the largest possible eigenvalue as a measure of centrality (see Borgatti et al., 1992).

14. For clique identification, conflict and alliance networks were combined and analyzed; the assumption was made that information travels equally well through alliance and conflict links. It could well be that it does not; however, field interviews with gang members and Boston Police Department gang officers indicate that gangs pay close attention to the activities of their rivals. The links in these analyses were not valued according to the intensity of the conflict or the presence of an alliance (values assigned: conflict or alliance=1, no conflict or alliance=0).

15. As these analyses were exploratory, we selected a recommended technique. Researchers and practitioners may want to explore other techniques, such as k-cores, m-cores, k-plex, cliques, and n-cliques, to identify cohesive subgroupings within networks (see Knoke and Kiklinski, 1982; Scott, 1991).

16. The interpretation of the n-clan technique and the concept "cohesive subgroupings" is not straightforward when the links between nodes represent hostilities rather than lines of communication or association. The transmission of information in groups is traditionally represented as communication between willing partners, such as brokers or liaisons in a fencing operation. Although a "partnership" does not exist, we suggest that information can also travel through groupings of gangs in conflict due to their sensitivity to the actions of their rivals. It is likely that a deterrent message can diffuse through a clique of gangs when the illicit activities of one gang have been halted by an intensive enforcement effort. Further, the deterrent message can be amplified to other gangs in the identified clique if all are visited by law enforcement officers and edu-

cated on their behavior (violence) that triggered the intervention on the targeted gang.

17. We would like to thank Charles Ellis of MaconUSA for his generous help in facilitating certain of the mapping tasks in this project.

18. In estimating how "overrepresented" crime is in these gang areas relative to the rest of the city, we compared the crime rates in gang areas to what would be expected if crime were evenly distributed across the city. The proportion of the city occupied by gang areas is 3.6%; the neighborhoods in which there is at least one gang area comprise 8.1% of the area of the city. The expected crime rates for the gang areas were calculated by: subtracting the total crime in gang areas from the total crime in the city; multiplying by .036 to estimate the crime that would be expected in the areas if it was not gang turf; adding this estimate of "base" crime in the areas to the total crime in the city; and multiplying by .036. The same procedure was used to estimate the expected crime rates for the 8.1% of the neighborhoods with at least one gang area.

19. The standardization per square mile was necessary to prevent distortions caused by aggregating the data. If the thematic shading of "hotter" RAs was based on raw totals, those areas that had the highest counts would be designated as the "busiest" areas. These findings, however, would necessarily be biased by the size of the RA. Boston's reporting areas are not proportional; certain RAs are more than ten times the size of others. Thus, the greater geographic expanse increased the likelihood of experiencing a gun assault or shot fired, and thematic shading based on raw counts of incidents per RA were more influenced by size than intensity of activity.

20. Areal analyses were used only to exhibit the distribution of gun assaults and shots-fired calls around gang areas. Although thematic mapping was very useful for preliminary research into the relationship between crime and gang turfs, we caution others from making policy decisions or designing interventions on the basis of such techniques. As noted, areal analyses suffer from interpretation problems, such as aggregation bias (Brantingham and Brantingham, 1984) and spatial autocorrelation (Roncek and Montgomery, 1993; Odland, 1988).

21. The STAC analyses were conducted for the entire city of Boston (area=419,676,777 sq. meters), with a search radius of 325 square meters (the minimum search size STAC would allow for a city-wide analysis). Both analyses yielded significant Nearest Neighbor Index scores (shots fired=0.26, gun assault=.30), indicating that clustering exists within the geographic distribution.

22. See Kennedy et al., 1996. Briefly, three-quarters of both youth homicide victims and known youth homicide offenders had at least one arraignment in Massachusetts courts; of those with at least one arraign-

ment, more than 40% had ten or more arraignments, for a wide variety of offense categories.

23. One long-time gang crime prosecutor in the U.S. Attorney's office reacted to the network map of gang antagonisms by leaping to his feet and shouting, "Yes! That's it!"

REFERENCES

Ball, R. and G. D.Curry (1995). "The Logic of Definition in Criminology: Purposes and Methods for Defining 'Gangs.'" *Criminology* 33:225-245.

Bittner, E. (1970). *The Functions of the Police in a Modern Society*. Bethesda, MD: U.S. National Institute of Mental Health.

Black, D. (1970). "The Production of Crime Rates." *American Sociological Review* 35:733-748.

Block, C. R. (1993). "STAC Hot Spot Areas: A Statistical Tool for Law Enforcement Decisions." In: C.R. Block and M. Dabdoub (eds.), *Workshop on Crime Analysis Through Computer Mapping Proceedings*. Chicago, IL: Illinois Criminal Justice Information Authority.

—— and R. Block (1993). *Street Gang Crime in Chicago*. Research in Brief Series. Washington, DC: U.S. National Institute of Justice.

Block, C.R. (1996). Personal communication to the first author from the senior research analyst of the Statistical Analysis Center, Illinois Criminal Justice Information Authority.

Block, C.R. and L. Green (1994). *The GeoArchive Handbook: A Guide for Developing a Geographic Database as an Information Foundation for Community Policing*. Chicago, IL: Illinois Criminal Justice Information Authority.

Bonacich, P. (1972). "Factoring and Weighting Approaches to Status Scores and Clique Identification." *Journal of Mathematical Sociology* 2:113-120.

Borgatti, S., M. Everett and L. Freeman (1992). *UCINET IV Version 1.0*. Columbia: Analytic Technologies.

Braga, A.A., D.L. Weisburd, and L.A. Green (1995). "Identifying Violent Crime Hot Spots in Jersey City." Paper presented at the annual meeting of the American Society of Criminology, Boston, November.

Braga, A.A., L.A. Green, D.L. Weisburd, and F. Gajewski (1994). "Police Perceptions of Street-Level Narcotics Activity: Evaluating Drug Buys as a Research Tool." *American Journal of Police* 13:37-58.

Brantingham, P. and P. Brantingham (1984). *Patterns in Crime.* New York, NY: Macmillan.

Buerger, M. (1994). "The Problems of Problem-Solving: Resistance, Interdependencies, and Conflicting Interests." *American Journal of Police* 13:1-36.

Curry, G.D., R. Ball, and R. Fox (1994). *Gang Crime and Law Enforcement Recordkeeping,* Research in Action. Washington, DC:U.S. National Institute of Justice.

Durbak, A. and G. Rengert (1993). "More Than Just a Pretty Map: How Can Spatial Analysis Support Police Decisions?" In: C.R. Block and M. Dabdoub (eds.), *Workshop on Crime Analysis Through Computer Mapping Proceedings.* Chicago, IL: Illinois Criminal Justice Information Authority.

Ennis, B. and T. Litwack (1974). "Psychiatry and the Presumption of Expertise: Flipping Coins in the Courtroom." *California Law Review* 62: 693-752.

Esbensen, F.-A. and D. Huizinga (1993). "Gangs, Drugs, and Delinquency in a Survey of Urban Youth." *Criminology* 31:565-587.

Farrell, G. (1995). "Preventing Repeat Victimization." In: Michael Tonry and David Farrington (eds.), *Building a Safer Society: Strategic Approaches to Crime Prevention.* Crime and Justice: A Review of Research, vol. 19. Chicago, IL: University of Chicago Press.

Goldstein, H. (1990). *Problem-Oriented Policing.* Philadelphia, PA: Temple University Press.

Gould, P. and R. White (1974). *Mental Maps.* New York, NY: Penguin Books.

Katz, J. (1988). *The Seductions of Crime.* New York, NY: Basic Books.

Kennedy, D.M. (1993). "Closing the Market: Controlling the Drug Trade in Tampa, Florida." Program Focus series, National Institute of Justice, U.S. Department of Justice, Washington, DC.

—— and M. Moore (1995). "Underwriting the Risky Investment in Community Policing: What Social Science Should Be Doing to Evaluate Community Policing." *Justice System Journal* 17:271-291.

—— A.M. Piehl, and A.A. Braga (1996). "Youth Violence in Boston: Gun Markets, Serious Youth Offenders, and a Use Reduction Strategy." *Law and Contemporary Problems* 59:147-196

Klein, M. (1995). *The American Street Gang: Its Nature, Prevention, and Control.* New York, NY: Oxford.

Knoke, D. and J. Kuklinski (1982). *Network Analysis.* Beverly Hills, CA: Sage.

Krackhardt, D., M. Lundberg, and L. O'Rourke (1993). "KrakPlot: A Picture's Worth a Thousand Words." *Connections* 16(1&2): 37-47.

LeBeau, J. (1992). "Four Case Studies Illustrating the Spatial-Temporal Analysis of Serial Rapists." *Police Studies* 15:124-145.

Maltz, M. (1993). "Crime Mapping and the Drug Market Analysis Program (DMAP)." In: Carolyn R. Block and Margaret Dabdoub (eds.), *Workshop on Crime Analysis Through Computer Mapping Proceedings*. Chicago, IL: Illinois Criminal Justice Information Authority.

—— A. Gordon, and W. Friedman (1991). *Mapping Crime in Its Community Setting: Event Geography Analysis*. New York, NY: Springer-Verlag.

Maxson, C. and M. Klein (1990). "Street Gang Violence: Twice as Great or Half as Great?" In: C. Ronald Huff (ed.), *Gangs in America*. Newbury Park, CA: Sage.

McEwen, J.T. and F. Taxman (1995). "Applications of Computer Mapping to Police Operations." In: J.E. Eck and D. Weisburd (eds.), *Crime and Place*. Crime Prevention Studies, vol. 4. Monsey, NY: Criminal Justice Press.

Miller, W.B. (1975). *Violence by Youth Gangs and Youth Groups as a Crime Problem in Major American Cities*. Washington, DC: U.S. National Institute for Juvenile Justice and Delinquency Prevention.

Monahan, J. (1981). *Predicting Violent Behavior: An Assessment of Clinical Techniques*. Beverly Hills, CA: Sage.

Muir, W. (1977). *Police: Streetcorner Politicians*. Chicago, IL: University of Chicago Press.

Odland, J. (1988). *Spatial Autocorrelation*. Beverly Hills, CA: Sage.

Pierce, G., S. Spaar, and L. Briggs (1988). *The Character of Police Work: Implications for the Delivery of Services*. Boston, MA: Center for Applied Social Research, Northeastern University.

Rich, T. (1995). *The Use of Computerized Mapping in Crime Control and Prevention Programs*. Research in Action. Washington, DC: U.S. National Institute of Justice.

Roncek, D. and A. Montgomery (1993). "Spatial Autocorrelation Revisited: Conceptual Underpinnings and Practical Guidelines for the Use of Generalized Potential as a Remedy for Spatial Autocorrelation in Large Samples." In: Carolyn R. Block and Margaret Dabdoub (eds.), *Workshop on Crime Analysis Through Computer Mapping Proceedings*. Chicago, IL: Illinois Criminal Justice Information Authority.

Rosenbaum, D. and P. Lavrakas (1995). "Self Reports About Place: The Application of Survey and Interview Methods to the Study of Small Areas." In: John Eck and David Weisburd (eds.), *Crime and Place*.

Crime Prevention Studies, vol. 4. Monsey, NY: Criminal Justice Press.

Rossmo, D.K. (1995). "Place, Space, and Police Investigations: Hunting Serial Violent Criminals." In: John Eck and David Weisburd (eds.), *Crime and Place*. Crime Prevention Studies, vol. 4. Monsey, NY: Criminal Justice Press.

Rubinstein, J. (1973). *City Police*. New York, NY: Farrar, Straus, and Giroux.

Scott, J. (1991). *Social Network Analysis: A Handbook*. Newbury Park, CA: Sage.

Sherman, L. (1987). *Repeat Calls to Police in Minneapolis*. Washington, DC: Crime Control Institute.

—— and D. Weisburd (1995). "General Deterrent Effects of Police Patrol in Crime Hot Spots: A Randomized Controlled Trial." *Justice Quarterly* 12:625-648.

—— P. Gartin, and M. Buerger (1989). "The Hot Spots of Predatory Crime: Routine Activities and the Criminology of Place." *Criminology* 27:27-56.

Smith, C. and G. Patterson (1980). "Cognitive Mapping and the Subjective Geography of Crime." In: D. Georges-Abeyie and K. Harries (eds.), *Crime: A Spatial Perspective*. New York, NY: Columbia University Press.

Sparrow, M. (1991). "The Application of Network Analysis to Criminal Intelligence: An Assessment of the Prospects." *Social Networks* 13: 251-274.

—— M. Moore, and D. Kennedy (1990). *Beyond 911: A New Era for Policing*. New York, NY: Basic Books.

Spelman, W. (1995). "Criminal Careers of Public Places." In: J.E. Eck and D. Weisburd (eds.), *Crime and Place*. Crime Prevention Studies, vol. 4. Monsey, NY: Criminal Justice Press.

Spergel, I. (1995). *The Youth Gang Problem: A Community Approach*. New York, NY: Oxford University Press.

Terrill, W. and L. Green (1995). "Mapping and Identifying Hot Spots in Public Housing." Paper presented at the annual meeting of the American Society of Criminology, Boston, November.

Toch, H. and J.D. Grant (1991). *Police as Problem Solvers*. New York, NY: Plenum Press.

U.S. National Institute of Justice (1989). *Program Plan*. Washington, DC: Author.

262 — David M. Kennedy et al.

Weisburd, D. and L. Green (1994). "Defining the Street-Level Drug Market." In: D. MacKenzie and C. Uchida (eds.), *Drugs and Crime: Evaluating Public Policy Initiatives.* Thousand Oaks, CA: Sage.

—— (1995). "Policing Drug Hot Spots: The Jersey City DMA Experiment." *Justice Quarterly* 12:711-736.

Weisburd, D., L. Maher, and L. Sherman (1992). "Contrasting Crime General and Crime Specific Theory: The Case of Hot Spots of Crime." *Advances in Criminological Theory,* vol. 4. New Brunswick, NJ: Transaction Books.

[16]

A PROSPECTIVE TEST OF A CRIMINAL CAREER MODEL*

ARNOLD BARNETT
Massachusetts Institute of Technology

ALFRED BLUMSTEIN
Carnegie Mellon University

DAVID P. FARRINGTON
Cambridge University

In an earlier article in this journal, Barnett, Blumstein, and Farrington (1987) formulated a model that described the criminal careers of the multiple offenders in a cohort of London males that had been studied from their 10th to 25th birthdays. That model involved two subpopulations of offenders (denoted as "frequents" and "occasionals"), each characterized by a constant annual conviction rate (μ) and a constant probability (p) of terminating the career following a conviction. This article describes the results of a prospective and predictive test of the model using new data collected on the same offenders from their 25th to 30th birthdays. The original model accurately predicted the number of recidivists, the degree of recidivism risk, the total number of recidivist convictions, and the time intervals between recidivist convictions. However, the predictions for the frequents suffered some distortions introduced by a few "intermittent" offenders who seemed to have terminated their careers, but who re-initiated offending during the test period after a long gap.

A CRIMINAL CAREER MODEL

In a recent paper, Barnett, Blumstein, and Farrington (1987) (denoted hereafter as BBF87) developed a simple probabilistic model to describe youthful criminal careers. Their aim was to model the longitudinal sequence of convictions incurred by a "multiple offender" (one with two or more convictions) in a London cohort of males up to age 25.[1] Their general premise

---

* Barnett's research in this paper was supported in part by grant #86-IJ-CS-0070 of the National Institute of Justice. Blumstein's research was supported in part by grant #86-IJ-CS-0047 of the National Institute of Justice. Points of view are those of the authors and do not necessarily represent the position of the U.S. Department of Justice. Farrington's research was supported by the British Home office.
   1. Reference to an age such as "25" applies to the 25th birthday.

374   BARNETT, BLUMSTEIN, AND FARRINGTON

was that such an offender's career can be represented succinctly by two probabilistic processes: one reflecting his annual rate of offending and another reflecting his likelihood of ceasing to offend after each conviction.

The model was based on the following assumptions:

1.   Convictions occur according to a Poisson stochastic process. In other words, if an offender commits μ crimes per year on average, his probability of offending on any given day is $\mu/365$, and this probability is independent of whether he offends on any other day.[2]

2.   There are two distinct subpopulations of offenders, termed "frequents" and "occasionals."

3.   Frequents commit crimes at a higher rate (μ_1) than occasionals (μ_2). For each group, the average rate of offending is the same for all offenders and constant over age for those who continue to be active.

4.   Frequents have a probability (p_1) of terminating their criminal careers after each conviction, and occasionals have a corresponding probability (p_2). For each group, the probability of termination or desistance is the same after each conviction and is the same for all offenders in the group.

BBF87 showed that this simple mathematical model accurately fitted the conviction sequences of these London men from age 10 to age 25. There was no claim that there were, in reality, only two homogeneous subpopulations of offenders, but rather that this representation of the heterogeneous population fit the data quite adequately.

It was not necessary to assume that conviction rates varied with age. The aggregate decline in convictions at older ages could be explained by the increasing proportion of offenders who had reached the conviction at which they desisted. Frequents and occasionals differed greatly in their rates of offending but were quite similar in their average lengths of criminal careers (about 7 to 9 years). Hence, the factors that influence offending rates may well differ from those that influence career lengths.

One possible objection to BBF87 is that the model was developed and tested on the same data. Hence, the explanatory power of the model might have been overestimated. It is desirable to derive a model from one set of data and test its adequacy when applied to another set. Recently, new data on the same individuals' offending sequences between ages 25 and 30 have become available. The aim of this analysis is to assess the prospective and predictive accuracy of the model when applied to the new data.

THE LONDON COHORT

This analysis uses official conviction record data from the Cambridge study

---

2.   For ease of exposition, we use the terms "offense" and "conviction" interchangeably.

in delinquent development, which is a prospective longitudinal survey of 411 males. At the time they were first contacted in 1961-1962, all were living in a working-class area of London, England. The sample was selected by taking all boys who were then aged 8 to 9 and on the registers of six state primary schools that were within a 1-mile radius of a research office that had been established. Almost all the boys were white, most had parents who had been brought up in the United Kingdom or Ireland, and most were working class according to their fathers' occupations. They have been interviewed eight times between ages 8 and 32 (see Farrington, in press; West, 1969, 1982; West and Farrington, 1973, 1977).

Repeated searches were carried out in the national Criminal Record Office in London to obtain information about convictions. Convictions were counted only if they were for offenses normally recorded in this office, which are the more serious offenses. The most common offenses were thefts, burglaries, and taking motor vehicles. All traffic offenses and simple drunkenness were excluded, as were status offenses such as truancy, which are dealt with in civil rather than criminal proceedings in England. The category of crimes included here is slightly wider than index offenses in the United States, in that property damage, drug use, receiving stolen property, and sex offenses other than forcible rape are included. Convictions were only slightly less common than arrests in this sample; the vast majority of arrests were followed by a conviction.

The analyses reported here are based on the date of the offense, not the date of the conviction. Ages of offending were recorded to the nearest month. Periods when the youths were not at risk of offending (e.g., periods spent in penal institutions) were excluded. The minimum age for conviction in England is 10, and juveniles become adults for legal purposes on their 17th birthday. An advantage of this study is the ability to include both juvenile and adult convictions and thereby build a picture of the complete criminal career.

MODEL PARAMETERS

The BBF87 model was based on 82 men with two or more convictions for offenses committed up to age 25. In the most recent set of searches in the Criminal Record Office, ending in 1987, more convictions under age 25 were discovered, however. The number of men now known to have two or more convictions for offenses committed under age 25 is 88. The parameters of the model were therefore recalculated on the basis of those 88 men's convictions through age 25. A comparison with the BBF87 model shows that the corrected parameters differ only marginally from the original ones.[3]

According to the model, the *frequents* constitute 40% of the offenders and

---

3. The six additional offenders were all classified as occasionals. The classification of the original 82 offenders into 35 frequents and 47 occasionals was unchanged.

sustain convictions while free and active according to a Poisson probability process with an average annual rate (μ_1) of 1.14. This is equivalent to a 1 in 320 daily chance of offending. Immediately after conviction, their probability of terminating (p_1) is .10. The *occasionals* constitute 60% of the offenders and sustain convictions while free and active at an average annual rate (μ_2) of 0.40. This is equivalent to a 1 in 913 daily chance of offending. Immediately after each conviction, their probability of terminating (p_2) is .33.

Although it might not be immediately apparent, the above descriptions of frequents and occasionals imply similar average career lengths. Active frequents average one conviction every 10 months, each conviction having a 10% chance of leading to termination. Active occasionals have a 33% chance of termination per conviction, but their convictions are typically 2.5 years apart. Thus, compared with occasionals, frequents get opportunities to terminate about three times as often but are only one-third as likely to take any given opportunity. The two groups, therefore, have comparable mean career lengths of about 8 years.

The most recent searches in the Criminal Record Office extend knowledge about the conviction careers of these men through age 30. This analysis investigates the extent to which the model developed on data about offenders under age 25 is adequate in predicting offending between the 25th and 30th birthday. Because three offenders died under age 25, only 85 were at risk of offending during the follow-up period, and the model was tested on those 85.

For the purpose of this analysis, we define a *recidivist* as one of our multiple offenders who has one or more further convictions for offenses committed between his 25th and 30th birthdays.

EVALUATING PROBABILISTIC PREDICTIONS

The BBF87 model provides probabilistic predictions about convictions between ages 25 and 30, based on information accumulated before age 25. A probabilistic prediction does not purport to reveal exactly what will happen; rather, it suggests the relative likelihood of the various possibilities. That indeterminacy imposes limits on the assessment of probabilistic forecasts. If, for example, a weather forecaster predicts a 40% chance of rain, then neither rain nor its absence contradicts the forecast.

Yet, while it is hard to confirm or falsify a single forecast in isolation, the collective accuracy of a group of predictions can be explored. If the forecaster predicts a 40% chance of rain 30 times over a year, then, if those forecasts are sound, rain would be expected on about $40\% \times 30 = 12$ of the days in question. It would be unreasonable to insist on exactly 12, much as it would be unreasonable to expect 20 tosses of a fair coin to yield exactly 10 heads, but too great a discrepancy between the observed and predicted percentages would raise questions about the forecaster's skill.

CRIMINAL CAREER MODEL 377

The same principle applies when the forecast concerns the number of events of a certain kind. Suppose, for instance, that a model describes the number of accidents over a period as a variable with an average of 2.2 and a standard deviation of 1.3. Then, an observed outcome of one accident would not be inconsistent with the forecast. But if many such forecasts are examined together, the expected group sum should be close to the actual one.[4] Repeated underestimation, therefore, would be interpreted as a sign of predictive failure.

Such considerations dictate the form of the prospective tests that follow. Under various criteria, we divide the offenders into subgroups and assess whether the predicted outcomes in each subgroup are in harmony with the actual ones. We avoid the more ambiguous question of whether any particular offender's behavior was compatible with the forecast about it.

The last statement raises a point worth explicit attention. If a given offender is assigned, say, a 75% chance of recidivating by age 30 but does not do so, we should not classify the prediction as a "false positive." The term "false positive" is not easily applied to probabilistic predictions. So long as nonrecidivism among a group of offenders with the 75%—25% forecast takes a rate near 1 in 4, the nonrecidivists are as consistent with the prediction as are the recidivists. Indeed, it would be disconcerting if all such offenders recidivated, for that would imply that the 75% estimate should have been much closer to 100%.

ESTIMATING RECIDIVISM POSSIBILITIES

The BBF87 model generates an estimate of each offender's recidivism probability based on his classification as a frequent or an occasional offender and on his age at his last conviction prior to age 25. For an offender whose last conviction before age 25 was at age L, two explanations exist for the absence of convictions in the ensuing 25 − L years: (1) he terminated at that conviction or (2) he did not terminate, but sustained no new convictions by age 25 under the ongoing Poisson conviction process.

The relative plausibility of these two explanations depends on whether the offender is a frequent or an occasional and on the value of L. For a frequent with L = 18, for example, termination is overwhelmingly the more credible; to suggest otherwise is to require an offender who averages one conviction every 10 months to go 7 full years without being convicted. By contrast, for an occasional with L = 24.99, the absence of further convictions by age 25 is hardly surprising; the probability that the offender has terminated would stay at 33%, the chance of termination on any conviction.

Using the laws of conditional probability and the BBF87 model, we derive in the appendix a formula for $P_A(L)$, the probability that the offender is still

---

4. The central limit theorem quantifies the word "close" in particular settings.

378 BARNETT, BLUMSTEIN, AND FARRINGTON

active at age 25 given that his last previous conviction was at age L. (This is equivalent to the probability that the offender has not terminated at L.) Suppose that μ and p are, respectively, the offender's conviction rate and termination probability per conviction ($\mu = 1.14$, p = .10 for frequents; $\mu = .40$, p = .33 for occasionals). Then, in the appendix, we derive the following equation:[5]

$$P_A(L) = \frac{(1 - p)\, e^{-\mu(25 - L)}}{p + (1 - p)\, e^{-\mu(25 - L)}} \qquad (1)$$

Equation (1), of course, incorporates no information about behavior after age 25.

Equation (1) is consistent with the qualitative discussion above. As L approaches 25, the exponential factors in the numerator and denominator approach 1, and thus $P_A(L)$ approaches $1 - p$. That outcome simply means that, having so little follow-up time to witness more convictions, we can infer very little from their absence. As L decreases below 25, the "exponential decay" in the numerator pushes the whole expression toward 0. That indicates a period of inactivity which is so inconsistent with the Poisson conviction process that termination is the only reasonable explanation for it.

Figure 1 shows how $P_A(L)$ varies with L for frequents and occasionals separately. Because frequents have lower termination probabilities than do occasionals, they are the likelier to be still active when L is close to 25. However, because their annual conviction rates are far higher when they are active, frequents without convictions between an early age L and 25 are more likely to have terminated than comparable occasionals.

An offender who is still active at age 25 will in time commit a further offense, but it is not certain that that offense will be committed before he reaches age 30. For active frequents, the chance of recidivism by age 30 is .997 (299 out of 300).[6] However, for active occasionals who only average one conviction every 2.5 years, there is a 1 in 7 chance of no new convictions over a 5-year period. We now define the quantity $P_R(L)$ as the chance of at least one recidivist conviction between ages 25 and 30, given that the last pre-25 conviction was at age L. $P_R(L)$ is related to $P_A(L)$ by:

$$P_R(L) = \begin{cases} .997 \times P_A(L) \text{ for frequents} \\ .865 \times P_A(L) \text{ for occasionals} \end{cases} \qquad (2)$$

---

5. For ease of exposition, times not at risk of offending (e.g., periods of incarceration) are not explicitly included in the equations, but they were taken into account in the analyses. For example, an incarceration period of duration I years would be taken into account in equation (1) by replacing L by the quantity (L + I).

6. Assuming that the time at risk is 5 years, this probability is $(1 - e^{-5\mu})$, where $\mu = 1.14$ (see the appendix).

Figure 1.
Probability Still Active at Age 25 Based on Age at
Most Recent Conviction

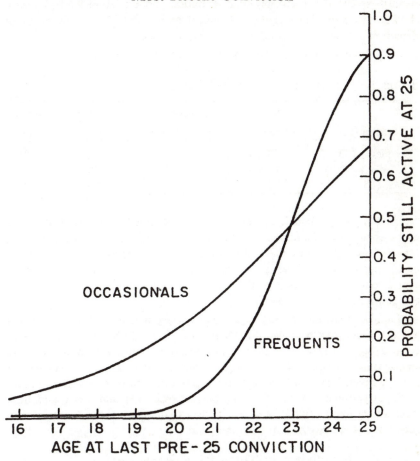

$P_R(L)$ is essentially $P_A(L)$ discounted by the chance that an offender who is active at age 25 will have no convictions by age 30.

PREDICTING THE NUMBER OF RECIDIVISTS

Taking account of whether each offender was a frequent or an occasional, and his value of L (age at the last conviction before age 25), $P_R(L)$ was estimated using equations (1) and (2). The calculated probabilities varied from 1 in 10,000 to 9 in 10, and averaged .28 for the 33 frequents and .29 for the 52 occasionals.

The element of uncertainty in the individual forecasts carries over to the group outcomes. Rather than pinpointing how many frequents or occasionals will recidivate, the model specifies probability distributions for those quantities. For the frequents, the distribution had a mean of 9.2 and a standard deviation of 1.8; for the occasionals, the mean was 15.1 and the standard deviation 3.0 (see the appendix for the derivation).

Table 1 shows how far the model succeeds in forecasting the number of

Table 1. Predicted and Actual Recidivism

	Number of Recidivists		Percent Recidivating	
Group (N)	Expected (S.D.)	Actual	Expected	Actual
Frequents (33)	9.2 (1.8)	12	28	36
Occasionals (52)	15.1 (3.0)	16	29	31
Total (85)	24.3 (3.5)	28	29	33

recidivists. As predicted, the proportion of offenders who recidivated was about one-third. The actual number with new convictions was higher than expected among both frequents and occasionals, but the excess was not statistically significant in either group, and neither was the overall excess of 28 actual recidivists over 24.3 predicted ones. The model's ability to predict in this respect seems quite satisfactory.

It is also important to investigate the correspondence between predicted and actual recidivism at the individual level. It would be surprising if those deemed highly likely to recidivate rarely did so, while recidivism was rife among those for whom it was thought almost inconceivable. In investigating this, we divided the offenders into three risk categories: low (with estimates of $P_R(L)$ between 0 and .333), middle (between .334 and .666), and high (between .667 and 1.0). Table 2 relates the extent of actual recidivism in each category to the amount that was predicted.

Table 2. Recidivism in Three Risk Categories

	Number of Recidivists		Percent Recidivating	
Risk Category (N)	Expected (S.D.)	Actual	Expected	Actual
Low (52)	6.5 (2.3)	11	13	21
Middle (26)	12.2 (2.5)	12	47	46
High (7)	5.7 (1.0)	5	81	71

Table 2 shows a clear correspondence between predicted and actual recidivism rates for individuals. The proportions with new convictions in the low, middle, and high categories were 21%, 46%, and 71%, respectively. There were more recidivists than expected in the low-risk category, but the excess was just within the two standard deviations margin of usual chance fluctuation.

PREDICTING THE NUMBER OF CONVICTIONS

The later years of the 5-year follow-up period have little effect in the above tests of the model. Frequents who recidivate, for example, should generally do so by age 26 and occasionals by age 28. Thus, a drop in the conviction rate after age 28 would scarcely be visible in Tables 1 and 2. The total number of new convictions, by contrast, is dependent on developments throughout the entire 5-year period.

Table 3 shows the predicted and actual numbers of new convictions (see

Table 3. Numbers of New Convictions

| | Total Number of New Convictions | |
Group (N)	Expected (S.D.)	Actual
Frequents (33)	37.7 (10.1)	29
Occasionals (52)	25.2 (6.2)	25
Total (85)	62.9 (11.9)	54

the appendix for the derivation). It can be seen that the frequents amassed fewer convictions than predicted (29 versus 38), but that this shortfall was not statistically significant. The predicted and actual numbers of convictions of the occasionals were remarkably similar.

TIME INTERVALS BETWEEN CONVICTIONS

A critic might wonder whether the slight shortfall of convictions among frequents was indicative of a decline in the individual rate (μ) of offending with increasing age. To explore whether μ changed with age, we investigated the time intervals between successive convictions. For a free and active offender whose conviction process has a Poisson distribution, the chance of a new conviction within the next 24 hours is independent of the time since the last one. Whether he was last convicted yesterday or 18 months ago, the expected time until his next conviction is the same. A corollary of this statement is that, for an offender known to be active for several years past age 25, the "street time" between his 25th birthday and his next conviction should on average equal the times between consecutive convictions in the future.

There were 13 recidivists in the London cohort with at least two convictions in the follow-up period, and 8 with at least three. (Only three offenders had four or more.) For each such person, we know the interval from age 25 to the next conviction (I_1), the time between that conviction and the subsequent one (I_2), and (where applicable) the time between the second conviction after age 25 and the third (I_3). If, as hypothesized, the conviction rate is invariant with age, then these intervals should on average be equal (see the appendix). But if offenders gradually slow down rather than terminate their offending abruptly, the successive intervals should increase.

We can restate these points a bit differently. Suppose that a given offender has his second post-25 conviction at, say, age 28. Then the model would lead us to expect his first post-25 conviction halfway between 25 and 28 (i.e., at age 26.5); only in that case, after all, would I_1 equal I_2. And if another offender had his third post-25 conviction at age 28, we would likewise expect that his first was at 26 (one-third through the 3-year period) and his second at 27 (two-thirds through). More generally, knowing the times until certain post-25 convictions allows us to "guess" the times of earlier ones. The adequacy of these guesses in depicting what actually happened measures the accuracy of the model that generated them.

Table 4 tests the model using the "backwards projection" method just

Table 4. Average Street-Times From Age 25 Until Post-25 Convictions

	Predicted (S.D.)	Actual
Offenders with ≥ 2 Convictions (N = 13):		
Time until First Conviction	1.23 (.22)	1.25
Offenders with ≥ 3 Convictions (N = 8):		
Time until First Conviction	1.00 (.27)	1.14
Time until Second Conviction	2.00 (.27)	1.94

described. Those offenders with two or more follow-up convictions averaged 2.46 years of street time between their 25th birthdays and the second conviction; hence, the expected time until the first conviction was 2.46/2 = 1.23 years. And those with three or more follow-up convictions averaged 3.00 years to reach the third, meaning that the first and second were expected at 1.00 and 2.00 years after 25, respectively. Table 4 shows that the actual times of the convictions under scrutiny were consistently close to the predicted ones. Moreover, in the case of offenders with three or more convictions, the first post-25 interval tended marginally to exceed the second one. The observed pattern is easily compatible with a constant conviction rate but clearly incompatible with a steadily declining rate.

Another prediction that can be tested is that, among recidivists, the average time from age 25 until the first new conviction should be less among

CRIMINAL CAREER MODEL 383

frequents than among occasionals. However, Table 5 shows that this prediction is seriously at fault. While the expected time for the frequents should

Table 5.   Time to First New Conviction among Recidivists

Group (N)	Expected Time[a] in Years (S.D.)	Actual Time in Years
Frequents (12)	0.88 (.25)	1.92
Occasionals (16)	1.72 (.43)	1.96

[a]This expected time is conditional on having the first recidivist conviction within 5 years, which reduces the expected time for the occasionals from the unconditional value of 2.5 years. The effect of the 5-year time boundary on the expected time for the frequents is negligible.

have been about half that of the occasionals, the actual average times were almost the same.

DO CRIMINAL CAREERS END AND RESTART?

Overall, the model performed satisfactorily in the tests in yielding predictions that were consistently quite accurate in both quantitative and qualitative terms. Recidivism in the London cohort involved a number of offenders close to that anticipated, and there was a strong, systematic relation between predicted and actual recidivism rates. The total number of recidivist convictions was also close to expectation. Further, the time intervals between convictions in the 25 to 30 age range remained fairly constant, as indeed they had before age 25 (as demonstrated by Table 4 in BBF87).

But while the results of the tests were generally satisfactory, there were a number of problems, all of which involved only the frequents. The observed number of recidivists among the frequents (Table 1) was higher than expected, but their observed number of recidivist convictions was lower than expected (Table 3). Further, the average time from age 25 to the first reconviction for those frequents who recidivated was longer than expected (Table 5). Also, Table 2 shows that the offenders classified as low-risk included more recidivists (11) than expected (6.5), almost 2 standard deviations more. We therefore investigated in some detail those deviations that seemed inconsistent with our predictions.

It emerged that the inconsistencies could be explained by the behavior of the 16 frequents with extremely low probabilities of recidivating (less than .10 each). Five of them actually became recidivists, in comparison with the expectation of only 0.31. We studied the five men closely and found some similarities among them. They all started offending relatively late (at an average age of 16.4, compared with 13.2 for all frequents); they then had several

384   BARNETT, BLUMSTEIN, AND FARRINGTON

convictions (an average of 5.8 convictions each) in quite a short period; and they then apparently ceased their criminal careers at age 19.4, on average. That is why they were classified as frequents, and why they had a very low probability of being active at age 25. However, after a period of 7 to 10 years with no convictions, they were all reconvicted at an average age of 27.3, and three of them in fact had yet another conviction at an average age of 29.4.

It is tempting to suggest that these men began and ended one criminal career in their late teens and then, after a period of nonoffending, restarted their criminal activities in their late twenties. These re-initiations could account for the larger number of frequent recidivists than predicted, and for the relatively long times to their first reconviction. The fact that the re-initiations occurred late in the follow-up period could also explain why there were fewer reconvictions per recidivist than expected. Hence, more elaborate models might incorporate the concept of intermittency, whereby offenders go into remission for several years and then resume their criminal careers.

We should not, however, overstate the importance of the observed intermittency. There is no comparable evidence of any such gaps in the offending careers of occasionals. Because occasionals have a lower offending rate, such gaps would be hard to detect. Nevertheless, if intermittency were prevalent among the occasionals, there could have been signs of gaps in the tables, but there were none. Even among the frequents, there were only 5 restarters out of 33, or about 15%, so the probability of restarting after any termination must be quite low.

CONCLUSION

The predictive validity of the BBF87 model was, in general, quite satisfactory in a series of prospective tests that explored the model's accuracy from a variety of distinct perspectives. Consequently, this model seems quite adequate in explaining the criminal careers of the London cohort. But given the limited number of offenders and the specific London setting, it would be highly desirable to test the model's validity with larger cohorts. The indication that a small number of offenders may have ended one criminal career and then restarted another after a hiatus suggests a direction in which criminal career models may be usefully extended in the future.

REFERENCES

Barnett, Arnold, Alfred Blumstein, and David P. Farrington
    1987   Probabilistic models of youthful criminal careers. Criminology 25:83–107.

Farrington, David P.
    In press Later adult life outcomes of offenders and non-offenders. In Michael
            Brambring, Friedrich Losel, and Helmut Skowronek (eds.), Children at Risk.
            Berlin: De Gruyter.

West, Donald J.
  1969   Present Conduct and Future Delinquency. London: Heinemann.
  1982   Delinquency: Its Roots, Careers, and Prospects. London: Heinemann.
West, Donald J., and David P. Farrington
  1973   Who Becomes Delinquent? London: Heinemann.
  1977   The Delinquent Way of Life. London: Heinemann.

Arnold Barnett is Professor of Operations Research at MIT's Sloan School of Management. His research specialty is applied probabilistic modeling, with particular attention to issues in criminal justice.

Alfred Blumstein is J. Erik Jonsson Professor of Urban Systems and Operations Research and Dean of the School of Urban and Public Affairs at Carnegie Mellon University. He has chaired the National Academy of Sciences Committee on Research on Law Enforcement and the Administration of Justice and the committee's panels on research on deterrent and incapacitative effects, on sentencing research, and on criminal careers.

David P. Farrington is Reader in Psychological Criminology at Cambridge University, England and Director of the Cambridge Study in Delinquent Development. His major research interest is in the longitudinal study of delinquency and crime.

APPENDIX
PREDICTING RECIDIVISTS, CONVICTIONS, AND OFFENSE INTERVALS

THE PROBABILITY THAT AN OFFENDER IS STILL ACTIVE AT 25

The probability that an offender is still active at age 25, given that his last conviction was at age L, denoted as $P_A(L)$, can be calculated as follows. For an offender convicted at age L ($L < 25$), the BBF87 model allows two possible reasons why no further convictions ensue by age 25: (i) termination at L or (ii) failure to terminate at L, but no new convictions before age 25 under the Poisson conviction process.

At age L itself, one would prospectively assign a probability of p to the first of these possibilities. In determining the probability of the second, denoted as P(ii), one would first note that, in a Poisson process with parameter μ, the chance of no events in a period of length x is $\exp(-\mu x)$. P(ii) would therefore be given by:

$$P(ii) = (1 - p) e^{-\mu x} \qquad (A1)$$

where, x = street time between ages L and 25.

In (A1), the factor of $(1 - p)$ specifies the failure to terminate, and the exponential factor indicates the absence of convictions despite continuation of the career. The offender's street time x would generally be $25 - L - I$, where I is any time spent incarcerated following the conviction at age L.

Of course, the possibilities still open at L include further convictions before 25. But if no such convictions emerge when the offender's record at age 25 is examined, then one assumes under the model that either (i) or (ii) has occurred. The law of conditional probability (Bayes' theorem) could then be used to obtain an expression for $P_A(L)$, the revised probability of being still active at 25, given no convictions between L and 25:

$$P_A(L) = P(ii)/[P(i) + P(ii)] \qquad (A2)$$

where,

$$P(i) = p \qquad \text{and}$$
$$P(ii) = (1 - p) e^{-\mu x}, \text{ as discussed.}$$

In effect, (A2) weights the two explanations for the observed outcome by their initial probabilities. If both possibilities had been deemed equally likely (i.e., if $P(i) = P(ii)$), then each would be assigned a probability of 50% when one of them is known to have occurred. If, however, termination had been deemed three times as probable as continuation but without convictions (i.e., if $P(i) = 3P(ii)$), then this factor-of-three difference would carry over to the revised assessment of $P_A(L)$, which would be 25% for continued activity at 25 and 75% for termination at age L.

CRIMINAL CAREER MODEL 387

PREDICTING THE NUMBER OF RECIDIVISTS

The predicted numbers in Tables 1 and 2 are based on the values of $P_R(L)$, the estimated probabilities of recidivism for each of the 85 offenders. The values of $P_R(L)$ likewise determined the standard deviations in these tables, which reflect the extent to which chance fluctuations can create differences between expected and actual outcomes.

More specifically, each of the offenders takes part in a Bernoulli probability process, in which he either recidivates or does not. (The Bernoulli process is discussed in most basic probability textbooks.) For the BBF87 model, the parameter of this process is the offender's value of $P_R(L)$. Using familiar rules for aggregating the outcomes of Bernoulli processes, we learn that (a) the expected number of recidivists in a group is just the sum of the $P_R(L)$ values of its members and (b) the variance of the number of recidivists is the sum over the members of $P_R(L) \times [1 - P_R(L)]$.

PREDICTING THE NUMBERS OF NEW CONVICTIONS

In BBF87 (p. 106), formulas are derived for the probability distribution, mean, and variance of an offender's number of convictions in the next T time units. These formulas assumed that the offender has just been convicted, and thus that the probability that he remains active is $1 - p$. Table 3 predicts the number of convictions in a forthcoming 5-year period; that period, however, starts not with a conviction but with the 25th birthday. Hence, the probability that the offender is still active is not $1 - p$, but rather $P_A(L)$.

The requisite changes in the formulas in BBF87 involve multiplying by $[P_A(L)/(1 - p)]$ the expressions for the mean number of convictions, the mean squared number, and the probability of exactly k convictions for the positive integer k. Thus, the mean number of follow-up convictions, E, becomes:

$$E = P_A(L) \times [1 - e^{-\mu p T}]/p$$

where, μ, p are the model parameters for the offender's status (as frequent or occasional) and T is the observation time (generally the full 5 years).

The probability of no convictions between 25 and 30 becomes:

$$Q = [1 - P_A(L)] + P_A(L) \times [1 - e^{-\mu T}]$$

where, $T = 5$ in most cases.

PREDICTING OFFENSE INTERVALS

Suppose that an offender known to be free and active between ages 25 and B had exactly one conviction during this period. Then, under a Poisson process with constant parameter μ, that conviction would be equally likely to have occurred at all times throughout the interval. (In statistical parlance, the time of the conviction would be uniformly distributed between 25 and B). Well-known results about the uniform distribution imply that the mean time

388   BARNETT, BLUMSTEIN, AND FARRINGTON

of the conviction would be $(25 + B)/2$ (i.e., the middle of the interval), and its variance around the middle would be given by $(B - 25)^2/12$.

Were there instead exactly two convictions between ages 25 and B, then the expected time of the earlier one would be given by $25 + [(B - 25)/3]$, and that of the later one would be given by $25 + 2(B - 25)/3$. (Note that these correspond, respectively, to one-third and two-thirds of the way through the interval.) The variance of the timing of each conviction around its mean time would be $(B - 25)^2/18$.

Aside from time not at risk of offending, these statistics would be relevant for an offender whose second conviction after age 25 was at, say, age 28. According to the model, this offender was clearly free and active between 25 and 28; hence, the expected age of his first post-25 conviction would be 26.5 (halfway between 25 and 28). If another such offender had his third post-25 conviction at 28, then his expected ages at the first two would be 26 and 27, respectively. Extending these ideas to other convictions, and allowing for time not at risk, is straightforward.

[17]

Micro-Models of Criminal Careers: A Synthesis of the Criminal Careers and Life Course Approaches via Semiparametric Mixed Poisson Regression Models, with Empirical Applications

Kenneth C. Land[1] and Daniel S. Nagin[2]

Much recent research and debate in criminology have centered around how to conceptualize and model longitudinal sequences of delinquent and criminal acts committed by individuals. Two approaches dominate this controversy. One originates in the *criminal careers paradigm*, which emphasizes a potential *heterogeneity of offending groups* in the general population—thus leading to a distinction between incidence and prevalence of criminal offending, a focus on the onset, persistence, and desistence of criminal careers, and the possibility that criminals are a distinctive group with constant high rates of offending. Another approach places criminal events within a broader context of *studies of the life course* by explicitly substituting the conceptualization of "social events" for that of "criminal careers." With respect to analytical models, this approach emphasizes a potential *heterogeneity of offenders with respect to order of criminal events* from first to second to higher orders and thus suggests an analysis of the "risks" or "hazards" of offending by order of offense. Some extant commentaries on the criminal careers and life course approaches to conceptualizing and modeling longitudinal sequences of delinquent and criminal events committed by individuals have emphasized their differences and incompatibilities. In contrast, we apply recently developed semiparametric mixed Poisson regression techniques to develop conditions under which the two conceptual/modeling approaches are formally equivalent. We also modify the semiparametric mixed Poisson regression model of criminal careers to incorporate information on order of the delinquent/criminal event and develop an empirical application. This modification demonstrates the complementarity of the criminal careers and life course approaches, even though they have somewhat different foci.

KEY WORDS: criminal careers; studies of the life course; Poisson models; hazards models.

[1]Department of Sociology, Duke University, Durham, North Carolina 27708-0088.
[2]Heinz School of Public Policy and Management, Carnegie–Mellon University, Pittsburgh, Pennsylvania 15213.

1. INTRODUCTION

Much recent research and debate in criminology have centered around how to conceptualize and model longitudinal sequences of delinquent and criminal acts committed by individuals. The persistence of criminal (and conversely noncriminal) behavior is well documented and accepted by all parties (e.g., Blumstein *et al.*, 1986; Gottfredson and Hirschi, 1990). To be sure, the positive association of past to future criminal behavior is susceptible to fundamentally different interpretations (e.g., Nagin and Farrington, 1992a, b; Nagin and Paternoster, 1991), but the observation that individuals have criminal careers in the sense that there are persistent differences across individuals in their rates of offending over time is unassailable. Debate about the notion of a criminal career, thus, does not stem from disagreement about the most basic empirical requirement for characterizing criminality as a career—the autocorrelation of criminal behavior. Rather, differences of opinion commence with respect to theoretical conceptualizations of criminal events ordered over the life course and associated analytical models and methodologies for analyzing data on criminal careers.

Two approaches dominate this controversy and are dealt with here. One originates in the *criminal careers paradigm* recently identified by Blumstein and associates (e.g., Barnett *et al.*, 1987, 1989). This approach emphasizes, among other things, a distinction between incidence (i.e., the frequency of offending of active offenders) and prevalence (i.e., the percentage of individuals who are active offenders) and focuses on constructs such as the onset, persistence, and desistence of criminal careers. It also raises the possibility that criminals are a distinctive group with constant high rates of offending. In the criminal career approach, the longitudinal pattern of offending is characterized as a stochastic process, with onset and termination of offending determined by processes distinct from those determining frequency of offending. During periods of active offending, the Poisson process commonly is used to characterize the stochastic character of actual offense events which, on average, occur at an *age-specific rate of offending*, called λ. This approach also emphasizes the potential *heterogeneity of offending groups* in the general population with respect to λ and age at onset and desistence. Another approach, more recently articulated by Hagan and Palloni (1988) and Polakowski (1990, 1994), places criminal events within a broader context of *studies of the life course* (Elder, 1985) by explicitly substituting the conceptualization of "social events" for that of "criminal careers." With respect to analytical models, this approach emphasizes a potential *heterogeneity of offenders with respect to order of criminal events* from first to second to higher orders and suggests an analysis of the "risks" or "hazards" of offending by order of offense.

Some extant commentaries on the criminal careers and life course approaches to conceptualizing and modeling longitudinal sequences of delinquent and criminal events committed by individuals have emphasized their differences and incompatibilities (see, e.g., Hagan and Palloni, 1988; Polakowski, 1994). In contrast, we apply recently developed semiparametric mixed Poisson regression modeling techniques (Nagin and Land, 1993; Land *et al.*, 1996) to demonstrate the complementarity of the criminal careers and life course approaches, even though they have somewhat different foci. We do this in two ways. First, we develop the conditions under which the Poisson regression and hazards regression models, corresponding, respectively, to the criminal careers and life course approaches, are formally equivalent. Second, we modify the semiparametric mixed Poisson regression model of criminal careers to incorporate information on order of the delinquent/criminal event and illustrate this modification with an empirical application.

2. THE THEORETICAL APPROACHES

2.1. The Criminal Careers Paradigm and Its Antagonists

The criminal careers concept in its controversial form—postulating that criminals are a distinctive group with respect to levels and lengths of offending sequences—dates back to the pioneering work of Sheldon and Eleanor Glueck (1937, 1940). The Gluecks believed that the study of the formation, development, and termination of criminal careers was an important research priority and that the causes of the initiation of crime were distinct from the causes of continuing crime and processes of desistence (Laub and Sampson, 1991). They argued that age at onset was a key factor in terms of etiology and policy and that career criminals (persistent serious offenders) started very young in life. In all of their longitudinal studies, the Gluecks found that, as the population of offenders aged, the crime rate and seriousness of offenses declined. Finally, the Gluecks advocated a multiple-factor theory of crime that was not exclusively tied to any of the traditional social science disciplines. The Gluecks' work stirred a debate at least as heated as its contemporary counterparts.[3]

Nagin and Land (1993, p. 329) noted that the current round of criminal careers research (and controversy) derives from the work of two engineers from New York City, Avi-Itzhak and Shinnar (1973). Concerned with the high levels of crime in New York City, they asked two questions: How much crime is avoided by the physical isolation of criminals in prison (i.e.,

---

[3]Edwin Sutherland became the leading opponent of the Gluecks from the late-1930s on. For an illuminating, insightful, and exhaustive historical account of the Glueck-Sutherland debate, see Laub and Sampson (1991).

incapacitation)? How sensitive is the incapacitation effect to variables susceptible to manipulation by public policy (e.g., sentence length)?

To study these questions, they posed a simple and elegant stochastic model. Active criminals commit crimes at a Poisson process rate, λ, and have a stochastically determined career length averaging τ time periods. This model and its extensions define the basic features of the *criminal career paradigm*. The Avi-Itzhak and Shinnar model has proven its usefulness for analyses of the questions with which they began. Controversy arises, however, from the question whether the model's defining structure—career onset followed by a period of active offending that ultimately comes to a halt with career termination—should also be the defining structure for theorizing about and analyzing data on the evolution of individual offending. In particular, this model includes the structural elements of *career onset* and *career termination*. These concepts suggest, in turn, that individuals can be distinctively characterized as belonging to one of two groups: criminals or noncriminals. The conception of criminals as a distinctive group is further reinforced by the argument of proponents of the criminal career paradigm that there may be distinctive social and psychological processes regulating the onset of active offending, the period of active criminality, and the termination of offending (Blumstein and Cohen, 1979; Blumstein *et al.*, 1986; Farrington, 1986; Farrington *et al.*, 1990).

An alternative to the sharp distinction between criminals and noncriminals has been put forward by Gottfredson and Hirschi (1990), the most vocal critics of the criminal career paradigm. They argued that criminal behavior, along with other self-destructive behaviors, is a reflection of a single, time-stable individual trait or behavioral propensity toward crime established early in life: *lack of self-control*. In their theory, lack of self-control is not a trait that is distinctive to a specific class of people. Rather, it is a trait that all people share to varying degrees. From the perspective of the Gottfredson and Hirschi theory, the population distribution of criminal involvement is simply a reflection of a continuous (but skewed) distribution of the population with respect to self-control. Chronic criminals are distinctive in degree, not kind; they simply have unusual levels of lack of self-control.

Greenberg (1991) and Rowe *et al.* (1990) contributed to this discourse on criminal careers by formulating mathematical models of the Gottfredson and Hirschi theory. Both their models and the standard criminal careers model adopt the assumption that individuals commit crimes according to a Poisson process at a rate λ. Unlike the criminal careers model, however, both drop the clean distinction between criminals and noncriminals: all individuals are potential criminals in the sense that they possess a positive λ. The pronounced skew in the distribution of offending within the population is accommodated by assuming that the population distribution of λ

follows the gamma distribution in the Greenberg model and the lognormal distribution in the Rowe *et al.* model. Both distributions have flexible shapes and can be highly skewed to the right. As a result, both models are compatible with the skewed distribution of offending in the population. Over a wide range of possible shapes, the γ and lognormal distributions predict that a large segment of the population will have small values of λ. Thus, the observation that a large fraction of the population commits no recorded crimes is not incompatible with the assumption that all individuals have a positive criminal potential (i.e., $\lambda > 0$).

Greenberg (1991) argued that this model framework, which does not resort to the concepts of onset and desistence, can explain many of the empirical findings that Blumstein and colleagues advance in support of the criminal career paradigm. Specifically, he argued that Blumstein and Cohen (1979) finding that the rate of offending is invariant with age may be a sample-selection artifact arising from their having based their calculation on individuals who actually committed at least two offenses. He also argued that empirical evidence of differing processes regulating the various aspects of the criminal career may again be an artifact of sample-selection biases.

2.2. The Crimes as Social Events in the Life Course Perspective

Developed in part as a commentary on one of the printed exchanges about the value of criminal careers research and longitudinal studies (Blumstein *et al.*, 1988a, b; Gottfredson and Hirschi, 1988), Hagan and Palloni (1988) reconceptualized the longitudinal sequences of delinquent and criminal acts committed by an individual within the broader context of *studies of the life course*. A central feature of this conceptualization is that it leads one away from a focus on restricted periods in the life course (e.g., the peak years of crime and delinquency in late adolescence to young adulthood) or on restricted groupings of persons (e.g., the constancy of criminality among high-rate offenders). Hagan and Palloni propose to do this by substituting the conceptualization of "social events" for that of "criminal careers." This redirects attention to the causes and consequences of events called crimes or delinquencies in the broader life course.

In putting forth this conceptualization, Hagan and Palloni (1988, p.90) criticized both the traditional criminal careers paradigm and the Gottfredson–Hirschi alternative. The former focuses attention too closely on relatively rare offenders who commit multiple crimes, while the latter neglects the impact of social events and circumstances throughout the life course. In contrast, a life course perspective emphasizes that social events that are termed delinquent or criminal are linked into life trajectories of broader significance, whether those trajectories are criminal or noncriminal in form. Key propositions of the life course perspective (Elder, 1985) are that "transitions are always embedded in trajectories that give them distinctive form and meaning" (p.31) and "the same event or transition followed by different adaptations can lead to very different trajectories" (p.35).

Hagan and Palloni (1988, pp. 96–97) further argued that the retention of information about the order of the delinquent or criminal event—first, second, and so forth—is essential to an analysis of its impact and meaning in the life course, because of the linkages of these events to each other and to other life course events and trajectories. The implication is that the underlying probabilities for events of different orders might be quite distinct. Polakowski (1994) followed up the conceptual developments of Hagan and Palloni by bringing a number of indicators of social and self-control and life course events together in an analysis of the risk of criminal convictions by age and order of criminal event for West and Farrington's (1973, 1977) London cohort data.

3. THE MODELING APPROACHES

3.1. Micro-Level Mixed Poisson Regression Models

In a commentary on an exchange between Blumstein and colleagues and Greenberg over the latter's model, Land (1992) made several recommendations for resolving certain of the points of contention in the criminal careers debate. First, he observed that formal statistical procedures for comparing the explanatory power of competing models (e.g., the likelihood-ratio test) require that the models be nested. Two models are said to be nested if one is a special case of the other. Because the Greenberg qua Gottfredson and Hirschi model with no onset and desistence is a special case of the criminal career model, in principle their comparative explanatory power and competing predictions can be tested in the context of a nested model formulation. Second, Land argued that models of criminal careers should be specified at the individual level and estimated using standard maximum-likelihood procedures so that their various parameters can be subject to conventional hypothesis testing. Third, Land pointed out that the Poisson γ-negative binomial model is just one example of a general class of mixed or compound Poisson models and that other specific models from this general class could be used to model criminal careers. Fourth, Land suggested allowing key model parameters to be a function of demographic and other characteristics of individuals or their environment in order to take into account measured heterogeneity among individuals.

Nagin and Land (1993) developed a new regression approach to micro-models of criminal careers based on mixtures of Poisson distributions that addressed these recommendations and applied the model to the London longitudinal cohort study of West and Farrington (1973, 1977). Further development of statistical methodology for this model and comparisons with conventional Poisson and negative binomial regression models are given by

Land *et al.* (1996). The latter paper also includes empirical applications to the second Philadelphia cohort study by Wolfgang and colleagues (Tracy *et al.*, 1990).

The mixed Poisson regression model of criminal careers represents a substantial departure from previous approaches. To present this model, assume that we have detailed count data for a sample of $i = 1, \ldots, N$ individuals followed for a sequence of $t = 1, \ldots, T$ time periods. Then the model can be written as a log-linear regression model:

$$\ln \lambda_{it} = X_i \beta + \varepsilon_i, \tag{1}$$

where ln denotes the natural logarithm, λ_{it} is the Poisson mean rate parameter for individual i in period t (i.e., the expected number of delinquent or criminal offenses for the ith individual in the tth time period), X_i denotes the ith row of an $N \times K$ regressor matrix X corresponding to observations on the K exogenous (explanatory, regressor) variables for the ith individual, β is the $K \times 1$ column vector of regression coefficients of the model, and ε_i is an error term included to account for unexplained randomness in λ_i. Note that the error term, ε_i, while specific to each individual i, does not vary across time periods. This error term could reflect a specification error due to the omission of an unobserved time-invariant exogenous variable (Gourieroux *et al.*, 1984a, b) or intrinsic randomness (Hausman *et al.*, 1984). In the former case, it represents the influence of what may be called "persistent" unobserved heterogeneity for individual panel members (Nagin and Farrington, 1992b). The direct incorporation of regressors or explanatory variables in the regression relationship of the conventional Poisson regression model is an effort to accommodate individual sources of variability of the Poisson rate parameter by taking into account *observed* sources of *heterogeneity* or differences among individuals. But no matter how extensive a list of explanatory variables the analyst may include on the right-hand side of model (1), there always is the possibility that other *unobserved* or *hidden* sources of *heterogeneity* may affect an individual's coefficient (Nagin and Land, 1993; Nagin and Farrington, 1992b).

Conventionally, model (1) is completed by specifying a parametric distribution for the error term. Denote by $g(\varepsilon_i)$ the probability density for ε_i. Assuming ε_i is independent of X_i, the marginal density of Y_{it}, a random variable denoting the number of delinquencies or crimes for the ith panel member in period t, can be derived by integrating with respect to ε_i:

$$\text{Prog}[Y_{it} = y_{it}] = \int \text{Prob}[Y_{it} = y_{it} | X_i, \varepsilon_i] g(\varepsilon_i) \, d\varepsilon_i$$

$$= \int \{\exp[-\exp(X_i\beta + \varepsilon_i)][\exp(X_i\beta + \varepsilon_i)]^{y_{it}}\}/y_{it}! g(\varepsilon_i) \, d\varepsilon_i \tag{2}$$

where $\text{Prob}[Y_{it} = y_{it}]$ denotes the probability that the random variable Y_{it}

takes on the specific integral value y_{it}. Equation (2) defines a *compound* or *mixed Poisson distribution*—with *mixing distribution* $g(\varepsilon_i)$—whose precise form depends upon the specific choice of $g(\varepsilon_i)$. For certain parametric forms, a closed-form expression for Eq. (2) can be obtained. For example, using the conventional γ-specification of $g(\varepsilon_i)$, or equivalently of λ_i, in Eq. (2) yields a closed-form solution in the form of a *negative binomial regression model*. This specification is popular because it is programmed in widely available statistical packages such as LIMDEP (Greene, 1992). It also can be seen to be a micro- or individual-level model version of the Greenberg (1991) specification of the Gottfredson–Hirschi model.

The main point is that mixed Poisson regressions provide a generalization of the conventional Poisson regression model which provide flexibility to accommodate hidden heterogeneity.[4] What is unique about the mixed Poisson model of Nagin and Land (1993) is that *no* parametric assumption is made about the distribution of the persistent unobserved heterogeneity, i.e., about the mixing distribution $g(\varepsilon_i)$ of Eq. (2). Rather, the underlying mixing distribution of hidden heterogeneity—whether discrete or continuous—is approximated nonparametrically in model estimation, and it is assumed only that this distribution is adequately represented in the sample data. Because the model thus combines a parametric specification of the regression component of the model with a nonparametric specification of the error term, it can be termed a *semiparametric mixed Poisson regression model*. This approach has several advantages compared to models, such as the negative binomial, that make a specific assumption about the parametric distribution of $g(\varepsilon_i)$. First, criminological theory does not provide specific guidance on the choice of $g(\varepsilon_i)$. Second, such a choice may impose restrictions that are inconsistent with the data. For example, while negative binomial regression provides more flexibility than simple Poisson regression, the former still imposes a restrictive functional form on the relationship of the sample mean and variance of the observed count data—namely, that the variance is a quadratic function of the mean. The nonparametric specification of $g(\varepsilon_i)$ avoids this constraint.

To illustrate informally how this semiparametric approach operates, suppose that Fig. 1A depicts the population distribution of persistent unobserved heterogeneity or, equivalently, of ε_i. Assuming that this underlying distribution has finite end points, Fig. 1B illustrates its approximation by a

---

[4]Hidden heterogeneity often is revealed by so-called *overdispersion* (*underdispersion*) in count data, i.e., by count data for which the sample variance is greater (smaller) than the mean. Using aggregate (sample-wide) data on offense counts by age, Greenberg (1991) demonstrated overdispersion and thus the utility of a group-level model based on the negative binomial. Land *et al.* (1996) provide a similar demonstration in an individual-level regression context.

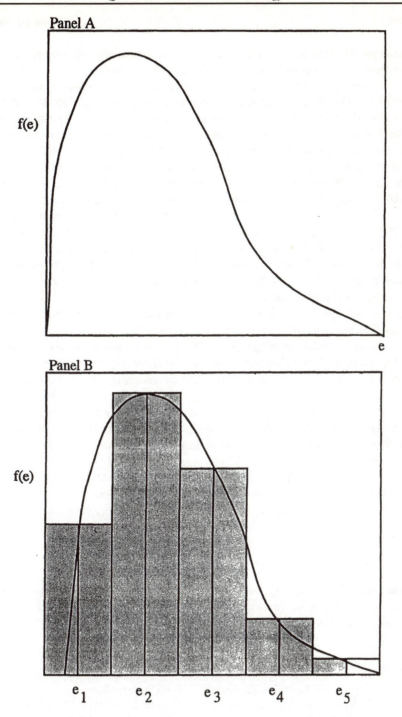

Fig. 1. Approximating a continuous mixing distribution nonparametrically.

discrete distribution (i.e., a histogram) or, alternatively, by a finite number of "points of support" (i.e., the dark-shaded columns).

To estimate the semiparametric mixed Poisson regression model, Nagin and Land (1993) used a *semiparametric maximum-likelihood* (SPML) estimator. Details on the statistical theory and methodology for the application of the SPML estimator to the semiparametric mixed Poisson regression model are available elsewhere (Land *et al.*, 1996; Nagin and Land, 1993) and are not repeated here. Suffice it to say that the semiparametric mixed Poisson model for delinquent/criminal careers includes, in addition to a nonparametric specification of the mixing distribution, parameters, denoted m_j, $j = 1, \ldots, J$, to estimate the percentages of the population at each point of support or grouping of individuals by career type, and an intermittency parameter, labeled π_{it}, to model the probability that individual $i = 1, \ldots, N$ will be actively offending during period $t = 1, \ldots, T$. The latter parameter enables the model to accommodate periods of active delinquency/criminal behavior (during which the mean offending rate parameter $\lambda_{it} > 0$) interspersed with periods of inactivity (during which $\lambda_{it} = 0$) and thus to capture some key features of the criminal careers paradigm.

For subsequent developments in Section 4, it will be useful to have a representation of the likelihood function for the semiparametric mixed Poisson model. To begin with, note that the probabilities of no crime and one or more crimes for individual i in period t are, respectively, $(1 - \pi_{it}) + \pi_{it} \cdot f(y_{it} = 0; \lambda_{it})$ and $\pi_{it} \cdot f(Y_{it} > 0; \lambda_{it})$. Note that these probabilities are conditional on the value of λ_{it}. In semiparametric mixed Poisson models, the distributions of such values are approximated by $j = 1, \ldots, J$ discrete points of support.

For each such point of support j, the likelihood of the sample observation for any given individual i can be formulated as follows:

$$p^j(y_{it} = 0) = (1 - \pi_{it}) + \pi_{it} \cdot f(y_{it} = 0; \lambda_i^j) \tag{3a}$$

and

$$p^j(y_{it} > 0) = \pi_{it} \cdot f(y_{it}; \lambda^j) \tag{3b}$$

where Eqs. (3a) and (3b) are specified at each point of support j. Equations (3a) and (3b) can be combined to form $p^j(y_{it})$ for both zero and positive values of y_{it} with the relationship

$$p^j(y_{it}) = (1 - I_{it}) \cdot p^j(y_{it} = 0) + I_{it} \cdot p^j(y_{it} > 0) \tag{3c}$$

Recall that $I_{it} = 1$ if individual i is active in period t. Thus, if $y_{it} = 0$, the second term is zero, and if $y_{it} = 1$, the first term is zero.

Let the vector $Y_i = \{y_{i1}, y_{i2} \cdots y_{it}\}$ denote individual i's longitudinal sequence of offending over the periods of observation and $P^j(Y_i | \Theta^j)$ denote the probability of that sequence at the jth point of support. Assuming that i is in the jth group:

$$P^j(Y_i) = \prod_t p^j(y_{it}) \tag{4}$$

The next step in formulating the likelihood is to aggregate the likelihood for i over the groupings j:

$$P(Y_i) = \sum_j m^j \cdot P^j(Y_i), \qquad m^j \geq 0, \qquad \sum_j m^j = 1 \tag{5}$$

where $P(Y_i)$ is the unconditional probability of observing i's longitudinal sequence of offending. This unconditional probability is simply the sum of the probability of Y_i at each point of support j, $P^j(Y_i)$, multiplied by the proportion of the population at that point of support, m^j. Thus, the log of the likelihood function is

$$\ln L = \sum_i \ln(P(Y_i)) = \sum_i \ln \left(\sum_j m^j \cdot P^j(Y_i) \right) \tag{6}$$

Maximization of this log-likelihood function yields estimates of the regression coefficients and their standard errors as well as asymptotic chi-square likelihood-ratio statistics for assessing model fit and to assist in making decisions about the optimal number of points of support (groupings) to utilize.[5] Further details on these methods are given by Land *et al.* (1996) and Nagin and Land (1993).

All of the foregoing discussion of the mixed model has assumed that the only distinction between the groupings is with respect to the intercepts of the ln λ functions in Eq. (1). In practice, Nagin and Land (1993) and Land *et al.* (1996) found it useful, in producing models that adequately represent the empirical patterns, to allow the age and age-squared regression coefficients to be specific to each of the groupings used in the analyses. This then permits each grouping to display different age trajectories of the mean rate of offending.

A key feature of the semiparametric mixed Poisson model approach is that individuals are not sorted *ex ante* among the specified number of groupings. After model estimation, however, as shown by Nagin and Land (1993), individuals can be sorted using the following *maximum probability procedure*: Based on the model coefficient estimates, the probability of

---

[5]A computer program for obtaining maximum-likelihood estimates of the semiparametric mixed Poisson regression model has been written in the special programming language GAUSS (Aptech Systems, 1992).

observing each individual's longitudinal pattern of offending is computed conditional on the individual's being in each of the respective groupings. The individual then is assigned to the grouping with the highest probability. Based on this procedure, an individual with a long history of offending at a high rate per period, in all likelihood, would be assigned to a high-rate offending group. On the other hand, an individual with a history of a low rate of offending likely would be categorized as a low-rate offender. Note that the maximum probability sorting rule does not guarantee perfect assignments. For example, based on this rule, individuals with no recorded offenses are always categorised as nonoffenders. Some such individuals may in fact be a member of one of the "active" offending groups but simply had no recorded offenses.

Based on empirical applications of the mixed Poisson regression model to the London cohort study (Nagin and Land, 1993) and the Second Philadelphia cohort (Land *et al.*, 1996), several empirical results have been obtained. First, in contrast to the aggregate criminal careers model of Blumstein and colleagues, these applications of the mixed model have found that groupings of the samples into two groups (offenders and nonoffenders) is not sufficient. Rather, four groupings are necessary: a nonoffender group, together with three groups ranging in offending levels from low to medium to high. Moreover, each grouping displays a unique age trajectory of the λ rates. Second, also in contrast to the aggregate criminal careers model, all of the age trajectories of offense rates, even those of the highest-rate offending group, exhibit quadratic age curves. That is, there is no evidence that the rate of offending of the high-rate offending group is invariant with age. Third, however, in support of the criminal careers paradigm, mixed Poisson regression models that incorporate the intermittency parameter, π, fit the data significantly better than do models that do not allow this parameter to vary. The intermittency parameter also displays a single-peaked age trajectory and varies across individuals as a function of observable characteristics and prior offending, but with parameter estimates distinct from those of λ. Fourth, also in support of the criminal careers paradigm, mixed Poisson regression models that allow more than one grouping of the samples fit better than those which assume only a single grouping. Moreover, using the extensive longitudinal data on parent and child characteristics at ages before delinquency/criminal careers began, Nagin and Land (1993) and Nagin *et al.* (1995) were able to find a number of such factors which distinguish the various groups they identified. Thus, while the models affirm that the mean offense rate varies continuously from individuals with zero mean offense rate to those with very high mean rates, there also is some utility to distinguishing groupings within the entire sample.

3.2. Hazards Regression Models and Associated Empirical Findings

Hagan and Palloni (1988, p.97) argued that the methods of event history analysis (see, e.g., Tuma and Hannan, 1984; Yamaguchi, 1991) are particularly well suited for the study of crime as social events in the life course. They argued that the modeling of criminal careers based on the Poisson process produces estimates of a summary hazard of criminal involvement which mixes crime order-specific hazards. That is, for all those involved in a first delinquent or criminal event, there is a hazard or risk of involvement in a second criminal event, possibly dependent on the time since the first event and other covariates. The same applies to those in later (third-, fourth-, or higher-order) events. In each case, the order-specific hazard characterizes the entire process. That is, while one can infer the value of the criminal careers λ from the combined order-specific λ's, one cannot generally infer event-specific hazards from lambda. This makes the criminal careers λ an ambiguous indicator of the dynamic processes underlying it. Accordingly, Hagan and Palloni (1988, p.97) argue that it might be more illuminating to retrieve the hazards by order of event and that this "would considerably bolster the power of hypothesis testing."

The simplest form of event history model is the *proportional hazards regression model* originally developed by Cox (1972). The *hazard or instantaneous risk function* of experiencing some event, say, a first criminal offense, at time t is given by

$$h(t, \mathbf{x}) = h_0(t) \exp(\mathbf{X}\beta) \tag{7}$$

where $h(t, \mathbf{X})$ is the instantaneous rate of offending at time t for an individual with a vector of covariates $\mathbf{X}_t$, $h_0(t)$ is a nonnegative but otherwise unspecified baseline hazard function (the "underlying hazard function") not dependent on the covariates, and β is a vector of unknown regression coefficients (including a constant) to be estimated.

A key assumption of the proportional hazards model, sometimes called the *proportionality assumption*, is that the effects of the covariates remain constant throughout all segments of the duration variable (time, age) under consideration (Allison, 1984; Kalbfleisch and Prentice, 1980; Trussell and Hammerslough, 1983; Yamaguchi, 1991). Under this assumption, the ratio of hazard functions for any two individuals with covariate vectors $\mathbf{X}_1$ and $\mathbf{X}_2$ is simply $\exp[(\mathbf{X}_1 - \mathbf{X}_2)]\beta$ independent of time t—which yields the "proportional hazards" label. *Nonproportional hazards models* can be formulated by allowing $h_0(t)$ to depend on $\mathbf{X}$ (i.e., by allowing one or more covariates to interact with the duration variable—that is, have different effects in different duration intervals) or by incorporating "time-varying covariates" that allow X to depend on t.[6]

Recent contributions to the analysis of data on delinquency/crime patterns over the life course by application of hazards regression have begun to appear. For example, a proportional hazards specification was employed by Tontodonato (1988) in her analysis of the rate at which officially detected juvenile offenders move from one crime type to another between age 10 and age 18 in the Second Philadelphia Cohort. Often, however, it is found empirically that the effects of one or more covariates have different effects on the risk of an event, such as delinquency or crime, in different age intervals. In other words, the proportionality assumption often is violated in hazards analyses of delinquency or criminality across extended age intervals. A conventional solution to this problem is to estimate a *semiparametric hazard regression model* in which the hazard function is assumed to be constant within time subintervals but allowed to vary (in an arbitrary, nonparametric form) across time intervals.[7] Potentially valuable information regarding the timing of events and the effects of covariates thereon is retained in this way.

The semiparametric hazard regression model recently has been applied by Polakowski (1994) to estimate hazard regressions for the transition to first conviction and the transition to second- and higher-order convictions (grouped) for the London cohort study by West and Farrington. After preliminary nonparametric estimation of survival and hazards functions for the entire sample and preliminary estimation of proportional hazards regression models, Polakowski found that, for the transition to first conviction, a semiparametric model with subintervals in which the hazard function is assumed constant provided the best empirical fit. In particular, he found that a total observation period from age 9 to age 32 was best treated by four 2- to 3-year sequences (within which the hazards are constant) from age 9 to age 21, after which the hazard again is constant to age 32. For the transition to second- and higher-order convictions, Polakowski's preliminary nonparametric analyses suggested that a five-period partition of the age range 10 to 32, with constant effects of covariates across all age periods (i.e., proportional hazards), was sufficient.

---

[6]As standard expositions of the maximum-likelihood and partial-likelihood estimation of proportional hazards and piecewise-constant hazards regression models are readily available in the literature cited, they are not repeated here.

[7]Sometimes this model also is called the *piecewise-constant hazards model* or the *piecewise-exponential survival function model*. As Yamaguchi (1991, p.76) notes, the pattern of time dependence in hazards regression models often does not conform well to a parametric form, such as the Gompertz or Weibull. In such cases, a piecewise-exponential model may well constitute the best approach.

4. CONDITIONS FOR FORMAL EQUIVALENCE OF THE MODELS

In the preceding sections we have reviewed two seemingly disparate approaches to the development of micromodels of sequences of delinquent and criminal acts ordered by age. As noted in Section 1, one approach, that based on traditional criminal careers notions and mixed Poisson regression analysis, emphasizes the importance of controlling for the potential heterogeneity of the population with respect to offending groups. According to this approach, not to do so results in the confounding of high-rate, low-rate, and nonoffending groups. The other approach, that based on the life course perspective and hazards regression analysis, emphasizes the need to control for heterogeneity of offenders with respect to order of criminal events and, also, for age. Not to do so results in a combining of hazards of criminal events of various orders and ages.

But are these approaches, in fact, discrete and different? We believe not. First, there has been a considerable amount of confusion about the different models. For instance, Nagin and Land's development of statistical methods for Poisson-based micromodels of criminal careers shows that the power of statistical foundations for hypothesis testing is just as available for this approach as Hagan and Palloni (1988, p.97) claimed for hazards regression. Second, under various conditions on the two classes of models, microlevel Poisson regression models can, in fact, be shown to be discrete-time equivalents of hazards regression models.

To demonstrate this claim for a particular class of model specifications, assume, first, that the focus of attention is on criminal events of a given order, say the first. Assume that a semiparametric hazard model without covariates is estimated for a given set of data, i.e., that an overall hazard for the transition to the first offense is estimated by specifying that the hazard is piecewise-constant (equivalently, that the survival functions are piecewise-exponential) within selected age intervals but varies between age intervals. This can be expressed as

$$\ln h_k = \beta_k \qquad (8)$$

for age intervals $j = 1, 2, \ldots, J$. The corresponding simple Poisson regression model (i.e., no heterogeneity or discrete groupings of the population), with a constant term but no covariates fitted piecewise over the same selected age intervals, is

$$\ln \lambda_k = \beta_k^* \qquad (9)$$

The equivalence of the constants β_k and β_k^* then follows from the facts that, under these specifications:

(a) the Poisson regression model has a representation as a log-linear model for the cell means of contingency tables with Poisson sampling distributions (see, e.g., McCullagh and Nelder, 1989; pp. 209–210);

(b) log-linear models for Poisson contingency table data are exactly equivalent to log-linear hazards for survival data; and

(c) the likelihoods for these two classes of models are also equivalent.

Propositions b and c were proven for the general case by Laird and Olivier (1981) and therefore need not be demonstrated here. Indeed, Laird and Olivier showed the model equivalence applies more generally when we specify (i) piecewise-exponential survival distributions and (ii) categorical covariates.

The argument for model equivalence can be taken beyond this special case. First, the equivalence does not require that $\ln h$ and $\ln \lambda$ be fixed constants. The previous argument holds for the case where these two quantities are functions of time-invariant covariates, say, $X\beta$. Second, the constraint to piecewise-exponential hazards regression models, which strictly speaking is incompatible with time-varying covariates, is not limiting, because discrete-time hazards regression models generally (i.e., not just the piecewise-exponential class of hazards models) have a logistic regression formulation (Cox, 1972; Yamaguchi, 1991; p.18), and as the measurement of the duration variable becomes finer and finer, the logistic regression form of the hazards regression model approaches (i.e., converges to) that of the corresponding continuous-time hazards regression model, as represented in Eq. (7) (Yamaguchi, 1991, p.18).[8]

While all of the foregoing equivalences pertain to Poisson and hazards regression models with homogeneous populations (i.e., unmixed models), Manton and Stallard (1981) gave a demonstration of properties similar to a–c above for mixed Poisson regression models of the negative binomial type, and their results apply straightforwardly to the semiparametric mixed Poisson regression model specified above.

In brief, by focusing on the duration time or age to criminal events of any order, the hazards and Poisson regression models of criminal careers become identical. A key part of this synthesis was the development by Land (1992) and Nagin and Land (1993) of micromodel versions of the conventional group-level Poisson criminal careers model. By specializing this model

[8]In fact, discrete-time hazards regression models provide adequate approximations of the corresponding continuous-time models only if the conditional probabilities of the event of interest are reasonably small. How small? Yamaguchi (1991, p.42) states that the approximation can reasonably be expected not to be adequate if the aggregate frequency data include a high proportion of situations where the conditional probability becomes much larger than 0.1. In the case of delinquency/crime events over the life course, it is rare to find more than one or two ages (usually ages 16 and 17) in which the proportions of, say, first police contacts, arrests, or convictions are greater than one-tenth of the at-risk members of a sample.

to criminal events of particular orders and a homogeneous population (no discrete groupings due to hidden heterogeneity), it then becomes equivalent to a piecewise-exponential hazards regression. Indeed, under the assumption that the observation time intervals (i.e., the time intervals between waves of a panel) are sufficiently short that no more than one event (e.g., arrest) occurs for any given individual in any discrete time interval, one can estimate a general hazard regression function using pooled data on events of all orders by allowing the regression function to vary for different orders of events [e.g., by constructing a set of dummy variables to represent the different events in a sequence (see Allison, 1982; p.93)].

But the more general mixed Poisson regression of Nagin and Land (1993) is capable of bringing additional analytic focus on crime event data. First, one can specify a parametric form of the time (age) dependence of the hazard of crime events (of a given order) such as the quadratic employed by Nagin and Land (1993). Second, even when the focus is on the duration time to the first delinquent or criminal event, the possibility of hidden heterogeneity within a population should be explored. This can be done within the mixed Poisson framework by allowing for a small number of groupings (say, two, three, or four) in the manner described above. In this elaborated form, the mixed Poisson model becomes, in fact, a discrete-time approximation to the continuous-time hazard regression model with a parametric hazard function and nonparametric hidden heterogeneity developed by Heckman and Singer (1982, 1984a, b).

To demonstrate this, note that, using notation similar to that defined above for the log-likelihood function for the mixed Poisson regression model with intermittency, the log-likelihood function for the Heckman–Singer (1984a; p.302) model may be expressed as

$$\ln L = \sum_i \ln\left(\sum_j m^j \cdot Pr^j(t)\right), \quad m^j \geq 0, \quad \sum_j m^j = 1, \quad m^j \geq 0, \quad \sum_j m^j = 1 \qquad (10)$$

First, to interpret this log-likelihood, note that, just as in the log-likelihood for the mixed Poisson regression model given in Eq. (6) above, the m^j-denote the proportions of the population at each point of support j and that these proportions sum to 1.0. Second, in the context of Heckman and Singer (1984a) the $Pr^j(t)$ function denotes the duration density for the event of interest at time t given membership in the jth point-of-support grouping. Heckman and Singer (1948b) generalize this to a Box–Cox class of functions—which includes the quadratic (in age or duration–time) hazards utilized in the delinquency/criminal careers models studied here. Given this explication of the notation, the structural similarity of the log-likelihood function of the Heckman–Singer hazard regression model in Eq. (10) to the log-likelihood function of the semiparametric Poisson regression model in Eq. (6) is apparent.[9]

To see this, recall that we are focusing here on the transition to the first delinquent or criminal offense. Thus, as the length of the discrete time period approaches 0 (i.e., as we move closer to continuous time), the vectors $Y_i = \{y_{i1}, y_{i2}, \ldots, y_{iT}\}$ defined earlier and which enter into the calculation of the log-likelihood in Eq. (6) consist of sequences of zeros with a single one corresponding to the age at which individual i makes the transition to the first offense. This is precisely the sample equivalent of the conditional probability function for a duration time of length t until individual i makes a transition to the first offense, as given in the log-likelihood of the Heckman–Singer model in Eq. (15). This result, of course, is that the maximization of the log-likelihood function of the mixed Poisson model approximates the maximization of the log-likelihood function of the Heckman–Singer model, as was claimed. We now turn to an empirical application which illustrates these calculations in the context of the semiparametric mixed Poisson regression model.

5. EMPIRICAL APPLICATION TO THE LONDON COHORT DATA

The foregoing points can be expanded upon and made more concrete in the context of an empirical application. For this, we use the panel data set assembled by David Farrington and Donald West. The panel is a prospective longitudinal survey of 411 males from a working-class area of London. Data collection began in 1961–1962, when most of the boys were about age 8. Criminal involvement is measured by convictions for criminal offenses[10] and is available for all individuals in the sample through age 32, with the exception of eight individuals who died prior to that age. To the extent possible,

[9]There are, of course, some key differences between the two models. For instance, as we have noted, the Heckman–Singer model is an intrinsically continuous-time hazards regression model [which subsumes the conventional proportional hazards regression model of Eq. (7) as a special case with no hidden heterogeneity], whereas our semiparametric mixed Poisson regression model is an intrinsically discrete-time model [which, nonetheless, is implied by several continuous-time models for recurrent events (see Allison, 1982, p.91)]. In addition, there is no counterpart in the Heckman–Singer hazards regression model of the intermittency component of the expanded semiparametric Poisson regression model defined above. Also, in the formulation of the latter model, we have assumed that the analyst specifies a priori a particular number of points of support and then estimates the parameters of the corresponding model, whereas in the most general version of the Heckman and Singer model, an optimal number of points of support is estimated simultaneously with all other model parameters (Heckman and Singer, 1984b, p.95). Despite these differences, the essential structural similarity of the two log-likelihood functions is evident.

[10]The conviction records do not include convictions for traffic offenses or for offenses deemed to be of minor seriousness (e.g., drunkenness or simple assault).

Table I. Average Annual Rate of Conviction (×10) by Age and Offender Type

Age	Offender type		
	High-level chronic	Adolescent-limited	Low-level chronic
10–11	2.1	0.8	0.0
12–13	5.0	2.4	0.5
14–15	9.0	5.5	1.7
16–17	14.6	5.7	1.7
18–19	16.5	4.9	1.8
20–21	11.5	1.0	3.1
22–23	7.5	0.0	3.6
24–25	5.6	0.0	2.6
26–27	3.8	0.0	3.3
28–29	5.2	0.0	2.4
30–31	3.5	0.0	2.6
(No. in sample)	(52)	(51)	(42)

all of the boys were interviewed at approximately 2-year intervals until they were age 18. Parents, teachers, and friends were also interviewed. Data are available on psychological characteristics (e.g., IQ, risk-taking behavior, and neuroticism), on socialization variables (e.g., parental supervision and attachment), and on family background variables (e.g., criminality of parents and siblings, income, separation from parents, and family size). Our analysis is based on the data for the 403 individuals for which a complete conviction history was available for ages 10 to 32. For a complete discussion of the data set, see West and Farrington (1973, 1977).

Our purpose is to provide an empirical demonstration of the capability of semiparametric mixed Poisson statistical models to control for "hidden heterogeneity" and also to allow the hazard to depend on the order of the event and age. The point of departure for the demonstration is Nagin and Land (1993), who used semiparametric mixed Poisson models to analyze this same data set. Nagin and Land identified four distinct groupings (i.e., points of support). A group who had never been convicted was labeled "nonconvicted." A group who ceased their offending (as measured by conviction) by their early 20's was labeled "adolescence-limiteds" (ALs) after Moffitt (1993). Also identified were two chronic offender groups: "high-level chronics" (HLCs), who offended at a high level through much of the observation period; and "low-level chronics" (LLCs), who offended at a low level throughout the observation period—ages 8 to 32.

Table I reports the average rate of conviction by age for the three groups with at least one conviction, the HLCs, LLCs, and ALs. Observe that the trajectory of offending differs dramatically across group. The HLC age–conviction curve follows the contour of the typical age–crime curve based on aggregate data—a rather steep rise to a peak at about age 18 and a gradual decline thereafter (Farrington, 1986). The rising proportion of the AL curve follows this conventional contour, but upon reaching a peak at about age 16, the rate begins a precipitous decline; by age 22 the rate is zero, where it remains for the rest of the observation period. The LLC curve is also distinctive. While there is a clear rise through early adolescence, it remains relatively stable after age 18. By age 20, the LLCs are more active than the ALs, and by age 30, the rates of the HLCs and LLCs have nearly converged. These results imply that explanations of the age–crime curve at the level of the individual cannot be the same as explanations of average population tendencies.

Nagin and Land identified these distinctive trajectories by estimating a model where λ at each point of support was specified as follows:

$$HLC: \qquad \ln(\lambda_{it}^a) = (\beta_0 + \bar{\varepsilon}_a) + \delta X_i + \beta_1^a \, age_{it} + \beta_2^a \, age_{it}^2 \qquad (11a)$$

$$AL: \qquad \ln(\lambda_{it}^b) = (\beta_0 + \bar{\varepsilon}_b) + \delta X_i + \beta_1^b \, age_{it} + \beta_2^b \, age_{it}^2 \qquad (11b)$$

$$LLC: \qquad \ln(\lambda_{it}^c) = (\beta_0 + \bar{\varepsilon}_c) + \delta X_i + \beta_1^c \, age_{it} + \beta_2^c \, age_{it}^2 \qquad (11c)$$

where the subscripts i and t, respectively, denote the ith individual in the sample and the tth observation period, age_{it} is i's age in t, age_{it}^2 is i's age squared ($\div 10$) in t, and TOT_i is a scalar index computed as the average of four binary indicator variables: low IQ, which equals 1 if i is in the lower quartile of the IQ distribution; criminal parents, which equals 1 if either of i's parents had a criminal conviction; daring, which equals 1 if i is in the upper quartile of a composite measure of risk-taking and adventurous behavior; and poor parenting, which equals 1 if i's parents were judged as having poor parenting skills (e.g., used harsh and erratic discipline). All of these variables were measured when the study male was between age 8 and age 10 and each has been consistently found to be associated with criminal and delinquent behavior in this and other data sets. Thus, higher values of TOT are expected to be associated with higher rates of offending.[11]

Two features of this model are noteworthy. First, the mean rate of offending is specified to be a function of age, specifically a quadratic function. Thus, for any given group j (HLC, AL, LLC), the hazard is age graded except for the special case where β^j_1 and β^j_2 are found to be equal to 0. In the case where $\beta^j_1 > 0$ and $\beta^j_2 < 0$, λ will rise and then fall with age just as

[11]The Nagin and Land and the present analyses include a fourth point of support to accommodate the never convicted. At this point of support, λ is set equal to a very small value (0.01).

Table II. Original and Extended Semiparametric Mixed Poisson Regression Models of Convictions in the London Cohort Data

Variable/parameter λ_{it}	Original model		Extended model	
	Coefficient estimate	t-ratio	Coefficient estimate	t-ratio
$\beta_0 + \bar{\varepsilon}_a$(HLC)	−2.55	−2.51	−2.12	−1.85
$\beta_0 + \bar{\varepsilon}_b$(AL)	−14.80	−3.28	−15.38	−3.27
$\beta_0 + \bar{\varepsilon}_c$(LLC)	−4.74	−2.21	−4.35	−1.84
TOT$_i$	1.34	4.47	2.10	4.21
Age (HLC)	2.76	2.63	1.39	1.24
Age**2 (HLC)	−0.79	−3.13	−0.50	−1.88
Age (AL)	19.20	3.30	18.94	3.17
Age**2 (AL)	−6.52	−3.49	−6.54	−3.45
Age (LLC)	2.70	1.20	1.32	0.56
Age**2 (LLC)	−0.59	−1.08	−0.29	0.50
O_{it}	—	—	1.18	2.57
$O_{it} * \text{TOT}_i$	—	—	−1.42	−5.21

in aggregate data. Because of the equivalence of Heckman–Singer hazard and semiparametric mixed Poisson regression models noted above, such age-graded variation in λ implies a parallel age gradation (or time dependence) in the hazard function. Second, observe that the coefficients of age$_{it}$ and age$_{it}^2$ are not constrained to be equal across offending groups, so that separate age trajectory coefficients were estimated for each such group. This allowed Nagin and Land to test for heterogeneity in *offending trajectories* within the population. As described above, such heterogeneity was indeed found.

Table II reports the intercepts and age coefficients for the three offender groups and also the coefficient of TOT$_i$ as estimated by Nagin and Land. These estimates are reported in the column "original model." Note that across groups there are large differences in these paper estimates. The very distinctive offending trajectories across group shown in Table I are a manifestation of these differences.

Consider next a modification of the model as estimated by Nagin and Land to accommodate structural shifts in the hazard *by order of the event*. To do so, we expand specifications of $\ln(\lambda^J_{it})$, Eqs. (11a)–(11c), for the three offending groups as follows:

$$HLC: \ln(\lambda^a_{it}) = (\beta_0 + \bar{\varepsilon}_a) + \delta X_i + \beta^a_1 \text{age}_{it} + \beta^a_2 \text{age}^2_{it} + \beta_3 O_{it} + \beta_4 O_{it} * TOT_i \quad (12a)$$

$$AL: \ln(\lambda^b_{it}) = (\beta_0 + \bar{\varepsilon}_b) + \delta X_i + \beta^b_1 \text{age}_{it} + \beta^b_2 \text{age}^2_{it} + \beta_3 O_{it} + \beta_4 O_{it} * TOT_i \quad (12b)$$

$$LLC: \ln(\lambda^c_{it}) = (\beta_0 + \bar{\varepsilon}_c) + \delta X_i + \beta^c_1 \text{age}_{it} + \beta^c_2 \text{age}^2_{it} + \beta_3 O_{it} + \beta_4 O_{it} * TOT_i \quad (12c)$$

The expanded specification includes two additional terms. One, O_{it}, is a binary variable equal to 1 if, in any period to the current period t, individual i had been convicted; O_{it} can be interpreted as an indicator of onset having occurred. The inclusion of this term allows for the possibility that onset of offending is associated with a change in the rate of offending.[12] Such a change is equivalent to allowing the hazard rate to depend on the order of the event and is a type of "state dependency" whereby prior behavior alters the probability of future outcomes (Nagin and Paternoster, 1991). The second term is the interaction of O_{it} with TOT_i. Like the main effect term O_{it}, inclusion of this interaction term allows the hazard rate to depend on order of event. Specifically, it allows for the possibility that the factors which predict onset (i.e., the first 2-year period in which an individual is convicted in the London data) are in some respects different from those that predict the probability of continued offending (i.e., the second- and higher-order periods in which an individual is convicted in the London data).

The coefficient estimates of this expanded specification are also reported in Table II, in the column labeled "extended model."[13] With two exceptions, the coefficient estimates across specification are similar. One exception concerns high-level chronics. For this group, the coefficients of the age_{it} and age_{it}^2 terms in the extended specification are smaller in (absolute) magnitude than the companion estimates in the original specification. This implies that the λ-age trajectory in the extended specification rises less quickly and falls more slowly (i.e., is "flatter") than in the original specification. Indeed, in the extended specification, the coefficient of age_{it} (but not age_{it}^2) is insignificant by conventional standards. A second notable difference pertains to the coefficient estimate of the composite index, TOT_i; the estimate from the extended specification is nearly 60% larger than in the original specification (2.10 vs 1.34).

Consider now the coefficient estimates of the two additional variables in the extended specification, O_{it} and $O_{it} * TOT_{it}$. Both are highly significant.[14] Specifically, the coefficient of the main effect of onset is positive, which implies that the post-onset offending hazard is higher than the pre-onset

[12]The effects of second and subsequent convictions on the rate of offending were pooled because the numbers of individuals convicted for distinct numbers of offenses beyond two becomes too small for the London cohort data to permit reliable estimation of separate effect coefficients.

[13]The full model defining the extended specification like the original specification includes parameters specifying the proportion of the population at each point of support and intermittence parameters. Because the parameter estimates pertaining to these aspects of the full model are not relevant to the points we wish to make here, they are not reported in Table II.

[14]A likelihood-ratio test of the comparative explanatory power of the two specifications shows that the addition of these two variables results in a highly significant improvement in goodness of fit ($\chi^2 = 31.47$, df = 2).

hazard. The coefficient of the $O_{it} * \text{TOT}_{it}$ interaction is negative. This implies that post-onset differences in the underlying hazard rate of individuals with different levels of TOT_i are smaller than pre-onset differences.

To illustrate further capacity of the semiparametric mixed Poisson method to estimate hazards that vary by grouping (point of support), order of event, and age, Table III reports estimates by age and grouping of the conditional probabilities of onset and of post-onset offending. Specifically, the age-dependent conditional probability of onset estimates the probability of onset during the 2-year period beginning at that age. Similarly, the age-dependent conditional probability of post-onset offending is the estimated likelihood of at least one conviction during the current age period given that onset had occurred by the prior age period. Also reported are survival probabilities by age for each group.

These probabilities are calculated as follows. First, given estimates of all of the regression coefficients for the λ_{it} and π_{it} functions of the model, and noting that for the Poisson density function $f(0; \lambda_{it}) = \exp\{-\lambda_{it}\}$, the probability of *zero* convictions for individual i during period $t = 1, \ldots, 11$, which we denote $P_{it,0}$, is given by Eq. (5) above. Note that in computing this $P_{it,0}$ for an individual with no prior convictions, the index $I_{i,t-1}$ in Eq. (7) equals zero. In calculating these probabilities, we also set TOT_i equal to 0.50. The probabilities of onset reported in the second column in Table III then are evaluated as $P_{it,1+} = 1 - P_{0it}$. Because $P_{it,1+}$ is the probability of no convictions for individual i in period t and is evaluated for $I_{i,t-1} = 0$, $P_{it,1+}$ is properly interpreted as the conditional probability of onset in period t. The post-onset conditional probabilities of conviction reported in the third column in Table III are calculated in the same fashion as $P_{it,1+}$, except that $I_{i,t-1} = 1$. Finally, the survival probabilities reported in the last column in Table III are simply the cumulative probabilities of no convictions (i.e., no onset) through each period. Thus, the age 12 survival probability of 0.615 equals 0.815 (the survival probability for age 10) times $P_{it,1+} = 1 - 0.245$, where $t = 12$ and 0.245 is the onset probability at age 12.

Consider first the resulting estimated conditional probabilities in Table III for the high-level chronics. At all ages, onset probability is highest for this group. Indeed, onset probabilities are so high that by age 16 the probability of a HLC having "survived" first conviction (i.e., not been convicted) is only 0.29. By age 22, the survival rate is reduced to 0.1. Once onset has occurred the HLC postonset offending probabilities at all ages are extremely high—more than 0.5 at most ages and never less than 0.25. Thus, for this group continued offending is a virtual certainty. Accordingly, they were labeled "high-level chronics."

The pattern of onset and post-onset probabilities for the adolescent-limiteds is again reflective of their group label. Until age 16, both of these

Table III. Predicted Probabilities of Onset, Post-onset Offending, and
Survival by Group for TOT=0.5

Age	Probability of onset	Post-onset offending probability	Survival probability
(A) High-level chronics			
10	0.185	—	0.815
12	0.245	0.606	0.615
14	0.293	0.664	0.435
16	0.321	0.695	0.295
18	0.328	0.702	0.198
20	0.315	0.684	0.136
22	0.283	0.643	0.097
24	0.237	0.578	0.074
26	0.184	0.492	0.061
28	0.129	0.390	0.053
30	0.081	0.282	0.049
(B) Adolescent-limiteds			
10	0.044	—	0.956
12	0.126	0.391	0.836
14	0.202	0.534	0.667
16	0.202	0.522	0.532
18	0.123	0.346	0.466
20	0.042	0.128	0.447
22	0.008	0.025	0.443
24	0.000	0.003	0.433
26	0.000	0.000	0.443
28	0.000	0.000	0.443
30	0.000	0.000	0.443
(C) Low-level chronics			
10	0.032	—	0.968
12	0.047	0.167	0.922
14	0.062	0.202	0.865
16	0.075	0.230	0.800
18	0.086	0.251	0.731
20	0.092	0.265	0.664
22	0.093	0.269	0.602
24	0.090	0.264	0.548
26	0.081	0.250	0.504
28	0.068	0.226	0.470
30	0.052	0.192	0.445

probabilities are only modestly lower than the companion estimates for the
HLCs. For example, at age 14 the probability of onset for the ALs is 0.2.
For the HLCs, it is 0.29. The post-onset offending probabilities at age 14
for the two groups are, respectively, 0.53 and 0.66. After age 16, however,
the offending probabilities of the two groups radically diverge. By age 22

Table IV. Predicted Versus Actual Survival
Probabilities

Age	Survival probability	
	Predicted	Actual
10	0.971	0.975
12	0.922	0.918
14	0.857	0.834
16	0.795	0.759
18	0.748	0.720
20	0.714	0.692
22	0.690	0.680
24	0.671	0.667
26	0.657	0.658
28	0.647	0.653
30	0.641	0.640

the probabilities of onset and of continued offending for ALs are near-zero. For the HLCs both remain high—0.28 and 0.64.[15]

Consider, finally, the low-level chronics. Compared to HLCs and ALs, the offending probabilities of the LLCs vary least with age. Until age 18, the probabilities of onset and continued offending are lowest for this group. By age 20, these two probabilities are higher for the LLCs than for the ALs. By age 30 the offending probabilities of the high- and low-level chronics have nearly converged.

As a final exercise to evaluate the model's goodness of fit to the data, we compared the "onset" survival probabilities predicted by the model aggregated over all groups with the actual sample survival rates. The results are reported in Table IV.[16] It can be seen that the fit is nearly perfect. Judged by its empirical fit, then, the semiparametric mixed Poisson model and the hazards (conditional probabilities of conviction) estimated from it appear to provide a most appropriate representation of the London data.

Viewed from a methodological perspective, the probabilities reported in Table III also nicely illustrate our contention that the semiparametric mixed Poisson estimation method has the flexibility to capture both age and order dependencies in hazard rates while also controlling semiparametrically for hidden heterogeneity. Specifically, for each grouping the offending probabilities are shown to depend on age and onset status, which thus illustrates the capacity to capture both age and order dependencies. Variation in

[15]The probability of onset applies only to those who have not previously been convicted. Thus, by age 22 this probability has little relevance for the high-level chronics since nearly all have previously been convicted.

[16]For this goodness-of-fit exercise we set TOT to the sample average of 0.25.

offending probabilities across groups controlling for age and onset status reflects the capacity of the mixed Poisson approach to capture hidden heterogeneity.

6. CONCLUSION

On the basis of the reviews reported above of the criminal careers and life course approaches to longitudinal sequences of delinquent and criminal acts committed by individuals—and the corresponding microlevel Poisson and Hazards regression models—several conclusions can be stated. The hazards regression model, which underlies event history analysis, and the Poisson regression model, which underlies the semiparametric mixed Poisson model, are analytically equivalent under conditions that are satisfied in most empirical applications to delinquent/criminal career data. Thus, whatever difference exist between the "criminal career" and the "life course" perspectives are not methodological; rather, they are substantive. In the end, such substantive differences can be resolved only by empirical tests of specific competing theories.

In addition, based on the model comparisons and analyses reported above, the semiparametric mixed Poisson approach described herein appears to have two specific advantages over the typical hazards regression model of time to the nth event employed in conventional event history analyses. First, in addition to allowing for the capacity to test for age and order dependencies in offending probabilities, it provides the capability to control for hidden heterogeneity. Second, by incorporating all orders of offenses within a single model specification, the semiparametric mixed Poisson model attains greater statistical power for these tests. Because hidden heterogeneity cannot generally be ruled out on an a priori basis with respect to any longitudinal delinquency/criminal careers data set, and because it generally is advisable to bring as much statistical power as possible to bear on the evaluation of substantive hypotheses, these would appear to be desirable attributes for advancing substantive research on micromodels of criminal careers.

These features were illustrated in our analysis of the London cohort data—for which we were able to estimate a positive effect of onset of offending on subsequent offending in the presence of previously identified latent groupings of offenders by age-specific offending patterns. We also found that post-onset differences in the underlying hazard rate of individuals with different levels of our TOT index are smaller than pre-onset differences. In particular, we estimated post-onset offending probabilities for the high-level chronic offender grouping of more than 50% at most ages—a virtual certainty.

In concluding, it should be noted that additional work on the semiparametric mixed Poisson modeling apparatus remains to be done. For instance, the models illustrated in this paper do not incorporate time-varying exogenous variables. They also do not allow for jointly endogenous variables (i.e., for endogenous variables that both affect and are affected by offenses). These and other generalizations will be necessary for the development of models that are more adequate to the task of modeling the development of delinquent/criminal acts across the life course.

ACKNOWLEDGMENTS

The research reported here was supported, in part, by National Science Foundation Grant SES-9210437. We thank two anonymous referees and the Editor of the *Journal of Quantitative Criminology* for helpful suggestions for revision of an early version of the manuscript.

REFERENCES

Allison, P. D. (1982). Discrete-time methods for the analysis of event histories. *Sociol. Methodol.* 1982: 61–98.

Allison, P. D. (1984). *Event History Analysis*, Sage, Beverly Hills, CA.

Aptech Systems (1992). *GAUSS 3.0 Systems and Applications Manual*, Aptech Systems, Inc., Maple Valley, WA.

Avi-Itzhak, B., and Shinnar, R. (1973). Quantitative models in crime control. *J. Crim. Just.* 1: 185–217.

Barnett, A., Blumstein, A., and Farrington, D. P. (1987). Probabilistic models of youthful criminal careers. *Criminology* 25: 83–108.

Barnett, A., Blumstein, A., and Farrington, D. P. (1989). A prospective test of a criminal career model. *Criminology* 27: 373–385.

Blumstein, A., and Cohen, J. (1979). Estimation of individual crime rates from arrest records. *J. Crim. Law Criminol.* 70: 561–585.

Blumstein, A., Cohen, J., Roth, J. A., and Visher, C. A. (eds.) (1986). *Criminal Justice and "Career Criminals,"* 2 vols., National Academy Press, Washington, DC.

Blumstein, A., Cohen, J., and Farrington, D. P. (1988a). Criminal career research: Its value for criminology. *Criminology* 26: 1–36.

Blumstein, A., Cohen, J., and Farrington, D. P. (1988b). Longitudinal and criminal career research: Further clarifications. *Criminology* 26: 57–74.

Cox, D. R. (1972). Regression models and life tables (with discussion). *J. Roy. Stat. Soc. Ser. B* 34: 187–220.

Elder, G. H., Jr. (1985). *Life Course Dynamics*, Cornell University Press, Ithaca, NY.

Farrington, D. P. (1986). Age and crime. In Tonry, M., and Morris, N. (eds.), *Crime and Justice: An Annual Review of Research, Vol. 7*, University of Chicago Press, Chicago.

Farrington, D. P., Loeber, R., Elliott, D. S., Hawkins, J. D., Kandel, D. B., Klein, M. W., McCord, J., Rowe, D. C., and Tremblay, R. E. (1990). Advancing knowledge about the onset of delinquency and crime. In Lahey, B., and Kazdin, A. E. (eds.), *Advances in Clinical Child Psychology, Vol. 13*, Plenum, New York.

Glueck, S., and Glueck, E. (1937). *Later Criminal Careers*, Commonwealth Fund, New York.

Glueck, S., and Glueck, E. (1940). *Juvenile Delinquents Grown Up*, Commonwealth Fund, New York.

Gottfredson, M., and Hirschi, T. (1988). Science, public policy, and the career paradigm. *Criminology* 26: 37–56.

Gottfredson, M., and Hirschi, T. (1990). *A General Theory of Crime*, Stanford University Press, Stanford, CA.

Gourieroux, C., Monfort, A., and Trognon, A. (1984a). Pseudo maximum likelihood methods: Theory. *Econometrica* 52: 681–700.

Gourieroux, C., Monfort, A., and Trognon, A. (1984b). Pseudo maximum likelihood methods: Applications to Poisson models. *Econometrica* 52: 701–720.

Greenberg, D. F. (1991). Modeling criminal careers. *Criminology* 29: 17–46.

Greene, W. H. (1992). *LIMDEP: User's Manual and Reference Guide*, Econometric Software, Inc., New York.

Hagan, J., and Palloni, A. (1988). Crimes as social events in the life course: Reconceiving a criminal controversy. *Criminology* 26: 87–100.

Hausman, J., Hall, B. H., and Griliches, Z. (1984). Econometric models for count data with an application to the patents-r&d relationship. *Econometrica* 52: 909–938.

Heckman, J. J. (1984a). A method for minimizing the impact of distributional assumptions in econometric models for duration data. *Econometrica* 52: 271–320.

Heckman, J. J. (1984b). Econometric duration analysis. *J. Econometr.* 24: 63–132.

Heckman, J. J., and Singer, B. (1982). Population heterogeneity in demographic models. In Land, K. C., and Rogers, A. (eds.), *Multidimensional Mathematical Demography*, Academic Press, New York, pp. 567–599.

Kalbfleisch, J., and Prentice, R. (1980). *The Statistical Analysis of Failure Time Data*, Wiley, New York.

Laird, N., and Olivier, D. (1981). Covariance analysis of censored survival data using log-linear analysis techniques. *J. Am. Stat. Assoc.* 76: 231–240.

Land, K. C. (1992). Models of criminal careers: Some suggestions for moving beyond the current debate. *Criminology* 30: 149–155.

Land, K. C., McCall, P. L., and Nagin, D. S. (1996). A comparison of Poisson, negative binomial, and semiparametric mixed Poisson regression models, with empirical applications to criminal careers data. *Sociol. Methods. Res.* 24: 387–442.

Laub, J. H., and Sampson, R. J. (1991). The Sutherland-Glueck debate: On the sociology of criminological knowledge. *Am. J. Sociol.* 96: 1402–1440.

Manton, K. G., and Stallard, E. (1981). Methods for the analysis of mortality risks across heterogeneous small population: Examination of space-time gradients in cancer mortality in North Carolina Counties 1970–75. *Demography* 18: 217–230.

Moffitt, T. E. (1993). Adolescent-limited and life-course persistent antisocial behavior: A developmental taxonomy. *Psychol. Rev.* 100: 674–701.

McCullagh, P., and Nelder, J. A. (1989). *Generalized Linear Models*, 2nd ed., Chapman and Hall, New York.

Nagin, D. S., and Farrington, D. P. (1992a). The onset and persistence of offending. *Criminology* 30: 501–523.

Nagin, D. S., and Farrington, D. P. (1992b). The stability of criminal potential from childhood to adulthood. *Criminology* 30: 235–260.

Nagin, D. S., and Land, K. C. (1993). Age, criminal careers, and population heterogeneity: Specification and estimation of a nonparametric, mixed Poisson model. *Criminology* 31: 327–362.

Nagin, D. S., and Paternoster, R. (1991). On the relationship of past to future delinquency. *Criminology* 29: 163–189.

Nagin, D. S., Farrington, D. P., and Moffitt, T. E. (1995). Life course trajectories of different types of offenders. *Criminology* 33: 111–137.

Polakowski, M. (1990). *Criminality, Social Control, and Deviance in a Life-Course Analysis,* Unpublished Ph.D. dissertation, University of Wisconsin–Madison.

Polakowski, M. (1994). Social and self control, life-course events, and crime: A hazard analysis of criminal convictions, Unpublished manuscript, School of Public Administration and Policy, University of Arizona, Tuscon, AZ 85721. Presented at the annual meeting of the American Society of Criminology, Miami, FL.

Rowe, D. C., Osgood, D. W., and Nicewander, W. A. (1990). A latent trait approach to unifying criminal careers. *Criminology* 28: 237–270.

Tontodonato, P. (1988). Explaining rate changes in delinquent arrest transitions using event history analysis. *Criminology* 26: 439–460.

Tracy, P. E., Wolfgang, M. E., and Figlio, R. M. (1990). *Delinquency in Two Birth Cohorts,* Plenum, New York.

Trussell, J., and Hammerslough, C. (1983). A hazards-model analysis of the covariates of infant and child mortality in Sri Lanka. *Demography* 20: 1–26.

Tuma, N. B., and Hannan, M. T. (1984). *Social Dynamics: Models and Methods,* Academic Press, New York.

West, D. J., and Farrington, D. P. (1973). *Who Becomes Delinquent?* Heinemann, London.

West, D. J., and Farrington, D. P. (1977). *The Delinquent Way of Life,* Heinemann, London.

Yamaguchi, K. (1991). *Event History Analysis,* Sage, Newbury Park, CA.

[18]

Desistance as a Developmental Process: A Comparison of Static and Dynamic Approaches

Shawn D. Bushway,[1,4] Terence P. Thornberry,[2] and
Marvin D. Krohn[3]

New research in the field of developmental criminology has led researchers to reconceptualize desistance as a behavioral process that unfolds over the life course. This approach puts more emphasis on the pathways by which people reach the state of non-offending, and less emphasis on the state of non-offending itself. This reconceptualization has implications for how we measure desistance in longitudinal data. In this paper, we suggest that the traditional measurement approach is inconsistent with this view, and we present an alternative measurement approach based on the premises of developmental criminology. Although not perfect, we argue that the dynamic measure better describes the key elements of the process of desistance. Both approaches are implemented using data from the Rochester Youth Development Study, a longitudinal study of youthful offenders. We demonstrate that the two approaches identify different people as desistors. Moreover, we argue that the dynamic definition of desistance has more promise for providing insight into the changes that are the behavioral focus of the desistance process.

KEY WORDS: desistance; behavioral change; developmental processes; offending.

1. INTRODUCTION

Of the three core dimensions of the criminal career—onset, maintenance, and desistance—desistance is the least studied. Despite the theoretical and policy importance of understanding why people stop offending, we do not have robust conceptual models or rich empirical investigations of desistance. This paper begins to address this imbalance in our understanding

[1]Department of Criminology and Criminal Justice, University of Maryland, 2220 LeFrak Hall, College Park, MD 20742.
[2]School of Criminal Justice, University at Albany, Albany, NY.
[3]Department of Sociology, University at Albany, Albany, NY.
[4]To whom correspondence should be addressed. E-mail: sbushway@crim.umd.edu

of criminal careers by developing a dynamic approach to the measurement and study of desistance and comparing it to the more traditional approach.

The key defining characteristic of desistance is behavioral change, change from one state—some non-trivial level of offending—to another state—that of non-offending (Uggen and Kruttschnitt, 1998). While desistance ultimately refers to a change in the person's pattern of behavior from involvement in crime to non-involvement in crime, the process of desistance can vary along a number of dimensions. For example, the change can be abrupt, as when someone stops "cold turkey," or it can be more gradual, as when someone slows down from a high rate of offending to lower and lower rates until they reach zero. It can begin either early or late in the person's criminal career and, independent of when it occurs in the criminal career, it can begin at younger or older ages.

Given this view, an ideal measure of desistance should be able to accomplish the following three objectives. First, it should be able to discriminate between people who continue to offend and people who, after some involvement in criminal behavior, stop offending. Second, it should be able to estimate whether the change to non-offending is permanent (or at least of long duration), as opposed to transient or fleeting. Finally, the measure should also be able to describe the transition from offending to non-offending. Doing so allows for the study of desistance that is more or less gradual. It also allows for the study of desistance at different stages of the person's criminal career and of their life course.

Unfortunately, it is virtually impossible to fully meet these objectives. Most previous studies of desistance have adopted what we will refer to as a "static" measure of desistance. This approach counts everyone who offends at least once before a specified cutoff but not afterwards as a desistor. Individuals who offend in both periods are termed persisters. Examples include the work of Farrington and Hawkins (1991), Ayers *et al.* (1999), Loeber *et al.* (1991), and Warr (1998). This static approach to measuring desistance has a number of appealing qualities. By focusing on the state of non-offending, the static approach provides a measure that is consistent with the basic meaning of the word desistance, that is, ceasing or stopping something. Also, since the static approach defines desistance as an absorbing state (that is, there are transitions into, but not out of it), it emphasizes the permanence of desistance, a characteristic that distinguishes it from related concepts such as de-escalation (LeBlanc and Loeber, 1998) or intermittency (Huizinga *et al.*, 1994). Despite these positive features, there are a number of serious weaknesses with the static approach that ultimately limit its ability to provide an acceptable measure of desistance. The weaknesses can be grouped into the following three criticisms.

1.1. Selection of the Cutting Point

First, the cutoff point between the pre and post periods is entirely arbitrary. It is usually chosen because of the nature of the sample. In Farrington and Hawkins (1991), for example, the cutoff of age 21 was chosen so as to split the available data roughly in half. In Warr (1998), the cutoff was not a particular age, but a particular wave of the National Youth Survey where the needed data were available. As a result, the cutoffs vary from study to study which, at the very least, makes comparisons across studies difficult. Given the variation across studies in how desistance is operationalized (Laub and Sampson, 2001), we think it is not at all surprising that there is little agreement in the literature about the prevalence of desistance, its timing, or correlates. More to the point, the arbitrariness of the cutoff points, and the fact that criminal actions are relatively rare events, leaves open the question of whether the results would be different if the cutoff were imposed at a different age.

In addition, the static approach does not provide the researcher with any way to link the onset of desistance to the point at which offending changed. In fact, in this approach, no thought is given to when either the onset of offending or the onset of the desistance process occurs for a given individual, since desistance begins at the same arbitrary cutoff point for everyone in the sample. If we want to look at factors in adolescence or early adulthood that might lead to desistance, there is no way to causally link the onset of desistance with the occurrence of these events. Yet, proper temporal ordering is crucial for any kind of causal study (Loeber and LeBlanc, 1990; Uggen and Piliavin, 1998).

1.2. Heterogeneity of Offenders

Second, individuals who have very different criminal careers in terms of length, seriousness, and frequency of offending are all treated the same when desistance is a state that one attains. Stopping after a "career" of only one or two relatively minor offenses may be both quantitatively and qualitatively different from stopping after a career of many offenses (Loeber and LeBlanc, 1990). Certainly the theoretical and policy implications associated with desistors who move from a high rate of offending to zero are much different from those associated with desistors who move from one or two offenses to zero.

Also, because low frequency offenders by definition have long periods between offenses, any particular observation period will observe more high-level offenders than low-level offenders. If someone only offended once before age 21, there is a good chance that we will not observe another offense before age 30, even if no behavioral change has occurred.[5] As a result, what we define as the "desistor" group could contain mainly low-level offenders who persist in their offending at widely spaced intervals. In contrast, the persister group could contain mostly high frequency offenders (Baskin and Sommers, 1997; Blumstein *et al.*, 1986).[6]

1.3. Onset of Desistance

Finally, there is no way to determine whether the chosen follow-up period is long enough to know whether someone has really stopped offending. Researchers recognize this as one of the key problems in the study of desistance and some even question the utility of the concept (Elliott *et al.*, 1989). The issue of permanence is not black and white. We can probabilistically identify people who are less likely (or more likely) to reoffend than other people, based on their offending patterns in the past and their current period of non-offending. It seems obvious that the longer the period of non-offending, the less likely it is that an individual will reoffend.[7]

Taken together, these problems raise questions about what exactly we are studying when we utilize a static definition of desistance. These problems can be at least partially addressed by reconceptualizing desistance within a developmental criminology framework.

Developmental criminology highlights the importance of studying within-individual changes in offending over the life course (LeBlanc and Loeber, 1998; Thornberry, 1997). When the change occurs, the level of offending before and after the change and even the nature of the change

---

[5]If we assume an exponential distribution with a lambda of 0.1 (1 offense in ten years), there is a 33% chance that we will not observe an offense in 11 years.

[6]An examination of the data in the Cambridge Study in Delinquent Development (Farrington, 1986) demonstrates this possibility. The average number of convictions before age 21 for the desistors is 2.3 convictions, while the average number of convictions for the persisters before age 21 is 4.4 convictions. Furthermore, 75% of all the desistors had 2 or fewer convictions before age 21, while only 45% of the persisters had 2 or fewer convictions. A comparison of persisters and desistors defined in this way could, as a result, be a comparison of *high-level* and *low-level* offenders, rather than of individuals who have not changed versus those who have changed. This type of comparison of levels could lead to mistaken conclusions about the factors that lead to desistance, especially if, as suggested by criminal career researchers like Blumstein and colleagues (Blumstein *et al.*, 1986; 1988), different causal processes govern onset, offending, and desistance.

[7]More formally, Barnett *et al.* (1989) have demonstrated that the length of time with no offenses, combined with the level of offending during the active career, provides excellent predictions about who might in fact reoffend in the future. This kind of information is not used, however, in a static definition of desistance in which the same follow-up period is imposed on all individuals. Acting as if information about permanence is entirely unknowable ignores information that might help us to assess the exact nature of the state of non-offending that we capture in our data.

itself (sudden or gradual) can indicate that different causal mechanisms may be at work. In this paper we implement a conceptual approach, summarized by Bushway *et al.* (2001), that views desistance as a developmental process that unfolds over time rather than as a static state that is achieved. This view emphasizes behavioral change as the defining characteristic of desistance and pays particular attention to capturing the timing of an individual's change in behavior. While this approach, like the static approach, cannot demonstrate with certainty that desistance is permanent, it uses more information about the history of offending and non-offending to classify individuals and to estimate the likelihood that the change is permanent. As we will argue below, this dynamic approach, while not perfect, provides a measure of desistance more closely linked to the conceptual definition of desistance as a process and one that allows for a fuller description of important dimensions of that process.

We also examine the empirical differences between the static and dynamic approaches to measuring desistance using data from the Rochester Youth Development Study. We are particularly interested in whether these two conceptually different methods identify the same individuals as desistors or as persistent offenders. If they do, and they are simply alternative ways of measuring desistance, parsimony would argue for the use of the static approach. If they do not identify the same individuals as desistors, however, researchers who study desistance will have to grapple much more seriously with the appropriateness of the various measures. We return to this issue in the discussion section, after the empirical evidence has been presented.

2. A DEVELOPMENTAL APPROACH

Bushway *et al.* (2001) define desistance as the *process of reduction in the rate of offending from a nonzero level to a stable rate empirically indistinguishable from zero.* The key to this definition is that it views desistance as a process, not a state, an insight first articulated by Fagan (1989) and expanded by Laub and Sampson (2001). In other words, this approach emphasizes the *transition* from offending to non-offending, rather than the *state* of non-offending. The transition can be characterized by the age range over which the change takes place and the levels of offending that occur during this process.

Since everyone does not offend at the same rate during their active career and everyone does not cease offending at the same time, the dynamic approach recognizes that there may, in fact, be different paths or trajectories to desistance. This emphasis on equifinality—the idea that there are multiple causal processes that can lead to the same outcome—is a central tenet of developmental psychopathology (Cicchetti and Rogosch, 1996) and developmental criminology (Loeber and LeBlanc, 1990). In our case, we believe that people who experience declines in offending at different ages, or who differ in their original levels of offending, should be differentiated since they may be experiencing different causal forces as they decline to low levels of offending. At a minimum, the probability of different causal forces should be able to be examined empirically. Measuring the rate of offending over time for multiple groups of offenders allows the data to describe the predominant patterns of offending, including multiple patterns of desistance.

Bushway *et al.* (2001) suggest that this measurement approach can be operationalized using semiparametric statistical models which identify trajectories of rates over time for different groups of individuals. This approach, initially developed by Nagin and Land (1993),[8] groups individuals so that rates can be estimated at each point in time over the observed portions of the life course. The model assumes that there are a finite number of discrete groups of individuals who follow some type of parametric pattern of behavior (such as the Poisson distribution). Each group of individuals is allowed to have its own offending trajectory (a map of offending rates throughout the life course) with a distinct intercept and slope for each group of offenders. This approach is particularly advantageous for the study of desistance, since we are interested in identifying individuals (or groups of individuals) whose offending rate changes over time to a stable rate indistinguishable from zero.

This type of model[9] has three key outputs: the slope parameters which describe the trajectory for each group, the estimated proportion of the population belonging to each group, and the posterior probability of belonging to a given group for each individual in the sample. The posterior probability, which is the probability of group membership *after* the model is estimated, is used to assign an individual to a group based on their highest probability. Despite the fact that we talk about groups, it is important to keep in mind that group assignments are made with error. In all likelihood, the groups only approximate a continuous distribution. In the present context, the identification of groups is advantageous because it allows us to identify desistors, which can then be compared with desistors identified through the more traditional approach. We provide more detail about how we implemented the trajectory approach in the next section.

[8]For additional information see also Nagin *et al.* (1995), Nagin (1999), Land *et al.* (1996), D'Unger *et al.* (1998), Nagin and Tremblay (1999), and Laub *et al.* (1998).
[9]What follows is a brief description of this approach. Those interested in a more detailed description should see Nagin and Land (1993), Land and Nagin (1996), or Nagin (1999).

3. METHODS

The analysis is conducted with data from the Rochester Youth Development Study (RYDS), a multi-wave panel study of the development of delinquent behavior among adolescents and young adults. Starting in 1988, sample members and an adult caregiver were interviewed and data from school, police, courts, and social service records were collected. The data span a period from when the average age of sample members was 13.5 to when the average age was 22.

All interviews were conducted by RYDS staff. For Waves 1 through 9, adolescents were interviewed in private rooms in the school setting. Students who could not be interviewed at school were interviewed at home. For Waves 10 through 12, interviews were generally conducted at home.

3.1. Sampling

The RYDS oversampled youth at high risk for serious delinquency and drug use since the base rates for these behaviors are relatively low (Elliott *et al.*, 1989; Wolfgang *et al.*, 1987). To accomplish this while still being able to generalize the findings to a population of urban adolescents, the following strategy was used. The target population was limited to seventh and eighth grade students in the public schools of Rochester, New York, a city that has a diverse population and a relatively high crime rate. The sample was then stratified on two dimensions. First, males were oversampled (75 vs. 25%) because they are more likely than females to be chronic offenders and to engage in serious delinquency (Blumstein *et al.*, 1986). Second, students from high crime areas of the city were oversampled on the premise that subjects residing in these areas are at greater risk for offending. To identify high crime areas, each census tract in Rochester was assigned a resident arrest rate reflecting the proportion of the tract's total population arrested by the Rochester police in 1986. In all but the highest arrest rate tracts, subjects were selected with a probability proportionate to the rate of offenders living in the tract. For the highest third of residential arrest rate census tracts, subjects were selected with certainty. Because the true distribution of seventh and eighth grade students in census tracts is known, and because the probability of each adolescent being selected into the sample is known, the sample can be weighted to represent all seventh and eighth graders in the Rochester public schools. All calculations are performed using the appropriate sample weights.

There are 1000 seventh and eighth grade adolescents in the base panel. The current analysis is based on 846 adolescents who were interviewed through Wave 12. This represents a retention rate of 84.6%. Comparing the characteristics of respondents included in this analysis with those of the total sample indicates that attrition did not bias the sample.[10] Not all 846 individuals were available in all waves, although rarely did they miss more than one wave. The trajectory model deals with the absence of information by simply not using the missing information in the likelihood function. The remaining information for that individual is used. The absence of complete information is more problematic for the traditional approach, in which people are categorized by their offending at every wave. Sensitivity analysis indicated that our way of dealing with this problem did not affect our results.

Individuals were interviewed nine times at approximately six-month intervals during adolescence (average age 13.5 to 17.5) and, after a 2.5-year gap, three annual intervals during young adulthood (average age 20 to 22). Because every effort was made to track individuals who failed to complete the interview on schedule, at each wave there is a small number of respondents who have a longer gap between interview dates. Also, even though they were held out of the next wave as long as possible, they often had to be interviewed before six (or twelve) months had elapsed. Thus there is a distribution around the average lag of six months between interviews. Averaged over the first nine waves though, 92% of the interviews were completed within eight months.

Not all subjects were the same age at the start of the study. They ranged from age 12 to age 15 at the first interview, with most (75%) being 13 or 14 years of age. The respondents were from age 20 to age 23 at the end of the panel. The existence of multiple age cohorts means that the observed trajectory will be spread out, using observations from the younger individuals to complete the trajectory in the early years, and using observations from the older individuals to complete the trajectory in the later years. We have chosen to start the lower range at age 13 and end the upper range at age 22.5. In this way, we model a trajectory for 9.5 years, although we only have 7.5 years of observations for any one person. This may limit our conclusions somewhat, because the trajectories at any point in time are only supported by the people who have data at that age. The trajectory at age 22.5, for example, is based on only 249 people. In contrast, we have 830 observations at age 16. To the extent that the younger (13 years old at the first wave) or older (15 years old at the first wave) sample members are different from the rest of the sample, the tails of the trajectory are not entirely representative of the whole sample. At the same time, the model weights the trajectory, and gives more emphasis to the years that have more data. Moreover, we have chosen to limit the spread by not including the full range of the data (12–23.5) to avoid having just a few people determine the shape of the trajectories at the tails.

---

[10]See Thornberry *et al.* (1993) and Krohn and Thornberry (1999) for a more complete discussion of the sample and attrition.

3.2. Measurement

One measure of delinquent behavior is included in this analysis. It is based on the self-reported delinquency inventory that has been asked at each wave of the Rochester study. We use the general offending index that includes 31 items covering a range of delinquent behaviors from status offenses, vandalism, and minor property crimes to serious violent and property crimes.[11] These offenses change somewhat as an individual ages (e.g., individuals are no longer asked about status offenses in the adult waves), but the changes are minor, and the construct of general offending is maintained throughout. Although this analysis can also be done with subsets of offenses, we seek here to discover baseline desistance trajectories for the broadest type of offending possible. Subsequent analyses will identify the ways in which other types of offending are embedded within the overall pattern of general offending.

We mentioned earlier that there is approximately a 2.5-year gap in data collection between the 6-month interviews conducted during adolescence (the last one at Wave 9) and the annual interviews conducted during early adulthood (the first one at Wave 10). The Wave 10 interview also included a self-reported delinquency inventory in which information about offending during the 1.5-year period between the Wave 9 interview and the beginning of the regular annual reference period for the Wave 10 interview was included. This measure used a categorical response set, which was converted into a count format so it could be used in the trajectory framework. Trajectories estimated with and without this gap year data are virtually identical. These data are included in the results reported below.

3.3. Trajectory Estimation

There are two software packages currently available that can estimate trajectories: Mplus, a proprietary software package, and Proc Traj, a special procedure for use in SAS, made available for free by the National Consortium on Violence Research.[12] We used Proc Traj, both because it is more flexible than Mplus, and because the authors of Proc Traj, Bobby Jones and Daniel Nagin, worked with us to modify Proc Traj to accommodate the special needs of our data set. A more detailed discussion of Proc Traj can be found in Jones *et al.* (2001).

---

[11]General offenses include: Running away from home, skipping classes, lying about one's age, hitchhiking, public disorder, begging, public drunkenness, vandalism, arson, avoiding paying for services, burglary, stealing things $5 or less, stealing things worth $5–$50, stealing things worth $50–$100, stealing things worth more than $100, fencing, taking a car without permission, auto theft, check fraud, credit card fraud, con games, serious assault, assault, gang fights, throwing objects at people, armed robbery, obscene phone calls, being paid for having sex, rape, selling marijuana, or selling hard drugs.

[12]The procedure, with documentation, is available at www.ncovr.heinz.cmu.edu.

There are three main choices that we had to make when estimating trajectories of count data: parametric form (Poisson vs. Zero-Inflated Poisson), functional form of the trajectory over time (quadratic vs. cubic), and number of groups. These choices were made (a) to maximize model fit using the Bayesian Information Criteria (BIC) and (b) to best describe the long-term processes of behavioral change so that we can identify individuals who have either desisted or appear to be on their way to desisting by early adulthood.

The Poisson distribution is a standard distribution used to estimate the frequency distribution of offending that we would expect given a certain unobserved offending rate λ (Osgood and Rowe, 1994). The Zero-Inflated Poisson (ZIP) builds on a Poisson by accommodating more non-offenders in any given period than predicted by the standard Poisson distribution. The zero-inflation parameter can be allowed to vary over time, and can be estimated separately for each group. It is sometimes called an intermittency parameter, since it allows people to have "temporary" spells of non-offending without recording a change in their overall rate of offending.

In the context of studying desistance, the ZIP model's differentiation between short-term and long-term change is problematic. With the ZIP model, "temporary" spells can last for 3 or 4 years, which is a fairly long period in a panel of only 9.5 years. As a result, the ZIP model describes relatively flat trajectories with significant intermittency parameters, a picture which runs the risk of obscuring meaningful change in offending rates over time, since we do not know anything about the timing or magnitude of the change captured by the intermittency parameter. The Poisson model, on the other hand, tracks movement in the rate of offending in one parameter, λ, allowing all relatively long-term change to be reflected in one place. We believe this trait of the Poisson model makes it the better model for modeling desistance, especially over relatively short panels, even though the ZIP model provides a better fit according to the BIC criteria used for model selection.[13]

We do recognize, however, that using the Poisson places a burden on the researcher not to overemphasize the stability of any given change to zero captured by the trajectories.[14] The choice of the Poisson also places a bur-

[13]We can imagine using the ZIP model in data sets covering longer periods of offending. With this type of offending pattern, the distinction between short-term and long-term change would be more distinct, and therefore meaningful. In a broader context, the choice of parametric form will undoubtedly impact the definition of desistors. In the present case, the choice was made on substantively meaningful grounds (we believe the ZIP model obscures substantively meaningful change) rather than on a pure model fit criteria. We advocate serious consideration of both substance and model fit in any decision about parametric form, and we encourage future research to be aware of the impact of parametric form on the identification of desistors (Brame *et al.*, in press).

[14]Fortunately, our definition of desistance (Bushway *et al.*, 2001) stresses stable near-zero offending rates, so we are sensitive to the problem of overstating the permanence of a two- or three-year move to zero without relying on the intermittency parameter.

den on the polynomial form of the trajectory over time. Given that the trajectory will be the only part of the model to describe the change in offending, it is important that the polynomial form of the trajectory be as flexible as possible. The quadratic functional form, which is used in most published research trajectories, only allows for one major directional change over the estimated time period. A cubic functional form, on the other hand, allows the trajectory to change direction and turn back up after reaching a level of zero offending—the original meaning of intermittency. As we will see, the cubic form of the trajectories identifies an upturn in several of the trajectories at the end of the observation period, an observation that we would not have been able to make with the predicted quadratic trajectories.[15] Although not identical to the intermittency parameter, the cubic form for each group allows us to observe relatively short-term changes in criminal offending that are consistent with the concept of intermittency.

As described above, the RYDS data has two unique features. First, it oversampled boys relative to girls. Since we want the trajectories to reflect the underlying population of public school children in Rochester, the data are weighted. The creators of Proc Traj expedited the development of a weighting function in order to allow us to use the appropriate sample weights. Second, the first nine waves each cover six months, and the last three waves each cover one year, with a gap covering one and half years. This means that the self-reported events, gathered from questions that cover behavior since the last interview, occurred over different exposure times. As a result, we needed to account for differential exposure time in the likelihood function. The creators of Proc Traj were able to accommodate this need, and there is now an exposure function available in Proc Traj.[16]

Our final estimation task involved choosing the number of groups. We chose the number of groups based on the Bayesian Information Criteria

[15] A comparison of the predicted and actual average curves for the quadratic models reveals the upturn in the actual curves not captured by the quadratic form. There is no longer any meaningful difference between the predicted and actual average offending rates when we move to the cubic model, and as a result, we will only report the predicted curves for the cubic model. The predicted and actual average trajectories are available upon request.

[16] Both functions have applicability beyond the RYDS data. Most longitudinal samples are stratified in some way, which implies that they have sampling weights. In addition, even surveys with standard times between interviews have some variation in exposure times between interviews. In fact, as noted above, the important effort to track down difficult-to-contact participants can have the unfortunate effect of creating substantial wave-to-wave variation in exposure time for self-reported offending. The exposure function allows the researcher to control for this unavoidable wave-to-wave variation in exposure time. Although not presented here, we found that trajectories estimated without the controls for wave-to-wave variation in exposure time had different shapes and group assignments. Since the RYDS has relatively little wave-to-wave variation compared with data sets like the National Longitudinal Survey of Youth, we encourage other researchers to use this exposure control when estimating trajectories with self-reported offending data.

because conventional likelihood ratio tests cannot be used to test whether the addition of a group improves the explanatory power of the model (D'Unger *et al.*, 1998). In the end, the exact number of groups is somewhat arbitrary, limited by the model's ability to make use of the information available. These models are highly complex, and researchers run the very real risk of arriving at a local maximum. The stability of the answer when providing multiple starting values should be considered in any model choice (McLachlan and Peel, 2000). In the final analysis, the utility of the groups is determined by their ability to identify distinct trajectories, the number of people in each group, and their relative homogeneity. Finding seven groups in which 90% of the sample is in one group, and 10% is spread over the remaining six groups is clearly not as interesting for analysis as finding four groups of roughly equivalent size and with high average probability of assignment.

4. RESULTS

The results are divided into three sections. The first identifies desistors using a measure based on what we have termed the static approach. The second uses the semiparametric trajectory measure based on the dynamic or developmental approach. Finally, we compare these two methods to see if the measures identify the same individuals as desistors.

4.1. The Static Approach

According to the static definition of desistance, desistors are people who have entered a period of non-offending. To identify desistors using this approach, we need to divide the sample into two time periods. Individuals can then be observed over each time period. Individuals who offend at least once in the first period but not in the second period are termed desistors. Individuals who offend at least once in both the first time period and the second time period are termed persisters. Individuals who offend in the second period only are considered late starters and, of course, the residual category is the group of non-offenders.

We have chosen age 18 as the cutoff. It falls roughly in the middle of the observations for our sample and has the added advantage of having some social significance as a marker for entrance into adulthood.[17] We have four age cohorts in our study (ages 12 to 15), so a cut point at age 18 means that the older groups have more waves of exposure after the cut point, while the younger groups have more waves of exposure before the cut point.

[17]We experimented with other cutoff ages and found that our main conclusion did not change.

Using this cutting point, 12.0% of the sample can be categorized as non-offenders according to the static method because they report no offending throughout the entire study. Recall that our measure of offending is based on self-report data; as a result, there are many fewer non-offenders than one would find based on official records. Another 6.5% can be categorized as late starters, because they report no offending before age 18, but at least one offense from age 18 onward. The bulk of the sample (53.9%) report at least some offending before and after age 18. We call these individuals persisters. Finally, 27.6% of the sample can be classified as desistors, having offended at least once before age 18, but not afterwards. The period of non-offending in this case is at least three years without even one minor self-reported offense.

4.2. The Developmental Approach

Based on offending information for the 846 individuals who were interviewed through Wave 12, we were able to fit a trajectory model identifying seven groups using Nagin and Land's semiparametric trajectory method. We used multiple starting values and report the model with the highest BIC. A model with eight groups converged with a better BIC score, but the solution appeared to be very dependent on starting values and most of the improvement from the seven-group model came from splitting two of the groups in the seven-group model into three fairly small groups. In the final analysis, we do not believe that the move to eight groups warranted the added complexity.

The results of the trajectory model are listed in Table I; the predicted curves are shown in Fig. 1. No group has less than 4.2% (about 36 people) of the sample nor more than 38.7% (328 people), providing excellent discrimination across the sample (see Table II). The groups are also remarkably well defined; no group has an average posterior probability of assignment of less than 98.1%. In fact, only 4.4% of the sample, 37 people, has a probability of assignment less than 90%. The small number of people with low probabilities of assignment to their designated group suggests that this discrete distribution is a reasonable approximation for this sample.[18]

---

[18]30 of the 37 individuals with less than 90% posterior probability of assignment belong to either the very low-level offenders or the low-level offenders. All 11 of the very low-level offenders with probability of assignment less than 0.9 have the next highest probability of assignment to the low-level offender group. Seven of the remaining eight low-level offenders with probabilities of assignment less than 0.9 have their loyalty divided with the late starter group. A quick glimpse at Fig. 1 demonstrates that these three groups are very close together, especially early in the observation period. Finally, it bears noting that some of the models with lower BICs had fewer people with probability of assignments less than 0.9, primarily because the low-level offender group was made up of only non-offenders with probability of assignment of 0.99.

The groups are very similar to those found using all 1000 members of the Rochester sample, a further indication that attrition bias in this sample is minor, a conclusion reached earlier by Thornberry *et al.* (1993) and Krohn and Thornberry (1999). The distribution of all posterior probabilities by group is given in Table II.

The shapes of the curves in Fig. 1 provide information about the types of offending trajectories that are identified and, therefore, the possible identification of desistors. Each group is discussed in turn, starting with the very low-level offenders.

The *very low-level offender* group contains 38.7% of the sample. These individuals basically do not offend throughout the observational period. The highest average level of offending is 0.5 general offenses per six months, and this decreases to 0.09 by the end of the period. Of this group, 102 subjects never report any offending at all. One way to interpret this combination of the non-offenders and very low-level offenders is that the respondents with very few offenses are statistically indistinguishable from the people who report zero offenses. There is another group of *low-level offenders* representing 22.5% of the sample (191 offenders). They start at 1.5 offenses at age 13, never increase above 2 offenses, and end up around 1 offense at age 22.5. From a descriptive stand point, the very low-level offenders and the low-level offenders are practically identical. Although it is tempting to call these individuals desistors, their rate is quite close to zero, even at its peak. The distinguishing characteristic of these people is stability; their offending rate starts low and stays low throughout the sample period. To call them desistors would imply change, yet we believe that their defining characteristic is the lack of change over time. As a result, neither group satisfies our definition of desistance.

At the other extreme, 4.2% of the sample can be identified as *high-level chronic offenders*. This group offends at a rate of over 20 offenses every six months until age 17. Their rate then declines to 8 offenses every six months followed by a rise at the end of the offending period to a rate of almost 20 offenses per six months by age 22.5.

Two groups start offending a bit later in the life course, but are at a fairly high level of offending in the adult years. The existence of these groups is somewhat unusual, and worthy of exploration (Blumstein *et al.*, 1986; Wolfgang *et al.*, 1987). We call the group that is indistinguishable from the low-level offenders until age 18 before accelerating to over 10 offenses by age 20 the *late starters* (9.7%), and the group that begins to accelerate around age 14 the *slow-uptake chronic offenders* (7.9%). At age 22.5, slow-uptake chronics commit 13 offenses per six months and the late starters 7 offenses.

Table I. Semiparametric Model with Seven Groups, Cubic Model

	Estimate	Error	*t* Statistic
Very low-level offenders (38.6%)[a]			
Intercept	−11.258	27.014	−0.417
Linear	27.891	47.331	0.589
Quadratic	−20.510	27.339	−0.750
Cubic	4.439	5.199	0.854
Low-level offenders (22.5%)			
Intercept	−30.821	26.064	−1.183
Linear	57.319	44.496	1.288
Quadratic	−33.311	24.951	−1.335
Cubic	6.255	4.601	1.360
Slow-uptake chronic offenders (7.8%)			
Intercept	−108.892	1.147	−94.950
Linear	181.627	1.740	104.392
Quadratic	−97.113	0.908	−106.951
Cubic	17.134	0.166	102.975
Late starters (9.8%)			
Intercept	124.760	5.246	23.783
Linear	−218.762	10.565	−20.662
Quadratic	125.928	6.734	18.699
Cubic	−23.477	1.371	−17.128
Intermittent offenders (8.6%)			
Intercept	−188.212	7.779	−24.194
Linear	358.638	14.701	24.396
Quadratic	−218.700	9.159	−23.879
Cubic	43.113	1.878	22.953
Bell-shaped desistors (8.5%)			
Intercept	−199.826	214.958	−0.930
Linear	331.141	318.149	1.041
Quadratic	−175.963	151.192	−1.164
Cubic	30.286	22.791	1.329
High-level chronic offenders (4.2%)			
Intercept	−83.618	2.140	−39.080
Linear	157.182	4.098	38.356
Quadratic	−92.040	2.573	−35.769
Cubic	17.519	0.525	33.353

BIC = −44673.5 (N = 846)

[a]These percentages are population estimates of the percentage of the population in each group. Since they are population parameters, they differ slightly from the sample proportions reported in Table II and Table III.

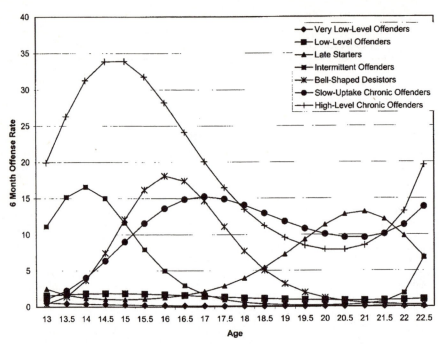

Fig. 1. Predicted trajectories for the 7-group Poisson cubic model.

Another group, *intermittent offenders* (8.6% of the sample), starts out with over 10 offenses every six months from age 13 to age 15. Their offending rate then declines to close to zero by age 18, and remains at that level for three years. There is then a noticeable upswing at the end of the observation period. This upswing is driven by roughly 15 members of the group with non-zero levels of offending, including several who have a very high number of offenses. Many of these offenses are drug sales, suggesting that some members of this group have returned to or begun to deal drugs. We have decided to call these offenders intermittent to reflect the fact that some of them appear to return to crime after a period of non-offending.

Finally, there is one group that declines to something that approaches zero near the end of the observation period and could potentially be called a desistance group. We call this group, which mimics the age-crime curve, the *bell-shaped desistors* (8.4%). Unlike the low-level offenders, this group has experienced real change and, unlike the intermittent offenders, they do not evidence an upswing of offending at the end of the period. We consider the members of this group desistors since they have experienced both statistically and substantively interesting amounts of change from offending rates of over 15 offenses every six months from age 15.5 to age 17, and then decrease to less than 1 offense per 6 months by age 20.5. However, because

Table II. Posterior Probability of Group Assignment

	Raw N	Weighted[a] B (%)	Mean (SD)	Minimum	Raw # below 0.90	Raw # below 0.80
Very low-level offenders	284	328 (38.7)	0.991 (0.0520)	0.580	11	7
Low-level offenders	181	191 (22.5)	0.981 (0.0658)	0.504	19	8
Slow-uptake chronic offenders	77	67 (7.9)	0.988 (0.0431)	0.793	2	1
Late starters	108	82 (9.7)	0.998 (0.0244)	0.628	1	1
Intermittent offenders	67	73 (8.6)	0.991 (0.0489)	0.596	2	2
Bell-shaped desistors	80	71 (8.4)	0.996 (0.0197)	0.832	1	0
High-level chronic offenders	49	36 (4.2)	0.998 (0.0129)	0.882	1	0
Total	846	848 (100.0)				

[a]The weights in this data set take into account the undersampling of girls in the RYDS data. The large discrepancy in group sizes between the raw and weighted data occurs because girls are more or less likely to belong to certain groups. For example, the girls are more likely to be low-level offenders and very low-level offenders relative to the boys. As a result, those groups are larger when the weights are included in the model. In contrast, the high-level chronic offenders, bell-shaped desistors, late starters, and slow-uptake chronic offenders are more likely to be boys, which causes the cell count to decrease when the weights are added. The girls and boys are about equally likely to be intermittent offenders, which causes the weighted and raw numbers to be roughly equivalent for this group.

we only observe them until age 22.5, we cannot firmly state that this end to offending is permanent.

4.3. Comparing the Two Approaches

The most important comparison between the two approaches is ultimately descriptive. The static definition provides the bare minimum of description. We know that 12.0% of the sample never offend (non-offenders), 6.5% of the sample start offending after age 18 (late starters), 53.9% of the sample report at least some offending before and after age 18 (persisters), and 27.6% of the sample offend at least once before age 18, but not afterwards (desistors). For the static desistor group we know nothing about the levels of their offending prior to age 18, or the nature and timing of the change from being an offender to being a non-offender. For example, we do not know if the change is sudden or gradual, occurred earlier or later, etc. As a result, the benefit that descriptive information may provide to an understanding of desistance is not provided by this method.

In contrast, the trajectory method not only tells us which individuals approach a zero rate of offending, but it also tells us how long they have been there. Furthermore, the trajectory method provides the approximate path by which members of these groups have arrived at the point of non-offending. More specifically, the trajectory method identifies four groups of people who are at very low levels of offending during the early twenties. Yet, two groups, the low-level and very low-level offenders, have experienced very little change. The bell-shaped desistor group and the intermittent offenders have experienced much larger amounts of change, although they have done so in very different ways. It is at least plausible that the causal mechanisms by which these individuals have arrived at this point are very different. Using the static method, we have no way to even pose the question, let alone approach it empirically. The trajectory method does a much better job of describing the offending patterns of the sample, at which point it is at least possible to explore alternative causal patterns which might explain, for example, why at least some of the intermittent offenders appear to reoffend.

The dynamic model is much more articulate than the static model about the nature of the desistance process. This point can also be made by looking at a cross-tabular comparison of the groups identified by the two methods (Table III). The static approach identified 27.6% of the sample as desistors. The dynamic model identified only 8.4% of the sample as desistors. Moreover, we found that of the 291 people identified by the two methods as desistors, there is only agreement by the two methods in 4.8% of the cases. The static method only identified 14 of the 71 people identified by the dynamic method as desistors. So, not only do the two methods identify different proportions of the sample as desistors, they also identify different people as desistors.

It is useful to think about why the two methods disagree. The bulk of the individuals (78.7%) categorized as desistors by the static method are included in the two low-level offender groups by the trajectory method. The predominant characteristic of these two groups is low (but not zero) levels of offending on a very broad measure of offending for the entire observation period. Categorizing any of these individuals as desistors places a great deal of emphasis on what is in effect a very small change, and ignores the larger

Table III. Cross-Comparison of Desistors Using the Static and Dynamic Definitions

Frequency[a] Row percent Column percent	Static definition				
	Non-offenders	Late starters	Persisters	Desistors	Total
Dynamic definition					
Very low-level offenders	102	38	55	133	328
	31.1	11.5	16.7	40.6	38.7
	100.0	68.3	12.0	57.0	
Low-level offenders	0	8	133	51	191
	0.0	4.1	69.4	26.5	22.5
	0.0	14.1	29.0	21.7	
Late starters	0	10	72	0	82
	0.0	11.9	88.1	0.0	9.7
	0.0	17.6	15.9	0.0	
Slow-uptake chronic offenders	0	0	67	0	67
	0.0	0.0	100.0	0.0	7.9
	0.0	0.0	14.6	0.0	
High-level chronic offenders	0	0	36	0	36
	0.0	0.0	98.9	1.1	4.2
	0.0	0.0	7.8	0.2	
Intermittent offenders	0	0	37	36	73
	0.0	0.0	51.3	48.7	8.6
	0.0	0.0	8.2	15.2	
Bell-shaped desistors	0	1	57	14	71
	0.0	0.6	80.4	19.6	8.4
	0.0	0.7	12.5	6.0	
Total	102	55	457	234	848
	12.0	6.5	53.9	27.6	

[a]Because the data are weighted, the frequencies are non-integers. To make this table easier to read, we have rounded all frequencies to the nearest integer. The row and column percentages, which are based on the true weighted frequencies, cannot be identically recaptured from the frequencies in the table.

point that these individuals have stable but very low levels of offending over time.

The absence of any consideration of overall levels of offending also means that the static approach is not very good at describing what is occurring in the sample with respect to patterns of change. More to the point, the static definition misses much of the interesting behavioral change that is occurring in the RYDS sample. The static definition of desistance only identifies 19.6% of the bell-shaped desistors as desistors, despite the fact that, on average, they move from 17 offenses every six months at age 16 to 0.27 offenses by age 22.5. The reason that the static method does not classify these individuals as desistors is obvious—much of the change occurs after age 18. The bell-shaped desistors are still averaging 8 offenses every six months by age 18. The age 18 cutoff forces us to miss much of the interesting change taking place in the sample.

Another problem with the static method can also be identified by the cross-tabulations in Table III. A static study of desistance would compare the desistors to the persisters. The static desistor group was dominated by the low-level offenders. The static persister group is much more heterogeneous, drawing people from every trajectory group. A minimum of 16.7% (51.3% if we exclude the very low-level offender group) of each of the trajectory offender groups is represented in the persister group, rendering it a melange of different offenders whose only distinguishing characteristic is that they self-report at least one offense before and after age 18. Given the heterogeneity in this group, it is hard to understand the meaning of comparisons with this group.

The point that the static method provides a poor measure of change is not limited to studies of desistance. The static approach also misses the substantial behavioral change associated with the late starters. Based on the static approach, which uses age 18 as the cutoff, only 6.5% of the sample are late starters. Yet, 82.4% of these individuals are actually very low or low-level offenders who never offend much even when they do offend. In contrast, the trajectory method identifies 9.7% of the sample as late starters. These people on average are indistinguishable from the low-level offenders until age 17, at which point they accelerate rapidly so that by age 21 they are at a rate of 13 offenses per six months, the highest rate at this age. They then decline somewhat over the next two years. The very existence of a group of offenders who follow this path is interesting, especially since it is not predicted by typological models of delinquency (e.g., Moffitt, 1993; Patterson *et al.*, 1991).

This leads to a larger point—an interest in processes of offending, whether they be desistance processes or onset processes, requires a method that allows the researcher to identify meaningful change in offending rates over the life course. Any such method relies on the grouping of offenders, requiring the researcher to assume homogeneity when in all likelihood the members of the group are not identical.[19] But, in our opinion, the comparison in this section highlights the importance of describing patterns of behavior over the life course, rather than concentrating on one act of offending in an arbitrarily defined period of time.

---

[19]Statistical techniques do exist which allow the uncertainty caused by heterogeneity within the group to be taken into account (Roeder *et al.*, 1999).

5. DISCUSSION

The study of desistance is concerned with understanding why the behavior of some offenders changes from active involvement in offending to a level of zero or near-zero involvement in crime. Understanding this type of behavioral change is important both to developmental theories of crime and to the formation of policies to reduce crime. Accordingly, research in this area has recently emphasized the importance of not only identifying who desists but also of identifying the processes by which offenders do so. For example, researchers like Baskin and Sommers (1997), Shover (1996), and Fagan (1989), among others, speculate about the speed of the transition, the timing of the transition in the criminal career, and the degree to which these features vary according to the seriousness of the offender's career. To address these and related issues, it is essential that we be able to measure desistance so that these processes can be identified.

With this objective in mind, this paper contrasted two strategies for measuring desistance. One is the traditional approach in which before and after periods are compared to identify offenders who stop. The other approach, rooted in developmental criminology, focuses attention on trajectories of offending over time. We have argued that the traditional approach is conceptually limited. For example, the selection of the cutting point to separate before and after periods is often arbitrary, the method tends to group dissimilar offenders within the desistance (or persistence) category, and the point at which desistance begins cannot readily be identified.

In contrast, the dynamic approach has the advantage of being inherently descriptive. A manageable number of group trajectories are distilled from the information provided by an entire panel of respondents. A basic picture of the level of behavior at each point in the life course is provided and individuals who have experienced meaningful change in offending and have arrived at or are approaching a low, near-zero rate of offending can be identified. In addition, plausible hypotheses about the stability of the near-zero state of offending can be tested, and the degree of change experienced by the offenders can be assessed empirically. All of these features enhance our ability to study desistance.

The dynamic approach is not, of course, without its own deficiencies. The chief advantage of this approach—that it provides estimates of rates of offending at different points of time—is also its major drawback. These estimates are obtained by grouping individuals into non-homogenous groups and the degree of heterogeneity within the groups is hard to quantify. While sophisticated users of this method undoubtedly understand that it is a discrete approximation of a continuous reality (Nagin, 1999), there is an undeniable desire to interpret the groupings as discrete entities. Finally, the statistical method is undoubtedly more difficult to implement than the traditional approach. The models are complex and routinely find local maxima, requiring the researcher to solve the models numerous times to find the best available solution. And, although the trajectory approach is data driven, the researcher needs to make choices regarding parametric and functional form which impact the final shape and membership of the trajectories. Just as an alternative choice of the cutoff point in the static method will lead to identification of different people as desistors, the selection of the ZIP model or the 8-group model would also have led to the identification of different people as desistors in this study.[20]

In order to determine if the additional complexity required by the trajectory method is valuable, we compared the two different approaches to measuring desistance using data from the Rochester Youth Development Study. For, if the more parsimonious static approach and the more complex dynamic approach identify the same individuals as persistent offenders and as desistors, there would be little reason to use the dynamic approach. Clearly though, in our analysis the two methods do not identify the same people as desistors. Indeed, there is remarkably little overlap in the two methods.

Moreover, we believe the comparison shows that the trajectory method is better able than the static approach to articulate the nature of the processes by which individuals reach non-offending. The trajectory method identified three groups of individuals—the bell-shaped desistors and the two low-level offender groups—who have zero or near-zero rates of offending by age 22.5. Each arrived at this point through a qualitatively different path of offending rates, however. The static definition of desistance draws people from each of these groups into its desistance group. As a result, the static method is unable to identify distinct causal paths to desistance for further study. More to the point, the majority of the offenders identified as desistors by the static method were in fact low-level offenders who experienced very little change over the ten years of study. As a result, the comparison of static persisters and static desistors is, in large part, a distinction between levels of offending, rather than changes in rates of offending.

This raises the possibility that much of the prior causal analyses of desistance based on the static method may not have studied individuals who have experienced meaningful change. This could have serious implications for the current debate about the relative role of static vs. dynamic factors in

---

[20]The choice of the quadratic form, in contrast, would have led to fairly similar groups, with a nearly identical Table III. The disadvantage is that the predicted curves would have missed the upturns at the end of the predicted trajectories. This failure on the part of the model might be less problematic in studies that do not focus on desistance, and the simpler form of the quadratic model might be advantageous in more general studies of offending processes.

the causation of desistance. If the method used to identify desistance does a better job of capturing levels of, rather than changes in, offending, the method might be predisposed to find more evidence for the importance of stable factors than is warranted.

In addition to comparing the persistent offenders and the desistors, a number of issues about those who desist can also be addressed using the dynamic approach. In the Rochester data, this method identified several groups of people who have substantial declines in offending over the observation period. These patterns of decline start at different ages with different rates of decline. We can now begin to think of the onset of desistance and whether different factors—either stable or time-varying—are associated with those who started earlier or later. In the examination of time-varying factors it is also possible to locate them more proximally to when the behavioral change occurred. It is possible, for example, that time-varying factors lead to the downturn in offending, but the specific time-varying factors could differ depending on the developmental stage in which the downturn occurred.

Similar issues can be raised about the speed of the change from the peak of offending to zero or near-zero rates. For example, we can now try to identify the stable and time-varying factors that account for the steepness of the decline. We can also see if they differ by the developmental stage during which the decline occurs, the seriousness of the criminal career, and related dimensions.

While these and other issues come to mind, we hope at this point that we have demonstrated the value of applying new statistical approaches such as the semiparametric trajectory approach to important criminological questions such as desistance. After a series of public debates in the late 1980s between criminal career researchers and Gottfredson and Hirschi (e.g., Blumstein *et al.*, 1988; Gottfredson and Hirschi, 1988), Hagan and Palloni (1988) called for the creation of new techniques that would allow for better modeling of developmental processes of offending. From our perspective the trajectory approach introduced by Nagin and Land (1993), along with other techniques such as HLM, have effectively answered this call. Nagin in particular has led an impressive effort to describe the process of offending on many of the longitudinal data sets now available (for a review, see Nagin, 1999). In our opinion, it is time for criminology as a field to take the next logical step and begin to use these techniques to answer some of the traditional questions in criminology regarding the causes of onset, desistance, and frequency of offending. In this paper, we have demonstrated that the trajectory approach leads to very different conclusions about who has desisted when compared with more traditional static approaches. We have every reason to believe, therefore, that we will also generate new insight when we move from this type of descriptive analysis to more analysis of the causes of desistance advocated by researchers such as Uggen and Piliavin (1998).

REFERENCES

Ayers, C. D., Williams, J. H., Hawkins, J. D., Peterson, P. L., Catalano, R. F., and Abbott, R. D. (1999). Assessing correlates of onset, escalation, deescalation, and desistance of delinquent behavior. *J. Quant. Criminol.* 15: 277–306.

Barnett, A., Blumstein, A., and Farrington, D. P. (1989). A prospective test of a criminal career model. *Criminology* 27: 373–385.

Baskin, D. R., and Sommers, I. B. (1997). *Casualties of Community Disorder: Women's Careers in Violent Crime*, Westview Press, Boulder, CO.

Blumstein, A., Cohen, J., and Farrington, D. P. (1988). Criminal career research: Its value for criminology. *Criminology* 26: 1–35.

Blumstein, A., Cohen, J., Roth, J. A., and Visher, C. A. (1986). *Criminal Careers and "Career Criminals"*, National Academy Press, Washington, DC.

Brame, R., Bushway, S. D., and Paternoster, R. (In press). Examining the prevalence of criminal desistence. *Criminology*.

Bushway, S. D., Piquero, A., Mazerolle, P., Broidy, L., and Cauffman, E. (2001). An empirical framework for studying desistance as a process. *Criminology* 39: 491–515.

Cicchetti, D., and Rogosch, F. A. (1996). Equifinality and multifinality in developmental psychopathology. *Dev. Psychopathol.* 8: 597–600.

D'Unger, A., Land, K. C., McCall, P. L., and Nagin, D. S. (1998). How many latent classes of delinquent/criminal careers? Results from mixed Poisson regression analyses. *Am. J. Sociol.* 103: 1593–1630.

Elliott, D. S., Huizinga, D., and Menard, S. (1989). *Multiple Problem Youth: Delinquency, Substance Use and Mental Health*, Springer-Verlag, New York, NY.

Fagan, J. (1989). Cessation of family violence: Deterrence and dissuasion. In Ohlin, L., and Tonry, M. (eds.), *Family Violence: Crime and Justice: An Annual Review of Research*, University of Chicago Press, Chicago, IL, pp. 377–425.

Farrington, D. P. (1986). Age and Crime. In Tonry, M., and Morris, N. (eds.), *Crime and Justice, Vol. 7*, University of Chicago Press, Chicago, IL, pp. 29–90.

Farrington, D. P., and Hawkins, J. D. (1991). Predicting participation, early onset, and later persistence in officially recorded offending. *Crim. Behav. Ment. Health* 1: 1–33.

Gottfredson, M., and Hirschi, T. (1988). Science, public policy, and the career paradigm. *Criminology* 26: 37–55.

Hagan, J., and Palloni, A. (1988). Crimes as social events in the life course: Reconceiving a criminological controversy. *Criminology* 26: 87–100.

Huizinga, D., Esbensen, F. A., and Weiher, A. W. (1994). Examining developmental trajectories in delinquency using accelerated longitudinal designs. In Weitekamp, E. G. M., and Kerner, H. (eds.), *Cross-national Longitudinal Research on Human Development and Criminal Behavior*, Kluwer Academic Publishers, Boston, MA, pp. 203–216.

Jones, B. L., Nagin, D. S., and Roeder, K. (2001). A SAS Procedure based on mixture models for estimating developmental trajectories. *Soc. Meth. Res.* 29: 374–393.

Krohn, M. D., and Thornberry, T. P. (1999). Retention of minority populations in panel studies of drug use. *Drugs and Society* 14: 185–207.

Land, K. C., McCall, P. L., and Nagin, D. S. (1996). A comparison of Poisson, negative binomial and semiparametric mixed Poisson regression models. *Sociol. Meth. Res.* 24: 387–442.

Land, K. C., and Nagin, D. S. (1996). Micro-models of criminal careers: A synthesis of the criminal careers and life course approaches via semiparametric mixed Poisson regression models, with empirical applications. *J. Quant. Criminol.* 12: 167–191.

Laub, J., Nagin, D. S., and Sampson, R. (1998). Good marriages and trajectories of change in criminal offending. *Am. Sociol. Rev.* 63: 225–238.

Laub, J., and Sampson, R. (2001). Understanding desistance from crime. In Tonry, M. (ed.), *Crime and Justice: A Review of Research, Vol. 28,* University of Chicago Press, Chicago, IL, pp. 1–69.

LeBlanc, M., and Loeber, R. (1998). Developmental criminology updated. In Tonry, M. (ed.), *Crime and Justice: Review of Research, Vol. 23*, University of Chicago Press, Chicago, IL, pp. 115–198.

Loeber, R., and LeBlanc, M. (1990). Toward a developmental criminology. In Tonry, M. and Morris, N. (eds.), *Crime and Justice: Review of Research, Vol. 12*, University of Chicago Press, Chicago, IL, pp. 375–473.

Loeber, R., Stouthamer-Loeber, M., Van Kammen, W. B., and Farrington, D. P. (1991). Initiation, escalation, and desistance in juvenile offending and their correlates. *J. Crim. Law and Criminol.* 82: 36–82.

McLachlan, G. J., and Peel, D. (2000). *Finite Mixture Models*, Wiley, New York.

Moffitt, T. (1993). "Life-course persistent" and "adolescent-limited" antisocial behavior: A developmental taxonomy. *Psychol. Rev.* 100: 674–701.

Nagin, D. S. (1999). Analyzing developmental trajectories: A semiparametric, group-based approach. *Psychol. Meth.* 4: 139–157.

Nagin, D. S., Farrington, D. P., and Moffitt, T. (1995). Life course trajectories of different types of offenders. *Criminology* 33: 111–139.

Nagin, D. S., and Land, K. C. (1993). Age, criminal careers, and population heterogeneity: Specification and estimation of a nonparametric, mixed Poisson model. *Criminology* 31: 327–362.

Nagin, D. S., and Tremblay, R. E. (1999). Trajectories of boys' physical aggression, opposition, and hyperactivity on the path to physically violent and nonviolent juvenile delinquency. *Child Devel.* 70: 1181–1196.

Osgood, D. W., and Rowe, D. C. (1994). Bridging criminal careers, theory, and policy through latent variable models of individual offending. *Criminology* 32: 517–554.

Patterson, G. R., Capaldi, D., and Bank, L. (1991). An early starter model for predicting delinquency. In Pepler, D. J. and Rubin, R. H. (eds.), *The Development and Treatment of Childhood Aggression*, Erlbaum, Hillsdale, NJ, pp. 139–168.

Roeder, K., Lynch, K., and Nagin, D. S. (1999). Modeling uncertainty in latent class membership: A case study in criminology. *J. Am. Stat. Assoc.* 94: 766–776.

Shover, N. (1996). *Great Pretenders: Pursuits and Careers of Persistent Thieves*, Westview Press, Boulder, CO.

Thornberry, T. P. (ed.) (1997). *Developmental Theories of Crime and Delinquency*, Transaction Publishers, New Brunswick, NJ.

Thornberry, T. P., Bjerregaard, B. E., and Miles, W. C. (1993). The consequences of respondent attrition in panel studies: A simulation based on the Rochester Youth Development Study. *J. Quant. Criminol.* 9: 127–158.

Uggen, C., and Kruttschnitt, C. (1998). Crime in the breaking: Gender differences in desistance. *Law Soc. Rev.* 32: 339–366.

Uggen, C., and Piliavin, I. (1998). Asymmetrical causation and criminal desistance. *J. Crim. Law Criminol.* 88: 1399–1422.

Warr, M. (1998). Life-course transitions and desistance from crime. *Criminology* 36: 183–215.

Wolfgang, M. E., Thornberry, T. P., and Figlio, R. (1987). *From Boy to Man, from Delinquency to Crime*, University of Chicago Press, Chicago.

[19]

TRAJECTORIES OF CRIME AT PLACES: A LONGITUDINAL STUDY OF STREET SEGMENTS IN THE CITY OF SEATTLE*

DAVID WEISBURD
  University of Maryland
  Hebrew University of Jerusalem
SHAWN BUSHWAY
  University of Maryland
CYNTHIA LUM
  Northeastern University
SUE-MING YANG
  University of Maryland

KEYWORDS: crime places, hot spots, crime drop, trajectory analysis, routine activities, spatial analysis

Studies of crime at micro places have generally relied on cross-sectional data and reported the distributions of crime statistics over short periods of time. In this paper we use official crime data to examine the distribution of crime at street segments in Seattle, Washington, over a 14-year period. We go beyond prior research in two ways. First, we view crime trends at places over a much longer period than other studies that have examined micro places. Second, we use

---

*   This research was supported by National Institute of Justice grant #2001-IJ-CX-0022 to the University of Maryland. Points of view in this paper are those of the authors and do not necessarily represent the U.S. Department of Justice. We want to express our gratitude for the cooperation of the Seattle Police Department, and especially to Chief Gil Kerlikowske for his interest and support of our work. We would also like to thank Lt. Ronald Rasmussen for his assistance in identifying and transferring data for the project, and Anthony Braga, John Eck, Elizabeth Groff, Daniel Nagin and Lorraine Mazerolle for their thoughtful comments and advice in revising our paper. We owe a special debt to Daniel Nagin for his guidance in applying the trajectory approach to micro crime places.

group-based trajectory analysis to uncover distinctive developmental trends in our data. Our findings support the view that micro places generally have stable concentrations of crime events over time. However, we also find that a relatively small proportion of places belong to groups with steeply rising or declining crime trajectories and that these places are primarily responsible for overall city trends in crime. These findings are particularly important given the more general decline in crime rates observed in Seattle and many other American cities in the 1990s. Our study suggests that the crime drop can be understood not as a general process that occurred across the city landscape but one that was generated in a relatively small group of micro places with strong declining crime trajectories over time.

Traditionally, research and theory in criminology have focused on individuals and communities (Nettler, 1978; Sherman, 1995), with communities examined primarily at larger geographic units such as states (Loftin and Hill, 1974), cities (Baumer et al., 1998) and neighborhoods (Bursik and Grasmick, 1993; Sampson, 1985). Recently, however, criminologists have begun to explore other units of analysis that may contribute to our understanding of the crime equation. An important catalyst for this work came from theoretical perspectives that emphasized the context of crime and the opportunities presented to potential offenders (Weisburd, 2002). In a groundbreaking article on routine activities and crime, for example, Cohen and Felson (1979) suggest the importance of recognizing that the availability of suitable crime targets and the presence or absence of capable guardians influence crime events. Researchers at the British Home Office in a series of studies examining "situational crime prevention" also challenged the traditional focus on offenders and communities (Clarke and Cornish, 1983). These studies showed that crime situations and opportunities play significant roles in the development of crime (Clarke, 1983).

One implication of these emerging perspectives is that micro crime places are an important focus of inquiry (Eck and Weisburd, 1995; Sampson and Groves, 1989; Taylor, 1997). While concern with the relationship between crime and place goes back to the founding generations of modern criminology (Guerry, 1833; Quetelet, 1842), the "micro" approach to places suggested by recent theories has just begun to be examined by criminologists.[1] Places in this "micro" context are specific locations within the larger social environments of communities and

---

1. It should be noted that a few early criminologists did examine the "micro" idea of place as discussed here (see Shaw et al., 1929). However, interest in micro places was not sustained and did not lead to significant theoretical or empirical inquiry.

neighborhoods (Eck and Weisburd, 1995). They are sometimes defined as buildings or addresses (see Green, 1996; Sherman et al., 1989), sometimes as block faces or street segments (see Sherman and Weisburd, 1995; Taylor, 1997), and sometimes as clusters of addresses, block faces or street segments (see Block et al., 1995; Weisburd and Green, 1995). Research in this area began with attempts to identify the relationship between specific aspects of urban design (Jeffrey, 1971) or urban architecture (Newman, 1972) and crime, but broadened to take into account a much larger set of characteristics of physical space and criminal opportunity (see Brantingham and Brantingham, 1975, 1981; Duffala, 1976; Hunter, 1988; LeBeau, 1987; Mayhew et al., 1976; Rengert, 1980, 1981).

Recent studies point to the potential theoretical and practical benefits of focusing research on micro crime places (Eck and Weisburd, 1995; Sherman, 1995; Taylor, 1997; Weisburd, 2002). A number of studies, for example, suggest that significant clustering of crime at place exists, regardless of the specific unit of analysis defined (see Brantingham and Brantingham, 1999; Crow and Bull, 1975; Pierce et al., 1986; Roncek, 2000; Sherman et al., 1989; Weisburd and Green, 1994; Weisburd et al., 1992). Lawrence Sherman (1995) argues that such clustering of crime at places is even greater than the concentration of crime among individuals. Using data from Minneapolis, Minnesota and comparing these to the concentration of offending in the Philadelphia Cohort Study (see Wolfgang et al., 1972), he notes that future crime is "six times more predictable by the address of the occurrence than by the identity of the offender" (1995:36-37). Sherman asks, "why aren't we doing more about it? Why aren't we thinking more about wheredunit, rather than just whodunit?"

The concentration of crime at place suggests significant crime prevention potential for such strategies as hot spots patrol (Sherman and Weisburd, 1995; Weisburd and Braga, 2003) which focus crime prevention resources at specific locations with large numbers of crimes. However, concentration itself does not provide a solid empirical basis for either refocusing crime prevention resources or calling for significant theorizing about why crime is concentrated at places. For example, if "hot spots of crime" shift rapidly from place to place it makes little sense to focus crime control resources at such locations, because they would naturally become free of crime without any criminal justice intervention (Spelman, 1995). Similarly, if crime concentrations can move rapidly across the city landscape, it may not make much sense to focus our understanding of crime on the characteristics of places. Sociologists, for example, have long recognized that the "opportunity for a criminal act" influences the occurrence of crime (Sutherland, 1947:5). However, if such opportunity is widespread with little geographic stability, a focus on criminal motivation would likely be a more productive concern of criminological inquiry.

While the geographic concentration of crime at place has been well documented in recent years, the stability of crime at hot spots over time has received little research attention. Studies of crime at micro places have generally relied on cross-sectional data and reported the distributions of crime statistics over short periods of time, usually just over a year or two (see Chakravorty and Pelfrey, 2000; Eck et al., 2000; Sherman and Rogan, 1995; Weisburd and Green, 1994). Even studies concerned with the possible stability or instability of the distribution of crime events at micro places have used only a few years of crime data or compared discrete periods separated by long gaps (see Spelman, 1995; Taylor, 1999).

In this paper we use official crime data to examine the distribution of crime at street segments in Seattle, Washington, over a 14-year time period. Our study allows us to go beyond prior research in this area in two ways. First, we are able to view crime trends over a much longer period than other studies that have examined micro crime places. Second, we utilize a group-based statistical technique drawn from developmental criminology that is tailor-made to uncover distinctive developmental trends in the outcome of interest (Nagin, 1999, in press; Nagin and Land, 1993). This technique has the added desirable characteristic of being easy to present in tables and graphs, not an insignificant feature given that our dataset has almost 30,000 units of analysis each with recorded crime for 14 years. While this approach, termed "trajectory analysis," has not been used to examine micro places in earlier studies, we think it particularly appropriate for gaining a fuller understanding of the development of crime at places over time.[2]

We begin our paper with a discussion of what is known about the nature of the distribution of crime at place over time. We then turn to a description of our data and methods and basic findings. The findings support the view that micro places generally have stable concentrations of crime incidents over time. However, we also find that a relatively small proportion of the total number of places belong to groups that have steeply rising or declining crime trajectories, and that these places are primarily responsible for overall city trends in crime. These findings are particularly important given the more general decline in crime rates observed in most American cities in the 1990s (Blumstein and Wallman, 2000; Hoover, 2000; Travis and Waul, 2002). Our study suggests that the crime drop can be understood not as a general process across the city landscape but one generated in a relatively small group of micro places

2. For a paper that is applying the trajectory approach to places at a higher geographic level of analysis, see Griffiths and Chavez, 2004.

with strong declining crime trajectories over time. In our discussion and conclusions, we discuss the implications of our findings for future study of crime at place and crime control policies that focus on crime hot spots.

DISTRIBUTION OF CRIME AT PLACE OVER TIME

Recent study of crime places has focused primarily on the question of the concentration of crime at micro places often defined as "hot spots." The first use of the term in the case of crime places was brought by Sherman et al. (1989), though the basic idea that crime events were clustered in specific places had been documented in earlier studies (see Abeyie and Harries, 1980; Crow and Bull, 1975; Pierce et al., 1986) and suggested by work in environmental criminology (Brantingham and Brantingham, 1975, 1981). Sherman et al. (1989) found that only 3 percent of the addresses in Minneapolis produced 50 percent of all calls to the police. Their proposal that crime was concentrated in hot spots in urban areas has now been confirmed in a series of studies conducted in different cities using different definitions of hot spot areas (see Brantingham and Brantingham, 1999; Eck et al., 2000; Roncek, 2000; Spelman, 1995; Weisburd and Green, 1994, 2000; Weisburd et al., 1992). For example, Weisburd and Green (2000) found that approximately 20 percent of all disorder crimes and 14 percent of crimes against persons were concentrated in 56 drug crime hot spots in Jersey City, New Jersey, that comprised only 4.4 percent of street segments and intersections in the city. Similarly, Eck et al. (2000) found that the most active 10 percent of places (in terms of crime) in the Bronx and Baltimore accounted for approximately 32 percent of a combination of robberies, assaults, burglaries, grand larcenies and auto thefts.

While scholars have provided a strong empirical basis for the assumption that crime is strongly clustered at crime hot spots, they have so far directed little attention to the question of the distribution of crime at micro places over time. We could identify only two published studies that specifically examined this issue longitudinally. One study conducted by Spelman (1995), looks at specific places such as high schools, public housing projects, subway stations and parks in Boston, using 3 years of official crime information. Dividing his data set into 28-day periods, Spelman used a pooled time series cross-sectional design to examine the sources of variability over time and across the types of sites examined. His findings again replicate the more general assumption of a concentration of crime at specific hot spots, with the "worst 10 percent of locations and times accounting for about 50 percent of all calls for service" (Spelman, 1995:129). But he also finds evidence of a very high degree of stability of crime over time at the places he examines. Long-run differences among locations were responsible for the largest source of variation in each of the analyses Spelman conducted, leading him to conclude that it "makes sense for the people who live and work in high-risk locations, and the police officers and other government officials who serve them, to spend the time they need to identify, analyze and solve their recurring problems" (1995:131).

Taylor (1999) also reports evidence of a high degree of stability of crime at place over time, examining crime and fear of crime at ninety street blocks in Baltimore, Maryland using a panel design with data collected in 1981 and 1994 (see also Robinson et al., 2003; Taylor, 2001). Data included not only official crime statistics, but also measures of citizen perceptions of crime and observations of physical conditions at the sites. Although Taylor and his colleagues observed significant deterioration in physical conditions at the blocks studied, they found that neither fear of crime nor crime showed significant or consistent differences across the two time periods.

The finding of stability of crime at micro places over time is mirrored in early research on the nature of longitudinal patterns of crime within communities. For example, Shaw and McKay (1942) found that patterns of delinquency in the city of Chicago remained relatively stable over time despite continuous population changes. They argued that the process of invasion and succession of individuals moving into and out of communities contributed to social disorganization, and that subcultures of delinquency were passed on from those leaving to those coming in through institutionalized mechanisms. In particular, the zones of transition were characterized not only by consistently high levels of delinquency but also by many other social ills, such as high infant morbidity, vacant housing and increased opportunities for illegitimate activities.

Calvin Schmid (1960) also identified evidence of stability of crime in communities over time when analyzing geographic patterns in Seattle using a panel approach. Using census tract boundaries and comparing relatively short time frames (from 1939 to 1941 and from 1949 to 1951) Schmid found that when comparing the frequency of homicide, rape, robbery and burglary in these two sets of years, zones that were high in crime remained high and zones that were lower in frequency also remained low. Crime concentrations in Schmid's research were most likely located at the center of the city within the "business district." Schmid also studied the city of Minneapolis from 1933 to 1936 and found similar evidence that areas of the city that had higher concentrations of crime in 1933 also evidenced high concentrations of crime across the four year period.

The assumption of a stability of crime over time in communities was challenged by Bursik and Webb in the 1980s (Bursik, 1986; Bursik and Webb, 1982; Heitgerd and Bursik, 1987). When re-analyzing Shaw and McKay's dataset as well as more recent data from the 1970s on delinquency in Chicago, they found that Shaw and McKay's argument of the stability of crime in communities with high levels of invasion, succession and population changes may have been a historical artifact, relevant only prior to 1950. Their data suggest that after 1950 there was evidence that large-scale demographic changes corresponded with changes in delinquency rates. They argue that dramatic changes in population can increase social disorganization in communities and that corresponding increases in delinquency rates will only begin to settle when communities reestablish themselves.

Bursik and his colleagues' work was to spark further thinking about how crime develops in communities that we think particularly relevant to understanding the development of crime at micro places over time. In particular, some scholars began to discuss the possibility of communities having "criminal careers." Schuerman and Kobrin (1986), for example, suggested the application of a developmental model to explain neighborhood crime characteristics over time. Although their research focused on the non-recursive relationship between physical deterioration and crime, it emphasized the move away from thinking about longitudinal crime patterns as stable towards explaining changing crime frequencies over geography (see also McDonald, 1987 who discusses the effect of gentrification on crime rates).

The idea that the developmental concept of criminal careers might also apply to micro crime places has recently been raised by Sherman (1995) and Weisburd (1997). They argue that a fuller understanding of crime places must examine the dynamics of change over time and look to innovations in developmental models of individual criminal careers for insights into the criminal careers of places. As we have described above, research on the distribution of crime at place over time has been restricted both by the data available and the statistical tools used. Below, we examine crime data over a much longer time series than available to other researchers to explore the nature of longitudinal crime trends in Seattle, Washington. We also employ a dynamic statistical model that permits identification of varying trajectories of criminal careers of places.

DATA AND UNIT OF ANALYSIS

The specific focus of our study is micro crime places, defined as street segments, over a 14-year period in Seattle, Washington. We chose that city after a careful screening of available crime data on American cities with populations of over 200,000. We found the Seattle Police Department to be among a small group of police agencies with a relatively long history of official data on crime trends collected in computerized format. Seattle was also chosen because it included a diverse population, significant levels of

290   WEISBURD ET AL.

crime during the study period, and was guided by a police administrator fully committed to aiding a basic research program on crime places.

Seattle spans approximately 84 square miles. According to the 2000 U.S. census, it is the 22nd most populous city (563,374) in the United States and its population has remained relatively constant from 1970 to 2000. Although Seattle's population is primarily Caucasian (70.1 percent), it has a substantial ethnic mix of African Americans (8.4 percent), Asians (13.1 percent), Hispanics (5.3 percent) and American Indians (1.0 percent). The number of crimes per 100,000 people in Seattle was 8,004 in 2002, 1.4 times the average for cities with populations between 100,000 and 1,000,000 (Federal Bureau of Investigation, 2002). Compared with cities in a narrower population range (±100,000 of Seattle's population), Seattle's crime rate was slightly higher than the average (7,640) and ranked eighth in sixteen jurisdictions in this category.

We used computerized records of written reports often referred to as "incident reports" to examine crime trends. Incident reports are generated in the Seattle Police Department by police officers or detectives after an initial response to a request for police service. In this sense, incident reports are more inclusive than arrest reports but less inclusive than calls for service. We chose not to use calls for service primarily because such data are kept by Seattle for only 4 years. Also, in a separate analysis on these data, Lum (2003) found that calls for service and crime reports often generate very similar distributions of crime across place. We did not use arrest reports because we thought they would screen too much crime from our field of observation.

The geographic unit of interest for this study is the street segment (sometimes referred to as a street block or face block) defined as the two block faces on both sides of a street between two intersections. We chose the street segment for a number of reasons. Scholars have long recognized its relevance in organizing life in the city (Appleyard, 1981; Jacobs, 1961; Smith et al., 2000; Taylor, 1997). Taylor, for example, argues that the visual closeness of block residents, interrelated role obligations, acceptance of certain common norms and behavior, common regularly recurring rhythms of activity, the physical boundaries of the street, and the historical evolution of the street segment make the street block or street segment a particularly useful unit for analysis of place (see also Hunter and Baumer, 1982; Taylor et al., 1984).

The choice of street segments over smaller units such as addresses (see Sherman et al., 1989) also minimizes the error likely to develop from miscoding of addresses in official data (see Klinger and Bridges, 1997; Weisburd and Green, 1994). We recognize however, that crime events may be linked across street segments. For example, a drug market may operate across a series of blocks (Weisburd and Green, 1995; Worden et al., 1994), and a large housing project and problems associated with it may transverse street segments in multiple directions (see Skogan and Annan, 1994). Nonetheless, we thought the street segment a useful compromise because it allows a unit large enough to avoid unnecessary crime coding errors, but small enough to avoid aggregation that might hide specific trends.

We decided at the outset to exclude those incidents that occurred at an intersection or could not be linked to a specific street segment. Of the 2,028,917 crime records initially obtained from the city from 1989 to 2002, 19 percent were linked to an intersection. Our decision to exclude these events was primarily technical. Intersections could not be assigned to any specific street segment because they were generally part of four different ones. However, it is also the case that incident reports at intersections differed dramatically from those at street segments. Traffic-related incidents accounted for only 4.5 percent of reports at street segments, but for 44 percent of reports at intersections. Places without specific geographic identifiers (for example, "University of Washington" or "Hay Street Market") that could not be linked to a specific street segment were also excluded. Such geographically undefined places accounted for 2 percent of the incident reports in our data base. After excluding intersections, generally defined places, and records without locations, we were left with 1,544,604 incident reports across the 14-year period requiring conversion into a Seattle street segment.

Linking incident reports with street segments was a two-step process: ensuring that the location recorded was legitimate and recognizable, and then converting it to its corresponding street segment. We identified 29,849 street segments from the street map of Seattle.[3] To convert event locations into a corresponding segment, we used both a geographic

---

3. Normally, a street segment in Seattle is delimited in multiples of 100. For example, addresses from 100 to 199 Main Street would most likely occur on one street segment, between two intersections or other divisions. However, there are cases in Seattle where segments could potentially extend from 100 to 299, without an intersection break. To ascertain which of Seattle segments were within the scope of a "hundred block" and which extended further would have required physically examining each street in Seattle, a task beyond the scope of this research. Even the computerized map used (from the City of Seattle's Information Technology Division) did not provide any clues regarding the extent of this problem. The database supporting the shapefile (computerized map) of Seattle's streets simply gave the street name and the beginning and ending house numbers for each street on the odd and even sides. To overcome this issue, the database supporting the Seattle street map was used to develop "hundred blocks" for each city street in Seattle. For example, if the base map listed a street as spanning house numbers 1 through 399, we created four segments from this range: 1-99, 100-199, 200-299, and 300-399.

information system (ARCGIS 8.2[4]) as well as data manipulation software (Visual Foxpro[5]). Geographic information systems (GIS) are designed to find the positions on the earth's surface of addresses in a database (a process known as "geocoding"), which can then be mathematically analyzed or electronically mapped. In our study we used ARCGIS both to verify whether addresses were legitimate and to help correct or "clean" addresses (interactively with Foxpro) that could not initially be matched to a computerized street map in Seattle.

Approximately 2.5 percent of the 1,544,604 records could not be matched to a legitimate address.[6] We exclude these and two other types of records: those whose location was given as a police precinct or police headquarters and those written for crimes that occurred outside city limits. The use of a police precinct's address as a location of a crime is common, according to the Seattle police department, when no other address can be ascertained by the reporting officer. This left 1,490,725 crime records that were then converted into their corresponding street segments so that crime frequencies for each of the 29,849 segments for each year could be calculated.

DESCRIBING THE OVERALL DISTRIBUTION

Table 1 provides the overall distribution of incident reports in our 14 observation years. The most common was property crime (49.3 percent) followed by disorder, drug and prostitution offenses (17 percent) and violent person-to-person crime (11.4 percent). Another 16.6 percent of the incident reports were defined in various related categories such as weapon offenses, violations, warrants, domestic disputes, missing persons, juvenile-related offenses, threats and alarms. The remaining events were coded as traffic-related or unknown.[7]

---

4. ARCGIS 8.2 is a product of Environmental Systems Research Institute.
5. Visual FOXPRO is a product of the Microsoft Corporation.
6. It should be noted that street segments could have been added or removed from the Seattle street map over the 14-year period. While the City of Seattle could only provide us with their most recent up-to-date street map as of the year 2001, we recognize that this issue could be a small source of error.
7. We were not able to distinguish for "traffic" and "unknown" cases whether incidents were crime related because the incident report database does not include details of the events recorded. According to the Seattle Police Department, traffic incident reports were most likely not traffic citations, but rather hit and run crimes, drunk driving and accidents involving injuries. In cases where events were clearly not crime related, such as reports of assistance or administrative activities of police, we excluded them.

TRAJECTORIES OF CRIME AT PLACES   293

Before we turn to our analysis of the dynamic patterns of crime at place over time, we wanted to examine our data in the context of the more general assumption of the concentration of crime at place. Of the 29,849 existing streets segments in Seattle, 23,135 had at least one incident over the 14-year period, leaving 6,714 segments with none. The mean number of incidents per segment was approximately 3.6 (sd = 11.8). Crime trends in Seattle overall followed the national pattern (see Blumstein and Wallman, 2000), with a decline in incident reports at least since 1992 (see Figure 1). Between 1989 and 2002, Seattle street segments experienced a 24-percent decline in the number of incidents recorded.

Table 1. Overall Distribution of Incident Reports

Type of Incident Report	%
Property Crimes (all theft, burglary, property destruction)	49.3%
Disorder, Drugs, Prostitution	17.0%
Person Crimes (homicide, all assault, rape, robbery, kidnapping)	11.4%
Other Nontraffic Crime Related Events (for example, weapon offenses, violations, warrants, domestic disputes, missing persons, juvenile-related offenses, threats and alarms)	16.6%
Traffic-related (hit and run, drunk driving, accidents with injuries)	4.7%
Unknown	1.0%
Total	100.0%

Figure 1. Seattle Street Segment Crime Trends

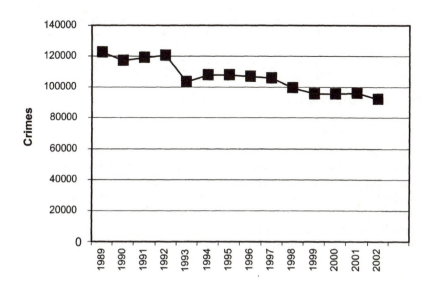

Examined year by year our data confirm findings from prior studies
that indicate a strong concentration of crime in "hot spots" (see Figure 2).
Moreover, they suggest that the general concentration of crime in hot
spots follows a consistent pattern over time. Sherman et al. (1989) report
that over a year 50.4 percent of all calls for service in Minneapolis
occurred at 3.3 percent of all addresses and intersections and that 100
percent of such calls occurred at 60 percent of all addresses. Very similar
findings for all reported incidents are found for each of the 14 years
observed in Seattle (see Figure 2). Between 4 and 5 percent of the street
segments account for about 50 percent of incidents in our data in each of
the years examined. All incidents are found in between 48 and 53 percent
of the street segments.

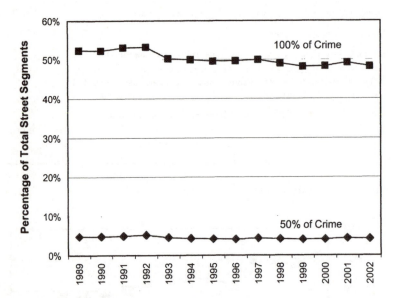

Figure 2. Crime Concentration in "Hot Spots"

A simple review of our data also suggests a significant degree of
stability of crime concentrations over time. In Figure 3 we report the
percentage of street segments in each year with a specific number of
incident reports. Though there is variability, the overall distribution is
fairly similar from year to year. For example, the percentage with no
recorded crime varies between 47 percent and 52 percent. Similarly, the
proportion of street segments with one to four incidents varies only

TRAJECTORIES OF CRIME AT PLACES 295

slightly, between 34 percent and 35 percent. The proportion with more than 50 recorded crime events in a year is approximately 1 percent across all 14 years.

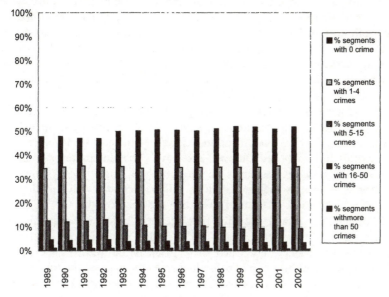

Figure 3. Crime Concentration Stability across Seattle Street Segments

Though the proportions of street segments with a specific threshold of crime activity remain fairly consistent year to year, it may be that the specific segments within each of these thresholds change. Accordingly, it is important to identify not only the general patterns over time but also how each of the 29,849 street segments' crime frequencies changed. This descriptive exercise on the aggregate data leads to two key questions. First, is the stability evidenced in our simple descriptive analysis of the proportion of places with a specific threshold of crime in a specific year replicated if we examine the developmental patterns of offending of places over time? Second, are there different patterns of crime over time for different groups of street segments?

TRAJECTORY ANALYSIS

We are unaware of any available technique in use in the criminology of place that would allow us to answer these questions, but such a technique—group based trajectory analysis—has been used in developmental social science more broadly (Nagin, 1999, in press; Nagin and Land, 1993). This technique and related complementary growth curve

296   WEISBURD ET AL.

techniques such as hierarchical linear modeling (Bryk and Raudenbush, 1987, 1992; Goldstein, 1995) and latent curve analysis (McArdle and Epstein, 1987; Meredith and Tisak, 1990; Muthen, 1989; Willet and Sayer, 1994) are designed to allow developmental researchers in the social sciences to measure and explain differences across population members as they follow their developmental path.[8] The need for such techniques arose in the 1980s as psychologists, sociologists and criminologists all began to turn to the study of developmental processes rather than to static events or states (see Bushway et al., 2001; Hagan and Palloni,1988; Laub et al., 1998; Loeber and LeBlanc, 1990; Moffitt, 1993).

The group-based trajectory model, first described by Nagin and Land (1993) and further elaborated in Nagin (1999, in press), is specifically designed to identify clusters of individuals with similar developmental trajectories and it has been utilized extensively to study patterns of change in offending and aggression as people age (see Nagin, 1999; Nagin and Tremblay, 1999). As such, we believe it is particularly well suited to our goal of exploring the patterns of change in the Seattle data.

Formally, the model specifies that the population is comprised of a finite number of groups of individuals who follow distinctive developmental trajectories. Each such group is allowed to have its own offending trajectory (a map of offending rates throughout the time period) described by a distinct set of parameters that are permitted to vary freely across groups. This type of model has three key outputs: the parameters describing the trajectory for each group, the estimated proportion of the population belonging to each group, and the posterior probability of belonging to a given group for each individual in the sample. The posterior probability, which is the probability of group membership after the model is estimated, can be used to assign an individual to a group based on their highest probability.[9]

This approach is less efficient than linear growth models but allows for qualitatively different patterns of behavior over time. There is broad agreement that delinquency and crime is one such case where this group-based trajectory approach is justified: not everyone participates in crime, and people appear to start and stop at very different ages (Muthen, 2001;

---

8. For an overview of these methods, see Raudenbush (2001), Muthen (2001), Nagin (1999) or Nagin (in press).

9. The group-based trajectory is often identified with typological theories of offending such as Moffitt (1993) because of its use of groups (see Nagin et al., 1995). But it is important to keep in mind that group assignments are made with error. In all likelihood, the groups only approximate a continuous distribution. The lack of homogeneity in the groups is the explicit trade off for the relaxation of parametric assumptions in random effects model (Bushway et al., 2003). For a different perspective on this issue, see Eggleston et al. (2003).

TRAJECTORIES OF CRIME AT PLACES 297

Nagin, 1999, in press; Raudenbush, 2001). Given that we have no strong expectation about the basic pattern of change, the group-based trajectory approach is an excellent choice for identifying major patterns of change in our data set.[10]

There are two software packages available that can estimate group-based trajectories: Mplus, a proprietary software package, and Proc Traj, a special procedure for use in SAS, made available at no cost by the National Consortium on Violence Research (for a detailed discussion of Proc Traj, see Jones et al., 2001).[11] We chose Proc Traj. When estimating trajectories of count data, Proc Traj requires that we make three decisions: parametric form (Poisson vs. Normal vs. Logit), functional form of the trajectory over time (linear vs. quadratic vs. cubic), and number of groups.

The Poisson distribution is a standard distribution used to estimate the frequency distribution of offending that we would expect given a certain unobserved offending rate (Lehoczky, 1986; Maltz, 1996; Osgood, 2000).[12] We found that the quadratic was uniformly a better fit than the linear model, and that the cubic model did not improve the fit over the quadratic in the case of a small number of groups. In choosing the number of groups we relied upon the Bayesian Information Criteria because conventional likelihood ratio tests are not appropriate for defining whether the addition of a group improves the explanatory power of the model (D'Unger et al., 1998). These models are highly complex, and researchers run the risk of arriving at a local maximum, or peak in the likelihood function, which represents a sub-optimal solution. The stability of the answer when providing multiple sets of starting values should be considered in any model choice (McLachlan and Peel, 2000). In the final analysis, the utility of the groups is determined by their ability to identify distinct trajectories,

---

10. Those interested in a more detailed description of the group-based trajectory approach should see Nagin (1999) or Nagin (in press).

11. The procedure, with documentation, is available at www.ncovr.heinz.cmu.edu.

12. Proc Traj also provides the option of estimating a Zero Inflated Poisson (ZIP) model. The ZIP model builds on a Poisson by accommodating more non-offenders in any given period than predicted by the standard Poisson distribution. The zero-inflation parameter can be allowed to vary over time, but cannot be estimated separately for each group. It is sometimes called an intermittency parameter, since it allows places to have "temporary" spells of no offenses without recording a change in their overall rate of offending. In this context, the ZIP model's differentiation between short-term and long-term change is problematic. The Poisson model, on the other hand, tracks movement in the rate of offending in one parameter, allowing all relatively long-term changes to be reflected in one place. We believe this trait of the Poisson model makes it the better model for modeling trends, especially over relatively short panels, even though the ZIP model provides a better fit according to the BIC criteria used for model selection. For a similar argument see Bushway et al. (2003).

298   WEISBURD ET AL.

the number of units in each group, and their relative homogeneity (Nagin, in press).

We began our modeling exercise by fitting the data to three trajectories. We then fit the data to four trajectories and compared this fit with the three-group solution. When the four-group model proved better than the three-group, we then estimated the five-group model and compared it to the four-group solution. We continued adding groups, each time finding an improved BIC, until we arrived at nineteen groups. We were unable, despite repeated attempts, to estimate the twenty-group solution and interpret this failure to mean that such a solution is not viable. The nineteen-group solution had a better BIC score than the eighteen-group, but proved very unstable, meaning that it did not converge to the same solution in multiple attempts with similar starting values. In each case, the model simply divided a larger group into two parallel curves. In contrast, the eighteen-group model found the same solution in at least four attempts from different starting values, and created a new group with a different shape than we found in the seventeen-group analysis.[13] We therefore chose the eighteen-group model with a BIC score of -626,182.42.

Figure 4 illustrates the final eighteen trajectories we obtained with the percentage of segments that fall within each trajectory. The figure presents the actual average number of incident reports found in each group over the 14 year time period. The main purpose of trajectory analysis is to identify the underlying heterogeneity in the population. What is most striking, however, is the tremendous stability of crime at places suggested by our analysis. Looking at the trajectories, it is clear that although many have different initial intercepts in terms of the level of criminal activity observed, most evidence relatively stable slopes of change over time.

This finding can be interpreted more easily if we classify our trajectories into common patterns. To simplify our description and to focus our discussion more directly on the question of stability of crime at place across time, we divided the trajectories from Figure 4 into three groups: stable, increasing and decreasing trajectories (Figures 5, 6 and 7, respectively). To aid in this classification, which does not depend on the quadratic term in the fitted trajectories, we fit a linear curve to the average number of offenses at each time point for each group. This created eighteen linear trend lines that were either basically stable, declining or

---

13. It is worth noting that this model was extremely complex because of the large number of segments. As a result, the model estimation was time and computer intensive. For example, the eighteen-group model took 8 hours and 15 minutes to converge using an AMD Athlon (TM) 2100 1.73 GHZ machine with 1.00 GB of RAM.

Figure 4. Eighteen Trajectory Solution for Seattle Street Segments

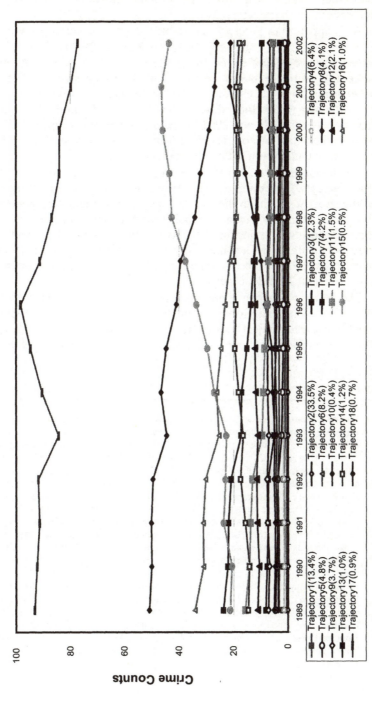

Note: The percentages in parentheses represent the proportion of street segments that each trajectory accounts for in the city of Seattle.

300   WEISBURD ET AL.

increasing. Under each figure, we provide the fitted linear slope and intercept for each trajectory.[14]

As is apparent in Figure 5, the stable trajectories had slopes very close to 0 (ranging from between -.0779 and +.1412). Eight of the eighteen trajectories we identified fit this pattern, and they represent fully 84 percent of all the segments we examined. This suggests that most of the street segments in the city did not follow the general crime decline found in Seattle as a whole. Indeed, there is a decrease of only 1,590 in incident reports between 1989 and 2002 in stable trajectories, a decline of only 4 percent. This may be contrasted with the overall decline of about 30,000 incidents in the city as a whole, a 24-percent drop.

It is important to note that these trajectories overall also had relatively low intercepts. For example, trajectories 1 and 2 account for almost half of all the street segments in the city, but may be classified more generally as "no crime" segments, given that their trajectories remain close to zero. In contrast, however, trajectory 12, accounting for about 2 percent of the street segments, shows a stable crime pattern of just over 10 incidents per year and trajectory 9, accounting for almost 4 percent of the segments, has a rate of about 7 incidents per year.

The number of street segments found in trajectories that represented noticeable increasing slopes during the study period is comparatively small. Only three trajectories of this type are identified in our study, and they account for only about 2 percent of the street segments in Seattle as a

---

14. We justify our use of a fitted linear trend to curves estimated using a quadratic functional form in the present case because we are primarily interested in differentiating between the simple direction of the trend, and not the shape of the downward or upward trend. Use of the simple linear slope makes this classification easier to present than if we provided the parameters of the quadratic curves. We also use the approach of presenting the actual number of events because of the unique nature of geographic, rather than individual data. In this case, we had a number of segments that routinely reported more than fifty crimes. This seems plausible in the case of places, but is unrealistic in the case of individuals, where the most likely explanation for such outliers is over reporting or data entry error. In most analyses of individuals (see Nagin and Land 1993; Jones et al. 2001), the distribution is truncated at approximately fifty to estimate Proc Traj, a practice done without loss of generality. In this case however, presenting the smoothed estimates using the data truncated at fifty would in fact be misleading because these types of high crime places are plausible, realistic and an important part of the crime story in Seattle. To get around the shortcomings of the parametric form without harming the descriptive story, we first estimated the groupings based on the truncated distribution, but report the graphs using the untruncated, actual data. This manipulation only affected approximately 1 percent of the segments over the 14 years.

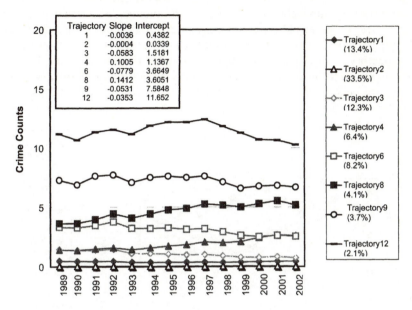

Figure 5. Stable Trajectories

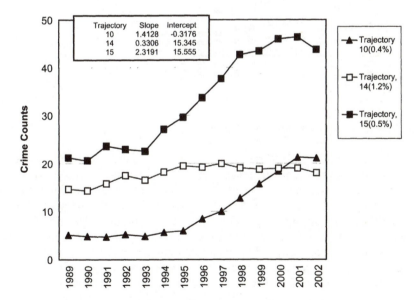

Figure 6. Increasing Trajectories

302   WEISBURD ET AL.

whole (see Figure 6). Nonetheless, the overall crime changes noted here
are generally relatively large. Trajectory 10, though beginning with a very
low rate of crime, increased its average crime rate more than four fold
during the observation period to more than 20 incident reports per year.
Trajectory 15 increased from about 20 to more than 40 incidents. Overall
these segments accounted for a 6,507 increase in incident reports between
the first and final observation years, a 42-percent increase in reported
crime over the period.

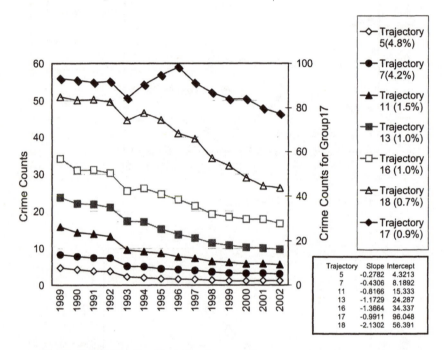

Figure 7. Decreasing Trajectories

Another seven trajectories identified in our analysis account for about
14 percent of the street segments in the city and can be classified as having
noticeably decreasing slopes (Figure 7). The extent of the declining slopes
varied a good deal across the segments identified here (between -2.1302 to
-.2782), as did the intercepts observed. It is significant that, despite the
variability of crime across these segments over time, the highest rate
trajectories remain relatively high throughout the observation period, and
the lower rate trajectories remain lower both in terms of their intercepts
and final estimates. For example, the highest rate trajectory begins at a
rate of almost 95 incidents and has at the end of our study an average rate
of more than 75 incidents. This is still a higher rate than any other

TRAJECTORIES OF CRIME AT PLACES 303

trajectory in our study. Similarly, the largest declining slope (trajectory 18) has an initial estimate of over 50 incidents and falls to about 25. Again, this is still higher than the final estimates for all lower intercept decreasing trajectories we examine.

Overall, as illustrated in Figure 8 these decreasing segments appear to account for the crime drop observed in Seattle during the study period. The area at the bottom of the figure represents crime that occurred in stable trajectories, and shows that the overall number of incident reports in these segments remains relatively stable throughout the 14 years examined in our study. The increasing trajectories, represented in the next shaded area, provide for a slight increase in crime. When combining both stable and increasing trajectories, representing about 86 percent of the street segments, we identify a small increase in crime between 1989 and 2002. In contrast, we can see that the shaded area associated with decreasing segments provides a fairly consistent degree of decline in the crime rate as measured by incident reports. Indeed, the decreasing trajectories, which show a decline of about 35,000 incidents between the first and last year of observation, can be seen as more than accounting for the overall crime drop in Seattle street segments of about 30,000 events during the study period.

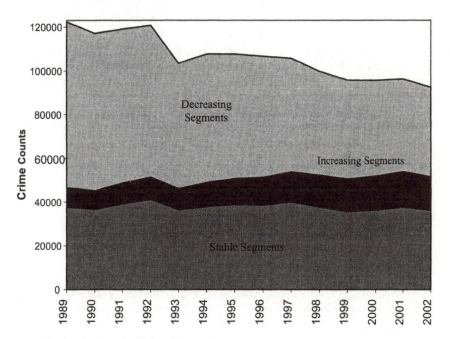

Figure 8. Seattle Crime Drop Analysis

THE GEOGRAPHY OF CRIME TRAJECTORIES

We think that the use of a micro place level of analysis has allowed us to examine crime trends at places with greater precision. It might be argued, however, that this choice has masked more general clustering of crime trends within neighborhoods or communities, or in terms of geographic analysis, that stable, increasing and decreasing trajectories may not be randomly distributed across space but rather exhibit some spatial dependence that might contribute to the trends. To examine this problem we developed kernel density maps for each of the three types of trajectories identified above (see Figure 9). Kernel density estimations provide a visual interpretation of the number of events across a geographic area, estimated at every point in that area. These estimates of intensity are created using a moving circular window around the region that measures the number of event locations from the center of the window outward at a specified distance, known as a "bandwidth."[15] The intensity is measured at every point to create a "smooth" estimate of the terrain of event locations. To estimate kernel densities of segments classified within stable, increasing or decreasing trajectories, equal bandwidths for each estimation were set at 5000 map units with equal output cell sizes of 500 map units. Equalizing bandwidths and output cell sizes allows for comparison among maps.

We recognize that this is only a general estimate of the concentration of segments within each grouping.[16] Overall, though, Figure 9 suggests that street segments of each of the three defined types are spread throughout the city. At the same time there are places of concentration. Segments classified into stable trajectories, for example (see Figure 9a), appear to have considerable diffusion across the entire city, but are especially prominent in more affluent and less densely populated areas in the north of the city.

---

15. Formally, the kernel density estimation function is represented by the following equation:

$$\hat{\lambda}_\tau(s) = \frac{1}{\delta_\tau(s)} \sum_{i=1}^{n} \frac{1}{\tau^2} k\left(\frac{s - s_i}{\tau}\right)$$

Here, the mean estimated intensity of a particular location is denoted by $\lambda_\tau(s)$. $k(...)$ is the probability density function, which is the function of intensity around a particular point, the radius of the kernel being the bandwidth, or τ and the center of the kernel, s. See Bailey and Gatrell (1995) for a full explanation of kernel density estimation.

16. While not the focus of this study, we are looking more carefully at the geography of crime trajectories in another paper (see Lum et al., in progress).

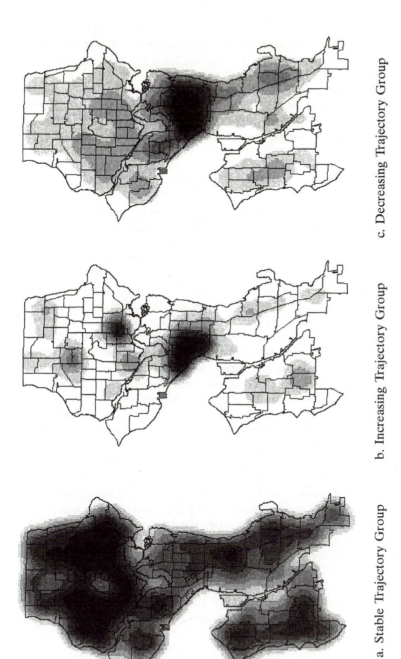

c. Decreasing Trajectory Group

b. Increasing Trajectory Group

Figure 9. Kernel Density Estimations

a. Stable Trajectory Group

Similarly, though a relatively small proportion of the street segments are increasing trajectories (Figure 9b), we find concentrations in most areas of the city. There is even greater spread of decreasing segments (Figure 9c), though this may be due in part to the larger number of segments in this grouping. At the same time, we do find that there are concentrations of increasing and decreasing trajectories in the urban center of the city. This is particularly interesting in part because it suggests that there may be similar causal processes underlying both types of trajectories.

DISCUSSION

In our introduction we argued that prior studies of concentration of crime at place do not provide a solid empirical basis for focusing either theory or practice on micro places. Even if there is tremendous concentration of crime at crime hot spots, as has been documented (see Brantingham and Brantingham, 1999; Crow and Bull, 1975; Pierce et al., 1986; Roncek, 2000; Sherman et al., 1989; Weisburd and Green, 1994; Weisburd et al., 1992), if there is little stability in such concentration across time, the underlying assumptions of this new area of research interest and practical crime prevention would be challenged. Our study enabled us to go beyond prior description of crime at micro places in two ways. First, we were able to examine assumptions about the stability of crime at place looking at a longer time series than has been available in prior research. Second, we were able to investigate whether different developmental trends are found across groups of places. Taking this approach we find strong support for the position of stability of crime at micro places across time.

Eighty-four percent of the street segments we examined could be grouped into what we defined as stable trajectories. That is, the vast majority of street segments in Seattle showed a remarkably stable pattern of crime over a 14-year period. Moreover, even in the case of the increasing and decreasing trajectories, changes in the rates of incident reports over time suggest a kind of stability of scale. For example, the two decreasing trajectories with the highest initial rates of more than fifty incident reports do not decline to fewer than twenty-five at the end of the study period—still placing these trajectories among the most active in our study. And the highest frequency increasing trajectory, which ended in an average count of more than forty incidents, still began with a rate of more than twenty.

It might be argued that the fact that trajectories that show the largest increases or decreases in the number of incident reports are also those with the highest crime frequencies to begin with, suggests that random

TRAJECTORIES OF CRIME AT PLACES 307

factors unlikely to be under the control of the police or the community might play an important part in the crime patterns found in our data. For example, "regression to the mean" could be one explanation for highly variable crime patterns. Very high levels of crime at a particular time might decline simply as part of a more general set of chance processes. While this explanation could apply to the trajectories with the very highest initial incident report rates, it does not explain why we do not find dramatic increases in incident reports over time at the very lowest rate places, which would be the other side of the regression to the mean phenomenon.

While we do not discount the workings of random fluctuations in our data (Spelman, 1995), we think the overall stability that we observe suggests that such fluctuations are much less important than systematic factors. Our data do not allow us to define directly these underlying causes of crime at place. Nonetheless, before concluding we would like to speculate on the potential mechanisms leading to the distributions we observe and discuss the types of studies that would help us to more fully understand crime trajectories at places.

Most study of crime hot spots has relied on routine activities theory (see Cohen and Felson, 1979) as an explanation for why crime trends vary at places and as a basis for constructing practical crime prevention approaches (see Eck, 1995; Sherman et al., 1989). The main assumptions of this perspective are that specific characteristics of places such as the nature of guardianship, the presence of motivated offenders, and the availability of suitable targets will strongly influence the likelihood of criminal events (see also Felson, 1994). Studies examining the factors that predict crime at micro places generally confirm this relationship (see Roncek and Bell, 1981; Roncek and Maier, 1991; Smith et al., 2000).

Routine activities theory does not necessarily predict stability of crime at place over time. Indeed, the theory was originally developed to explain changes in crime rates that were observed over long periods and that were related to changes in routine activities (Cohen and Felson, 1979). But most scholars advocating hot spots approaches have argued that the routine activities of places are likely to be fairly stable over relatively shorter periods of time such as the 14 years in this study (see Sherman, 1995; Weisburd, 2002). The availability of suitable targets, of capable guardians, and the presence of motivated offenders in this context are not expected to change rapidly under natural conditions in the urban landscape, though they are likely to change over longer periods as routine activities of offenders, victims and guardians change as well. Accordingly, the overall stability of crime at place we observe in our data is consistent with routine activities theory.

308   WEISBURD ET AL.

Although we can only speculate on changes in routine activities over time in Seattle, a theory of routine activities at crime hot spots (see Sherman et al., 1989) might also explain the variability in the increasing and decreasing trajectories. Those advocating hot spots approaches have assumed that the routine activities of places can be altered in the short term by interventions such as greater police presence (see Sherman and Weisburd, 1995; Weisburd and Green, 1995). Indeed, the short-term stability of crime at place predicted by routine activities theory and the assumed amenability of routine activities to change through police or community intervention is seen to provide a strong basis for crime prevention at hot spots (see Braga, 2001; Eck and Weisburd, 1995; Sherman, 1995; Sherman et al., 1989; Taylor, 1997; Weisburd, 2002). It may be that declining trajectories in our study are places where aspects of routine activities that prevent crime have been encouraged, perhaps because the police have focused more attention on them. Increasing crime trajectories could represent places where crime opportunities have increased, perhaps as a result of the introduction of new targets through urban renewal, or motivated offenders through the introduction of easy transportation access or perhaps the displacement of offenders from other crime hot spots that have been the focus of police or other crime prevention measures.

While routine activities theory has been a central feature of recent interest in crime hot spots, it is important to note that other theoretical approaches might also be consistent with our findings. Ecological theories of social disorganization used to explain the stability of crime patterns in communities (see Schmid, 1960; Shaw and McKay, 1942), for example, might also be applied to micro crime places (see Smith et al., 2000). In this case one might expect a stability of crime patterns because there is an underlying social and demographic stability at places (see Bursik, 1986). Conversely, relatively stable high crime rates at places may be explained by continuous social change that prevents the establishment of strong social bonds and community controls at the micro place level (e.g. see Shaw and McKay, 1942). Relatively high numbers of increasing and decreasing trajectories (representing on average higher overall rates of crime) in the urban center of Seattle are consistent with this perspective, as are the low rate stable trajectories showing higher concentrations in the less densely populated and more affluent northern parts of the city.

But if social disorganization variables explain the crime patterns we observe, formal social controls, such as hot spots policing, may have less potential for affecting the trajectories of crime at places. While the police may affect social disorganization at crime places by reinforcing forces of social organization and social control, the social disorganization perspective suggests emphasis on a much broader set of policies than increased police attention. If the primary causal mechanism underlying crime trajectories can be found in factors such as single family households, racial heterogeneity and economic deprivation, all linked to the social disorganization perspective, then a much wider set of social interventions would be required to change the form of trajectories at crime hot spots. Of course, it may be that a combination of routine activities and social disorganization variables influence crime patterns at micro places (see Smith et al., 2000), and thus a complex combination of interventions might be required to have a meaningful and long term impact on crime at hot spots.

Accordingly, while we think that our finding regarding the stability of crime at place across time is a robust one and is consistent with the theoretical arguments underlying crime prevention practice at hot spots, our study suggests that more analysis of crime trajectories at places drawing from a much more comprehensive set of data is needed. Future studies should examine changes in the social and demographic characteristics of places over time, and in the characteristics of their routine activities and guardianship, including the role of police activities in altering crime trajectories. Such data would be needed to tease out the characteristics of places that encourage stability and those which lead to change in crime rates, and would provide a basis for testing directly the relevance of routine activities theory and theories of social organization for understanding trajectories of crime at micro places over time.

Because different causal mechanisms may underlie different types of crime (Clarke, 1983) examination of crime trajectories of specific types of crime might also lead to new insights. It may be for example, that homicide or robbery trajectories at places differ markedly from those we observed here, though of course such studies might encounter new problems in defining trajectories when the occurrence of such crime events is relatively rare at micro units of analysis. In turn, while focusing on general trends, such as those represented by stable, increasing and decreasing trajectories, has allowed us to examine assumptions underlying hot spots approaches, more specific analyses of specific trajectories would likely increase our understanding of the dynamics of crime at place.

Finally, while our study has examined a longer time series than has been available to other scholars, it is still relatively short when one considers the overall developmental patterns of crime at places. Theories of routine activities and social disorganization are often concerned with changes that occur over decades or even longer time periods (e.g. see Bursik, 1986; Bursik and Webb, 1982 Cohen and Felson, 1979). Our analysis accordingly, may have underestimated dynamic elements of change over the long run and thus provides only a part of the story of crime trajectories at places. Although such long-term longitudinal data

310   WEISBURD ET AL.

may prove extremely difficult to identify, they would provide key insights
into the nature of trajectories of crime at places and the underlying
theoretical mechanisms that explain such change.

CONCLUSIONS

Our analysis of crime at street segments in Seattle over a 14-year period
and our use of the trajectory approach allowed us to fill an important gap
in our understanding of crime at micro places. Our study confirms prior
research showing that crime is tightly clustered in specific places in urban
areas, and that most places evidence little or no crime. But we also are
able to show that there is a high degree of stability of crime at micro places
over time. This stability is evident in the vast majority of street segments in
our study of 14 years of official data. Moreover, for those trajectories that
evidenced decreasing or increasing trends, we still found a stability of scale
with the highest rate segments generally remaining so throughout the
observation period.

Our data however, also suggest that crime trends at specific segments
are central to understanding overall changes in crime. The crime drop in
Seattle was confined to very specific groups of street segments with
decreasing crime trajectories over time. If the trends in Seattle are
common to other cities, the crime drop should be seen not as a general
phenomenon common to places across a city but rather as focused at
specific places.[17] Such places in our study are also street segments where
crime rates are relatively high. This reinforces a public policy approach
that would focus crime prevention resources on hot spots of crime (Braga,
2001; Sherman and Weisburd, 1995; Skogan and Frydl, 2003; Weisburd
and Braga, 2003; Weisburd and Eck, 2004).

These observations are of course preliminary given the nature of our
data. Our more general findings must be subjected to examination in other
contexts and across other micro place units (for example, see Griffiths and
Chavez, 2004). To understand the etiology of crime trajectories at micro
places we also need more insight into the nature of such places and their

---

17. One reader, Anthony Braga, has suggested that our finding that specific trajectories
account for the overall crime drop in Seattle is consistent with broader trends in
crime and violence across American cities. While the national trends illustrate an
overall decrease in crime during the 1990s, there was a good deal of variability
across cities (Blumstein, 2000; Travis and Waul, 2002). When looking at specific
crimes there has also been acknowledgement of important differences across
populations. For example, Cook and Laub (1998, 2002) observe that the youth
violence epidemic was concentrated among minority males who resided in poor
neighborhoods, used guns and engaged in high risk behaviors such as gang
participation (see also Braga, 2003).

TRAJECTORIES OF CRIME AT PLACES 311

experiences across the periods of study. Nonetheless, our examination of trajectories of crime at micro places over time suggests the importance of a developmental, criminal career perspective in the study of micro crime places (Sherman, 1995; Weisburd, 1997).

REFERENCES

Abeyie, Daniel and Keith D. Harries (eds.)
  1980   Crime: A Spatial Perspective. New York: Columbia University Press.

Appleyard, Donald
  1981   Livable Streets. Berkeley: University of California Press.

Bailey, Trevor and Anthony Gatrell
  1995   Interactive Spatial Data Analysis. Harlow, England: Pearson Education Ltd.

Baumer, Eric, Janet Lauritsen, Richard Rosenfeld and Richard Wright
  1998   The influence of crack cocaine on robbery, burglary, and homicide rates: a cross–city, longitudinal analysis. Journal of Research in Crime and Delinquency 35(3):316–340.

Block, Carolyn, Margaret Dabdoub and Suzanne Fregly (eds.)
  1995   Crime Analysis Through Computer Mapping, Washington, DC: Police Executive Research Forum.

Blumstein, Alfred
  2000   Disaggregating the Violence Trends. In Alfred Blumstein and Joel Wallman (eds.), The Crime Drop in America. Cambridge: Cambridge University Press.

Blumstein, Alfred and Joel Wallman (eds.)
  2000   The Crime Drop in America. Cambridge: Cambridge University Press.

Braga, Anthony A.
  2001   The effects of hot spots policing on crime. The Annals of American Political and Social Science 578:104–125.
  2003   Serious youth gun offenders and the epidemic of youth violence in Boston. Journal of Quantitative Criminology 19(1): 33–54.

Brantingham, Patricia L. and Paul J. Brantingham
  1975   Residential Burglary and Urban Form. Urban Studies 12(3):273–284.
  1981   Notes on the Geometry of Crime. In Paul J. Brantingham and Patricia L. Brantingham (eds.), Environmental Criminology. Beverly Hills, CA: Sage Publications.

312   WEISBURD ET AL.

1999   Theoretical model of crime hot spot generation. Studies on
        Crime and Crime Prevention Volume 8(1):7–26.

Bryk, Anthony S. and Stephen W. Raudenbush.
   1987   Application of hierarchical linear models to assessing change.
           Psychology Bulletin 101:147–158.
   1992   Hierarchical Linear Models for Social and Behavioral Research:
           Application and Data Analysis Methods. Newbury Park, CA:
           Sage Publications.

Bursik, Robert J. Jr.
   1986   Ecological Stability and the Dynamics of Delinquency. In
           Albert Reiss, Jr. and Michael Tonry (eds.), Communities and
           Crime. Crime and Justice: A Review of Research 8. Chicago:
           The University of Chicago Press.

Bursik, Robert J., Jr. and Harold G. Grasmick
   1993   Neighborhoods and Crime. San Francisco: Lexington.

Bursik, Robert J. Jr. and Jim Webb
   1982   Community change and patterns of delniquency. American
           Journal of Sociology 88(1):24–42.

Bushway, Shawn D., Alex Piquero, Lisa Broidy, Elizabeth Cauffman and
Paul Mazerolle
   2001   An empirical framework for studying desistance as a process.
           Criminology 39(2):491–515.

Bushway, Shawn D., Terence P. Thornberry and Marvin D. Krohn
   2003   Desistance as a developmental process: a comparison of static
           and dynamic approaches. Journal of Quantitative Criminology
           19(2):129–153.

Chakravorty, Sanjoy and William Pelfrey
   2000   Exploratory Data Analysis of Crime Patterns: Preliminary
           Findings from the Bronx. In Victor Goldsmith, Philip McGuire,
           John Mollenkopf and Timothy Ross (eds.), Analyzing Crime
           Patterns: Frontiers of Practice. Thousand Oaks, CA: Sage
           Publications.

Clarke, Ronald V.
   1983   Situational Crime Prevention: Its Theoretical Basis and
           Practical Scope. In Michael Tonry and Norval Morris (eds.),
           Crime and Justice: An Annual Review of Research 14. Chicago:
           University of Chicago Press.

Clarke, Ronald V. and Derek B. Cornish
   1983   Crime Control in Britain: A Review of Policy Research. Albany,
           NY: State University of Albany Press.

Cohen, Lawrence E. and Marcus Felson
 1979 Social change and crime rate trends: a routine activity approach. American Sociological Review 44:588–605.

Cook, Philip J. and John H. Laub
 1998 The Unprecedented Epidemic of Youth Violence. In Michael Tonry and Mark H. Moore (eds.), Youth Violence. Crime and Justice: A Review of Research 24:27–64. Chicago: The University of Chicago Press.
 2002 After the Epidemic: Recent Trends in Youth Violence in the United States. In Michael Tonry (ed.), Crime and Justice: A Review of Research 29:1–17. Chicago: The University of Chicago Press.

Crow, W. and J. Bull
 1975 Robbery deterrence: an applied behavioral science demonstration—Final Report. La Jolla, CA: Western Behavioral Science Institute.

Duffala, Dennis C.
 1976 Convenience stores, armed robbery, and physical environmental features. American Behavioral Scientist 20(2):227–246.

D'Unger, Amy, Kenneth Land, Patricia McCall and Daniel Nagin
 1998 How many latent classes of delinquent/criminal careers? results from mixed poisson regression analysis. American Journal of Sociology 103:1593–1630.

Eck, John
 1995 Examining routine activity theory: a review of two books. Justice Quarterly 12(4): 783–797.

Eck, John E and David Weisburd (eds.)
 1995 Crime and Place: Crime Prevention Studies 4. Monsey, NY: Willow Tree Press.

Eck, John, Jeffrey Gersh, and Charlene Taylor
 2000 Finding Crime Hot Spots Through Repeat Address Mapping. In Victor Goldsmith, Philip McGuire, John Mollenkopf and Timothy Ross (eds.), Analyzing Crime Patterns: Frontiers of Practice. Thousand Oaks, CA: Sage Publications.

Eggleston, Elaine P., John H. Laub, and Robert Sampson
 2003 Methodological Sensitivities to Latent Class Analysis of Long–Term Criminal Trajectories. Journal of Quantitative Criminology (in press).

314   WEISBURD ET AL.

Federal Bureau of Investigation
  1995   Crime in the United States, Uniform Crime Reports—1995.
         Washington, DC:.

Department of Justice.
  2002   Crime in the United States, Uniform Crime Reports—2002.
         Washington, DC: U.S. Department of Justice.

Felson, Marcus
  1994   Crime and Everyday Life: Insights and Implications for Society.
         Newbury Park, CA: Pine Forge Press.

Goldstein, Harvey
  1995   Multilevel Statistical Models. (2nd ed.). London: Arnold.

Green (Mazerolle), Lorraine
  1996   Policing Places with Drug Problems. Thousand Oaks, CA: Sage
         Publications.

Griffiths, Elizabeth, and Jorge M. Chavez
  2004   Communities, Street Guns, and Homicide in Chicago, 1980–
         1995: Merging Methods for Examining Homicide Trends Across
         Space and Time, 1980–1995. Unpublished manuscript.

Guerry, Andre-Michel
  1833   Essai sur la Statisticque morale de la France. Paris: Crochard.

Hagan, John and Alberto Palloni
  1988   Crimes as social events in the life course: reconceiving a
         criminological controversy. Criminology 26(1):87–100.

Heitgerd, Janet L. and Robert J. Bursik, Jr.
  1987   Extracommunity dynamics and the ecology of delinquency.
         American Journal of Sociology 92:775–787.

Hoover, Larry
  2000   Why the Drop in Crime? Crime and Justice International
         16(38): 11–29.

Hunter, Ronald D.
  1988   Environmental Characteristics of Convenience Store Robberies
         in the State of Florida. Paper presented at the annual meeting of
         the American Society of Criminology. Chicago.

Hunter, Albert and Terry L. Baumer
  1982   Street traffic, social integration and fear of crime. Sociological
         Inquiry 52: 122–131.

Jacobs, Jane
  1961 The Death and Life of Great American City. New York: Vintage Books.

Jeffrey, Clarence R.
  1971 Crime Prevention Through Environmental Design. Beverly Hills, CA: Sage Publications.

Jones, Bobby, Daniel S. Nagin and Kathryn Roeder
  2001 A SAS procedure based on mixture models for estimating developmental trajectories. Sociological Methods and Research 29(3):374–393.

Klinger, David and G. Bridges
  1997 Measurement error in calls–for service as an indicator of crime. Criminology 35(4):705–726.

Laub, John, Daniel S. Nagin and Robert J. Sampson
  1998 Trajectories of change in criminal offending: good marriages and the desistance process. American Sociological Review 63(2):225–238.

LeBeau, James
  1987 The methods and measures of centrography and the spatial dynamics of rape. Journal of Quantitative Criminology 3:125–141.

Lehoczky, John
  1986 Random Parameter Stochastic Process Models of Criminal Careers. In Alfred Blumstein, Jacqueline Cohen, Jeffrey A. Roth, and Christy A. Visher (eds.), Criminal Careers and Career Criminals. Washington, DC: National Academy of Sciences Press.

Loeber, Rolf and Marc Le Blanc
  1990 Toward a Developmental Criminology. In Michael Tonry and Norval Morris (eds.), Crime and Justice: A Review of the Research 12:375–473. Chicago: The University of Chicago Press.

Loftin, Colin and Robert H. Hill
  1974 Regional subculture and homicide: an examination of the Gastil–Hackney thesis. American Sociological Review 39(5):714–724.

Lum, Cynthia
  2003 The Spatial Relationship between Street–Level Drug Activity and Violence. Ph.D. Dissertation. College Park, MD: University of Maryland.

316   WEISBURD ET AL.

Lum, Cynthia, David Weisburd and Sue-Ming Yang
   In Progress The Spatial Distribution of Trajectories of Crime Places.

Maltz, Michael
   1996   From poisson to the present: applying operations research to
           problems of crime and justice. Journal of Quantitative
           Criminology 12(1):3–61.

Mayhew, Patricia, Ronald V. Clarke, A. Sturman and Mike Hough
   1976   Crime as Opportunity. Home Office Research Study 34.
           London: H.M. Stationery Office.

McArdle, J. and D. Epstein
   1987   Latent gross curves within developmental structural equation
           models. Child Development 58:110–133.

McDonald, Scott
   1987   Does Gentrification Affect Crime Rates? In Albert Reiss, Jr.
           and Michael Tonry (eds.) Communities and Crime. Crime and
           Justice: A Review of Research 8: 163–201. Chicago: The
           University of Chicago Press.

McLachlan, Geoffrey and David Peel
   2000   Finite Mixture Models. New York: Wiley.

Meredith, W. and J. Tisak
   1990   Latent Curve Analysis. Psychometrika 55:107–122.

Moffitt, Terrie E.
   1993   Adolescence-limited and life-course persistent antisocial
           behavior: a developmental Taxonomy. Psychological Review
           100:674–701.

Muthen, Bengt
   1989   Latent variable modeling in heterogeneous populations.
           Psychometrika 54:557– 585.
   2001   Second-generation Structural Equation Modeling With a
           Combination of Categorical and Continuous Latent Variables:
           New Opportunities for Latent Class-Latent Growth Modeling.
           In Linda M. Collins and Aline G. Sayers (eds.), New Methods
           for the Analysis of Change. Washington, DC: American
           Psychological Association.

Nagin, Daniel S.
   1999   Analyzing developmental trajectories: a semiparametric,
            group-based approach. Psychological Methods 4:139–157.
   In Press Group-based Modeling of Development Over the Life
            Course, Cambridge, MA: Harvard University Press.

TRAJECTORIES OF CRIME AT PLACES 317

Nagin, Daniel and Kenneth C. Land
  1993 Age, criminal careers, and population heterogeneity: specification and estimation of a nonparametric, mixed poisson model. Criminology 31(3):327– 362.

Nagin, Daniel and Richard Tremblay
  1999 Trajectories of boys' physical aggression, opposition, and hyperactivity on the path to physically violent and nonviolent juvenile delinquency. Child Development 70:1181–1196.

Nagin, Daniel S., David P. Farrington and Terrie E. Moffitt
  1995 Life-course trajectories of different types of offenders. Criminology 33(1):111–139.

Nettler, Gwynn
  1978 Explaining Crime (2nd ed.). New York: McGraw Hill.

Newman, Oscar
  1972 Defensible Space: Crime Prevention Through Environmental Design. New York: Macmillan.

Osgood, D. Wayne
  2000 Poisson-based regression analysis of aggregate crime rates. Journal of Quantitative Criminology 16(1): 21–43.

Pierce, Glenn, S. Spaar and L.R. Briggs
  1986 The Character of Police Work: Strategic and Tactical Implications. Boston, MA: Center for Applied Social Research, Northeastern University.

Quetelet, Adolphe J.
  1842 A Treatise of Man. Gainesville, FL: Scholar's Facsimiles and Reprints (1969 ed.)

Raudenbush, Stephen
  2001 Toward a Coherent Framework for Comparing Trajectories of Individual Change. In Linda M. Collins and Aline G. Sayers (eds.), New Methods for the Analysis of Change 35–63. Washington, DC: American Psychological Association.

Rengert, George
  1980 Theory and Practice in Urban Police Response. In: Daniel Georges-Abeyie and Keith Harries (eds.), Crime: A Spatial Perspective. New York, NY: Columbia University Press.
  1981 Burglary in Philadelphia: A Critique of an Opportunity Structural Model. In Paul J. Brantingham and Patricia L. Brantingham (eds.), Environmental Criminology. Beverly Hills: Sage Publications.

318   WEISBURD ET AL.

Robinson, Jennifer B., Brian A. Lawton, Ralph B. Taylor and
Douglas D. Perkins.
   2003   Multilevel longitudinal impacts of incivilities: fear of crime,
          expected safety, and block satisfaction. Journal of Quantitative
          Criminology 19(3):237–274.

Roncek, Dennis
   2000   Schools and Crime. In Victor Goldsmith, Philip McGuire, John
          Mollenkopf, and Timothy Ross (eds.), Analyzing Crime
          Patterns Frontiers of Practice. Thousand Oaks, CA: Sage
          Publications.

Roncek, Dennis and Ralph Bell
   1981   Bars, blocks, and crimes. Journal of Environmental Systems
          11(1):35–47.

Roncek, Dennis and Pamela Maier
   1991   Bars, blocks and crimes revisited: linking the theory of routine
          activities to the empiricism of "hot spots". Criminology
          29(4):725–754.

Sampson, Robert
   1985   Neighborhood and crime: the structural determinants of
          personal victimization. Journal of Research in Crime and
          Delinquency 22(1):7–40.

Sampson, Robert and W. Byron Groves
   1989   Community structure and crime: testing social disorganization
          theory. American Journal of Sociology 94:774–802.

Schmid, Calvin
   1960   Urban crime areas: Part II. American Sociological Review
          25(5):655–678.

Schuerman, Leo and Solomon Kobrin
   1986   Community Careers in Crime. In Albert Reiss, Jr. and Michael
          Tonry (eds.), Communities and Crime. Crime and Justice: A
          Review of Research 8. Chicago: The University of Chicago
          Press.

Shaw, Clifford, Frederick Zorbaugh, Henry McKay and Leonard Cottrell
   1929   Delinquency Areas. Chicago: The University of Chicago Press.

Shaw, Clifford and Henry McKay
   1942   Juvenile Delinquency and Urban Areas: A Study of Rates of
          Delinquents in Relation to Differential Characteristics of Local
          Communities in American Cities. Chicago: The University of
          Chicago Press.

TRAJECTORIES OF CRIME AT PLACES 319

Sherman, Lawrence
   1995   Hot Spots of Crime and Criminal Careers of Places. In John Eck
          and David Weisburd (eds.), Crime and Place: Crime Prevention
          Studies 4. Monsey, NY: Willow Tree Press.

Sherman, Lawrence and Dennis Rogan
   1995   Deterrent effects of police raids on crack houses: a randomized,
          controlled experiment. Justice Quarterly 12(4):755–782.

Sherman, Lawrence and David Weisburd
   1995   General deterrent effects of police patrol in crime "hot–spots":
          a randomized controlled trial. Justice Quarterly 12:626–648.

Sherman, Lawrence, Patrick R. Gartin, and Michael E. Buerger
   1989   Hot spots of predatory crime: routine activities and the
          criminology of place. Criminology 27(1):27–56.

Skogan, Wesley and Sampson Annan
   1994   Drugs and Public Housing: Toward and Effective Police
          Response. In Doris Mackenzie and Craig Uchida (eds.), Drugs
          and Crime: Evaluating Public Policy Initiatives. Thousand Oaks,
          CA: Sage Publications.

Skogan, Wesley and Kathleen Frydl
   2003   Effectiveness of Police Activity in Reducing Crime, Disorder
          and Fear. In Wesley Skogan and Kathleen Frydl (eds.), Fairness
          and Effectiveness in Policing: The Evidence: 217–251. National
          Research Council.

Smith, William, Sharon Frazee, and Elizabeth Davidson
   2000   Furthering the integration of routine activity and social
          disorganization theories: small units of analysis and the study of
          street robbery as a diffusion process. Criminology 38(2):489–
          524.

Spelman, William
   1995   Criminal Careers of Public Places. In John E. Eck and David
          Weisburd (eds.), Crime and Place: Crime Prevention Studies 4.
          Monsey, NY: Willow Tree Press.

Sutherland, Edwin H.
   1947   Principles of Criminology: A Sociological Theory of Criminal
          Behavior. New York: J.B. Lippincott, Company.

Taylor, Ralph
   1997   Social order and disorder of street blocks and neighborhoods:
          ecology, microecology, and the systemic model of social
          disorganization. Journal of Research in Crime and Delinquency
          34 (1):113–155.

320 WEISBURD ET AL.

1999 Crime, Grime, Fear, and Decline: A Longitudinal Look. Research in Brief. Washington, DC: National Institute of Justice.

2001 Breaking Away From Broken Windows: Baltimore Neighborhoods and the Nationwide Fight Against Crime, Grime, Fear, and Decline. Boulder, CO: Westview Press.

Taylor, Ralph, Steven Gottfredson, and Sidney Brower
1984 Block crime and fear: defensible space, local social ties and territorial functioning. Journal of Research in Crime and Delinquency 21(4):303–331.

Travis, Jeremy and Michelle Waul
2001 Reflections on the Crime Decline: Lessons for the Future? Proceedings from the Urban Institute Crime Decline Forum. Washington, DC: The Urban Institute.

Weisburd, David
1997 Reorienting Crime Prevention Research and Policy: From the Causes of Crime to the Context of Crime. National Institute of Justice Research Report. Washington, DC: U.S. Government Printing Office.

2002 From criminals to criminal contexts: reorienting criminal justice research and policy. Advances in Criminological Theory 10:197–216.

Weisburd, David and Anthony Braga
2001 Hot Spots Policing. In H. Kury and J. Obergfell–Fuchs (eds.), Crime Prevention: New Approaches. Manz: Weisser Ring.

Weisburd, David and John E. Eck
2004 What can police do to reduce crime, disorder and fear? Annals of American Political and Social Science 593:42–65.

Weisburd, David and Lorraine Green (Mazerolle)
1994 Defining the Drug Market: The Case of the Jersey City DMA System. In Doris Layton MacKenzie and Craig D. Uchida (eds.), Drugs and Crime: Evaluating Public Policy Initiatives. Newbury Park, CA: Sage Publications.

1995 Policing drug hot–spots: the Jersey City drug market analysis experiment. Justice Quarterly 12:711–735.

2000 Crime and disorder in drug hot spots: implications for theory and practice in policing. Police Quarterly 3(2):152–170

Weisburd, David, Lisa Maher, and Lawrence Sherman
1992 Contrasting crime general and crime specific theory: the case of hot-spots of crime. Advances in Criminological Theory 4:45–70.

Willet, J. and A. Sayer
  1994 Using covariance structure analysis to detect correlations and predictors of individual change over time. Psychological Bulletin 116:363–381.

Wolfgang, Marvin E., Robert Figlio, and Thorsten Sellin
  1972 Delinquency in a Birth Cohort. Chicago: The University of Chicago Press.

Worden, Robert, Timothy Bynum, and James Frank
  1994 Police Crackdowns on Drug Abuse and Trafficking. In Doris Layton Mackenzie and Craig Uchida (eds.), Drugs and Crime: Evaluating Public Policy Initiatives. Thousand Oaks, CA: Sage Publications.

David Weisburd is a professor in the Department of Criminology and Criminal Justice at the University of Maryland and in the Institute of Criminology at the Hebrew University Law School in Jerusalem. His major research interests are in the areas of policing, crime at place, white collar crime and research methods.

Shawn D. Bushway is an assistant professor in the Department of Criminology and Criminal Justice at the University of Maryland and a Fellow with the National Consortium of Violence Research. His current research focuses on developing methods that deal with selection bias, understanding the developmental process of change in offending over time, and explaining variation in sentencing outcomes.

Cynthia Lum is an assistant professor at the College of Criminal Justice at Northeastern University. Her current research interests include the spatial analysis of crime, international and domestic policing concerns and the relationship between drugs and violence.

Sue-Ming Yang is a doctoral student in the Department of Criminology and Criminal Justice at the University of Maryland. Her current research interests include criminological theory testing, etiology of violent behavior, and understanding the relationships between crime and place over time.

Part V
Causal Modelling

[20]

MEASURING POSITIVE EXTERNALITIES FROM UNOBSERVABLE VICTIM PRECAUTION: AN EMPIRICAL ANALYSIS OF LOJACK*

IAN AYRES AND STEVEN D. LEVITT

Lojack is a hidden radio-transmitter device used for retrieving stolen vehicles Because there is no external indication that Lojack has been installed, it does not directly affect the likelihood that a protected car will be stolen There may, however, be positive externalities due to general deterrence. We find that the availability of Lojack is associated with a sharp fall in auto theft. Rates of other crime do not change appreciably At least historically, the marginal social benefit of an additional unit of Lojack has been fifteen times greater than the marginal social cost in high crime areas Those who install Lojack, however, obtain less than 10 percent of the total social benefits, leading to underprovision by the market.

I. INTRODUCTION

The enormous resources devoted to the criminal justice system are well documented. Prison populations have more than tripled in the last two decades, with roughly 1.5 million Americans now behind bars. Total government spending on criminal justice in 1995 was almost $100 billion dollars. Often overlooked, however, is the fact that private expenditures on self-protection potentially dwarf public spending. Sources cited in Philipson and Posner [1996], for instance, estimate that private expenditures to reduce crime are $300 billion annually.[1] Laband and Sophocleus [1992] come to a similar conclusion. The opportunity cost associated with crime-related distortions to behavior (e.g., avoiding Central Park after dark or moving to the suburbs), while difficult to quantify, is also likely to be substantial.

Understanding the impact of private efforts taken to avoid criminal victimization is important not only because of their

* We would like to thank Gary Becker, Omri Ben-Shahar, Daniel Farber, Henry Farber, James Heckman, Louis Kaplow, Lawrence Katz, Eric Maskin, James Poterba, Steven Shavell, Joel Waldfogel, and numerous seminar participants for extremely helpful comments We are indebted to James Spiller for the National Insurance Crime Bureau, and the Lojack company for their generous provision of data Financial support of the National Science Foundation is gratefully acknowledged This work was not funded in any manner by Lojack, nor do the authors have any financial stake in Lojack All remaining errors are our own.

1 Victim precaution expenditures also appear to be growing at a rate faster than public spending For example, Sherman [1995] cites a *Wall Street Journal* report that the security guard industry grew 11 percent in 1994, more than twice the rate of police expenditures in recent years.

magnitude, but also because of the potential externalities associated with such actions. Many forms of victim precaution, such as highly visible car alarms or home-security systems, may serve primarily to redistribute crime across victims rather than to reduce crime. Consequently, those who engage in observable self-protection may impose a cost on those who do not.[2] In contrast, other forms of precaution such as silent alarms and passive disabling devices in automobiles may provide positive rather than negative externalities. Criminals cannot identify who has engaged in unobservable precaution, providing benefits to all potential victims.

The first formal treatment of externalities associated with victim precaution dates to Clotfelter [1978]. Subsequent theoretical work includes Friedman [1984], Cook [1986], Shavell [1991], De Meza and Gould [1992], Harel [1994], Hui-Wen and Png [1994], and Ben-Shahar and Harel [1995]. Empirical analysis of victim precaution, however, is almost nonexistent, with the exception of gun ownership and right-to-carry laws which have recently become the subject of heated debate [Black and Nagin 1997; Duggan 1996; Lott and Mustard 1997].[3] These studies, however, cannot differentiate between direct benefits to gun owners and externalities.

In this paper we provide the first thorough empirical examination of the externalities associated with self-protective efforts, focusing our attention on the Lojack car retrieval system. With Lojack, a small radio transmitter is hidden in one of many possible locations within a car. When the car is reported stolen, the police remotely activate the transmitter, allowing specially equipped police cars and helicopters to track the precise location and movement of the stolen vehicle. From an economic perspective, what makes Lojack most interesting is that there is no

---

2. Shavell [1991] notes that observable self-protection may also have a general deterrent effect. For instance, if there are fixed costs to engaging in criminal activities or search costs in finding suitable victims, then increases in observable self-protection may deter criminals and consequently may provide positive externalities. At least in the auto theft case, where there are a large number of available targets that are close substitutes, the magnitude of this deterrent effect is likely to be outweighed by the negative externality associated with crime displacement.

3. Crime-shifting in response to changes in the level of public law enforcement is somewhat better documented. For instance, Mayhew et al [1976] find that the installation of surveillance cameras in selected London subway stations did not increase crime in other stations. Wilson [1983] reports that increased evening police patrols in New York City subways led to a rise in daytime subway robberies. Eck [1993] and Hesseling [1994] review the existing literature.

indication anywhere on a Lojack-equipped vehicle that Lojack is installed.[4] Thus, Lojack is a prototypical example of the positive externality-generating unobservable self-protection.[5] An individual car owner's decision to install Lojack only trivially affects the likelihood of his or her own vehicle being stolen since thieves base their theft decisions on mean Lojack installation rates. Thus, to the extent that Lojack has any impact on lowering auto theft rates, these reductions are purely an externality from the perspective of the car owner installing Lojack. The only internalized benefits of Lojack are higher retrieval rates and lower theft damages once a vehicle is stolen.

There are various reasons why the presence of Lojack makes auto theft riskier and less profitable, leading to a reduction in the number of such crimes. First and foremost, Lojack disrupts the operation of "chop-shops" where stolen vehicles are disassembled for resale of parts. In the absence of Lojack, identifying chop-shops requires time-consuming, resource-intensive sting operations. With Lojack, police following the radio signal are led directly to the chop-shop. In Los Angeles alone Lojack has resulted in the breakup of 53 chop-shops. Second, data collected in California suggest that the arrest rate for stolen vehicles equipped with Lojack is three times greater than for cars without Lojack (30 percent versus 10 percent). Since most thieves are repeat offenders [Visher 1986; DiIulio and Piehl 1991], arrests that lead to incarceration may also provide social benefits via reductions in victimizations while the criminal is behind bars.[6]

Empirically, we find strong support for the argument that Lojack reduces auto theft. According to our estimates, one auto theft is eliminated annually for every three Lojacks installed in

4. Lojack executives report that law enforcement agencies condition their acceptance of the Lojack technology on the product being unidentified Insurance boards make insurance premium discounts conditional on a vehicle owner not privately identifying the presence of Lojack (for example, by a decal) Lojack owners may or may not individually benefit from concealing the presence of Lojack in their cars Signaling the presence of Lojack may reduce the likelihood that a vehicle is stolen, but will also increase the chances that a criminal will search for and successfully disable Lojack, reducing the likelihood that the stolen car is recovered Even if a Lojack owner wanted to signal the presence of Lojack, it may be difficult to do so in a credible manner.

5 Ben-Shahar and Harel [1995] also note the unobservability of Lojack and use it to illustrate their theoretical arguments.

6. Other possible benefits of Lojack include the elimination of the need for high-speed chases in Lojack-equipped vehicles. In 1993, 238 fatal accidents resulted from high-speed chases with police in pursuit according to data from the Fatal Accident Reporting System. Also, to the extent that the availability of a stolen vehicle facilitates the commission of other crimes, Lojack may reduce the rate of such crimes.

46   *QUARTERLY JOURNAL OF ECONOMICS*

high-crime central cities. There is little evidence that the reductions in central city auto thefts are simply being displaced either geographically or to other categories of crime. Auto theft rates also fall in the remainder of the state (much of which is typically also covered by Lojack, but at a lower penetration rate). There is little systematic change in the rates at which other crimes are committed in these cities. One form of substitution that is observed, however, is toward older vehicles, which are less likely to have Lojack.

An important issue is whether the negative association that we observe between Lojack and auto theft truly reflects a causal relationship. For instance, if cities grant regulatory approval to Lojack when they decide that it is time to get tough on auto theft, it may be that the observed reduction in auto theft is due not to Lojack, but rather to other actions the city takes coincident with the arrival of Lojack. We address this concern in a number of ways. First, if cities adopting Lojack shift police resources away from other crimes to fight auto theft, then one would expect to observe both an increase in the arrest rate for auto theft and a rise in those other crimes from which resources have been diverted.[7] Neither of these predictions are borne out in the data. Second, in an attempt to address the possibility of selection bias in the set of cities that grant regulatory approval to Lojack, we instrument for our measures of Lojack using the number of years that have elapsed since Lojack began the regulatory process in a state.[8] The resulting instrumental variables estimates are larger than the ordinary least squares estimates, implying that Lojack is more likely to be approved in cities where the auto theft problem is expected to worsen. Finally, we analyze whether the arrival of Lojack precedes or follows the declines in auto theft. Given lags of two to seven years in gaining regulatory approval for Lojack in a particular market, if Lojack systematically targets cities that are getting tough on auto theft, one would expect to observe falling auto theft rates immediately prior to the introduction of Lojack. Once again, such a pattern is not apparent.

Nor can our results be easily explained by the omission (due to lack of available data) of other measures of victim precaution

---

7 As will be discussed later, increased arrests do not appear to be the primary channel through which Lojack reduces auto theft.

8 It is also possible that there is sample selection in the set of cities that Lojack attempts to enter, which would not be addressed by this instrument As discussed in Section III, the direction of this bias is uncertain.

such as expenditures on antitheft devices, the locking of car doors, or not parking in dangerous neighborhoods. The presence of Lojack reduces the incentives for these other forms of victim precaution, both for car owners with Lojack, who suffer less harm when their vehicle is stolen, and for other car owners, who face lower theft rates as a consequence of Lojack's positive externality. Thus, the omission of these factors is likely to lead our estimates to understate the true effect of Lojack.

Our calculations suggest that an individual-Lojack owner who does not have theft insurance will benefit from installing Lojack in high crime areas due to the increased recovery rate of and lessened damage to Lojack-equipped stolen vehicles. For vehicle owners who have theft insurance, the internalized benefit of Lojack is much smaller since most of the costs associated with vehicle theft are borne by the insurer. In either case, the direct benefit to the Lojack-owner/insurer represents less than 10 percent of the social benefits of Lojack installation since almost all of the benefit results from the positive externality of reduced auto theft. Consequently, Lojack is likely to be dramatically undersupplied by the free market, suggesting a role for public policy. One form of government intervention currently in place is state-mandated insurance discounts; the current levels of such discounts, however, are far below the socially optimal levels.

The remainder of the paper is organized as follows. Section II provides background on Lojack and the data used in the paper. Section III contains the empirical estimates of the impact of Lojack. The fourth section discusses the results and considers numerous extensions. Section V presents a rough accounting of the private and social costs and benefits of Lojack. The final section offers a brief set of conclusions.

II. Background on Lojack and Data Sources

As noted above, Lojack is a radio-transmitter device hidden inside a car in order to allow fast and near-certain recovery of the vehicle if stolen. Virtually all Lojack systems are installed in new cars at the time of purchase. Installation involves a one-time fee of roughly $600. There are no additional maintenance costs or annual fees. According to statistics collected by the Lojack company, 95 percent of stolen vehicles equipped with Lojack are

48   *QUARTERLY JOURNAL OF ECONOMICS*

recovered, compared with roughly 60 percent of vehicles that do not have Lojack.[9]

The Lojack company has followed the strategy of entering markets sequentially. Approval for entry into a market by Lojack requires the cooperation of the state police organization, the state Attorney General, and local police departments. Time elapsed in waiting for approval into markets has ranged historically from fourteen weeks to almost a decade. A full list of markets covered by Lojack as of December 1994 and dates of entry into those markets is presented in Table I.[10] Lojack was first introduced in Massachusetts in 1986, and Massachusetts remains Lojack's strongest market today.[11] Lojack was subsequently introduced in South Florida in 1988 and in three additional markets in 1990. As of December 1994, Lojack served twelve markets. Lojack is the only widely available product for the remote tracking of stolen vehicles currently on the market.

The percentage of cars equipped with Lojack differs greatly across markets. Because installation is almost exclusively in new cars, initial penetration into markets tends to be slow (new car sales in a given year represent less than 10 percent of total cars registered). While the installed base increases over time, the fraction of cars equipped with Lojack generally remains small. After five years in a market, Lojack's typical coverage rate is less than two percent of registered vehicles.[12]

---

9 All data on vehicle recovery rates, chop-shops eliminated, and arrest rates for cars equipped with Lojack are from the internal reports generated monthly by Bob Montoya, Lojack's law enforcement liaison in California, in cooperation with various California police departments Data on Lojack installations, dates of entry into markets, and types of vehicles protected are drawn from internal Lojack records. Other Lojack information cited in the paper is based on discussions with Lojack executives.

10 The latest UCR crime data available at the time of this analysis covered 1994, so markets entered after 1994 (Connecticut, Orange County, and San Diego County) are not included as having Lojack coverage in our analysis.

11 Two factors contributing to Lojack's success in Massachusetts are ti aditionally high rates of auto theft (in 1985, the year before Lojack became available there, Boston ranked first among large cities in stolen vehicles per capita) and substantial insurance discounts to cars with Lojack Installation of Lojack provides a mandatory 20 percent discount on the comprehensive portion of Massachusetts auto insurance Lojack in conjunction with selected antitheft devices increases that discount to 35 percent Insurance discounts in other states are typically capped at 20 percent and are often at the discretion of individual insurance companies.

12. Confidentiality agreements with Lojack prohibit us from revealing penetration rates into individual markets. Estimates of the percent of total cars equipped are derived from data provided by Lojack on the percent of new car registrations equipped with Lojack and authors' calculations of new car sales as a function of total registrations, factoring in typical rates of removal of cars from the road.

LOJACK **49**

TABLE I
MARKETS SERVED BY LOJACK AS OF DECEMBER 1994

Market	Cities > 250,000 covered	Date of entry
Massachusetts	Boston	July 1986
South Florida	Miami	December 1988
New Jersey	Newark	March 1990
Los Angeles County	Los Angeles	July 1990
	Long Beach	
Illinois	Chicago	November 1990
Georgia	Atlanta	August 1992
Virginia	Norfolk	August 1993
	Virginia Beach	
Michigan[a]	Detroit	February 1994
New York	New York City	June 1994
Rhode Island	None	June 1994
Tampa/St Petersburg	Tampa	July 1994
District of Columbia	Washington, DC	September 1994

a Lojack was available in parts of Michigan beginning in April 1990, but service in Detroit did not begin until 1994.

When entering a market, the coverage range of Lojack varies. In some cases, an entire state is covered; in other instances, only an extended metropolitan area. On average, in states where Lojack is available, roughly 60 percent of the population is in coverage range. While no estimates of the geographic breakdown of Lojack installations within a market are available, installation rates are probably highest in the areas with the highest auto theft rates, which are invariably large cities. Auto theft rates per capita in cities with populations over 250,000 are three times higher than in cities with populations under 250,000 and more than ten times higher than in rural areas. For that reason, the primary focus of our analysis is on cities with a population greater than 250,000, although we also provide estimates for the remainder of the state as well. As of December 1994, Lojack was available in 13 of the 57 U. S. cities with population greater than 250,000.

Data on auto theft rates per capita, as well as for other crime rates, arrest rates, and number of police officers, are available annually on a city-level basis from the FBI's *Uniform Crime Reports*. UCR data include only those crimes reported to the police. Reported auto theft figures are considered more reliable than data for most other crimes because insurance companies

50   *QUARTERLY JOURNAL OF ECONOMICS*

require that auto thefts be reported to police to be eligible for reimbursement.[13]

In addition to the theft data, a number of economic and demographic variables are used as control variables in the analysis. These measures (unlike the theft data) are generally not available on a yearly basis at the city-level, necessitating a number of data compromises. Unemployment rates are available annually at the SMSA level; these values are used as proxies for city-level unemployment. State per capita income is measured on an annual basis at the state level, as are data on the age distribution of the population. The percent of a city's residents who are black is linearly interpolated between decennial census years. Year dummies and city-fixed effects are also included as control variables.

Summary statistics are presented in Table II, both for all central cities with populations greater than 250,000 in 1981 and for the subset of those cities served by Lojack by December 1994. It is important to note that cities served by Lojack differ systematically from the other cities in the sample. Lojack cities tend to be larger and have not only higher auto theft rates, but also more crime generally. Consequently, in our empirical analysis we focus exclusively on specifications that include city-fixed effects so that our parameter identification comes from within-city changes over time rather than from cross-city comparisons.

III. EMPIRICAL ESTIMATES OF THE IMPACT OF LOJACK

Figure I presents per capita auto theft rates over the period 1981–1994 for the six cities with population over 250,000 in markets Lojack entered before or during 1990.[14] Mean auto theft rates per capita for all non-Lojack U. S. cities with population over 250,000 are also shown. The vertical line in each picture represents the year in which Lojack became available in the market. Boston has experienced a 50 percent decline in auto theft rates

---

13 Victimization data from the National Crime Victimization Survey shows that 75 percent of all auto theft attempts (including 92 percent of all completed thefts) are reported to the police, compared with only 53 percent of burglaries, 51 percent of robberies, and 27 percent of larcenies [Bureau of Justice Statistics 1994].

14. For the purposes of the figure, Los Angeles and Long Beach, which share an SMSA, are combined These cities are entered separately in the regressions.

The regression results that follow are not sensitive to using 1981 as the starting point for our sample Using a later beginning date has almost no effect on the Lojack coefficients or standard errors, but somewhat increases the precision with which other parameters are estimated.

LOJACK 51

TABLE II
SUMMARY STATISTICS

Variable	Mean	Standard deviation	Minimum	Maximum
All cities in sample:				
Lojack share				
(% of all vehicles)	.05	33	0	4.95
Years of Lojack	17	85	0	9
City population	764,268	1,045,791	250,720	7,375,097
Auto theft per capita	.012	.008	002	.054
Robbery, burglary, larceny per capita	.078	.021	033	.156
Assault, rape,				
murder per capita	008	004	.001	025
SMSA unemp	6 3	2.1	2.2	15 9
State per capita real income ($1994)	19,911	2,821	13,720	31,228
% Black	26 0	18.7	1.2	80 7
% Aged 0–17	26.3	2.0	19.7	31 7
% Aged 18–24	11.5	1.3	8.4	15.1
% Aged 25–44	31.4	2.1	26.1	36 4
Sworn officers per capita (×1000)	2 47	96	1.32	7 81
Cities with Lojack coverage by 12/94				
Lojack share				
(% of all vehicles)	.21	.67	0	4 95
Years of Lojack	.83	1.71	0	9
City population	1,402,239	1,959,315	257,617	7,375,097
Auto theft per capita	018	.011	.002	.05
Robbery, burglary, larceny per capita	.0881	.025	.044	156
Assault, rape,				
murder per capita	011	.006	.001t	
SMSA unemp	6.5	2.1	2 7	15 9
State per capita real income ($1994)	20,843	3,370	13,932	31,228
% Black	37.5	21.0	10.4	80 7
% Aged 0–17	24.9	2.2	19 7	31 7
% Aged 18–24	11.5	1.5	8.4	15 1
% Aged 25–44	32.0	2.3	26 1	36.4
Sworn officers				
per capita (×1000)	3.20	1 33	1 40	7 81

Data cover the period 1981–1994 for the 57 U cities with a population greater than 250,000 in 1981 For the thirteen cities with Lojack coverage, data presented are for the entire period 1981–1994, not just for the years with Lojack Lojack data were provided by the Lojack company Crime, police, and city population data are from the FBI's *Uniform Crime Reports* Demographic data are from the U S Bureau of the Census and the *Statistical Abstract* Unemployment data are from *Employment and Earnings* State per capita income is in 1994 dollars, deflated using the CPI.

since the introduction of Lojack, going from nearly twice the rate for large cities to only slightly higher than average. There is, however, some evidence of a declining trend before the arrival of Lojack. Newark (−35.0 percent) and Los Angeles/Long Beach

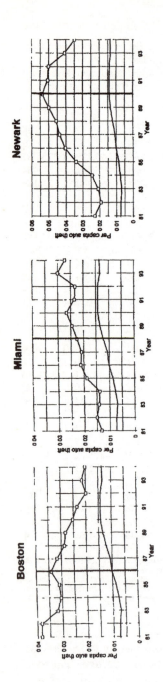

FIGURE I

Auto Theft Patterns in Cities Adopting Lojack before 1991

(−19.6 percent) have also seen substantial declines since the introduction of Lojack. In both cases, the post-Lojack declines represent a break from past trends. Auto theft rates continued to rise in Miami (11.4 percent) after the introduction of Lojack, although preliminary data released by the FBI (not included in the figure or subsequent analysis) show a 15 percent decline in auto theft in 1995, leaving present auto theft rates in Miami below those at the time of Lojack's introduction. There is little apparent impact of Lojack in Chicago where Lojack market shares are extremely low—less than one-twentieth as large as Boston. The low penetration rates in Chicago appear to be attributable to the fact that until 1996 Illinois law prohibited insurance companies from giving discounts for Lojack.

Figure II combines the information for these six cities into one figure. Because the level of auto theft varies across cities, the figure is expressed in terms of changes in auto theft, using five years prior to the entry of Lojack as a baseline. Since Lojack enters cities at different times, the horizontal axis is years pre- or post-Lojack entry; e.g., year 0 is 1986 for Boston and 1990 for Los Angeles. For comparison, Figure II also reports a simple average of changes in auto theft rates for all non-Lojack cities for the relevant years.[15] In the years preceding Lojack's arrival, the cities that will be served by Lojack experience slightly greater increases in auto theft. Directly coinciding with the introduction of Lojack, that trend reverses. In the four years after the introduction of Lojack, auto thefts per capita decline by .0051, or 17.4 percent. There is little apparent change in non-Lojack cities.

While it is true that the cities Lojack enters tend to have both higher than average levels of auto theft and faster rates of increase in advance of entry, the subsequent declines in auto theft do not appear to simply reflect mean reversion. The cities targeted by Lojack were perennially high auto theft cities. In 1973, for instance, almost two decades before Lojack entered most of these markets, per capita auto theft rates were 64 percent higher than average for big cities. There is evidence, however, that short-run *changes* in auto theft are partially offset in ensuing years. In our

---

15. For instance, year $t − 1$ in Figure II corresponds to 1985, 1988, 1989, 1989, and 1990 for the five Lojack cities Thus, the value of the non-Lojack cities is the average change in auto theft in those years for the 44 large U. S. cities that do not adopt Lojack in our sample period. Note that the 1989 value would carry twice the weight of the other years because there are two relevant observations in that year.

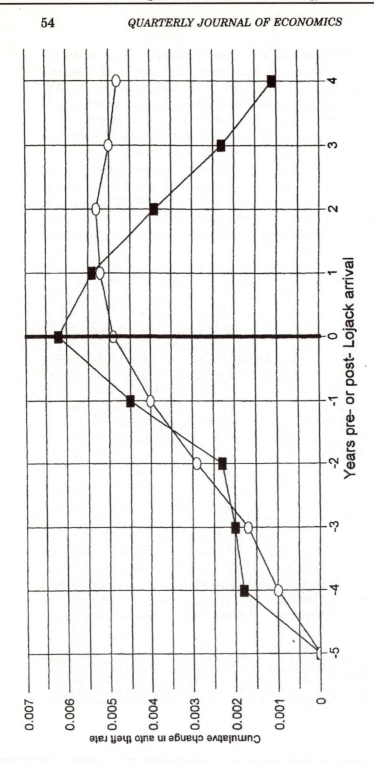

FIGURE II
Auto Theft and Lojack Availability
Lojack Cities versus non-Lojack Cities

LOJACK 55

data, roughly one-sixth of recent changes in auto theft per capitaare undone in the subsequent two years.[16] This effect, however, explains only a small fraction of the decline in auto theft rates after the introduction of Lojack since rates of growth in auto theft are not very different before Lojack arrives. Also, given the long regulatory delays often encountered by Lojack in entering a market, it is difficult to tell a compelling story that Lojack entry is driven by short-term fluctuations in auto theft rates.

In the analysis that follows, we employ two alternative measures of Lojack's market presence. The first measure is simply the number of years that Lojack has been available in a market. Since Lojack is installed almost exclusively in new vehicles, its market share grows steadily over time. This simple proxy has the advantages of being straightforward to interpret and also allows for the possibility that criminals learn about Lojack over time in a manner not based solely on the number of Lojacks installed. The disadvantage of this measure is that it sacrifices much of the variation in the data since penetration rates vary widely across markets. Consequently, we also consider the fraction of total car registrations equipped with Lojack in a given market and year as a proxy for Lojack's presence. This estimate is derived from Lojack's internal data on installation rates in new cars and authors' estimates of the hazard rates for autos being removed from the road.[17] There are two major drawbacks of this measure. First, due to data limitations, it can only be defined for the market as a whole, rather than, just for the central city. Since auto theft rates are higher in large cities, it is likely that Lojack's penetra-

16 This estimate of mean reversion is obtained by regressing the change in a city's auto theft rate between years t and $t + 2$ on the change in that city's auto theft rate between years $t - 2$ and t, including year dummies in the specification. Cities that adopt Lojack are excluded from the regression The coefficient of interest is $- 159$ with a standard error equal to .065 If city-fixed effects are included in the regression, the coefficient rises to $- 250$ (standard error equal to 060).

17. Our estimates of the hazard rates for removal of cars from the road are based on data for passenger cars in use published in compact disc form by the Polk Company under the title *National Vehicle Population Profile* Based on a census of currently registered passenger vehicles and light trucks, this data source provides information on the number of cars on the road annually by model year. The authors' calculations using these data show that roughly 3 percent of vehicles are removed from the road annually in the first five years of operation, with that hazard growing to 8 percent between years six and ten, and approximately 15 percent thereafter. Our estimates ignore the fact that some vehicles will move away from the Lojack coverage area, leading our estimated market shares to overstate the true Lojack presence.

tion rates are greater in these cities than in outlying areas, and thus are measured with error. In order to interpret the coefficients, one must make an assumption about the relative installation rates in central cities and outlying areas. A second problem with this measure is that market share may be endogenously determined. Cities where auto theft is expected to be high and increasing will tend to have higher installation rates. This may lead the estimates to understate the true magnitude of the impact of Lojack.

The form of the equations estimated in the basic specifications is as follows:

$$(1) \quad \ln{(AUTO\_THEFT)}_{it} = \beta LOJACK_{it} + X'_{it}\Gamma + \lambda_t + \theta_i + \epsilon_{it},$$

where I indexes cities and t corresponds to years. $AUTO\_THEFT$ is the auto theft rate per capita, $LOJACK$ is one of the two Lojack proxies described earlier, and X is a vector of controls for SMSA unemployment rates, the state age distribution, and the number of city police per capita.[18] Chiricos [1987] and Freeman [1996] report that property crime is negatively related to labor market conditions. Blumstein et al. [1986] find that the prevalence of criminal involvement drops off sharply after the teenage years. Levitt [1997] and Marvell and Moody [1996] find that increased numbers of police reduce crime. λ_t are year indicators and θ_i are city-fixed effects. Because the dependent variable is logged, β is roughly interpreted as the percent change in auto theft rates associated with a unit change in the Lojack proxy.

If the timing of regulatory approval of Lojack by cities is endogenous (e.g., cities approve Lojack at the same time other steps are taken to reduce auto theft), then the OLS estimates of equation (1) will be inconsistent. Consequently, in some specifications we instrument for the Lojack variables using the number of years that have elapsed since Lojack initiated the often lengthy regulatory approval process. Included in the construction of this variable are the three cities (Baltimore, Philadelphia, and Pittsburgh) where Lojack had begun the regulatory process, but had not yet been granted approval by the end of our sample. This variable is highly correlated with our two measures of Lojack

---

18. There is no strong theoretical justification for our choice of a log-linear functional form The primary rationale for this specification is the ease of interpretation of the coefficients. The findings with the dependent variables in levels are completely consistent with the results reported using the log-linear specification.

presence,[19] but does not exploit any of the potentially endogenous variation in the timing of regulatory approval.[20]

Estimation results are presented in Table III. Columns (1) and (2) include the number of years that Lojack has been available as a regressor; columns (3) and (4) use the Lojack market share. Odd numbered columns are OLS estimates with White-standard errors in parentheses. Even columns are 2SLS estimates using years since Lojack initiated the regulatory approval process as an instrument for the Lojack variables. The full set of demographic and economic controls are included in Table III, along with year dummies and city-fixed effects. The bottom row of Table III also provides the corresponding coefficient on the Lojack variable from specifications where only year dummies and city-fixed effects are included as controls.

In all specifications the coefficient on the Lojack variable is

---

19. The first-stage regression results are as follows (White-standard errors are in parentheses)

$$LOJ\_YEARS = 418*YEARS\_APPLY + YEAR DUMMIES$$
$$+ CITY\text{-}FIXED EFFECTS \quad N = 796 \quad Adj. R^2 = 703$$

$$LOJ\_SHARE = 142*YEARS\_APPLY + YEAR DUMMIES$$
$$+ CITY\text{-}FIXED EFFECTS \quad N = 796 \quad Adj. R^2 = 545.$$

Each additional year elapsed since the regulatory approval process began is associated with an additional .418 years of Lojack availability and an extra .142 percentage points of market share. For simplicity in displaying the results, the specification above omits demographic and socioeconomic covariates. When the covariates described below are included, the coefficients on years elapsed since initiating the regulatory approval process are virtually unchanged: 408 (standard error = .043) for LOJ_YEARS and .138 (standard error = .022) for LOJ_SHARE. The only covariate that is a statistically significant predictor of Lojack in both first-stage regressions is real income per capita, which is negatively related to Lojack.

20. One may also worry about possible sample selection in the set of cities where Lojack chooses to initiate the regulatory approval process. It is probably in Lojack's interests to enter markets where auto theft is high and is expected to remain high (to sustain consumer demand), which suggests that any bias should work against finding that Lojack reduces auto theft. The contrary possibility that Lojack would try to enter markets in which it expected auto theft to fall—in order to demonstrate to other markets Lojack's effectiveness—is belied by Lojack's belief that it is primarily selling a stolen vehicle retrieval service that reduces the expected damages if a vehicle is stolen (The corporation has never attempted to measure how increased market penetration affects the auto theft rate.)

In an attempt to control for sample selection in the cities Lojack enters, we estimated a logit predicting Lojack adoption by the year 1994 as a function of lagged auto theft rates, city population, per capita sworn officers, and state per capita income. We then limited our sample to those cities with above average propensity scores for Lojack adoption. The coefficient estimates obtained were slightly larger than those in Table III, suggesting that sample selection in the set of cities entered is unlikely to explain our findings.

58   *QUARTERLY JOURNAL OF ECONOMICS*

TABLE III
IMPACT OF LOJACK ON CITY AUTO THEFT RATES

Variable	(1)	(2)	(3)	(4)
Years of Lojack availability	−.109	− 157	—	—
	(.013)	(021)		
Lojack share	—	—	−.242	−.463
			(031)	(.065)
Unemployment rate	019	.026	.017	.028
	(009)	(010)	(009)	(010)
State real per capita income (×1000)	022	028	016	022
	(014)	(015)	(.014)	(016)
% Black	−.005	− 005	− 002	001
	(008)	(.008)	(009)	(.009)
% Aged 0–17	.106	115	102	.118
	(.030)	(.026)	(.030)	(.027)
% Aged 18–24	.003	−.005	−.004	− 027
	(039)	(039)	(039)	(041)
% Aged 25–44	028	059	008	056
	(039)	(038)	(039)	(039)
ln (sworn officers/per capita)	.044	060	− 001	− 009
	(.130)	(.133)	(131)	(137)
Instrument w/years since Lojack began regulatory process?	No	Yes	No	Yes
Adjusted R^2	.883	—	882	—
Coefficient on Lojack excluding covariates from the specification	− 086	−.113	−.200	−.333
	(.012)	(018)	(.028)	(053)

Dependent variable is ln(reported auto thefts per capita) Data cover the period 1981–1994 and include all 57 U S central cities with a population greater than 250,000 in 1981 Lojack share is the estimated percent of total vehicles registered that have Lojack installed in the market Number of observations is equal to 751 in all columns as a result of occasional missing data In columns (2) and (4) the number of years elapsed since Lojack began the regulatory approval process is used as an instrument for the Lojack variables All columns include year dummies and city-fixed effects in addition to the variables shown Unemployment is the annual SMSA unemployment rate % Black is linearly interpolated between decennial census years Age categories refer to state age distributions, the omitted category is percent of the population over age 45 White standard errors are in parentheses The bottom row of the table presents the coefficient on the Lojack variable in specifications that include only year dummies and city-fixed effects as covariates.

negative and highly statistically significant. In column (1) each additional year of Lojack availability in a market is associated with roughly a 10 percent decline in auto theft. The 2SLS estimate in column (2) are even larger. Column (3) shows that each additional percentage point of Lojack in the market is associated with a greater than 20 percent reduction in auto theft in central cities. This coefficient is deceptively large, however, since Lojack is disproportionately installed in central cities. Assuming that Lojack penetration rates are three times higher in cities than in the overall market, each percentage point of Lojack installation translates into a 7 percent decline in auto theft. 2SLS estimates column (4) are once again larger than OLS estimates.[21]

Increases in the unemployment rate are associated with rising auto theft rates as expected. Each percentage point increase in unemployment raises auto theft by about 2 percent. There is also some evidence that high incomes are associated with higher auto theft rates, presumably due to an increase in the pool of attractive automobiles available to be stolen. The coefficient on percent black is substantively small and statistically insignificant. The age category variables generally have the expected positive sign relative to the omitted category (over age 44), but are statistically significant only for the 0–17 age range. The coefficient on sworn officers, as is typically the case in correlational analyses [Cameron 1988], is small and sometimes carries a counterintuitive sign. The generally weak performance of the control variables is not surprising given the inclusion of year dummies and city-fixed effects. After removing year and city means, there is relatively little variation remaining in the controls, especially for the race and age variables. Coefficients on the Lojack variables from specifications that include only year dummies and city-fixed effects as controls are presented in the bottom row of Table III. The estimated impact of Lojack is somewhat smaller, but still highly statistically significant.

IV. DISCUSSION AND EXTENSIONS

Given the large estimated impact of Lojack, it is worth considering whether the magnitude of the effect is plausible. As noted above, a one percentage point increase in the Lojack share of the entire market is likely to be associated with a much greater increase in the share of vehicles protected by Lojack in the central city. Even so, it does not seem likely that changes in the aggregate likelihood of arrest for auto theft can account for the large effects: if arrests are three times as likely with Lojack-equipped cars (30 percent versus 10 percent), a 3 percent Lojack market share would increase the likelihood of arrest only 6 percent (i.e., from 0.10 to 0.106). Levitt [1998] estimates the elasticity of auto theft

21. As a further check on the potential endogeneity of the timing of Lojack adoption in a city, we ran specifications identical to those in Table III, but adding in leads of the Lojack variables to test whether the declines in auto theft precede the arrival of Lojack. There is no evidence of systematic patterns in auto theft rates in the three years preceding the arrival of Lojack. The signs on the leads of the Lojack variables flipped across specifications and were not statistically significant.

with respect to the auto theft arrest rate to be roughly -0.10, which implies that the increase in aggregate arrest rates can explain only a small fraction of the overall Lojack-related decline. Empirically, when we replicate the specifications in Table III using the auto theft arrest rate (defined as the number of auto theft arrests divided by the number of reported auto thefts) as the dependent variable, we obtain small, negative, and statistically insignificant coefficients on Lojack. These estimates are consistent with the argument that changes in the arrest rate are not the primary channel through which Lojack reduces auto theft.

However, if there is a subset of professional auto thieves who steal large numbers of vehicles with virtually no likelihood of being caught in the absence of Lojack, then the introduction of Lojack may have a dramatic impact on their activities. For example, a professional thief stealing 100 cars a year who has only a three-tenths of 1 percent chance of arrest per theft without Lojack, but a 10 percent chance of arrest when Lojack is installed, sees the annual chance of arrest increase from 26 percent to 45 percent. The incapacitation effect from this heightened chance of arrest is also substantial: prisoners surveyed in DiIulio and Piehl [1991] self-report committing a mean of 141 nondrug, serious crimes in the year prior to imprisonment. Sources cited in Clarke and Harris [1992] estimate that roughly 60 percent of vehicles are stolen with the intention of stripping, VIN-switching, or exporting. If much of this activity is done by professional thieves, a large fraction of our results can plausibly be explained through this channel.

The most important effect of Lojack, however, may not be its direct impact on the auto thief, but rather the disruption it creates for chop-shop operations. Without Lojack, it is extremely difficult to break such auto theft rings without expensive, time-consuming stings. By leading police directly to the site where cars are stripped, Lojack makes the detection of chop-shops routine.[22] The Lojack company reports that their product has led police to 53 chop-shops in the Los Angeles area, the only area for which complete data are available. Given the large number of vehicles processed by a typical auto theft ring, a small Lojack presence

22 One anecdote emphasizes this point in a particularly telling way The FBI had been conducting a year-long sting operation and was finally on the verge of shutting down an auto theft ring that it had under observation As FBI agents engaged in the stakeout watched, a single local police cruiser, following a Lojack signal, stumbled onto the chop-shop in question, leading to multiple arrests and the dissolution of the auto theft ring.

translates into a high likelihood that at least one Lojack-equipped vehicle will be encountered. For instance, assuming a 3 percent Lojack market share, if 50 cars are stripped annually, the likelihood that at least one of these cars has Lojack is 78 percent. If 100 cars are stripped, this value rises to 95 percent. As evidence that the threat Lojack poses to auto theft rings is real, in cities where Lojack has a presence, professional auto thieves drive stolen vehicles for no more than a few miles before temporarily abandoning them. They return to the spot later; if the stolen car is still there, they presume it does not have Lojack and only then proceed to the chop-shop.[23] Thus, even if Lojack does not lead to the dismantling of a given auto theft ring, it greatly increases the time costs and inconvenience of conducting such an operation.

One indirect piece of evidence supporting the argument that Lojack's primary impact is on professional thieves and chop-shops comes from allowing for nonlinearities in the impact of Lojack's market share. Figure III presents a plot of the curve traced out in a specification identical to that of column (3) of Table III, except that squared and cubic values of Lojack's market share are also included in the regression.[24] Over the range in which most of the available data lie (i.e., 0–2 percent Lojack penetration), the function is concave, implying sharply decreasing marginal returns to Lojack installation. The decline associated with the first percentage point of Lojack market share is two and a half times larger than that of the second percentage point, and seven times that of the third percentage point. While there is some hint of an upturn in the high penetration ranges, only Massachusetts has experienced such penetration levels, making inference based on this portion of the curve suspect. One interpretation of these sharply declining marginal returns is that those who are most affected by Lojack's presence, namely professional car thieves and chop-shops, alter their practices in response to relatively low concentrations of Lojack. Having changed their behavior (e.g., temporarily abandoning stolen vehicles in parking lots, substituting toward other crimes, or moving out of central cities), there is little crime-reduction benefit from higher concentrations of Lo-

---

23 The police, however, have responded to this practice by staking out some stolen Lojack-equipped vehicles rather than immediately recovering them. If the thief returns, he or she is trailed by undercover police.

24. The squared and cubic terms are jointly, but not individually, statistically significant at the .05 level (F-statistic = 3 25 with degrees of freedom equal to 2 in the numerator and 672 in the denominator) In regressions using years of Lojack in place of Lojack's share, the nonlinear terms are not statistically significant.

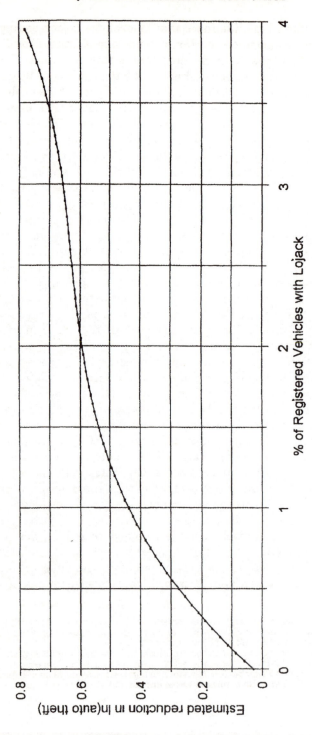

FIGURE III

Estimated Auto Theft Decline with Lojack Allowing for Nonlinearities

jack. In contrast, one would expect the crime-reducing impact of Lojack market share on joyriders to be roughly linear (and, as argued above, of second-order importance).

A. *Displacement*

Assuming that the observed decline in central city auto theft is real, it is important to explore whether this reflects a true reduction in crime or is simply a displacement. It is possible that crime shifts either geographically or toward other criminal acts such as burglary or robbery.[25]

The first possibility we explore is that crime shifts geographically, falling in central cities and rising in other parts of the state. Table IV explores this hypothesis by replacing per capita *city* auto theft rates with the corresponding variable for the remainder of the state, excluding any cities with Lojack coverage and population over 250,000. Because the dependent variable in Table IV is defined at the state level, the covariates in the table are also state-level variables. Otherwise, the specifications in Table IV mirror those in Table III. Each year of Lojack availability is associated with 3–6 percent declines in rest-of-state auto theft rates, or roughly one-third that observed in central cities. The effect of Lojack market share is also negative and substantially smaller than that observed in central cities. The smaller magnitudes outside of central cities is consistent with Lojack installations being disproportionately concentrated in large cities where the auto theft threat is greatest, and with the fact that only 50 percent of the outlying areas in these states are actually covered by Lojack.

A more skeptical interpretation of Table IV is that the decline in auto theft outside of the central cities is evidence not of the effectiveness of Lojack (which is likely to be installed in relatively few cars), but rather of a spurious correlation between Lojack and declining auto theft rates that may also be tainting the central city estimates. Incorporating this perspective, a potential lower bound on the true effect of Lojack in central cities may be obtained by subtracting the estimates of Table IV from those of Table III, which would reduce the magnitudes of the coefficients by roughly 30 percent.

An alternative form of displacement is across crime catego-

25. Cornish and Clarke [1987] and Clarke and Harris [1992] survey studies that examine both types of displacement in auto theft.

TABLE IV
IMPACT OF LOJACK ON OUTLYING AREA AUTO THEFT RATES

Variable	(1)	(2)	(3)	(4)
Years of Lojack availability	− 041	− 058	—	—
	(.011)	(019)		
Lojack share	—	—	− 056	− 173
			(019)	(.059)
Unemployment rate	.000	004	− 004	.006
	(007)	(009)	(007)	(.009)
State real per capita income (×1000)	004		− 002	001
	(016)	(015)	(015)	(015)
% Black	− 0004	− 0005	− 0002	− 0004
	(0003)	(.0003)	(0003)	(.0003)
% Aged 0–17	128	.134	.118	.126
	(.022)	(.026)	(.022)	(.026)
% Aged 18–24	.089	.086	.089	.076
	(.035)	(.036)	(.036)	(.038)
% Aged 25–44	.070	.083	.052	082
	(.034)	(034)	(035)	(035)
ln (police/per capita)	136	131	123	068
	(113)	(119)	(112)	(126)
Instrument w/yrs. since Lojack began regulatory process?	No	Yes	No	Yes
Adjusted R^2	874	—	907	—
Coefficient on Lojack excluding covariates from the specification	− 027	− 032	− 045	− 092
	(009)	(012)	(019)	(035)

Dependent variable is ln(reported auto theft per capita) for all areas in the state *except* central cities with population greater than 250,000 that are covered by Lojack by the year 1994 Data cover the period 1981–1994 Only states with at least one city with a population greater than 250,000 are included in the sample Lojack share is the estimated percent of total vehicles registered that have Lojack installed in the market covered within this state In columns (2) and (4) the number of years since Lojack began the regulatory approval process is used as an instrument for the Lojack proxy Number of observations is equal to 403 in all columns All columns include year dummies and state-fixed effects in addition to the variables shown Unemployment, % Black, police, and age categories refer to the entire state, not just the outlying areas White-standard errors are in parentheses The bottom row of the table reports the Lojack coefficient from a specification with only year dummies and state-fixed effects as controls.

ries rather than across geographic areas. The economic model of crime [Becker 1968] predicts that rising punishments or reduced rewards for one crime will lead criminals to increase their involvement in substitutable crimes. If reductions in auto theft are accompanied by increases in burglaries and robberies—crimes that entail a much greater likelihood of injury to the victim than auto theft—then Lojack may be socially costly. On the other hand, there are numerous scenarios in which Lojack leads to reductions in other crimes. For instance, if stealing a car facilitates the commission of other crimes and Lojack impedes the acquisition of a vehicle, then fewer crimes of all kinds may occur. Similarly, if some criminals do not attribute the increased ability of police to fight auto theft to a specific technological advance, then a "halo deterrence" effect can emerge, with criminals mistakenly perceiving a general increase in police capabilities and consequently reducing all criminal activities. Finally, if Lojack allows the apprehension of professional criminals who are both generalists [Beck 1989] and otherwise difficult to catch, there may be incapacitation effects as well.

Table V presents estimated impacts of Lojack on crimes other than auto theft. These crimes are divided into two categories: "substitutable" and "nonsubstitutable." Substitutable crimes (burglary, larceny, robbery) are those whose primary motivation is financial; nonsubstitutable crimes (murder, rape, aggravated assault) are those where financial gain is generally not the primary motive. The specifications in Table V are identical to those of Table III, except that the dependent variable has changed.[26] The regressions suggest that Lojack has only a small impact on crimes other than auto theft. While the Lojack coefficients are consistently negative, the estimates are statistically different from zero at the .05 level in only one of eight cases. Even the largest coefficients are only about one-fourth of the magnitude of the estimates for auto theft, increasing our confidence that the observed decline in auto theft reflects real effects of Lojack. If the fall in other crimes was commensurate with that of auto theft, it would call into question the causal role of Lojack. While theory would predict a greater shift toward financially motivated crimes, there is little evidence of a differential effect of Lojack across substitutable and nonsubstitutable crimes.[27]

Another form of auto theft displacement is away from newer, expensive vehicles that are more likely to have Lojack toward older, cheaper models. While we do not have detailed Lojack penetration rates by make, aggregate data on Lojack installations shows that Mercedes and BMWs are, respectively, four times and two times as likely as the typical car to have Lojack. The fact that Lojack is installed almost exclusively in new vehicles allows us to test the degree of substitution toward older models by auto

26 Specifications utilizing two-stage least squares, omitted from Table V, are consistent with those presented.

27. Replicating the specifications in Table V, but replacing city nonauto theft crime rates with the equivalent crime rates from the rest of the state yielded an even mix of positive and negative coefficients on the Lojack variable, none of which were statistically significant.

TABLE V

IMPACT OF LOJACK ON CRIMES OTHER THAN AUTO THEFT

Variable	Substitutable crimes (robbery, burglary, larceny)		Nonsubstitutable crimes (assault, rape, murder)	
	(1)	(2)	(3)	(4)
Years of Lojack availability	−.015	—	− 005	—
	(.009)		(.006)	
Lojack share	—	−.059	—	− 015
		(.015)		(.016)
Unemployment rate	024	025	−.022	−.022
	(005)	(.004)	(.006)	(.006)
State real per capita income (×1000)	− 019	−.019	003	.003
	(009)	(.009)	(010)	(.010)
% Black	−.005	−.004	− 001	−.001
	(.004)	(.004)	(006)	(006)
% Aged 0–17	− 065	−.064	−.015	−.016
	(.013)	(013)	(.018)	(.018)
% Aged 18–24	−.037	−.041	−.019	− 020
	(.022)	(022)	(.029)	(029)
% Aged 25–44	.099	102	−.012	−.012
	(.024)	(024)	(.023)	(022)
ln(sworn police per capita)	.077	070	.398	396
	(.064)	(063)	(.090)	(090)
Adjusted R^2	.819	839	.928	936
Coefficient on Lojack excluding covariates	.005	− 016	−.016	− 040
	(.006)	(011)	(.005)	(.008)

Dependent variable is the natural log of the crime categories named Substitutable crimes are those that are presumed to be close substitutes for auto theft, i e , robbery, burglary, and larceny Nonsubstitutable crimes are murder, rape, and aggravated assault In both cases, the sum of the reported crime rates within the various crime categories is used Data cover the period 1981–1994 and include all 57 U S central cities with a population greater than 250,000 in 1981 Number of observations varies between 742 and 767 based on the number of missing observations All columns include year dummies and city-fixed effects in addition to the variables shown Lojack share is the estimated percent of total vehicles registered that have Lojack installed in the market Unemployment is the annual SMSA unemployment rate % Black is linearly interpolated between decennial census years Age categories refer to state age distributions, the omitted category is percent of the population over age 45 White-standard errors are in parentheses The bottom row of the table presents estimates of the Lojack coefficient from specifications including only year dummies and city-fixed effects as covariates .

thieves. Annual data on the breakdown of motor vehicle thefts by city and model year were provided to us by the National Insurance Crime Bureau (NICB). The NICB database includes information on roughly 30 percent of vehicles stolen annually. The sample of vehicles included in the NICB figures are those for which member insurance companies voluntarily provided data. Consequently, these data are not representative of all auto thefts since many vehicles (particularly older ones) do not carry comprehensive auto insurance. These data are available only back to 1989.

Table VI presents simple tabulations of the raw data breaking down auto theft by vehicle age for the years 1989 and 1994 for the cities in our sample without Lojack and the cities that adopted Lojack by 1990 (the same cities included in Figures I and II).[28] Vehicles are assigned to one of three age categories: less than four years, four to six years, and more than six years old. Columns 1 and 2 compare non-Lojack and Lojack cities in 1989, at which time the percent of cars equipped with Lojack (denoted in the table by the number in brackets), even among new cars, was extremely low. The proportion of stolen vehicles in each category is nearly identical in non-Lojack and Lojack cities. Roughly 44 percent of the cars stolen in 1989 had been on the road for three years or less. Columns 3 and 4 present the same comparison for 1994. The fraction of new cars stolen declines sharply between 1989 and 1994 in both sets of cities due to a decline in the relative number of new cars on the road in the latter period.[29] The fall in the fraction of new vehicles stolen in Lojack cities, however, is almost five percentage points greater. This finding is consistent with the pattern of Lojack penetration: new vehicles are four times as likely to be equipped with Lojack as vehicles that are four to six years old. Vehicles older than this are very unlikely to have Lojack. A two-tailed test of the equality of means for the 1994 fraction of stolen vehicles less than four years old in Lojack and non-Lojack cities rejects equality at the .10 level. Regression estimates of the impact of Lojack market share on the fraction of stolen vehicles less than four years old (not shown in tabular form) confirm the patterns in Table VI. Using data for the period 1989–1994, we ran a range of specifications (with and without year dummies, city-fixed effects, demographic covariates, and instrumenting using years elapsed since Lojack initiated the regulatory approval process). In ten of twelve cases the coefficient on Lojack market share was negative and statistically significant. In the other two cases, the point estimate was positive, but statistically insignificant.

---

28. Miami is excluded from this analysis because of wild inconsistencies between NICB and UCR data The NICB data, which matched closely with UCR data for all other cities, implied three times as many auto thefts in Miami as did the UCR data When Miami is included in the following analysis, similar trends are observed, but the magnitude of the effect is diminished.

29 According to *National Vehicle Population Profile,* published on compact disc by the Polk company, in 1989 30.6 percent of cars on the road had been built in the last three years. By 1994 this fraction had fallen to 17.7 percent.

TABLE VI
FRACTION OF STOLEN VEHICLES BY VEHICLE AGE NON-LOJACK
VERSUS LOJACK CITIES

Vehicle age	1989		1994	
	Non-Lojack cities	Cities with Lojack by 1990	Non-Lojack cities	Cities with Lojack by 1990
Three or fewer years	44.3	44.6	28 5	23.9
	(1.4)	(1.3)	(1 4)	(2.3)
	[0.0]	[0.63]	[0 0]	[5 60]
Four to six years	29.5	28.7	26 9	28.3
	(0 7)	(1.5)	(0.6)	(1.0)
	[0 0]	[0.0]	[0 0]	[1.66]
Seven or more years	26.2	26 8	44.6	47.8
	(1 4)	(1 2)	(1.6)	(2.8)
	[0 0]	[0.0]	[0.0]	[0 02]
Total	100.0	100.0	100.0	100 0

Data on ages of stolen vehicles were provided by the National Insurance Crime Bureau (NICB) and represent roughly 30 percent of the stolen vehicles Cities with Lojack coverage by 1990 are Boston, Newark, Los Angeles, Long Beach, and Chicago Data for Miami are not included due to apparent inconsistencies between the *Uniform Crime Report* data used throughout the paper and NICB data used in computing this table Breakdowns by vehicle age are not available prior to 1989 Numbers reported in the table are the means across cities in the percentage of all vehicles stolen in the named year that fall within a given age category The standard error of the mean is reported in parentheses The mean Lojack market share among cars of a given age category is reported in brackets.

B. Robustness

Table VII presents a range of additional specifications as a means of assessing the sensitivity of our results to alternative sets of assumptions. The four columns in Table VII correspond to city auto theft rates, outlying auto theft rates, substitutable crimes in cities, and nonsubstitutable crimes in cities. Rows in Table VII represent different specifications. Each cell entry, therefore, is the regression coefficient on years of Lojack availability from a separate regression. The pattern of estimates using Lojack's market share, rather than years of Lojack, is similar in all instances. The regressions include the full set of covariates from earlier tables. Full regression results are available on request from the authors.

The first row of Table VII simply replicates results from Tables III–V to provide a baseline for evaluating the alternative specifications. The second row of Table VII adds region-year interactions to the basic specification to control for any region-specific shifts in crime. Adding region-year interactions has little effect on the auto theft point estimates. The coefficients on other

LOJACK   69

TABLE VII
SENSITIVITY OF LOJACK COEFFICIENTS TO ALTERNATIVE SPECIFICATIONS

	Coefficient on years of Lojack for			
Specification	Central city auto theft	Rest of state auto theft	Substitutable crimes	Nonsubstitutable crimes (from earlier tables)
Baseline (from earlier tables)	−.109	− 041	−.015	− 005
	(.013)	(.011)	(.009)	(006)
Region-year interactions	−.100	−.044	.013	−.009
	(.013)	(.014)	(.007)	(.008)
City-trends	−.065	− 073	−.022	− 031
	(.017)	(.032)	(.009)	(.014)
Only cities with population greater than 500,000	− 149	−.042	−.030	008
	(.012)	(.014)	(.009)	(008)
Only cities with above average auto theft in 1985	− 077	−.049	−.003	013
	(.021)	(.014)	(.011)	(.008)
Include once- and twice-lagged dependent variable as regressor	−.031	−.024	−.004	− 001
	(.009)	(.013)	(.004)	(.005)
Instrument for police per capita using mayoral and gubernatorial elections	−.158	−.049	−.020	−.012
	(.026)	(.029)	(.014)	(021)
Excluding Boston from sample	−.077	−.037	.008	−.003
	(.015)	(020)	(.009)	(009)
Excluding Newark from sample	−.112	− 038	−.018	−.001
	(.014)	(.011)	(.008)	(007)

All table entries are coefficients on years of Lojack availability in a market from separate regressions The dependent variable in each case corresponds to that listed in the column heading In all cases, the full set of covariates listed in previous tables is employed in addition to the listed changes in specification The first row of values represents baseline estimates from previous tables for comparison purposes.

crimes remain statistically insignificant. The third row adds city-specific trends to take into account that cities may systematically differ not only in the level of crime (which city-fixed effects control for), but also in the rate of change. Including trends reduces the estimated impact of Lojack on city auto theft, but makes the estimates more negative for the other three crime classifications. Auto theft falls more in outlying areas than in central cities in this specification, the only instance where this is the case among all the estimates presented in this paper.

Rows 4 and 5 limit the sample such that the group of control cities more closely matches the characteristics of cities that actually adopted Lojack, which tend to be larger and have higher rates of auto theft. Restricting the sample to the 28 cities with greater than 500,000 in population, or those with above average auto theft in 1985 (the year before Lojack was first introduced) does not substantively change the conclusions. Although the coefficient in row 6, which allows for an autoregressive component in motor vehicle theft, is smaller than those in the other rows, it is important to recognize that it is not directly comparable. When lagged dependent variables are included in the specification, the Lojack variable captures only the direct effect of Lojack on auto theft, missing the dynamic feedback effects operating through the lags of the dependent variable.[30] When the full impact of Lojack is calculated over a five-year period, the implied decrease in auto theft due to Lojack in row 6 is roughly two-thirds as large as the magnitude in the base specification.

In the seventh row we instrument for the police variable using the timing of mayoral and gubernatorial election years. Levitt [1997] demonstrates that police hiring is disproportionately concentrated in election years, and argues that the exclusion of elections from the second-stage regression seems plausible. Instrumenting for police once again leads to more negative Lojack coefficients on auto theft. The elasticity of crime with respect to police, which is small and positive in most of the OLS specifications, ranges between $-.20$ and $-.58$ in the instrumented regressions. While large standard errors make the police coefficients statistically insignificant, the magnitude of the estimates is similar to those obtained in Levitt [1997].

The final two rows of Table VII are estimates of the basic specification eliminating, respectively, Boston and Newark, the two cities that have experienced the greatest auto theft declines after Lojack's introduction. Dropping those cities has only a small impact on the point estimates.

V. ANALYZING THE PRIVATE AND SOCIAL COSTS AND BENEFITS OF LOJACK

The preceding analysis suggests that increases in Lojack market penetration are associated with large declines in city auto theft rates and smaller percentage declines in outlying area auto theft rates, with little apparent impact on other types of crime. In this section the social welfare implications of Lojack are exam-

---

30. The coefficient on once- and twice-lagged auto theft in column 1 of Row 6 are .708 (standard error equal to .137) and $-.005$ (standard error equal to -112), respectively.

ined, paying special attention to differentiating between direct benefits to those who install Lojack (or their insurers) and externalities associated with auto theft reductions. Our cost-benefit analysis is admittedly incomplete. Omitted from our calculations is any consideration of criminals' welfare, increases in the price of used auto parts, or diversion of auto theft across state lines, all of which will exaggerate the apparent social benefit of Lojack. On the other hand, we also ignore the reduction in expenditure on other forms of victim precaution (as well as the reduction in negative externalities associated with observable victim precaution), and the fact that substitution toward older, cheaper vehicles will reduce the average loss per theft, both of which lead us to understate the benefits of Lojack.

As our benchmark for determining social benefits, we use the characteristics of the six large cities that Lojack has served for at least five years, evaluated at the city mean in the fifth year of coverage. In all cases we base our estimates on the coefficients from the uninstrumented regression using Lojack's market share (i.e., column (3) of Table III). These estimates imply smaller effects than the 2SLS estimates or the coefficients on years of Lojack availability and thus provide more conservative conclusions with respect to the social benefits of Lojack. We begin by analyzing the direct benefits to Lojack owners and their insurers and then proceed to calculate the externalities associated with Lojack's general deterrence effect.

Three factors are critical in determining the direct benefits of Lojack to those car owners who install it: the value of the vehicle, the auto theft rate, and the presence or absence of comprehensive auto insurance. While the first two factors have an obvious and direct impact on the calculations, the role of comprehensive auto insurance is less straightforward. The comprehensive portion of auto insurance covers theft, vandalism, and fire damage.[31] Car owners are not required to carry such coverage if they own their vehicles outright, but it is commonly required for vehicles that are financed. Standard deductibles range from $100 to $500. If a car owner does not choose to have comprehensive insurance, all of the direct benefits of higher Lojack retrieval rates accrue to the car owner. However, if a car owner has comprehensive insurance, Lojack provides little direct financial benefit except for insurance

---

31 Much of the information that follows regarding comprehensive insurance is drawn from the Insurance News Network's web page and links available on the internet at http:\ \ www insure.com

premium discounts since recovered vehicles will typically sustain damage greater than the deductible. Thus, with comprehensive insurance, it is the insurer rather than the insured who reaps the direct benefits of Lojack.

We examine first the case of a car owner who does not have comprehensive insurance coverage. The mean loss per stolen vehicle for cars not equipped with Lojack, based on self-reported losses in the National Crime Victimization Survey, is roughly $4000 per vehicle [Cohen 1988]. According to company estimates, vehicles equipped with Lojack sustain slightly less than $1000 worth of damage on average.[32] The mean auto theft rate per capita in the baseline cities is 0.025.[33] With roughly one vehicle per every two people, this implies a theft rate per vehicle of 0.05 annually. Assuming that Lojack cars are stolen at the same rate as non-Lojack cars, uninsured Lojack-installed vehicle owners receive an expected benefit of $150 per vehicle per year in reduced auto theft losses from Lojack installation. This figure will, of course, depend crucially on the value of the car being protected from theft loss. Given that Lojack entails a one-time $600 fee, whether Lojack is worth installing for a given car owner depends also on the discount rate, the length of time that the vehicle will be owned, and the increment to resale value associated with having Lojack. As a benchmark, amortizing the initial cost over a ten-year period at 10 percent interest rate yields a yearly Lojack cost of approximately $97.[34]

With comprehensive insurance coverage, the Lojack owner

32. This estimate of the mean loss for Lojack vehicles appears to be reasonable. Approximately 60 percent of non-Lojack-equipped stolen vehicles are recovered according to the National Insurance Crime Bureau. Cohen's estimates of the loss per vehicle does not separately distinguish losses to vehicles recovered and those not found Assuming an average of $750 in damages for the typical recovered vehicle, this implies a $9000 loss for vehicles that are never recovered Because Lojack-equipped vehicles are found more quickly, they tend to sustain less damage Assuming a value of $500 in losses for vehicles recovered by Lojack and applying a $9000 value to the 5 percent of Lojack-equipped vehicles that are never recovered, yields an average loss of $925 with Lojack.

33 This value is roughly 60 percent above the average for large cities in the sample during the 1990s since Lojack tends to enter high auto theft cities It is twice as high as the overall sample average due both to the cities Lojack chooses and to large increases in auto theft during the 1980s As a consequence, the scenario outlined here provides larger estimates of the benefits of Lojack than would be obtained using the sample mean as the benchmark.

34. The consumer's price is likely to overstate the true marginal social cost for two reasons First, some fraction of that price accrues as profit to Lojack shareholders. Second, that price is likely to reflect an average rather than a marginal cost and thus also reflects the fixed costs of establishing Lojack in a market and providing the physical equipment required to make the system operational.

weighs the cost of installation against the value of the available insurance discounts.[35] The real value of these discounts varies widely as a consequence of differences in comprehensive insurance premiums and state regulations concerning discounts. The mean annual comprehensive insurance premium for automobiles in the United States is roughly $100, although this number varies dramatically by geographic location and vehicle type. In high-theft urban areas, comprehensive insurance is much more expensive. For instance, these costs are almost ten times higher in sections of the Bronx and three times higher on average in Miami. Insurance premium discounts for Lojack also vary widely. In Massachusetts, for instance, state law mandates a 20–35 percent reduction in comprehensive insurance premiums for vehicles with Lojack installed, depending on what antitheft devices are also present in the vehicle. In most other states, insurance discounts are capped at 20 percent. In some states, discounts are at the discretion of the insurer rather than mandatory. Back-of-the envelope calculations suggest that insurance discounts are well below the cost of Lojack installation for most vehicle owners. Even in Boston, which offers the most generous discounts, the dollar value of such discounts is likely to be only $70 per year for the typical car. In Miami and Los Angeles the discount for Lojack is typically no more than 10 percent, yielding an average benefit of $30. These estimates suggest that insurance companies capture most of the benefit of Lojack, calculated as $150 per vehicle per year above.

Given these results, it is not surprising that insurance companies have been very supportive of Lojack. It is common for insurers to donate the funds necessary for equipping police cruisers with Lojack detection devices. In Massachusetts insurers lobbied the state insurance board to increase the comprehensive insurance deduction for Lojack from a maximum of 20 percent to 35 percent. In South America insurance companies have even gone a step farther, purchasing Lojack directly and installing it into customer vehicles free of charge. Half of all Lojack units installed in Colombia were purchased by insurance companies. It is surprising, however, that in areas of the United States where discounts are discretionary, competition has not led insurers to offer larger discounts.

---

35 The damage sustained by a recovered stolen vehicle almost always exceeds the deductible on most comprehensive insurance policies We ignore the psychic benefits of vehicle recovery via Lojack, which may also be substantial.

While higher retrieval rates provide direct benefits to those who install Lojack, installing an individual Lojack will have no practical impact on the likelihood that the protected car will be stolen. The impact of aggregate Lojack installations on a city's auto theft rates is consequently purely external to a car owner's individual decision whether to purchase Lojack.[36] Assuming that Lojack installation rates are three times greater in cities than in the market as a whole, a one percentage point increase in Lojack for the market as a whole corresponds to a three percentage point increase in Lojack installation in the central city. Using a baseline auto theft rate of 0.05 per vehicle per year and a regression coefficient of $-.24$, that three percentage point increase in Lojack is associated with roughly a one percentage point decrease $(.05 * -.24)$ in the auto theft risk. Put another way, one auto theft is eliminated each year for every three Lojacks.[37] Using a loss per stolen vehicle of $4000 from Cohen [1988], each Lojack yields an annual externality of over $1300. Note that this externality is almost ten times the magnitude of the direct benefit to the owner/insurer from Lojack installation.

Combining the direct benefits of Lojack with the externality associated with reduced auto theft yields an estimated social benefit from each marginal unit of Lojack of roughly $1500 per year. In comparison, an upper bound on the social cost of a marginal unit of Lojack is the consumer's one-time outlay of $600, which discounted over the life of a vehicle, equates to roughly $97 per year. The marginal social benefit of Lojack, at least historically, appears to be fifteen times greater than the marginal social cost.

VI. Conclusions

Lojack is a real-world example of an unobservable victim precaution measure that yields positive externalities. Increases in the fraction of Lojack-equipped vehicles are associated with substantial declines in auto theft, without any evidence of in-

36. Large insurers are able to internalize a fraction of the auto theft reduction externality consistent with their market share, making the failure of insurers to offer greater premium discounts to those installing Lojack even more puzzling.

37. If there are decreasing returns as in Figure III, the reduction in auto theft will be sensitive to the amount of Lojack that is present. The estimate we use here (from the linear specification) corresponds roughly to the marginal effect assuming a starting Lojack concentration of 0.5 percent in Figure III. At higher (lower) starting concentrations, the marginal benefit would be reduced (increased).

creases in other crime categories. From the perspective of the car owner who installs Lojack, this auto theft decline is a pure externality. Because Lojack is unobservable, auto theft rates are affected by thieves' perceptions about the mean Lojack installation rate, which are only imperceptibly affected by a given car owner's choice. Combining this externality with the direct benefit of an increased likelihood of successful vehicle recovery for those with Lojack, the estimated marginal social benefit of Lojack installation has been roughly fifteen times greater than the marginal social cost. Lojack appears to be one of the most cost-effective crime reduction approaches documented in the literature, providing a greater return than increased police, prisons, jobs programs, or early educational interventions [Donohue and Siegelman 1996]. The car owner who installs Lojack internalizes only 10 percent of the total social benefit, however, implying that Lojack will be undersupplied by the free market. The current system of insurance premium discounts is far less generous than the apparent social optimum.

An important consideration is the extent to which the estimates of this paper can be generalized. Lojack tends to enter markets with high auto theft rates. Extrapolating to other markets with lower initial levels of crime, we would predict smaller, but not categorically different benefit-cost ratios. It is more difficult to extrapolate from our results to a determination of the optimal level of Lojack penetration within markets. If criminals did not engage in behavior designed to offset Lojack, it would appear that auto theft could be all but eradicated with Lojack penetration rates of 10–20 percent. It is clear, however, that Lojack affects criminal behavior, even at low penetration rates.[38] The apparent presence of decreasing marginal returns to Lojack in Figure III is consistent with the argument that low levels of Lojack penetration are sufficient to provide a costly disruption of operations for professional thieves. From the perspective of social welfare, expansion of the geographical coverage of Lojack at relatively low levels of vehicle installation is likely to be preferable to large increases in Lojack penetration rates in existing markets.

The magnitude of the externalities associated with Lojack points to the importance of conducting parallel research on other

---

38. One would also expect that thieves would engage in heightened technology development designed to thwart Lojack.

76   *QUARTERLY JOURNAL OF ECONOMICS*

types of self-protection which, unlike Lojack, are observable to criminals and therefore carry negative externalities. In the extreme case of perfect substitutability across targets, such self-protection actions may represent pure deadweight loss.

YALE LAW SCHOOL
UNIVERSITY OF CHICAGO AND AMERICAN BAR FOUNDATION

REFERENCES

Beck, Allen, "Recidivism of Prisoners Released in 1983," Bureau of Justice Statistics Special Report, 1989.
Becker, Gary, "Crime and Punishment· An Economic Approach," *Journal of Political Economy,* LXXVI (1968), 169–217.
Ben-Shahar, Omri, and Alon Harel, "Blaming the Victim Optimal Incentives for Private Precautions against Crime," *Journal of Law, Economics, and Organization,* XI (1995), 434–455.
Black, Dan, and Daniel Nagin, "Do 'Right-to-Carry' Laws Deter Violent Crime?" mimeo, Carnegie Mellon University, 1997.
Blumstein, Alfred, Jacqueline Cohen, Jeffrey Roth, and Christy Visher, eds., 1986, *Criminal Careers and "Career Criminals"* (Washington DC: National Academy of Sciences, 1986).
Bureau of Justice Statistics, *Criminal Victimization in the United States, 1992* (Washington, DC Department of Justice, 1994).
Cameron, Samuel, "The Economics of Crime Deterrence· A Survey of Theory and Evidence," *Kyklos,* XLI (1988), 301–323.
Chiricos, Theodore, "Rates of Crime and Unemployment· An Analysis of Aggregate Research Evidence," *Social Problems,* XXXIV (1987), 187–211.
Clarke, Ronald, and Patricia Harris, "Auto Theft and Its Prevention," in Michael Tonry, ed , *Crime and Justice· A Review of Research,* XVI (1992), 1–54.
Clotfelter, Charles, "Private Security and the Public Safety," *Journal of Urban Economics,* V (1978), 388–402.
Cohen, Mark, "Pain, Suffering, and Jury Awards· A Study of the Cost of Crime to Victims," *Law and Society Review,* XXII (1988), 537–555.
Cook, Philip, "The Demand and Supply of Criminal Opportunities," *Crime and Justice,* VII (1986), 1–27.
Cornish, Derek, and Ronald Clarke, "Understanding Crime Displacement An Application of Rational Choice Theory," *Criminology,* XXV (1987), 933–947.
De Meza, David, and J. R Gould, "The Social Efficiency of Private Decisions to Enforce Property Rights," *Journal of Political Economy,* C (1992), 561–580.
DiIulio, John, and Anne Piehl, "Does Prison Pay? The Stormy National Debate over the Cost-Effectiveness of Imprisonment," *The Brookings Review* (Fall 1991), 28–35.
Donohue, John, and Peter Siegelman, "Is the United States at the Optimal Rate of Crime?" American Bar Foundation mimeo, 1996.
Duggan, Mark, "Guns, Violence, and Public Policy," Harvard University Department of Economics mimeo, 1996.
Eck, John, "The Threat of Crime Displacement," *Criminal Justice Abstracts,* XXV (1993), 527–546.
Freeman, Richard, "Why Do So Many Young American Men Commit Crimes and What Might We Do about It?" *Journal of Economic Perspectives,* X (1996), 25–42.
Friedman, David, "Efficient Institutions for the Private Enforcement of Law," *Journal of Legal Studies,* XIII (1984), 379–398
Harel, Alon, "Efficiency and Fairness in Criminal Law The Case for a Criminal Law Principle of Comparative Fault," *California Law Review,* LXXXII (1994), 1181–1229.
Hesseling, Rene, "Displacement A Review of the Empirical Literature," in R Clarke, ed , *Crime Prevention Studies,* III (1994), 197–230.

Hui-Wen, Koo, and I P L Png, "Private Security. Deterrent or Diversion?" *International Review of Law and Economics,* XIV (1994), 87–101.

Laband, David, and John Sophocleus, "An Estimate of Resource Expenditure on Transfer Activities in the United States," *Quarterly Journal of Economics,* CVII (1992), 959–983.

Levitt, Steven, "Using Electoral Cycles in Police Hiring to Estimate the Effect of Police on Crime," *American Economic Review,* LXXXVII (1997), 270–290.

____, "Why Do Increased Arrest Rates Appear to Reduce Crime Deterrence, Incapacitation, or Measurement Error?" *Economic Inquiry* (1998), forthcoming.

Lott, John, and David Mustard, "Right-to-Carry Concealed Guns and the Importance of Deterrence," *Journal of Legal Studies,* XXVI (1997), 1–68.

Marvell, Thomas, and Carlisle Moody, "Police Levels, Crime Rates, and Specification Problems," *Criminology,* XXXIV (1996), 609–646.

Mayhew, Patricia, Ronald Clarke, Andrew Sturman, and J Mike Hough, "Crime as Opportunity," Home Office Research Study No. 34, London, 1976.

Philipson, Tomas, and Richard Posner, "The Economic Epidemiology of Crime," *Journal of Law and Economics,* XXXIX (1996), 405–433.

Shavell, Steven, "Individual Precautions to Prevent Theft Private versus Socially Optimal Behavior," *International Review of Law and Economics,* XI (1991), 123–132.

Sherman, Lawrence, "The Police," in *Crime,* in J Q. Wilson and J. Petersilia, eds (San Francisco Institute for Contemporary Studies, 1995).

Visher, Christy, "The RAND Inmate Survey A Reanalysis," in A Blumstein et al , eds , *Criminal Careers and "Career Criminals,"* Volume II (Washington, DC National Academy Press, 1986).

Wilson, James Q , *Thinking About Crime* (New York: Basic Books, 1983).

[21]

A COMPARATIVE STUDY OF THE PREVENTIVE EFFECTS OF MANDATORY SENTENCING LAWS FOR GUN CRIMES*

DAVID McDOWALL, COLIN LOFTIN, BRIAN WIERSEMA**

I. INTRODUCTION

No policy designed to prevent firearm violence is more popular than mandatory sentence enhancements for gun crimes. By providing stiff and certain penalties when a gun is involved in an offense, sentence enhancement laws[1] promise to reduce the use of firearms by criminals. Because the laws apply only when a crime is committed, they impose no direct costs on legitimate gun owners. Opinion polls find that a large majority of the public favors mandatory sentence enhancements, and more than half the states have adopted them.[2] If these laws deliver their expected crime preventive effects, they are an especially attractive approach to regulating the use of firearms.

We previously conducted case studies to estimate the preventive effects of mandatory sentencing on firearm offenses in Detroit, Jacksonville, Tampa and Miami.[3] Based on the findings of these

* Portions of this research were supported by National Institute of Justice award 84-IJ-CX-0044. Computer time was provided by the University of Maryland Computer Science Center.

** Members of the Violence Research Group of the Institute of Criminal Justice and Criminology, University of Maryland at College Park.

[1] Examples include: HAW. REV. STAT. § 706-660.1 (1985 & Supp. 1991); MINN. STAT. ANN. § 609.11 (West 1987 & Supp. 1992); N.H. REV. STAT. ANN. § 651:2, II-b (1986 & Supp. 1991); S.D. CODIFIED LAWS ANN. § 22-14-12 (1988); WASH. REV. CODE ANN. § 9.94A.125 (West 1988).

[2] See JAMES D. WRIGHT ET AL., UNDER THE GUN: WEAPONS, CRIME, AND VIOLENCE IN AMERICA 235 (1983); Franklin E. Zimring, Firearms, Violence and Public Policy, 265 SCI. AM. 48, 52 (1991).

[3] The Detroit research is reported in Colin Loftin et al., Mandatory Sentencing and Firearms Violence: Evaluating an Alternative to Gun Control, 17 LAW & SOC'Y REV. 287 (1983), and in Colin Loftin & David McDowall "One With A Gun Gets You Two": Mandatory Sentencing and Firearms Violence in Detroit, 455 ANNALS AM. ACAD. POL. & SOC. SCI. 150 (1981)

earlier studies, we concluded there was little evidence that sentence enhancement laws are successful in reducing violent crime. More recently, we completed similar studies in Philadelphia and Pittsburgh (Allegheny County), Pennsylvania. In this paper, we pool together the individual results to obtain a combined estimate of the impact of the laws. The pooled results lead to very different conclusions from the city-specific case studies. The analyzed data suggest that the mandatory sentencing laws substantially reduced the number of homicides; however, any effects on assault and robbery are not conclusive because they cannot be separated from imprecision and random error in the data.

Part II of this article describes the earlier case studies. Part III explains the methodology for combining the individual results and presents the pooled estimates. Part IV discusses our interpretation of the findings and Part V provides suggestions for future research.

II. Case Studies

A.   Mandatory Sentencing Laws in Three States

Our analysis is based on six city-specific case studies, which monitored the effects of mandatory sentencing on violent crime in Detroit, Jacksonville, Tampa, Miami, Philadelphia and Pittsburgh. The key features of the laws were the same in each area.[4] First, each law required judges to impose a specified sentence on defendants convicted of an offense involving a gun. Second, mitigating devices such as probation, suspended sentences and parole were prohibited. In theory, all sentences specified by the laws had to be served in full.

[hereinafter Loftin & McDowall, *One With a Gun*]. The Florida studies are reported in Colin Loftin & David McDowall, *The Deterrent Effects of the Florida Felony Firearm Law*, 75 J. Crim. L. & Criminology 250 (1984) [hereinafter Loftin & David McDowall, *The Deterrent Effects*]. The effect of the Detroit law on the processing of court cases is also evaluated in Milton Heumann & Colin Loftin, *Mandatory Sentencing and the Abolition of Plea Bargaining: The Michigan Felony Firearm Statute*, 13 Law & Soc'y Rev. 393 (1979).

[4] Specifically, the Florida law, Fla. Stat. Ann. § 775.087(2) (West 1976 & Supp. 1992), required a three-year sentence for persons convicted of committing any of 12 specified felonies while in possession of a firearm. The law went into effect on October 1, 1975. Michigan's law, Mich. Comp. Laws Ann. § 750.227b (West 1991 & Supp. 1992), went into effect on January 1, 1977. It mandated a two-year sentence for the possession of a firearm while committing any felony. Pennsylvania's law, 42 Pa. Cons. Stat. Ann. §§ 9712-9714 (1982), adopted in June 1982, required a five-year minimum sentence for any of seven violent crimes if (1) the offense was committed with visible possession of a firearm; (2) the defendant had been convicted of the same offense within the past seven years; or (3) the crime was committed in or near public transportation facilities. In Florida and Michigan, the mandatory sentences were to be served consecutively to the sentence for the triggering felony. In all three states, suspended, deferred and withheld sentences were explicitly prohibited, and parole was not possible until the firearm sentence was served.

Finally, all three states used advertising campaigns involving radio and television commercials, posters, bumper stickers and billboards to communicate the message that offenders would receive additional punishment if they used a gun to commit a crime. The laws are therefore similar enough in purpose and content that they can be regarded as replications of approximately the same experiment.

B. DESIGN OF THE CASE STUDIES

Each earlier city-specific case study used an interrupted time series research design[5] that compared the level of violent crime before and after the statutes were adopted. This comparison provides an estimate of the aggregate preventive effect of the announcement of the laws.[6] If the laws were effective in reducing firearm crimes, the number of gun offenses should decrease in the post-intervention period.

To further strengthen the basis for causal inference, our design incorporates several other features. First, to increase the precision of the estimates in each city, we examined long, monthly pre-intervention series (54 to 150 months) for three violent crimes: homicides, assaults and robberies.[7]

Second, because the statutes apply specifically to gun crimes, we analyzed companion series of gun offenses and non-gun offenses.[8] This additional analysis narrows the range of extraneous

---

[5] *See* THOMAS D. COOK & DONALD T. CAMPBELL, QUASI-EXPERIMENTATION: DESIGN AND ANALYSIS ISSUES FOR FIELD SETTINGS 207-32 (1979).

[6] The results thus represent the net influence of deterrence, incapacitation and other preventive mechanisms. Because we cannot model individual behavior, it is not possible to isolate the specific mechanisms that might be responsible for an observed change in crime. This places some limits on the conclusions that can be drawn, but it is offset by the fact that the interrupted time series is among the strongest quasi-experimental designs. JACK P. GIBBS, CRIME, PUNISHMENT, AND DETERRENCE 29-93 (1975) provides an extensive discussion of the mechanisms through which a legal change might influence criminal behavior.

[7] The length of each pre-intervention series was dictated by data availability. In Detroit, the pre-intervention series included 96 monthly observations for homicides and 120 monthly observations for assaults and robberies. There were 93 monthly pre-intervention observations for all crimes in each of the three Florida cities. For homicides in Pittsburgh and Philadelphia, the pre-intervention series included 150 monthly observations. For assaults and robberies in the state of Pennsylvania, there were 54 monthly pre-intervention observations.

[8] In Florida, data for robbery and assault were drawn from the Uniform Crime Report (UCR) Return A tapes for January 1968 through December 1980 (156 monthly observations). Florida homicide data were taken from the UCR's Supplementary Homicide Report tapes for January 1968 through December 1978 (132 observations). In Detroit, robberies and assaults from January 1967 through December 1979 (156 observations) were taken from the Detroit Police Department's Computerized Monthly Reports. Detroit homicides were collected from Vital Statistics data tapes provided by

variables that could be confounded with the intervention. Another causal variable would be confounded with the law only if it influenced gun and non-gun crimes differently, and if it changed markedly at the intervention point. The contrast between the gun and non-gun series is also helpful in identifying displacement or substitution effects. Outcomes of this type would occur if offenders switched from guns to other weapons after the laws were implemented.[9]

Third, systematic within-series variation (nonstationarity and autocorrelation) was removed from each series using an autoregressive integrated moving average (ARIMA) noise model.[10] If the noise model is correctly specified, it will account for causes of violent crime (poverty, age structure, etc.) that operate consistently throughout a series. Unless these other variables change in an unusual way at the time of the intervention—a threat that Cook and Campbell call "history"—the noise model cannot explain an observed impact.[11]

After an appropriate noise model was separately developed for each series, an intervention model was added to represent the effects of the gun law.[12] We considered three types of intervention models: an abrupt permanent change model, a gradual permanent

---

the Michigan Department of Public Health for January 1969 through December 1978 (120 observations). The Pennsylvania Commission on Crime and Delinquency provided state-level robbery and assault data for January 1978 through December 1984 (84 observations), and the Pennsylvania Department of Health supplied homicide data for Allegheny County (Pittsburgh) and the city of Philadelphia for January 1970 through December 1984 (180 observations).

All the homicide series are defined similarly: the number of gun homicides versus the number of homicides by other means. Because robberies were defined only as "armed" and "unarmed" in the Uniform Crime Reporting program prior to 1975, all the robbery series, except those for Pennsylvania, are the number of armed and the number of unarmed robberies. In Pennsylvania, it was possible to distinguish gun robberies from robberies with other weapons. The Detroit and Pennsylvania assault series are defined as gun assaults versus assaults by other means. In Florida, gun assaults are compared to knife assaults.

[9] Substitution effects have been reported in similar contexts. *See, e.g.*, Lee R. McPheters et al., *Economic Response to a Crime Deterrence Program: Mandatory Sentencing for Robbery with a Firearm*, 22 ECON. INQUIRY 550 (1984); Glenn L. Pierce & William J. Bowers, *The Bartley-Fox Gun Law's Short-Term Impact on Crime in Boston*, 455 ANNALS AM. ACAD. POL. & SOC. SCI. 120 (1981); and Charles L. Rich et al., *Guns and Suicide: Possible Effects of Some Specific Legislation*, 147 AM. J. PSYCHIATRY 342 (1990).

[10] G. E. P. BOX & G. JENKINS, TIME-SERIES ANALYSIS: FORECASTING AND CONTROL (1976).

[11] COOK & CAMPBELL, *supra* note 5, at 211.

[12] G. E. P. Box & G. C. Tiao, *A Change in Level of a Non-Stationary Time-Series*, 52 BIOMETRIKA 181 (1965); G. E. P. Box & G. C. Tiao, *Intervention Analysis with Applications to Economic and Environmental Problems*, 70 J. AM. STAT. ASS'N 70 (1975).

change model and an abrupt temporary change model.[13] For each series, the abrupt permanent change model provided the best fit to the data.[14]

C. RESULTS OF THE CASE STUDIES

The results of the city-specific case studies are summarized in Table 1 (homicides), Table 2 (assaults) and Table 3 (robberies).[15] The intervention coefficient for each offense, ω_0, represents the change in the number of monthly crime reports following the announcement of the statutes. The analyses for Detroit and the three Florida cities are presented in detail elsewhere,[16] and our major interest is in combining the estimates. Therefore, the individual case studies are only briefly discussed here.

In Detroit, there was a statistically significant decrease in gun homicides, but no significant change in any other offense. We concluded from this study that the results best fit a model in which the mandatory sentencing law did not have a preventive effect on crime.[17] Similarly, in Florida, there were significant decreases in Tampa gun homicides and Jacksonville gun assaults. Unarmed robberies increased significantly in Tampa and Miami, but armed robberies did not change. In addition, there was a significant increase in Tampa gun assaults. Again, we concluded that the results did not support a preventive effect model.[18]

Alone, the Pennsylvania estimates do not strongly challenge the conclusion that the statutes have no preventive effect. There were statistically significant decreases in gun homicides in both Pittsburgh and Philadelphia. The decrease in Philadelphia gun homicides was mirrored by a reduction in non-gun homicides, however,

---

[13] *See* DAVID McDOWALL ET AL., INTERRUPTED TIME SERIES ANALYSIS (1980) for details.

[14] *See id.* at 83-85 for the criteria used to select the best-fitting model.

[15] An appendix that describes the intervention analyses in more detail is available from the authors. Since the studies were originally conducted over several years using a variety of computer programs and machines, we have re-estimated the models to verify the results in a common computing environment. All of the series were re-estimated using BMDP88's P2T algorithm on an IBM 3081 running VM/CMS Release 5. Variations in the computing environments are responsible for most differences from previously published estimates, but an error in the earlier analysis is responsible for a change in Jacksonville gun assaults.

[16] Loftin et al., *supra* note 3; Loftin & McDowall, *One With a Gun, supra* note 3; Loftin & McDowall, *The Deterrent Effects, supra* note 3.

[17] Loftin et al., *supra* note 3, at 309-10; Loftin & McDowall, *One With a Gun, supra* note 3, at 162.

[18] Loftin & McDowall, *The Deterrent Effects, supra* note 3, at 256-57.

and there was no change in gun assaults or robberies in the state of Pennsylvania.

Although the results of the case studies are complex, no individual study provides clear support for the proposition that mandatory sentencing reduces firearm violence. If the studies are considered together, however, the no-effect conclusion is less certain. This is especially so for homicide. Gun homicides decreased in all six of the cities, significantly in four (Detroit, Tampa, Pittsburgh and Philadelphia) and insignificantly in two (Jacksonville and Miami). The argument for a preventive effect is stronger when the three crimes are compared across cities than when the findings for each city are examined separately.

The immediate goal in each city-specific case study was to obtain an unbiased estimate of the policy's impact in a given area. Yet the ultimate objective was not simply to describe what happened at a particular site, but rather to predict what would occur if other cities enacted mandatory sentencing statutes for gun crimes.

From this point of view, each city-specific case study represents a sample observation drawn from a population of studies that could be conducted under similar circumstances. If the effects of mandatory sentencing vary with features unique to a site's setting or law, a single case may provide an untrustworthy basis for inference. A more desirable approach would be to combine the results from several replications. An estimate based on combining several sites would be less sensitive to the characteristics of any particular area, and it would more precisely measure the expected impact in the population.

III. Comparative Analysis

To estimate the combined impact of the laws, we pooled the results from the six cities. This analysis treats the impact-estimate for each city as an observation from a distribution of possible responses to mandatory sentencing laws. The major motivation for pooling is to obtain an overall estimate of the effect of the statutes on each type of crime. Pooling, however, has other advantages as well. First, in conjunction with the case study designs, pooling makes it extremely unlikely that the estimates are confounded with other variables. Second, the pooled data make it possible to measure variation in the response across cities. Finally, pooling increases statistical power and efficiency, allowing the influence of the laws to be determined more precisely.

A. PROCEDURES USED FOR THE COMPARATIVE ANALYSIS

We obtained a combined estimate of the effect of the statutes on each type of violent crime using statistical methods developed for synthesizing the results from multiple studies.[19] Since the level of crime varies greatly among the cities, we first standardized the individual estimates by dividing each intervention coefficient by the standard deviation of its error term:

$$d_j = \frac{\omega_{0j}}{\sqrt{RMSE_j}}$$

Here, ω_{0j} is the estimate of the change in a crime for city j; d_j is the standardized estimate of the change; and $RMSE_j$ is the residual mean square error from the intervention model.

Standardization is necessary because the cities vary greatly in the number of violent crimes per month. For example, a decrease of ten gun homicides has a different meaning in Detroit than it would in Jacksonville. Many more homicides occur each month in Detroit than in Jacksonville, and an unweighted comparison of crime counts in the two cities would be misleading. The standardized effects measure the change in crime attributable to the intervention, expressed in standard deviation units.

To pool the individual standardized effects for each offense, we used a variance components model. This model is most easily understood by comparing it with a simpler approach, called a fixed effects model. The fixed effects model involves computing the mean of the standardized coefficients for each crime. The fixed effects model can be written as:

$$d_j = \gamma + e_j \qquad e_j \sim N(0,V)$$

In the fixed effects model, γ measures the change in crime attributable to the laws, and e_j is a random error term. The e_j vary from city to city because only a portion of the time series process generating crime is observed. The e_j are assumed to be distributed Normally with a mean of zero and a variance of V.

The fixed effects model is limited by assuming a common impact, γ, that holds across all cities. In other words, after removing random errors in sampling over time, the effect of the laws on a particular type of crime is identical in each area. This is probably

---

[19] This type of synthesis is often referred to as a "meta-analysis." The specific methods we use are described in LARRY V. HEDGES & INGRAM OLKIN, STATISTICAL METHODS FOR META-ANALYSIS 189-203 (1985), and Stephen W. Raudenbush & Anthony S. Bryk, *Empirical Bayes Meta-Analysis*, 10 J. EDUC. STAT. 75 (1985).

unrealistic. More likely, the effects will vary because of differences in the details of the laws, implementation, publicity and other factors specific to a given setting. In this case, there will be a distribution of effects instead of one common impact.

The variance components model that we estimate incorporates the site-specific effects. The variance components model can be written as:

$$d_j = \delta_j + e_j \qquad\qquad e_j \sim N(0,V)$$
$$\delta_j = \gamma + u_j \qquad\qquad u_j \sim N(0,\tau)$$

or:

$$d_j = \gamma + u_j + e_j$$

In the variance components model, γ may be interpreted as the average effect of the laws. No city may actually experience this average effect because the impact will vary from one setting to another depending on local conditions. The value for γ is a meaningful quantity, however, because it provides an estimate of the change in crime across the population of cities. In other words, holding unique characteristics and random error constant, γ is the expected impact of the announcement of the laws.

Besides the average impact, the variance components model provides an estimate of the dispersion of the effects across settings (τ). The larger the value of τ, the larger the expected variation in the effects. If τ is equal to zero, the variance components model reduces to a fixed effects model.

To estimate the variance components model, it is necessary to make an assumption about the probability distribution from which the site-unique effects are drawn. Following conventional practice, we assume that the operation of numerous random variables will generate a Normal distribution of effects. Given this assumption, the variance components model can be estimated in a variety of ways. We used an empirical Bayes algorithm developed by Raudenbush and Bryk.[20]

The analysis will allow us to select among three general theoretical models of community response to the announcement of the sentencing laws. If the reported number of gun crimes declines after the laws are implemented, and there is no similar decline in crimes without guns, then the data fit a preventive effect model. An

---

[20] Raudenbush & Bryk, *supra* note 19. The algorithms are available in ANTHONY S. BRYK ET AL., AN INTRODUCTION TO HLM: COMPUTER PROGRAM AND USERS' GUIDE (1989) (manual and software distributed as *HLM Distribution Package Version 2.20*, April 1991, for DOS 3 and later, by Scientific Software, Inc., 1525 E. 53rd St., Suite 906, Chicago, Ill. 60615). We also assume that the replications are independent. Because cities from the same state are included in the analysis, this is probably only approximately correct.

increase in non-gun crimes and a decrease (or an increase of smaller magnitude) in gun offenses would be compatible with both a preventive effect model and a weapon substitution model. While weapon substitution may influence the pattern of injuries resulting from crimes, it will not reduce the total number of offenses that are committed. Other outcomes favor a model in which there is no preventive effect. The no effect model, like the preventive effect model, subsumes several different micro-level processes. Most notably, it does not distinguish between the case where the policy produces no change in sanctions and the case where a change in sanctions does not influence criminal behavior.

B. RESULTS OF THE COMPARATIVE ANALYSIS

The pooled analysis for homicides (Table 1) provides exceptionally strong support for the preventive effect model. The intervention estimates (ω_0) for gun homicides are negative in all six cities and statistically significant in Detroit, Tampa, Pittsburgh and Philadelphia. The estimate of the average standardized effect (γ) is .69. This implies that the expected reduction in gun homicides is about two-thirds of a standard deviation.[21]

To illustrate the magnitude of this effect, we can reverse the standardization procedure and express the reduction in terms of the number of homicides rather than in standardized units. For example, consider Detroit, a city with a pre-intervention mean of forty gun homicides per month and a standard deviation of eight. Here, a decrease of .69 standard deviation units represents an average of 5.5 lives saved each month, a fourteen percent reduction.

In contrast, there was little change in non-gun homicides. The signs of the intervention effects were positive in four cities (Detroit, Jacksonville, Tampa and Miami) and negative in two (Philadelphia and Pittsburgh). While the decrease in Philadelphia non-gun homicides was statistically significant, it was smaller than the reduction in homicides committed with a gun. The average standardized effect across all the cities is only $-.03$. It is hard to imagine data that would fit the preventive effect model better than these series.

Table 2 describes a similar analysis for assaults.[22] In this case,

---

[21] A rule of thumb, suggested in JACOB COHEN, STATISTICAL POWER ANALYSIS FOR THE BEHAVIORAL SCIENCES 24-27 (rev. ed. 1977), is that standardized effects of 0.2 may be regarded as small, 0.5 as medium and 0.8 as large. By these guidelines, the impact on gun homicides is substantial.

[22] The assault series consist of aggravated assaults as defined by the Uniform Crime Reporting program: "Aggravated assault is an unlawful attack by one person upon another for the purpose of inflicting severe or aggravated bodily injury. This type of as-

the fit to the crime preventive model is poor. Gun assaults decreased significantly in Jacksonville, but they increased significantly in Tampa. Although there were also decreases in gun assaults in Detroit, Miami and the state of Pennsylvania, they were not large enough to be statistically significant. The average standardized change in gun offenses is small ($\gamma = -.36$) and not significantly different from zero. Other weapon assaults did not change appreciably in any of the areas, and the average standardized impact of $-.06$ is also statistically insignificant. The results, therefore, provide little solid evidence of a reduction in gun assaults that can be attributed to the statutes.

As with assaults, the robbery[23] data, presented in Table 3, do not fit the preventive effect model well. Armed robberies did not decrease significantly in any area following the introduction of the laws; in fact, the intervention coefficients are negative for only two of the five series. The estimate of γ is .08 and not statistically significant. For unarmed robbery, however, there were two cities, Tampa and Miami, that experienced large and significant increases following the laws' adoption. The average effect across all cities for unarmed robbery is a significant increase of two-thirds of a standard deviation. At best, one might argue that the sentencing laws prevented armed robberies from increasing in the same way as unarmed robberies.

The estimates of τ measure the amount of variation in the standardized effects across the cities. Chi-square tests[24] led to a rejection of the null hypothesis of zero variation in the effects for each crime. We conclude, therefore, that the impact of the laws differs from one setting to another. Because of this variation, the experience of any single city may not be an accurate guide to the average effect across the population of cities as a whole.

IV. Discussion

The results are a logical puzzle because different conclusions are reached depending on the weight given to the homicide data as

---

sault is usually accompanied by the use of a weapon or by means likely to produce death or great bodily harm. Attempts are included. . . ." *See* FEDERAL BUREAU OF INVESTIGATION, UNIFORM CRIME REPORTS FOR THE UNITED STATES 22 (1989). For Pennsylvania, we analyzed assaults for the entire state because weapon-specific monthly data were not available for Philadelphia and Pittsburgh.

[23] The robbery series are defined according to the conventions of the Uniform Crime Reporting program: "Robbery is the taking or attempting to take anything of value from the care, custody, or control of a person or persons by force or threat of force or violence and/or by putting the victim in fear." *Id.* at 17.

[24] HEDGES & OLKIN, *supra* note 19, at 197-98.

opposed to the data for robbery and assault. In interpreting the earlier case studies in Detroit and the three Florida cities, we placed equal emphasis on each type of crime. The homicide estimates fit the prevention model in Detroit and Tampa, but the estimates for the other offenses were not consistent with a preventive effect. Because of this apparent irreconcilability, we attributed the homicide findings to chance and concluded that the data best fit the no effect model. That preliminary conclusion is now at odds with the results of the pooled homicide analysis.

It is not possible to select a single model if each type of crime is equally weighted. That is, across the three offenses, the findings are incompatible with *both* the preventive effect model and the no effect model. The consistency of the effects on gun homicide virtually rules out the possibility that factors confounded with mandatory sentencing could account for the reductions in this crime. Such an explanation would require that confounded factors reduce gun homicides, but not other types of homicides, in different years and in six different cities. Therefore, the accumulating evidence forces us to reject the no effect model as a general explanation of the results. There is clear and convincing evidence of preventive effects for homicide.

At the same time, the preventive effect model does not adequately fit the robbery and assault data. This result is perplexing because a reduction in homicides caused by the laws should be accompanied by a more general decrease in gun violence. In a sense, homicide is not a separate offense; it is a measure of the severity of injury associated with other assaultive crimes. Accordingly, one would not expect a mandatory sentencing law for gun offenses to have an effect on homicides without influencing either assaults or robberies.

Faced with this pattern of outcomes, it is necessary to consider a wider range of explanations. The simplest alternative is to assume that homicides are more completely and accurately reported than robberies and assaults. As a result, the effect of the laws is detected for homicide, but lost in the noise of the less sensitive robbery and assault series.

There is independent reason to believe that the homicide data are more precise than the data for robberies and assaults. First, homicides are uniformly serious, and they command attention in reporting and recording.[25] Variation in the seriousness of the other

---

[25] *See* Michael J. Hindelang, *The Uniform Crime Reports Revisited*, 2 J. CRIM. JUST. 1 (1974).

offenses produces discretion in reporting, and there is less consistency over time or between jurisdictions in recording practices.[26] Second, our experience in modeling the robbery and assault data suggests inconsistent and erratic patterns of recording. The homicide series were easy to model and the noise components were simple and fit well. The assault and robbery series, on the other hand, required complex models whose fit was relatively poor. This outcome would be expected in the presence of irregular shifts in the recording process. Finally, the Uniform Crime Reports did not permit us to distinguish between robbery offenses with and without guns. Accordingly, we compared armed with unarmed robberies for Detroit, Tampa, Jacksonville and Miami, and this necessarily introduced imprecision in the estimates. These considerations lead us to the working hypothesis that mandatory sentencing laws have a preventive effect on homicide, and probably on other gun crimes as well. However, the available data contain measurement errors that mask the preventive effects on assault and, perhaps, robbery.

Beyond the substantive findings, the analysis also illustrates the desirability of using replications to identify variation in the effects of a legal innovation in different areas. There is evidence that features of the local setting affected the magnitude of the preventive effects. The impact of the laws on homicide was negative in all the cities that we studied, but it varied greatly from case to case. If there were a measure of data quality (or any other factor that might explain the variation), it could be included in the variance components model.[27] Such measures are not available, however, and any explanation of the heterogeneity remains speculative.

Although the comparative analysis cannot account for the variation across cities, it shows the importance of considering these differences in studying the influence of the laws. Each case study provided an unbiased estimate of the impact of the law in a particular jurisdiction. Yet if areas differ in characteristics related to the law, individual estimates are of relatively limited value. These estimates will be drawn from a probability distribution of possible ef-

---

26 *See* WRIGHT ET AL., *supra* note 2, at 154-56 for a summary of sources of error in the UCR data. For some of the sources of error, *see* Richard Block & Carolyn R. Block, *Decisions and Data: The Transformation of Robbery Incidents into Official Robbery Statistics*, 71 J. CRIM. L. & CRIMINOLOGY 622 (1980); Richard McCleary et al., *Uniform Crime Reports as Organizational Outcomes: Three Time Series Experiments*, 29 SOC. PROBS. 361 (1982); Victoria W. Schneider & Brian Wiersema, *Limits and Use of the Uniform Crime Reports*, *in* MEASURING CRIME: LARGE-SCALE, LONG-RANGE EFFORTS 21 (D. L. MacKenzie et al. eds., 1990); and David Seidman & Michael Couzens, *Getting the Crime Rate Down: Political Pressure and Crime Reporting*, 8 LAW & SOC'Y REV. 457 (1974).

27 *See* Raudenbush & Bryk, *supra* note 19, at 88-93.

fects, and a single case will be inadequate to characterize the population response.

Because of heterogeneous effects, crime might even increase in some settings despite a strongly negative average impact in the population. For example, we found a mean decrease in gun homicides of .69 standardized units following the introduction of the laws. The variance of the estimates was .22, however, implying substantial differences from one city to another. Because of the dispersion, any city with an impact-estimate more than 1.47 standardized units above the mean would register an increase in gun homicides following the law.[28] Given that the effects are drawn from a Normal distribution, increases of this type would be expected about seven percent of the time. If one examined a single city and was unfortunate enough to select such a case, it would appear that the laws were responsible for higher levels of homicide.

V. CONCLUSIONS

There is reason for both confidence and caution in our findings. The confidence follows from the strength of the research design and the quality of the homicide data. The consistency of the homicide estimates across the six locations requires that we modify our earlier conclusions. The only plausible interpretation of the results is that the reductions in gun homicides are due to the announcement of the laws. Since there were no compensating increases in the number of homicides committed with weapons other than guns, these effects can be interpreted as truly preventive of homicides.

For reasons that we cannot directly evaluate, the robbery and assault series do not reflect the preventive effects. It seems likely, however, that this result is due to a lack of precision in the data. Assault and robbery may respond to the policy in different ways, but we cannot distinguish between the no effect model and measurement errors in these crimes.

There are several reasons for caution in interpreting the results. First, despite the powerful research design, the estimate of the average impact is probably not very precise. This is because only six cities were examined, and substantial heterogeneity existed in the size of the intervention coefficients. There is little doubt that the average effect is negative, at least for homicides. However, addi-

---

[28] That is, $\dfrac{D-(-.69)}{\sqrt{.22}} = 1.47.$

Any impact estimate more than 1.47 standard deviations above the mean of the distribution will therefore be positive in sign.

tional research is necessary to identify characteristics of the organizational environment and conditions of implementation that explain the variation in the impacts.

Second, we did not examine a probability sample of cities that have instituted mandatory sentencing laws. The cities were selected fortuitously as our interest in the topic progressed. We began with Detroit because it was convenient. We then examined Florida because news reports suggested that its law had reduced gun homicides. Pennsylvania was added because its law was enacted and widely publicized while we were working on the issue. The sample is thus composed of areas in which the policy change was heavily advertised, and inferences should be limited accordingly. Future research should select a probability sample of cities and study the effects of factors such as the form of the publicity campaign on the size of the preventive effects.

Third, the post-intervention periods were all relatively short, ranging from twenty-four months for Detroit to sixty-three months for assaults and robberies in the Florida cities. Our analysis thus addresses only short-term changes, and it does not allow inferences about the impact over a long period. The effects of the laws may decay, and it would be desirable to extend the study periods to examine this possibility.

Finally, we do not know what features of the policy are responsible for the preventive effects. Given the evidence that preventive effects exist, future research also should investigate the specific behavioral mechanisms responsible for the effects, factors that influence their magnitude and their temporal trajectory.

Table 1

SUMMARY OF ANALYSIS FOR HOMICIDE IN SIX CITIES

City	Parameter	Gun Homicide	Other Homicide
Case Studies: Intervention Estimates			
Detroit	ω_0	−10.5700*	.0016
	d	−1.3893	.0049
Jacksonville	ω_0	−.8577	.1822
	d	−.3058	.0968
Tampa	ω_0	−1.1950*	.1167
	d	−.6165	.0875
Miami	ω_0	−.3441	.8031
	d	−.1253	.3258
Pittsburgh	ω_0	−1.0700*	−.3500
	d	−.4613	−.1772
Philadelphia	ω_0	−6.8300*	−2.2500*
	d	−1.2973	−.5507
Meta-Analysis: Variance Components Model			
All Cities	γ	−.6904	−.0316
	σ_γ	.2108	.1236
	γ/σ_γ	−3.28*	−.26
	τ	.2225	.0516
	χ^2 (5 df)	28.79*	11.47*

ω_0 = Impact-estimate from intervention model
d = Standardized impact-estimate
γ = Grand mean standardized effect
σ_γ = Standard error of grand mean standardized effect
τ = Estimate of variance of parameters
χ^2 = Test of H_0: $\tau = 0$

* $p < .05$

Table 2
SUMMARY OF ANALYSIS FOR ASSAULT

Jurisdiction	Parameter	Gun Assault	Other Assault
Case Studies: Intervention Estimates			
Detroit	ω_0	−.9967	.0327[a]
	d	−.0506	.3132
Jacksonville	ω_0	−20.9500*	−2.4650[b]
	d	−1.8830	.2937
Tampa	ω_0	10.2400*	−4.2750[b]
	d	1.1862	−.4732
Miami	ω_0	−9.5400	−3.6720[b]
	d	−.6856	−.3415
Pennsylvania	ω_0	−12.2500	36.0700[c]
	d	−.3862	.6064
Meta-Analysis: Variance Components Model			
All Jurisdictions	γ	−.3641	−.0567
	σ_γ	.4959	.2039
	γ/σ_γ	−.734	−.28
	τ	1.1913	.1740
	χ^2 (4 df)	130.87*	23.35*

ω_0 = Impact-estimate from intervention model
d = Standardized impact-estimate
γ = Grand mean standardized effect
σ_γ = Standard error of grand mean standardized effect
τ = Estimate of variance of parameters
χ^2 = Test of H_0: $\tau = 0$

* $p < .05$
[a] Non-gun assault
[b] Knife assault
[c] Non-gun weapon assault

Table 3
SUMMARY OF ANALYSIS FOR ROBBERY

Jurisdiction	Parameter	Armed Robbery	Unarmed Robbery
Case Studies: Intervention Estimates			
Detroit	ω_0	.0778	.0207
	d	.7044	.1844
Jacksonville	ω_0	2.5300	3.5580
	d	.1308	.4136
Tampa	ω_0	-3.7230	9.6590*
	d	$-.3415$	1.2361
Miami	ω_0	1.9440	30.1700*
	d	.0825	1.4541
Pennsylvania	ω_0	-19.0300[a]	3.4590[b]
	d	$-.2264$	.0987
Meta-Analysis: Variance Components Model			
All Jurisdictions	γ	.0763	.6809
	σ_γ	.1826	.2787
	γ/σ_γ	.42	2.44*
	τ	.1351	.3539
	χ^2 (4 df)	21.75*	45.68*

ω_0 = Impact-estimate from intervention model
d = Standardized impact-estimate
γ = Grand mean standardized effect
σ_γ = Standard error of grand mean standardized effect
τ = Estimate of variance of parameters
χ^2 = Test of H_0: $\tau = 0$

* $p < .05$
[a] Gun robbery
[b] Other weapon robbery

[22]

Time Series Analysis of Crime Rates

David F. Greenberg[1]

A methodological critique of Cantor and Land's (1985) approach to the time series analysis of the crime–unemployment relationship is developed. Error correction models for U.S. homicide and robbery rates for the years 1946–1997 are presented to illustrate procedures for analyzing nonstationary time series data. The critique is followed by a discussion of methodological problems in work by Devine *et al.* (1988), Smith *et al.* (1992), and Britt (1994, 1997) that builds on Cantor and Land's approach.

KEY WORDS: time series; crime; unemployment; age; divorce; cointegration.

1. INTRODUCTION

David Cantor and Kenneth Land's (1985) analysis of the relationship between annual unemployment rates and crime rates in the United States has served as a paradigm for subsequent criminological time series analyses. Though Hale and Sabbagh (1991) and Hale (1991) have raised questions about their approach, Cantor and Land (hereafter C-L) (1991) have defended their work vigorously (Land *et al.*, 1995). Here I raise further questions about the C-L procedures. I then update their data set, add additional variables to it, and carry out further analyses of homicide and robbery rates in the United States during the years 1946–1997. Finally, I discuss the work of several other researchers who have used the C-L approach.

2. THE CANTOR–LAND APPROACH

C-L (1985) argue that earlier research dealing with the impact of unemployment on crime rates has led to weak and inconsistent findings because it has failed to take into account two possible ways unemployment might

[1]Sociology Department, New York University, 269 Mercer Street, Room 402, New York, New York, 10003. E-mail: david.greenberg@nyu.edu. (This paper has been cut to accommodate *JQC*'s space limitations. The longer version will be sent on request.)

influence crime. Although the unemployed are expected to have greater motivation to violate the law, they might also spend more time at home, preventing burglaries and reducing their vulnerability to robbery, assault, and homicide[2] (an opportunity effect). C-L note that the two possibilities need not be mutually exclusive: unemployment could reduce the opportunities to violate the law while, at the same time, increasing the motivation to do so. If both effects are instantaneous, a coefficient representing the net effect of unemployment on crime might be small and insignificant even though both effects are substantial.

A linear relationship between the rate at which individual i commits crimes (C_i), and that individual's lawful opportunities and motivation at time t can be represented in the form of a regression equation with residual e_i:

$$C_{it} = a + b_1(\text{opportunity}) + b_2(\text{motivation}_{it}) + e_{it} \tag{1}$$

If opportunity at time t and motivation at time t are both proportional to unemployment at time t (U_t), a regression of C_t against U_t will yield an estimate of the sum $b_1 + b_2$. Without additional information, there is no way to estimate the individual coefficients b_1 and b_2.

C-L break the underdetermination by suggesting that opportunity effects should be instantaneous, while motivational effects are likely to be lagged. This is because most workers will have savings and welfare benefits to sustain them for a time after they lose a job. C-L represent the motivational factor with a term involving the difference in the unemployment rate, $\Delta U_t = U_t - U_{t-1}$, arguing that people will compare their current employment status with what it was in the past. Thus one can measure the motivational and opportunity effects of unemployment by using the expression $b_1 U_t + b_2 \Delta U_t$ to predict the crime rate at time t. The coefficient b_1 should be negative, while b_2 should be positive.

Analyzing nationally aggregated annual data for the years 1946–1982, C-L find evidence for trends in the crime rates, which they eliminate by taking first or second differences. The equations they consider thus take the form of

$$\Delta C_t = a + b_1 U_t + b_2 \Delta U_t + e_t \tag{2}$$

or

$$\Delta^2 C_t = a + b_1 U_t + b_2 \Delta U_t + e_t \tag{3}$$

C-L present results for both logged and unlogged crime rates. Values of adjusted R^2 for these models range from 0 (assault) to .1979 (larceny).

---

[2]A similar argument was presented by Cook and Harkin (1985).

Evidence of the predicted opportunity and motivational effects is found primarily for offenses involving illegal acquisition. In a subsequent analysis, Land *et al.* (1995) extend the time series to 1990, obtaining similar results. In Section 2, I point out several problems associated with the C-L procedures. Because there is something of a disconnect between the narrative in which C-L present their theoretical ideas and the equations they use to represent those ideas, I discuss both.

2.1. The Lag Structure of Unemployment

2.1.1. Distinguishing Between Opportunity and Motivation Effects

The validity of the C-L strategy for distinguishing motivational from opportunity effects rests on the accuracy of the proposition that most workers have savings and welfare benefits to sustain them for a time on losing a job. This may well be true of some workers, but it is surely not true of all. Evidence to this effect can be found in Conley's (1999) study of a cohort of subjects in the Panel Study of Income Dynamics. Among blacks with an income of $15,000 or less in 1992, the median net worth of the family was zero (i.e., no assets). In the entire black subsample, the median assets excluding housing equity were $2000. In 1998, the bottom 40% of households in the Federal Reserve Board's Survey of Consumer Finances had a mean net worth of $1100 and a mean annual income of $13,500. Among non-Hispanics, 14.8% of whites and 27.4% of African Americans had zero or negative net worth (Wolff, 2001). Clearly, many would face serious financial difficulties very quickly after losing a job.

In an unpublished study[3] using monthly crime and unemployment data, C-L (1987) found that changes in unemployment were positively related to changes in burglary and larceny just 1 month later. Longer-lagged effects were absent, apart from negative effects with a lag of 2 months. These results suggest that analyses of annual data may be insufficiently fine-grained to detect the motivational effects of unemployment and that lags as long as a year are too long to model them. If the various motivational effects of unemployment are felt very quickly, then it will be impossible to distinguish opportunity effects from motivational effects with annual data because they will both appear as contemporaneous effects.

If the motivational effect is indeed lagged, so that loss of a job in year $t - 1$ increases the motivation to violate the law in year t, then one could represent the motivational effect with a term in U_{t-1}, and the underdetermination of coefficients would no longer be a problem. This is not the strategy C-L adopt, but it would appear to be a straightforward translation of

---

[3] I know its contents only through the summary by Land *et al.* (1991).

the ideas in their narrative into a statistical model. Because C-L found evidence that motivational effects have a time lag much shorter than a year, it is questionable whether they should be studied by introducing a term in unemployment lagged by as long as a year, though they could legitimately be modeled with much shorter lags (e.g., weekly or monthly). However, the procedure would still be substantively dubious.

To see this, consider three sets of individuals. Members of the first set lose their jobs at the end of year t and remain unemployed through the following year. Members of the second set are employed in year t but lose their jobs during year $t + 1$. Members of the third set become unemployed at the start of year t but find jobs a year later and keep them. If the motivational effect of unemployment were to be expressed through an unemployment rate lagged by 1 year, members of all three groups would have low motivation to violate the law in year t because they would both be living on earnings until they lost their jobs (groups 1 and 2) or on savings and welfare (group 3). Groups 1 and 2 would have equally low motivation to violate the law in year $t + 1$, even though members of the first group are unemployed for the entire year, while members of the second group are working part of the year. On the other hand, members of group 3 would have higher motivation to violate the law in year $t + 1$, even though they are working throughout that year, because they were unemployed the previous year.

These implications seem implausible. A current job will provide income to meet the present needs, as well as a stream of income in the future that the job-holder may not want to jeopardize (however, see the discussion of low-wage jobs below). To be sure, someone who is currently unemployed and who was also unemployed in the previous year might have greater financial need than someone who had been employed for a long time prior to the current spell of unemployment. Such a person might be more likely to have debts or needs that cannot be met with current income. But that would also be true of some people in the year they become unemployed. Very likely a distributed lag dependence of motivation on unemployment is needed, or a nonlinear expression in which the coefficient expressing the effect of contemporaneous unemployment on motivation depends on earlier levels of unemployment.

Ignoring these complications, one would operationalize Eq. (1) by writing

$$C_t = a + b_1 U_t + b_2 U_{t-1} + e_t \tag{4}$$

Making use of the identity $\Delta U_t = U_t - U_{t-1}$, and grouping terms, we have

$$C_t = a + (b_1 + b_2)U_t - b_2 \Delta U_t + e \tag{5}$$

Examination of Eq. (5) shows that the coefficient of the contemporaneous unemployment term is the sum of the opportunity and motivation effects, while the coefficient of the differenced term enters with opposite sign from the coefficient of the lagged term in Eq. (4).

Because Eq. (5) follows logically from C-L's discussion of motivational effects, even if it is not their own mathematical formulation, the implications of this equation are worth considering. Ignore for a moment the fact that the left-hand member of Eq. (5) is a crime rate and not a difference in crime rate, and consider the Cochrane–Orcutt estimates that C-L (1991, p. 329) present for robbery and burglary in light of the present discussion. They estimate the contemporaneous coefficient for the effect of unemployment to be −8.3501 for robbery and −41.685 for burglary; the corresponding coefficients for the change in unemployment are 7.2727 and 36.613. They interpret the positive coefficients as consistent with motivational theory, but based on the reasoning just presented, both coefficients have the wrong sign. Moreover, the coefficients representing opportunity effects are not −8.3501 and −41.685 but −8.3501 + 7.2727 = −1.0774 and −41.685 + 36.613 = −5.072. Both coefficients are negative, consistent with opportunity theory, but they are much smaller in magnitude than the coefficients C-L identify with opportunity effects. Because I doubt that a lagged unemployment rate is the best way to capture the motivational effect of unemployment on crime rates, I do not want to stress this finding too much; I mention it to highlight a problem in the way C-L translate verbal expressions of their ideas into equations.

Now consider not the C-L narrative, but its mathematical representation. Instead of representing the motivational effect of unemployment by lagging unemployment, C-L represent it by a difference score, ΔU_t. Two points may be made about this procedure. The first is the implausibility of representing motivation with a difference score.[4] This procedure would imply that the motivation to commit crime is as strong among those who have been unemployed for a long time as among those who have been continuously employed for a long time. In each case, there is no change in unemployment status from 1 year to the next. C-L's suggestion that motivation arises through a comparison with one's previous employment status seems off the mark here. Whatever standard one uses for a mental comparison, unemployment leads to real needs among some people that may be expected to affect criminal motivation. Moreover, someone who is unemployed at time t but who finds a job the next year would, by virtue of the

---

[4]After completing my paper, I discovered that Pyle and Deadman (1994) have also expressed reservations about Cantor and Land's specification, commenting, "It is not apparent why motivation should be related to the change in unemployment rather than its level in a previous period" (p. 341).

improvement, be less motivated to commit a crime in year $t+1$ than someone who had always been employed. This implication, too, is implausible.
It is also at variance with C-L's suggestion that unemployment is more
criminogenic when it has lasted awhile than when it first occurs.

Next, suppose that the equation to be estimated is Eq. (2). If the motivational effects are represented by ΔU_t, then the equation represents change
in unemployment as causing change in crime rates without a lag, contrary
to the C-L narrative. A lagged model would use ΔU_{t-1} as a predictor, not
ΔU_t. It follows that the mathematical representation of motivational effects
is no more satisfactory than the narrative version.

To determine empirically whether the influence of change in unemployment might be lagged rather than contemporaneous, I updated C-L's data
set and examined the cross-correlation function for ΔU_t and the differenced
murder rate for the United States, for the years 1946–1996. There were
suggestions that an increase in unemployment might reduce the murder rate
with a lag of a year or 2, but none of the correlations was statistically
significant at the .05 level, and in a regression of change in the murder rate
on ΔU_{t-1} alone or in a model that also includes ΔU_{t-2}, the F statistic for the
regression was not significant. Nor were any of the individual coefficients.

2.1.2. Motivation and the Duration of Unemployment

C-L were probably on the right track in suggesting that long-term
unemployment may be a more powerful motivater of crime than short-term
unemployment, as several studies have found that long-term unemployment
increases involvement in crime, while short-term unemployment does not.
To take account of this one needs a variable representing the duration of
unemployment. Neither a difference score nor a lagged aggregate unemployment variable can substitute for such a measure. Conceptually they are quite
distinct.

One can have a constant level of unemployment with no one's employment status changing between time 1 and time 2 or with such a high level
of turnover in unemployment that no one is unemployed at both times.
Where aggregate unemployment has increased between time 1 and time 2,
the increase establishes a floor on the number of people who have been
unemployed for just a short time, but the number could be substantially
larger. If, for example, the unemployment rate in one year is 5% and that
in the next year it is 6%, the number of people who lost jobs in the intervening year could be anywhere between 1 and 6%. For this reason, neither
change in unemployment nor aggregate unemployment is a good proxy for

Table I. Cochrane–Orcutt Estimates of Coefficients and Summary Statistics for the Effects of Unemployment on Crime Rates, 1946–1996[a]

Dependent variable	Intercept	U_t	DUR_t	Adj. R^2	$\hat{\rho}$	DW
Dhomicide	1.325*	.049	−.120*	.310	.39	1.90
Drape	2.725*	−.022	−.151	.030	.41	1.88
Drobbery	41.988*	4.127	−5.009*	.439	.36	1.85
Dassault	24.029*	3.676*	−2.950*	.127	.32	2.02
Dburglary	221.788*	14.378	21.798*	.330	.40	1.69
Dauto	80.242*	−1.133	−4.989*	.300	.59	2.02

[a]All dependent variables are first-differenced crime rates, measured as numbers of crimes per 100,000 population. Intercepts and coefficients for U_t and DUR_t (duration of unemployment) are metric coefficients.
*$p < .10$.

duration of unemployment.[5] Were strength of motivation to be measured by the numbers of people who are unemployed, no matter for how long, this would not be an issue, but when long-term unemployment is assumed to increase motivation, then it is an issue.

Using the updated data set, I replicated C-L's regressions using the duration of unemployment, rather than change in unemployment, as a measure of motivation.[6] The results of such analyses for six index offenses (homicide, rape, robbery, assault, burglary, auto theft) are shown in Table I, which is constructed parallel to C-L's (1985) Table II.[7] None of the contemporaneous unemployment coefficients is both negative and statistically significant, as predicted by opportunity theory. In addition, all of the coefficients of DUR (duration of unemployment) are negative, five of them significantly. Motivation theory predicts that these coefficients should be positive. Thus, using these procedures there is no support for either motivational theory or opportunity theory. However, in the remaining part of this article I argue that the procedures themselves are flawed, so that the lack of support for either theory has little meaning.

[5]Empirically, the two variables are quite weakly related. Using data from the Executive Office of the President (1998) I computed the correlation between average number of weeks unemployed and the difference in levels of civilian unemployment using annual data for the United States for the period from 1950 to 1997. It was .17.
[6]Because the duration of unemployment does not provide information on how many people are experiencing unemployment of that duration, it is not an ideal measure of motivation. The product of the level of unemployment and the duration of unemployment would be a better measure. However, in our data set, the correlation between the product variable and the level of unemployment is .940; empirically it would be difficult to distinguish the two.
[7]As definitions of larceny–theft changed during the period of study, I elected to omit this offense from the analysis rather than adjust for the change, as C-L did.

Table II. Error Correction Model Estimates of Models for Homicide Rates, 1946–1997[a]

Independent variable	Model						
	A	B	C	D	E	F	G
Constant	−.14	−.17	−.18	.68	.76	.41	.47
	(.39)	(.50)	(.54)	(1.97)	(1.82)	(.94)	(.92)
ΔDivorce	.29***	.34**	.32***	.28*	.29*	.29*	.29*
	(4.72)	(5.75)	(5.48)	(2.57)	(2.56)	(2.65)	(2.61)
Error	−.15	−.29**	−.26**	−.22*	−.22*	−.24*	−.25*
	(1.74)	(3.34)	(2.80)	(2.51)	(2.48)	(2.69)	(2.63)
PCTM1529	4.52*	5.16**	5.75**	1.90	1.39	3.38	3.00
	(2.45)	(2.94)	(3.22)	(1.28)	(.66)	(1.60)	(1.11)
U_t	−.16***	—	−.07	—	.02	—	.02
	(4.15)		(1.41)		(.36)		(.23)
U_{t-1}	—	−.18***	−.13*	—	—	−.07	−.07
		(4.92)	(2.67)			(.99)	(.94)
DUR	—	—	—	−.09**	−.09**	−.06	−.07
				(4.73)	(3.31)	(1.87)	(1.60)
R^2	.48	.53	.55	.56	.56	.57	.57
DW	1.65	1.70	1.65	1.51	1.49	1.52	1.52

[a] Coefficients are unstandardized regression coefficients; figures in parentheses are values of Student's *t*.
*$p < .05$.
**$p < .01$.
***$p < .001$.

2.2. The Treatment of Trends

During the years covered by the C-L and Land–Cantor–Russell studies, crime rates rose. Because trends in time series pose problems for statistical estimation, statisticians remove them before carrying out further analyses. C-L (1985) and Land *et al.* (1991) do this by taking first or second differences, a standard procedure. To show that this differencing poses a problem for the interpretation that Land and his collaborators give to their findings, assume for the sake of simplicity that the trend in crime rates is linear. If we add a term linear in *t* to Eq. (1), the terms involving opportunity and motivation represent the degree to which variation in these variables raises or lowers the crime rate above or below the trend line. Assuming that the opportunity effects are proportional to U_t and that the motivational effects are proportional to the duration of unemployment, estimation of this equation for the six offenses listed in Table I yields coefficients for the effect of unemployment that are consistently positive, and for the effect of duration of unemployment that are consistently negative, except for rape, where both estimates fail to achieve statistical significance. Because C-L (1985) found the best-fitting models for all six offenses we are considering to be ones in which the crime rates were differenced twice, I reestimated the equation after adding a quadratic term in year.[8] Except for burglary, none of the quadratic terms was statistically significant. All coefficients for the contemporaneous unemployment rate were positive and statistically significant at the .05 level; all those for the duration of unemployment were negative and statistically significant.[9]

These conclusions were reached by estimating regression equations containing deterministic linear or quadratic terms in time. Although this is a perfectly acceptable procedure, the trends can also be eliminated by taking first differences (or second differences if needed). If this is done, the intercept in the regression equation drops out, and the term in t becomes a constant. We are thus left with an equation in which a difference in the crime rates is predicted by a difference in the opportunity variable and a difference in the motivation variable. This is what is expected theoretically. Corresponding to a given level of opportunity and motivation there should be, in equilibrium, a corresponding level of illegality. A change in opportunity or in motivation should lead to a change in the volume of crime.

Contrast the procedure just outlined with the one that C-L adopt. They difference the crime rates in Eq. (1) once or twice to eliminate trends but carry out no differencing of the independent variables. This procedure is mathematically unacceptable. If one accepts Eq. (1) as a theoretical representation of the processes of interest, then operations that transform the left-hand member of Eq. (1) must also be performed on the right-hand member if the equality is to be preserved.

The equations on which Land and his collaborators base their conclusions lead to absurd implications because they difference only the crime rates, and not their predictors. Suppose that the trend being eliminated is linear, that it is Eq. (2) being estimated, and that there are no motivational effects. However, there are opportunity effects, so that b_1 is negative. Equation (2) says that a constant level of unemployment would lead to a steady drop in the crime rate. If the crime rates require second-differencing, Eq.

---

[8] To reduce multicollinearity between *year* and *year²*, I subtracted 1972 from *year*, and used this centered variable and its square in the regression.

[9] For purposes of comparison with C-L (1985), I also estimated these models using U_t, ΔU_t, as well as the linear and quadratic terms in year as predictors. In this set of estimates, all the linear and quadratic terms in time were significant except for rape, where the quadratic term was not significant. Four of the six coefficients for U_t were negative, but only two of the six were statistically significant at the .10 level: the coefficient for rape was positive; the coefficient for auto theft was negative. Of the six coefficients for change in unemployment, only the coefficient for rape was negative (not significant); the remaining five were positive, with the coefficients for murder, robbery, and auto theft being statistically significant at the .10 level. Discrepancies from the results reported by C-L (1985) may be due to differences in the years covered.

(3) would be estimated. It would say, under the same conditions, that a constant rate of unemployment will lead to a deceleration in the increase of crime rates. In a world in which there are no opportunity effects, only motivational effects, Eqs. (2) and (3) also predict that a constant level of unemployment will lead to an increasing or decreasing crime rate [Eq. (2)] or an accelerating or decelerating crime rate [Eq. (3)], as long as the constant term in the regression, a, is different from zero. These predictions do not correspond to any reasonable notion of the way unemployment should affect crime rates.

In responding to criticism from Hale and Sabbagh, C-L (1991) offer a justification for differencing crime rates not given in their original paper: differencing could eliminate omitted variables responsible for the upward trend in crime rate, allowing them to concentrate on the effects of unemployment. Yet differencing undertaken for this reason must still be carried out for both left- and right-hand members of an equation if logical consistency is to be maintained and the equations are to retain their original meaning. In addition, Hale (1991) has pointed out that this procedure works only if the omitted variable has a constant trend but does not contribute at all to fluctuations around the trend line. Should an omitted variable have a random component as well as a deterministic trend, the differencing procedure will not eliminate it. Residuals for the differenced equation will have a negative first-order serial correlation, and estimates for the effects of, unemployment will be biased if the random component is correlated with unemployment. Because virtually every imaginable social variable that might contribute to a trend in crime rates will have a random component, differencing cannot be considered a satisfactory way of eliminating omitted variables responsible for trends. One must, therefore, echo Hale's (1991) observation that "differencing is no substitute for modeling." If there are variables responsible for trends in crime, it is desirable that they be identified and introduced into one's model whenever possible.

2.3. Cointegration Issues

2.3.1. Nonstationarity and Unit Root Tests

When a time series is not stationary, classical statistical theory breaks down (Granger and Newbold, 1974; Phillips, 1986) and special procedures are needed. Consequently, one of the very first issues a researcher must confront when analyzing a time series is the question of whether it is stationary. "Unit root" tests allow one to determine whether a series is stationary, and if it is not, whether it is a random walk, a random walk with drift, or a random walk with drift and trend (Banerjee *et al.*, 1993; Holden and Perman, 1994; Harris, 1995, pp. 27–39; Charemza and Deadman, 1997, pp. 98–122; Greene, 1997, pp. 847–851; Johnston and DiNardo, 1997, pp. 223–228) . These tests consider whether the coefficient a in the equation $y_t = ay_{t-1} + \cdots + e_t$, $y_t = \mu + ay_{t-1} + \cdots + e_t$, or $y_t = \mu + ay_{t-1} + bt + \cdots + e_t$ is significantly different from 1. Equations in which the coefficient a is equal to 1 represent "unit root" processes.

When I carried out two such tests, the Augmented Dickey–Fuller test and the Phillips–Perron test, for the six crime rates (homicide, forcible rape, robbery, assault, burglary, auto theft) for the years 1946–1997, the tests failed to reject the null hypothesis of a unit root for each offense, consistent with each series being nonstationary.[10] When the tests were repeated on the differenced rates, the unit root hypothesis was rejected in each instance, suggesting that no further differencings were needed. The same tests for unemployment indicated that it was stationary, and required no differencing.

A question could be raised whether it is really possible for a crime rate to be a realization of a random walk process. The variance of a random walk time series increases without limit over time, and this seems implausible for crime. It is unrealistic to suppose, however, that the same generating process responsible for temporal changes in crime will continue unchanged forever. A random walk seems to fit these offenses over the half-century for which we have data. Changes in the causes of crime (including social control strategies) or in the strength of their effects could change the structure of the crime rate series in the future.

Before proceeding to discuss cointegration, it is worth reflecting on the theoretical importance of the finding that crime rates appear to be realizations of a unit root process. This means that there are no effective social processes tending to reduce crime rates if they grow too large or to increase them if they fall too low. Instead, they bounce about randomly, uninfluenced by the instantaneous level of crime, and without tending to return to an equilibrium level.

If a time series requires d differencings to achieve stationarity, it is said to be integrated of order d, denoted $I(d)$. Logical consistency requires that if crime rates are a realization of a unit root process, they must be explained by a unit root process. It is thus mathematically impossible for a crime rate that is $I(1)$ to be caused only by a function that is $I(0)$. If a crime rate is $I(1)$, at least one of the explanatory variables must also be $I(1)$, though additional predictor variables can be $I(0)$. This knowledge can help focus a search for explanatory variables.

If one estimates the effect of an $I(1)$ series X_t on an $I(1)$ series Y_t by regressing Y_t on X_t, one runs the risk of spurious regressions. Until recently,

[10] I treat a failure to reject the null hypothesis as equivalent to accepting the null hypothesis.

differencing both sides of the regression equation to eliminate the non-stationary, and then analyzing the stationary differences, was the recommended way to proceed. Yet this is not a satisfactory procedure because it removes all information about the long-run tendencies of the differenced variables. Often it is the long-run trends that are of much greater interest than short-time fluctuations; yet researchers following procedures needed to avoid spurious regressions focused all their attention on the short-run, ephemeral fluctuations, rather than the long-run tendencies. In criminology this has meant ignoring the causes of the large rise in crime rates between the early sixties and the early seventies, while focusing on year-to-year fluctuations in crime rates around the rise. Recent developments in statistical theory based on the concept of cointegration offer an appealing way to avoid this loss of information.

2.3.2. The Cointegration of Crime and Divorce

Cointegration theory is based on the insight that even if the series X_t and Y_t are individually nonstationary, a linear combination of the two series may be stationary. If there exists a constant β such that $Y_t - \beta X_t$ is $I(0)$, the two series are said to be cointegrated. Cointegrated series will tend to move together. If a disturbance leads to a short-run increase in the distance between them, an equilibrating force will tend to bring them back together again. The relationship between the two variables thus tends to maintain itself over the long term. Even though each variable drifts, they drift together and do not grow farther apart, as they would were they not cointegrated, and were random-walking independently of one another. Information about this long-term relationship is what is lost when the series are differenced (Banerjee *et al.*, 1993, pp. 136–140; Harris, 1995, pp. 52–75; Greene, 1997, pp. 851–859).

To consider cointegration for each of the six index offenses would extend the length of this paper unduly. Instead, I analyze just the homicide rate and the robbery rate in this light. Visual inspection of graphs for the homicide rate, the robbery rate, and the divorce rate strongly suggests that each crime rate is cointegrated with the divorce rate:[11] both crime rates move roughly in parallel with the divorce rate, although the parallel movement may have weakened some in recent years (see Figs. 1 and 2). Augmented Dickey–Fuller and Phillips–Perron tests confirm that the divorce rate is $I(1)$, and that when the homicide rate and the robbery rate are each

---

[11]I was encouraged to examine divorce by a graph showing the divorce rate and the robbery rate given by LaFree (1998, pp. 140–144). LaFree rests his argument on the relationship between various crime rates and other social indicators on the basis of general trends, without conducting any statistical analyses to test their relationships.

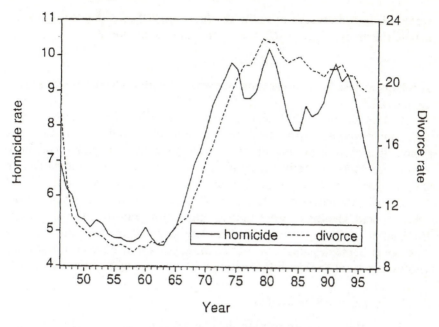

Fig. 1. Homicide rates and divorce rates.

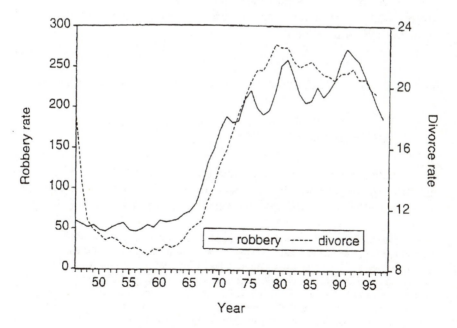

Fig. 2. Robbery rates and divorce rates.

regressed on the divorce rate, the residuals are $I(0)$, i.e., stationary. If we denote the divorce rate by D_t, the cointegrating equation is

$$C_t = \alpha + \beta D_t + v_t \tag{6}$$

A Johanssen test for cointegration is consistent with each pair of series being cointegrated.

It does not seem likely that this relationship is a direct, causal one or that people who are divorcing have exceptionally high divorce rates. More likely, divorce is an indicator of a strain in a fundamental social institution—the nuclear family. It is this strain that leads some individuals to kill, whether or not they themselves divorce. The divorce rate in the United States rose dramatically between 1960 and 1980, a time when gender relations and ideologies were undergoing major transformations, putting great strain on many families and leading some of them to divorce. The upsurge in homcides and robberies in those years may have been responses to strains related to this shift experienced by people who did *not* divorce.[12]

2.3.3. Error Correction Models

Fluctuations around equilibrium can be assessed statistically through a transformation of a dynamical equation. For illustrative purposes, suppose that the crime rate C is influenced by the lagged and contemporaneous divorce rates, a contemporaneous term in unemployment, and a lagged crime rate. We thus write

$$C_t = \gamma_0 + \gamma_1 C_{t-1} + \gamma_2 D_t + \gamma_3 D_{t-1} + \gamma_3 U_t + e_t \tag{7}$$

Writing $C_t = C_{t-1} + \Delta C_t$ and grouping terms, we can express this equation as

$$\Delta C_t = \gamma_0 \gamma_2 \Delta D_t + (\gamma_1 - 1)\left[C_{t-1} - \left(\frac{\gamma_2 + \gamma_3}{1 - \gamma_1} \right) D_{t-1} \right] + \gamma_4 U_t + e_t \tag{8}$$

By evaluating Eq. (8) at its equilibrium ($C_t = C_{t-1}$, $D_t = D_{t-1}$) and comparing with Eq. (6), we see that the ratio $(\gamma_2 + \gamma_3)/(1 - \gamma_1)$ can be identified with the coefficient β, and that the expression in brackets is the deviation

---

[12]Because unmarried women are more likely than married women to hold jobs (Nakosteen and Zimmer, 1989), one might wonder whether some or all of the divorce effects are related to women's greater labor force participation, a possibility that is given particular relevance to the present analysis by research indicating that women's employment is positively related to crime in Australia (Kapuscinski *et al.*, 1998). Although women's labor force participation and the divorce rate are positively correlated in the Unted States, they behave rather differently, and the women's labor force participation does not move together with the homicide rate or the robbery rate; the divorce rate does.

of the series from its equilibrium in the cointegration model. Equation (8) can thus be written more compactly as

$$\Delta C_t = \gamma_0 + \gamma_2 \Delta D_t + \varphi v_{t-1} + \gamma_4 U_t + e_t \qquad (9)$$

where $\varphi = \gamma_1 - 1$ and v represents the quantity in brackets in Eq. (8). This "error correction" representation of Eq. (7) expresses short-run change in crime rates as an additive function of short-run change in the divorce rate, an error correction term that maintains the long-run tendencies of the model, and the exogenous variable U_t. Additional independent variables, such as a term in U_{t-1} or ΔU_t, can be added to the equation if that is appropriate, so long as they are $I(0)$.

Two points regarding Eq. (9) are noteworthy. First, if the coefficient φ is nonvanishing, the omission of the error correction term could lead to omitted variable bias. This term would be absent were one naively to write a simple regression equation in which a differenced divorce rate causes a differenced crime rate. Thus, differencing to deal with nonstationarity is not the recommended procedure when a pair of variables is cointegrated. Second, because all the variables in Eq. (9) are stationary, the equation can be estimated using OLS.

Equation (9) is the basis for the Engle–Granger two-step estimation procedure: one first estimates Eq. (6) to obtain the residuals, then uses them to estimate Eq. (9) (Engle and Granger, 1987). I carried out Engle–Granger estimations for various models involving, in addition to divorce, several stationary variables that might be expected to influence either criminal motivation or opportunity or both. For this purpose I chose the percentage of males between age 15 and age 29, the unemployment rate (various combinations of contemporaneous, lagged and differenced, but never all three at once, as only two of the three are linearly independent), and the duration of unemployment. This list of variables could, obviously, be extended, but with 51 observations, there are limits to what is practical. OLS estimates of these models are shown in Table II (homicide) and Table III (robbery).[13] F tests for those sets of models that are nested show that the most parsimonious and best-fitting models for both homicide and robbery are B (unemployment lagged by 1 year) and D (duration of unemployment). Adding additional measures of unemployment fails to yield a significant improvement in fit to these models.

The graphs in Figs. 3 and 4 show the actual changes in homicide rates and robbery rates alongside the rates predicted on the basis of model B.

---

[13]On the basis of LaFree's (1998, pp. 115–132) discussion of inflation, I also considered models in which percentage change in the consumer price index was used as a predictor, but it did not make a statistically significant contribution to the regressions. Estimates for these models are not listed in Tables II and III.

Table III. Error Correction Model Estimates of Models for Robbery Rates, 1946–1997[a]

Independent variable	Model						
	A	B	C	D	E	F	G
Constant	−.72	−2.33	−1.71	22.15	31.65*	−1.24	5.38
	(.95)	(.24)	(.17)	(1.98)	(2.38)	(.10)	(.34)
ΔDivorce	7.69**	7.21**	7.42**	2.61	2.85	3.95	4.00
	(3.00)	(3.62)	(3.58)	(.76)	(.83)	(1.23)	(1.24)
Error	−.13	−.11	−.12	−.02	−.02	−.12	−.11
	(1.51)	(1.70)	(1.73)	(.22)	(.22)	(1.43)	(1.34)
PCTM1529	105.41	174.30**	164.86**	90.13	32.40	204.97**	166.38*
	(1.52)	(3.34)	(2.87)	(1.74)	(.48)	(3.31)	(2.05)
U_t	−3.71*	—	.60	—	2.63	—	1.44
	(2.59)		(.42)		(1.30)		(.74)
U_{t-1}	—	−6.27***	−6.60***	—	—	−6.69**	−6.28**
		(5.97)	(4.99)			(2.91)	(2.64)
DUR	—	—	—	−3.10***	−3.97***	−.36	−1.00
				(4.74)	(4.29)	(.32)	(.71)
R^2	.34	.58	.58	.53	.54	.61	.61
DW	1.43	1.35	1.36	1.12	1.39	1.32	1.31

[a] Coefficients are unstandardized regression coefficients; figures in parentheses are values of Student's *t*.
*$p < .05$
**$p < .01$
***$p < .001$

The models do a fairly good job at predicting changes in both rates, while failing to predict the sharp drop in the rates that occurred after 1993. Significantly, the increases of the 1960s are explained without any criminal justice system variables in the model. There is little here to suggest, for example, that Supreme Court decisions entitling indigent defendants to attorneys (*Gideon* v. *Wainwright*, 1963; *Escobedo* v. *Illinois*, 1964) and requiring the police to issue warnings to suspects (*Miranda* v. *Arizona*, 1966), had anything to do with those increases. Nor is there an unexplained increase in crime associated with the suspension of executions between 1967 and 1976 while the constitutionality of capital punishment was being challenged in the courts. I do not mean to imply that law enforcement variables had no effect on crime whatsoever, only that they do not seem to have been responsible for major shifts in levels of crime in these years.

The value in Tables II and III show that short-run increases in the divorce rate tend to produce short-run increases in both homicide and robbery (though in model D for robbery, the coefficient for divorce is not statistically significant). As expected, the error correction terms are negative in all the models, indicating that divorce and crime tend to move together—

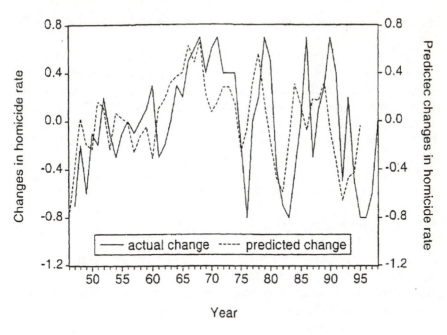

Fig. 3. Actual and predicted changes in homicide rates.

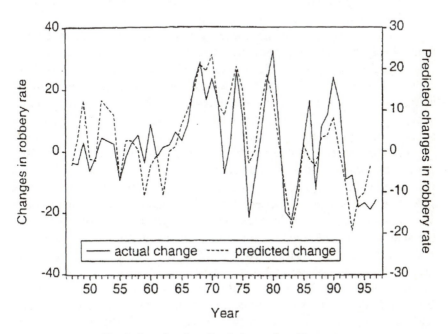

Fig. 4. Actual and predicted changes in robbery rates.

though in model D for robbery the coefficient is very small and not statistically significant.

The negative signs of the terms involving lagged unemployment and unemployment duration are opposite to what is expected of motivational effects, consistent with other studies (Ruhm, 1999; Raphael and Winter-Ebmer, 2001). Possibly the greater collective hardships of high or protracted unemployment strengthen social solidarity, reducing crime. Or it may be that unemployed people—especially those who have been unemployed for a long time—spend more of their time in public places, socializing in parks, and loitering and begging on the streets, discouraging crime by their presence. Consumption of alcohol rises in times of prosperity and drops when unemployment rises (Ruhm, 1995). Alcohol is a known disinhibitor and induces belligerence in some individuals. Unemployment might, then, curb violent crime by reducing the consumption of alcohol.

If the contemporaneous effect of unemployment measures the opportunity effect of unemployment, there is no unequivocal evidence for such an effect. Once the duration of unemployment or the lagged effect of unemployment is controlled, contemporaneous unemployment does not make a significant contribution.

How do these results compare with those of C-L (1985) and Land *et al.* (1995)? They found, in their first-differenced model incorporating both U_t and ΔU_t, that the instantaneous effect of unemployment was significantly negative, while the effect of change in unemployment was not. They also found a negative contemporaneous effect for robbery. If the Land *et al.* (1995) results are reparametrized in terms of U_t and U_{t-1} rather than U_t and ΔU_t to facilitate comparison of the estimates, their results are entirely consistent with mine: as discussed above, they find a contemporaneous effect that is positive, but very small and not statistically significant, and an appreciable negative effect of U_{t-1}.

For reasons that should be obvious from what has already been said, the results presented here are more credible and more informative than those presented by C-L (1985) and Land *et al.* (1995). The equation on which I base my analysis better represents a plausible theoretical model. The estimation procedure does not eliminate the drift in crime rates from the analysis but explains it. The resulting models reproduce the homicide and robbery rates reasonably well except that they do not predict the sharp drop in crime rates of the past few years.

That said, I do not want to exaggerate the strength of my findings. Because the correlations among unemployment, lagged unemployment, and duration of unemployment are high (between .75 and .80), it is difficult to assess their simultaneous effects with just 50 observations. The Durbin–

Watson statistics in Tables II and III lie in the "inconclusive" region, so the potential for omitted variable bia exists.[14]

3. USERS OF THE PARADIGM

The procedures developed by C-L for analyzing time series have been put to use by several researchers, notably Devine *et al.* (1988), Smith *et al.* (1992), and Britt (1994, 1997). Devine *et al.* use time series to study the impact of several variables on U.S. crime rates between 1948 and 1985. Following the standard recipe, Devine *et al.* difference the crime rates to eliminate what they consider trends. Probably the trends are actually manifestations of drift, but that is a distinction without a consequence here, as drift can be eliminated by differencing. In one set of models they introduce as independent variables change in the rate of male unemployment, the rate of inflation, the change in public relief, and the change in the imprisonment rate. Because all independent variables are measures of change, these models take the form of "change causes change" and do not raise problems of interpretation. In another set of models, Devine *et al.* add a static measure of opportunity and find that it makes a significant contribution to homicide, robbery, and some of the burglary models. However, as I have already argued, the use of a static measure of opportunity to explain change in the crime rate makes little sense.

Britt (1994) and Smith *et al.* (1992) apply the C-L paradigm to study the age-specific effects of unemployment on crime. This is a potentially valuable undertaking because recent crime rate changes have been highly age specific: increases in the murder rate in the years immediately after 1985 were restricted largely to people younger than age 25 (Blumstein and Rosenfeld, 1998), and recent decreases have been confined largely to the same age bracket (Butts, 2000). In these circumstances, an aggregate analysis that did not distinguish younger from older offenders could be quite misleading. Both studies take the number of arrests as a measure of the number of crimes committed, and regress it on the unemployment rate and the change in unemployment rate. Britt restricts his analysis to 16–19 year olds between 1958 and 1990 and considers all index crimes; Smith *et al.* consider four age categories—16–19, 20–24, 25–34, and 35–44—examining homicide, robbery and burglary. Each measures the crime rate by the arrest rate, and regresses it on the unemployment rate and the change in unemployment

---

[14]However, I did carry out Cochrane–Orcutt estimations of the error correction models that included first-order autocorrelations among the residuals, and the results were very similar to those presented in the text. Omitted variables often lead to serially correlated errors.

rate. Denoting arrests by A, and age and year by the subscripts i and t, this implies the estimation of an equation that takes the form

$$\Delta A_{it} = b_0 + b_1 U_{it} + b_2 \Delta U_{it} + e_{it} \tag{10}$$

Their findings are consistent: the contemporaneous effect of unemployment is negative, and the change effect positive, for all offenses. I comment on these studies below.

3.1. Britt's Analysis of the Age–Crime–Unemployment Relationship

In a further extension of this line of research, Britt (1997) analyzes age-specific U.S. arrest rates for the seven index offenses for the years 1958–1995 to test two propositions concerning the impact of unemployment on crime found in Greenberg's (1977, 1985) theoretical treatment of the age–crime relationship. Quoted verbatim from Britt's paper, the two propositions are as follows: (H1): "The unemployment–crime relationship will vary by age group, where youth and young adults are expected to show a greater motivational (positive) effect of unemployment on criminal behavior" and (H2) "The unemployment–crime relationship will vary over time, especially for youth and young adults, where the motivational (positive) effect of unemployment is expected to increase over time."

For several reasons, Britt's research does not provide a satisfactory test of Greenberg's ideas or these propositions. Here I summarize and then criticize Britt's research. My discussion deals with the following issues: (a) the extraction of propositions to be tested from Greenberg's narrative, (b) the translation of the discursive propositions into regression equations, (c) the operationalization of the variables in the regression equations, (d) the use of aggregate data to test propositions about individuals, and (e) the choice of a time frame for conducting the analysis.

3.1.1. The Extraction of Propositions from Greenberg's Narrative

Greenberg's (1977, 1985) model for the age dependency of crime draws on two major pillars of criminological theory to explain the age distribution of crime and the manner in which it has changed historically: strain theory and control theory. The model posits three types of institutional involvement or lack of involvement as sources of strain. It asserts that adolescent theft "occurs as a response to the disjunction between the desire to participate in social activities with peers and the absence of legitimate sources of funds needed to finance this participation" (p. 197). This is the first source of strain.[15] Greenberg argued that the intensity of this strain depends on age. Because adolescents lack the institutional affiliations that provide adults with alternative sources of self-esteem, participation in peer-focused social activities is expected to be more important to adolescents than to older adults.[16] The age stratification of American society has increased over time, so that this sort of strain should be greater now than in the past. These last two sentences form the basis of the two propositions Britt tests.

The model posits that a second source of strain—the denial of autonomy and the exposure to status degradation inflicted on students in school—is relevant primarily to the explanation of joy-riding, vandalism, acts of interpersonal violence, and seemingly irrational thefts in which the objects stolen are discarded or destroyed. Delinquency in response to this type of strain is also posited as contingent. It is primarily students who do not find compensating rewards and benefits from school (such as gratification from learning, extracurricular activities such as sports and clubs, socializing with peers, and future occupational rewards) who are expected to rebel against the restrictions and status degradations they encounter in school. Students who find school to be rewarding on balance, or who anticipate that it will enable them to achieve valued occupational goals, will tend to put up with its restrictions and status degradations. Any test of the theory must take these interaction effects into account. A third source of strain in the model is "masculine status anxiety," which intensifies at the end of the transition from adolescence to adulthood, when young males find that they cannot obtain jobs or discover that the jobs they can obtain pay badly and offer poor prospects for advancement. This source of strain is asserted to be relevant primarily to violent offenses. The control theory component of the argument focuses on the shift from juvenile court jurisdiction to the criminal court, which creates a substantially enhanced risk of serious punishment,

---

[15]Though not discussed by Greenberg (1977), the sale of illegal narcotics is another offense to which this reasoning might reasonably be expected to apply. Several studies have linked the sale of drugs by young people to their limited opportunities for earning income lawfully (Reuter *et al.*, 1990; Fagan, 1992; Myers, 1992; Hagedorn, 1994).

[16]This line of reasoning could be criticized on theoretical grounds for what it omits. Leisure-time social activities are usually considered discretionary. Someone—even a teenager—who cannot afford these activities might be unhappy but can survive: for most adolescents, paying for rent and food is not a serious problem, no matter what their employment status or personal finances may be, because someone else is paying for them. Homeless adolescents, who may have to steal to survive, would be exceptions (McCarthy and Hagan, 1992). In contrast, an adult who lacks financial resources may be unable to pay the rent or buy groceries. One might think that the strain induced by inability to pay for life necessities would be greater than the strain induced by inability to pay for leisure-time social activities. Greenberg's omission of this source of strain was intentional; a focus on life necessities would suggest that the peak age of involvement in theft should be in adulthood, not in adolescence, where it is in fact.

Quantitative Methods in Criminology

and on the informal sources of control associated with the institutions juveniles are able to establish or enter when they become adults: marriage and employment.

Several features of this argument are relevant to the present discussion. First, the relationship between strain arising from lack of income and employment is not simple, because employment is not the only source of legitimate income. Greenberg (1977, pp. 196, 198) remarks that as long as parents pay for their children's leisure-time social activities, children will not be strapped for cash even though they do not derive income from a job. It follows that if one wants to test Britt's propositions, one must assess variations in the extent to which parents subsidize their children. Parental ability and willingness to do this may well depend on their own employment circumstances.

When considering youths' aspirations toward conventional careers, the same problem arises. Fifteen-year-olds' aspirations may be influenced by the level of unemployment adults in their community experience, quite independently of their own employment statuses. If, for example, adolescents see that older adults in their communities are unable to find lawful jobs, they are likely to dismiss lawful employment as a possibility for themselves in the future. It follows that youthful involvement in crime may depend not only on their own employment, but on their parents' employment and income. Unfortunately, a model that incorporated the age-specific unemployment rates for both youths and individuals who belong to an older generation would be difficult to estimate with aggregate data because of severe multicollinearity: Britt notes that the correlation between the total annual unemployment rate and the unemployment rate for persons ages 16 to 19 between 1958 and 1990 is .98. This high correlation means that when Britt reports the effect of unemployment variables, we cannot be confident that the effects are those of the relevant age-specific unemployment rate, rather than those of the overall unemployment rate, or the unemployment rate for middle-aged workers who are parents of the 16- to 19-year-olds.

Second, the theory makes different predictions about the effects of unemployment for different kinds of crime. Unemployment is predicted to have the strongest effect on theft in adolescence but on interpersonal violence in young adulthood. For this reason, Britt's conclusion that the motivational effect of unemployment on homicide is greater at ages 18–24 (his Table III) than in earlier and later years is not at odds with Greenberg's theoretical model: quite the contrary (see further discussion below). Third, Greenberg's theory is explicitly multivariate. Estimating the effect of unemployment alone on illegality does not provide an appropriate test of a multivariate theory, unless the independent variables in the model are uncorrelated. The results reported in this paper suggest that the effect of unemployment on crime cannot be studied without taking into account the other factors that might influence crime rates.

In addition, a number of researchers have suggested that there is a relationship between adolescent employment and school experience. When high school students work long hours, their school performance may suffer, increasing their involvement in some kinds of illegal activities. Deficiencies in school performance may also lead some juveniles to take jobs. Because the Greenberg model posits irritating experiences in school to be crimino-genic, these influences must be taken into account if the effect of unemployment is to be assessed. Regrettably, information about the relevant subjective variables is not to be found in nationally aggregated data sets. A better test of the model would use longitudinal data for individuals.

3.1.2. Formulating the Regression Equation

To test the two hypotheses reproduced above, Britt estimates equations in which differences in the age- and period-specific arrest rates are regressed on the age- and period-specific unemployment rates and on differences in these unemployment rates [see Eq. (10) above]. Each coefficient in the regression equation is expressed as the sum of a constant term and terms representing fixed effects for age and year. As written here, the subscripts for the regression coefficients arising from the fixed effects are omitted.

On carrying out the estimation, Britt finds no significant age dependence of the unemployment and differenced-unemployment coefficients for rape, larceny, and motor vehicle theft. For homicide and assault he finds the opportunity effect of unemployment, represented by b_1, to be negative for persons age 16 through 24 and positive for adults who are 25 or older. None of the motivational effects are significant for assault, but for homicide they are positive for ages 16–24, with the strongest effect at ages 18–19; at ages 25–34 they are negative but not significant.[17] Britt considers these homicide and assault findings to be "at odds with Greenberg's hypothesis that youth and young adults will have greater motivation to commit crimes in response to unemployment." Actually, Greenberg formulated no hypotheses about the age dependence of the opportunity effect; moreover, findings about the opportunity effect have no bearing whatsoever on the existence or nonexistence of a motivational effect, or about its strength.

---

[17]In fact, this is not exactly what Britt says about his findings. He says that the motivational effects for homicide have "a greater motivational effect on adults (25 years and older)." This statement is inconsistent with the figures in Britt's Table III. I strongly suspect that the reference to a motivational effect in this passage reflects an attention lapse while writing and base my remarks on the table, rather than the text.

Britt finds weak support for the motivational effect of unemployment on larceny being stronger for 16–17 year olds than for older people. The motivational effects of unemployment for rape, larceny, and motor vehicle theft did not vary significantly by age. For homicide, they were higher at ages 18–24 than at younger and older ages; for robbery and burglary they were higher at ages 20–24 than at earlier and older ages. Britt summarizes these findings by saying that they are generally consistent with the hypothesis that younger persons who are more likely to be excluded from the labor market will be more motivated to commit acts of theft. In contrast, the effect of unemployment on homicide and aggravated assault shows a greater motivational effect for older persons, suggestive of the possibility that adults may be faced with additional psychological pressures immediately upon being unemployed, which are not as pressing for younger individuals but lead to increased chances of homicide for adults. In fact, the homicide effects (strongest at ages 18–24) are exactly what Greenberg (1977) predicted as a consequence of masculine status anxiety.

Tests of the second hypothesis can be summarized more briefly: Britt finds no evidence that the impact of unemployment has been increasing over time. All these conclusions rest on the validity of Britt's translation of the discursive formulations of opportunity theory and motivational theory into the regression equation given in Eq. (10). In Section 2 I argue that this specification does not satisfactorily represent motivation theory; those arguments apply here as well. The equations that Britt and Smith *et al.* (1992) estimate, then, are not the equations that are appropriate for testing the theoretical ideas they wish to test. The coefficients they obtain are not measures of motivational effects or of opportunity effects.

This is not the only difficulty. It is implicit in Eq. (10) that opportunity effects are age specific. That is, the motivational contribution to the arrest rate in a given age bracket is assumed to be influenced only by unemployment levels of individuals in the same age bracket. This is as dubious theoretically as the notion that the motivational effects of unemployment are age specific (discussed earlier). Residences left unattended when a resident takes a job are easier to burglarize than residences where someone is cleaning and cooking during the day. People who are working at a job outside the home may have increased exposure to assault at the hands of strangers. These effects, however, are not expected to be age specific. Thus, if someone of a given age takes a job, leaving her apartment unattended while she is working, she is increasing her vulnerability to burglary and assault by perpetrators of all ages.

Of course, some opportunity effects of unemployment may be age specific. If teenagers are unemployed because they are attending school, they will be spending a sizable fraction of their waking hours in the company of others of roughly the same age, who are unemployed for the same reason. Their vulnerability to assault or theft at the hands of their peers may be influenced by the unemployment rate of their peers, but not so much by the unemployment rate of persons in other age brackets. Likewise, people who are working have opportunities to engage in employee theft that should be relatively uninfluenced by the unemployment rates of people in other age categories. But these possibilities do not refute my argument that for many kinds of crime, the unemployment rate in a given age bracket should affect opportunities of persons in all age brackets to commit crimes. These cross-age effects of unemployment must be taken into consideration in constructing a model. Failure to do so makes the interpretation of findings uncertain.

3.1.3. Operationalization of Variables

In testing a theory empirically, it is important that the variables be operationalized in such a way that they reasonably represent the variables in the theory. Serious discrepancies inevitably raise questions about the meaningfulness of the test. Britt justifies his use of arrests as a measure of crimes committed by citing studies that the age distribution of arrests is similar to the age distribution of offenses, However, the age categories used in some of these studies are crude (e.g., 21 and over), and so provide only a limited basis for assessing the accuracy with which the age distribution of arrests parallels that of offending behavior. In a study that Britt does not cite, Patterson and Arguer (1993) conclude on the basis of self-reports that the age distribution of arrests is not the same as the distribution of offenses.

The possibility that the probability of an arrest following the commission of a crime could be influenced by unemployment rates must also be taken seriously. Using data from the National Longitudinal Study of Youth, Glasser and Sarcerdote (1999) find that the effect of the local unemployment rate on whether the subject stole something worth less than $50, shoplifted in the last year, or had income from crime in the last year was negative but not statistically significant. The effect on whether the subject was charged with a crime or ever convicted (also negative), however, was highly significant. This result suggests the possibility that local enforcement practices are in some way influenced by the level of unemployment in a community. If this is so, a regression of arrest rates on unemployment might actually be measuring changes in enforcement practices, not changes in motivation or opportunities.

The operationalization of unemployment in all these studies is also problematic. Without discussion, Britt, like C-L and Devine *et al.*, simply takes unemployment rates produced by the U.S. Department of Labor's

Bureau of Labor Statistics as valid representations of unemployment as a theoretical variable. A closer examination of the way unemployment rates are defined demonstrates that this equivalence cannot be taken for granted.

As summarized above, in Greenberg's model, theft is a response to the strain associated with the exclusion of juveniles from the world of full-time adult work. When they get older, this strain diminishes for those young adults who are able to find full-time jobs. This claim cannot be tested adequately with unemployment rates produced by the Bureau of Labor Statistics. The Bureau of Labor Statistics derives unemployment rates from responses to the Current Population Survey of the civilian noninstitutional population that is 16 years of age or older. Respondents are counted as unemployed if they did not hold a job during a particular calendar week (Sunday through Saturday of the week that includes the 12th day of the month), "were available for work, except for temporary illness, and had made specific efforts, such as contacting employers, to find employment sometime during the 4-week period ending with the reference week," or "were waiting to be recalled to a job from which they had been laid off" even if they were not looking for a job (U.S. Department of Labor, 1997, p. 5). These criteria exclude from the ranks of the unemployed discouraged individuals who have given up looking for a job or who never sought one because they thought it unlikely that a search would be successful. Housewives and students who are not working or looking for a job because they are in school are not classified as unemployed. Part-time workers who are underemployed because they want a full-time job but cannot find one are not counted. Youths who are less than 16 years old are not counted because in most states they would be barred by law from most jobs (Nixon, 1968; U.S. Department of Labor, 1997). Individuals who are working for very low wages are also not counted. Moreover, some youth may be employed part-time at jobs that could hardly qualify as part of "the world of adult work" (e.g., babysitting, mowing lawns). From the point of view of testing the Greenberg model, many of these individuals should be counted as unemployed because they will not earn enough from their jobs to meet their subjectively defined target level of expenditures. But they are not counted by the Bureau of Labor Statistics criteria.

Many criminals hold such jobs. In the RAND study of persons arrested in Washington, DC, for selling drugs (the great majority of them being young black males), roughly two-thirds were employed at the time of their arrest, but at low-wage jobs in which the median pay was $800 a month. Narcotics trafficking supplemented this income (Reuter *et al.*, 1990). Other studies have reached similar conclusions (Greenberg, 2001). Crutchfield and Pitchford (1997) found that young adults employed in the secondary sector, where wages were low and employment irregular, had higher levels of criminal involvement than those employed in the primary sector. Workers who expected their employment to be of long duration were less likely to engage in crime. To complicate matters further, some of those counted as unemployed, along with many who are considered outside the labor market, may be working "off the books," in the so-called informal economy, or at illegal occupations, such as prostitution or drug selling (Sassen-Koob, 1989; Reuter *et al.*, 1990; Fagan, 1992, 1994, 1997; Edin and Lein, 1997, pp. 145–146, 172–178). The number of state and federal prisoners serving sentences for drug offenses—277,859 in 1997—most of them for selling (Mumola, 1999, p. 2), suggests that the number of individuals earning money illegally may be quite large.

The lack of correspondence between a theoretically relevant conception of unemployment and the definition employed by the Bureau of Labor Statistics becomes evident when one computes the correlation between the proportion of the total civilian population that is employed and the civilian unemployment rate. One might think, naively, that, by definition, the employment rate and the unemployment rate would be negatively correlated. If one drops, the other should rise correspondingly. Yet the correlation between these variables between 1950 and 1997 is a *positive* .513. This is possible because someone who is not working will not be counted as unemployed if not considered to be in the labor market. When large numbers of people are newly entering the labor market (as women have been doing in the past few decades), it is possible for the employment rate and the unemployment rate to rise simultaneously (Cook and Harkin, 1985).

Were the undercount to be uniform across age categories and years, it would make no difference that officially defined unemployment failed to coincide with exclusion from the world of full-time adult work: the two variables would be exactly proportional. However, there is no reason to think that this is so (Bowen and Finegan, 1965; Tella, 1965; Dernberg and Strand, 1966). The proportions of individuals who are defined as not in the labor force because they are in school, or keeping house, or retired surely vary by age. To use the official unemployment statistics is, therefore, to risk serious systematic bias in the analysis.

Realizing that the employment–unemployment contrast might be inadequate, Phillips *et al.* (1972) analyzed age-specific U.S. arrest rates for property offenses for the years 1952–1967 using this contrast and, also, using the contrast "in the labor force–not in the labor force." Models based on the latter contrast had quite a bit more explanatory power. Phillips *et al.* note that the labor force measure may be less transitory, as it is based on past as well as current work status. This measure merits further exploration.

3.1.4. The Level of Analysis

All the authors under discussion here use nationally aggregated data in their analyses. When one simply wants to determine whether changes in certain variables characteristic of a nation affect other variables characteristic of that nation, this procedure is unexceptional. It is more problematic, however, when adopted as a means of testing theories about individuals.[18] Criminal motivation theory is a theory about individuals, and opportunity theory, though it involves features of a community, rests on arguments about how those features affect the behavior of potential offenders, making it easier or more difficult for them to violate the law.

It has been understood for decades that relationships found in aggregated data may not hold for individuals (Robinson, 1950; Langbein and Lichtman, 1978). Evidence that arrest rates are high when unemployment is high, for example, need not imply that the unemployed have a higher rate of arrest than the employed. Conversely, a relationship found for individuals need not appear in aggregate data. Teenagers and young adults have a higher likelihood of committing homicide than those who are younger or older, yet national homicide rates for nations are not always elevated when the percentage of the population in these age brackets is high (Gartner, 1990; Gartner and Parker, 1990; Marvel and Moody, 1991; Pampel and Gartner, 1995). Males are more likely than females to commit crimes of violence, but in American cities, the sex ratio does not significantly influence the violent crime rate (Messner and Sampson, 1991). Some analyses of crime rates in SMSAs have found that the percentage of young males in the population either has a *negative* effect on crime (Crutchfield *et al.*, 1982; Messner and Blau, 1987) or fails to make a significant contribution (DeFronzo, 1983), contrary to what is found in studies of individuals. Someone who failed to find an aggregate relationship between the percentage of young people and the crime rate, and inferred that among individuals age was unrelated to crime, would reach a mistaken conclusion.

One can see why this might happen by considering the propensity to steal C_{ij} of individual i in community j as a function of his or her own wealth W_{ij} and the mean wealth of the community. We allow for the possibility that the effect of an individual's wealth might depend on the mean wealth of the jurisdiction in which he or she lives. Writing a regression equation for these

---

[18]In a private communication, Ken Land mentioned to me that his papers were not intended to test theories about individuals, only to examine the relationships among macro variables. The discussion of motivation in his papers involves reasoning about individuals. Motivation in the Cantor and Land papers is conceptualized as a characteristic of individuals. To the extent that his findings are interpreted as bearing on motivation to commit crime, they are tests of ideas about individuals.

effects, letting a bar over a variable represent its mean in jurisdiction j, and letting u represent the residual, we have

$$C_{ij} = a + b_1 W_{ij} + b_2 \bar{W}_j + b_3 W_{ij} \bar{W}_j + u_{ij} \tag{11}$$

Summing over individuals in each jurisdiction and dividing by the number of individuals in each jurisdiction gives us

$$\bar{C}_j = a + b_1 \bar{W}_j + b_2 \bar{W}_j + b_3 W_j^2 + \bar{u}_j = a + (b_1 + b_2)\bar{W}_j + b_3 W_j^2 + \bar{u}_j \tag{12}$$

With aggregate data alone, the individual coefficients b_1 and b_2 are not identified (only their sum is), and the interaction term in Eq. (11) cannot be distinguished from a quadratic contextual variable. As a result of these limitations, aggregate data alone cannot distinguish between the effect of an individual's unemployment on his or her own criminal behavior and that of the unemployment rate in the community. Moreover, nonlinear terms, product terms, and ratios do not aggregate in any simple way. That is, if an equation for individuals involves terms such as X_{ij}^2, $X_{ij} Y_{ij}$, and X_{ij}/Y_{ij}, aggregation to the level of the jurisdiction will not, in general, lead to an equation with corresponding terms involving the powers, products, or ratios of the averaged variables in each jurisdiction (Greenberg and Kessler, 1981). This has immediate implications for analyses of crime rates and unemployment rates, each of which is defined as a ratio.

It follows that when one wants to test a theory formulated for individuals, it is preferable to obtain data for individuals, not just data for aggregates. Social scientists have sometimes avoided doing so because it is difficult, but also because they have been misled by Durkheim's (1951) fallacious argument that a rate characteristic of a jurisdiction is a collective phenomenon that cannot be explained by the individual characteristics of the people living in that jurisdiction. A rate is computed by adding up the contributions of individuals. Those contributions may, of course, be affected by characteristics of the aggregate. It is possible to work with individual data and yet incorporate contextual effects into one's model, as is done in Eq. (11). Thus, methodological individualism need not imply a rejection of the sociological axiom that the collective properties of the groups in which people live are consequential.

When contextual effects are considered, it will often be the case that the relevant context is something smaller than the nation. In studying the opportunity effects of unemployment, for example, it is likely to be the local unemployment rate that is relevant; few prospective criminals will be enabled to commit crimes by opportunities arising from changes in unemployment in distant regions. Nor need the collection of individual data imply that individual behaviors are statistically independent of one another. With appropriate data, one could take into account the influence that respondents (e.g., best friends or fellow gang members) have on one another's activities.

Whether an individual-level model explains variation among aggregate units, such as SMSAs, states, or nations, is a question separate from the validity of the model. A theory about individuals might be correct in the sense that every assertion it makes about the effects of variables in the theory is valid, but it might be incomplete, failing to incorporate additional variables or effects that are also important. It might, for this reason, fail to explain aggregate-level variation fully. When one wants to see whether an individual-level equation accounts for aggregate differences, one must first estimate the individual-level equation, use it to generate predictions for the dependent variable that can be aggregated, and then compare the predictions for the aggregate with the reality. This is not the same as estimating a regression equation with the aggregated variables.

Another disadvantage to the use of aggregate data in criminological analyses concerns the distinction between rates of participation (whether someone violates the law) and frequency of violation on the part of the violators (Blumstein *et al.*, 1986, p. 55, 1988). The number of crimes committed is the product of the number of violators and the mean frequency at which they violate the law. The two can vary independently. When analyzing aggregate crime rates it is possible to study only the product. With individual data it is possible, at least in principle, to study both.

A second issue is not inherent in the use of aggregate data but is frequently characteristic of it: information about the mechanisms by which independent variables bring about their outcome is often lacking. C-L noted that they did not have direct information about criminal motivation and opportunities. Their analyses, like those by Devine *et al.* and Britt, make assumptions about the effects of unemployment on individual behavior yet cite no evidence to support these assumptions. Is it true that unemployment increases the time people spend at home? Studies of individuals have the potential for collecting this sort of information.

3.1.5. The Time Span of the Study

To determine whether there is a trend in the effect of unemployment on crime, as hypothesized in H2, it would be necessary to examine the relevant time period. Greenberg's discussion does not make the ahistorical claim that there is a general tendency for unemployment to influence crime more and more strongly as one decade follows another until the end of time. He claims that specific, historically located developments have had that effect. In arguing that the exclusion of juveniles from the world of adult work is of greater importance now than in the past, Greenberg called attention to the particular importance of child labor laws and mandatory school attendance legislation adopted during the first few decades of the twentieth century, as well as post-World War II affluence, with its culture of consumerism, and marketing targeted to adolescents (Greenberger and Steinberg, 1986). All these developments were in place by 1958, the first year in Britt's time series. Outside the South, for example, high school enrollment rates and graduation rates rose rapidly between 1910 and 1940, then leveled off (Goldin, 1998; Goldin and Katz, 1998). To study the effect of these developments it would be necessary to start the time series much earlier.

To be sure, college attendance rose substantially during the years of Britt's study, but one would not expect this trend to have the same consequences for the crime rate as the earlier increase in high school attendance, some of which was required by state law. Many college students work or are supported by parents, scholarships, and loans. Almost all are in college because of its immediate and long-term rewards. Historically, this has not been as true of high school attendance.

In explaining the historical trend toward a greater concentration of criminality in the youthful years, Greenberg notes that exclusion of juveniles from the world of adult work had been going on gradually for a long period of time—perhaps a century—and therefore might plausibly be explained not merely as the result of child labor and mandatory school attendance laws but, rather, as a consequence of a capitalist economy's failure to generate sufficient employment to put youth and adults to work. Recent research allows us to flesh out this sketchy explanation. Compulsory school attendance legislation, combined with child labor laws, did increase school attendance at the start of the twentieth century (Margo and Finegan, 1996). Child labor dropped very substantially over a period of several decades, starting around 1870 or 1880 (Carter and Sutch, 1996), though only in part because of legislation or a weakening demand for labor. Silberman (1965) charts the declining labor force participation of teenagers in the first half of this century, noting that by far the largest component of the drop occurred for farm workers. The decline of the family farm, accompanied by migration to the city, eliminated their jobs. In addition, as parents' incomes rose, they increased their investment in their children's future by educating them for longer periods, in the process, deferring their entrance into the labor market.

Though in recent decades the American economy has endured large numbers of plant closings and downsizings (Sordius *et al.*, 1981), resulting in the loss of millions of jobs, unemployment rates have not trended upward because an even larger number of new jobs has been created. Many of the new jobs, however, are in the service sector, teach few skills, pay badly, are repetitive and boring, carry few or no benefits or opportunities for advancement, and offer only irregular employment (Bluestone and Harrison, 1982;

Kasarda, 1988, 1989, 1990, 1992; Burtless, 1990; Reubens *et al.*, 1981; Taylor, 1997). The proportion of students working at such jobs has increased in recent decades: in the 1950s, about 5% of high school students worked after school; in the 1990s, this figure increased to about 25%. Possibly in response to the increased supply of teenage workers, teen wages have fallen relative to adult wages. There is also evidence that employers have substituted young workers for older ones in response to the wage differential (Kalachek, 1969; Hills and Reubens, 1983; Greenberger and Steinberg, 1986, pp. 65–68; Rothman, 1992). According to one observer, the youths taking these jobs are largely "media-savvy teenagers hungry for designer clothes and cellular phones, or saving for the rising costs of college" (Thomas, 1998).

Black males are the one exception to the upward trend in high school students holding part-time jobs; for them the trend has been downward. Greenberg noted that the trend in labor force participation had been different for black and white youths: black teenage labor market participation dropped dramatically between 1950 and 1973, while for white teenagers it remained stable. After noting this difference, Greenberg did not comment further on it. This article provides an occasion for doing so. For the years 1958–1995 (the time spanned by Britt's data), black male labor force participation rates continued to decline for 16–19 year olds, while for white males they *rose*. This racial difference in employment trends calls for an explanation (Adams and Mangum, 1978) that goes beyond Greenberg's off-hand reference to the "disaccumulationist" phase of the capitalist mode of production. Developments such as the loss of manufacturing jobs to low-wage foreign countries, cuts in public sector employment, increases in the minimum wage, skill deficits among youth educated in center-city public schools, spatial mismatch between jobs and potential workers, and the high incomes now available to youths selling illegal narcotics must figure in such an explanation (Goodman and Dolan, 1979, pp. 170–171; Wilson, 1987; Hagedorn, 1988; Hughes, 1989; Fagan, 1992, 1997; Fernandez, 1992; Kasarda, 1992; Peterson and Vroman, 1992; Hagan, 1997; Taylor, 1997).

With employment trends differing for black and whites youths, it is essential that a statistical analysis examine crime trends separately for blacks and whites, lest important effects be washed out in the mix. That the increases in homicide rates in the late eighties were larger for black males than for white males (Blumstein and Rosenfeld, 1998) may be related to the racial differences in employment trends. Presumably it is because of their more limited legitimate labor market prospects that black males were disproportionately drawn into street-level crack distribution, where unregulated competition has been accompanied by high levels of violent crime

(Fagan and Chin, 1990; Blumstein, 1995; Cook and Laub, 1998; Grogger and Willis, 1998).

4. CONCLUSION

I have identified numerous difficulties in the attempts to study the impact of unemployment on crime rates by analyzing nationally aggregated data. The regression equations in these efforts do not adequately represent the theoretical ideas they are designed to test, and the variables in the theory are not adequately represented by those available in official unemployment statistics. Nationally aggregated data are less than ideal when estimating relationships posited by theory to hold for individuals. For this reason, it is doubtful that much confidence can be placed in the conclusions reached in the studies discussed here.

The issues raised in this discussion transcend the handful of studies I reviewed. Recent advances in the econometric analysis of nonstationary time series suggest that many—perhaps most—sociological analyses of crime rate time series (and, very likely, other kinds of rates as well) suffer from serious methodological deficiencies. The methods they have used fail to reveal long-run tendencies or rely on misspecified models and improper estimation procedures. The cointegration revolution provides a solution to these difficulties. Researchers making use of this solution will still have to grapple with the other issues raised here, such as the operationalization of variables, the translation of ideas into mathematical representations, and the limitations of aggregate data for purposes of testing theories about individuals. Some of these difficulties may be harder to solve than the purely statistical problems posed by nonstationarity.

ACKNOWLEDGMENTS

I am grateful for Chris Hale and Robert Yaffee for helpful comments, to Thomas Marvell for furnishing data, to Nitsan Chorev for assistance in data collection, and to Susan Carlson for statistical advice.

REFERENCES

Adams, A. V., and Mangum, G. L. (1978). *The Lingering Crisis of Youth Unemployment*, W. E. Upjohn Institute for Employment Research, Kalamazoo, MI.
Banerjee, A., Dolado, J. J., Galbraith, J. W., and Hendry, D. F. (1993). *Co-Integration, Error Correction, and the Econometric Analysis of Non-Stationary Data*, Oxford University Press, New York.
Bluestone, B., and Harrison, B. (1982). *The Deindustrializing of America: Plant Closings, Community Abandonment, and the Dismantling of Basic Industry*, Basic, New York.

Blumstein, A. (1995). Youth violence, guns, and the illicit-drug industry. *J. Crim. Law Criminol.* 86: 10–36.

Blumstein, A., and Rosenfeld, R. (1998). Explaining recent trends in U.S. homicide rates. *J. Crim. Law Criminol.* 88: 1175–1216.

Blumstein, A., Cohen, J., Roth, J. A., and Visher, C. A. (eds.) (1986). *Criminal Careers and "Career Criminals,"* National Academy Press, Washington, DC.

Blumstein, A., Cohen, J., and Farrington, D. P. (1988). Criminal career research: Its value for criminology. *Criminology* 26: 1–35.

Bowen, W. G., and Finegan, T. A. (1965). Labor force participation and unemployment. In Ross, A. M. (ed.), *Employment Policy and the Labor Market*, University of California Press, Berkeley, pp. 115–161.

Britt, C. L. (1994). Crime and unemployment among youths in the United States, 1958–1990. *Am. J. Econ. Sociol.* 53: 99–109.

Britt, C. L. (1997). Reconsidering the unemployment and crime relationship: Variation by age group and historical period. *J. Quant. Criminol.* 13: 405–417.

Burtless, G. (ed.) (1990). *A Future of Lousy Jobs? The Changing Structure of U.S. Wages*, Brookings Institution, Washington, DC.

Butts, J. A. (2000). *Youth Crime Drop*, Urban Institute Justice Policy Center, Washington, DC.

Cantor, D., and Land, K. C. (1985). Unemployment and crime rates in the post-World War II United States: A theoretical and empirical analysis. *Am. Sociol. Rev.* 50: 317–332.

Cantor, D., and Land, K. C. (1987). Unemployment and crime rates: A bivariate seasonal ARIMA analysis of monthly data, 1969–1985. Unpublished paper.

Carter, S., and Sutch, R. (1996). Fixing the facts: Editing of the 1880 U.S. census of occupations with implications for long-term labor force trends and the sociology of official statistics. *Hist. Methods* 29: 5–24.

Charemza, W. W., and Deadman, D. F. (1997). *New Directions in Econometric Practice: General to Specific Modelling, Cointegration and Vector Autoregression*, Edward Elgar, Lyme, MA.

Conley, D. (1999). *Being Black: Living in the Red: Race, Wealth, and Social Policy in America*, University of California Press, Berkeley.

Cook, P. J., and Harkin, G. A. (1985). Crime and the business cycle. *J. Legal Stud.* 14: 115–28.

Cook, P. J., and Laub, J. H. (1998). The unprecedented epidemic in youth violence. In Tonry, M., and Moore, M. H. (eds.), *Youth Violence. Crime and Justice: A Review of Research*, Vol. 15. University of Chicago Press, Chicago, pp. 27–64.

Crutchfield, R. D., and Pitchford, S. R. (1997). Work and crime: The effects of labor stratification. *Social Forces* 76: 93–118.

Crutchfield, R. D., Geerken, M., and Gove, W. R. (1992). Crime rate and social integration: The impact of metropolitan mobility. *Criminology* 20: 467–478.

DeFronzo, J. (1983). Economic assistance to impoverished Americans: Relationship to incidence of crime. *Criminology* 21: 119–136.

Dernberg, T., and Strand, K. (1966). Hidden unemployment 1953–1962: A quantitative analysis by age and sex. *Am. Econ. Rev.* 55: 71–95.

Devine, J. A., Sheley, J. F., and Smith, M. D. (1988). Macroeconomic and social-control policy influences on crime rate changes, 1948–1985. *Am. Sociol. Rev.* 53: 407–420.

Durkheim, E. (1951). *Suicide* (G. Simpson, trans.), Free Press, New York.

Edin, K., and Lein, L. (1997). *Making Ends Meet: How Single Mothers Survive Welfare and Low-Wage Work*. Russell Sage Foundation, New York.

Engle, R. F., and Granger, C. W. J. (1987). Cointegration and error correction: Representation, estimation and testing. *Econometrica* 55: 251–276.

Executive Office of the President (1997). *Economic Report of the President*, US Government Printing Office, Washington, DC.

Fagan, J. (1992). Drug selling and licit income in distressed neighborhoods: The economic lives of street-level drug users and dealers. In Harrell, A. V., and Peterson, G. E. (eds.), *Drugs, Crime and Social Isolation*, Urban Institute Press, Washington, DC, pp. 99–146.

Fagan, J. (1994). Women and drugs revisited: Female participation in the cocaine economy. *J. Drug Issues* 24: 179–226.

Fagan, J. (1997). Legal and illegal work: Crime, work, and unemployment. In Weisbrod, B. A. and Worthy, J. C. (eds.), *The Urban Crisis: Linking Research to Action*. Northwestern University Press, Evanston, IL, pp. 33–80.

Fagan, J., and Chin, K. L. (1990). Violence as regulation and social control in the distribution of crack. In de la Rosa, M., Gropper, B., and Lambert, E. (eds.), *Drugs and Violence*, National Institute on Drug Abuse Research Monograph No. 103, U.S. Public Health Administration, Rockville, MD, pp. 8–39.

Fernandez, R. M. (1997). Spatial mismatch: Housing, transportation, and employment in regional perspective. In Weisbrod, B. A., and Worthy, J. C. (eds.), *The Urban Crisis: Linking Research to Action*. Northwestern University Press, Evanston, IL, pp. 81–99.

Gartner, R. (1990). The victims of homicide: A temporal and cross-national comparison. *Am. Sociol. Rev.* 55: 92–106.

Gartner, R., and Parker, R. N. (1990). Cross-national evidence on homicide and the age structure of the population. *Social Forces* 69: 351–371.

Glasser, E. L., and Sacerdote, B. (1996). Why is there more crime in cities? *J. Polit. Econ. Suppl. S* 107: S225–S258.

Goldin, C. (1998). America's graduation from high school: The evolution and spread of secondary schooling in the twentieth century. *J. Econ. Hist.* 58: 345–374.

Goldin, C., and Katz, L. (1998). Human capital and social capital: The rise of secondary schooling in America, 1910 to 1940. *J. Interdisc. Hist.* 29: 683–723.

Goodman, J. C., and Dolan, E. G. (1979). *Economics of Public Policy*, West, Minneapolis, MN.

Granger, M. C. W. J., and Newbold, P. (1974). Spurious regressions in econometrics. *J. Economet.* 2: 111–120.

Greenberg, D. F. (1977). Delinquency and the age structure of society. *Contemp. Crisis* 1: 189-223.

Greenberg, D. F. (1985). Age, crime, and social explanation. *Am. J. Sociol.* 91: 1–21.

Greenberg, D. F. (2001). Novus ordo saeclorum? *Punish. Soc.* 3: 81–93.

Greenberg, D. F., and Kessler, R. C. (1981). Aggregation bias in deterrence research: An empirical analysis. *J. Res. Crime Delinq.* 18: 128–137.

Greenberger, E., and Steinberg, L. D. (1986). *When Teenagers Work: The Psychological and Social Costs of Adolescent Employment*, Basic Books, New York.

Greene, W. H. (1997). *Econometric Analysis*, Prentice–Hall, Upper Saddle River, NJ.

Grogger, J., and Willis, M. (1998). The introduction of crack cocaine and the rise in urban crime rates. Working Paper 6353, National Bureau of Economic Research, Cambridge, MA.

Hagan, J. (1997). Crime and capitalization: Toward a developmental theory of street crime in America. In Weisbrod, B. A., and Worthy, J. C. (eds.), *The Urban Crisis: Linking Research to Action*, Northwestern University Press, Evanston, IL, pp. 287–308.

Hagedorn, J. M., with Macon, P. (1988). *People and Folks: Gangs, Crime, and the Underclass in a Rustbelt City*, Lake View, Chicago.

Hagedorn, J. M. (1994). Homeboys, dope fiends, legits, and new jacks. *Criminology* 32: 197–220.

Hale, C. (1991). Unemployment and crime: Differencing is no substitute for modeling. *J. Res. Crime Delinq.* 28: 426–429.

Hale, C., and Sabbagh, D. (1991). Testing the relationship between unemployment and crime: A methodological comment and empirical analysis using time series data from England and Wales. *J. Res. Crime Delinq.* 28: 400–417.

Harris, R. I. D. (1995). *Using Cointegration Analysis in Econometric Modeling*, Prentice–Hall, New York.

Hills, S. M., and Reubens, B. G. (1983). Youth employment in the United States. In Reubens, B. G. (ed.), *Youth at Work: An International Survey*, Roman and Allanheld, Totowa, NJ, pp. 269–318.

Holden, D., and Perman, R. (1994). "Unit roots and cointegration for the economist." In Rao, B. B. (ed.), *Cointegration for the Applied Economist*, St. Martin's, New York, pp. 47–112.

Hughes, M. A. (1989). Misspeaking truth to power: A geographical perspective on the "underclass" fallacy. *Econ. Geogr.* 65: 187–207.

Johnston, J., and DiNardo, J. (1997). *Econometric Methods*, 4th ed., McGraw-Hill, New York.

Kalachek, E. (1969). *The Youth Labor Market*, Policy Papers in Human Resources and Industrial Relations No. 12, Institute of Labor and Industrial Relations, University of Michigan–Wayne State University, Ann Arbor.

Kapuscinski, C. A., Braithwaite, J., and Chapman, B. (1998). Unemployment and crime: Toward resolving the paradox. *J. Quant. Criminol.* 14: 215–244.

Kasarda, J. D. (1988). Jobs, migration and emerging urban mismatches. In McGeary, M. G. H., and Lynn, L. E., Jr. (eds.), *Urban Change and Poverty*, National Academy Press, Washington, DC, pp. 148–198.

Kasarda, J. D. (1989). Urban industrial transition and the underclass. *Ann. Am. Acad. Polit.-Soc. Sci.* 501: 26–47.

Kasarda, J. D. (1990). Structural factors affecting the location and timing of urban underclass growth. *Urban Geogr.* 11: 234–264.

Kasarda, J. D. (1992). The severely distressed in economically transforming cities. In Harrell, A. V., and Peterson, G. E. (eds.), *Drugs, Crime, and Social Isolation: Barriers to Urban Opportunity*, Urban Institute Press, Washington, DC, pp. 45–97.

LaFree, G. (1998). *Losing Legitimacy: Street Crime and the Decline of Social Institutions in America*, Westview, Boulder, CO.

Land, K. C., Cantor, D., and Russell, S. T. (1995). Unemployment and crime rate fluctuations in the post-World War II United States: Statistical time series properties and alternative models. In Hagan, J., and Peterson, R. D. (eds.), *Crime and Inequality*, Stanford University Press, Stanford, CA, pp. 55–79.

Langbein, L. A., and Lichtman, A. J. (1978). *Ecological Inference*, Sage, Beverly Hills, CA.

Margo, R. A., and Finegan, T. A. (1996). Compulsory schooling legislation and school attendance in turn-of-the-century America: A "natural experiment" approach. *Econ. Lett.* 53: 103–110.

Marvell, T. B., and Moody, C. E., Jr. (1991). Age structure and crime rates: The conflicting evidence. *J. Quant. Criminol.* 7: 237–273.

McCarthy, B., and Hagan, J. (1992). Mean streets: The theoretical significance of situational delinquency among homeless youth. *Am. J. Sociol.* 98: 597–627.

Messner, S. F., and Blau, J. R. (1987). Routine leisure activities and rates of crime: A macro-level analysis. *Social Forces* 65: 1035–1052.

Messner, S. F., and Sampson, R. J. (1991). The sex ratio, family disruption, and rates of violent crime: The paradox of demographic structure. *Social Forces* 69: 693–713.

Mumola, C. (1999). *Substance Abuse and Treatment, State and Federal Prisoners, 1997*, Bureau of Justice Statistics, U.S. Department of Justice, Washington, DC.

Myers, S. L., Jr. (1992). Crime, entrepreneurship, and labor force withdrawal. *Contemp. Policy Issues* 10: 84–97.

Nakosteen, R. A., and Zimmer, M. A. (1989). Minimum wages and labor market prospects of women. *South. Econ. J.* 56: 302–314.

Nixon, R. A. (1968). An appreciative and critical look at official unemployment data. In Herman, M., Sadofsky, S., and Rosenberg, B. (eds.), *Work, Youth, and Unemployment*, Thomas Y. Crowell, New York, pp. 29–43.

Pampel, F. C., and Gartner, R. (1995). Age structure, socio-political institutions, and national homicide rates. *Eur. Soc. Rev.* 11: 243–260.

Peterson, G. E., and Vroman, W. (1992). *Urban Labor Markets and Labor Mobility*, Urban Institute, Washington, DC.

Phillips, L., Votey, H. L., and Maxwell, D. (1972). Crime, youth, and the labor market. *J. Pol. Econ.* 80: 491–504.

Phillips, P. C. B. (1986). Understanding spurious regressions in econometrics. *J. Econometr.* 33: 311–340.

Pyle, D. J., and Deadman, D. F. (1994). Crime and the business cycle in post-war Britain. *Br. J. Criminol.* 34: 339–357.s

Raphael, S., and Winter-Ebmer, R. (2001). Identifying the effect of unemployment on crime. *J. Law Econ.* (in press).

Reubens, B. G., Harrison, J. A. C., and Rupp, K. (1981). *The Youth Labor Force 1945–1995: A Cross-National Analysis*, Allenheld, Osmun, Totowa, NJ.

Reuter, P., MacCoun, R., and Murphy, P. (1990). Money from Crime: A Study of the Economics of Drug-Dealing in Washington, DC., Report R-3894, Rand, Santa Monica, CA.

Robinson, W. S. (1950). Ecological correlations and behavior of individuals. *Am. Sociol. Rev.* 15: 351–357.

Rothman, R. A. (1992). Working youths in the United States. In Warme, B. D., Lundy, K. L. P., and Lundy, L. A. (eds.), *Working Part-Time: Risks and Opportunities*, Praeger, New York, pp. 119–130.

Ruhm, C. J. (1995). Economic conditions and alcohol problems. *J. Health Econ.* 14: 583–603.

Ruhm, C. J. (1999). Are recessions good for your health? Unpublished paper.

Sassen-Koob, S. (1989). New York City's informal economy. In Portes, A., Castells, M., and Benton, L. A. (eds.), *The Informal Economy: Studies in Advanced and Less Developed Countries*, Johns Hopkins University Press, Baltimore, pp. 60–77.

Silberman, C. E. (1965). What hit the teenagers? *Fortune* April: 130–134, 228–230, 232, 234.

Smith, M. D., Devine, J. A., and Sheley, J. F. (1992). Crime and unemployment: Effects across age and race categories. *Sociol. Perspect.* 35: 551–572.

Sordius, J. P., Jarle, P., and Ferman, L. A. (1981). *Plant Closings and Economic Dislocation*, W. E. Upjohn Institute for Employment Research, Kalamazoo, MI.

Taylor, I. (1997). The political economy of crime. In Maguire, M., Morgan, R., and Reiner, R. (eds.). *The Oxford Handbook of Criminology*, Clarendon Press, Oxford, pp. 265–303.

Tella, A. (1965). The relation of labor force to employment. *Industr. Lab. Rel Rev.* April: 76.

Thomas, J. (1996). Experts take a 2d look at virtue of student jobs. *New York Times* May 13: A16.

U.S. Department of Labor (1997). *Bureau of Labor Statistics Handbook of Methods*, U.S. Government Printing Office, Washington, DC.

Wilson, W. J. (1987). *The Truly Disadvantaged*, University of Chicago Press, Chicago.

Wolff, E. N. (2001). Recent trends in wealth ownership, 1983–1998. In Shapiro, T. M., and Wolff, E. N. (eds.), *Assets and the Disadvantaged: The Benefits of Spreading Asset Ownership*, Russell Sage Foundation, New York (in press).

[23]

Poisson-Based Regression Analysis of Aggregate Crime Rates

D. Wayne Osgood[1]

This article introduces the use of regression models based on the Poisson distribution as a tool for resolving common problems in analyzing aggregate crime rates. When the population size of an aggregate unit is small relative to the offense rate, crime rates must be computed from a small number of offenses. Such data are ill-suited to least-squares analysis. Poisson-based regression models of counts of offenses are preferable because they are built on assumptions about error distributions that are consistent with the nature of event counts. A simple elaboration transforms the Poisson model of offense counts to a model of per capita offense rates. To demonstrate the use and advantages of this method, this article presents analyses of juvenile arrest rates for robbery in 264 nonmetropolitan counties in four states. The negative binomial variant of Poisson regression effectively resolved difficulties that arise in ordinary least-squares analyses.

KEY WORDS: Poisson; negative binomial; crime rates; aggregate analysis.

1. INTRODUCTION

The purpose of this paper is to introduce a statistical approach to analyzing aggregate crime rates that solves problems arising from small populations and low base-rates. In aggregate analyses, the units of the sample are aggregations of individuals, such as neighborhoods, cities, and schools, and the researcher is interested in explaining variation in crime rates across those units. These crimes rates are defined as the number of crime events (e.g., arrests, victimizations, crimes known to the police) divided by the population size, often reported as crimes per 100,000.

The standard approach to analyzing per capita rates such as these is to use the computed rates for each aggregate unit (or a transformed version of them) as the dependent variable in an ordinary least-squares (OLS) regression. For reasons discussed below, this least-squares approach is inappropriate when rates for many of the units must be computed from small

[1]Crime, Law and Justice Program, Department of Sociology, 201 Oswald Tower, Pennsylvania State University, University Park, Pennsylvania 16802. e-mail: wosgood@psu.edu.

numbers of events. The present paper demonstrates how to resolve this problem through Poisson-based regression models that are well suited to such data. The statistical basis of this analytic approach is well established (e.g., Cameron and Trevedi, 1998; Gardner *et al.*, 1995; King, 1989; Liao, 1994; McCullagh and Nelder, 1989; Land *et al.*, 1996). In criminology, Poisson-based regression models have become common in analyses of criminal careers (Greenberg, 1991; Land *et al.*, 1996; Nagin and Land, 1993; Rowe *et al.*, 1990), but they have rarely been applied to aggregate analysis of crime or other social phenomena (for examples see Bailey *et al.*, 1994; Sampson *et al.*, 1997). In the hope of making these techniques accessible to a broader range of researchers, the present article is devoted to articulating the special advantages of these models for solving problems in analyzing aggregate data.

1.1. The Problem

Because arrests are discrete events, the possible crime rates for any given population size are those corresponding to integer counts of crimes. For instance, in a county of 200,000 individuals, every additional crime increases the crime rate by half an arrest per 100,000, while in a neighborhood of 5000 each crime corresponds to 20 crimes per 100,000. If the population sizes of the aggregate units are large relative to the average arrest rate, then the calculated rates will be sufficiently fine-grained that there is no harm in treating them as though they were continuous and applying least squares statistics. For almost any measure of offending, populations of several hundred thousand should prove adequate in this regard. When populations are small relative to offense rates, however, the discrete nature of the crime counts cannot be ignored. Indeed, for a population of a few thousand, even a single arrest for rape or homicide might correspond to a high crime rate. Low counts of crimes are common for offense-specific analyses, samples of small towns and rural areas, and analyses of subpopulations, such as females versus males or specific age categories.

Crime rates based on small counts of crimes present two serious problems for least squares analysis. First, because the precision of the estimated crime rate depends on population size, variation in population sizes across the aggregate units will lead to violating the assumption of homogeneity of error variance. We must expect larger errors of prediction for per capita crime rates based on small populations than for rates based on large populations. Second, normal or even symmetrical error distributions of crime rates cannot be assumed when crime counts are small. The lowest possible crime count is zero, so the error distribution must become increasingly skewed (as well as more decidedly discrete) as crime rates approach this lower bound. As populations decrease, an offense rate of zero will be observed for a larger and larger proportion of cases. Thus, there is an effective censoring at zero that is dependent on sample size, which has considerable potential for biasing the resulting regression coefficients.

The standard solution to the problems of low offense counts has been to increase the level of aggregation, such as analyzing only large cities or combining specific offenses into broad indices. For instance, one rarely see analyses of homicide for populations less than several hundred thousand. Not only does this strategy preclude analyses about many interesting questions, it leads to coarser measurement of important explanatory variables, such as being forced to assume that a single poverty rate applies equally well to all neighborhoods in a city. Fortunately, there is an alternative data analytic approach that resolves these problems.

2. THE POISSON REGRESSION MODEL

The Poisson distribution has been useful for many problems in criminology and criminal justice. Indeed, Poisson originally derived the distribution for analyzing rates of conviction in France during the 1820s (see Maltz, 1994). Maltz (1994) reviews many uses of the Poisson distribution for modeling phenomena related to crime, such as assessing the potential for selective incapacitation, projecting prison populations, and estimating the size of the criminal population. The present paper focuses specifically on Poisson-based regression models, which relate explanatory variables to dependent variables that are counts of events. These models can solve the problems described above because they allow us to recognize the dependence of crime rates on *counts* of crimes. Several good, nontechnical descriptions of Poisson regression are now available (e.g., Gardner *et al.*, 1995; Liao, 1994; Land *et al.*, 1996), so my description of these models is brief, emphasizing the features most relevant to aggregate analysis.

The Poisson distribution characterizes the probability of observing any discrete number of events (i.e., $0, 1, 2, \ldots$), given an underlying mean count or rate of events, assuming that the timing of the events is random and independent. For instance, the Poisson distribution for a mean count of 4.5 would describe the proportion of times that we should expect to observe any specific count of robberies $(0, 1, 2, \ldots)$ in a neighborhood, if the "true" (and unchanging) annual rate for neighborhood were 4.5, if the occurrence of one robbery had no impact on the likelihood of the next, and if we had an unlimited number of years to observe. Figure 1 shows the Poisson distribution for four mean counts of arrests. When the mean arrest count is low, as is likely for a small population, the Poisson distribution is skewed,

with only a small range of counts having a meaningful probability of occurrence. As the mean count grows, the Poisson distribution increasingly
approximates the normal. The Poisson distribution has a variance equal to
the mean count. Therefore, as the mean count increases, the probability of
observing any specific number of events declines and a broader range of
values have meaningful probabilities of being observed.

Our interest is in per capita crime rates rather than in counts of offenses, and Fig. 2 demonstrates the correspondence between rates and counts.
Figure 2 translates the Poisson distributions of crime counts in Fig. 1 to
distributions of crime rates. Given a constant underlying mean rate of 500
crimes per 100,000 population, population sizes of 200, 600, 2000, and
10,000 would produce the mean crime counts of 1, 3, 10, and 50 used in
Fig. 1. For the population of 200, only a very limited number of crime rates
are probable (i.e., increments of 500 per 100,000), but those probable rates
comprise an enormous range. As the population base increases, the range
of likely *crime rates* decreases, even though the range of likely *crime counts*
increases. The standard deviation around the mean rate shrinks from 500
crimes per 100,000 for a population of 200 to 71 crimes per 100,000 for a
population of 10,000. Thus, Fig. 2 illustrates the effect of population size
on the accuracy of estimated crime rates.

The basic Poisson regression model is

$$\ln(\lambda_i) = \sum_{k=0}^{K} \beta_k x_{ik} \tag{1}$$

$$P(Y_i = y_i) = \frac{e^{-\lambda_i} \lambda_i^{y_i}}{y_i!} \tag{2}$$

Equation (1) is a regression equation relating the natural logarithm of the
mean or expected number of events for case i, $\ln(\lambda_i)$, to the sum of the
products of each explanatory variable, x_{ik}, multiplied by a regression coefficient, β_k (where β_0 is a constant multiplied by 1 for each case). Equation
(2) indicates that the probability of y_i, the observed outcome for this case,
follows the Poisson distribution (the right-hand side of the equation) for the
mean count from Eq. (1), λ_i. Thus, the expected distribution of crime
counts, and corresponding distribution of regression residuals, depends on
the fitted mean count, λ_i, as illustrated in Fig. 1. The role of the natural
logarithm in Eq. (1) is comparable to the logarithmic transformation of the
dependent variable that is common in analysis of aggregate crime rates. In
both cases, the regression coefficients reflect proportional differences in
rates. Liao (1994) provides a detailed discussion of the interpretation of
regression coefficients from Poisson-based models.

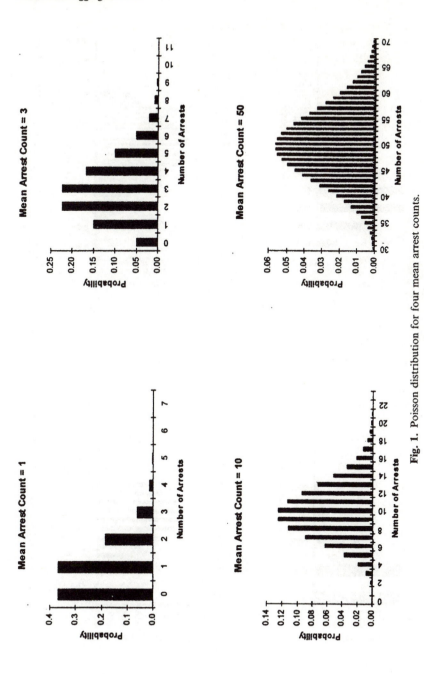

Fig. 1. Poisson distribution for four mean arrest counts.

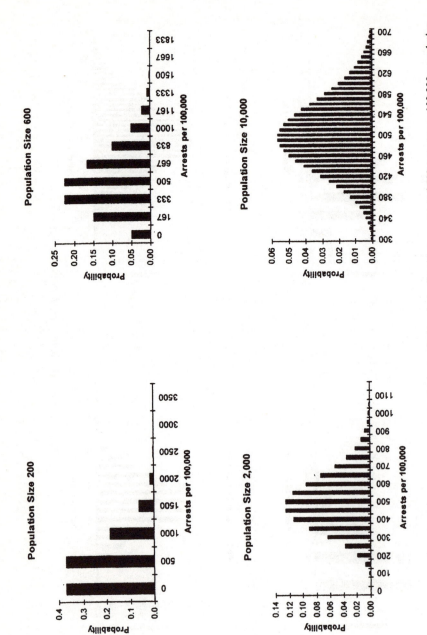

Fig. 2. Poisson distribution of arrest rates for four population sizes, given a mean rate of 500 arrests per 100,000 population.

Next we must alter the basic Poisson regression model so that it provides an analysis of per capita crime rates rather than counts of crimes. If λ_i is the expected number of crimes in a given aggregate unit, then λ_i/n_i would be the corresponding per capita crime rate, where n_i is the population size for that unit. With a bit of algebra, we can derive a variation of Eq. (1) that is a model of per capita crime rates:

$$\ln\left(\frac{\lambda_i}{n_i}\right) = \sum_{k=1}^{k} \beta_k x_{ik}$$

$$\ln(\lambda_i) = \ln(n_i) + \sum_{k=0}^{K} \beta_k x_{ik} \tag{3}$$

Thus, by adding the natural logarithm of the size of the population at risk to the regression model of Eq. (1), and by giving that variable a fixed coefficient of one, Poisson regression becomes an analysis of rates of events per capita, rather than an analysis of counts of events. The same strategy can be used to standardize event count models for other sources of variation across cases, such as the length of the period of observation. Accordingly, computer programs for Poisson regression routinely incorporate this feature.

A Poisson-based regression model that is standardized for the size of the population at risk acknowledges the greater precision of rates based on larger populations, thus addressing the problem of heterogeneity of error variance discussed above. This becomes apparent when we translate the known variance of the Poisson distribution to a standard deviation for the corresponding crime rates. Because the variance of the Poisson distribution is the mean count, λ, its standard deviation will be $SD_\lambda = \sqrt{\lambda}$. The mean count of crimes, in turn, equals the underlying per capita crime rate, C, times the size of the population: $\lambda = Cn$. When a variable is divided by a constant, its standard deviation is also divided by that constant. Therefore, it follows that the standard deviation of a crime rate, computed from a population of size n, will be

$$SD_C = \frac{\sqrt{\lambda}}{n} = \frac{\sqrt{Cn}}{n} = \frac{\sqrt{C}\sqrt{n}}{n} = \frac{\sqrt{C}}{\sqrt{n}}$$

This equation shows that, in the expected distribution of observed crime rates around the fitted mean crime rates produced by Eq. (3), the standard deviation is inversely proportional to the square root of the population size. Thus, Poisson regression analysis explicitly addresses the heterogeneous residual variance that presented a problem for OLS regression analysis of crime rates.

2.1. Overdispersion and Variations on the Basic Poisson Regression Model

The basic Poisson regression model is appropriate only if the probability model of Eq. (2) matches the data. Equation (2) requires that the residual variance be equal to the fitted values, λ_i, which is plausible only if the assumptions underlying the Poisson distribution are fully met by the data. One assumption is that λ_i is the true rate for each case, which implies that the explanatory variables account for all of the meaningful variation among the aggregate units. If not, the differences between the fitted and true rates will inflate the variance of the residuals. It is very unlikely that this assumption will be valid, for there is no more reason to expect that a Poisson regression will explain all of the variation in the true crime rates than to expect that an OLS regression would explain all variance other than error of measurement.

Residual variance will also be greater than λ_i if the assumption of independence among individual crime events is inaccurate. Dependence will arise if the occurrence of one offense generates a short-term increase in the probability of another occurring. For aggregate crime data, there are many potential sources of dependence, such as an individual offending at a high rate over a brief period until being incarcerated, multiple offenders being arrested for the same incident, and offenders being influenced by one another's behavior. These types of dependence would increase the year-to-year variability in crime rates for a community beyond λ_i, even if the underlying crime rate were constant.

For these two reasons, "overdispersion" in which residual variance exceeds λ_i is ubiquitous in analyses of crime data. Applying the basic Poisson regression model to such data can produce a substantial underestimation of standard errors of the β's, which in turn leads to highly misleading significance tests. There are several ways to allow for the possibility of overdispersion (Cameron and Trevedi, 1998; Land *et al.*, 1996). Perhaps the simplest is the quasi-likelihood approach (Gardner *et al.*, 1995), which retains coefficient estimates from the basic Poisson model but adjusts standard errors and significance tests based on the amount of overdispersion. Other approaches explicitly incorporate a source of overdispersion in the probability model, typically by adding a case-specific residual term to the regression model [Eq. (1) or (3)], comparable to the error term in OLS regression. These versions of Poisson regression are distinguished by the specific assumptions made about the distribution of the residual variation in underlying rates, which may be continuous or discrete (Cameron and Trevedi, 1998).

We illustrate this approach with the negative binomial regression model, which is the best known and most widely available Poisson-based

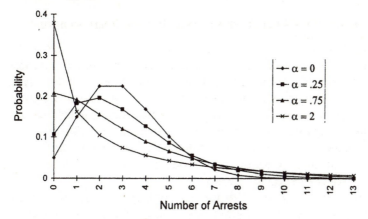

Fig. 3. Negative binomial distributions with mean count of 3, for four levels of residual variance.

regression model that allows for overdispersion. Negative binomial regression combines the Poisson distribution of event counts with a gamma distribution of the unexplained variation in the underlying or true mean event counts, λ_i. This combination produces the negative binomial distribution, which replaces the Poisson distribution of Eq. (2). The formula for the negative binomial is

$$P(Y_i = y_i) = \frac{\Gamma(y_i + \phi)}{y_i! \Gamma(\phi)} \frac{\phi^\phi \lambda_i^{y_i}}{(\phi + \lambda_i)^{\phi - y_i}} \tag{4}$$

where Γ is the gamma function (a continuous version of the factorial function), and ϕ is the reciprocal of the residual variance of underlying mean counts, α (Gardner *et al.*, 1995, p. 400).

Figure 3 demonstrates the impact of residual variance on the resulting distribution for a mean count of three crimes. With α equal to zero, we have the original Poisson distribution. For the Poisson, 5.0% of cases would have zero crimes and 1.2% would have eight or more crimes. As α increases, the distribution becomes more decidedly skewed as well as more broadly dispersed. Even for a moderate α of 0.75, the change from the Poisson is dramatic: 20.8% of cases would have zero crimes and 8.8% would have eight or more crimes.

In negative binomial regression (as in almost all Poisson-based regression models), the substantive portion of the regression model remains Eq. (1) for crime counts or Eq. (3) for per capita crime rates. Thus, though the response probabilities associated with the fitted values differ from the basic Poisson regression model, the interpretation of the regression coefficients does not.

3. AN EXAMPLE: SOCIAL DISORGANIZATION AND RURAL YOUTH VIOLENCE

I illustrate the use of Poisson-based regression to study aggregate crime rates with an analysis of rates of juvenile violence in nonmetropolitan counties of four states. This is an elaboration of part of the results presented by (Osgood and Chambers, 2000), and the present article is intended as a methodological companion to that article. Osgood and Chambers (2000) provide a rationale for these analyses in terms of social disorganization theory, offer a full description of the sample and measures, and present analyses for a variety of specific offenses.

The sample consists of the 264 nonmetropolitan counties of Florida, Georgia, South Carolina, and Nebraska, which have total populations ranging from 560 to 98,000. The average population of these counties is roughly 10,000, which is comparable to average neighborhood populations in research comparing neighborhoods within urban centers (Sampson *et al.*, 1997; Warner and Pierce, 1993).

The measure of offending for these illustrative analyses is the number of juveniles (ages 11 through 17) arrested for robberies in each county, pooled over the 5-year period of 1989 through 1993. The measures of the explanatory variables are based primarily on 1990 census data (United States Department of Commerce, 1992). They include (1) *residential instability*, defined as the proportion of households occupied by persons who had moved from another dwelling in the previous 5 years; (2) *ethnic heterogeneity*, computed as the index of diversity (Warner and Pierce, 1993), based on the proportion of households occupied by white versus nonwhite persons; (3) *family disruption*, indexed by female-headed households, expressed as a proportion of all households with children; (4) *poverty*, defined as the proportion of persons living below the poverty level; (5) the *unemployment* rate (coded as proportion of the workforce); (6) *proximity to metropolitan counties*, as indicated by a dummy variable with 1 being adjacent to a metropolitan statistical area and 0 being nonadjacent.[2] Also included in the analysis was the number of youth 10 to 17 years of age, which is the *population at risk* for juvenile arrests. Because states may differ in their statutes and in the organization, funding, and policies of their justice systems, it was important to eliminate from our analysis all variation between states and

---

[2]To ensure that single cases did not have undue influence on our results, we recoded some extreme values to values less deviant from the distribution as a whole. We set the maximum for residential stability to 0.6 (formerly 0.76; three cases recoded), that for female-headed households to 0.35 (formerly 0.42, four cases recoded), and that for unemployment to 0.12 (formerly 0.14; three cases recoded). This recoding had no substantive impact on the results, and it increases our faith in their reliability.

Table I. Descriptive Statistics

	Mean	SD
Robbery arrest rate per 100,000 per year	25.28	48.65
Population at risk in person/years	11,346	10,776
Log population at risk	8.89	1.04
Residential instability	0.39	0.07
Ethnic heterogeneity	0.26	0.20
Female-headed households	0.18	0.08
Poverty rate	0.16	0.06
Unemployment	5.64	2.60
Adjacent to metropolitan area	0.45	0.50
N of counties	264	

assess only within-state relationships pooled across the states. Therefore the model includes dummy variables representing states (with Florida serving as the omitted reference category).

3.1. The Distribution of Crime Rates

Table I presents descriptive statistics for all measures. During this 5-year period, there were 1212 arrests of juveniles for robbery in this sample of counties, which corresponds to an annual arrest rate of 40.5 per 100,000, or one arrest in 5 years for every 494 juveniles. The distribution of arrest rates is highly skewed, with zero robbery arrests of juveniles recorded in 52% of the counties, while the highest annual arrest rates were 338 and 390 per 100,000. Counties with smaller populations tended to have lower arrest rates, so the mean of robbery arrest rates across counties, 25.3, is lower than the overall arrest rate. There were zero arrests in all but one of the 47 counties with the smallest populations (700 or less). The exception is a county with two arrests in a population of 289 youths, which constitutes the seventh highest annual arrest rate. With a population this small, even a single arrest would place this county among the top 12% for arrest rate. It is clear that the data provide very crude estimates of arrest rates for any single county with a small juvenile population. Yet the lack of arrests across many small counties is strong evidence that the per capita robbery rate is lower in these counties than in counties with larger juvenile populations.

3.2. Ordinary Least-Squares Analysis

To demonstrate the purposes and use of Poisson-based regression models, I compare five analyses of the same data. The results appear in Table II. The first is an OLS regression analysis of the computed arrest rates (per 100,000 per year) for each county. The full model explains 28.4% of

Table II. Five Statistical Models of Juvenile Arrest Rates for Robbery in Nonmetropolitan Counties of Four States

Explanatory variable	OLS, rate/100,000	OLS, log(rate + 1)	OLS, log(rate + 0.2)	Basic Poisson	Negative binomial
Log population at risk					
b	11.220	0.749	1.102	1.501[a]	1.718[a]
SE	3.838	0.128	0.177	0.061	0.188
t	2.923	5.852	6.226	8.213	3.819
P	0.004	0.000	0.000	0.000	0.000
Residential instability					
b	35.573	3.017	4.366	1.567	0.162
SE	48.790	1.628	2.255	0.567	2.026
t	0.729	1.853	1.936	2.764	0.080
P	0.467	0.065	0.054	0.005	0.936
Ethnic heterogeneity					
b	63.839	2.461	3.325	2.069	2.861
SE	32.711	1.091	1.512	0.419	1.156
t	1.952	2.256	2.199	4.938	2.475
P	0.052	0.025	0.029	0.000	0.013
Female-headed households					
b	22.765	0.533	0.192	3.919	3.739
SE	71.679	2.391	3.313	1.030	2.937
t	0.318	0.223	0.058	3.805	1.273
P	0.751	0.824	0.954	0.000	0.203
Poverty rate					
b	39.474	1.405	2.181	0.499	0.021
SE	81.162	2.708	3.752	1.009	3.381
t	0.486	0.519	0.581	0.495	0.006
P	0.627	0.604	0.561	0.621	0.995
Unemployment					
b	−42.658	5.246	8.137	−1.338	0.432
SE	203.957	6.804	9.428	1.810	6.568
t	−0.209	0.771	0.863	−0.739	0.066
P	0.834	0.441	0.389	0.466	0.948
Adjacent to metropolitan area					
b	−3.944	−0.211	−0.267	−0.247	−0.458
SE	6.372	0.213	0.295	0.071	0.215
t	−0.619	−0.991	−0.905	−3.479	−2.130
P	0.537	0.322	0.365	0.000	0.034
Constant					
b	−66.020	−6.645	−11.560	−13.750	−15.243
SE	43.732	1.459	2.022	0.630	1.722
t	−1.510	−4.554	−5.717	−21.825	−8.852
P	0.132	0.000	0.000	0.000	0.000

Table II. Continued.

	Statistical method				
Explanatory variable	OLS, rate/100,000	OLS, log(rate + 1)	OLS, log(rate + 0.2)	Basic Poisson	Negative binomial
Model fit					
Method specific criteria					
Baseline model[b]					
MSE[c]	1853.9	2.419	4.729	α^e	1.263
R^2	0.226	0.328	0.332	0.484[f]	0.456[f]
$-2LL^d$				1584.5	950.8
Full model					
MSE	1760.6	1.960	3.762	α	0.852
R^2	0.284	0.471	0.483	0.585	0.548
$-2LL$				1420.9	901.5
Spearman r	0.653	0.708	0.710	0.671	0.687

Note: The models also included dummy variables representing differences between the four states.
[a] t and P values computed for difference of b from 1 rather than difference of b from 0.
[b] The baseline model controls for differences between states and, in the Poisson and negative binomial models, includes log population at risk, with a fixed coefficient of 1.
[c] Mean squared error for the OLS regression models.
[d] -2 times the log likelihood for the Poisson and negative binomial models.
[e] Reflects residual variance in true crime rates, which is overdispersion beyond that expected from a simple Poisson process.
[f] See footnote 5 for a description of the computation of R^2 values for the Poisson and negative binomial analyses.

the variance in these robbery rates, which is 5.9% more than a baseline model that includes only differences between states [$F(7,253) = 2.97$, $P = 0.005$].

There are several indications that this OLS model is very poorly suited to the data. Though an arrest rate below zero would be impossible, this model yielded negative fitted values for 42 cases, and these negative values fall as much as 0.61 standard deviations below zero. Under this OLS model, the two counties with the highest arrest rates constituted extreme outliers with standardized residuals of 7.2 and 6.1, both far too large to be acceptable at any sample size. These are strong indications that the fitted values do not accurately track actual mean crime rates, so it is clear that a linear model severely distorts the relationship between these explanatory variables and county level arrest rates.

The critical assumption for the accuracy of standard errors and significance tests in OLS analysis is that the residual variance does not vary systematically across cases, and White's test for heteroscedasticity (McClendon, 1994, pp. 178–181) provides a simple and direct means of testing this assumption. This test involves an OLS regression analysis in which the squared values of the residuals serve as the dependent variables, and the fitted values of that regression will reflect mean levels of squared residuals. The independent variables in this residual analysis can be any factors suspected to be related to heterogeneity of the residuals. Because I expect that residual variance will depend on population size, but not in a linear fashion, I chose linear, squared, and cubed terms for population size as independent variables. Using absolute values of residuals rather than squared residuals as the dependent variable provided a better summary of the data. (When squared, residuals of the outliers dominated the entire sample.) This analysis indicated that the magnitude of residual variance varied widely by population size: The squared values of the fitted absolute residuals ranged from 94 to 1162 [$R^2 = 0.050$, $F(3,260) = 4.51$, $P = 0.004$].[3]

3.3. Ordinary Least-Squares Analysis of Logged Crime Rates

The most drastic shortcomings of the OLS model stem from the highly skewed distribution of arrest rates. A common strategy for addressing this problem is to transform the data so that they become less skewed. The logarithmic transformation is a common choice for this purpose because it reduces the skew and it also yields a straightforward conceptual interpretation. Under a linear model of the untransformed data, the regression coefficients indicate the difference in the mean of the dependent variable that is associated with a unit difference on the explanatory variable. After the logarithmic transformation, the regression coefficients reflect proportional differences in the mean of the dependent variable, given a 1-unit difference on the explanatory variable. For crime rates, proportional differences would appear more plausible than constant differences. We do not expect a factor that raises a crime rate from 40 per 100,000 to 60 per 100,000 to also raise a crime of 1 per 100,000 to 21 per 100,000, as would be the case for a linear model of the untransformed data. Under the proportional model produced by the logarithmic transformation, the same percentage increase would hold for both, such as 40 versus 60 and 1 versus 1.5.

The third column in Table II presents an OLS regression analysis with the natural logarithm of the arrest rate as the dependent variable. One has been added to the rates (per 100,000) before taking the logarithm because the logarithm of zero is undefined (corresponding to minus infinity). The OLS analysis of logged rates is a far better match to the data in several respects. First, in this analysis the full model accounts for 47.1% of the

---

[3]Strictly speaking, White's test uses the squared residual as the dependent variable and uses a χ^2 significance test due to the likely heteroscedasticity of the residuals themselves. This test would also be significant for this residual analysis [$\chi^2(3) = 13.2$, $P = 0.004$] as well as for the comparable analysis reported below [$\chi^2(3) = 28.5$, $P = 0.000$].

variance, which is a clear indication that the transformation puts the data in a form that has a closer linear correspondence to these explanatory variables. Also, in this altered metric a larger share of the explained variance is attributable to the explanatory variables rather than to differences between states [increase in $R^2 = 0.142$, $F(7,253) = 9.761$, $P < 0.001$]. Second, the range of the fitted values is not problematic under this model because negative fitted values correspond to logarithms of crime rates between zero and one. Third, the transformation also reduces problems of outliers, with the most extreme standardized residual for the OLS analysis of the transformed arrest rates now 3.2. The change in metric means that the coefficients of these first two analyses are not comparable, but the benefit of the improved correspondence between model and data is apparent in the higher t values for the three variables most strongly related to crime rates (population size, residential instability, and ethnic heterogeneity).

Though the logarithmic transformation renders the data more suitable for OLS analysis, it also makes apparent the inherent problems that require Poisson-based regression. First, rather than solving the problem of heteroscedasticity, the error variance has become even more strongly related to population size. The cubic model of the absolute residuals now acounts for 10.8% of their variance [$F(3,260) = 10.52$, $P < 0.001$], with fitted values corresponding to squared residuals that range from 0.01 to 1.98. Furthermore, the specific cases that constitute outliers also have changed. In the OLS analysis of untransformed rates, the two most extreme outliers were the counties with the highest crime rates, both of which have larger than median juvenile populations. The most extreme outlier in the OLS analysis of the transformed rates is the smallest population with any recorded arrests. The OLS assumption of homogeneity of residual variance implies that the predictive accuracy of the model is independent of population size. As we would expect from the inevitable unreliability of crime rate estimates based on small population sizes, that assumption is clearly in error.

Second, the discrete and skewed nature of crime rates for small populations presents a special problem for analyzing log transformed crime rates. Observed rates of zero will be common for small populations, in which case the transformation can be computed only after adding a constant. The common choice of adding one is highly arbitrary. The value could as easily be 1 per 1000 or 1 per 1,000,000 as the 1 per 100,000 used in the analysis just discussed, yet the choice of this constant may drastically effect the results. To see this compare Columns 3 and 4 in Table II, which differ only in that Column 3 reports an analysis resulting from adding a constant of 1 per 100,000 while the constant for Column 4 is 0.2 (corresponding to 1 arrest per 100,000 for the 5 years covered in the study, rather than for one year). This arbitrary choice results in an increase of roughly 40% in most of the regression coefficients, which is a large difference in the implied effects of these explanatory variables on mean crime rates. The reason for this change is that decreasing the constant increases the variance of the dependent variable by inflating the difference between the transformed value for the rate of zero and the transformed value for the next higher observed rate. Thus, the choice of this constant has great potential for biasing the coefficient estimates. Interestingly, changing the additive constant had minimal consequence for significance testing because standard errors grew proportionately with the coefficients, with the result that t values were essentially unchanged.

3.4. Poisson-Based Analyses

Poisson-based regression analyses successfully address the most serious problems that arise in the OLS analyses. As discussed above, Poisson-based models do not assume homogeneity of variance. Instead, residual variance is expected to be a function of the predicted number of offenses, which is in turn a function of population size. Furthermore, even though a logarithmic transformation is inherent in Poisson-based regression, observed crime rates of zero present no problem. Unlike the preceding OLS analyses of log crime rates, Poisson-based regression analyses do not require taking the logarithm of the dependent variable. Instead, estimation for these models involves computing the probability of the observed count of offenses, based on the fitted value for the mean count. As Figs. 1 and 2 demonstrate, observed rates of zero become increasingly likely as the estimated mean rate approaches zero.

The last two columns in Table II present results from a basic Poisson regression and a negative binomial regression, both estimated with the LIMDEP statistical package (Greene, 1995). Because these are maximum-likelihood estimates, likelihood-ratio significance tests can be used to determine whether more complex models provide better fit to the data than do simpler models. The test statistic is minus twice the difference between the log likelihoods for the models, and the significance level is determined by comparing this value to the χ^2 distribution with degrees of freedom equal to the number of additional parameters in the more complex model.

3.4.1. Poisson versus Negative Binomial

The negative binomial model differs from the basic Poisson by the addition of the residual variance parameter, α. The likelihood-ratio test value for the comparison between these models is 519.4 with 1 degree of freedom, indicating that the data are far more consistent with the negative binomial model than with the basic Poisson ($P < 0.001$). This result means that, on average, differences between fitted and observed crime rates are considerably larger than specified by the Poisson distribution. This overdispersion reflects some combination of unexplained variation in counties' true crime rates and positive dependence among crime events.

Comparing the fifth and sixth columns in Table II makes clear the consequence of ignoring that overdispersion. The basic Poisson model gives the impression of far greater precision in the estimated relationships than is justified. The standard errors for the basic Poisson model average only about one-third the size of the standard errors for the negative binomial, so the basic Poisson model would produce highly erroneous significance tests for the coefficients. In this example, the basic Poisson would lead us to conclude that residential instability and female-headed households are significantly related to rates of arrests of juveniles for robbery, while the negative binomial would not.

3.4.2. Fit of the Negative Binomial Model

I examined residuals from the negative binomial model to check the match between the model and data in terms of potential outliers. Standardized residuals are less useful here because the residuals are not expected to follow a normal distribution. Instead, an appropriate strategy is to use the negative binomial distribution of Eq. (4) to compute the probability of obtaining a value at least as extreme as the observed value, based on the fitted values, λ_i, and the estimate of residual variance in true crime rates, α. Because this is a tedious calculation, even using a spreadsheet program, I first computed standardized residuals[4] to identify the cases most likely to constitute outliers, and then computed probabilities for those cases. The most extreme outlier was a county with three recorded arrests. Its fitted value, λ, was 0.204, which yields a probability of 0.0043 of observing three or more arrests. Only 1 in every 233 cases should have a probability this small, but that is quite acceptable in our sample of 264. Probabilities for four cases were less than 0.02, which is no more than would be expected by chance in a sample of this size. It is especially encouraging that these four counties varied widely in population size, from the eighth to the eightieth percentile. Thus, there are good indications that the assumptions of the negative binomial model are a good match to these data and that this model

---

[4]Standardized residuals can be computed on the basis of the variance of the negative binomial, which is $\lambda_i + \alpha\lambda_i^2$ (Gardner *et al.*, 1995). Though the Poisson rapidly approaches the normal distribution as λ increases, this is far less true of the negative binomial with the moderate value of α obtained in this example. For instance, even with a value of λ as large as 32, standardized residuals could differ from the normal deviates corresponding to negative binomial probabilities by over 50%.

successfully addresses the confounding of population size and accuracy of crime rate estimates.

How well does the negative binomial model account for crime rates, in comparison to the OLS analyses? The R^2 values in Table II are not very helpful for this purpose because they reflect scaling differences in the dependent variable as much as differences in the success of the models. Thus, the higher R^2 values for the Poisson and negative binomial models are partly a reflection that the outcome variable in these analyses is not the crime rate, but rather the count of offenses. The Spearman rank order correlation, which is unaffected by scaling, indicates that the five models have similar success in ordering the counties by crime rate (values range from 0.66 to 0.71). When taking the metric of the outcome measure into account, we find that the negative binomial model explains substantial portions of variance in both untransformed crime rates (22.2% for negative binomial versus 28.4% for the OLS analysis of these rates) and log-transformed crime rates (22.8% for negative binomial versus 47.1% for this OLS analysis).[5] In sharp contrast, each of the OLS analyses is surprisingly unsuccessful in accounting for variance in the other metric: Fitted values from the OLS analysis of log-transformed rates account for only 8.8% of the variance in untransformed rates, while fitted values from OLS analysis of untransformed rates account for only 5.2% of the variance in log-transformed rates. It is likely that these mismatches reflect the shortcomings of both OLS approaches. A direct linear model is unsuitable for the untransformed rates, as evidenced in the impossible negative fitted values that result. Yet the OLS analysis of log-transformed rates yields fitted values that poorly match the original crime rates, despite a strong rank order correlation between the two. It appears that the arbitrary constant required for OLS analysis of log-transformed rates results in a seriously distorted metric. Poisson-based models avoid these problems and, as a result, generalize well to either response metric.

3.4.3. Results from the Negative Binomial Model

The likelihood-ratio test can be used to assess the overall contribution of the explanatory variables, comparable to the test for increase in R^2 in

---

[5]I computed these percentages of explained variance by transforming fitted values from each model to the metric of the observed scores, summing the squared differences between these and the observed scores, and calculating one minus the quotient of that sum divided by the total sum of squares for the observed scores. This computation corresponds to the definition of R^2 in OLS regression. Because R^2 is not part of the maximum-likelihood estimation of the basic Poisson and negative binomial models, this procedure was also used to compute the R^2 values for those models. Negative fitted values from the OLS analysis of untransformed crime rate were set to zero in order to compute the fit of that model to log-transformed crime rates. The additive constant of 1 per 100,000 was used for all log transformations of crime rates.

OLS models. For the Poisson-based analyses, the baseline model includes not only dummy variables to control for differences between states, but also the log of the population at risk with a fixed coefficient of one, as in Eq. (3). This control for population size is necessary so that the regression will be a model of per capita crime rates rather than a model of counts of crimes. For the negative binomial, the full model yields a likelihood-ratio value of 49.4 in comparison to the baseline model, which is statistically significant (df = 7, $P < 0.001$). Thus, we can conclude that the explanatory variables account for more variation in crime rates than would be expected by chance alone.

By the conventional 0.05 standard of statistical significance, the negative binomial analysis indicates that higher juvenile arrest rates for robbery are associated with larger populations at risk, greater ethnic heterogeneity, and being adjacent to a metropolitan area.[6] To interpret the regression coefficients for these variables, we must take into account the logarithmic transformation that intervenes between the linear model and fitted crime rates [in Eqs. (1) and (3)]. Liao (1994) explains several useful strategies for interpreting these coefficients. One relatively straightforward approach to this task follows the implication of Eqs. (1) and (3) that an increase of x in an explanatory variable will multiply the fitted mean crime rate by the $\exp(bx)$. Thus, given the coefficient of 2.861 for ethnic heterogeneity in the negative binomial model, a 10% increase in ethnic heterogeneity would multiply the rate by $\exp(0.286)$, which is 1.33. In plain English, a 10% increase in ethnic heterogeneity is associated with a 33% increase in the juvenile arrest rate for robbery. Because being adjacent to a metropolitan area is coded as a dummy variable, an increase of one in this variable corresponds to the contrast between adjacent and nonadjacent counties. Thus, the statistically significant coefficient of -0.458 indicates that counties adjacent to metropolitan areas have a 37% lower rate of robbery than those that are not because $\exp(-0.458 * 1)$ equals 0.63. [This surprising result does not replicate for analyses of other offenses reported by Osgood and Chambers (2000).]

In interpreting the results for population size, we must take into account the special role of this variable in Poisson-based analyses of aggregate rates. When the coefficient for the log of the population at risk is fixed at one [as in Eq. (3)], per capita crime rates are constant across counties with different population sizes, controlling for the other explanatory variables. The analyses reported in Table II treat that coefficient as estimated

---

[6]In the more extensive analyses reported by Osgood and Chambers (2000) population at risk, ethnic heterogeneity, residential instability, and female-headed households proved to be associated with most offenses, but adjacency to metropolitan areas did not.

rather than fixed, which allows for the possibility that crime rates differ with population size. In this case, however, it is necessary to subtract the value of one from this coefficient in order to determine its implications for the relationship of population size to per capita crime rates. Similarly, the statistical significance of the relationship is gauged by comparing the estimate to the value of one, rather than to zero as is the usual case.[7] A coefficient greater than one would indicate that counties with larger populations have higher per capita crime rates, while a coefficient less than one would indicate the opposite. Thus, the coefficient of 1.718 from the negative binomial analysis agrees quite closely with the value of 0.749 from the OLS analysis of the transformed crime rates. The first indicates that a doubling of the population is associated with a 64% increase in per capita robbery rates $[\exp(0.718 * \log(2)) = 1.645]$, while the second implies a 68% increase $[\exp(0.749 * \log(2)) = 1.680]$.

I have argued that the coefficients and significance tests based on the negative binomial (or another Poisson-based regression model that allows for overdispersion) are preferable because the other models I have reviewed rely on assumptions that are inconsistent with the data. Yet how much difference does the choice of model make? We can get some idea by comparing the coefficients and t values for the negative binomial analysis with those for the other analyses in Table II. Other than the OLS analysis of untransformed rates, all models specify a logarithmic relationship between fitted values and mean crime rates, so coefficients have comparable meanings across those models. In general, one would not expect an incorrect model to introduce any systematic bias, so it is surprising that estimates for many of the coefficients differ dramatically across the models. The absolute values of coefficients for residential instability, poverty rate, and unemployment are far larger in the OLS analyses than in the negative binomial analysis, while the opposite is true for female-headed households. Differences of this sort most likely are due to the role of population size in Poisson-based analyses. OLS analyses place as much weight on small counties as on large ones, but Poisson-based regression models expect error distributions in small counties to have greater variance, with the consequence that results are less influenced by small counties. This differential weighting has considerable potential for changing results in a sample such as ours, where there is a large range of population sizes.

The standard errors for the negative binomial model are most similar to those of the OLS analysis of log transformed rates, using the additive constant of one. Even here, however, standard errors for four of the seven

---

[7]In other words, the test statistic to be compared to the normal distribution is not the usual b/SE_b, but rather $(b-1)/\mathrm{SE}_b$.

substantive variables are at least 20% larger in the negative binomial analysis. There are far greater discrepancies in standard errors for the other models, so it is clear that significance tests may be seriously affected by applying an appropriate statistical model to aggregate data for small populations.

4. CONCLUSIONS

Using Poisson-based regression models of offense counts to analyze per capita offense rates is an important advance for research on aggregate crime data. Standard analytical approaches require that data be highly aggregated across either offense types or population units. Otherwise offense counts are too small to generate per capita rates that have appropriate distributions and sufficient accuracy to justify least-squares analysis. Poisson-based regression models give researchers an appropriate means for more fine-grained analysis. Poisson-based models are built on the assumption that the underlying data take the form of nonnegative integer counts of events. This is the case for crime rates, which are computed as offense counts divided by population size. In our example analysis of juvenile arrest rates for robbery, the Poisson-based negative binomial model provides a very good fit to the data, while OLS analyses produce outliers and require arbitrary choices that have a striking impact on results.

Poisson-based regression models free researchers to investigate a much broader range of aggregate data because they are appropriate for smaller population units and less common offenses. Yet these models are not magic. The reason they are appropriate is that they recognize the limited amount of information in small offense counts. The price one must pay in this trade-off is that the smaller the offense counts, the larger the sample of aggregate units needed to achieve adequate statistical power. For example, this sample of 264 counties proved too small for a meaningful analysis of juvenile homicide, the least common offense examined in this study (Osgood and Chambers, 2000).

Though this article has concentrated on two of the most common Poisson-based regression models, this approach to analyzing aggregate crime rates can be implemented with virtually any of the Poisson-based regression analyses. The numerous Poisson-based models reviewed by Cameron and Trevedi (1998) offer many choices for finding a model with assumptions that best match one's data. Some models expand the range of research questions that can be addressed, such as using finite-mixture models to identify homogeneous groups of counties. Other Poisson-based models have been developed for designs with repeated measures or nested data, such as counties nested within states or multiple subpopulations nested within a sample of geographic areas. The semiparametric model of Nagin and Land (1993), which has been so influential in research on criminal careers, would be appropriate for such cases. Also, the recent version of Bryk and co-workers' (1996) HLM program implements a Poisson version of their hierarchical linear modeling approach to analyzing nested data (Bryk and Raudenbush, 1992). Thus, Poisson-based regression models should have broad applicability for the study of crime at the aggregate level.

ACKNOWLEDGMENTS

This research was supported by Grant 94-JN-CX-0005 from the Office of Juvenile Justice and Delinquency Prevention, Office of Justice Programs, U.S. Department of Justice. The author thanks Jeff Chambers for his assistance with this study, Chet Britt for comments on an early draft, and Gary Melton and Susan Limber for their support of the entire project. Points of view or opinions in this document are those of the authors and do not necessarily represent the official position or policies of the U.S. Department of Justice.

REFERENCES

Bailey, A. J., Sargent, J. D., Goodman, D. C., Freeman, J., and Brown, M. J. (1994). Poisoned landscapes: The epidemiology of environmental lead exposure in Massachusetts. *Soc. Sci. Med.* 39: 757–766.

Bryk, A. S., and Raudenbush, S. W. (1992). *Hierarchical Linear Models: Applications and Data Analysis Methods*, Sage, Newbury Park, CA.

Bryk, A. S., Raudenbush, S. W., and Congdon, R. (1996). *HLM: Hierarchical Linear and Nonlinear Modeling with the HLM/2L and HLM/3L Programs*, Scientific Software International, Chicago.

Cameron, A. C., and Trivedi, P. K. (1998). *Regression Analysis of Count Data*, Cambridge University Press, Cambridge.

Gardner, W., Mulvey, E. P., and Shaw, E. C. (1995). Regression analyses of counts and rates: Poisson, overdispersed Poisson, and negative binomial. *Psychol. Bull.* 118: 392–405.

Greenberg, D. F. (1991). Modeling criminal careers. *Criminology* 29: 17–46.

Greene, W. H. (1995). *LIMDEP: Version 7.0 Users Manual*, Econometric Software, Plainview, NY.

King, G. (1989). *Unifying Political Methodology: The Likelihood Theory of Statistical Inference*, Cambridge University Press, Cambridge.

Liao, T. F. (1994). *Interpreting Probability Models: Logit, Probit, and Other Generalized Linear Models*, Sage University Paper Series on Quantitative Applications in the Social Sciences, 07–101, Sage, Newbury Park, CA.

Maltz, M. D. (1994). Operations research in studying crime and justice: Its history and accomplishments. In Pollock, S. M., Rothkopf, M. H., and Barnett, A. (eds.), *Operations Research and the Public Sector, Volume 6 of Handbooks in Operations Research and Management Science*, North-Holland, Amsterdam, pp. 200–262.

McClendon, McK. J. (1994). *Multiple Regression and Causal Analysis*, F. E. Peacock, Itasca, IL.

McCullagh, P., and Nelder, J. A. (1989). *Generalized Linear Models*, 2nd ed., Chapman and Hall, London.

Nagin, D. S., and Land, K. C. (1993). Age, criminal careers, and population heterogeneity: Specification and estimation of a nonparametric, mixed Poisson model. *Criminology* 31: 327–362.

Osgood, D. W., and Chambers, J. M. (2000). Social disorganization outside the metropolis: An analysis of rural youth violence. *Criminology* 38: 81–115.

Rowe, D. C., Osgood, D. W., and Nicewander, W. A. (1990). A latent trait approach to unifying criminal careers. *Criminology* 28: 237–270.

Sampson, R. J., Raudenbush, S. W., and Earls, F. (1997). Neighborhoods and violent crime: A multilevel study of collective efficacy. *Science* 177: 918–924.

United States Department of Commerce (1992). Summary Tape Files 1 and 3, 1990 Census.

Warner, B. D., and Pierce, G. L. (1993). Reexamining social disorganization theory using calls to the police as a measure of crime. *Criminology* 31: 493–517.

Name Index